Photo: Franz Gingele

Wiencke Island

The Belgica expedition 1897-1899

The first expedition to winter in Antarctic waters
A tale of extraordinary scientific achievements and human endurance

Patrick De Deckker

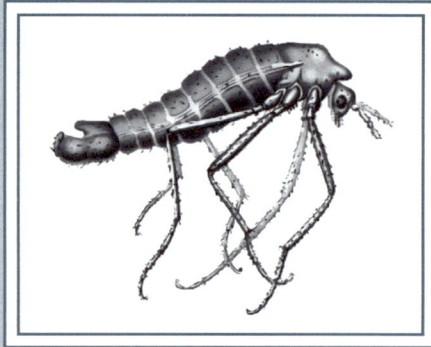

Belgica antarctica ♂

Sketch of the flightless chironomid fly *Belgica antarctica* discovered in the de Gerlache Strait, a possible emblem of the expedition for its **ability to survive under harsh conditions**.

TEXT, PHOTOGRAPHS (with due acknowledgements of origin) AND DIAGRAMS BY:
Patrick De Deckker (patrick.dedeckker@anu.edu.au)

DESIGN BY: Jo Hoadley (johodesign@icloud.com)

PLANTIN fonts were used in places in the layout of this book, not only because of their elegant appeal, but also because Christoffel Plantin was the second printer of books in Europe and was based in Antwerp where his extraordinary house and printing equipment can still be visited. This is to celebrate the city of Antwerp that supported this expedition so much and even recently had an exhibition on the Belgica expedition.

COVER PHOTO: The *SY Belgica* trapped in the sea ice with an onlooker emperor penguin.

PHOTO OPPOSITE: The *SY Belgica* trapped in the sea ice with large blocks of ice on the starboard side of the ship. For more details refer to the caption of Fig. 8.10.1D. Photograph 'colorized' using palette.fm/color/filter.

INSIDE BACK COVER PHOTO: Amundsen and Cook on the sea ice near the tent they designed.

BACK COVER PHOTO: Members of the Belgica crew in the process of lowering a probe below the sea ice to sample plankton, other organisms, sea floor sediments and water.

A catalogue record for this book is available from the National Library of Australia

Acknowledgements

The preparations of this book took several years, primarily through travels to examine archives in countries where the Belgica scientists and personnel originated from, as well as to meet many enthusiasts of the Belgica expedition.

IN BELGIUM:

1. The MAS (Museum aan de Stroom) in Antwerp where I received help from Rita Jalen, Natalie Wagemans, Jan Parmentier and Waander Devillé; the latter provided many useful information and links to important web sites;

2. The Felixarchief (Stadsarchief Antwerpen) and through correspondence with Nelle Van Bedts and Danny Teurelincx;

3. Professor Claude De Broyer at the Royal Belgian Institute of Natural Sciences who guided me in many ways over the years, and made available a lot of unpublished correspondence and archives belonging to members of the Belgica expedition;

4. At the same institution, numerous people helped me examine numerous collections: Linda Maurisse, Nicolas Gillan, Sebastien Bruaux, Thierry Hubin, assisting Dr Yves Samyn and Dr Oliver Pauwels, and Tommy D'heuvaer assisting Dr Marleen De Ceukelaire. In addition, Marie Depris the RBINS librarian helped me scan numerous Belgica Résultats illustrations;

5. Professor Paul Bettens, Secrétaire Adjoint of the Société Royale de Géographie de Belgique at the ULB in Brussels;

6. Eddy Stuer and the late Helge Seifert for providing much information on the Belgica expedition and also taking me to see the 'new' *Belgica* replica ship being constructed; they were also assisted by Willy Versluys who enabled me to get a replica of the *Belgica* ship;

7. Governor Dr Cathy Berx for support in Antwerp;

8. Frederik Leliaert of the Herbarium of the Meise Botanic Garden for facilitating access to digitised photographs of plants collected during the Belgica expedition.

9. Jozef Verlinden for information as well as a copy of his book entitled: 'Discovery and Exploration of Gerlache Strait'.

10. Fons Verheyde, librarian at the Vlaams Institut voor de Zee (VLIZ) for his continuous and generous help to obtain digitized copies of archives held in his institute.

IN ROMANIA:

1. in Bucharest: Emeritus Professor Dumitru Murariu of the Grigore Antipa Museum for allowing me to examine many Racovitza archives and overall support and also for commenting on the appendix on seals; Professor Nicolae Panin of GeoEcoMar in Bucharest for support and interest;

2. In Cluj: Dr Ioana Meleg of the Emil. G. Racoviță Institute at Babeş-Bolyai University, and Bogdan Craciun of the Romanian National Archives (whom I visited twice) and where I was able to examine and copy many Racovitza archives.

IN NORWAY:

1. Anne Melgård and Guro Tangvald from the National Library of Norway allowed me to examine many photographs belonging to Roald Amundsen;

2. Anne Melgård also for taking me to the National Archives of Norway and for correspondence with Kristin Brattelid, the Archivist there;

3. Anders Bache from the Roald Amundsens Hjem Museene i Akershus for correspondence and access to archives;

4. Geir O. Kløver of the Fram Museum for discussions.

IN POLAND:

5. Dagmara Bożek and Katarzyna Dąbkowska, co-authors of the recently published book on Henryk Arctowski for numerous enthusiastic discussions and enabling me to visit the Polish Academy of Science Archives in Warsaw, including Arctowski's diary and helping me visit the graves of H. Arctowski and A. Dobrowolski in Warsaw;

6. Dr Agnieszka Pietrzak of the Ziemi Museum in Warsaw for allowing me to examine the Dobrowolski archives and permitting me to copy many of them.

IN THE US:

7. Carol Smith and Aldo Troiani of the Sullivan County Museum in Hurleyville, New York where many of the Frederick Cook archives and photographs are held. Both gave me many top quality photographs taken by Cook;

8. Dr Oana-Elena Marcu in California for many discussions and allowing me to have access to many of the Racovitza archives prepared by her family in Romania;

9. For correspondence with Laura Kissel of Ohio State University for enabling me to obtain some of the stunning photos taken by F. Cook that are held in the University archives.

In addition, I am grateful to Professor Robin Robertson for calculating the potential temperatures in Drake Passage based on Arctowski data, and Dr John Rogers for providing Ocean Data View profiles of Drake Passage. I also wish to thank several other people who helped me during the preparation of this book: the Late Franz Gingele for access to his wonderful photographs he took of Antarctic wildlife and also his friend Mikołaj Golachowski for photographs of penguins and seals from de Gerlache Strait. Dr Karsten Gohl from the Alfred Wegener Institute for Polar and Marine Research (AWI) in Germany for providing a map showing the track of the *Belgica* ship over a recently-obtained bottom topography map of the Bellingshausen Sea; also from AWI are Hannes Grobe for permission to use one of his images and Christoph Held for his photo of the small jellyfish near Racovitza Island. I am indebted to R. Fenstermacher for searching the Frederick Cook archives in the Library of Congress in Washington, Librarian Kirsty Summers at Sydney University for facilitating my examination of the *Belgica* Résultats volumes as well as those from the Charcot expedition. The many librarians at the National Library of Australia in Canberra for continuous access to so many books and maps held in that amazing institution. Ian Myers for applying his superb computing skills to enhance all the crew photographs in Figure 5.1 which were later on 'colorized' by myself using palette.fm/color/filters. Dr Claus-Dieter Hillenbrandt from the British Antarctic Survey for discussions on the absence of sea ice in the Bellingshausen Sea. Professor Thierry Corrège for advice on the colours of the flags hanging over the *Belgica* in Antwerp harbour.

Thank you also very much to Dace De Deckker for her superb and imaginative sketches of the little penguins that adorn the start of every chapter. I have been very fortunate to have had Jo Hoadley as book designer. She simply did an amazing job at satisfying my picky requirements for this book. She was a pleasure to work with.

Finally, sincere thanks to Charlotte and Olivier De Schrevel, as well as Terence Lecointe in Brussels for friendship and help with obtaining documents and information on the Belgica expedition. I also owe a great debt to Dr Toni Noble for going through the first draft of this extensive manuscript and providing many very useful comments on how to improve its format.

"Un tout grand merci" also to my family Kim, Stephen, Peter and Dace for their support over the years and allowing me to pursue my interests in science subjects. Thank you to all.

Writing a book can be a very satisfying job, but is at times a lonely affair. Luckily, I was able to be accompanied by the music of many wonderful artists such as Haroula Rose, Shawn Colvin and Alison Krauss, Laura Wright, Amy Macdonald, Paul Simon, The Coors, Alexis French, Ludovico Einaudi, Arvo Pärt and Julos Beaucarne, to name a few.

Patrick De Deckker

Canberra
17 March 2025

Dedication   *To the memory of my beautiful Kerry*

Introduction

This book documents the extraordinary tale of a sea journey to Antarctica at the end of the 1890s that took two and half years and occurred over 125 years ago.

It is a story of great scientific exploration as well as human endurance as the ship became trapped in the sea ice for nearly 13 months. The scientists and crew were the first to endure the debilitating harshness of the dark, long Antarctic winter and uncertainty of survival. Yet, the entrapment also yielded a unique opportunity for the scientists and crew on board to collate ground-breaking scientific data about the ocean and land near the Antarctic Peninsula. Funded by Belgium, the ship was called the *S.Y. Belgica* (see previous page) and departed from Antwerp in August 1897, 17 years before the better known and celebrated Shackelton expedition. The Belgica expedition was affiliated with the Antwerp Yacht Club and the original aim of the expedition was to spend winter at Cape Adare in Victoria Land on the edge of Antarctica. But this did not happen; instead, the voyage first led to the charting of the deep Drake Passage and eventually the discovery of many new islands bordering the Antarctic Peninsula as well as a new passageway frequented today by many tourist ships. This was eventually called 'de Gerlache Strait', named after the Commander of the ship.

At the end of the nineteenth century, little was known about Antarctica including whether it was even a continent and the south magnetic pole was still unchartered. The oceanographic and meteorological investigations carried out during the *Belgica's* long journey by the scientists on board now provide a significant baseline that informs our understanding today of climate change. The Antarctic Peninsula is one place on Earth facing the largest changes and challenges due to global warming. The expedition's remarkable scientific investigations also extended to a vast collection of geological, glaciological, meteorological, biological (flora and fauna) and anthropological data.

The *Belgica's* expeditioners gained international fame on their return and for the rest of their careers. Yet, despite this recognition, the numerous scientific reports (totalling 3767 pages) from the expedition have largely been ignored in the English-speaking world. This book documents the expeditioners' significant and comprehensive scientific findings and celebrates the outstanding scientists of the Belgica expedition.

Facing page: photograph of the *S.Y. Belgica* in Antwerp Harbour. Note the Belfry on the right and the Steen Castle at the very left of the photograph. The insert shows the original flag of the Yacht Club of Antwerp used during the expedition and gifted back by A. de Gerlache to the Club, now called 'Royal Yacht Club of Belgium' where the flag is on display. The original photograph of the ship originates from the MAS collections featuring an album of photographs entitled: "Expédition antarctique belge" 1897-1899, catalogue 29.718.02, with permission from Waander Devillé. The photo was 'colorized' using 'palette.fm/color/filters/

This book describes much of the science gathered during the expedition, and also looks at what we know of the area visited by the *Belgica* since. It draws on recent, alarming findings that will force us to revisit the area so as to document all the significant changes, and also aim at predicting the future of this 'fragile' part of the globe.

The chapters describe concisely what each topic discusses in the book.

Over the centuries, Antarctica has become more than just a frozen territory at the edge of the world. It is a precious and vulnerable ecosystem, a barometer of global climate change and, above all, a reminder of our responsibility to our planet, our home.

Heïdi Sevestre in the Preface of the book by Dominique Brechon 2024

Patrick De Deckker is a geologist with a doctorate in zoology. He was educated in Belgium, Switzerland and Australia. He commenced working on microcrustaceans (ostracods) and salt lakes, then used the remains of microorganisms to determine environmental change in large lacustrine systems through time. Using the same approach, he continued his investigations with the aim of identifying changes in all three oceans surrounding Australia, and spent much time investigating the Australian sector of the Southern Ocean. Patrick spent one summer season sampling lakes in the vicinity of the Australian Antarctic Casey base, and also examined the possible record of Australian dust in Antarctic ice cores (with results published). He is a Member of the Order of Australia and Officier de l'Ordre de Leopold II awarded by Belgium.

He published over 250 articles in peer-reviewed international scientific journals and edited/co-edited 8 books and journal volumes. Patrick is a Fellow of the Australian Academy of Science and also the recipient of several distinguished awards, including the Christoffel Plantin Medal bestowed by the Governor of the Antwerp Province in Belgium.

Patrick travelled extensively to research for this book: on several occasions to Belgium (Antwerp, Brussels, Ghent), twice to Romania (Bucharest and Cluj) and Poland (Ziemi Museum and Polish Academy of Sciences, Warsaw), USA (Sullivan County Museum, New York), Norway (National Library and National Archives, Fram Museum) and UK (Cambridge Polar Institute).

Currently, he is Emeritus Professor in the Research School of Earth Sciences at the Australian National University in Canberra, Australia.

Contents

PART ONE

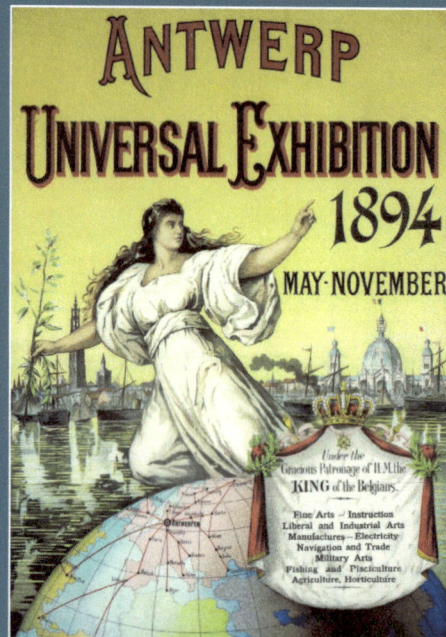

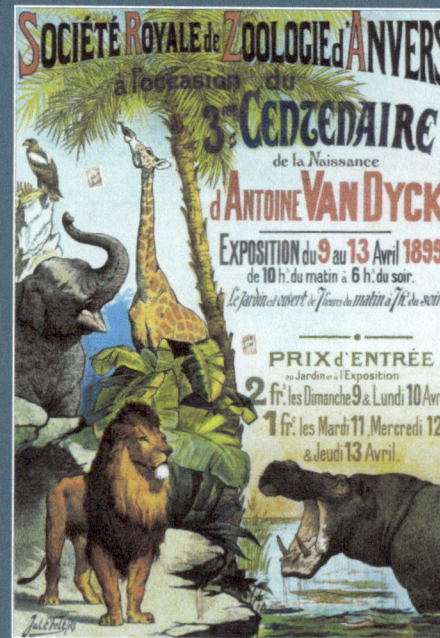

Figure 1.1 On left, poster advertising the International Exhibition in Antwerp in 1894, Wikimedia Commons, Belgium. On the right, poster advertising the zoological exhibition in Antwerp in 1899, published with permission of the Royal Zoological Society of Antwerp. Both posters demonstrate the international opening of the city of Antwerp to the world and its wealth.

Chapter 1

Setting the scene for exploration of the 'unknown Antarctica'

KEY POINTS

- Late in the 19th century little was still known about the Antarctic continent. In fact, very few people considered it to be a continent. Several people referred to it as 'Antarctide'.

- In the late 1890s, an accrued interest was acquired by geographers and scientists on Antarctica, with people urging for the exploration of that landmass. Sir John Murray, famous for the *Challenger* exploration achievements, listed important reasons for the exploration of Antarctica. He provided important maps to help lead the interest in that continent. This was endorsed by Sir Clements Markham at the International Geographical Congress in 1895 in London.

- At that Congress, the adventurer Carsten Borchgrevinck announced that he had been able to land at Cape Adare in Antarctica, and that this was an ideal place to overwinter on the Antarctic mainland. The race for exploring Antarctica had begun!

- Mention is made of the first attempts at crossing the Antarctic Polar Circle by James Cook in 1774 and Fabian Gottlieb von Bellingshausen 1820-1821 and sailing in Antarctic waters.

- The discovery of rocks in Adélie Land by Dumont d'Urville and his crew documented that Antarctica was a 'true' landmass/continent as rocks were found there.

BELGIUM, AN EMERGING INDUSTRIALISED NATION

At the end of the 19th century, Belgium was a very young country, only achieving independence from The Netherlands in 1830. The following year, the Belgian people welcomed King Leopold I, originally Prince of Saxe-Coburg from Germany to Brussels. Thirty five years later, Belgium had a new King, Leopold II who stated in the Senate that "Belgium, in order to participate to the colonial expansion of Europe, the ocean permitted access to markets all over the world", thereby offering opportunities to expand Belgium's colonial empire. By 1885, the German Chancellor Bismarck formally acknowledged that King Leopold II was the "sovereign proprietor" of the independent State of Congo, a country 80 times the size of Belgium! It is by then that Belgium had become a prosperous, industrialised nation which exported one third of its national products, in contrast to France which exported only one seventh of his products, and Great Britain one fourth. By 1900, Antwerp was a vibrant city with a harbour from which coal machines, industrial products and sugar were exported. Antwerp citizens were brokers, sometimes industrialists and many possessed large warehouses (Dumont, 1977).

In 1894, the city of Antwerp hosted the Universal Exhibition for five months, to show its entrepreneurial capabilities, where numerous items were featured like electricity, manufactured products, military, arts, fishing, agriculture among others (see Fig. 1.1 left). In 1899 also, the Zoological Garden in Antwerp organised a large exhibition (see Fig. 1.1 right). This testified that Antwerp was a vibrant city with much wealth and also international in ambition.

AN EVOLVING EUROPEAN INTEREST ON ANTARCTICA

The first geographical congress was held in Antwerp in 1871 and was entitled "Congrès des Sciences géographiques, cosmographiques, et commerciales", but only once among the 1212 pages published from the congress was the word 'Antarctica' mentioned, and this in relation to the approaching transit of Venus.

A search through the 1152 pages of the recording of Berne Congress held in 1891 indicates that its discussions listed 25 pages in which the word 'Antarctica' was mentioned. However, it is London that hosted in 1895 the sixth International Geographical Congress which was 'commandeered' by the President of the Geographical Society of London,

Sir Clements Markham. He personally organised a day of discussion on Antarctic exploration during which he listed the following important issues concerning Antarctica:

- The key to the future knowledge of terrestrial magnetism lies in the determination of the exact position of the south magnetic pole; for we are not within 300 miles of a guess of its exact position;

- The meteorology of the Antarctic area, of which we know the barest outlines only;

- The geology of the regions in question … reasons to believe that interesting fossils exist.

Also in 1895, Markham stated in the Nineteenth Century magazine that an 'Antarctic expedition must be a naval expedition … because by no other means can the work be effectively done'.

The maps originally produced by the British cartographer and geographer J.G. Barthlomew shown in Fig. 1.2 that have been assembled from the publication of Mills (1905) show the progressive investigations around Antarctica over 145 years until 1905 that aimed at defining its periphery. The blackened areas display the uncharted areas. It shows that even in 1905 little was known about the nature and extent of this continent.

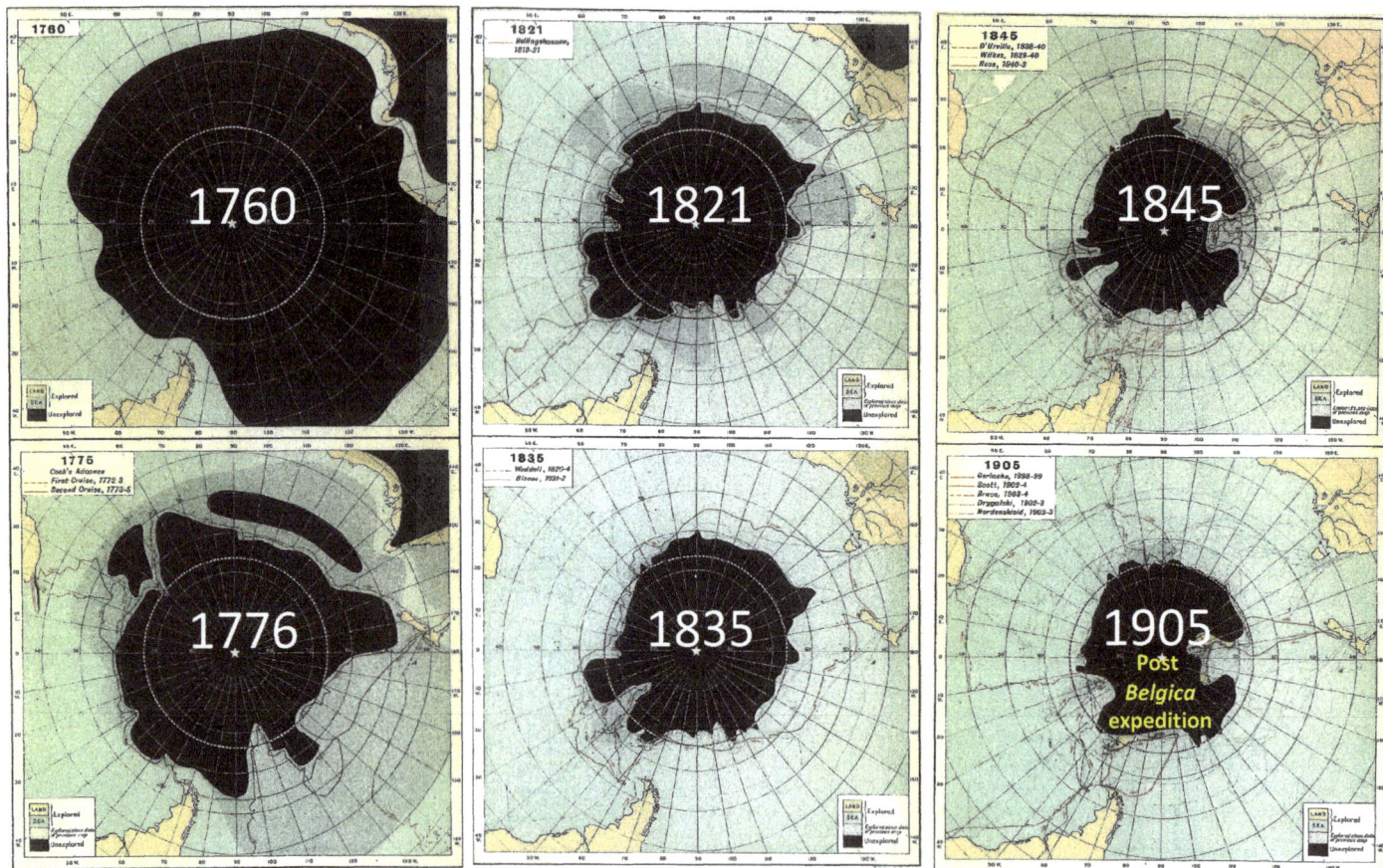

Figure 1.2 Collage of several of the maps prepared by the cartographer and geographer J.G. Bartholomew that accompany the publication by Mills (1905). The black areas clearly show that over 245 years before 1905, little was known about the Antarctic continent.

AN IMPORTANT LANDING ON THE ANTARCTIC CONTINENT

Present at the 1895 Congress was Carsten Borchgrevink who had just returned from Antarctica on-board the *Antarctic* whaling ship with the Norwegian businessman and whaler Henryk Bull. Borchgrevink made a presentation titled: 'The Voyage of the "Antarctic" to Victoria Land' where he stated that they had left Melbourne on 20 September 1894 and sighted Cape Adare on Victoria Land, Antarctica on 16 January 1895, and then landed on Cape Adare on January 23. He explained that *"The peninsula on which we landed at Cape Adare must be some 40 acres in extent…I made a thorough investigation … I believe it to be a place where a future scientific expedition might safely stop even during winter months … At this place, there is a safe situation for houses, tents, and provisions".* This statement obviously attracted much attention. We note that, among the 1212 attendees at the London Congress, there were 19 Belgians, 7 of whom were government delegates, and this included Jean Du Fief, the President and Secretary of the Royal Belgian Geographical *Society* and two members of the Royal Belgian Observatory, M.A. Lancaster and M.J. Vincent. Borchgrevinck talked about returning to Cape Adare, and this started the race to reach Antarctica and spend winter there. In the final report of the London Congress, the secretaries expressed their opinion that the exploration of Antarctic regions, was the greatest piece of geographical exploration still to be undertaken. They believed that such scientific exploration would contribute knowledge in almost every branch of science. The Congress also recommended that this work be undertaken before the close of the century.

SIGNIFICANT STATEMENTS BY SIR JOHN MURRAY

However, prior to this 1885 Congress, Sir John Murray, the highly-regarded Canadian and Scottish oceanographer, marine biologist and limnologist and whose fame was to have been responsible for the publication of some 50 scientific volumes after the 1872-1876 Challenger expedition had presented an address at the Royal Geographical Society in London entitled: 'The renewal of Antarctic Exploration'. In it, he stated that *"our knowledge of the meteorology of the Antarctic regions is limited to a few observations during the summer months in very restricted localities and is therefore most imperfect. One of the most remarkable features in the meteorology of the globe is the low atmospheric pressure, maintained in all seasons, in the Southern Hemisphere south of latitude 40°S, with its inevitable attendant of strong westerly winds, large rain and snowfall, all round the globe in these latitudes".* He also wrote that *"the general result of all the sea-temperatures observed by Cook, Wilkes, Ross, and the Challenger, in the Antarctic Ocean shows that a layer of cold water underlies in summer a thin warm surface stratum and overlies another warm but deeper stratum towards the bottom".* In addition, he said that *"no land animal, and no trace of vegetation - not even a lichen or a piece of seaweed - has been found on land within the Antarctic circle".* He also recorded what the German Professor Neumayer had so long advocated for South Polar exploration: *"it is certain that without an examination and a survey of the magnetic properties in the Antarctic regions, it is utterly hopeless to strive, with any prospect of success, at the advancement of the theory of the Earth's magnetism".*

Murray finally stated that *"it demands rather a steady, continuous, laborious, and systematic exploration of the whole southern region with all the appliances of the modern investigator. This exploration should be undertaken by the Royal Navy. Two ships, not exceeding one thousand tons, should, it seems to me, be fitted out for a whole commission, so as to extend over three summers and two winters. Early in the first season a wintering-party of about ten men should be landed somewhere to the south of Cape Horn, probably about Bismarck Strait at Graham's Land. The expedition should then proceed to Victoria Land, where a second similar party should winter, probably in Macmurdo Bay [sic] near Mount Erebus.* All these statements confirm, that at the Sixth International Geographical Congress, Markham repeated the statements made by Murray a year earlier.

Accompanying Murray (1894)'s publication is a very important map prepared by the best Scottish cartographer at the time, J.G. Bartholomew who provided not only a map around the South Pole showing a poorly delineated Antarctic Continent, but also prominent tracks of ships that had sailed in the region. It is noteworthy that another map appeared posthumously in 1891 in the August Peterman Stieler's Hand Atlas no. 11 and produced by the German publisher Justus Perthes of Gotha. This map, part of which is shown in Fig. 1.3, is by far more detailed than Bartholomew's map and shows many more shipping tracks around Antarctica and also shows the location of Cape Adar [misspelt on that map]. It is very likely that A. de Gerlache had access to this map during the Belgica expedition on which the tracks of the voyages of F. von Bellinsghausen in 1821 (see details further on) are shown as well as that of John Biscoe in 1832 in the vicinity of Graham Land.

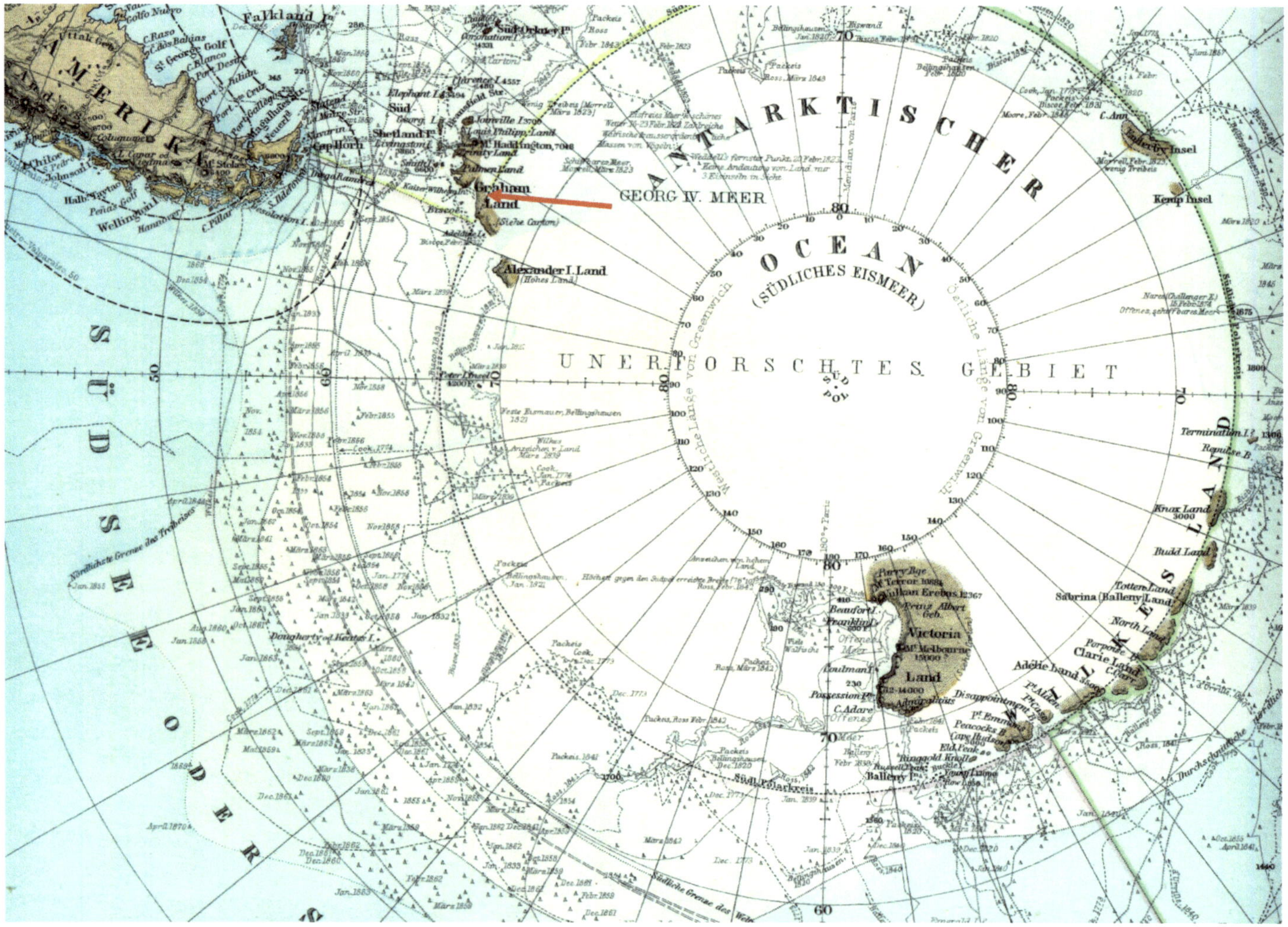

Figure 1.3 Detail of the map produced in 1891 by the publisher Justus Perthes of Gotha in the Stieler's Hand Atlas no.11 that was produced by August Peterman and published posthumously. It clearly shows Graham Land (shown by the red arrow) and the nearby tracks of both expeditions by von Bellinsghausen and Biscoe. This map is more detailed than the one produced in 1895 in Murray's publication. The full map can be downloaded at the Australian National Library web site: https://nla.gov.au/nla.obj-232283422/view.

Next to the main map of Bartholomew, there are five small detailed maps showing (1) oceanic deposits, (2) ice limits and currents, (3) mean temperature February, (4) isobars and winds February, and (5) annual rainfall (Fig. 1.4). In addition, there are also four smaller maps detailing magnetic phenomena after Neumayer (1891) such as inclination (variation), inclination, horizontal intensity and total intensity. The smaller maps 3 and 4 relied on those published in 1891 by Alexander Buchanan based on data acquired during the Challenger expedition.

It is noteworthy also that, prior to his presentation, Murray had written to several eminent scientists such as Professors Alexander Agassiz, a marine zoologist, oceanographer and curator of the Harvard Museum, Ernst Haeckel a German marine biologist, naturalist and famous biological illustrator[1], Julien Thoulet, French mineralogist, naturalist and oceanographer, to solicit their opinion about continuing "the great and noble task of discovering the secrets of the Antarctic regions" (sic Thoulet in Murray 1894)[2]

1 Emil Racovitza paid a visit to Haeckel during the preparation of his participation on the Belgica expedition and exchanged correspondence with him]

2 Henryk Arctowski co-published with J. Thoulet a report on seawater density, and Thoulet himself wrote a report on the determination of seawater density. Both publications appeared in the Résultats du voyage de la Belgica en 1897-1899.]

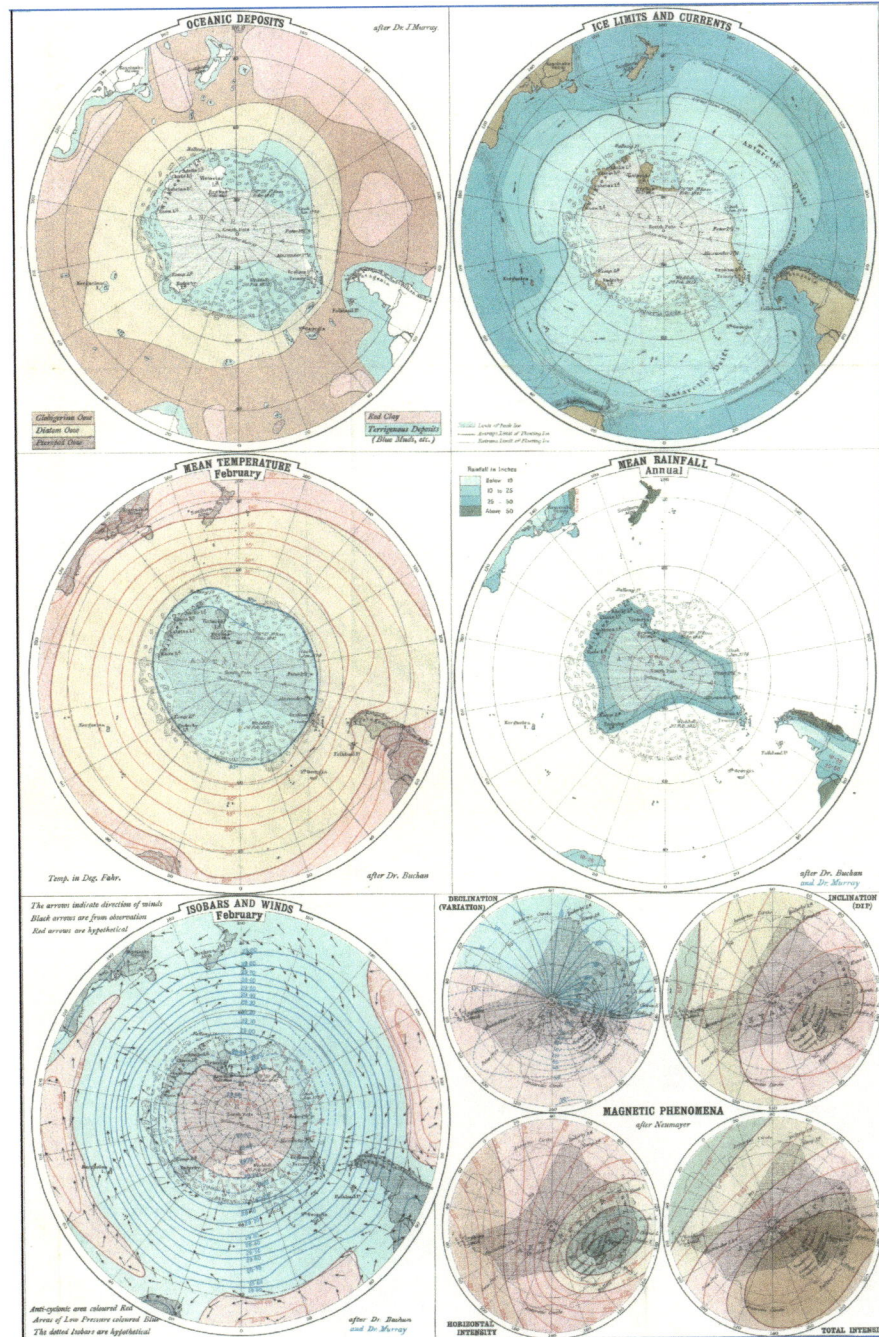

Figure 1.4 Maps extracted from Murray's set of maps prepared by the British cartographer and geographer J. G. Bartholomew in 1894 to document knowledge at the time on regions surrounding the South Pole. Note that some of the information was taken from the meteorological publication by Buchanan (1891) which originally appeared on a Miller projection. John Murray had added further information based on his observations made during the Challenger expedition. The four smaller maps in the bottom right hand corner were based on Georg Neumayer's magnetic maps that appeared in the Atlas of Earth Magnetism (Neumayer, 1891).

and Georg Neumayer, Director of the Oceanic Observatory in Hamburg, a long-term advocate for polar research, who stated that: *"it is certain that without an examination and a survey of the magnetic properties in the Antarctic regions, it is utterly hopeless to strive, with prospects of success, at the advancement of the theory of the Earth's magnetism"* [3].

Buchanan in his new isobaric charts which accompany his *Challenger* Report stated that *"in the Northern Hemisphere the land almost completely surrounds the Arctic Ocean; in the Southern Hemisphere the open ocean completely surrounds the Antarctic continent, and this open ocean carries with the low barometric pressure all round. Now if the low pressure still farther deepened with increase of latitude towards the South Pole, it is certain that the prevailing winds over all these high latitudes would be north-westerly and northerly. But the observations made by Ross, the Challenger, and more recently in latitudes higher than 60° S, by the Dundee whalers and others, quite unanimously tell us that, in these high southern latitudes, the predominating winds are southerly and south-easterly. Thus during the winter of 1892-93, in latitudes higher than 60° S, half of the whole winds recorded by the Diana were south, south-east and east, being directions opposite to the winds which would certainly prevail if pressure diminished steadily to the South Pole. Such surface currents as have been observed in the Antarctic Ocean come also from south and south-east".*

3 Note that Neumayer chaired the International Polar Commission in 1879 and also founded the International Polar Year in 1882-83. There is no indication that Belgians attended those meetings (Lüdecke, 2004).

Figure 1.5 Illustration of the *HMS Endeavour* in the 'Ice Islands' seen on January 17, 1773 and drawn by W. Hodges and engraved by BT Pouncy that appears in Cook's volume 1. Scanned image provided by the Australian National Library with the following catalogue reference: 550672.

THE FIRST ATTEMPTS AT CROSSING THE ANTARCTIC POLAR CIRCLE (67°30'S)

The first expedition to cross the Antarctic Circle was led by Lieutenant James Cook in 1773 (Fig. 1.5). On January 17, 1773 he wrote in his diary: *"At about a ¼ past 11 o'clock we cross'd the Antarctic circle … and are undoubtedly the first and only ship that ever cross'd that line"* (Fig.1.7). *He also added: "Metal and shivers froze fast in the blocks so that it required our utmost effort to get a top-sail down and up; the cold so intense as hardly to be endured, the whole Sea in a manner covered with ice, a hard gale and a thick fog."* (Cook, 1777, volume 1). He crossed the Circle again on January 26, 1777, having reached a latitude of 71°10´S and longitude of 106°54´W. His ship was named '*HMS Endeavour*' (Fig. 1.5), a name that remained over the centuries in the annals of sea exploration.

Fabian Gottlieb von Bellingshausen (Fig. 1.6), the Russian explorer, who discovered the Alexander I Coast in 1821, had two vessels, Vostok and Mirnyi, which sailed on the edge of the sea ice that extended from 69° 10' S, 76°46› W to 68° 30' S, 75°29' W. In fact, examination of Bellingshausen's route map produced by Debenham (1945) shows that the two ships crossed the Antarctic Circle on two occasions (see Fig. 1.7).

Figure 1.6 Portrait of Fabian Gottlieb von Bellingshausen. Modified from Debenham (1945).

Фаддей Фаддеевич Беллинсгаузен
1778- 1852

Figure 1.7 Map showing the route taken by the Russian ships *Vostok* and *Mirnyi* under the command of Fabian Gottlieb von Bellingshausen and Mikhail Lazarev (commander of the *Mirnyi*) during their voyage of circumnavigation around Antarctica. In red is the route when both vessels crossed the Antarctic Circle (shown here in mauve) on two occasions and were in what is now called the Bellingshausen Sea. The two Islands (Peter I and Alexander) were first seen and named during this expedition. Part of the route taken by Captain James Cook in 1774 during which time he crossed the Antarctic Circle and was halted by the pack ice (shown here in pale blue). Map modified from Debenham (1945).

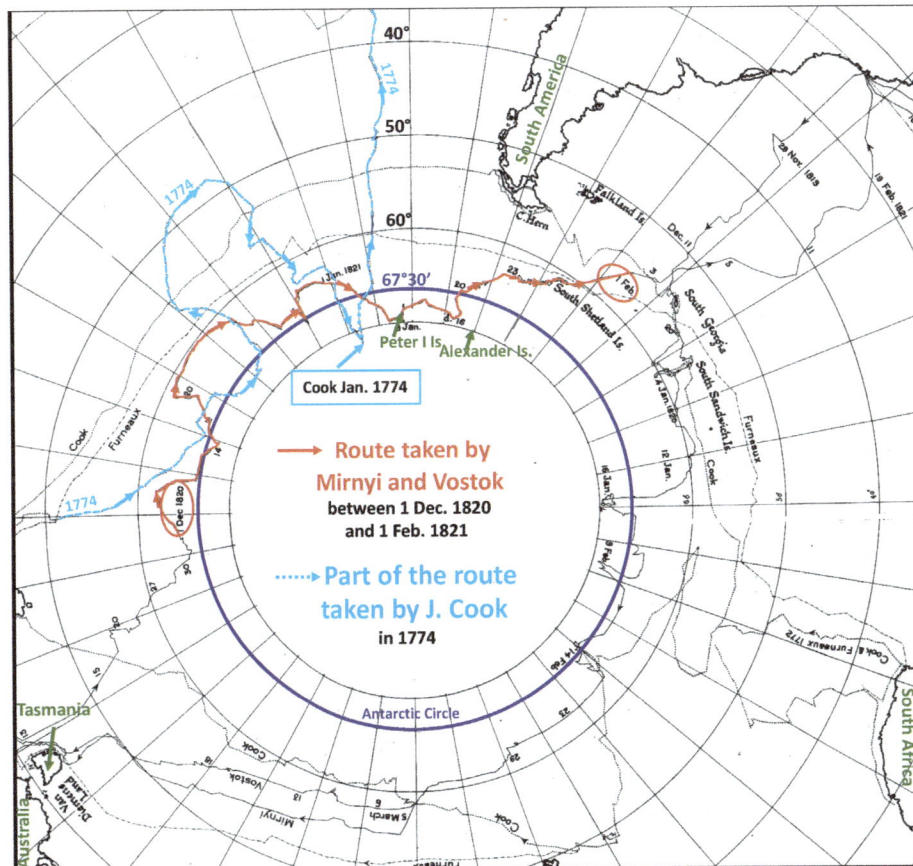

In his diary translated into English, Bellingshausen stated the following paraphrased statements: *"On December 14, 1820 the Antarctic Circle was crossed for a short period of time, but he then returned to it after January 1, 1821.The ships remained below the Circle for 20 days having seen Peter I Island (which was named) between January 9 and 16. On December 9, 1820, the ships were at 64°48'28"S 171°42'46"W and already a large number of icebergs were seen and their number progressively increased. On the 12th, icebergs were 100-120 feet high, and the following day their number decreased but eventually 148 icebergs were seen at 66°04'40"S 165°39'14"W. Once the Antarctic Circle was crossed at 7.30. At that stage, an ice field was seen with a number of large icebergs. On the 14th, at 161°27'30"S 67°15'30"W the ships were in an icefield with flat pieces of ice 5, 6 and 7 feet piled up on each other"*. For more details refer to the review by Tammiksaar (2016) who examined achievements of the Russian polar sailing expedition.

On January 22, 1840, the French Jules Sébastien César Dumont d'Urville reached Antarctica at a location now called Adélie Land and he collected rocks there (date corrected in Hunt et al., 2002). He had two ships, *L'Astrolabe* (Fig.1.8) and *La Zélée*. His position was 66°39'S 140°00'E and is now close to the location of the French Antarctic base called 'Dumont d'Urville Station'. The story tells that Dumont d'Urville risked the life of his crew as well as his ships while sailing in among icebergs and during a storm, but he was determined to reach the continent, which he did. This was the first time that rocks had been collected from Antarctica and thus helped argue that this was a 'true' landmass/continent.

Figure 1.8 (opposite) Sketch of the *Astrolabe* by L. Le Breton and lithographed by E. de Laplante and labelled as 'Astrolabe faisant de l'eau sur un glaçon. 6 Février 1838'. Note also the second vessel *'La Zélée'* in the background on the right. Photo of a print in the author's collection.

Figure 1.9 Sketch of Dumont d'Urville's vessels near Adélie Land with l'*Astrolabe* on the left and *La Zélée* on the right produced by Jean Baptiste Sabatier after a sketch made by Louis le Breton. From Dumont-d'Urville (1846). Published with permission of the National Library of Australia.

Details of figure 1.10 showing on the left people carrying the French flag to claim the site (and its inhabitants, the penguins!); on the right penguins on icebergs.

Figure 1.10 Sketch of Dumont d'Urville's expeditioners taking possession of Terre Adélie on rocky outcrops at Adélie Land waving the French flag to claim the land and its inhabitants (penguins!). Produced by Jean Baptiste Sabatier after a sketch made by Louis le Breton. From Dumont-d'Urville (1846). Published with permission of the National Library of Australia.

Figure 2.1 *HMS Challenger* in the Southern Ocean as painted on February 16 in 1874 (66° 40′ S, 78°15′ E) by Herbert Swire who was a 22 year old Royal Navy sub-lieutenant navigator on the ship during the scientific voyage of 1872-1876. (copied with permission from the State Library of Victoria, with the following caption: 'sailing ship in full sail in waters surrounded by ice floes, sea birds flying low over water on right, penguins jumping off ice floe on left').

Figure 2.2 Sketch of *HMS Challenger* moored on August 28, 1873 at St Paul's Rocks in the Atlantic Ocean, With permission of use from the University of Edinburgh Library Heritage Collections. http://lac-archivesspace-live4.is.ed.ac.uk:8081/repositories/2/digital_objects/168. ADO-2018-0011.

Chapter 2

The Challenger expedition 1873–1876; the first exploration of the world's ocean

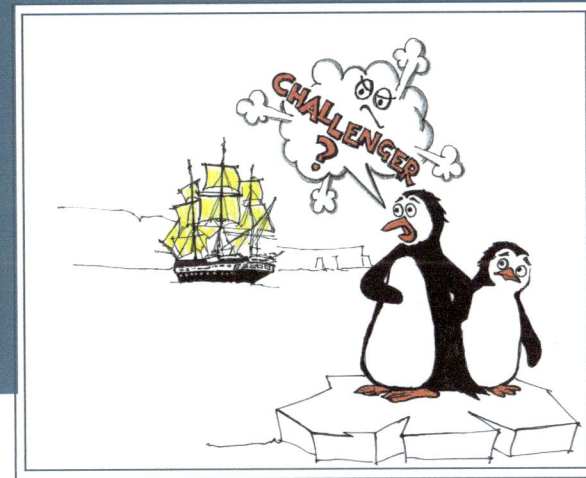

KEY POINTS

- The Challenger expedition of 1873–1876 was the first exploration of the world's oceans and resulted in a huge amount of scientific volumes published detailing all the findings and were written by experts at the time.

- Several of the experts who contributed to the publication of the results from the Challenger expedition were Belgian scientists, and these people played a very important role later on in supporting and guiding the Belgica expedition. These were Paul Pelseneer, Alphonse-Auguste Renard and Edouard Joseph Van Beneden. The latter, soon after the Belgica expedition ended, was in fact the President of the 'Commission de la "Belgica"' that oversaw the publication of all its results. Pelseneer and Renard were also members of that "Commission".

- It is of no surprise therefore that the format of the publications of the Belgica expedition were modelled on the Challenger reports.

Before discussing the Belgica expedition, it is important to set the scene about early exploration in the Southern Ocean and what are now known as Antarctic waters.

The British conducted the first ever global oceanographic expedition that left Portsmouth in December 1872 using a sailing ship from the Royal Navy, re-baptised the *HMS Challenger*. This corvette class vessel was 68.6 m long (Figs. 2.1, 2.2). It was also able to clear its propeller out of the water. During its three and a half year voyage, it sailed 68,890 nautical miles (~127,000 km) with 243 officers, sailors and scientists. This was truly an extraordinary expedition that took several years to prepare. Before the expedition, the ship was transformed to host laboratories, storage areas and accommodation for the large crew.

The objectives of the expedition were:

1. Investigate the physical components of the deep sea;

2. Determine the chemical composition of seawater at all depths, its saline constituents such as dissolved organic matter and particles in suspension; and

3. Ascertain the physical and chemical nature of deep-sea deposits, to trace their origin; and to examine the distribution of organic life, in the deep ocean and at different depths.

The vessel was extremely well equipped with 2 specialised laboratories, one for seawater chemical analyses (Figure 2.3) and the other for sorting, examining and preserving biological specimens (Figure 2.4).

Figure 2.3 The chemical laboratory on-board the *Challenger*, illustrated by Thomas Henry Tizard (1885), and used principally by J.Y. Buchanan to measure seawater density and consequently salinity (Wikimedia Commons).

Figure 2.4 The biology laboratory on-board the *Challenger*, used to process all the biological material collected during the expedition (Wikimedia Commons).

REPORT

ON THE

SCIENTIFIC RESULTS

OF THE

VOYAGE OF H.M.S. CHALLENGER

DURING THE YEARS 1873-76

UNDER THE COMMAND OF

CAPTAIN GEORGE S. NARES, R.N., F.R.S.

AND THE LATE

CAPTAIN FRANK TOURLE THOMSON, R.N.

PREPARED UNDER THE SUPERINTENDENCE OF

THE LATE

Sir C. WYVILLE THOMSON, Knt., F.R.S., &c.

REGIUS PROFESSOR OF NATURAL HISTORY IN THE UNIVERSITY OF EDINBURGH
DIRECTOR OF THE CIVILIAN SCIENTIFIC STAFF ON BOARD

AND NOW OF

JOHN MURRAY, LL.D., Ph.D., &c.

ONE OF THE NATURALISTS OF THE EXPEDITION

DEEP-SEA DEPOSITS

Published by Order of her Majesty's Government

PRINTED FOR HER MAJESTY'S STATIONERY OFFICE

AND SOLD BY

LONDON :—EYRE & SPOTTISWOODE, EAST HARDING STREET, FETTER LANE
EDINBURGH :—JOHN MENZIES & CO.
DUBLIN :—HODGES, FIGGIS, & CO.

1891

Figure 2.5 Cover of the 668 pages volume by J. Murray and A.-F. Renard (1891) on 'Deep-sea deposits'. All volumes and fascicules have the same large format (23 cm x 30.5 cm, being slightly larger than A4).

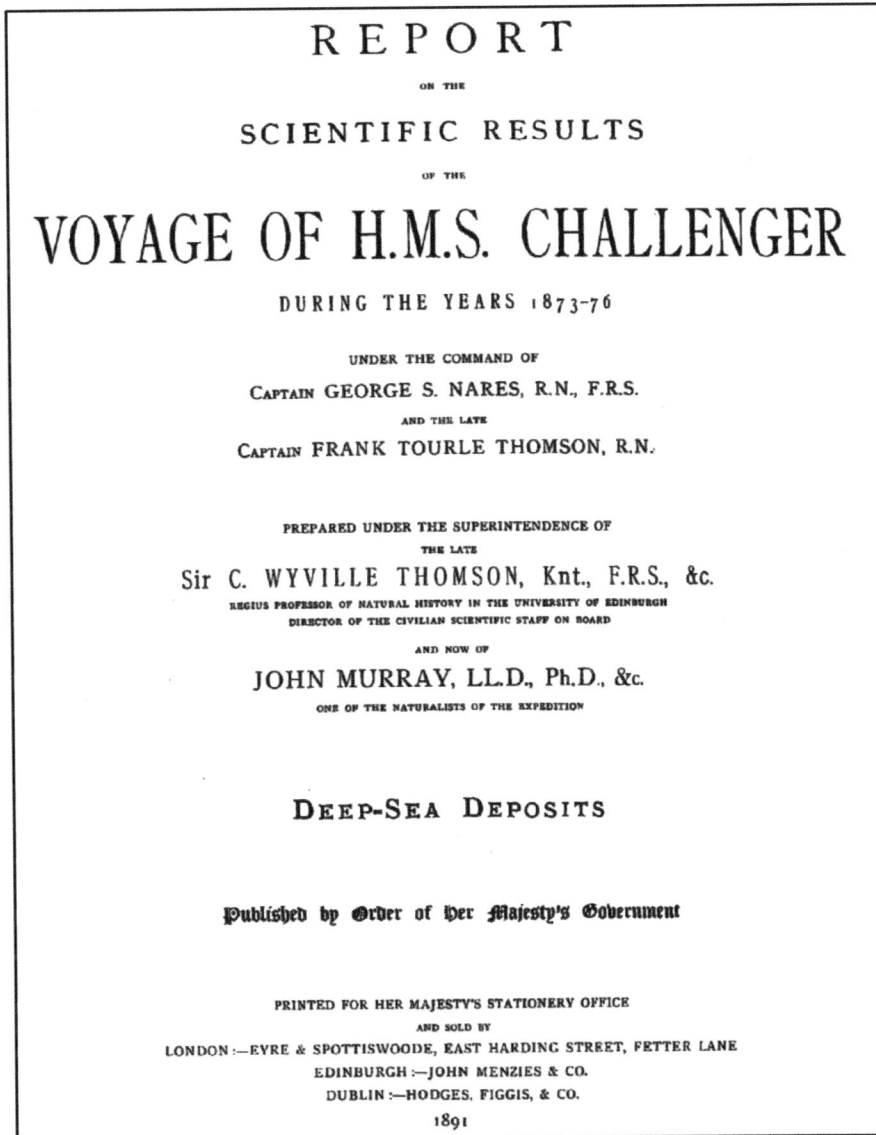

In total, the expedition performed some 492 deep sea soundings, 133 bottom dredges, 151 open water trawls and 263 serial water temperature observations were taken. In addition, about 4,700 new species of marine life were discovered. And more importantly, the results of the expedition were published in a set of 50 volumed reports in the same format (see front page of Murray and Renard (1881) for example in Fig. 2.5) over a twenty year period amounting to a total some 29,572 pages published by some 75 authors. The scientists who analysed the specimens and data amassed during the Challenger expedition were from Britain, Europe and the United States. These reports are currently available in an electronic format at the following web site: http://www.19thcenturyscience.org/HMSC/HMSC-INDEX/index-illustrated.htm

Note that many of these reports contain numerous superb illustrations, charts, surveys, and descriptions of many biological specimens which were new to science at the time. Maps of seawater density for example (Fig. 2.6) and significant investigations of geological material (Fig. 2.7) from the deep sea were published. The publication of these data revolutionised knowledge of the global ocean, which before the expedition was thought to be flat.

Of relevance here (and as will be discussed later) is that several imminent Belgian biologists (who were not on the expedition) contributed to various aspects of organisms and sediments collected during the HMS Challenger expedition. These are: Professor Paul Pelseneer (University of Ghent and Museum of Natural History in Brussels) who contributed three volumes on Pteropoda, one on *Sprirula* and one on deep-sea small molluscs. Professor Alphonse Renard (University of Ghent), who contributed to the large volume on deep-sea deposits with John Murray (op. cit.) after spending several months in Edinburgh. He also published in 1882 a report of the petrology of volcanic rocks from St Paul in the Atlantic Ocean (Renard, 1882). Renard also translated in French books by Charles Darwin on geological investigations in the Beagle Channel.

In addition, the well-known Professor Edouard Van Beneden, who made significant discoveries in cytology, was also an expert on tunicates and was the one to identify their links to chordates. He was obviously in contact with Professor W.S Herdman from the University of Liverpool who contributed three volumes on tunicates as listed among the Challenger reports. In 1895, Pelseneer contributed a large report on the free swimming mollusc *Sprirula* with TH Huxley. In addition, he wrote three volumes on free swimming pteropods (Pelseneer 1887, 1888) and one additional one on deep-sea Mollusca (Pelseneer 1888).

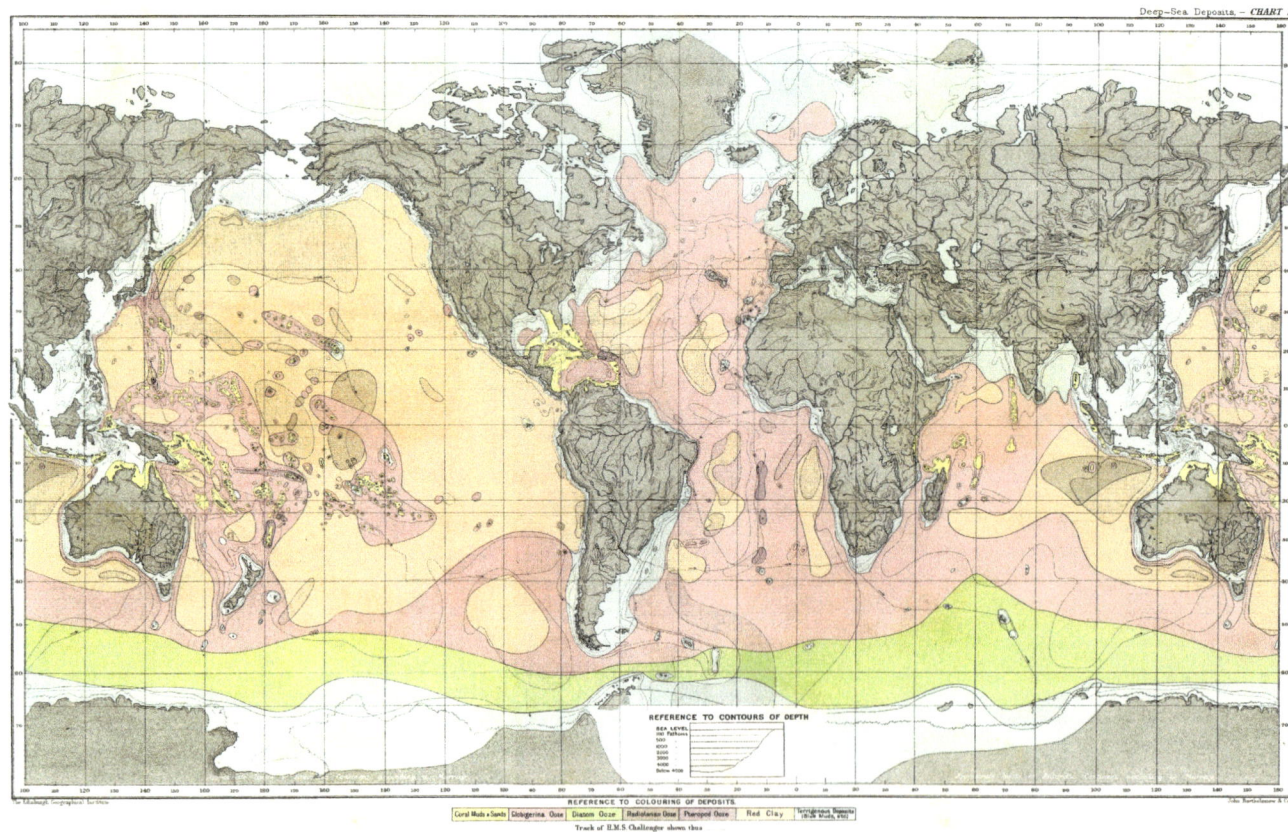

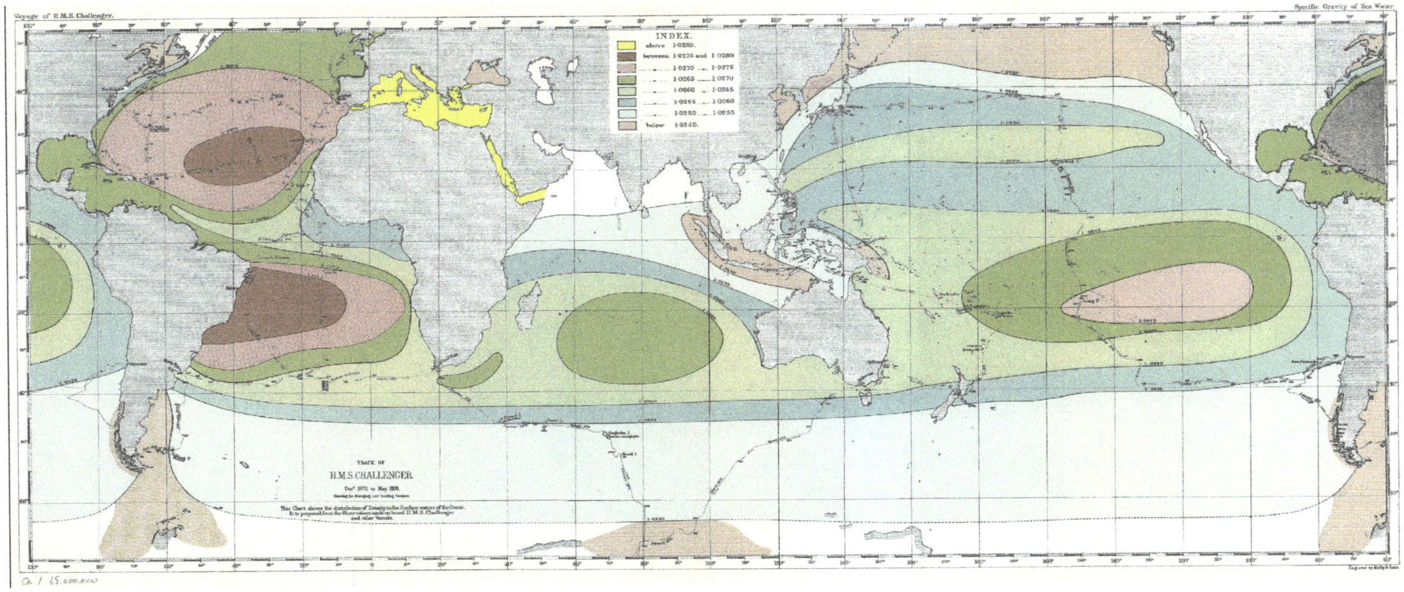

Voyage of H.M.S. Challenger.
Specific Gravity of Sea Water.
INDEX.
TRACK OF
H.M.S. CHALLENGER

Figure 2.6 Map above prepared by the chemist J.Y. Buchanan showing the distribution of seawater density at the surface based mostly on data collected on-board *HMS Challenger*, as well as its track during its three-year ocean-wide voyage. Taken from Buchanan, J.Y. (1884).

Figure 2.7 Map to the left showing for the first time the nature of the sediments and deposits on the world deep oceans. Taken from Murray, J. and Renard, A. F. (1891). Scanned image acquired from the Library of Ghent University, courtesy of Mr Frank Vanlangenhove. Colour schemes at bottom of map, from left to right, are 'Coral Muds & Sands', 'Globigerina Ooze', 'Diatom Ooze', 'Radiolarian Ooze', 'Pteropod Ooze', 'Red Clay', and 'Terrigenous Deposits (Blue Muds etc.)'. Note the lack of information near the Antarctic Peninsula. A substantial summary of the findings shown in this map appeared in French in 1894 in a publication written by Renard in J. Murray J. and A.-F. Renard (1894). Note that Renard spent several months in Edinburgh in 1881-1882 with Murray partly to work on the deep-sea deposits book.

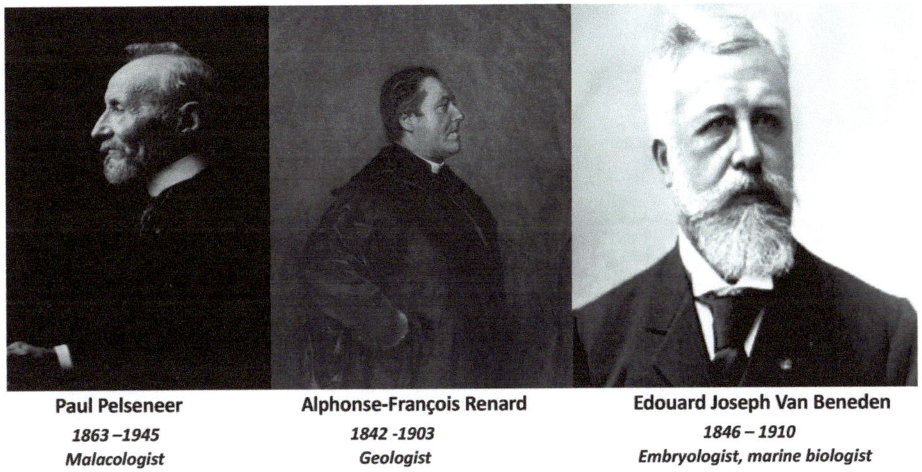

Paul Pelseneer
1863 –1945
Malacologist
Alphonse-François Renard
1842 -1903
Geologist
Edouard Joseph Van Beneden
1846 – 1910
Embryologist, marine biologist

Figure 2.8 Photographs of three of the eminent Belgian scientists who contributed to scientific reports of the *HMS Challenger* (Courtesy of Fons Verheyde, Librarian at VLIZ in Ostend), https://www.ugentmemorialis.be/catalog/000000198, and from the University of Liège Archives. Subsequently they became important advisers for the Belgica expedition by advising the Commander A. de Gerlache and for helping select scientists on the expedition.

Photograph of people downloading snow from the ship to prevent it from sinking due to the extra weight.
Photo obtained from the Emil Racovitza Archive, Library of the Romanian Academy, Cluj-Napoca Branch
and published with permission; 'colorized' using palette.fm/color/filter.

Chapter 3

A dream to conduct a Belgian Antarctic expedition

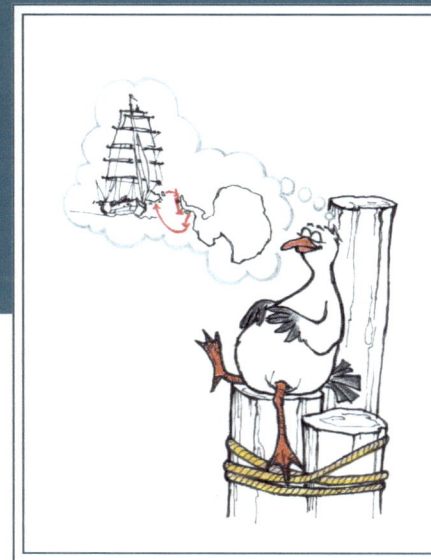

At a young age, the Belgian Adrien de Gerlache de Gomery (from now on refered to as Adrien de Gerlache) made three voyages to the United States as a cabin boy on an ocean liner in 1883 and 1884.

He was only 17 years old and had become fascinated by the sea. After completing one year of studies in Engineering at the University of Brussels, he changed direction and joined the Belgian navy and later graduated from the nautical college in Ostend in Belgium. After that he sailed as a seaman on the British ship *Craigie Burn* to San Francisco in 1887. He also spent time in South America and, upon his return to Europe, he sailed to the Black Sea via Constantinople. Following that he worked for the Holland-America Line and eventually returned to the Belgian navy and worked on the Ostend-Dover ferries where he was promoted to Captain in 1894. He offered his services to the Belgian King Leopold II for an expedition to the Congo, but this was refused. He also wrote a letter to the polar explorer Otto Nordenskjöld asking to join his expedition to Patagonia in 1885-1887, but received no reply.

This non-eventuality led de Gerlache to conceive a private Antarctic expedition. He first consulted Belgian scientists about his proposal to conduct a national expedition in the 'Antarctic Ocean' (sic de Gerlache, 1938). In 1894, he informed several Belgian scientists of his plans. His first 'confidantes' were Paul Pelseneer and A.-F. Renard. Later on, he contacted Edouard Van Benneden and Charles Lagrange. All were very well respected Belgian scientists. In his note to them, he defined a program to make hydrological observations, reckoning and describing coasts, surveys, meteorological observations including that of the aurora australis, plus dredges and observations of the nature of the sea floor, as well as on the pelagic fauna and flora, magnetic observations and photography.

Three of those 'distinguished' Belgian scientists had previously worked on material collected during the famous 'Challenger' expedition that circumnavigated the globe during a 3-year period (see chapter 2). One of them was Professor Paul Pelseneer who was an internationally respected expert malacologist and member of the Belgian Academy of Science. Another Belgian scientist was the geologist-mineralogist Alphonse-François Renard, who was Professor at Ghent University, as well as the biologist Edouard Van Beneden from the University of Liège. de Gerlache also eventually contacted the mathematician and astronomer Charles Henri Lagrange who had a joint astronomy appointment at the Royal Observatory in Uccle, Brussels.

As a result of discussions with those people listed above, de Gerlache wrote in September 1894 a long proposal titled 'Project to organise a Belgian expedition to explore the Antarctic Ocean' seeking support from the Royal Belgian Geographical Society and also to several members of the Royal Academy of Belgium. On January 7, 1895, a non-official reunion was held in the Palais des Académies that was chaired by Lieutenant General Henri-Alexis Brialmont (a politician, military architect and designer of fortifications, who also eventually was on the "Commission de la *Belgica*"). The replies to de Gerlache's proposal were overall favourable, but it remained for him to find sufficient funds, a ship and personnel. Soon after that, de Gerlache went to Sandefjord in Norway. He had been offered a berth on

the *Castor* ship to go from the end of March to early August in the vicinity of Greenland to gain training in high latitude (icy) waters and find out on the practices of chasing seals and whales. In January 1896, a call for funds under a subscription aiming at financially supporting an Antarctic expedition was made under the auspices of the Royal Belgian Geographical Society. Already, in 1895, the industrialist Ernest Solvay, a strong supporter of Belgian science, had donated 25,000 francs [today equivalent to ~US$1 million]. Eventually, in May 1896, the sum of 100,000 francs for an Antarctic expedition was obtained through military fairs, concerts, balloon rides, conferences and support from the Belgian Press. In addition, various cities and provinces donated funds (numbers that follow are in Belgian francs) such as Antwerp: 10,000, Liège: 1,500, Brussels: 1,000, Gent: 1,000, Schaerbeek: 500, Louvain: 300, Ostend: 200, Saint-Josse: 200, Saint-Gilles 200, Molenbeek: 100, plus Brabant and Liège Provinces: 1,000 and 500 respectively (Cabay, 1996). de Gerlache, together with friends, eventually obtained another sum of 100,000 francs from the Belgian government.

By the end of 1894, de Gerlache had contacted Scottish and Norwegian sealing and whaling companies searching for a boat. It is during this voyage that he saw the ship *Patria* which, after numerous negotiations, became available. It was eventually purchased on February 1896 for the sum of 50,000 Norwegian kroner and 'baptised 'with the name of *Belgica*.

THE *PATRIA – BELGICA*

The whaling ship *Patria* was originally built in Svelvig near Drammen in Norway. After its purchase by de Gerlache in 1895, it went to the Christensen Dockyard of Sandefjord in Norway for transformations to be readied for the Belgian polar expedition. de Gerlache remained in Norway during the works and he was accompanied by Emile Danco who was later to join the Belgica expedition. Both learned to ski and prepared themselves for polar conditions.

Figure 3.1. Photograph of Adrien de Gerlache taken in a studio in Christiania (Oslo) which he dedicated to Emil Racovitza (original held in National Romanian Archives, Cluj). de Gerlache would have been 30 years old at the time. Photo 'colorized' using palette.fm/color/filters.

Figure 3.2 Photograph of the *Y.S. Belgica*. Note the chimney linked to a 150 HP motor and the 'crows nest' at the top of the middle mast. The dimensions of the ship were: 34.6 m x 7.54 m x 4.09 m, and when loaded she displaced 590 m³ and was 172 T. Photo courtesy of Dr Pietrzak Agnieska, Ziemi Museum, Warsaw, Poland.

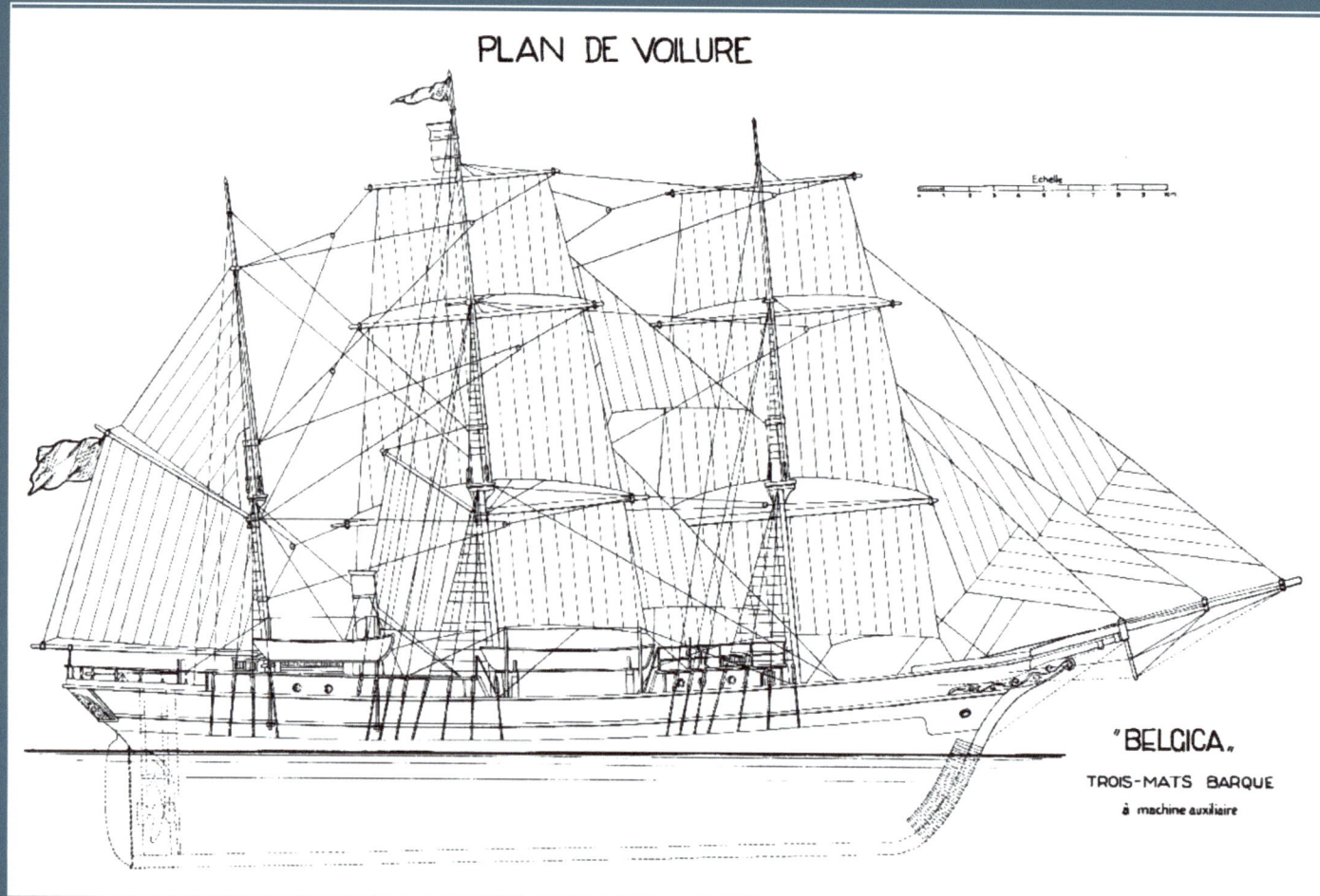

PLAN DE VOILURE

Echelle

"BELGICA."

TROIS-MATS BARQUE

à machine auxiliaire

Figure 4.1 Sketch of the *S.Y. Belgica* showing the characteristic 3-masts sloop with its sails and an auxiliary machine. The total length of the scale represents 10 m (taken from the posthumously-published report of de Gerlache (1938) and edited by Antoni Dobrowolski. The sketches and description of the ship were prepared by G. Verhofstadt, engineer of nautical constructions from the Cockerill worksite in Loboken, Antwerp. Details concerning the transformations of the ship from the original *Patria* are presented in this volume.

Chapter 4
Preparations for the voyage to Antarctica

KEY POINTS

- Description of the *S.Y. Belgica* is provided with sketches that only appeared in 1938. There were no drawings of the ship when she was purchased in Norway by A. de Gerlache on behalf of the Royal Belgian Geographical Society.

- Funds had to be raised to pay, not only for the purchase of the ship, but for the entire operation of the expedition. These were obtained from the Belgian government, benefactors, and though donations from cities, towns as well through organized fairs all across Belgium.

- The money raised from all sources amounted to approximately US$ 15 Million, and the ship cost ~ US$ 3 Million and the expedition ~ US$ 12.5 Million.

- The two scientists Emil Racovitza and Henryk Arctowski spent well over one year to prepare the expedition by visiting numerous experts and facilities in Europe.

- Racovitza was involved in much of the purchasing of equipment. There was even a possibility that a hot air balloon would be purchased but this did not eventuate. Likewise, Danco also spent time not only purchasing equipment but also trained to use them in several locations such as Vienna, Berlin, Hamburg, Wilhelmshaven and Paris.

- The socialite Mrs Léonie Osterrieth of Antwerp was the major benefactor who also organized events to raise funds.

- Soon after the expedition, King Leopold II signed a royal degree to form a 'Commission de la Belgica' so as to order the Belgian Government to fund the publication on the results of the expedition. The membership of this commission consisted of well-known scientists and dignities from Belgium. This secured the publication of all the results of the expedition which amounted to well over 3,000 pages.

After many negotiations, on July 4, 1896 the *Belgica* arrived on July 4, 1896 in Sandefjord in Norway at its Christensen shipyard displaying a Belgian flag.

THE *S.Y. BELGICA*

During the summer and autumn of that year, modifications were carried out on the ship. Work was interrupted during winter but by June 1897, the ship was ready to sail for a period of six years as approved by the Norwegian Veritas Bureau. During those preparations, de Gerlache negotiated with the Director of the Danish hydrographic office for obtaining deep-sea fishing equipment which was granted to him. Material consisted of a galvanised iron 2,000 m long cable, steam winch, pulleys etc. Already during that time, three recruited members of the expedition (Henryk Arctowski, Emil Racovitza and Emile Danco) were given tasks to prepare for the expedition (see information later).

PLAN D'ENSEMBLE

COUPE EN ELEVATION

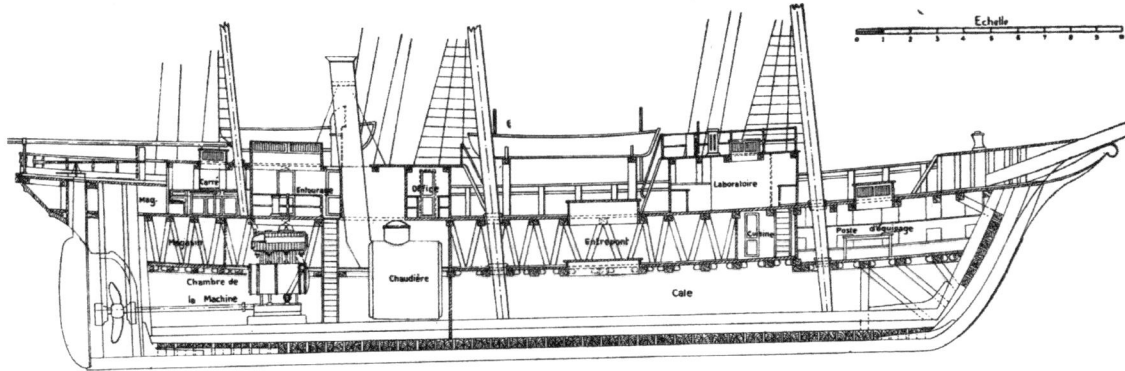

VUE EN PLAN

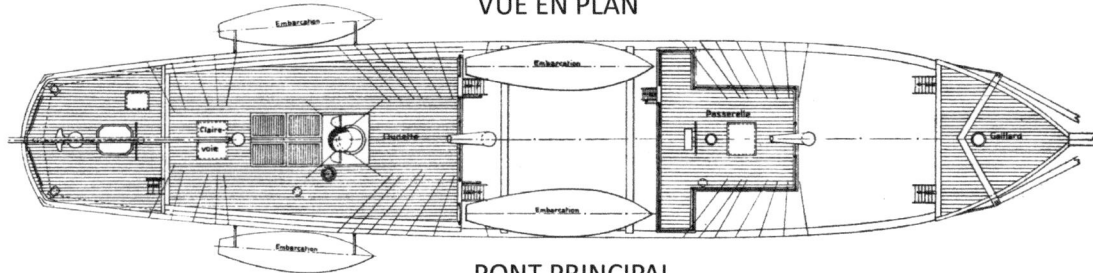

PONT PRINCIPAL

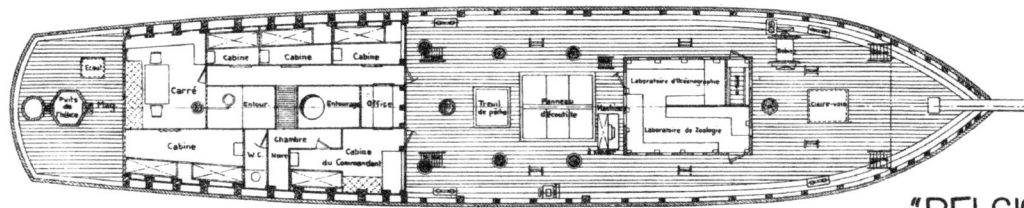

"BELGICA„

TROIS-MATS BARQUE

à machine auxiliaire.

ENTREPONT

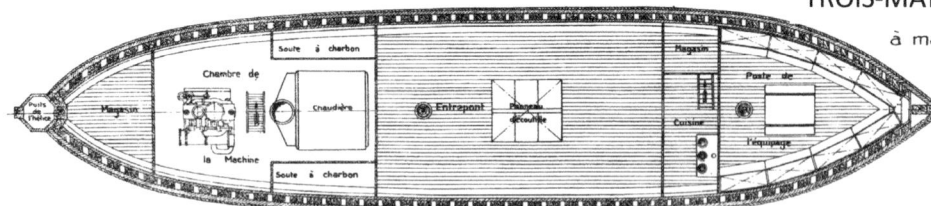

Figure 4.2 Sketches of the *Belgica* showing at the top details of the interior seen inside view; below is the view from above, followed by details of the main deck and finally below the lower deck. The total length of the scale represents 10 m (taken and slightly modified from the posthumously published report of de Gerlache (1938) and edited by Antoni Dobrowolski. The sketches and description of the ship were prepared by G. Verhofstadt (see caption for Fig. 4.1).

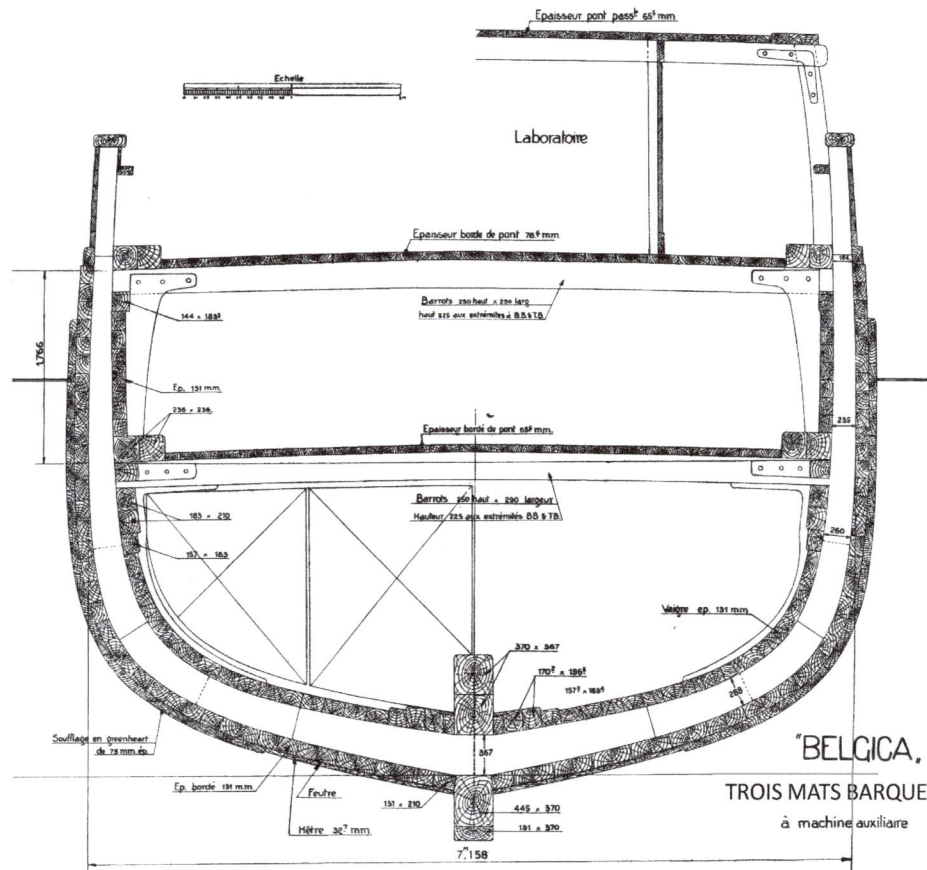

COUPE AU MAITRE

"BELGICA
TROIS MATS BARQUE
à machine auxiliaire

Figure 4.3 Cross section through the ship's hull to show the important double hull especially made to sail through icy conditions. On the bottom left hand corner, three significant features are labelled: (1) soufflage en greenwood 75 mm thick (an outer wall of greenheart wood which is a very dense and strongest hardwood sourced from South America); (2) feutre (felt); (3) hêtre 32.7 mm thick (beech tree) at the very bottom of the hull; and Ep. bordé 131 mm (Pine) above the felt. In addition the inner wooden frame labelled 'vaigre' is 131 mm thick; no type of wood is listed. The entire scale at the top represents 2 m. (Taken and slightly modified from de Gerlache, 1938). Later, some strips of cast iron (fonte) were placed to cover the bow to enable to go through sea ice. The bow was shaped so as to climb over sea ice and break it with its weight. The ship was also carrying four small boats, two of which were whaling boats. At the top, there is also a crow's nest as an observation post.

Importantly, two laboratories were installed, one dedicated for oceanography and the other for zoology. At the front are the kitchen and store, plus the sailors' quarters. At the back are the captain's cabin, four staff cabins, a quarter (carré) room, an office and a dark room. At the extreme end of the ship there is a lid giving access to the propeller. On the bridge, there is a hand-held machine to move the rudder by means of chains and rods.

In June 1897, Sir Clements Markham visited the shipyard to inspect the ship as did Fridtjof Nansen, Otto Sverdrup and Hjalmar Johansen who had all participated in the *Fram* expedition in 1893-1896. de Gerlache in his book stated that Nansen had provided him with much advice and very useful information about venturing in polar waters, clothing and food for the expedition.

In Sandefjord, de Gerlache also arranged for two demountable huts to be built. These were to be used at Cape Adare for the wintering party (see chapter 5). Eventually, one of those huts was displayed on the wharf in Antwerp to show visitors who visited the ship (Fig. 4.4) (see mention in the following section).

De Gerlache also managed to purchase at a good price from the Danish Government much of the fishing/dredging equipment that had been used previously on the ship *Ingolf* during oceanographic campaigns in Greenland waters in 1895 and 1896.

On its way from Norway to Antwerp, the *Belgica* ran aground on a sand bank and was stranded there. Such an event was mentioned by E. Danco in a letter to E. Racovitza written on June 29, 1897 from Den Helde when the weather was very foggy[2].

2 Examination of Dutch rescue archives reports that on June 30, 1897 the tug Titan (owned by the company Wijsmuller) pulled the *Belgica* off grounds called "*Noordergronden*". However, these are shallows off the barrier island Terschelling, two islands east of Texel. (*pers. comm.* Klaas C. Kikkert to J-B. Stuut, NIOZ and passed onto P. De Deckker). Delays were caused because the *Belgica* had to pay for the costs of the rescue, some 6000 Florins at the time.

Table 4.1 Details of the finances of the Belgica expedition as presented by Adrien de Gerlache in the 1st edition of his book published in 1902. It has proven very difficult to 'translate' those costs in today's dollars for the equivalence from the Belgian currency (francs) in 1897. Broad variations unfortunately differ between different banks.

Figure 4.4. (Opposite) One of the prefabricated huts on display in Antwerp Harbour when the public and dignitaries were able to visit the ship and some of its displayed equipment. The hut was to be used at Cape Adare but several panels were instead used to provide extra shelter when the ship was trapped in sea ice. Original from the MAS in Antwerp (AS1962.024.002) provided by Rita Jalen.

The ship was able to carry some 160 tonnes of coal, 40 to be used for heating, and about 40 tonnes of food, most of which was packed in some 10,000 tin (fer blanc) boxes.

FUNDS RAISED FOR THE EXPEDITION AND COSTS

Funding the expedition proved to be a challenging task. The first person to donate funds was the industrial Ernest Solvay who sponsored many scientific activities in Belgium. His donation of a hefty 25,000 Belgian francs at the very beginning proved a very important move so as to encourage not only the Belgian government but also cities, towns and people and dignitaries. The Belgian King Leopold II at first gave no money, but only his blessing, His interests lied in his 'private' property that was the Congo, 80 times the size of Belgium, where he could make profits, especially through the rubber industry. He did not support an expedition to Antarctica as he could not see this expedition returning a profit.

There were numerous fêtes, fairs and solicited donations, several of which occurred as the departure of the *Belgica* was approaching and, in particular in Antwerp, a distinguished socialite Mrs Léonie Osterrieth (Fig. 4.5, and check Janzing J., 2020), who was an art collector and patron of numerous organisations. She readily organised fund raising activities (Figs. 4.6 to 4.8).

Funding of the *Belgica* expedition

INTAKE:		Belgian francs in 1897	Equivalent in US$ in 2020
Initial subscription [Ernest Solvay, Dec 1894]		25,000	
Subscriptions of scientific societies and individuals		67,476	
Subsidy from the Belgian Government		201,000	
Subsidies from Provincial Councils		1,500	
Subsidies from Provincial shires [communes]		16,000	
Profits from raising funds activities [fêtes]		16,007	
Subscriptions obtained on the ship before departure		6,520	
Subscriptions obtained during the voyage		256	
Subscriptions from members of the expedition		11,211	
	TOTAL:	344,971	≈ $15 Million
EXPENSES:			
Vessel, inventory, engines, instruments		142,444	Ship: ≈ $3 Million
Personnel (salary, clothes etc)		63,871	
Food		31,839	
Repairs of ship and material		16,232	
Coal, oil etc		19,265	
Port fees, pilotage etc		1,767	
Administration (travel, ports, entry fees, telegrams)		7,167	
Costs of exploration in Patagonia		6,028	
	SUB-TOTAL:	282,617	≈ 12.5 Million
SURPLUS spent on:			
Belgica Prize		41,000	
Gratuities to 13 members of the expedition		13,000	
Various gifts to charities		854	
Gift to the Belgian Maritime League		1,500	
	TOTAL:	344,971	

Figure 4.5 Photograph of the socialite Mrs Léonie Osterrieth who generously supported the Belgica expedition. She was a resident of Antwerp and she left a huge amount of documents in the city of Antwerp Felix Archief about whom she met, supported over the years and who visited her. She was affectionately called 'Madame O.' or 'Madame Antarctique' by members of the Belgica expedition as written in letters addressed to her. Photo from the MAS Museum archives (AS1955.111.002) and used with permission and 'colorized' using palette.fm/color/filters.

Figure 4.7 (Opposite) Copy of a poster advertising the Venitian Fair in support of the Belgica expedition that was to be help on August 12, 1898, just five days before the departure of the expedition. It involved nautical games, explosion of underwater mines, making a 400 m bridge, gymnastic exercises, living pictures, lampoon parade, luminous fountains, concerts, luminous projections and fireworks. The Antwerp belfry is visible in the background. Copied with permission from FelixArchief, Antwerp City Archives (1114#17).

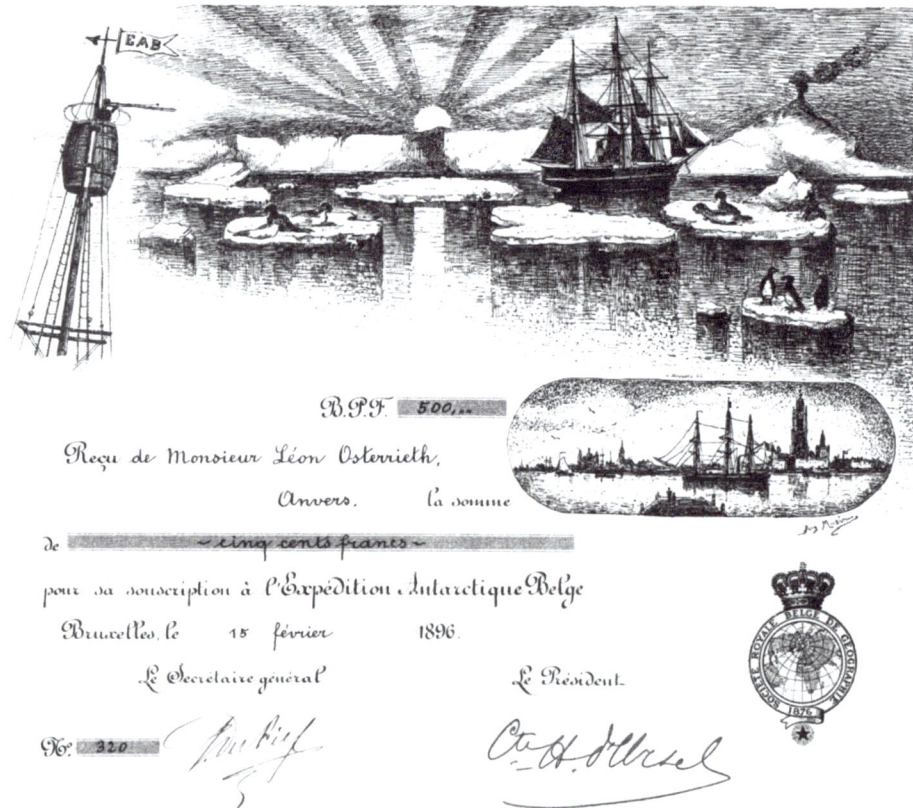

Figure 4.6 Copy of one of the receipts found in Mrs Osterrieth's archives held in the Felix Archief in Antwerp that testifies of the amount of money donated towards the Belgica expedition. In this case, 500 Belgian francs gifted by Léon Osterreith. Note the preempted view of the ship in Antarctic waters, the ship and its crows nest above which the initials EAB refer to the 'Expédition Antarctique Belge'. The small window on the right shows the ship in Antwerp harbour with its belfry in the background. The signatures are those of Jean Du Fief Secretary General of the Royal Belgian Geographical Society and that of its President Count Hippolyte d'Ursel. Note the sketch of an active volcano, likely eluding to Mount Erebus found near Cape Adare where the ship was meant to go. Copied with permission from FelixArchief, Antwerp City Archives (1114#26-021).

PREPARATIONS FOR THE EXPEDITION

Emil Racovitza, after having been appointed as a member of the Belgica expedition, spent well over one year to help towards the preparations of the expedition. It is understood that it was Henryk Arctowski, through advice of two Polish friends in Paris who had heard of the reputation of the biologist Emil Racovitza, that he suggested to A. de Gerlache that he be selected to participate in the expedition (Marinescu, 2019). Racovitza's mentor Professor Henri de Lacaze-Duthiers also recommended Racovitza to his colleague in Liège Professor Edouard Van Beneden about the scientific prowess of the Romanian biologist.

On numerous occasions Racovitza travelled across Europe in search of information, guidance and purchasing the best possible and suitable equipment. This effort contributed to the eventual success of the expedition. In among the archives held in the Museum of Natural History Museum in Brussels, the Antipa Museum and the National Romanian Archives held in Cluj, there is ample evidence that he corresponded with Adrien de Gerlache on numerous occasions, especially concerning the purchasing of equipment. For example, he went to Kiel in Germany to examine Hansen nets, to Monaco to examine the Prince of Monaco's yacht, to Naples to learn techniques to preserve marine animals and on how to perform deep-sea dredgings. He also visited Professor E. Haeckel in Leipzig to discuss about plankton collections and relevant collecting tools. In Jena in Germany, he visited Professor Johannes Walther to discuss general concepts in oceanography. He also went to the Zeiss factory to discuss special microscopy and camera tele-objective lenses, one to be built especially for the expedition, and which was a gift to the expedition.

Racovitza also travelled to Vienna to see Professor Edward Suess the geologist where Henryk Arctowski also had been at least twice. He spent much time in Belgium talking to Professors Van Beneden and Pelseneer (see reference to them in chapter 3 for discussions on how to prepare the laboratory on the ship). Having studied in Paris for his PhD, it was not difficult for him to meet people there and to order many items of equipment for collecting plankton as well as making numerous purchases to equip not only people but also the ship that was to go in Antarctic waters.

Among his numerous trips to Paris, he aimed at examining the possibility of purchasing a hot air baloon and on how to make a suitable gas for it. The idea was eventually abandoned due to the large quantity of acid and iron to make gas, the weight and volume of the balloon and also the prohibitive costs for such a purchase. He also linked numerous times with Henryk Arctowski concerning the purchasing of the equipment, such as nets purchased from Copenhagen. Originally, Racovitza been designated as the expedition photographer after having purchased much of the photographic equipment. The medical doctor Frederick A. Cook, who eventually joined the expedition in Rio de Janeiro, took on the role of phototographer for the expedition. He also developed all the photos on the ship. Interestingly, a copy of all the photos taken by Cook during the expedition were to have been given to the Royal Geographical Society in Brussels as stipulated by the latter before the expedition departed, but such photos have not been found. I am aware also that several items that were in store among the collections of the Society have disappeared, sadly (Professor Paul Bettens, pers. comm. to the author).

GRANDE
FÊTE VÉNITIENNE
au PARC.

Le Jeudi 12 Août, de 6 à 11 heures du soir

en faveur de l'expédition de " LA BELGICA "

sous la présidence d'honneur de Monsieur le Lieutenant général Chevalier Marchal, commandant de la 2e circonscription militaire, Monsieur le baron Osy de Zegwaert, gouverneur de la province, Monsieur J. Van Ryswyck, bourgmestre de la ville d'Anvers, Monsieur le général Constant Willaert, commandant supérieur de la garde civique d'Anvers.

PROGRAMME

Jeux Nautiques

Explosion de mines sous marines et fouganes
par la compagnie de télégraphistes de place et artificiers du génie.

Pont de 400 mètres
par la compagnie de pontonniers d'artillerie

Exercices Gymnastiques
par les sociétés Anversoises de la Fédération Belge de gymnastique

Tableaux Vivants

Lanterne Parade
par les sociétés cyclistes de la ville; tour du parc et traversée du pont de bateaux.

Fontaines Lumineuses

Des Concerts
seront donnés de 6 à 10 1/2 heures
sur le grand kiosque.
sur un second kiosque près de l'Ile et sur un pont flottant.

Illumination.

Projections Lumineuses.
par la compagnie de télégraphistes de place et d'artificiers du génie.

FEU D'ARTIFICE

Figure 4.8 Copy of a poster in both languages (Flemish version overleaf) advertising the Venitian Fair in support of the Belgica expedition, listing all the planned activities in the Parc in Antwerp on August 12, 1897. Copied with permission from FelixArchief, Antwerp City Archives (1114#17-002).

GROOT
✦ AVONDFEEST ✦
in het PARK.

Op Donderdag 12 Augustus, van 6 tot 11 uren

ter bestrijding der reiskosten van het schip " BELGICA "

onder het eerevoorzitterschap van den heer Ridder Marchal, generaal bevelhebber van het 2e krijgsgebied, van den heer baron Osy van Zegwaert, gouverneur der provincie, van den heer Jan Van Ryswyck, burgemeester van Antwerpen, van den heer Constant Willaert, generaal bevelhebber der burgerwacht van Antwerpen.

PROGRAMME

Waterspelen.

Ontploffing van Watermijnen

door de telegraphisten en vuurwerkers der genie.

Brug van 400 meters op booten

door de pontonniers der artillerie

Turnoefeningen

door de leden der Antwerpsche maatschappijen van den Belgischen Turnbond.

Levende Tafereelen

Wielrijders Lichtstoet

door de Antwerpsche maatschappijen van wielrijders.

Verlichte Waterstralen

Muziek uitvoeringen van 6 tot 10 ¹/₂ u.

op het groot kiosk.
op een tweede kiosk nabij het eiland,
en op een vlot.

Verlichtingen en Lichtstralen

VUURWERK.

Henryk Arctowski was originally appointed to be the scientific leader of the expedition. He had studied at the University of Liège in Belgium and his mentor, Professor Walthère Victor Spring, who was a well-known experimental chemist and already in 1885-6 was a forerunner in the study of the Greenhouse Effect (Spring and Roland, 1886; Demarée and Verheyden, 2016), advised him on sea water chemistry and lent him many instruments for the expedition. Arctowski also spent much time to calibrate thermometers and hygrometers which he used during the expedition (see Chapter 8). He spent quite a bit of time in London, and it is likely that he must have spent quite some time with people such as Clements R. Markham (President of the Royal Geographical Society) and John Murray (the oceanographer involved with the Challenger expedition) (refer to Chapters 1, 2). We are aware that the British 'establishment' also provided some 200 maritime maps to Adrien de Gerlache to help with his expedition. The Royal Society of London gave the 50 volumes of the Challenger expedition, and these must have been held in Racovitza's biological laboratory on the ship. He also purchased privately some 100 scientific volumes to aid in his study of organisms (Marinescu, 2019). Finally, Marinescu (2019) stated that many books of all kinds were also brought to the ship for relaxation such as novels in numerous languages. Emile Danco also spent time not only purchasing equipment but also trained to use them in Vienna, Berlin, Hamburg, Wilhelmshaven and Paris.

Some 6 large saws were also bought to cut the sea ice. Among the exhibits on the Belgica expedition in the Museum of Natural History Museum in Brussels, there is a display of the original plans of the scientific laboratories on the ship designed by Arctowski.

All these facts clearly indicate that the expedition was not only well equipped with scientific equipments, but extremely well prepared.

At the return of the expedition, the Belgian King Leopold II signed a royal decree on December 4, 1899 thus forming the 'Commission of the Belgica' that would organise and fund the publication of the results of the Belgian Antarctic Expedition. This was to be paid by the Belgian Government. The list of members of that Commission was tabled in the decree; it consisted of many well-known scientists and dignities from Belgium, as well as some members of the expedition (see list in de Gerlache, 1938, p. 249-250).

Figure 4.9 Pages detailing some of the purchases made by E. Racovitza in preparation for the expedition. The left panel lists chemicals he ordered and that must have been received just three days before the start of the expedition. The right panel lists some equipment that must have been delivered just two days before departure (published with permission from the National Archives of Romania in Cluj).

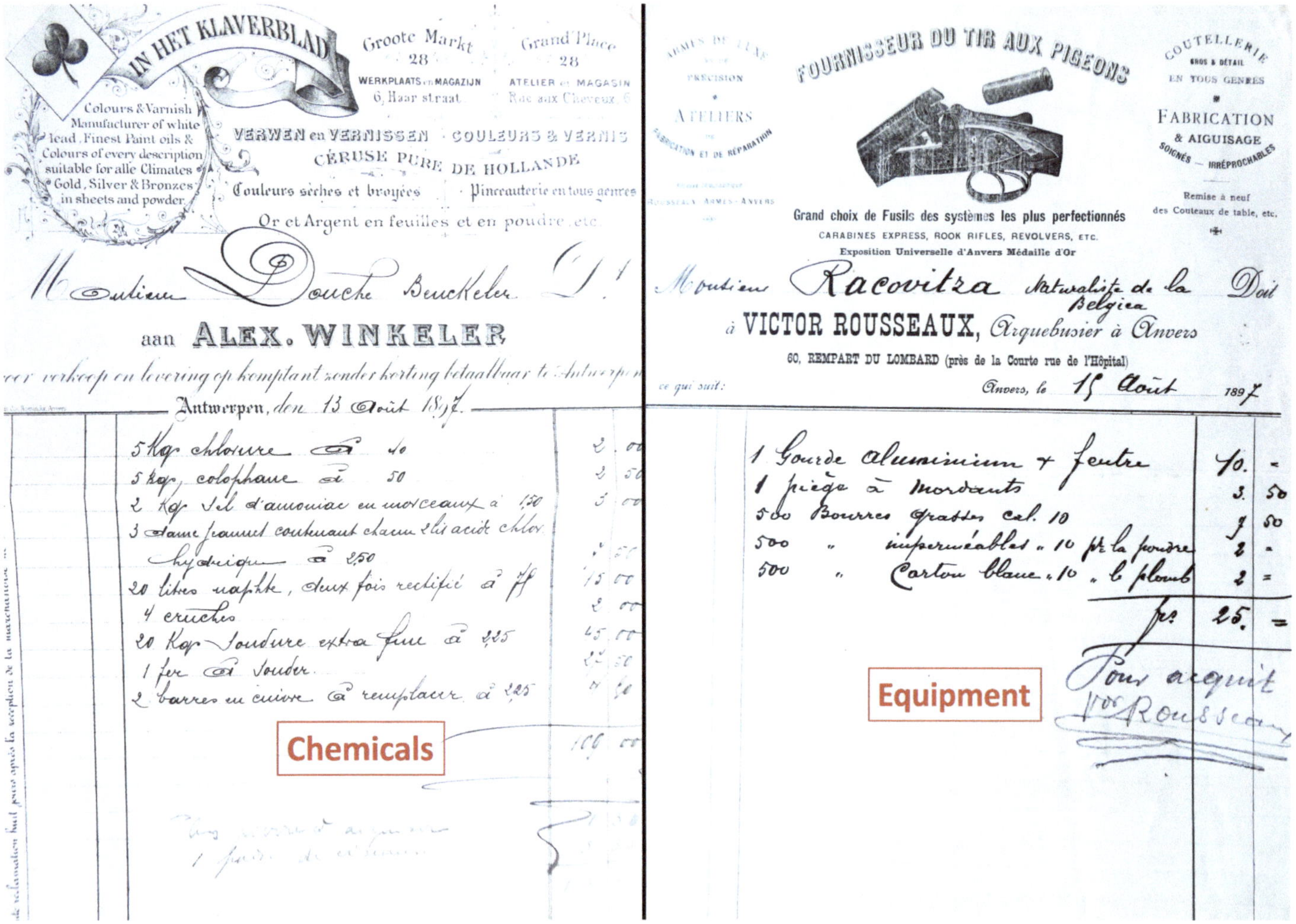

Figure 4.10 The left panel details Racovitza's order for a gun and accessories made through A. Guinard, a firm in Paris. In the right panel, there is a list of oceanographic equipment ordered by Racovitza such as cables, plankton nets, dredges as well as 8,000 glass tubes and 1,500 litres of alcohol, both for preserving biological material. This included also harpoons and related equipment (published with permission from the National Archives of Romania in Cluj).

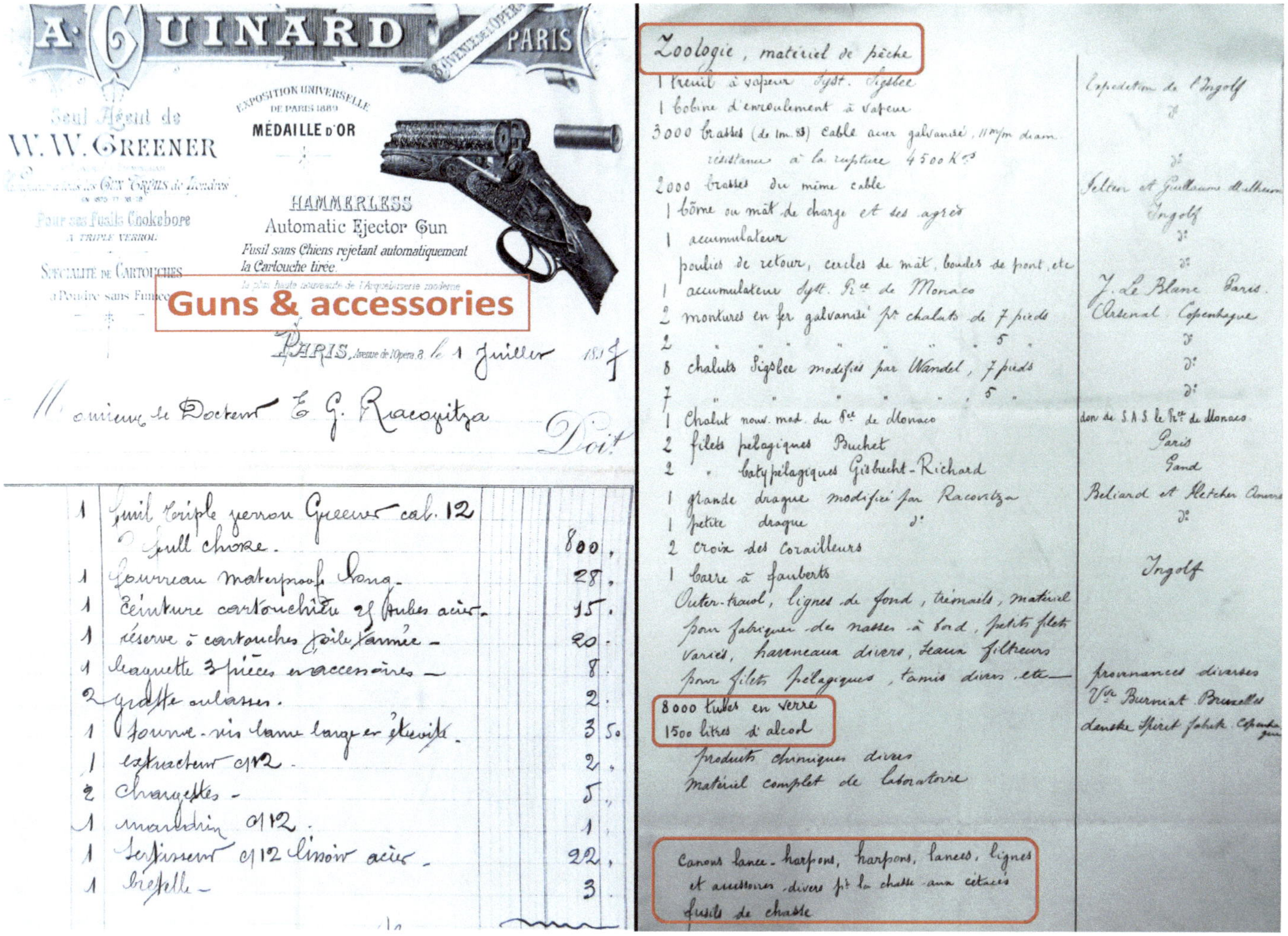

Photographs of the scientists who took part in the Belgica expedition, as well as Commander A. de Gerlache and first mate R. Amundsen. Those photos were taken before departure, except for F. Cook who joined the ship in Rio de Janeiro and A. Dobrowolski who was hired at the last minute. Most photos were obtained from the MAS in Antwerp, catalogue 29.178 04-11 and used with permission, and processed with Photoshop©, and 'colorized' using palette.fm. For more details check the caption of fig. 5.1.

Chapter 5

The Belgica personnel, celebrations in Antwerp prior to departure and departure for Antarctic waters

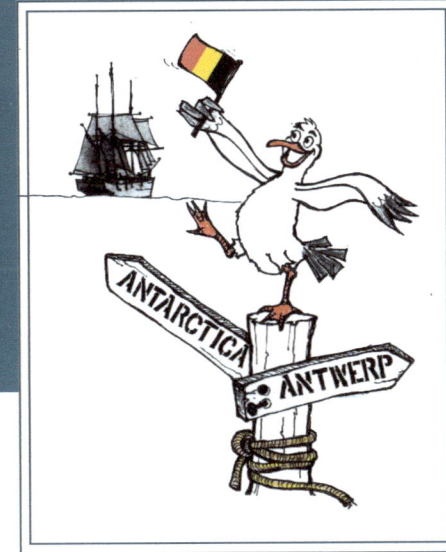

KEY POINTS

- The list of the personnel of the Belgica expedition is provided. There were 19 people, 9 Belgians: de Gerlache, Lecointe, Danco, Melaerts, Somers, Van Rysselberghe, Michotte, Dufour and Van Mirlo; 6 Norwegians: Amundsen, Tollefsen, Johansen, Knudsen, Koren and Wiencke; 2 Polish: Arctowski and Dobrowolski; 1 Romanian: Racovitza and 1 American: Cook. It was therefore a truly international expedition.

- There were several festivities organised in Antwerp before departure with many dignitaries and supporters attending and much needed money was still being raised at this time

- The original plan as agreed by the Royal Geographical Society of Belgium in Brussels is shown on a map, with another one detailing where the ship eventually went.

Members of the Belgica expedition

The original contingent of the expedition was much larger than when the ship departed from Punta Arenas on its way to the Beagle Channel and eventually Antarctic waters. Reasons for those decreased numbers are several, but when the ship left Antwerp on August 14 1897, it eventually had to stop in Ostend due to mechanical failure and repairs, several sailors had already left the ship. Later on, during the voyage in the Atlantic Ocean down to Rio de Janeiro in Brazil and eventually Punta Arenas in Chile, other sailors were asked to leave due to insubordination and poor behaviour caused by drunkedness. Importantly, the cook was asked to leave and a replacement had to be found. The medical doctor was offered a place on the expedition as it was about to leave Antwerp because the selected doctor withdrew at the last minute. Another medical doctor had been selected by the Geographical Society, but de Gerlache refused to take him on. The final medical officer (F.A. Cook) was North American and eventually joined the expedition in Rio. He had prior experience in the Arctic region. Due to the resignations of several sailors in Antwerp, the Polish Antoni Dobrowolski, who had originally been rejected for participation on the expedition, was offered a last minute placement on the ship. He joined as a sailor, but later was promoted to associate scientist.

The Commander of the expedition was obviously **Adrien de Gerlache de Gomery** (from now on called Adrien De Gerlache for simplicity) who had conceived the expedition, purchased the ship in Norway with funds assembled by the Royal Belgian Geographical Society and re-baptised it from 'Patria' to 'Belgica'.

He also spent much time in Norway consulting Arctic explorers such as Fridtjof Nansen (who was also a zoologist) and visited shipyards so as to determine what equipment to install on the ship and on how to strengthen it for sailing in icy waters and possibly frozen ones in the pack-ice. He also liaised with the executives of the Royal Belgian Geographical Society that had endorsed the expedition.

The second-in-command was **Georges Lecointe**, who is referred to as Captain*, who was an expert on sea navigation, and was the executive officer and a skilled hydrographer. Like de Gerlache, he was a Belgian citizen. Prior to the expedition, Lecointe had been seconded for three years to the French Navy, at the end of which he published a course on navigation for navy students of the École Polytechnique who, at the time of his appointment, was attached to the Observatory of the Bureau des Longitudes at Montsouris near Paris in France. He entered the Belgian Royal Military Academy in 1886 and the Military Cartographic Institute. He was a Lieutenant in the Belgian artillery. Lecointe had published in 1897 two important monographs prior to the expedition entitled: *"La navigation astronomique et la navigation estimée"* and *La création d'une marine nationale belge*. Lecointe was awarded the French Légion d'Honneur for his first publication. He had to seek permission from the Belgian King Leopold II to accept this award.

The entire contingent of the Belgica expedition consisted of the following 19 people, with ages in brackets at the time of departure:

Officers:	
	Adrien de Gerlache Commander (32)
	Georges Lecointe 2nd in command[1], executive officer, hydrographer (29)
	Henryk Arctowski geologist, oceanographer, meteorologist (26)
	Frederick A. Cook medical officer, photographer (32)
	Emile Danco geophysicist [died 5 June 1898] (29)
	Antony B. Dobrowolski assistant meteorologist (25)
	Emil G. Racovitza biologist (29)
	Roald Amundsen 1st mate (26)
	Jules Melaerts 2nd mate (21)
Engineers:	
	Henry Somers chief engineer (34)
	Max Van Rysselberghe 2nd engineer (18)
Crew:	
	Adam Tollefsen boatswain (31)
	Louis Michotte stewart, eventually became cook (28)
	Ludvig H. Johansen seaman (25)
	Engelbret Knudsen seaman (21)
	Gustave Dufour ordinary seaman (21)
	Johan Koren ordinary seaman (17)
	Jan Van Mirlo ordinary seaman (21)
	Karl-Auguste Wiencke ordinary seaman [died 22 January 1898] (19)

This was a **truly international crew** consisting of:

9 Belgians:	de Gerlache, Lecointe, Danco, Melaerts, Somers, Van Rysselberghe, Michotte, Dufour and Van Mirlo
6 Norwegians:	Amundsen, Tollefsen, Johansen, Knudsen, Koren and Wiencke
2 Polish:	Arctowski and Dobrowolski
1 Romanian:	Racovitza
1 American:	Cook

1 Also refered to as Captain, but several errors appeared in the literature stating him to only be a first mate
*(see H. de Gerlache who refered to him as 'eerste stuurman') in the Dutch version of 'L'Antarctique en Héritage', Nevicata Press (2009).

A collage of photographs of the entire contingent is shown in Fig. 5.1

Communication, especially at the start of the expedition, would have been a significant issue due to language barriers. de Gerlache spoke French, Norwegian and English; Lecointe only spoke French and Flemish; both Arctowski and Dobrowolski spoke French since they studied in Liège and also Arctowski in Paris. Arctowski also spoke German and Russian. Racovitza not only spoke Romanian, but also had a perfect command of the French language since he studied in Paris where he also completed a PhD in zoology. Amundsen spoke Norwegian and was obviously the interpreter to the Norwegian sailors. He spoke English as well as French (based on letters written in French to Racovitza found in the Romanian archives in Cluj). Cook only spoke English and when boarding the ship in Rio de Janeiro he exclaimed that he would have had to speak Latin to communicate with the officers. He must have learned at least some French during the expedition. He became a close friend of Amundsen and both must have conversed in English. They remained friends for life. Melaerts was an accomplished sailor who spoke French (evidenced by a letter he wrote to Racovitza found in the same archives listed above) and likely English as his passport indicated he worked in Folkestone in the UK. Koren spoke English as shown by a letter addressed to Racovitza (same archive).

Figure 5.1 Collage of photographs of all the Belgica contingent. The top two rows were obtained from the photo album entitled: 'Expédition antarctique belge' held by the MAS Museum archives in Antwerp, Belgium and bear the following reference numbers 29.781-1 to 29.781-8 and used with permission granted by Waander Devillé. The bottom two rows of photos (except the two bottom right hand corner ones) originate from the 'Expédition belge au pôle sud: la Belgica et son equipage' held in the Limburgensia Collection of Bibliotheek Hasselt Limburg,Hasselt, Belgium with permission for use granted by Raf Verheist.

From left to right for all rows are: 1st row: Adrien de Gerlache, Georges Lecointe, Henryk Arctowski, Emil Racovitza; 2nd row: Roald Amundsen, Emile Danco, Frederick Cook, Jules Melaert; 3rd row: Karl Wiencke, Johan Koren, Ludvig Johansen, Gustave Dufour, Jan Van Mirlo, Louis Michotte, ; 4th row: Adam Tollefsen, Henry Sommers, Engelbret Knudsen, Max Van Rysselberghe (modified photo of Max at his wedding in 1905 and used with permission from Enrique Van Rysselberghe Herrera), and Antoni Dobrowolski (modified photo taken after the expedition and taken from Forum Akademickie, with permission from Mariusz Karwowski). All photos were enhanced with all backgrounds blackened by Ian Myers and eventually 'colorized' using palette.fm/color/filters.

Note that Amundsen took a role as 'guardian' of the Norwegian sailors and even visited the family of the sailor Karl-Auguste Wiencke after his return to Norway to report on his death.

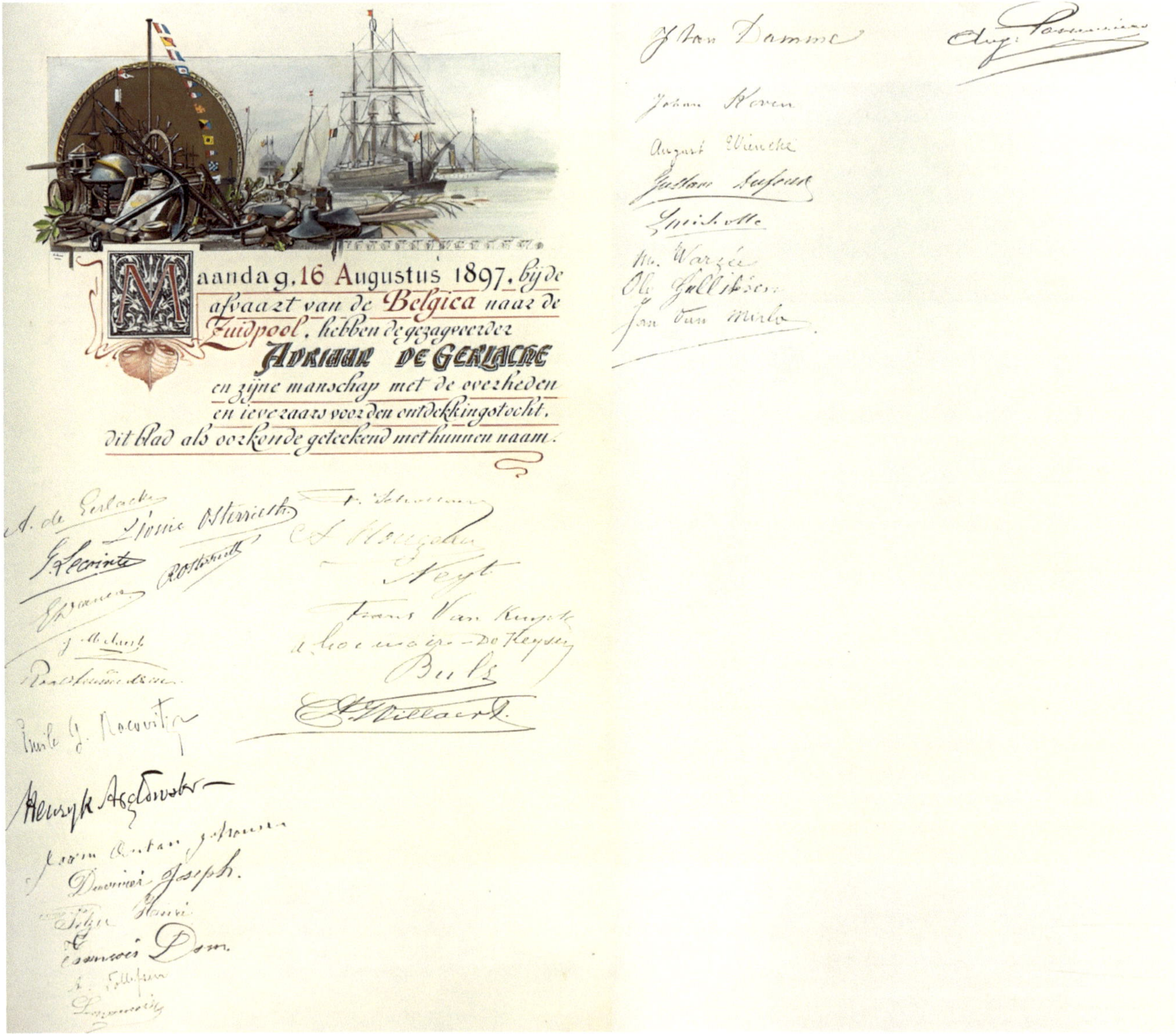

Maandag.16 Augustus 1897. bij de afvaart van de Belgica naar de Zuidpool, hebben de gezagvoerder ADRIAAN DE GERLACHE en zijne manschap met de overheden en ieverzaars voor den ontdekkingstocht, dit blad als oorkonde geteekend met hunnen naam.

Figure 5.2 Copy of the 2 pages in the City of Antwerp Gold Book celebrating the departure of the *S Y Belgica* on August 16, 1897. Signatures consist mostly of officers and members of the Belgica crew, some of whom left the ship on its way to Antarctic waters. The signature of Léonie Osterrieth and her son Robert, as well as long-time supporters of the expedition such as Charles Buls, Mayor of Brussels, and Général Neyt appear in the list. Copied with permission from Nelle Van Bedts, FelixArchief, Antwerpen.

Conversation on the ship at the start for the expedition must have been real cacophony!

The **Belgica expedition was therefore truly international** in comparison with British expeditions, for example, at about the same epoch that only consisted of members of the Commonwealth. The same for the two French Charcot expeditions that occurred a few years later. Nevertheless, the **Belgica expedition remained a Belgian effort** since it was funded by the Belgian government, some benefactors like the industrialist Ernest Solvay, private funds from Emile Danco and also the Belgian people themselves through money raised by cities, communities and also a multitude of fairs (see previous chapter). Many individuals also donated funds, even just a few days before the ship's departure.

ACTIVITIES AND CELEBRATIONS BEFORE DEPARTURE

Prior to departure, between July 26 and August 2, 1897 members of the public as well as dignitaries visited the ship. Visits were free but people were encouraged to make financial donations and this proved a success. Among the visitors were Edouard Van Beneden, Auguste-François Renard, Albert Lancaster, Elisée Reclus, as well as senators, governors of various provinces, generals and superior officers and diplomats. Money was still wanting (Marinescu, 2019).

There were numerous celebrations the day before departure. A banquet was held and also an entry was placed inside the city of Antwerp Gold Book to commemorate the event.

Figure 5.3. Copy of the banquet menu organized by the Yacht Club in Antwerp on August 15, 1897 for the commander and officers of the *S Y Belgica*. The menu reads: Varied hors d'oeuvres, St Vincent Rhine salmon, Boeuf filet Parisian sauce, Foularde in jelly, Roman sauce, Antarctic ice cream, Fruit, Desserts. Copied with permission from Nelle Van Bedts, FelixArchief, Antwerpen.

The original plan

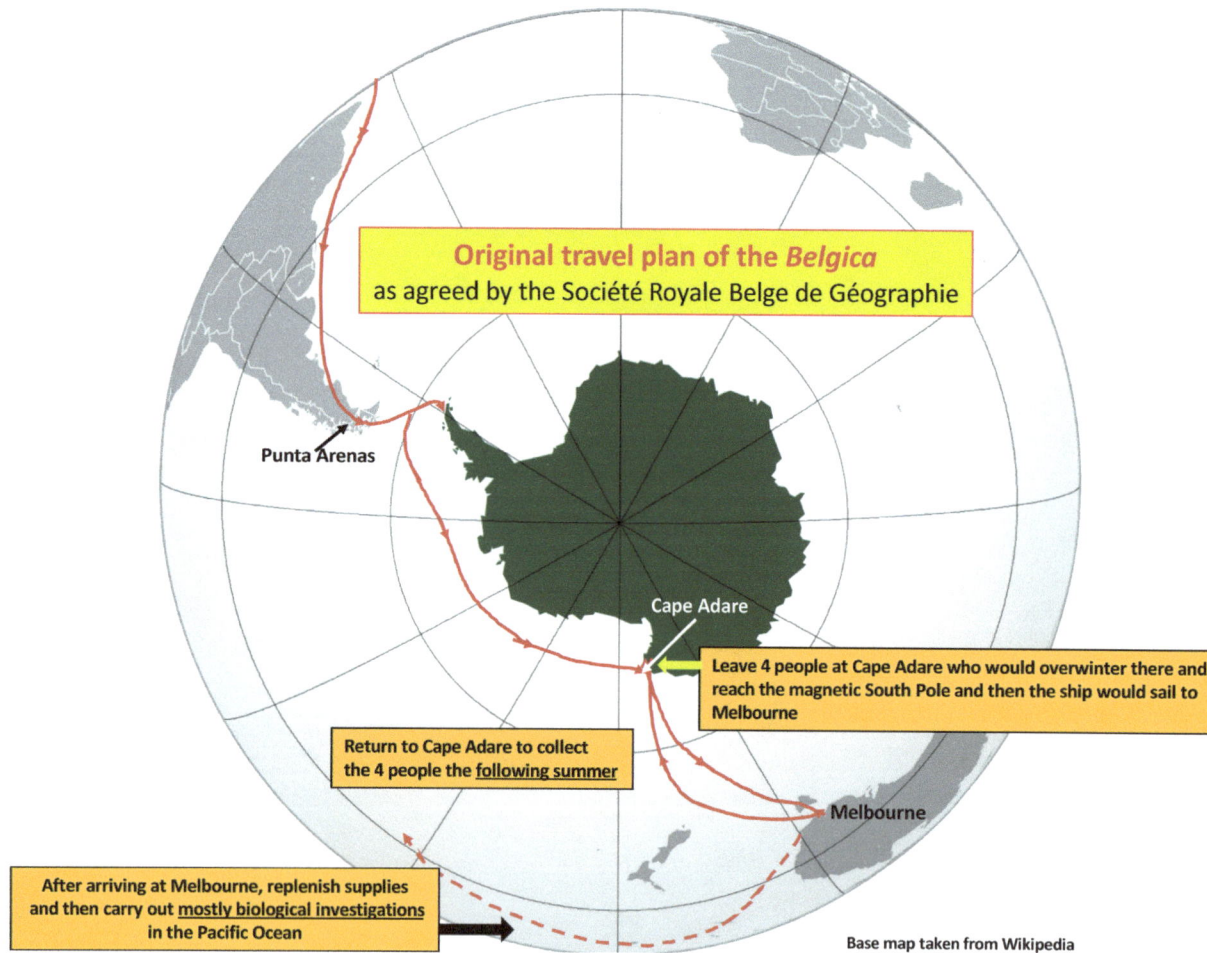

Original travel plan of the *Belgica*
as agreed by the Société Royale Belge de Géographie

Punta Arenas

Cape Adare

Leave 4 people at Cape Adare who would overwinter there and reach the magnetic South Pole and then the ship would sail to Melbourne

Return to Cape Adare to collect the 4 people the <u>following summer</u>

Melbourne

After arriving at Melbourne, replenish supplies and then carry out <u>mostly biological investigations</u> in the Pacific Ocean

Base map taken from Wikipedia

Figure 5.4 Map showing the original plan set by the Royal Geographical Society in Brussels which the *Belgica* was to follow.

Figure 5.5 Photograph of the *SY Belgica* in Antwerp harbour.

Note the Belfry on the right the Steen Castle on the left, for more details refer to the caption of Fig. 1.1.

EXPÉDITION ANTARCTIQUE BELGE
(1897-99)
Commandée par le Cap. A. de GERLACHE.

ITINÉRAIRE DE LA „BELGICA"
———— Aller. ————— Retour.
------- Dérive dans la banquise.

Figure 5.6 Map showing the route taken by the *SY Belgica* during its 1897-1899 Antarctic expedition. Map supplied by Professor Claude De Broyer from the Royal Belgian Museum of Natural History. The map originally appeared in Declerc and De Broyer (2001, p. 17) but is here modified using Photoshop©. Note that the return voyage took a different direction when sailing in the North Atlantic Ocean as it had insufficient coal for its steam engine due to the lack of funds. A copy of this map appears on the back of the book by de Gerlache published in 1938.

PART
TWO

Labels on map:

Punta Arenas

Beagle Channel

Staten Isl.

Cape Horn

1
2
3
4

Drake Passage

5

6

Elephant Isl.

7
8

South Shetland Islands

Bransfield Strait

de Gerlache Strait

9

Legend:
Approximate track of the *SY Belgica*
Sampling profile

Satellite image (from Google Earth©) to show the path followed by the *SY Belgica* between the tip of South America and the Antarctic Peninsula where the crew discovered and mapped the de Gerlache Strait. The dotted line shows the approximate path of the ship and also the various stations where deep water profiles were taken. Note the deeper the blue colour of the sea floor, the deeper the water is, reaching in places well over 4,500 m. Before the Belgica expedition, people thought it was a shallow strait with the Andes mountain chain continuing below sea level.

Chapter 6
Drake Passage

KEY POINTS

- The Belgica expedition was the first to document that the Andes mountain range does not extend underwater into the Drake Passage, which instead consists of a deep ocean basin.

- The temperature profiles obtained in a N-S transect in the Drake Passage in 1898 are the first of their kind and have been ignored by oceanographers since then. These data are very relevant to assess oceanographic changes in the region over the last 125 years. Indeed, they are very different.

- On 22 January 1898, sailor Carl-August Wiencke fell overboard and drowned in the Bransfield Strait despite a rescue attempt by G. Lecointe. Wiencke was only 20 years old.

After leaving the harbour of Punta Arenas in Patagonia, the expedition truly started.

The ship and its crew left on December 14, 1897 after some tumultuous events during which some members of the crew were asked to leave the ship. There were now only 19 people who formed the expedition. The itinerary saw the ship going first through the Beagle Channel but this will be discussed in great detail in chapters 13 and 16. Priority goes for the time spent in Antarctic waters as this was the original aim of the expedition and forms the most significant parts of the expedition. After leaving Staten Island at the southern tip of South America, the ship ventured into the poorly known Drake Passage. One pertinent question was meant to be answered by H. Arctowski: 'do the Andes continue below sea level in Drake Passage?'.

6.1 Discovery of a very deep passage, deep water profiling and the first icebergs

On January 14, 1898, the *Belgica* passed in front of Saint-Jean Bay at the western side of Staten Island located at the tip of South America. On that day, the first sounding was performed down to a depth of 296 m. In the afternoon, a second sounding reached a depth of 1564 m. The following day, the ship encountered three sailing boats, and three more in the afternoon. These were the last ships to be seen. The depth of the ocean was reached at 4040 m. This was sounding number 3 (see Fig. 6.1). The following soundings taken during a transect towards the South continued to return substantial depths 4: 3850 m; 5: 3800 m; 6: 3620 m; 7: 2900 m, and 9 nautical miles further south: 1800 m. This was on January 20, 1898. Reversed thermometers were used for the purpose of measuring temperature at depth along the profiles (Fig. 6.2) and Sigsbee bottles (Sigsbee, 1880) used to sample water for density measurements made by Arctowski. Unfortunately, the latter have not been recorded in the 'Résultats' of the expedition. Nevertheless, an important finding was made in that Drake Passage was in fact very deep. Hence, the hypothesis which Arctowski wanted to prove that the Andes continued at shallow depth in Drake Passage was unsubstantiated; it proved to be a very deep and rugged basin instead (Fig. 6.2).

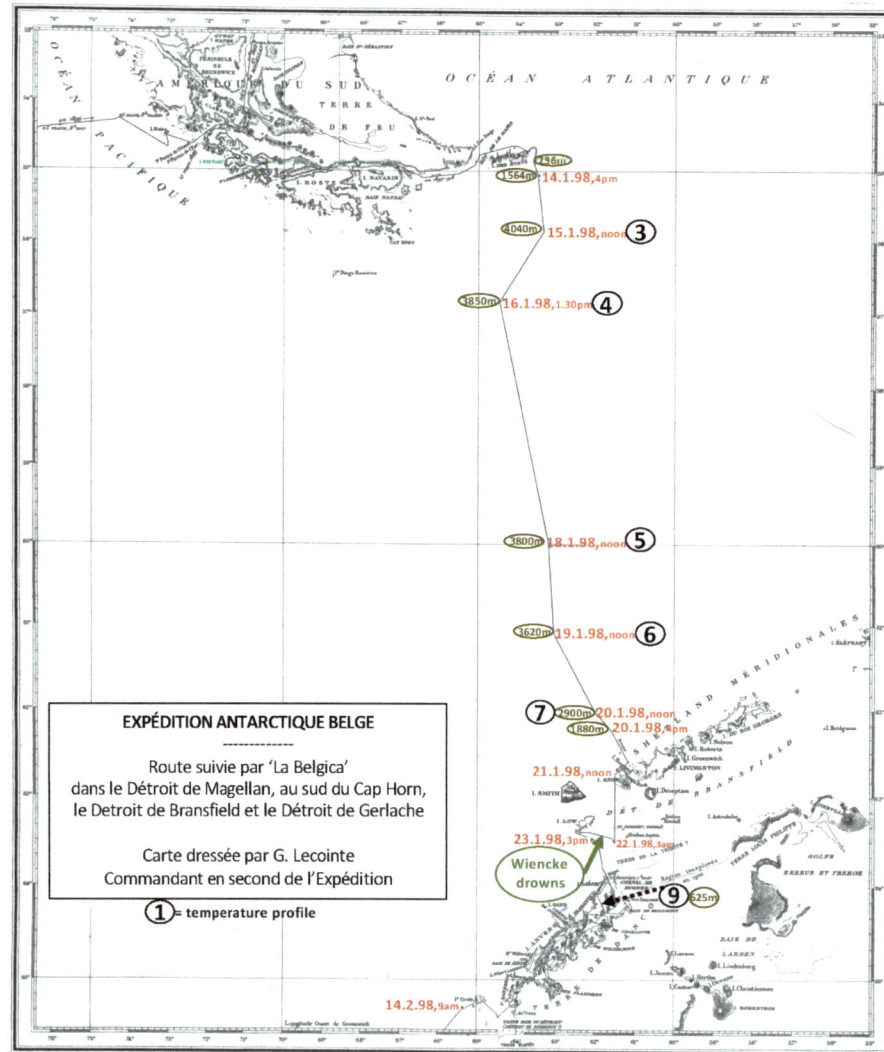

Figure 6.1 Map of Drake Passage (labelled 'Détroit de Bransfield') prepared by Georges Lecointe in 1903 showing the route followed by the *Belgica* and the location of the depth profiles (circled numbers in black) for which Arctowski measured temperature profiles *in situ*. Numbers in brown ovals are the depths reached in metres.

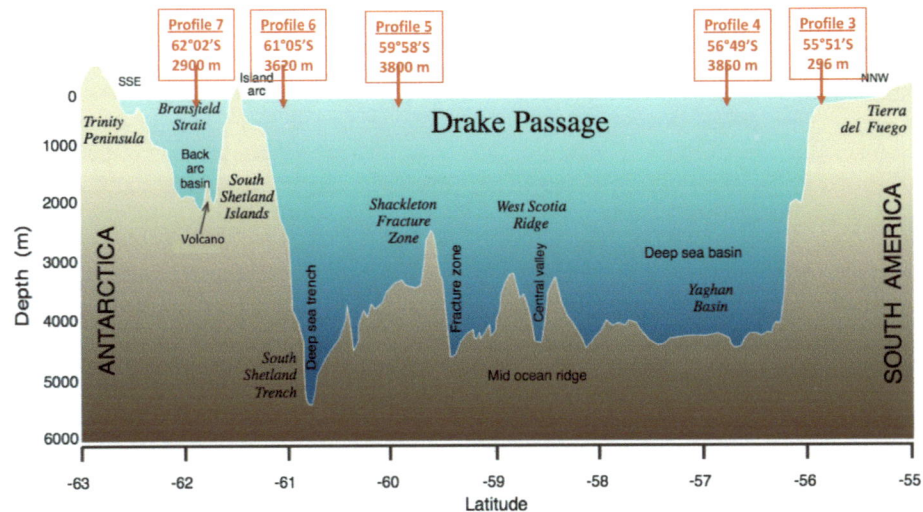

Figure 6.2 Profile of Drake Passage showing the deep nature of the sea floor as already proven by H. Arctowski during the profiling made in January 1898. Image modified from H. Grobe and used with his permission. The location of the depth profiles is indicated at the top of the figure with information on water depth reached. Note that sediments taken on the sea floor were taken at these stations (see chapter 11 for more details).

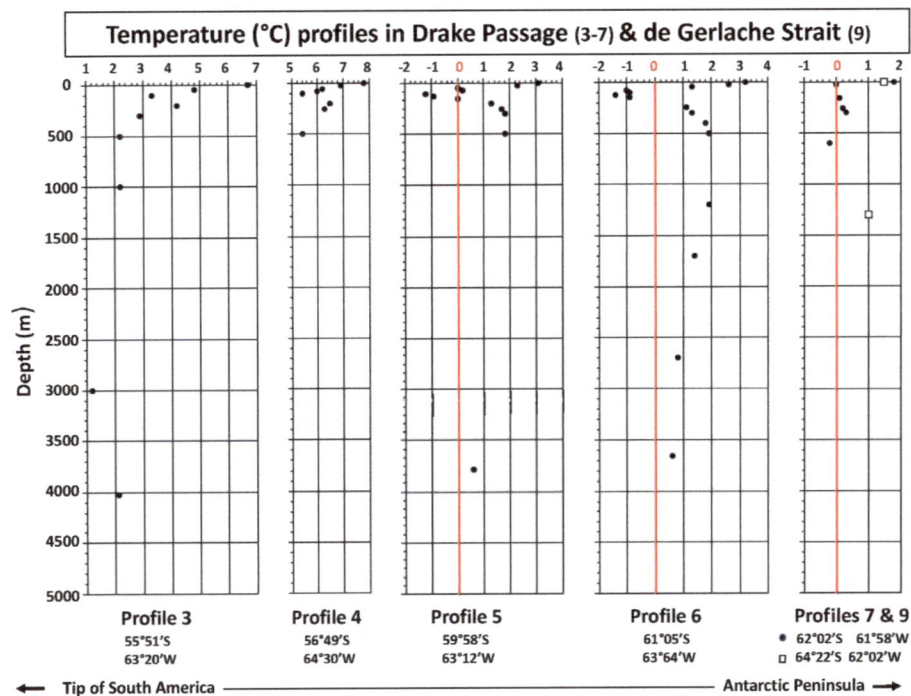

Figure 6.3 Temperature profiles in °C made by Arctowski in Drake Passage (stations 3, 4, 5, 6, 7) and the de Gerlache Strait (9). The red vertical lines indicate the 0°C value. Note that as the profiles extend towards the South, near-surface temperatures become colder.

45

During the transit in Drake Passage, the Belgica crew saw numerous albatrosses, the black-browed albatross *(Thalassarche melanophris)* and the snowy albatross *(Diomedea exulans)*, and several of the seamen caught several of them with fish hooks so as to make pipe tubes with their bones. On January 19, de Gerlache noted in his book (de Gerlache, 1902) that they saw for the first time the phenomenon called *'iceblink'*, for the white glow in the sky resulting from vast ice fields at a distance. This time he thought it was more of a *'landblink'* caused by the reflection of snow-covered land on the horizon. This is the day when they saw their first iceberg at 61°S, some 10 miles away (Amundsen, 1999), as well as a snow storm during which time they also saw sterns, albatrosses and Cape pigeons. The following day, more icebergs were seen. On January 21, they hit the base of an iceberg and also saw several rock outcrops, some of which they hit. A portion of the false keel was peeled off. More rocky outcrops were seen further south, likely to be Cattle Rock. Continuing in a southerly direction, they encountered many icebergs and numerous penguins. Land became visible with the South Shetland Islands seen at a distance.

On January 22, near Snow Island, in a demounted sea, seaman Carl-August Wiencke fell overboard. He did not have a harness despite recommendations from his superiors. While in the water, Wiencke managed to grab the lock line that hangs overboard and Frederick Cook (the doctor) managed to pull him close to the ship but it seemed that the seaman was already unconscious. Georges Lecointe, fully dressed and attached to a rope, jumped in the water with two men holding the rope. He eventually reached Wiencke but a strong wave separated them and Wiencke eventually let go the line and drifted away to eventually sink in the very cold waters. (For more details, refer to de Gerlache (1902), Lecointe (1904) and Amundsen (1999)). The atmosphere on the ship was very dreary and sombre, especially since Wiencke was very much liked by his peers and the commanding officers appreciated his intelligence, his devotion and outstanding character. We know that after the cruise Roald Amundsen visited Wiencke's family in Norway to pay his respect to his parents.

Photo 'colorized' using palette.fm/color/filters

Figure 6.4 Photo of Carl-August Wiencke wearing the *Belgica* seaman's hat. Photo courtesy of MAS Museum in Antwerp, AS.1988.078.006.002, reproduced with permission from Jan Parmentier. He was only 20 years old when he died.

6.2 Temperature profiles in Drake Passage and comparison with today's temperatures

On January 23, 1898 the *Belgica* entered Hughes Bay and named its first site as Cape Neyt, after the General who had been the first subscriber in the financial call by the Geographical Society of Brussels. Eventually, the ship discovered a new passage which became known as 'de Gerlache Strait' (see next chapter).

As illustrated below, Arctowski took numerous *in situ* temperature measurements using reversed thermometers along several profiles in Drake Passage (Figs. 6.1 to 6.3, Table 6.1). Today, with a better knowledge of oceanography, temperature measured at depth in the ocean has to be translated into what is called 'potential temperature' which is a measure of the temperature of a water parcel that is raised adiabatically to the sea surface. Intricate software is now used to calculate potential temperature and salinity of the water for each temperature measurement is required (see Jackett and McDougall, 1997).

As mentioned earlier, it seems that Arctowski took water samples for density/salinity measurements, but the results are not tabulated in Arctowski and Thoulet (1902). However, there is brief mention by de Gerlache (1938) that during the transect from Cape Horn to the Shetland Islands to the south, encountered bottom salinities were 34.32, 34.34, 34.33 and 34.34.

Table 6.1 Temperature measurements against depth in metres obtained by H. Arctowski (Arctowski and Mill, 1908) for 5 profiles in Drake Passage (3, 4, 5, 6, 7, 9). Shown in red are potential temperature values calculated by Dr R. Robinson with estimated salinities that are required to calculate the values. Unfortunately, Arctowski's salinity data are not available in the *Belgica* monograph by Arctowski and Thoulet's (1902) on sea water densities.

Profile 3 Depth (m)	Profile 3 Temp. °C	Profile 3 * Potential temp. °C @ 34.6 S	Profile 4 Depth (m)	Profile 4 Temp. °C	Profile 4 * Potential temp. °C @ 34.4 S	Profile 5 Depth (m)	Profile 5 Temp. °C	Profile 5 * Potential temp. °C @ 34.2 S	Profile 6 Depth (m)	Profile 6 Temp. °C	Profile 6 * Potential temp. °C @ 33.9 S	Profile 7 Depth (m)	Profile 7 Temp. °C	Profile 7 * Potential temp. °C @ 33.9 S	Profile 9 Depth (m)	Profile 9 Temp. °C	Profile 9 * Potential temp. °C @ 33.9 S
0	6.7	6.70	0	7.8	7.80	0	3.1	3.10	0	3.2	3.20	0	1.5	1.50	0	1.8	1.80
50	4.8	4.80	25	6.9	6.90	25	2.3	2.99	25	2.6	2.60	1300	1.0	0.93	25	0.0	0.00
100	3.3	3.29	50	6.2	6.20	50	0.0	0.00	50	1.3	1.30				150	0.1	0.09
200	4.2	4.02	75	6.0	5.99	75	0.2	1.97	75	-1.0	-1.00				250	0.2	0.09
300	2.9	2.88	100	5.4	5.39	100	-1.2	-1.20	100	-0.9	-0.90				300	0.3	0.29
500	2.2	2.17	150	6.5	6.48	125	-0.9	-0.93	125	-1.4	-1.40				600	-0.2	-0.22
1000	2.2	2.14	200	6.3	6.28	150	0.0	-0.01	150	-0.9	-0.90						
3000	1.2	0.99	250	5.4	5.38	200	1.3	1.29	250	1.1	1.09						
4025	2.1	1.75	300	4.4	4.38	250	1.7	1.69	300	1.3	1.29						
			500	3.8	3.77	300	1.8	1.78	400	1.8	1.78						
			1850	2.2	2.07	500	1.8	1.77	500	1.9	1.29						
			2850	1.9	1.69	3785	0.6	-0.33	1200	1.9	1.79						
			3850	1.2	0.90				1700	1.4	1.29						
									2700	0.8	0.62						
									3660	0.6	0.34						

* Potential temperature is the temperature of a water parcel that is raised adiabatically (without heat gain or loss) to the sea surface.

S: Salinity is estimated as no value was given by H. Arctowski

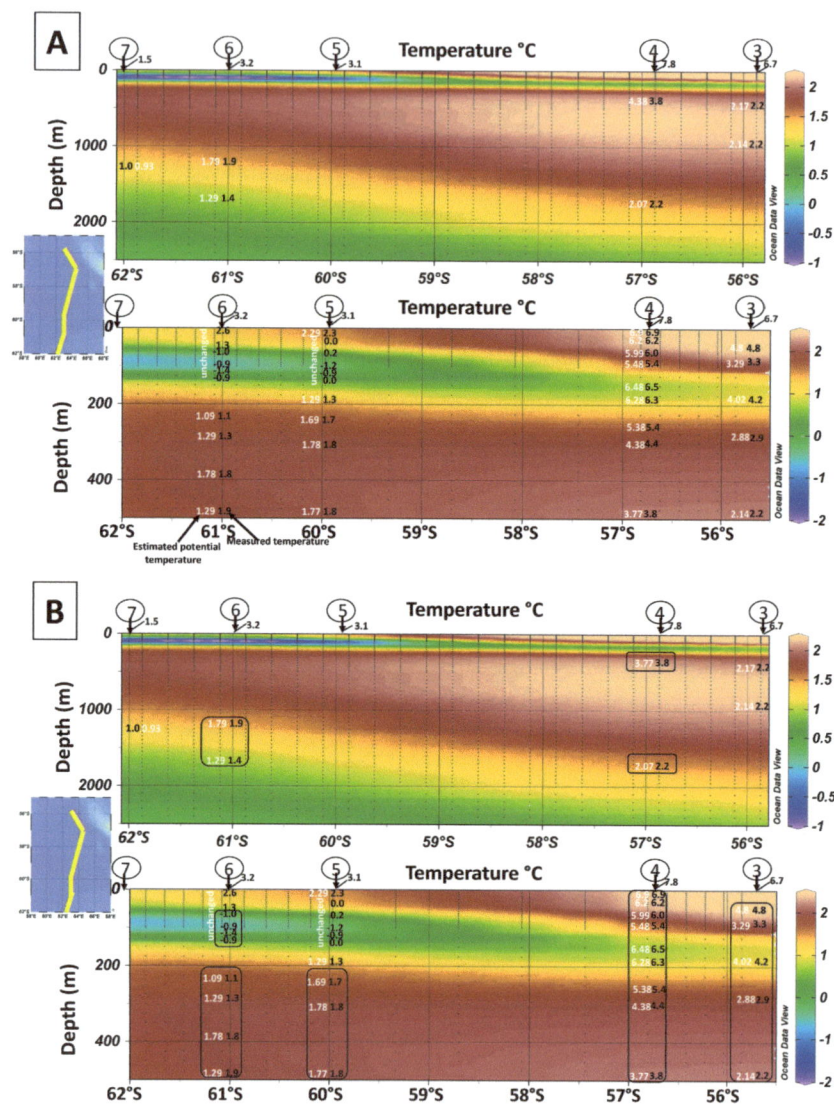

Figure 6.5 Transects of ocean temperatures in Drake Passage obtained from the software package 'Ocean Data View' used for the visualization of oceanographic data along a N-S transect shown with yellow lines in the small mauve inserts on the left. Those temperature profiles represented by different colours rely on numerous data sets obtained over many years (https://odv.awi.de/data/ocean/). Temperatures are calibrated against the colour scheme in the bars on the right. A: the 5 profiles overlaid here (3, 4, 5, 6, 7) gathered by H. Arctowski and respective temperatures are shown in black. Next to these numbers are others shown in white which represent calculated potential temperatures (see Table 6.1 for more information). To help with visualization, two depth transects are displayed, with the top ranging from 0 to 2500 m, the one below ranges between 0 and 500 m. B: this is the same figure as in A on which temperatures measured by Arctowski (and calculated potential temperatures) are shown with those values that depart from today's values are shown in black rectangles. The Ocean Data View profiles were generated by Dr J. Rogers.

Calculations of potential temperatures for all the temperature profiles obtained by Arctowski (Arctowski and Mill, 1908) were made by Dr Robin Roberston who estimated different salinities for the profiles. These are presented in Table 6.1. Although we will never know what the salinity data gathered by Arctowski for the 1898 transect were, it is still possible to estimate the potential temperatures for the different profiles. One attempt was made here by guessing salinities (Table 6.1 in combination with Fig. 6.5) and it is clear that comparison with the Ocean Data View plots (Fig. 6.4) with the Belgica data that significant changes have occurred in Drake Passage over 125 years. It is disappointing therefore to read that several important studies concerning the oceanography of Drake Passage and its recent changes have simply ignored the original work of Arctowski. These are, for example, Cunninghan et al (2003), Sprintall (2008), Xu et al. (2020) and Gutierrez-Villanueva et al. (2023) and references therein. Equally, in their important review of the circumpolar characteristics of Antarctic waters published in the Antarctic Folio Series, Gordon and Goldberg (1970) failed to mention the work of the Belgica expedition in Drake Passage. Let us hope that in the future oceanographers will revisit the data acquired by the Belgica expedition in 1898 as the Belgica data provide highly significant oceanographic information so as to assess the impact of climate change in the region since the onstart of the industrial revolution and its impact on global CO_2 emission.

6.3 Another look at temperature profiles in the upper 1000 m in Drake Passage

The recently available website Copernicus Marine Environment Monitoring Service (https://data.marine.copernicus.eu/viewer) that allows to plot high-quality sea temperature profiles anywhere on the globe for the last two years was used to compare temperature profiles in Drake Passage with those obtained by Arctowski in January 1898. These are plotted in Fig. 6.6.

Examination of this figure shows clear differences over 125 years: in 1898, Arctowski's profiles (see top left insert) inform us that temperature at the sea surface (as well as the upper 50 m of the water column) at each of the four sites that, from North to South, temperature was much higher than today, going from 7.8°, 3.1°, 3.2°, and 1.8° C (for the sea surface)

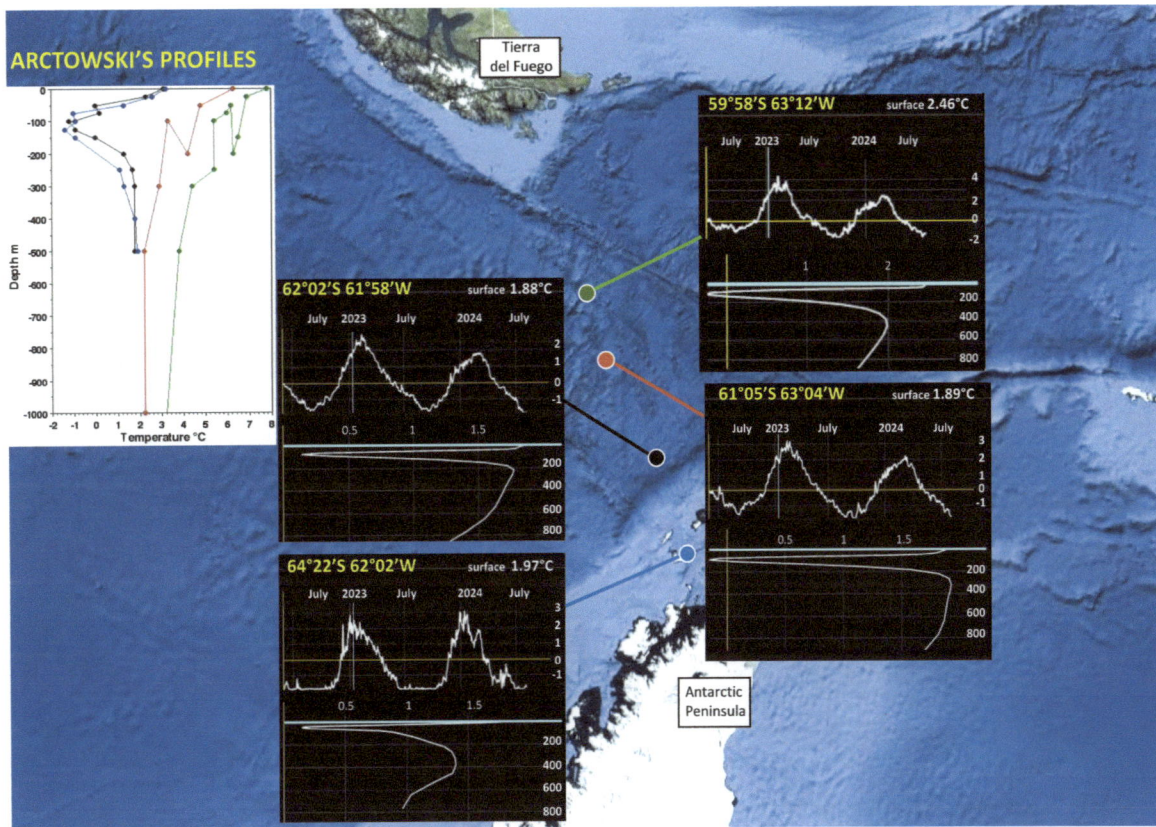

Figure 6.6 Sea temperature profiles for four sites in Drake Passage measured by Henryk Arctowski in January 1898 (top left diagram) compared to profiles obtained for the same sites using the Copernicus Marine Service program only for the upper 800 m of the water column, spanning the period January 1, 2023 to July 27, 2024. The plots for the four sites are shown in different colours used also in the top left diagram and refer to the coloured locations (dots) in the Passage. The coordinates for the four sites shown in the Copernicus diagrams in the centre are those for Arctowski's station but the plots are for sites located very close to Arctowski's stations. The surface temperatures (next to the coordinates) are for January 1, 2023.

de Gerlache Strait where 20 landings occurred between 23.1.1898 and 12.2.1898
Up to new 68 names were coined for his region by the crew (not all shown here)

This involved the study of fauna and flora [on land & at sea], geology, geophysics, glaciology, mapping, meteorology & oceanography

Flandres Bay
Anvers Is.
Wiencke Is.
Osterrieth Range
Wauvermans Isl.
Gand Is.
Brabant Is.
Du Fief Sierra
Solvay Mts
Liège Is.
C. Renard
Beneden H.
Cap Anna
Andvord Bay
Buls Bay
Cap Neyt
de Gerlache Strait
Wilhelmina Bay
Pelseneer Is.
Cobalcescu Is.
Gaston Is.
Cape Murray
Charlotte Bay
Danco Coast
Brialmont Cove

Satellite image obtained from Google Earth© to show the de Gerlache Strait and its surroundings over which many of the names provided by all members of the Belgica crew are pasted. This image was tilted to better display the topography.

Chapter 7
The de Gerlache Strait

KEY POINTS

- Twenty landings were made in the newly discovered de Gerlache Strait and a variety of geodesic instruments were used as well as the Mouchez method for reconnoitring features of the landscape.

- Lecointe's scientific legacy consists in the maps he generated during the expedition, especially the detailed map of the de Gerlache Strait. With all the information on the biota collected during the expedition in that Strait, comparison in the future at the same 20 landings will be of great importance to determine changes that have occurred over 125 years since the visit of the *Belgica* ship in 1898.

- In this chapter also there are sections on (1) flowering plants, (2) the chironomid fly *Belgica antarctica*, (3) acarid mites, (4) mosses, (5) lichen, (6) bryophytes, (7) seals and penguins, and geological observations.

This chapter describes the discovery of the de Gerlache Strait, its chartering as well as the ample collections made during some 20 landings over only 21 days. The mapping of the Strait was made using a variety of geodesic equipments that are briefly described, as well as geological collections that were eventually described in great detail after the expedition.

7.1 Discovery of a very deep passage, deep water profiling and the first icebergs

After crossing Drake Passage and taking several deep-sea profiles to measure water salinity and more importantly water temperature profiles (see chapter 6), the *Belgica* continued its voyage South during which time they already saw icebergs, and entered Bransfield Strait. A little later, the ship entered a new area and discovered a new passage where she and its contingent spent 20 days in a strait which later on became known as the de Gerlache Strait. Between January 23 and February 12, 1898, they made some 20 landings (called 'débarquement', meaning 'getting off the ship') (Table 7.1). Some landings barely lasted one hour. At times, on some days, two separate parties landed at different locations. During the January 30 - February 6, 1898 period (= 8 days), a group consisting of 5 people (Amundsen, Arctowski, Cook, Danco and de Gerlache) who were also assisted during the landing by Lecointe and two of the sailors Johansen and Tollefsen spent time exploring the large Brabant Island. Another sailor, Koren who was very interested in natural history (see chapter 14), made an 8 hour-long outing with Lecointe and Racovitza on Cape Van Beneden. Racovitza, on the other hand, participated in 15 of the 20 landings. In fact, 6 of those landings were made on the Antarctic continent *per se* (see Fig. 7.1.3); the others were on islands, all during that expedition.

In 1873–74, the German explorer Eduard Dallman had already made his first Antarctic whaling voyage aboard *Groenland,* and had already discovered and charted the west coasts of Anvers Island (on January 9, 1874

which he called 'Palmer Land') as well as Brabant and Liège Islands, named later by the Belgica crew (Barr et al., 2004). Being whalers, Dallman and his crew had already killed 120 seals and salted their skins by January 6! On January 12 1874, the ship passed Brabant Island and eventually Liège Island. In the process, Dallman corrected the British Admiralty charts available at the time. Of interest also is that on January 20, Dallman had noticed that eight sailors were suffering from scurvy. A crew member (Küper) in his log book reported that the best possible remedy was to eat raw penguin meat and drink their blood (quoted by Pawlik (1966) in Barr et al. (2004). For more details on how to combat scurvy, refer to chapter 13.

When the crew of the *Belgica* explored de Gerlache Strait, there would have been ample sun light (~20 hours per 24 hours) as this was the Summer period. This permitted much work and many observations to be accomplished.

Lecointe, with the help of de Gerlache, was responsible for the cartography of the Strait and adjacent islands. Despite that important task, Lecointe still participated in 13 of the landings. His final maps were eventually published in 1903. Originally, the Strait was named 'Belgica Strait' but eventually correspondence by Lecointe to de Gerlache on January 28, 1900 clearly indicates that Lecointe was the one who decided the name change and suggested this to the Belgica Commission. Nevertheless, before the 1903 publication, Cook (1900) in his book produced

a map of the 'Belgica Strait'. Similarly, Arctowski (1901) in his report on the expedition to the Royal Geographical Society in London, a map drafted by the Society gives the name of Belgica to the Strait. Again, Lecointe (1900) provided a map of the 'Belgica Strait' (Fig. 26.2) when he reported on the expedition to the Royal Belgian Geographical Society a year after its return to Belgium. Johan Koren, the sailor turned naturalist, traced in his diary a draft of the map prepared by Lecointe while at sea (Fig. 7.1.2) (Koren, no date).

Figure 7.1.1 (oppisite) Map drawn by Georges Lecointe in 1900 showing details of the 'Belgica Strait' which was presented to the Royal Belgian Geographical Society in Brussels. The name of the Strait was later on changed to 'de Gerlache Strait' at the request of Lecointe to the Belgica Commission.

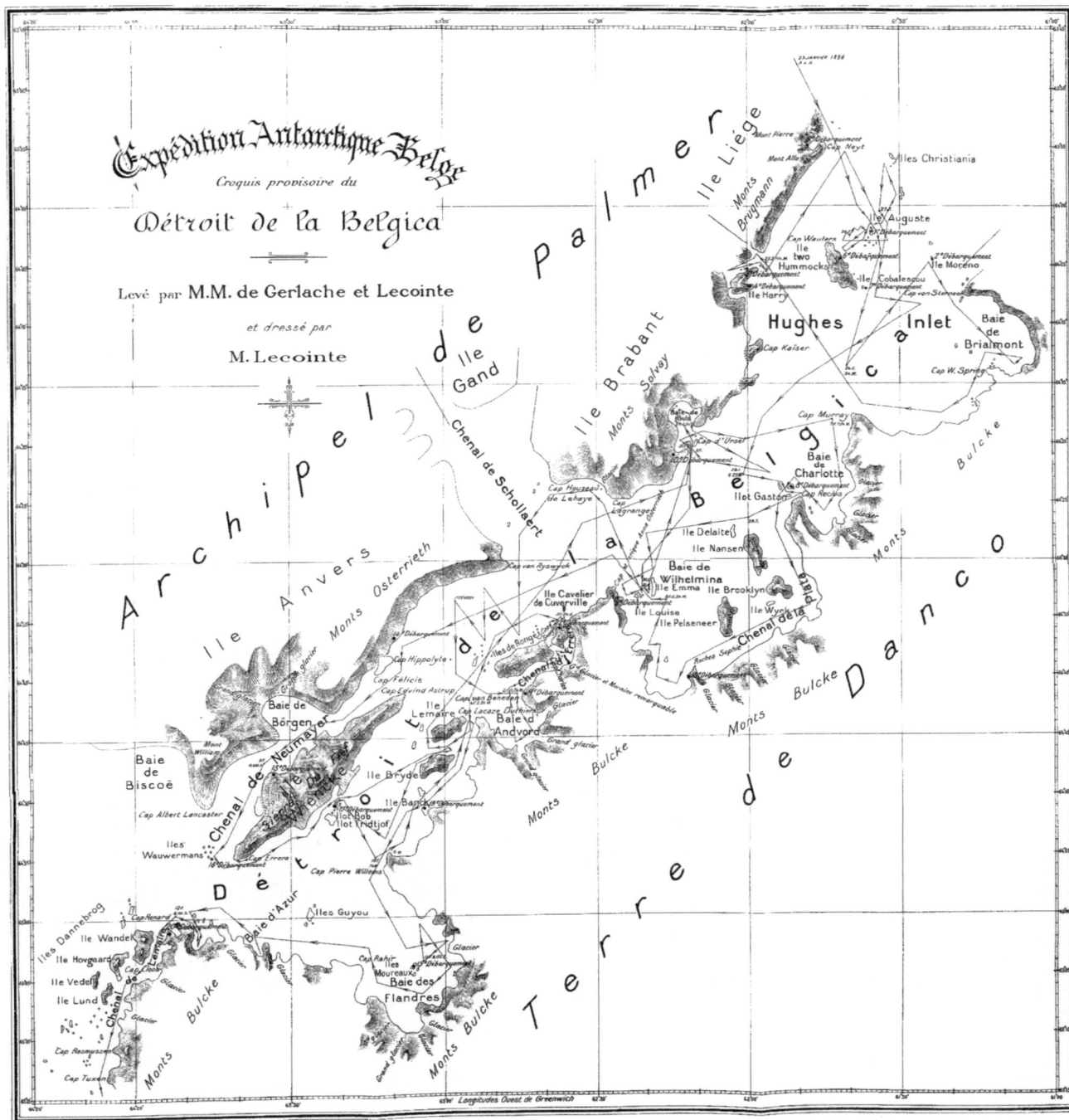

Expédition Antarctique Belge

Croquis provisoire du

Détroit de la Belgica

Levé par M.M. de Gerlache et Lecointe

et dressé par

M. Lecointe

Archipel de Palmer

Détroit de la Belgica

Terre de Danco

Hughes Inlet

Baie de Brialmont

Baie de Charlotte

Baie de Wilhelmina

Baie d'Andvord

Baie de Börgen

Baie de Biscoë

Baie d'Azur

Baie des Flandres

Chenal de Schollaert

Chenal de Neumayer

Chenal de la Plata

Ile Liége

Ile Brabant

Ile Gand

Ile Anvers

Monts Osterrieth

Monts Solvay

Monts Brugmann

Monts Bulcke

Iles Christiania

Ile Auguste

Ile two Hummocks

Ile Harry

Ile Moreno

Ile Cobalescou

Ile Delaite

Ile Nansen

Ile Emma

Ile Brooklyn

Ile Louise

Ile Wyck

Ile Pelseneer

Ile Cavelier de Cuverville

Iles de Rongé

Ile Lemaire

Ile Bryde

Ile Banck

Iles Wauwermans

Ile Wandel

Iles Hovgaard

Ile Vedel

Ile Lund

Iles Dannebrog

Iles Guyou

Ilot Gaston

Ilot Bob

Ilot Hidtjof

Cap Neyt

Cap Wauters

Cap von Sterneck

Cap Kaiser

Cap W. Spring

Cap Murray

Cap d'Ursel

Cap Houzeau de Lehaye

Cap Lagrange

Cap van Beneden

Cap Lacaze Duthiers

Cap Hippolyte

Cap Félicia

Cap Edvind Astrup

Cap Albert Lancaster

Cap Pierre Willems

Cap Rahir

Cap Henarw

Cap Cloos

Cap Roomussen

Cap Tuxen

Mont Pierre

Mont Allo

Mont William

Longitudes Ouest de Greenwich

53

Figure 7.1.2 Sketch found in the Norwegian sailor Johan Koren's dairy. The note at the top left hand corner says that this is a direct sketch from Georges Lecointe's map being prepared on the ship. Reproduction of this map was granted by the Norwegian Archive Library. A link to the diary can be found at: https://media.digitalarkivet.no/view/77494/45, although the map is incomplete at that website.

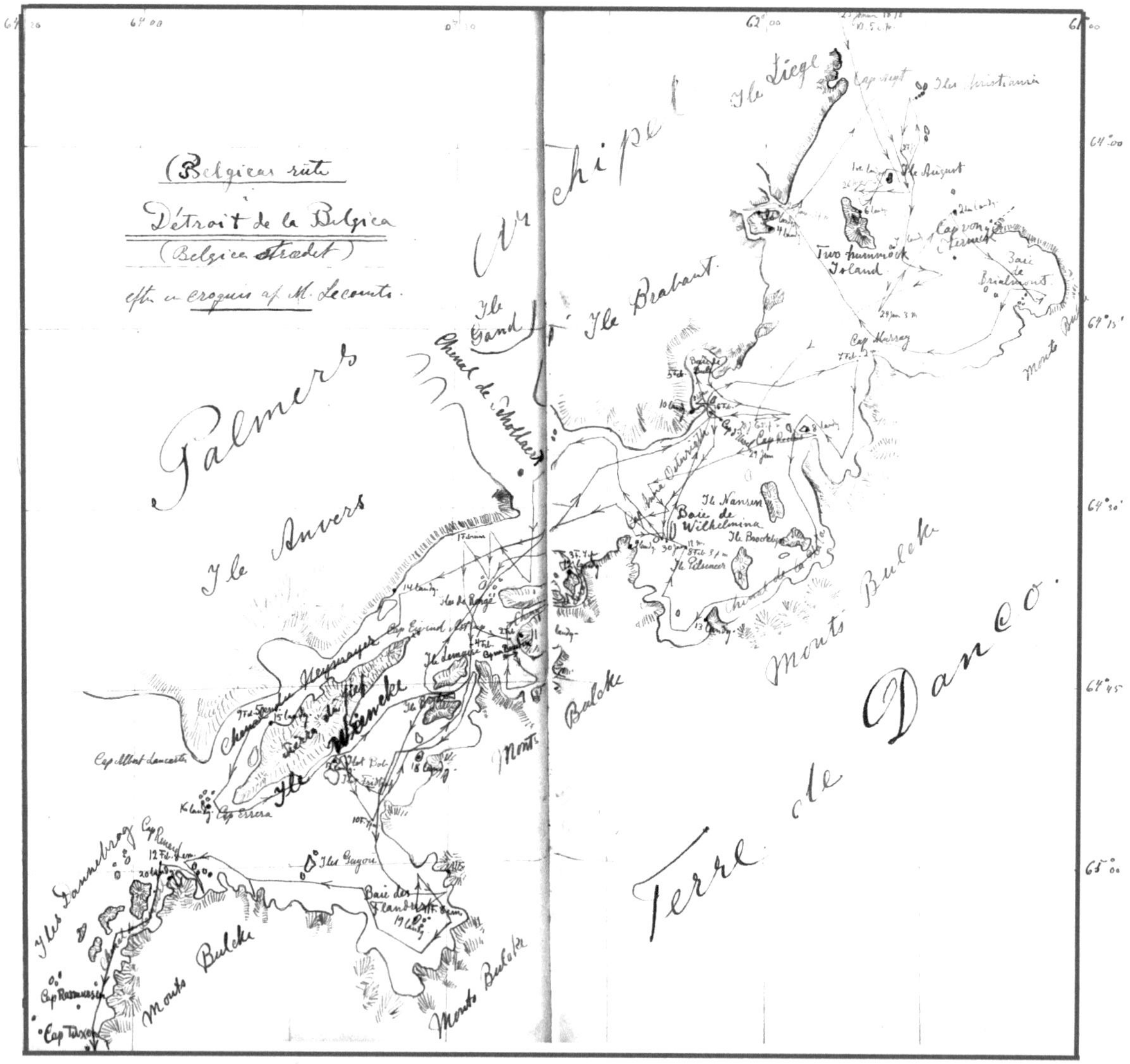

Figure 7.1.3 (Opposite) Copy of the original map by Georges Lecointe (Lecointe 1903, map 3) of the de Gerlache Strait on which information was placed such as where the iconic flightless chironomid fly *Belgica antarctica* was found (see section 7.3), as well as photographs published by H. Arctowski (1908) and F.A. Cook (1900) to illustrate the diversity of the landscape in this region. The unaltered map can be found in Lecointe (1903) and in De Deckker (2018, supplement).

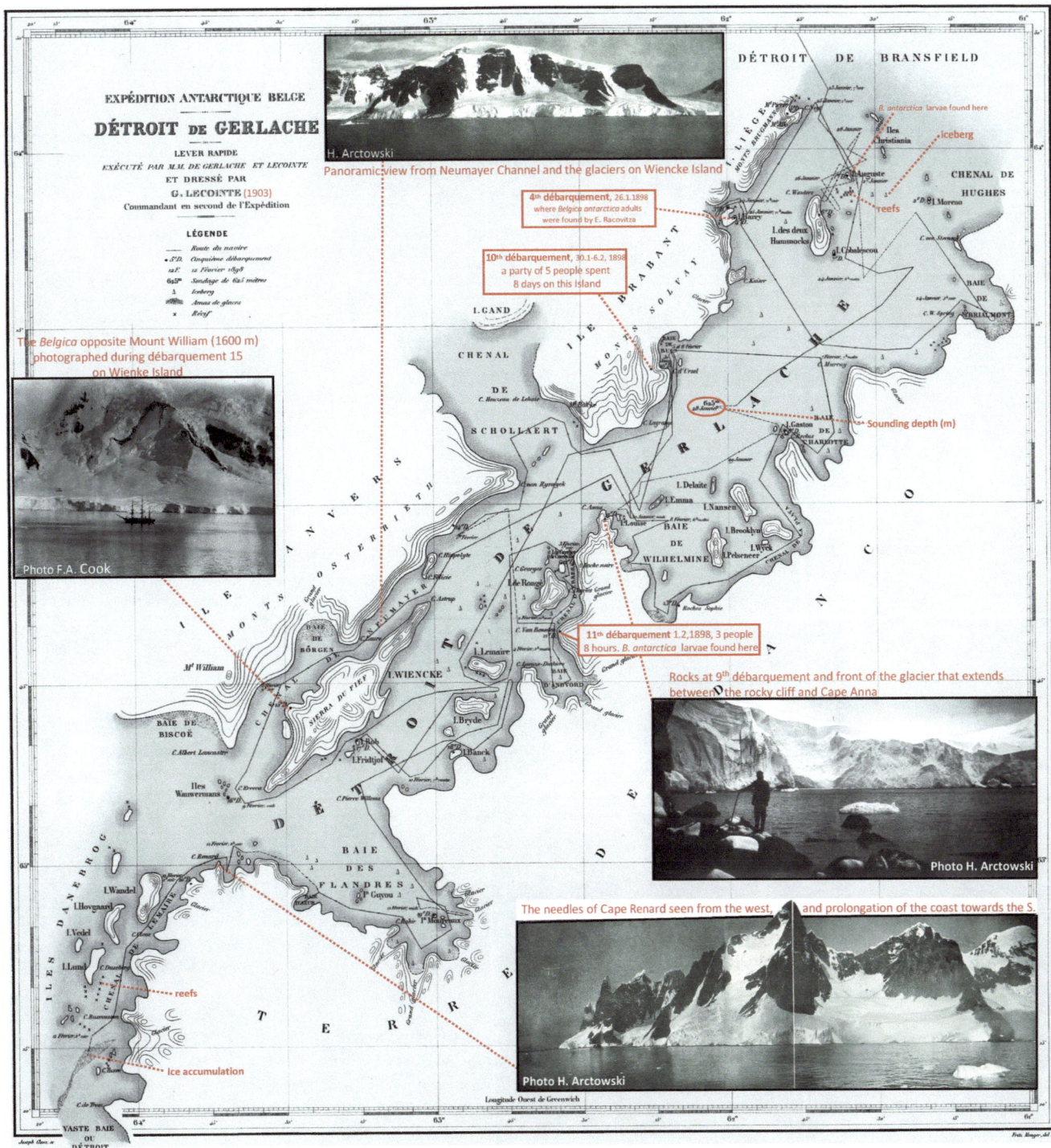

EXPÉDITION ANTARCTIQUE BELGE

DÉTROIT DE GERLACHE

LEVER RAPIDE

EXÉCUTÉ PAR M.M. DE GERLACHE ET LECOINTE

ET DRESSÉ PAR

G. LECOINTE (1903)

Commandant en second de l'Expédition

LÉGENDE

- Route du navire
- 5ᵉ D. Cinquième débarquement
- 12 F. 12 Février 1898
- 625ᵐ Sondage de 625 mètres
- Iceberg
- Amas de glaces
- × Récif

Panoramic view from Neumayer Channel and the glaciers on Wiencke Island

H. Arctowski

B. antarctica larvae found here

iceberg

4ᵗʰ débarquement, 26.1.1898 where *Belgica antarctica* adults were found by E. Racovitza

10ᵗʰ débarquement, 30.1-6.2, 1898 a party of 5 people spent 8 days on this Island

reefs

The *Belgica* opposite Mount William (1600 m) photographed during débarquement 15 on Wienke Island

Sounding depth (m)

Photo F.A. Cook

11ᵗʰ débarquement 1.2,1898, 3 people 8 hours. *B. antarctica* larvae found here

Rocks at 9ᵗʰ débarquement and front of the glacier that extends between the rocky cliff and Cape Anna

Photo H. Arctowski

The needles of Cape Renard seen from the west, and prolongation of the coast towards the S.

reefs

Ice accumulation

Photo H. Arctowski

Longitude Ouest de Greenwich

DÉTROIT DE BRANSFIELD

CHENAL DE HUGHES

BAIE DE SOLVAY

BAIE DE WILHELMINE

CHENAL DE SCHOLLAERT

ILE ANVERS

I.WIENCKE

BAIE DE BISCOE

ILES WANWERMANS

BAIE DES FLANDRES

ILES DANEBROG

DÉTROIT DE GERLACHE

VASTE BAIE OU DÉTROIT

55

Débarquement (landing) no.	Date 1898	Location	Débarquement (landing) no.	Date 1898	Location
I	23.1.	Auguste Island	X	30.1-6.2	Brabant Island (S of Buls Bay and Cape Ursel)
II	24.1	Moreno Island	XI	1.2	**Cape Van Beneden**
III	24.1	Harry Island (Hughes Inlet)		2.2	**Cape Van Beneden** (Danco Land, N of Andvord Bay)
Iv	25.1	Harry Island Cape Neyt (NE of Liège Island)	XII	3.2	Cuverville Island
V	25.1	Auguste Island, Two Hummock Island	XIII	7.2	**Sophie Rocks** (Danco Land, S of Wilhelmina Bay)
	26.1	Auguste Island	XIV	8.2	Anvers Island
VI	26.1	Two Hummock Island	XV	9.2	**Wiencke Island** (Neumayer Channel side)
VII	27.1	Cobalcescu Island (S of Two Hummock Island)	XVI	9.2	Island east of the Wauvermans Islands group
VIII	29.1	Gaston Island (Charlotte Bay)	XVII	9.2	Bob Island (proximity of the east coast of Wiencke Island)
IX	29.1	**Cape Anna Osterrieth** (NO of Wilhelmina Bay)	XVIII	10.2	**Banck Island**
	29.1	Louise Island	XIX	11.2	In the island the most westward of the Moureaux Islands group
	30.1	Louise Island	X	11.2	**S of Cape Renard (Danco Land, near the Lemaire Channel)**

Names in bold are located on the Antarctic mainland

Table 7.1 List of the 20 débarquements (landing) stations carried out in the de Gerlache Strait. Information obtained from a letter from Lecointe addressed to Racovitza found in the Racovitza family archives combined with the table on page 23 of Verlinden (2008).

The Belgica contingent listed some new 68 new names for features discovered around the de Gerlache Strait. Each crew member was able to suggest one name (such as 'Brooklyn' by F.A. Cook for the district of New York where he lived, and Cobalcescu by E. Racovitza for his former geology teacher who had reached international fame). A complete list of those names with respective coordinates and their justification is available in 3 languages (English, French and Flemish) on a 4 pages map (Federaal wetenschapsbeleid, 2008). A reproduction of the principal map listing all the names featured in the de Gerlache Strait is shown at the end of this chapter in Fig. 7.9.6. In addition, Verlinden (2008) provides a more extensive description of many of the islands and other sites in the de Gerlache Strait with numerous comments from the expeditioners as provided in their diaries. We note that since the original map (listing the new names) was published by Lecointe in 1903, several travel agencies have produced maps and have modified some of those names, a contravention to the formal international convention of listing geographical names.

It is noteworthy that the cartography achieved by Lecointe with the help of de Gerlache relied on (at the time) state-of-the art surveying equipment and techniques such as the Admiral Mouchez method. Derwael (2013, 2023) first of all reminded us that Lecointe was not only a 'navigation officer' and a 'hydrographer', eminently qualified to carry out a survey of the region. Lecointe's (1905) monograph detailing his hydrographic work discusses the imperfections of his measurements caused by several issues: short time allowed for the measurements to be made, poor weather conditions and the absence of visible landmarks. Derwael (2023) also discusses the surveying tools used by Lecointe. These are: a Hurliman Paris 1895 sextant (Fig. 7.1.4A), a Brunner magnetic theodolite (Figs. 7.1.4B, 7.1.5), three types of barometers (Fortin, marine barometer and several aneroid barometer), and a marine torpedo chronometer (7.1.4C). The barometers were giving a ~4 m error (Derwael 2023). In addition, in order to check the veracity of the chronometers, Lecointe relied on the eclipse of Jupiter, occultation of stars by the moon, and the method of lunar distances. Lecointe also used four chronometers and a torpedo boat watch (Derwael, 2023). In total, 11 points were used to survey the Strait and measurements were made with the sextant. Nevertheless, Lecointe had encountered several difficulties because the moon was not visible, the declination of the sun was low and poor weather conditions. Derwael (2023) estimated that comparison of Lecointe's map with the 2017 British Antarctic Survey maps that relied on satellite images, there were in some instances 3 km differences. Nevertheless, it is necessary to admit that the Lecointe (1903)'s map was an outstanding achievement, knowing that only 21 days were available to survey the entire de Gerlache Strait. Additional details on Lecointe's surveying technique and ample details on these are presented in Cornet and Derwael (2023); this paper discusses all measurements and mapping done also in the Bellingshausen Sea (see Chapter 8).

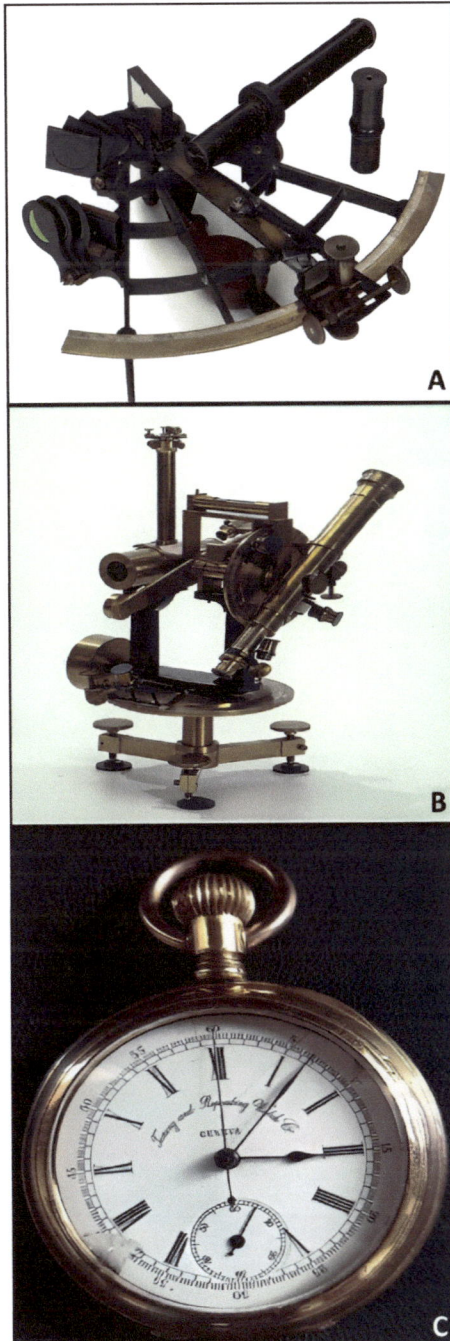

Figure 7.1.4

A: Photograph of a Lorieux Hurlimann Paris-1895 sextant copied from Derwael (2023). Refer also to https://sextantbook.com/?s=hurlimann+sextant for more details and photos;

B: Photograph of a Brunner magnetic theodolite used by Lecointe copied from Derwael (2023), Refer also to https://www.pop.culture.gouv.fr/notice/memoire/IVR93_19950600137ZA;

C: Photograph of a Marine Torpilleur Chronometer similar to the once used by Lecointe on the *Belgica;* copied with permission from Derwael (2023). More details at: https://www.etsy.com/au/listing/1242902208/working-dubois-marine-torpilleur?show_sold_out_detail=1&ref=nla_listing_details.

The longest landing lasting 8 days was achieved by de Gerlache, accompanied by Danco, Arctowski, Amundsen and Cook) who climbed the Solvay Mountains on Brabant Island on February 2, 1898 to reach a nunatak at 315 m in altitude] (see Fig. 7.1.6). Danco established the magnetic declination (20°43'13"NE) there and additional measurements helped towards the making of the map. This 5-men party was unable to go higher to make additional measurements due to poor meteorological conditions (de Gerlache, 1902). Nevertheless, during their excursion, the Admiral Mouchez method was utilised to help with the cartography. Derwael (2013) clearly and amply describes the principles behind this method which was used to measure the distance to and position of the coast from an elevated location.

The equipment used during this excursion was transported in two sleds and included a theodolite, skis and snow shoes, an oiled silk tent, a stove with fuel, sleeping bags made of reindeer skins, and food for 15 days. On the first day, this party was helped by Lecointe, Tollefsen and Johansen (see fig. 7.1.6) as the slope bordering the ocean was very steep (35 to 40°) and eventually the five men set up camp at ~300 m on a flat area. The second

day they went up further to eventually reach 315 m. At some stage, Danco fell in a crevasse but was rapidly rescued. On the 3rd day, on a nunatak at 315 m in altitude, they used the Mouchez method to survey various points in the de Gerlache Strait. However, the tent was torn in many places on that day and they could not repair it. Amundsen in his diary (edited by Decleir, 1999) discussed the inadequacy of the oiled silk material, and this eventually led him and Cook to design a new type of tent (see Fig. 15.3). The weather while on Brabant Island (Fig. 7.1.7 F) was most of the time unfavourable for surveying work and eventually they returned to the ship.

While in the de Gerlache Strait, Arctowski collected numerous rocks and examined glaciers and icebergs, and their vestiges. These are discussed in section 7.8. Racovitza collected a vast amount of biological material now described in chapter 9. The most extraordinary find was a wingless chironomid fly (*Belgica antarctica*) and two flowering plants (for more information, consult sections 7.2 and 7.3 and Racovitza 1900a, b). Of note is that Racovitza also made observations on penguins, sea birds, seals and whales. On one day (January 31, 1898), for example, he counted 100 humback whales and 50 blue whales, the only two species seen during the *Belgica* visit (Fig. 9.2.1). In addition, he identified Weddell seals and crabeater seals (Figs. 9.3.7, 9.3.11). Overall, most of Racovitza's observations of the whales were made during the time spent in the de Gerlache Strait (see chapter 9.2 and Racovitza, 1903).

Figure 7.1.5 Geological and geodetic investigations on Solvay Island. The person on the right is using a Brunner theodolite as identified by J-J. Derwael. Photo provided by Eddy Stuer and 'colorized' using palette.fm/color/filters.

Figure 7.1.6 Photograph of the team that explored Brabant Island obtained from Anders Bache from the MIA Museum near Oslo (from a photographic album given to R. Amundsen by G. Lecointe) and published with permission. Photograph enhanced using Photoshop© and then 'colorized' using palette.fm/color/filters.

Included here also are some photographs of features from de Gerlache Strait taken in recent times (Fig. 7.1.7).

In the chapters that follow I will present specific findings made in the de Gerlache Strait in early 1898. However, whales which Racovitza studied extensively were principally observed in the de Gerlache Strait but will be discussed in chapter 8.

Figure 7.1.7 Recent photographs of the spectacular landscapes seen in the de Gerlache Strait.

A: Flanders Bay;

B: Lemaire Channel;

C: Wiencke Island;

D: Peak in Lemaire Channel;

E: Danco Island;

F: Sunset on Brabant Island;

G: Neumayer Channel and Anvers Island.

All photos were provided by the late Dr Franz Gingele who granted permission to reproduce them here. For more photos taken by the Belgica crew refer to Fig. 7.1.3

7.2 Flowering plants

KEY POINTS

- Racovitza's scientific legacy is the discovery of the two flowering plants in Antarctica.

- Both *Deschampsia antarctica* and *Colobanthus* quitensis are flowering plants adapted to extreme conditions experienced on the Antarctic Peninsula.

- This adaptation and speciation are likely to have resulted from a long history of glacial conditions that have prevailed in the Antarctic region over a long period of time, perhaps one to two million years.

- Both plants are now found in more localities than in the de Gerlache Strait since first found by E. Racovitza.

- With the Antarctic Peninsula already undergoing climatic 'amelioration', we can be assured through physiological studies of both plants that they will survive and also expand their niches.

- Birds are seen to be the passive transport agents of the plants to new areas, but we should not ignore the fact that the plants have a fungal association on their roots. Again, plant fragments transported by birds would contribute to the transport of root fungal material as well.

- A new threat is the potential arrival of new pathogens to some of the Antarctic sites and islands by tourists that may affect the plant endemics discussed here.

Emil Racovitza made several important discoveries in the de Gerlache Strait. One was to find the first flowering plants to be recorded in the Antarctic region and the other was the first insect, a flightless chironomid fly. It was named *Belgica antarctica* and should perhaps should be treated as the emblem of the Belgica expedition.

The astonishing surprise in that De Wilderman (1905), who wrote a long monograph on phanerogams collected by E. Racovitza, did not comment on the presence of those two flowering plants on the Antarctic Peninsula, viz. *Deschampsia antarctica* (also called Antarctic hair grass) and *Colobanthus quitensis* (also called the Antarctic pearlwort) (Fig. 7.2.1). These plants were also found in the Beagle Channel area, but were the first occurrence of flowering plants in Antarctica, and some 1300 km from the Beagle Channel. Seeds of those plants would have had to travel across an ocean (Drake Passage) where winds are extremely strong and predominantly travel latitudinally (East West). Surprising also is the lack of comment from De Wilderman knowing what Racovitza exclaimed at public conferences published in 1900 such as: "on a particularly well-sheltered ledge, we found a small herb, a grass, the only flowering plant in this inhospitable region. All other terrestrial plants collected are part of the group of mosses, lichens and algae, lower plants..." (Racovitza 1900a, pp. 37-38). Also, Racovitza in 1900b (p. 189) said: *"a single flowering plant, Aira antarctica, a tiny grass hiding between tufts of moss and seeking well-sheltered ledges on the side of cliffs"*. These arose much

interest indeed as well as by the discovery of the first chironomid fly in the Antarctic region, *Belgica antarctica*. See section 7.3.

Indeed, the presence of these two flowering plants have attracted much interest in recent years because they are found in extreme environments. For example, Xiong et al. (1999), who examined the photosynthetic temperature response of both plants (C. *quitensis* and D. *antarctica*) near the US Palmer Station (64°46'27"S 64°03'10"W) found that the optimal leaf temperature for net photosynthetic rates were 14 and 10°C, respectively. These authors suggested that the temperature optima for growth for both plants may be in the range of 16 to 20°C, and therefore global warming in the region ought to place these species close to their growth temperature optima. The same authors also did other *in vitro* experiments to determine that the plants were able to maintain a substantial temperature optimum at near-freezing temperatures. Upson et al. (2008) examined root-associated fungi of both plants found in the Shetland Islands and Léonie Islands, adjacent to the southern end of the Antarctic Peninsula around 67°S 68°W, and found low numbers the arbuscular mycorrhizal fungi compared to other conspecific plants collected further north in South Georgia. Furthermore, endophytic symbiont yeasts were also studied on the roots of the same two species on King George Island, one of the South Shetland Islands, by Santiago et al. (2017) showing the interests generated by these plants. Disappointingly, in none of these publications, is it acknowledged that Emil Racovitza was the discoverer of those plants in Antarctica.

Figure 7.2.1 Recent photographs of the two flowering plants and surrounding associations.

A-B: *Colobanthus quitensis* with flowers in A;

C: two *Colobanthus quitensis* plants (green) surrounded by *Deschampsia antarctica* grasses;

D: a large tuft of *Deschampsia antarctica*;

E: view of a large assemblage of marine bivalves collected by kelp gulls and dumped on the nest with only a few visible live tuffs of *D. antarctica,* Graham Coast, North part of Petermann Island, 2020;

F: large patch of *D. antarctica* being the location of a kelp gull nest with bivalve debris left by the birds on the edge of its nest, Graham Coast, Argentine Islands, Galindez Island, 2021.

(A-D: Photographs courtesy of the late Dr Franz Gingele; E-F: photographs courtesy of Dr Ivan Parnikoza).

Recent investigations were also made by Nuzhyna et al. (2019) comparing the anatomy of distant Antarctic plants from Argentine Islands on the Antarctic Peninsula and others from the South Shetland Islands, using also cultivated plants. This study followed on from the work of Parnikoza et al. (2011) which showed that the two species discussed here have adapted through time to live under extreme Antarctic conditions and are the bi-product of a successful history of migration that eventually led to speciation. Further, Kozeretska et al. (2011) who studied the development of the tundra vegetation near Arctowski station on King George Island, South Shetland Island, determined the various growth stages of *D. antarctica* from juvenile to subsenile plans across three different regions (coastal, intermediate and periglacial). These authors argued that new environments, likely to become available through the disappearance of glaciers, will easily become the sites of new 'colonizing' plants such as *D. antarctica*.

Near the coast, on the other hand, the plants appear more stressed due to sea spray. In another study, Parnikoza et al. (2012), studied vegetation on the Argentine Islands (65°15'S, 64°16'W adjacent to the Antarctic Peninsula) where birds, principally the kelp gull (*Laurus dominicanus*) (See fig. 9.4.4A) nests on plants such as *D. antarctica* and mosses (*Sainiona georgicoincinata*) or use the latter two as nest material. These authors postulated that floral material lost by the birds in flight can help towards their propagation. Perhaps, these plant species have been in this region for a very long time during which climatic conditions in Antarctica 'deteriorated' over one to two millions years. The study of the pollen of these two plants in old sedimentary sequences ought to provide an answer to those suggestions.

In addition, with climatic conditions changing rapidly in the Antarctic Peninsula region, both plants are more than likely going to prosper and invade new niches. Xiong et al. (1999), through experiments, indicated that

these plants have a much higher optimal net photosynthetic rate (op. cit.). Are birds the likely agent to help with the migration is a question worth asking? Pernikoxa (op. cit.) already provides us with the answer. But the fungal association on plant roots as mentioned by Upson et al. (2008) and Podolich et al. (2021) needs to be also considered; are birds or even wind in this instance the likely passive agents to the 'colonisation' of new niches? Again, as Parnikoza et al. (2012, 2018) commented on, with the birds dropping plant fragments, the root fungi are likely to accompany those fragments. In addition, a new threat is envisaged by Yevchun et al. (2021) by the arrival of many tourists on some of the Antarctic sites who may bring new pathogens that may affect the plants discussed above. These authors are urging to have a code of conduct to prevent plant diseases to become introduced and caused significant long-term damage.

7.3 The amazing chironomid fly: *Belgica antarctica*

KEY POINTS

- Another of Racovitza's scientific legacies has been the discovery of the flightless chironomid fly *Belgica antarctica*

- It is endemic to the Antarctic Peninsula where it was discovered by Emil Racovitza in 1898 in the de Gerlache Strait.

- This chironomid is equipped to survive in extreme environments and has been extensively studied to determine its ability to survive/live/thrive in such environments. This must result from a long history of the organism in the Antarctic region and Its biological adaptation/modification is a testimony of this.

- Over 100 scientific papers have been dedicated to the study of *B. antarctica* with a thorough review of many of the papers discussed in Kozeretska et al. (2022).

- *B. antarctica* could well be the emblem of the Belgica expedition, an exemplar of survival in extreme environments.

Emil Racovitza made a significant find on islands in the de Gerlache Strait region: a flightless chironomid fly barely a few mm long; the first insect in the Antarctic region! In the same area, Racovitza had found the only two flowering plants (*Deschampsia antarctica and Collobanthus quitensis*), but these are also found in the Beagle Channel. See previous chapter.

In his conference paper presented to the 'Société belge de Géographie on December 22, 1899 (only a few months after the return of the expedition to Antwerp), Racovitza (1900a) briefly described a small insect he had found in the de Gerlache Strait by saying: *'the most highly organized animal is a poor fly, which has almost completely lost its wings. It hangs out a miserable existence near small pools of water in which wriggle its tiny larvae which are its offsprings'*. Also, on February 23, 1900, Racovitza (1900b) presented another talk, this time at the Zoological Society of France in La Sorbonne, and described a *'weak and delicate fly which desperately struggles to escape the deadly embraces of three ferocious spiders which want to suck its blood'*. In his recently published diary Racovitza (1998) mentions that on January 25, 1898 when he found the small chironomid fly that he saw two males mating with a single female. His observations were made at 30 m above sea level. These are the brief description of the extraordinary flightless chironomid fly he had found; the only insect so far found on the Antarctic Peninsula. There is another chironomid fly (also commonly refered to as a 'midge') called *Parochlus steinenii* (Gerke) that is found on the Shetland Islands near the Antarctic Peninsula. This species, on the other hand, possesses wings and can fly. It was described in 1889 by Gerke from a collection on South Georgia in 1882-1883.

The chironomid fly *Belgica antarctica* (Figs. 7.3.1, 7.3.2) found by Racovitza perhaps ought to be the 'emblem' of the Belgica expedition, not only because its name association *Belgica antarctica*, but because it is exceptional, so much like the scientific achievements of the expedition. *B. antarctica* is exceptionally well adapted to live in an extreme environment such as in the de Gerlache Strait. It is equipped to survive under very low temperatures and sometimes in low oxygen conditions (see more information below). The point to make is that its physiology is such that it must have evolved over a long period of time in order to live on the fringe of Antarctica. It is now found also on Lynch Island and the Byers Peninsula, both part of the Shetland Islands (Usher and Edwards, 1984 and Richard et al., 1994).

Disappointingly, many authors who refer to those species never mention their discoverer, Emil Racovitza (Kozeretska et al., 2022 being an exception). Even in the important Antarctic Map Folio Series, produced by the American Geographical Society of New York, and in Folio 5 published in 1967 (Greene et al., 1967), the map that details the presence of dipterans and fleas in Antarctica provides a poor and incorrect illustration of *B. antarctica*. Why not use the superb drawings made by the Belgian entomologist (and medical doctor) J.-Ch. Jacobs who described it as shown here in Fig. 7.3.2 This is puzzling.

Knowing that there was potential competition with the *Southern Cross* expedition (also refered to as the British Antarctic expedition) to Cape Adare in 1898-1900 led by C. Borchgrevink, in that the biologist on that expedition Nicolai Hanson could possibly find insects and fish, the entomologists who were asked to describe some of the collections made by E. Racovitza, and the fish expert Louis Dollo who was to describe fish from that expedition, relied on a customary rule in taxonomy: 'publish a diagnosis for your new species with the new name so as to retain priority: publish the full descriptions later'. This is exactly what the entomologists did by publishing a quick note in the *Annales de la Société entomologique de Belgique* in 1900 (volume 44; with authors followed by page numbers: André E. 105, Bourgeois J. 105, Brunner von Wattenwyl C. 112-113, Fairmaire L. 111-112, Jacobs J.-Ch. 106-107, Lameere A. 112, and Tosquinet W. J 112), and equally L. Dollo in four short publications (Dollo 1900a,b,c,d) in the *Académie royale de Belgique, Bulletin de la Classe des Sciences* provided the new fish names and their respective diagnoses.

Since the flightless midge *B. antarctica* was collected and described, over 100 papers have been published on this exceptional insect, reasons being that it is an amazing organism that lives under extreme conditions. Photos of this chironomid are shown in Fig. 7.3.1 and an assemblage of the original drawings made by Jacobs is shown in Fig. 7.3.2. Note that *B. antarctica* has atrophied wings as shown in Figs. 7.3.2 A,B.

Kozeretska et al. (2022) who recently reviewed knowledge on *B. antarctica* which they called 'a natural model organism for extreme environments' identified that as of January 10, 2021 there had been 3,750,000 Google search results on this organism! This clearly demonstrates a wide interest in this chironomid which has been discussed in so many publications (for many of them refer to the list in Kozeretska et al. (2022).

Among the many studies is the work of Michailova et al. (2023) who produced a chromosome map of *B. antarctica*, including chromosome variability. Also, the recent study by Ihtimanska et al. (2023) examined larvae in great details and also discussed larval deformities, in particular the mouth pieces. I note that for this work some 176 larvae were dissected! Are there plenty of biological material available for such studies?

One suggestion perhaps is to search for subfossil mandibles of this chironomid that are strongly sclerotized (Fig. 7.3.2 F; see figs. 2,3 in Ihtimanska et al. (2023)) in lacustrine sediments on the Antarctic Peninsula to determine how long they have occupied those habitats. Chironomid mandibles have long been recovered from lake sediments; the recent paper by Courtney-Mustaphi et al. (2024) is an example among many. In addition, radiocarbon

dates can be easily obtained from analysis of such mandibles. The issue is that *B. antarctica* could be transported to new site via human activities. This needs to be further investigated.

Here are some of the findings about *B. antarctica*:

1. it can survive the freezing of its body fluids
2. it has a 2 years life span, with 2 growing seasons
3. it can accumulate the energy needed to reproduce;
4. egg development takes 16 days at 4°C
5. adults live 7 to 10 days
6. it has a deep purplish black coloration that allows heat absorption and protects against UV light
7. it can tolerate large changes in salinity and pH
8. it can survive without oxygen for 2–4 weeks
9. it burrows at depth to cope for freezing temperatures and can survive down to -15°C
10. it has the lowest genome of any insects
11. its sex ratio is 1:1 at eclosion
12. females are slightly larger (1.5 to 3.2 mm in length) than males (1.6 to 2.5 mm), and
13. its larvae are freezing-tolerant during the austral summer and elaborate a complex of cryoprotectants including erythritol, glucose, sucrose and trehalose.

More information is available in Kozeretska et al. (2022).

Figure 7.3.1 Recent photographs of *Belgica antarctica* generously supplied by Professor Richard Lee.

A: adult male;

B: male and female mating;

C: fourth instar of larvae.

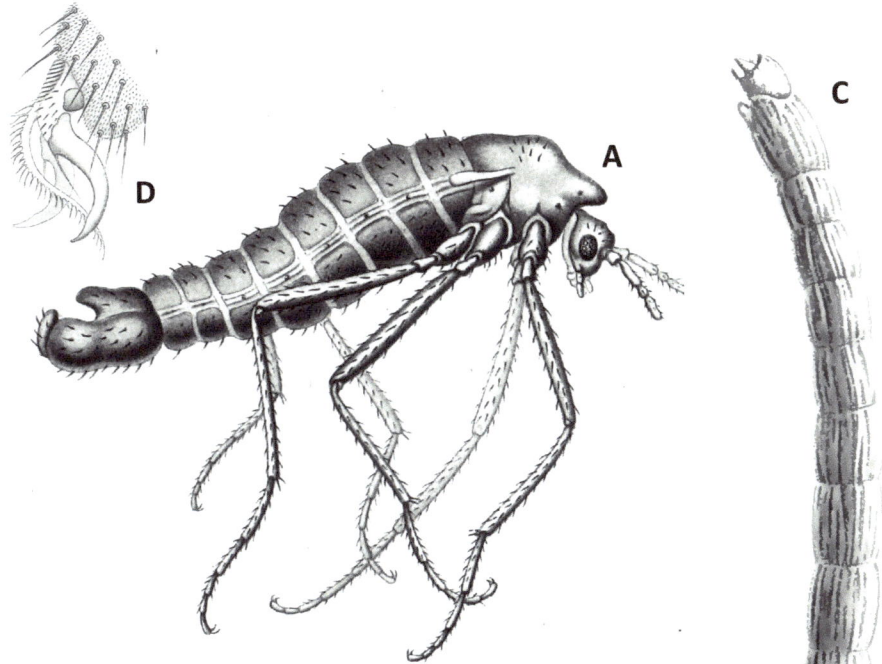

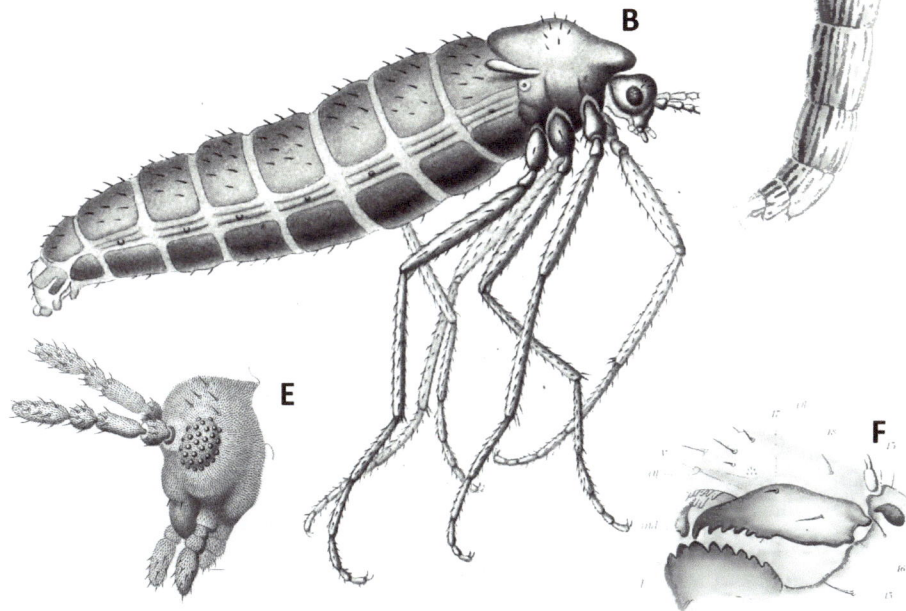

Figure 7.3.2 Illustrations of *Belgica antarctica* made by J.-Ch. Jacobs (1906).

A: adult male;
B: adult female;

C: larva:

D: end of foot;

E: head;

F: enlarged end of the head seen at an angle to show the strongly sclerotized mandibles.

7.4 Acarid mites

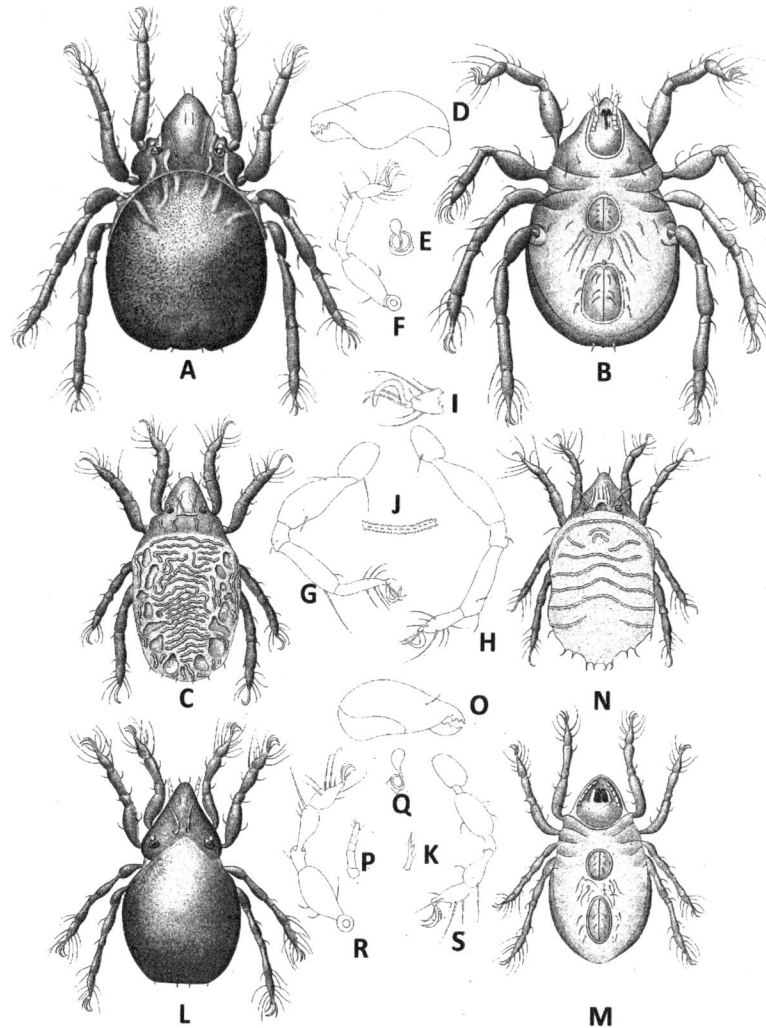

Racovitza collected two species of acarid mites in the de Gerlache Strait, plus a small one too damaged to warrant description. These were described by Michael (1903) but the latter did not provide the details of the collections apart from saying they come from between 64°23' S and 67°59' S and 62°02' to 70°39'W. In his recently published dairy, Racovitza (1998) mentions finding mites (referred to as 'podurelles' by him) on January 25, 1898 in the same location as the flightless chironomid fly. This location must have been Auguste Island or the adjacent Two Hummocks Island, both sites visited on that day (landing V). Illustrations by Michael (1903) of those two species are reproduced here in Fig. 7.4.1. Since then, Wallrock (1962) argued for a change of generic name to *Alaskozetes*, but it appears from this latter publication that the taxonomy of these two Antarctic species requires further revision. Wallrock (1962) provided a redescription of that genus that is accessible at: https://www.marinespecies.org/aphia.php?p=taxdetails&id=508180 on 2024-07-09.

Dalenius (1965) has since confirmed Wallrock (1962)'s taxonomic revision. Nevertheless, Wallrock (1962) broadened the distribution of those two mites to the Chilean Base Gonzales Videla, Penguin Island, FIDS Base in Admiralty Bay on King George Island, Livingston and Deception Islands, all last three in the South Shetland group. He also listed a few additional findings in localities such as Palmer and Ross Islands (for more details see Wallrock, 1963). In 2002, Hogg and Stephens compiled a list of mites from the maritime and continental Antarctic regions and argued for the potential changes that are to occur in the region where the terrestrial arthropods are found, that include climate change and habitat destruction.

It is worth mentioning that the distribution of those mites all around the Antarctic Peninsula must certainly be caused through passive transport by birds between sites. With climate change over the last few decades, one could ask if the mites are likely to broaden their distribution. Interestingly, nobody seems to have checked the avifauna for mites, either in among their feathers, feet and nostrils, or in their guts.

7.5 Mosses

KEY POINTS

- Racovitza collected mosses in the de Gerlache Strait, many of which are now known to also occur in the northern hemisphere polar regions.

- Climate amelioration over the last few decades that is affecting the Antarctic Peninsula already sees significant changes, such as an expansion of moss fields.

Emil Racovitza collected a substantial amount of mosses during the 20 landings in the de Gerlache Strait with specimens obtained from only 10 sites. The specimens were well preserved and eventually studied by the French bryologist Jules Cardot in 1902. He had already written a preliminary note on his investigations (Cardot, 1900). It is of interest that Cardot's manuscript was completed in just a year (28.11.1900) after the return of the Belgica expedition. Fig. 7.5.1 displays several of specimens which are now housed at the the Herbarium of the Meise Botanic Garden in Belgium. These had been digitised and permission was granted by Dr F. Leliart to display them here. It is fortunate that these Belgica specimens were returned to Belgium after their study as Cardot's collections and books were thrashed in his absence during the German occupations in WWI (refer to: https://plants.jstor.org/stable/10.5555/al.ap.person.bm000001274). Nevertheless, Cardot (1902) discussed at length the distribution of the mosses, not only in the southern end of South America but also looked at mosses described from South Georgia and Kerguelen Islands, and he also discussed mosses elsewhere in the Pacific region. Concerning the collections made in the de Gerlache Strait, over a period of 21 days, Cardot identified 27 species, all obtained by Racovitza. Cardot stated that the mosses were generally well developed and some quite large and, except for the species grouped under two genera (*Bryum*, 5 species and *Webra, 2 species*), all were sterile. Cardot (1902) claimed that all the species returned by Racovitza have affinities with northern hemisphere taxa that are found in temperate and cold regions. He went on to discuss that some species are also found in New Zealand and Australia, but also in South Georgia and Kerguelen. In a away, this is a surprise finding as the Antarctic Peninsula has so many endemic taxa, plants as well as invertebrates. This needs to be further examined. In 1900, Cardot claimed that among the species he examined from the de Gerlache Strait, six are 'absolutely identical' to Arctic species. These are: *Distichium alpinum, Webera cruda, Pogonatum alpinum, Polytrichum strictum, Hypnum uncinatum and H. revolutum*. Cardot (1902) further noted that the taxon *Hypnum uncinatum* was found at 6 localities, followed by 4 for *Bryum gerlachei* and *Pogonatum alpinum*, with less occurrences for the other species. I was unable to determine if the widespread *Hypnum uncinatum* ought to be synonymised with *Sanionia uncinata* and will therefore keep Cardot's original nomenclature.

The monograph by Cardot (1902) is nevertheless a very impressive one as it comprises numerous detailed illustrations of mosses in some 13 plates of specimens collected by Racovitza, not only in the de Gerlache Strait but also along the Beagle Channel and nearby regions. The last plate 14 also shows photographs of two mosses, over 30 cm across each, but these are of insufficient quality to be reproduced here.

Examination of Fig. 7.5.1 shows that many of the well pressed specimens have subsequently been examined by several experts; types have subsequently been selected and comments written on those cards. These are indeed very valuable specimens.

Figure 7.4.1 (opposite) Acarid mites sketches by Michael (1903). *Alaskozetes antarctica*

A: adult female dorsal view;

B: adult male, ventral view;

C: nymph;

D-K: various parts of the anatomy (for more details refer to Michael, 1903); *Alaskozetes belgicae*

L: adult female dorsal view;

M: adult male, ventral view,

N: nymph;

O-S: various parts of the anatomy (for more details refer to Michael, 1903).

Note the length of *A. antarctica* is 1.05 mm and that of *A. belgicae* is 0.56 mm.

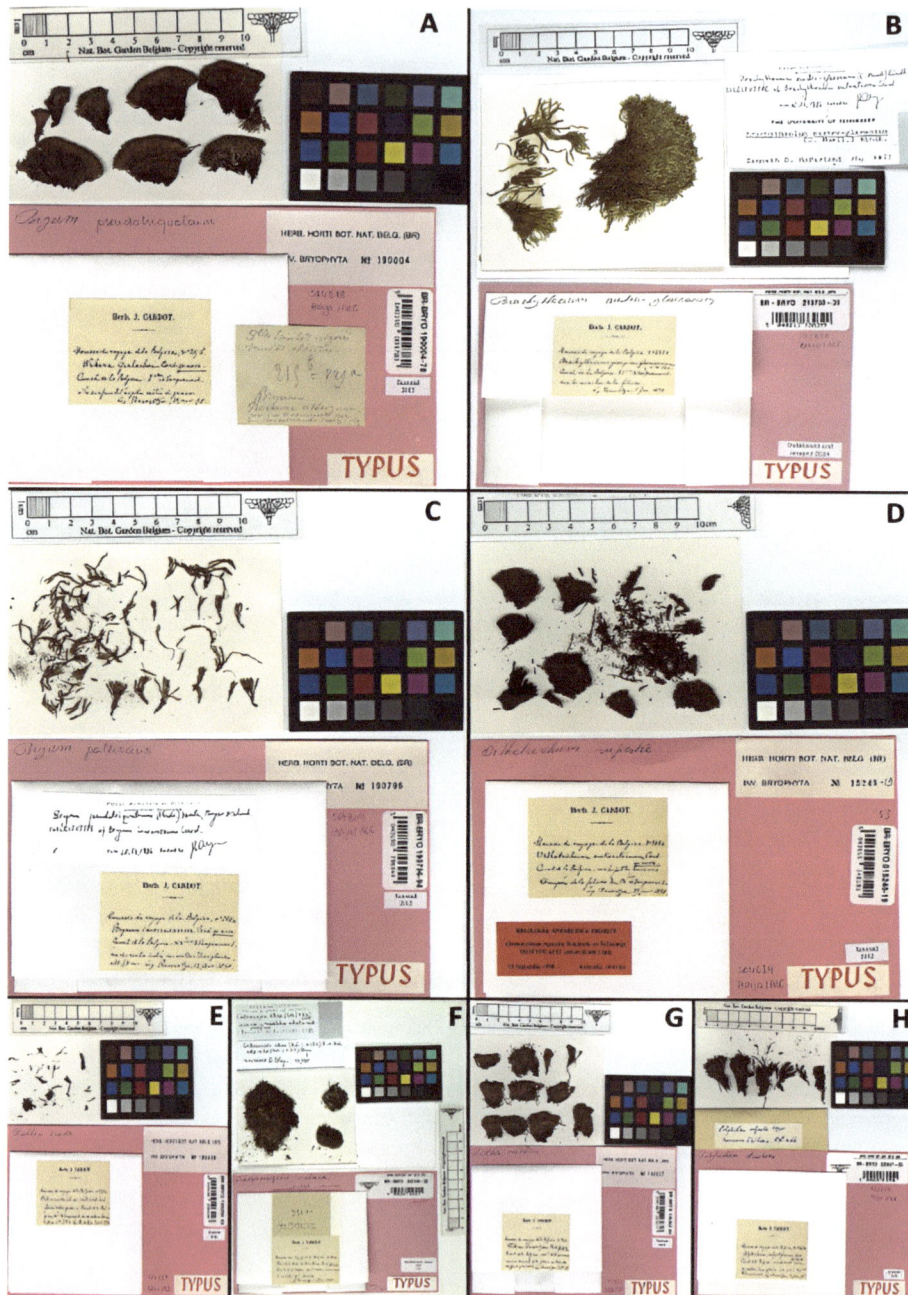

Figure 7.5.1 Mosses from the de Gerlache Strait and collected by Emil Racovitza.

A: *Bryum pseudotriquetum*, Landing I (Auguste Island), at the surface of clay mixed with guano 28.1.1898;

B: *Brachytherium austro-glareosum*, Landing XI (Terre de Danco, near Cap Anna Osterreith), on the cornice (corniche) of the cliff, 1.2.1899;

C: *Bryum pseudotriquetum*, Landing XX (Danco Land, at the entrance of the Lemaire Channel), on isolated rocks in the middle of a glacier, altitude 50 m, 12.2.1898;

D: *Orthotrichum rupestre*, Landing XX (Danco Land, at the entrance of the Lemaire Channel) on small moist terraces of the cliff, 29.1.1898;

E: *Bohlia cruda* stunted form, Landing X (Brabant Island near Buls Bay), on rocks surrounded by ice, altitude 350 m, 30.1.1898;

F: *Cratoneuropsis relaxa,* Landing XI (Danco Land, near Van Beneden Cape), on the cornices of the cliff, 2.2.1898;

G: *Bohlia nutans,* de Gerlache Strait, Landing XII (Cavelier du Cuverville Island), on the cornice of the cliff around graminae tuffs, 2.2.1898;

H: *Polytrichun strichum,* Landing XX (Danco Land, at the entrance of the Lemaire Channel), on isolated rocks in the middle of a glacier, 12.2.1898.

Roland et al. (2024) recently published the results of an important and alarming study based on Landsat archive images - spanning the period of 1986 to 2021 - that show a clear widespread greening across the Antarctic Peninsula that is leading to a major change in moss-dominated ecosystems and therefore also complete terrestrial ecosystems. These authors did not discuss the taxonomy of those mosses. A question remains: are the current moss taxa expanding their range, or are new taxa going to invade the Antarctic Peninsula, especially since ecotourists could be instrumental in introducing new taxa, some of which could become very invasive? We ought to consider that flowering plants could fall under the same regime.

7.6 Lichen

KEY POINT

The lichen collected by E. Racovitza are found in both polar regions in contrast with other plant taxa.

Emil Racovitza among his collections did not ignore lichen; an important group that principally grows on rocks and trees. His collections went for study to Edvard August Wainio, the eminent Finnish lichenologist at the time. Wainio in 1919 adopted the modern Finnish spelling for his name now known as Vainio. For more information on his tumultuous career, visit the following web site: https://en.wikipedia.org/wiki/Edvard_August_Vainio.

Wainio (1903) in his monograph stated that Racovitza had collected 55 lichen taxa, 38.18% of which are also found in the Arctic and temperate regions of Europe. Nine species (16.36%) are endemic to the Antarctic and Magellanic land. In addition, three species in the Antarctic are common with American ones. He also concluded that the lichen flora of the Antarctic Peninsula shared more species with the Arctic one compared to the Magellanic flora. In Wainio (1903)'s 51 pages monograph, there are 4 plates illustrating lichen, one of which is reproduced here. In addition, to accompany the description of the taxa are diagnoses presented in Latin and for each individual taxon, Wainio (1903) provides details for all the localities where the lichen were found. It would be interesting to return to the 20 landing sites in the de Gerlache Strait and see if additional taxa have now been found after Racovitza's collecting in 1898. In addition, another question remains:

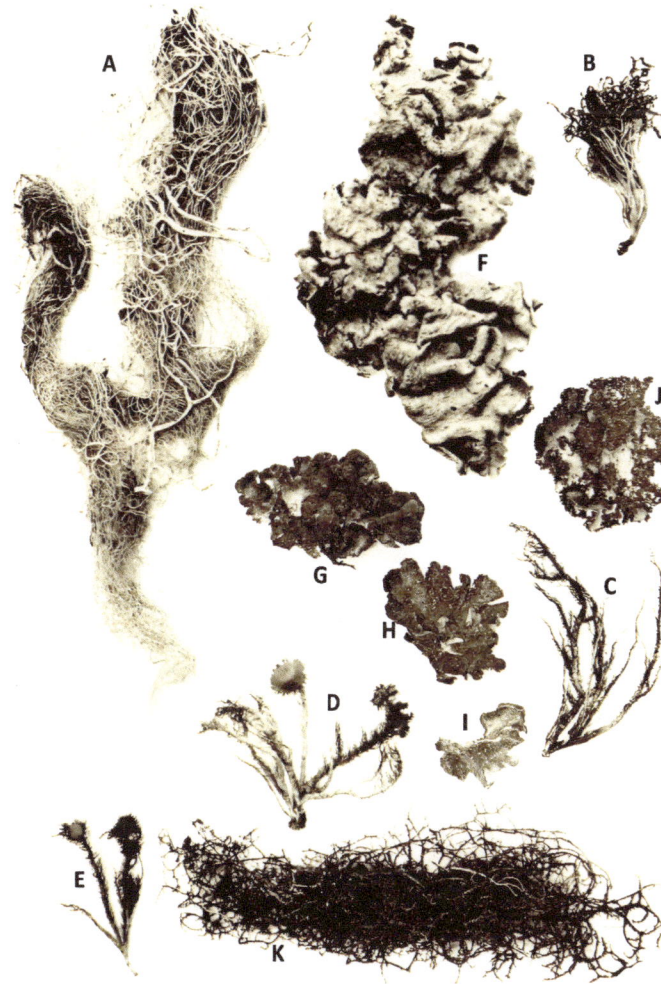

Figure 7.6.1 Lichen.

A. *Usnea cavernosa*;

B. *U. sulphurea* var. *sorediifera*;

C-E. *U. trachycarpa* var. *trachycarpoides*;

F. *Pseudocyphellaria albidopallens*;

G-I. *Stricta hypochra*;

K. *Umbilicaria cylindrica* Dub. f. *propagulifera*;

L. *Cetraria gracilent*.

All illustrations modified and processed using Photoshop© from Wainio, 1903, plate 3).

how is it possible that many of the lichen found in de Gerlache Strait also occur in the Arctic? Is plain morphological identification sufficient, or should genetic studies be used to differentiate between the various taxa?

7.7 Bryophytes
(Hépatiques - Liverworts)

KEY POINT

Emil Racovitza collected several bryophytes that have since been revised by Bednarek-Ochyra et al. (2000).

The bryophytes collected during the Belgica expedition were examined by the German Franz Stephani. His notes are brief as they only give the names of 29 taxa linked to localities (listed in Latin), from the Beagle Channel and surrounding areas as well as the de Gerlache Strait. Only three originate from the latter area. Stephani (1901) stated that none of the taxa were new as they had already been described by C.M. Gottshe (1890) from South Georgia. We have to assume that these species names are correct, despite the fact that the work of Stephani has been severely criticised by Gradstein (2006), since Stephani related his taxonomy to that previously published by Gottsche (1890).

Nevertheless, an important monograph by Bednarek-Ochyra et al. (2000) that appeared since acknowledged the collections made by Emil Racovitza and rapidly identified by Stephani (1901), and provided the following revision: the taxon identified by Stephani as *Lophozia hatcheri* is now synonymised to *Barbilophozia hatcheri, L. propagulifera* is synonymized to *L. exisa and Cephalozia varians* is now synonymized to *Cephaloziella varians*. Bednarek-Ochyra et al. (2000) state that these three species are the most widespread liverworts in the *Antarctic* biome. They also remarked that *C. varians* that was collected by E. Racovitza was subsequently described by Douin (1920) as a separate species, *Cephaloziella antarctica*. I have to assume that the Belgica material belongs to *C. antarctica* following Douin (1920)'s remark and not *C. varians*.

7.8 Seals and penguins in the de Gerlache Strait

The de Gerlache Strait is well known today for the presence of whales, penguin colonies as well as several species of seals. These are discussed at length in chapters 9.2 to 9.4. In those, distribution maps of seals and penguins as recorded by Emil Racovitza are produced for the first time. One figure of photographs (Fig. 7.8.1) provided by Mikołaj Golachowski (aka Miko) is shown here. These are reproduced here with his permission.

Figure 7.8.1. Animals recently photographed in the de Gerlache Strait by M. Golachowski.

A: Gentoo penguin colony on Couverville Island;

B: Weddell seal and Chinstrap penguins on Hydrurga Rocks;

C: Weddell seal in common curved postion;

D: Moulting Gentoo penguins on Couverville Island.

7.9 Geological observations in the de Gerlache Strait

KEY POINTS

- Arctowski, during his visit to some 14 island sites and 3 sites in Antarctica, collected a vast quantity of rocks, both *in situ* and erratics.

- Disappointingly, Aphonse-François Renard, who was to analyse and interpret these rocks, died prematurely. Hence, no geological map was made as a result of Arctowski's collections.

- A. Pelikan (1909) in Prague took on the analyses and descriptions of the *in situ* rocks collected by Arctowski.

- These are published in the monograph series dealing with the results of the Belgica expedition. Geologists who followed on from the Belgica expedition either failed to refer to Pelikan's work or did not discuss his geochemical and petrograpic results.

- A small set of photographs taken by staff from the Royal Belgian Institute of Natural Sciences (=RBINS) are presented here to show the quality of the 700 thin sections of the rocks collected by Arctowski.

Henryk Arctowski took part in 17 of the 20 landings in the de Gerlache Strait (Table 7.1). On Brabant Island, he spent a total of 168 hours. His aim was to collect rocks and also make geological and geomorphological observations. The original aim was to provide all that information and rock specimens to Professor Alphonse-François Renard from the University of Ghent in Belgium. We must remember that Renard was very influential in advising the scientific program of the Belgica expedition, and in particular the idea to spend much time in Magellan Strait and the Beagle Channel. Sadly, Renard died in July 1903 aged 60 and never got to publish the geological results of the Belgica expedition. For more information, refer to chapter 10. Nevertheless, he organized for up to 700 rock specimens collected by Arctowski to be thin sectioned, a process that enables a geologist to identify minerals and structure from a rock under a petrological microscope having made an almost transparent section of the rock that is only 60 microns thick. Renard apparently had written many notes having observed the sections, but his death prevented him to publish his results. At the recommendation of the Belgica Commission as well as by H. Arctowski, it was agreed to send all the thin sections with some descriptions made by Renard of their provenance to the Austrian Professor Anton Pelikan who held a post at Karl Ferdinand University in Prague. The latter stated in the introduction on the rocks of de Gerlache Strait (Pelikan 1909) that he was given Renard's notes but had discarded them as he disagreed with some of the original views. He recognised that there were a vast number of rocks called 'erratics' which mean that they were not *in situ*, more than likely having been transported by glaciers and dumped elsewhere after glacial melt. This is well interpreted as we know that Arctowski spent quite some time examining ancient glacial deposits such as moraines and tills, and by identifying the composition of the erratic rocks, one may be able to determine their original location and therefore estimate the distance and directions traveled by the glaciers. We note also that Arctowski collected sandy material, resulting from the weathering of rocks, likely with the aim to identify minerals, some possibly exotic and/or precious. This remains untouched but much material can be found in the collections at the Institut royal des Sciences naturelles de Belgique in Brussels where many of the material collected by the Belgica expedition are housed and curated (Fig. 7.9.1).

Overall, Pelikan (1909) identified several rock types which are listed in Table 7.9.1. He also provided extensive geochemical analyses for 7 samples but they will not be listed here. Disappointingly, as discussed later on, none of the investigations following from the study of Pelikan (1909) refer to those detailed analyses.

Débarquement (landing) no.	Location	Rock types/lithologies
I	Auguste Island	diabase = basalt gabbro
II	Moreno Island	quartz augite, diorite, augite (pyroxene) diorite
III	Harry Island	quartz-free augite diorite
VI	Two Hummock Island	quartz diorite, melaphyre, micropegmatite, granite, porphyrite
VII	Cobalescu Island	gabbro like at landing X
VIII	Gaston Island opposite Reclus Cap	diorite, porphyrite
IX	Cap et crique Osterrieth	quartz diorite, aplite, gangue with porphyritic diorite = large crystals in fine matrix
X	Brabant Island, foot of Mt Solvay	olivine gabbro, porphyritic vein rock
XI	Cape Beneden, Andvord Bay	porphyritic diorite, orthoclase porphyrite
XII	Coast of Danco Land between XI & XII Ile Rougé	porphyrite, lapilli tuff (trachytic and andesitic character)
XIII	SE on Danco Land	pegmatite, sandstone, shale 'family' and clayey slate
XIV	Anvers Island	gabbro, lamprophyritic (= K-rich biotite, K felspar) gangue, odinite and oddinite transiting between diabase melaphyre and lamprophyre
XV	Wiencke Island, west side	quartz diorite, gangue diabase
XVI	Wauvermanns Island	as above
XVII	Bob Island	gabbro, gangue rock consisting of porphyritic diorite
XVIII	Banck Island	granite, malachite
XIX	Flanders Bay, small group of islands "Moureaux'	granite, malachite
XX	Danco Land	decomposed porphyrite, quartz diorite granite.

Table 7.9.1 List of lithologies identified by A. Pelikan (1909) for rocks which were collected *in situ* by Arctowski.

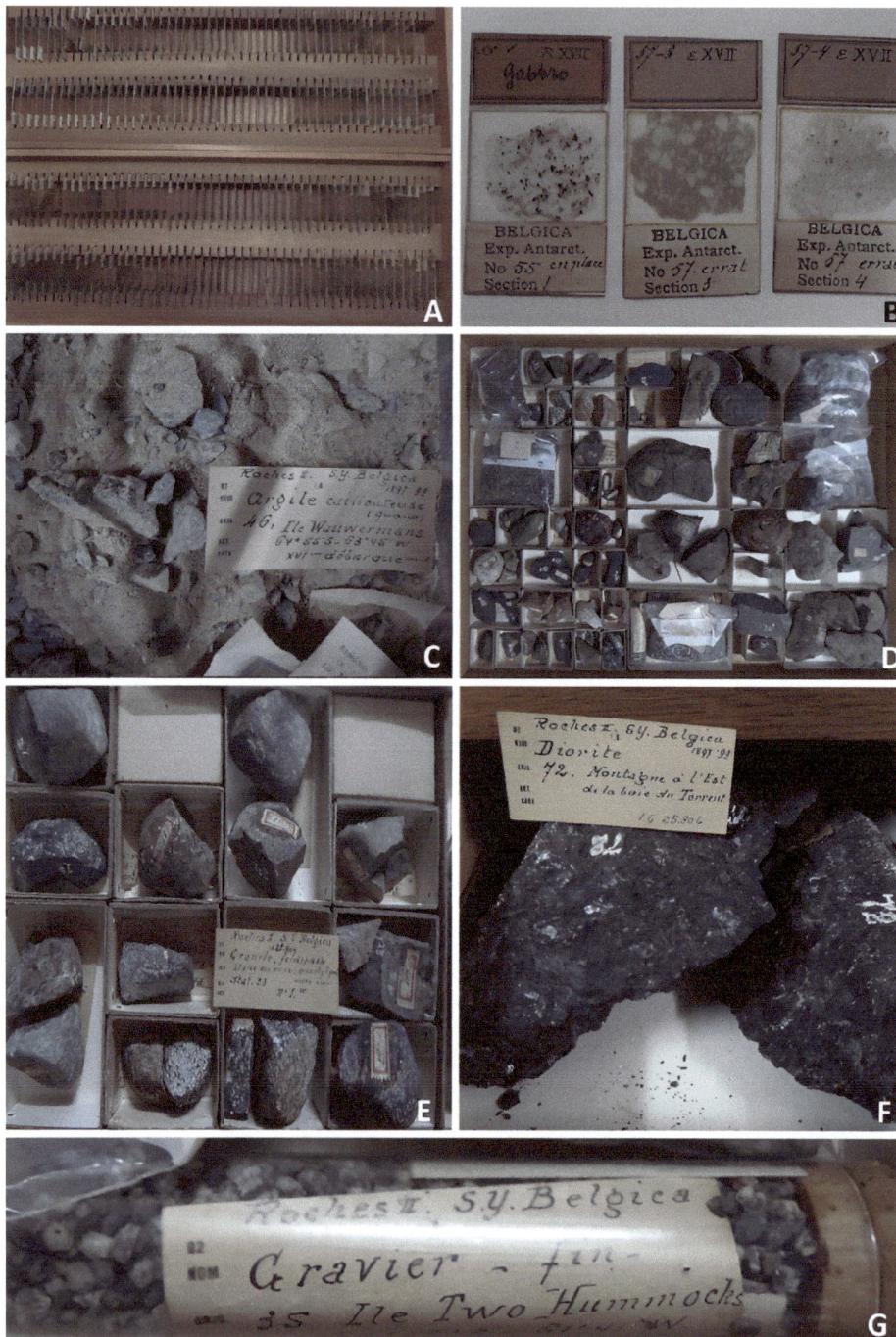

Figure 7.9.1 Collage of photographs showing:

A: tray containing the numerous thin sections (~700 in total in the RBINS' collections) of both the *in situ* as well as erratic rocks from both de Gerlache Strait and the Magellan Strait collected by H. Artowski.

B: example of three thin sections made of the rocks; left: gabbro, middle: erratic, right: erratic, all from landing XVII on Bob Island, de Gerlache strait;

C: shaley rocks, sand and guano from Wauvermans Island, landing XVI, de Gerlache Strait;

D: tray containing numerous racks collected by H. Arctowski during the Belgica expedition;

E: rocks from the Belgica expedition, one of which is labelled as granite with pink or white feldspars, quartz and black mica;

F: diorite from the eastern mountain at Torrent Bay, Magellan Strait;

G: fine gravel, from Two Hummock Island, landing IV, de Gerlache Strait.

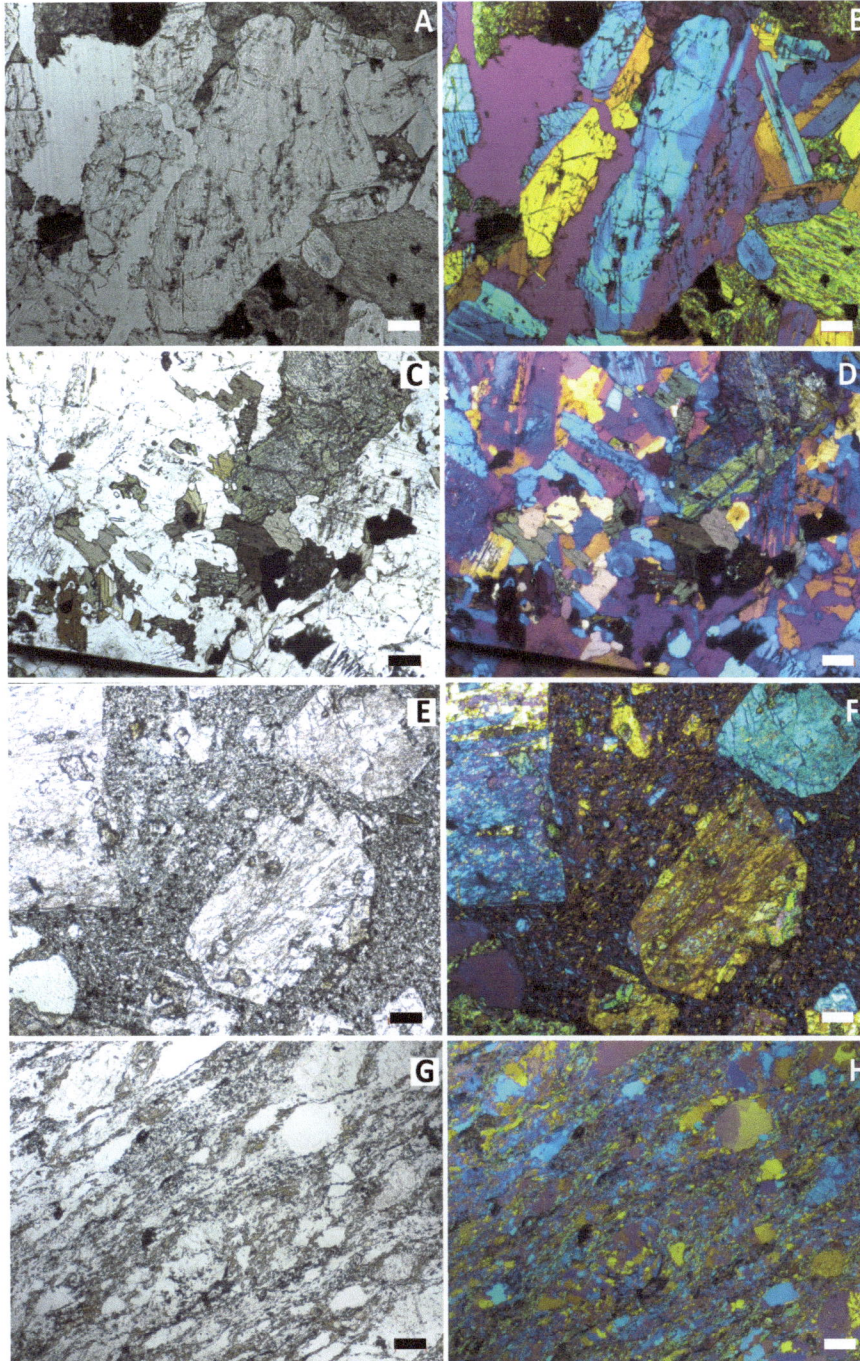

Figure 7.9.2 Thin sections (60 μm thick) of rocks collected by H. Arctowski in the de Gerlache Strait. On the left are slides photographed in normal light and on right are slides the same slides this time photographed in polarized light to help distinguish the different crystals. All the bars at the bottom right hand corner of each photo represent 200 μm.

A-B: gabbro (slide 55.1) from Banck Island, landing XVIII;

C-D: quartz diorite (slide 32) from landing VI;

E-F: erratic boulder (slide 57.3), Bob Island, landing XVII;

G-H: Erratic boulder (slide 36.17), from landing VI. All rocks from de Gerlache Strait.

Determination of some of the crystals seen in polarised light are:

B: the large mauve crystal on the top left hand corner is a pyroxene, the yellow in the centre is also a pyroxene with its twin on the left coloured pale blue.

D: the matrix consists primarily of quartz and plagioclase, and the dark, almost mineral consists of biotite (the same minerals are coloured brown to pale brown in **C**).

F: the pale blue crystal near the top right hand corner is olivine, and the large golden crystal near the centre consists of pyroxene; the small pale blueish-green crystal inside the golden one near the bottom is epidote; the matrix is altered.

H: the mauve crystal (centre top) is quartz and so are the orangey-brown crystals; the pale brown crystals best seen in

G consist of biotite. The whole slide displays strong schistosity as a result of deformation. Information on the mineralogy was provided by Professor DJ Ellis. Photographs provided by Tommy D'heuvaert from RBINS.

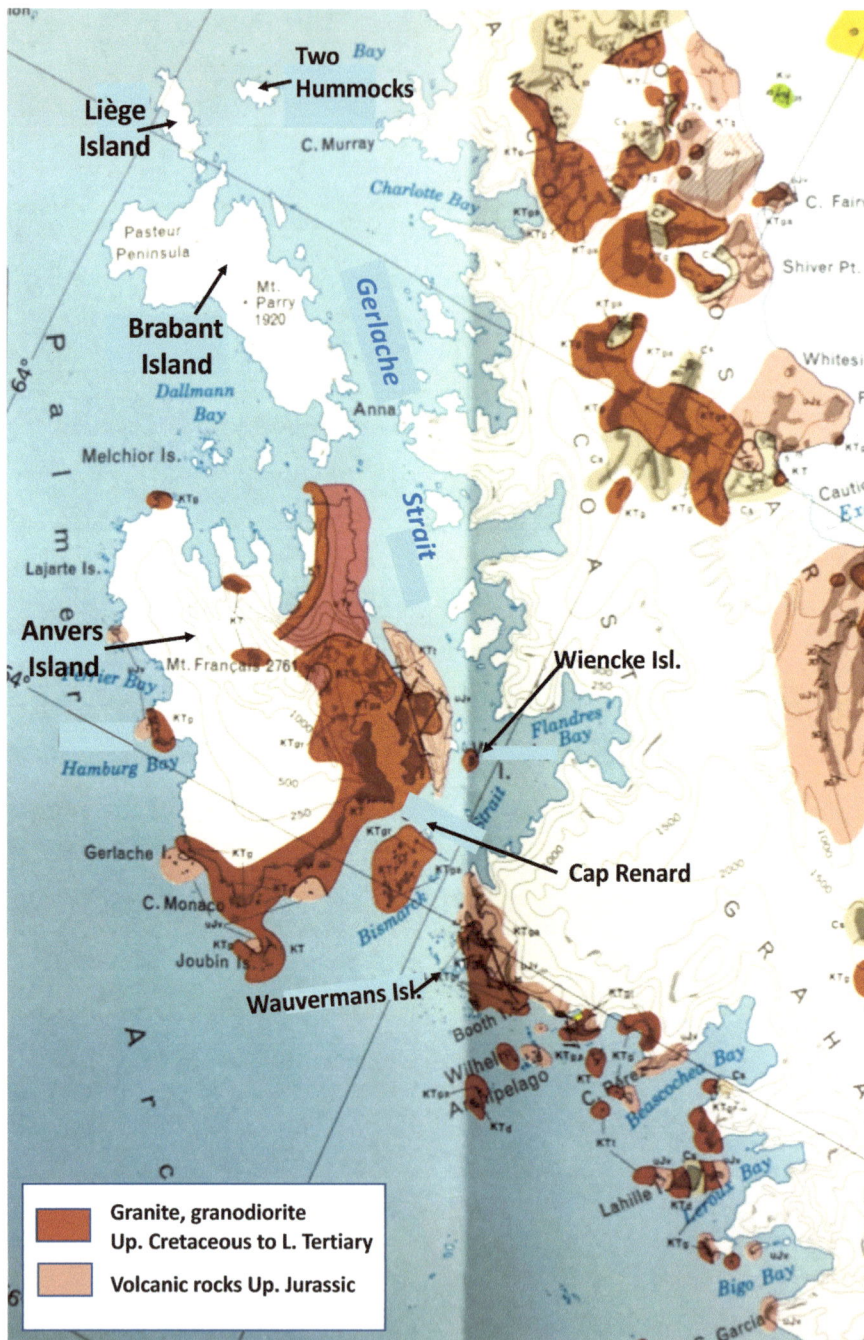

At first, the geologist R.J. Adie who completed his PhD at Cambridge University in 1953 on the 'Rocks of Graham Land' published the first map describing some of the geology of the Antarctic Peninsula. It appeared in the Antarctic map folio series edited by V.C. Bushnell and published over several years by the **American Geographical Society of New York**. Adie's map was published in 1969-1970 in the volume edited by C. Craddock et al. (1969-1970) (see detail to the left).

Disappointingly, the map on fig. 7.9.3 shows that Adie did not refer to many of the rock identifications made by Pelikan (1909); comparison of the map on the left and Table 25.1 which lists all the lithologies from the 20 landings in de Gerlache Strait clearly points out to the missing information in Adie's map. A subsequent set of maps was prepared by the British Antarctic Survey in 1979.

Hooper (1962) examined the petrology of rocks from Anvers, Wiencke and the Wauvermans Islands among others. He identified Upper Jurassic volcanics of andesitic composition on Wiencke Island as well as on islands of the NW coast of Anvers Island. An Andean Intrusive Suite and intermediate hybrid rocks, ranging from anorthite-gabbro to granodiorite from the greater part of Anvers Island. He also provided geochemical analyses of the Andean rocks, but disappointingly he did not compare his results with those of Pelikan (1909), despite acknowledging that publication in his reference list. Finally, he discussed the presence of post-Andean basaltic volcanics on the NE corner of Anvers Island.

Figure 7.9.3 Detail of the map produced by Adie (1969-1970) in the Antarctic Folio series no. 12 (Craddock C. et al.1969-1979) concentrating here on the islands which Arctowski had visited and for which Pelikan (1909) had described rocks. The map has been modified for clarity.

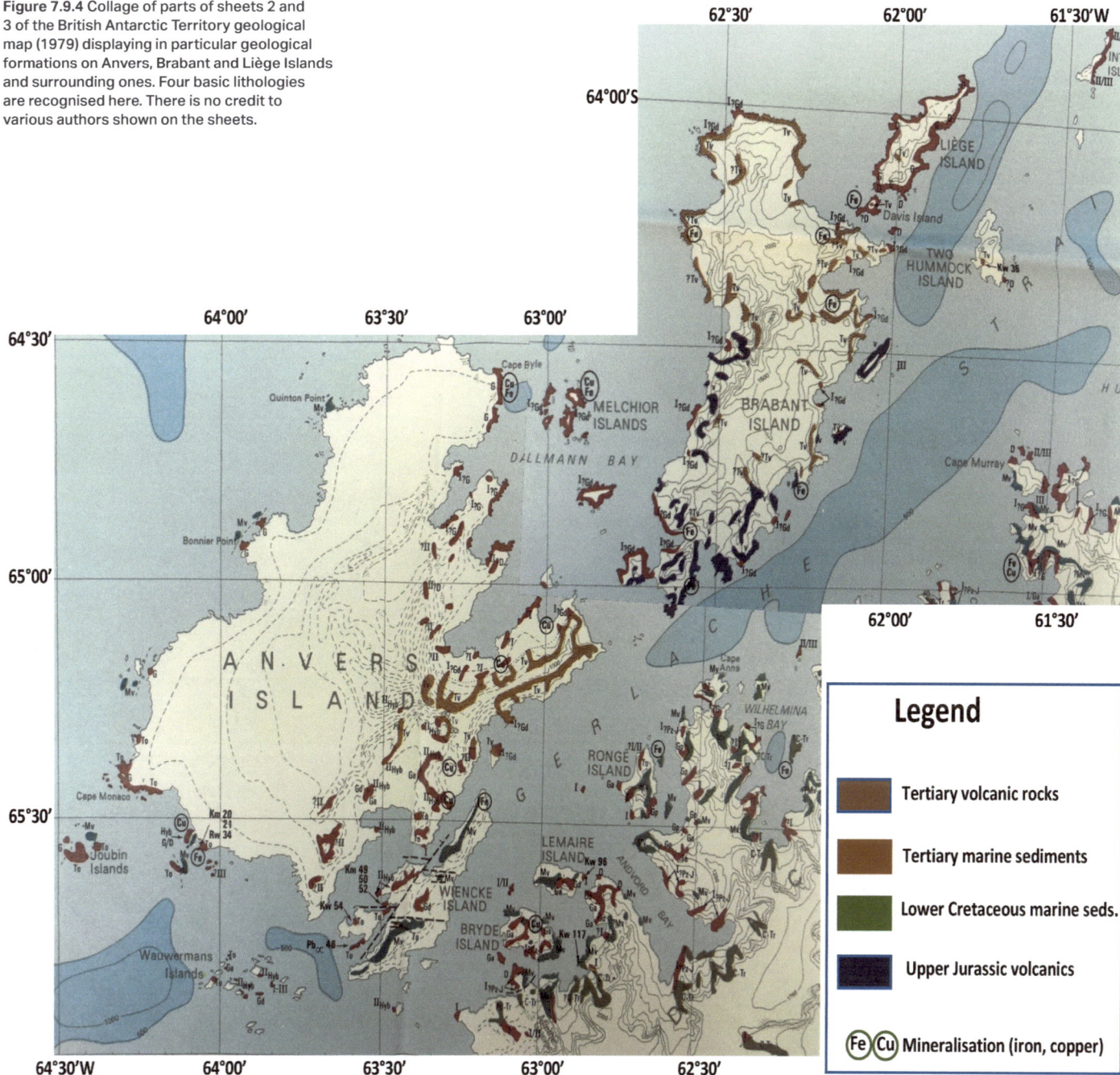

Figure 7.9.4 Collage of parts of sheets 2 and 3 of the British Antarctic Territory geological map (1979) displaying in particular geological formations on Anvers, Brabant and Liège Islands and surrounding ones. Four basic lithologies are recognised here. There is no credit to various authors shown on the sheets.

Legend

■ Tertiary volcanic rocks

■ Tertiary marine sediments

■ Lower Cretaceous marine seds.

■ Upper Jurassic volcanics

(Fe)(Cu) Mineralisation (iron, copper)

The Polish geologist K. Birkenmajer participated in several Polish Geodynamic Expeditions in 1984-1985 and 1987-1988 that were organised by the Polish Academy of Sciences. These resulted in numerous publications with often Birkenmajer as the first author, six of which are listed here in the reference list (Birkenmajer 1987, 1988, 1994, 1995, 1999, 2001). The last publication summarises the accomplishments of the Polish geological research in the Antarctic Peninsula region. The original investigations of H. Arctowski in the de Gerlache Strait are acknowledged, but once again the petrological investigations by A. Pelikan (1909) receive no mention in none of the publications by Birkenmajer listed here.

Figure 7.9.5 (below) Tectonic map of the islands surrounding de Gerlache Strait prepared by Birkenmajer (1999) and slightly modified herewith.

Two types of faults are shown: (1) *longitudinal faults* which are SW-NE-trending and seen in the Neumayer Channel and also Wiencke Island; it probably continues offshore Anvers and Brabant Islands. (2) *transverse faults* striking predominantly E-W to SE-NW. This is recognised on Wiencke and Brabant Islands. These are mainly strike-slip faults. Overall, four fault-bound tectonic blocks are recognised and these are **A**: the Danco Coast block; **B**: the Brabant Island block; **C**: the Neumayer Channel block; and **D**: the Anvers-Melchior block (Birkenmajer, 1999). Numbers in boxes denote radiometric ages in millions of years.

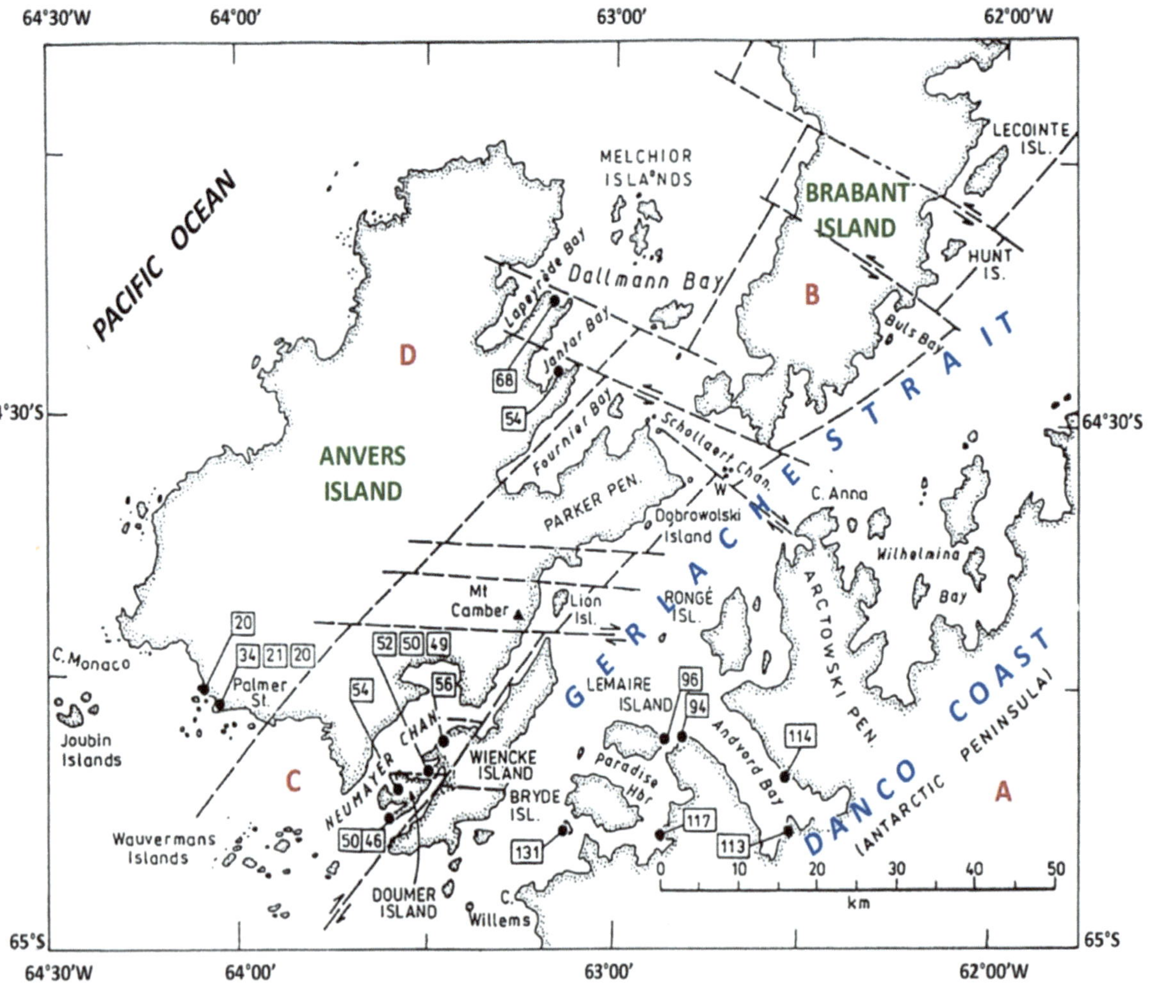

Figure 7.9.6 Slightly modified map of de Gerlache Strait showing all the names given to sites in the area by members of the Belgica expedition. Partly modified from https://www.belspo.be/belspo/BePoles/publ/poster%20antarctique_3.pdf

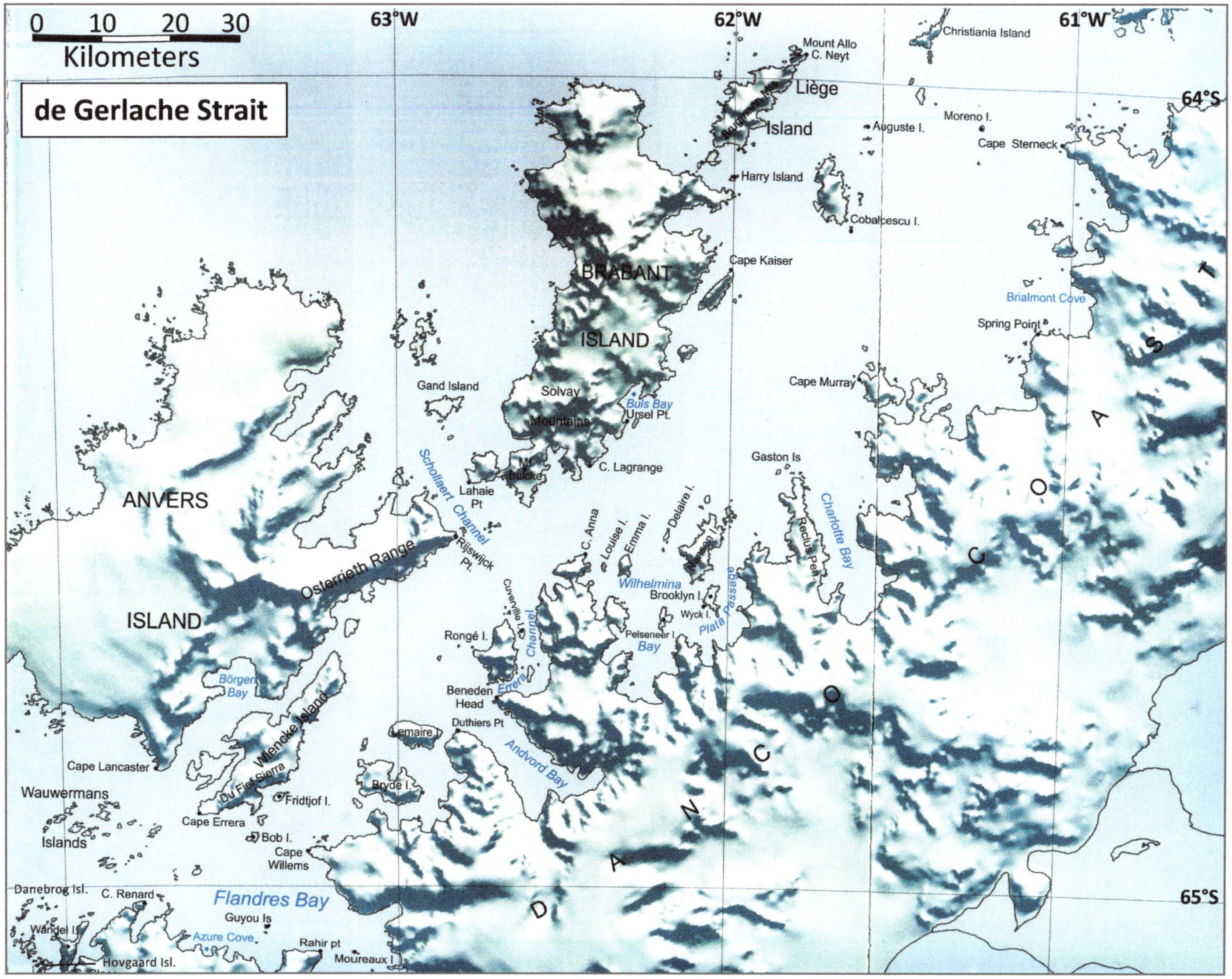

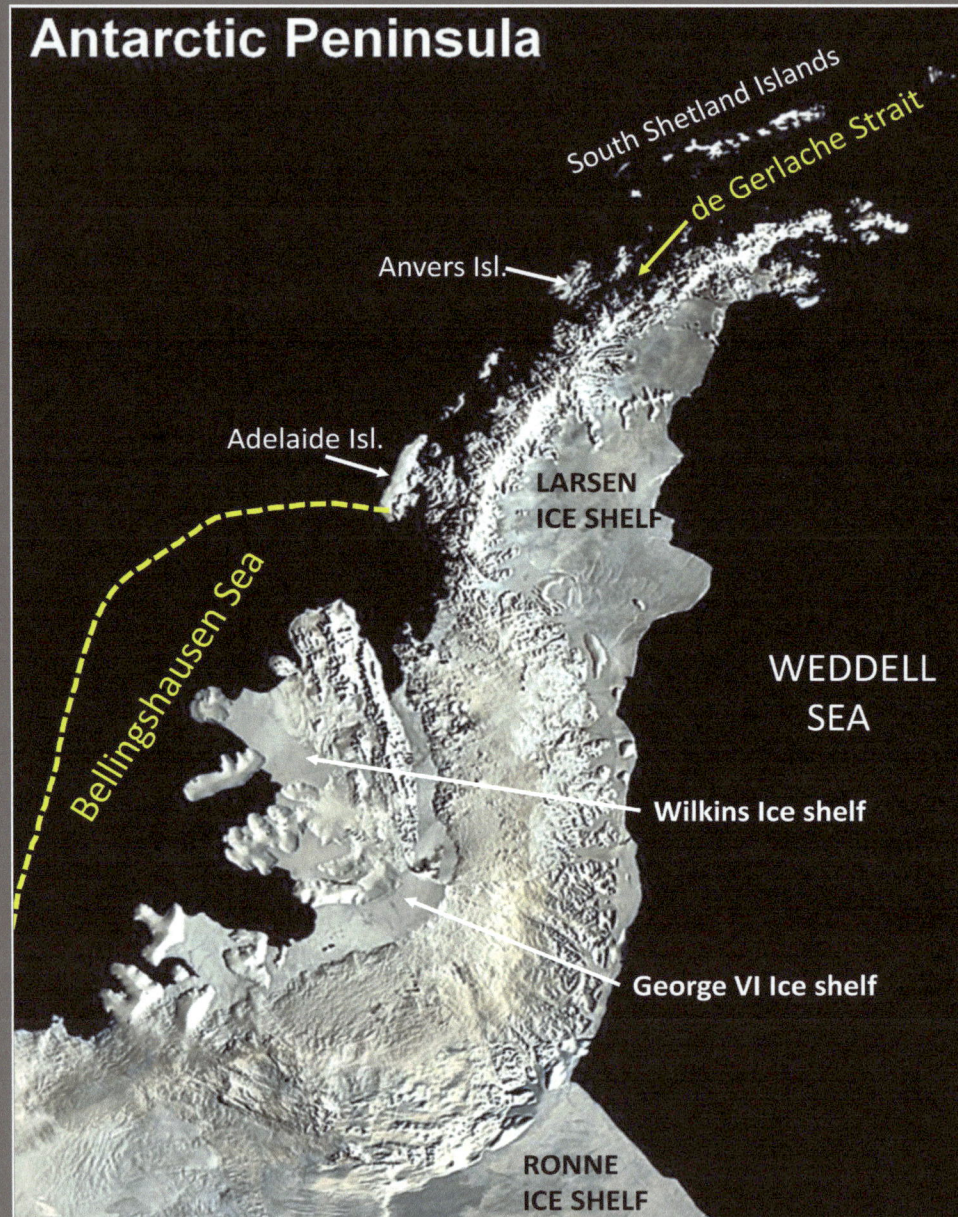

Antarctic Peninsula

South Shetland Islands

de Gerlache Strait

Anvers Isl.

Adelaide Isl.

LARSEN
ICE SHELF

Bellingshausen Sea

WEDDELL
SEA

Wilkins Ice shelf

George VI Ice shelf

RONNE
ICE SHELF

Satellite image of the Antarctic Peninsula showing the approximate boundaries of the Bellingshausen Sea as well as the location of the de Gerlache Strait discovered and surveyed by the Belgica expedition. Image obtained from Wikimedia Commons (https://upload.wikimedia.org/wikipedia/commons/a/ad/Antarctic_Peninsula_satellite_image.jpg) with additional details added by P. De Deckker.

Chapter 8

In the Bellingshausen Sea – Physico-chemical observations

This chapter describes what happened when the *Belgica* left the de Gerlache Strait and eventually became trapped in sea ice. No other ship had been stuck before in sea ice for a long period of time, reasons being that the extent of sea ice does vary from year to year. Conditions were more favourable when Bellingshausen and his two vessels sailed in the area in 1820-1821.

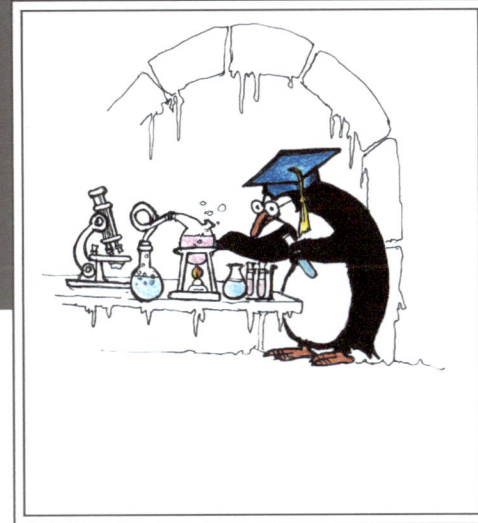

8.1 Trapped in the sea ice

When the *Belgica* left the de Gerlache Strait it passed the Dannebrog Islands, and on February 13, 1898 it started to encounter a very thick haze. It passed the Biscoe Islands and icebergs became quite common. The ship eventually crossed the Antarctic Polar Circle (Fig. 8.1.2) but the haze continued to be prevalent. At some stage during the day 85 icebergs were seen near the ship which later increased to 147. Iceblink caused by low clouds reflecting light off an ice field over the horizon became common. At this stage, the ship still managed to move freely and two soundings were performed (Fig. 8.1.2).

Figure 8.1.1 Photograph of the front to the ship piercing through the sea ice. This photo would have been taken from the crows nest. Photo reproduced with permission from the Emil Racovitza Archive, The Library of the Romanian Academy, Cluj-Napoca Branch and 'colorized' using palette.fm/color/filters.

Figure 8.1.2 Original map prepared by Georges Lecointe showing the course taken by the ship after leaving the de Gerlache Strait on February 13, 1898. Highlighted are atmospheric conditions (in black) encountered by the ship as well the number of icebergs (in pale blue) seen in the vicinity of the ship. Note the ship crossed the Antarctic Polar Circle (red line).

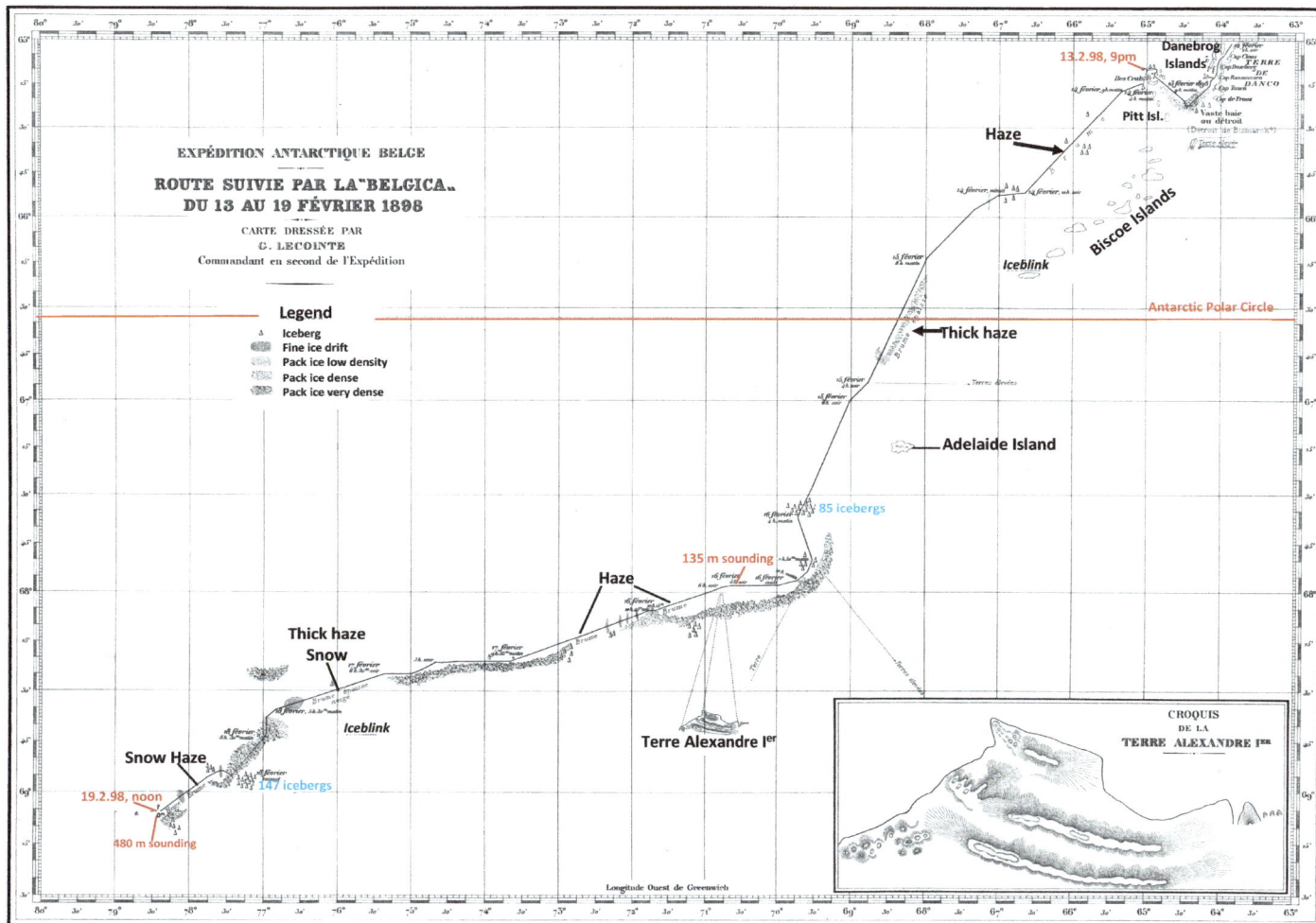

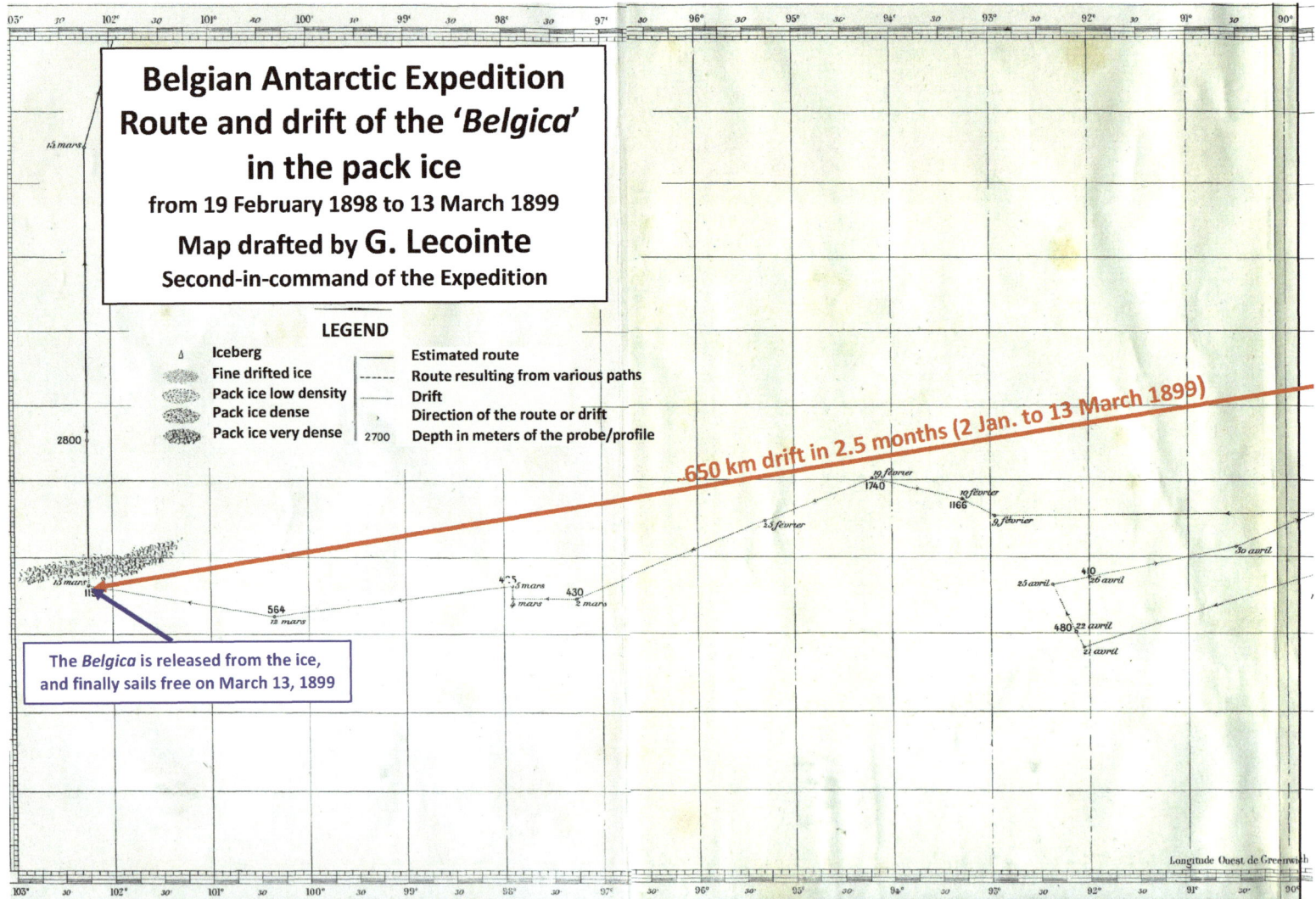

Figure 8.1.3 Modified map 3 of Lecointe (1903) that shows the 'route' of the *Belgica* in the sea ice after having left the de Gerlache Strait. Distances are approximated and shown in red is the zigzaging path of the ship during the period of complete winter darkness. Note the location of dense sea ice and the position of iceberg fields.

The *Belgica* becomes entrapped in the pack ice on February 28, 1898, to be finally blocked on March 13, 1899

>240 km in 8 days normal sailing

Note: the ship drifted in October-November 1898 back to where is was in February 1898

Drift during period of total darkness 22 May- 22 July 1988

March 3

Emile Dando dies and is buried at sea

It is only in mid-December 1899 that air temperature was close to 0°C and remained almost the same until March 2, 1899 (see Fig. 8.1.3). The mild temperatures likely facilitated the cutting of several channels in the sea ice. During the same months, most winds originated from the West and the ship was able to drift in the sea ice in an almost unidirectional westward direction (Fig. 8.1.6).

It is important to note that, during that entire period between February 28, 1898 and March 13, 1899, the ship was permanently 'trapped' in the sea ice and followed its course. During this first period, the crew saw a vast amount of icebergs (numbers in blue and mauve colours) shown by triangular symbols (Fig. 8.1.4). Several icebergs were so big that they were 'ploughing' through the sea ice and even at some stages

threatened to collide with the ship. The second period shown in red identifies the track of the ship in the sea ice between August 18, 1898 and January 12, 1899 and amazingly, this shows that she returned very close to the original track in February 1898. The obvious zigzagging course (shown especially in red around 82° and 84°W is interpreted here as being caused by the sea ice being entrained

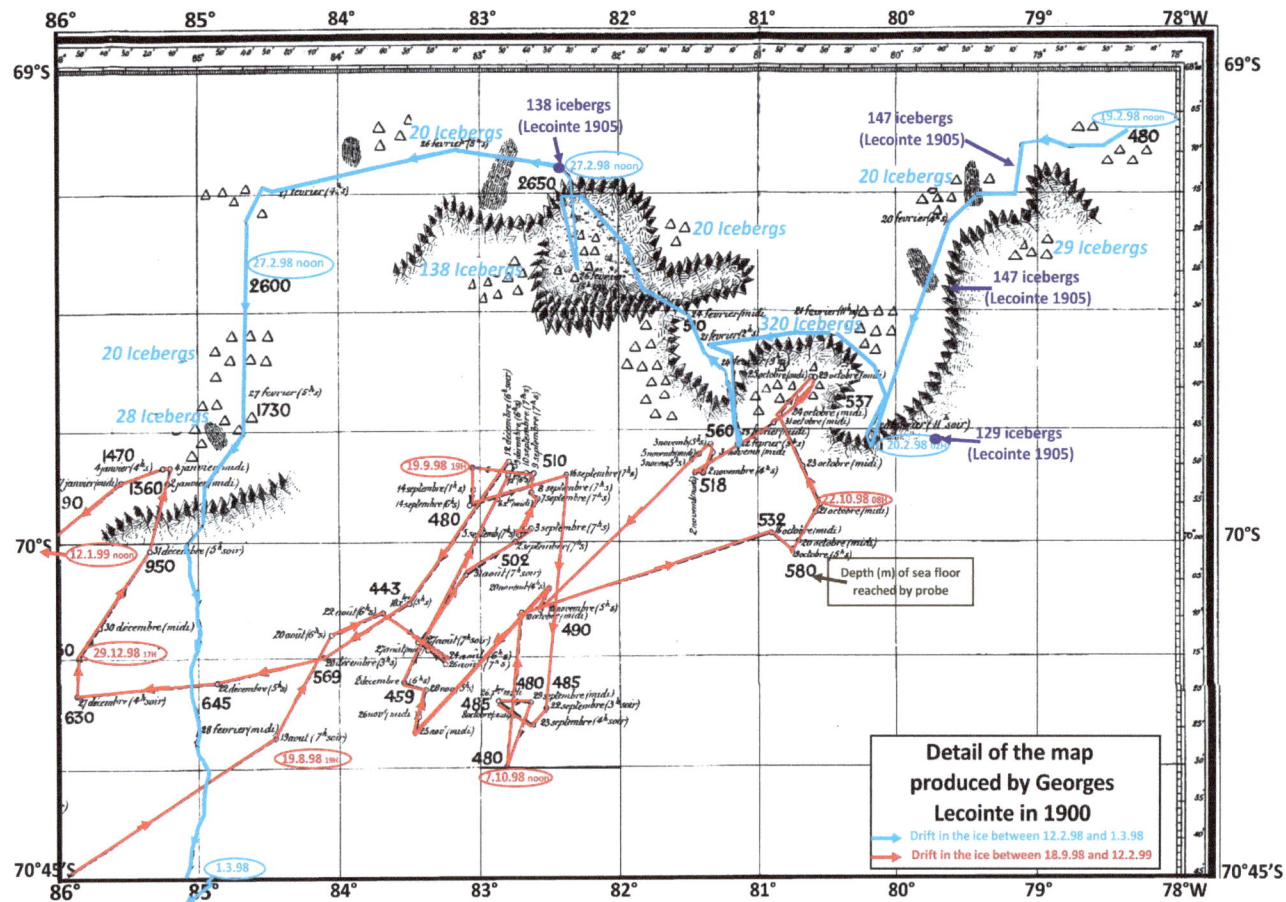

Figure 8.1.4 Detail of the map by Georges Lecointe (Fig. 8.1.4) which shows the continuous position changes of the ship between February 19, 1898 and March 1, 1898 shown by the pale blue track line; in red is the drift during the 18.9.1898 to 12.2.1899. Note the position of the iceberg fields, the number of icebergs seen by several members of the expedition and the sounding depths shown in black.

by large underwater eddies that would have formed above vast undersea features such as the Latady and Belgica Troughs (see Fig. 8.1.10). See more discussion in the text.

G. Lecointe (portrayed in Fig. 8.1.6) used a variety of techniques to reconnoitre the ship's position, in particular, the eclipses of Jupiter's satellites, the occultations of stars by the moon, and the methods of lunar distances (Lecointe, 1901). These methods are described in great detail in Lecointe (1901). A long telescope (lunette *sic* Lecointe, 1901) was used for these observations (see figure on page 24 in Lecointe 1901). Nevertheless,

Lecointe in his monograph stated that in 1898 the position of Jupiter had a weak austral declination and therefore was very close to the equator and was not often visible, and frequently its height was only just above the horizon. During the expedition, the eclipses of Jupiter's satellites were only seen three times

On February 28, 1898 a major storm forced the pack ice to shift and Ice blocks lifted up by the stormy sea were hitting one another (see Fig. 8.10.1D). Nevertheless, the *Belgica* was still able to move and the wind was blowing from E-N-E. At this stage, it would have been easy to move out of the pack ice. However, de Gerlache

and Lecointe made the fateful decision to sail in a southern direction with unknown consequences for the ship and its crew. On March 2, the ice pack that had opened up due to the storm closed around the ship. With great difficulty, the ship managed to move a further 2 miles to the South. Observations indicate that the ship (and pack ice) were moving in a southerly direction before the ship became completely 'locked' in the pack ice (see Fig. 9.4). Finally on March 4, the ship was trapped in the pack ice and remained so for almost 13 months. All around, icebergs and ice were hitting one another. New ice was forming and seals and penguins were also seen on the ice.

Figure 8.1.5 Photograph of Georges Lecointe standing on the deck of the ship. Photo provided by Terence Lecointe and used with his permission. The photo was 'colorized' using palette.fm/color/filters.

Figure 8.1.6 Photographs of the *Belgica* in the pack ice;

A: the ship is still in a melt pool, with a penguin spectator;

B: The ship is completely encircled by pack ice.

Note a small melt pool with floating ice in the front. Members of the crew used to climb to the crows nest on the middle mast in an attempt to assess how far the open sea was. Both photos reproduced with permission from the Emil Racovitza Archive, The Library of the Romanian Academy, Cluj-Napoca Branch.

Based on the map drafted by Lecointe (Figs. 8.1.5, 8.1.8), it is possible to discern that the pack ice (and entrapped ship) drifted in many directions over one year and 9 days. At times, it appeared that the ship was following a very large eddy (see red lines between longitudes 84° and 82°W in Fig. 8.1.4), or zig-zagging in a E-W direction (see pale blue lines between longitudes 87° and 92°W in Fig. 8.1.7) and, at others it moved in almost a single direction, as seen to the last 2 and a half months (green lines in Fig. 8.1.7).

More details on the entrapped ship's significant drifts follow:

1. On August 10, 1898 the pack ice and enclosed ship drifted in the NE direction until September 3.

2. After that date, the pack moved straight South until September 22.

3. The ship turned round and then moved straight South as if under the influence of a large eddy located under the ice. Coinciding with this eddy is the largest concentration of very dense pack ice as shown in Lecointe's map between meridian 85° and 86°W (see more comments below).

4. The pack ice and ship eventually returned to the same area they had been in February (about 9 months before), before eventually drifting towards the West, with another round turn and finally heading West from January 2, 1989. The drift then was in an almost straight (western) direction and was rather rapid as it only took 2 ½ months to travel some 650 km; this is equivalent to 9.7 km per 24 hours or 0.4 km per hour (equivalent to ~0.22 knot/hour).

Note also that in a number of locations (black numbers in Figs. 8.1.4, 8.1.5), crew members took water samples, as well as plankton and bottom samples. These were obtained through a hole in the sea ice. It is very likely that it was always through the same hole that instruments were lowered down and that it was located very close to the ship. The numbers identify the depth of the sea floor at each location.

The present interpretation is that the drift of the pack ice and ship could not have been caused by winds after examining the rose winds calculated by Arctowski (see Fig. 8.4.3), but instead by underwater coastal currents. In fact, an examination of the today's coastal currents in the Bellingshausen Sea, referred to as the Antarctic Coastal Current (AACC), indicate a broad flow in a western direction (Schubert et al., 2021). However, Schulze Chretien et al. (2021), measured currents directly that were resolved by velocity observations between December 27, 2018 and January 8, 2019. These data show several different directions (see dotted pink arrows in Fig. 8.1.8) that are partly controlled by the bottom topography of the area, with two salient features occurring above

Figure 8.1.7 Simplified map of the original one by Georges Lecointe to clearly show the position of the ship and movement of the sea ice it was 'trapped' in over different periods of time.

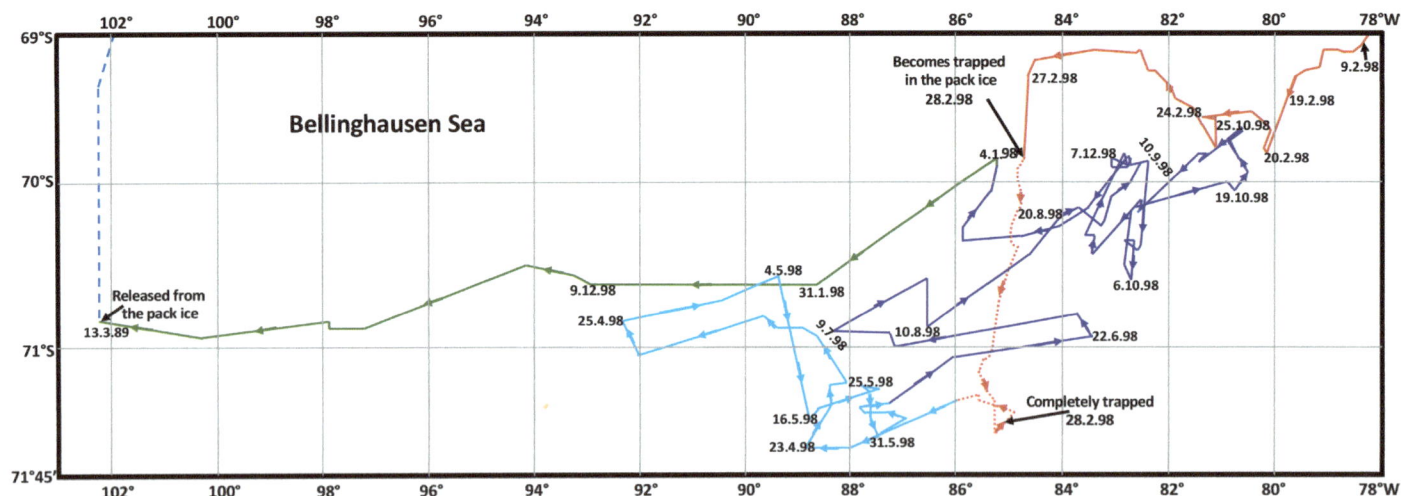

the Belgica Trough and the Latady Trough (see Fig. 8.1.10). The densest concentration of pack ice mentioned above in the map of Lecointe (Fig. 8.1.3) in fact sits directly above the Belgica Trough. One could postulate that cooler water from local upwelling in this Trough would have generated such a formation of dense pack ice. For more information on the underwater topography, refer to both figs. 1 in Schulze Chretien et al. (2021) and Schubert et al. (2021).

Figure 8.1.8 Summary of part of the course followed by the *Belgica* between early February 1898 and March 1899. Different colours are used to help visualize where the ship went, particularly when entrapped in the sea ice. The continuous red line shows the course when the ship was still able to move freely until February 25, 1898. The dotted red line shows the drift of the ship in sea ice until late March 13, 1898. The pale blue line indicates that the drift the ship followed a contorted trajectory from March 13 to June 30, 1898 to eventually return to where it was in February 1898. Note that the locations where the course of the ship zigzagged were in the vicinity of both the Latady and Belgica Troughs. The pinks arrows broadly indicate today's underwater currents defined by Schulze Chretien et al. (2021) and which, in the past, would have caused the 'erratic motion' of the sea ice and entrapped ship.

Figure 8.1.9 Map showing the bottom topography of the Bellingshausen Sea adjacent to the Antarctic continent defined by the green line. Of interest here are the two depressions, the Belgica and Latady Troughs, over which near surface currents are recognised today (see Fig. 8.1.9) that would have forced the sea ice in 1898 to take a very contorted course. Figure adapted from Graham et al. (2011).

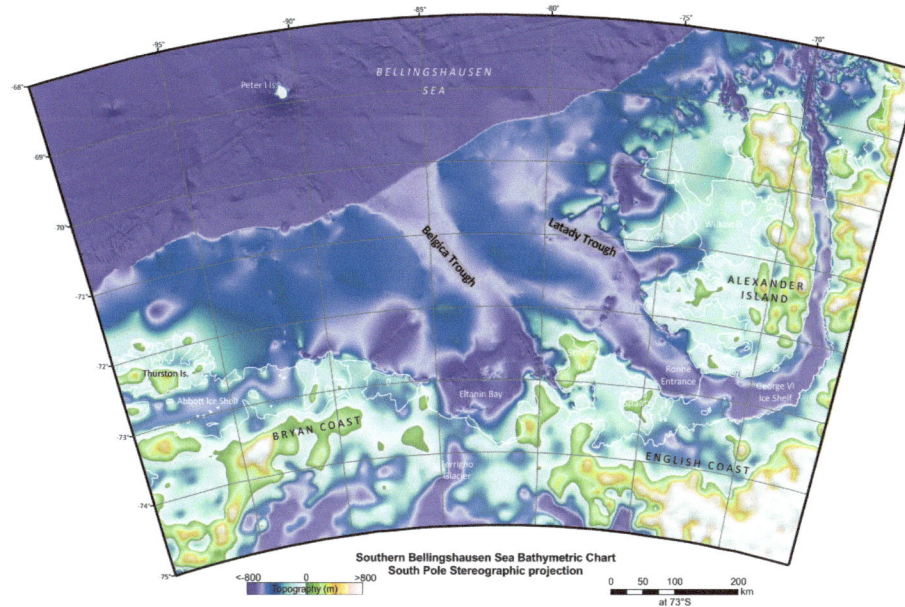

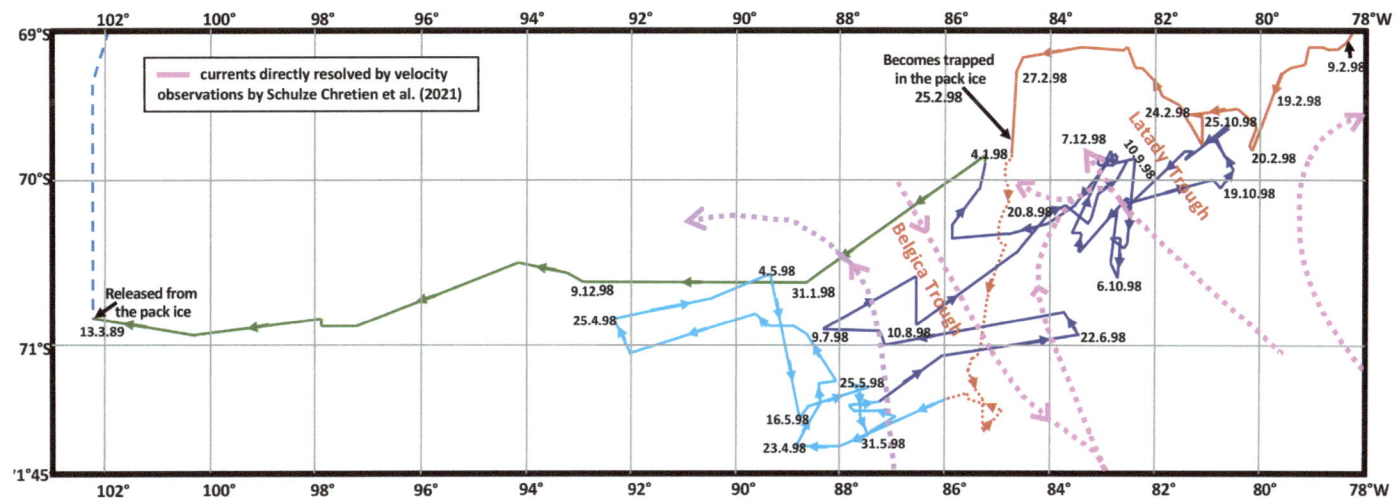

With today's knowledge of the topography in the region, it is now possible to understand why the ship became trapped in the dense pack ice along meridians 85° and 86°W directly above the now known Belgica Trough. In fact, today's near-surface current flows in a southerly direction, which is the direction of the *Belgica* drift (see Figs. 8.1.4, 8.1.7). The *Belgica's* zig-zagging drift appears to be a part of a gigantic eddy located above the western side of the Latady Trough where today's currents near the sea surface diverge (see dotted pink arrows in Fig. 8.1.9). This area is where the *Belgica* was almost encircled at times by a large number of icebergs; this area is at least 1,000 m deep and faces the deeper Bellingshausen Sea (see Fig. 8.1.10 from Graham et al. (2010) and Schubert et al. (2021)).

It is noteworthy that originally the ship and pack ice drifted parallel to the coastline, first in an easterly direction for 14 days (8 to 22 June 1898) and then in the opposite direction for 17 days (23 June to 9 July 1898) during the height of winter (when there was almost complete darkness). Finally, the last period of the *Belgica's* drift in the pack ice (green lines in Fig. 8.1.8), follows almost a straight westerly line which is the direction of the Antarctic Counter Current. In his publication on sea ice (glace de mer et banquise) in 1908, Arctowski reported that Captain Lecointe was to comment on the drift of the ship in the sea ice, but this was never published. Arctowski himself therefore did not tackle the subject.

A recent program of the German vessel *Polarstern* featuring its voyage in the Bellingshausen Sea in 2022/2023 can be consulted at https://125yearsbelgica.wordpress.com/ and https://epic.awi.de/id/eprint/57905/1/BzPM_0777_2023.pdf. The *Polarstern* did not encounter sea ice in contrast to the Belgica expedition some 124 years before! This indicates a major shift in climatic conditions in the area.

Finally, for the period starting January 7, 1899 until the ship eventually escaped from the pack ice on March 13, 1899, she drifted an estimated distance of 650 km over 2.5 months. This represents an average 'speed' of 420 m per hour (equivalent to ~10 km per 24 hours) over that period. During that time, the sea ice became fragmented at times and all the Belgica crew members contributed to cut the ice in large slabs so as to create a 'canal' to enable the ship to escape and become free (Fig. 15.8). This period coincided also with a significant increase in temperature (in the vicinity of zero °C) that would have aided in softening and or melting the sea ice (see section 8.4 on temperatures).

Finally, the period of entrapment and having to live in total darkness for several months took a toll on all members of the Belgica expedition. This will be discussed in chapter 12.

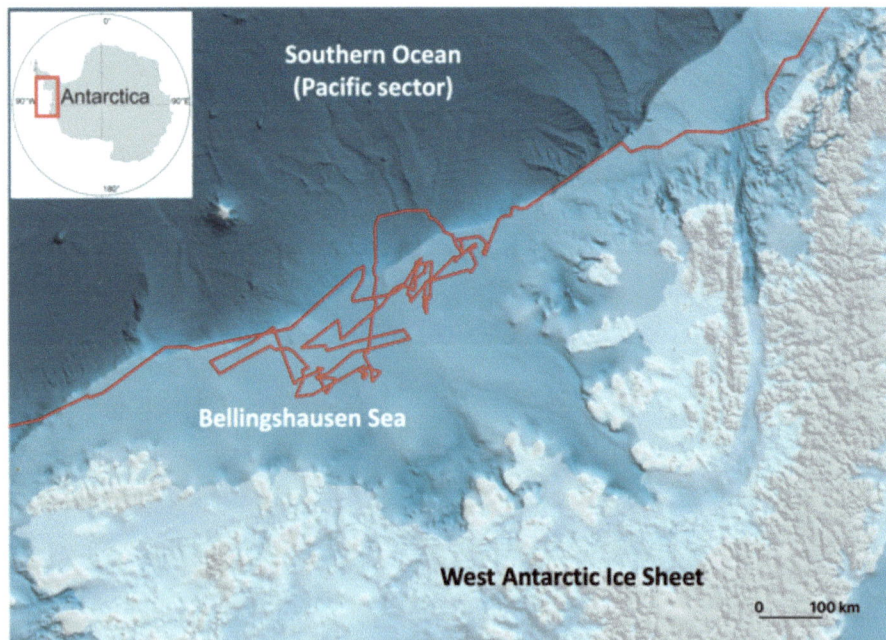

Figure 8.1.10 Complete track of the *Belgica* shown in red (after it left the de Gerlache Strait) placed over the bottom topography of the Bellingshausen Sea as we know it today. It is clear that when the sea ice in which the ship was trapped zigzagged continuously that its position was above the two deep-water basins (Belgica and Latipa). Consult figs. 8.1.8 and 8.1.9 for more information. Map produced by Dr Karsten Gohl from AWI and used here with his permission.

8.2 On oceanic temperature measurements made by Henryk Arctowski

KEY POINTS

- Henryk Arctowski measured water temperatures for 17 profiles in the Bellingshausen Sea by piercing a hole through the sea ice that would have been located close to the ship as it drifted with the sea in which it was enclosed.

- One profile was also performed in the de Gerlache Strait, and another in the open ocean outside the sea ice. The near-surface temperature in the de Gerlache Strait was above 1°C, but then rapidly dropped around 0°C down to 625 m.

- For the 17 profiles, the temperature was around -2°C at the sea surface and remained the same down to approximately 100 m before progressively increasing to 0°C when reaching 300 m, and below 400 m, the temperature remained around 1°C.

- Three profiles were deeper, reaching 950, 1360 and 1740 m, with always water temperature remaining around 1°C from around 500 m and downward.

- Note these measurements did not take into account salinity nor water pressure.

- Arctowski's legacy here is figure 8.2.1 that shows numerous temperature profiles mostly in the Bellingshausen Sea that can be compared with today's profiles. Such comparison indicates a significant warming of the upper few 100 m of the water column over 125 years. This has significant implications for sea ice formation, sea-surface salinity and the welfare of the biota such as seals and plankton (see chapter 9.3).

One of the tasks set by the scientists of the *Belgica* was to obtain much information on the oceanography of the regions she visited. Ocean temperature, both at the surface as well as at depth proved important as there was, at that time, no information from the Antarctic Ocean, nor Drake Passage between the tips of South America and the Antarctic Peninsula, only known at the time to be a set of islands associated with Graham Land. The section below details what Arctowski was able to unveil.

Some 60 profiles were obtained by lowering thermometers through a hole dug in the sea ice. The first 2 profiles are not discussed in Arctowski and Mill's (1908) publication and this is not explained. Profiles 3-7 were obtained from Drake Passage over the period of 15 to 29 of January 1898 (see Fig. 6.1). Arctowski and Mill (1904) list profile 6 obtained on January 16, 1898, which reached a depth of 3850 meters at which depth temperature was 1.2°C. The deepest profile reached a depth of 4,040 m for which the last temperature measurement was taken at a dept of 4,025m. Two other profiles at depths 3,800 and 3,690 m both returned temperatures of 0.6° C. These were the first ever temperature measurements taken in Drake Passage and these were made in Summer. A single sounding was made in the de Gerlache Strait down to a depth of 625 m, with 3 tries at greater depths but all attempts failed.

When the ship was 'trapped' in the pack ice, another 48 soundings were made and were all located South of the Antarctic Circle. The area covered a broad rectangle from 78°W to 103°W and 69°S to 71° 45'S. Only 7 of the soundings reached depths greater than 1,000 m, with the deepest of 2,700 m reached on February 25, 1988. We note that no soundings were made during the austral winter period (between May 27 and September 1, 1988), especially when there was no or little light and air temperatures were extremely low. Two additional soundings were made after the ship was in open water. The last sounding (no. 60) was taken down to a depth of 4,800 m but temperature measurements were only taken down to 1,000 m.

Arctowski in 1899, when he first reported preliminary results from the Belgica expedition to members of the Geographical Society in Brussels, tried to explain the temperature inversions noticed in the upper 300 m of all the profiles (Fig. 8.2.1) measured below the sea ice. He considered the possibility of vertical circulation and that the waters travel slowly towards the South in the bottom and return northward near the surface. We now have a better explanation of water masses movements and circulation near the Antarctic margin as clearly displayed by Martinson in 2012 (Fig. 8.2.2).

Nevertheless, Arctowski and Mill (1908) did not discuss the temperature inversions with temperatures characteristically below 0°C in the upper ~300 m of the water column, below which all temperatures were negative (Fig. 8.2.1), but the last two plates in their monograph showed various transects linking temperature profiles at depth. It is noteworthy that recent publications dealing with temperature profiles around the Antarctic Peninsula and Bellingshausen Sea never refer to the early publication of Arctowski and Mill (1900), despite the fact that that the latter authors discuss at length on how they critically and very carefully calibrated their instruments and measurements. These are papers by Jacobs and Comiso (1997), Schmidtko et al. (2014), Venables et al. (2017), Schulze Chretien et al. (2021) and Schubert et al. (2021) to name a few recent ones. Surely, examining archival records would be of great importance to assess temperature and salinity changes over the last 125 years. It is a great pity that Fogt et al. (2022) in their comparative study of the sea ice extent in the Ross, Amundsen and Bellingshausen Seas since 1900 do not mention the Belgica observations. They only account for Antarctic weather stations record since 1958 and for earlier records refer to the data assimilation of Dailaden et al. (2021) that goes back to 1800, but do not refer to the Belgica observations as a way of testing their compilation, at least for the year 1898 when the ship was trapped in sea ice. Disappointingly also is the work of Bigg (2024) who examined the circumnavigation records of James Cook (1772-1775) and Fabian Gottlieb Bellingshausen (1819-1821) (see Fig. 1.7) and related to the sea ice extent during those two periods, did not make any mention of the Belgica expedition record. A lot could have been learned concerning changes of sea ice extent over those periods.

Jacobs and Comiso (1997) had already informed the scientific community that satellite imageries had indicated a 20% decrease in sea ice extent between 1973 and 1993 and that this was negatively correlated with surface air temperatures on the west side of the Antarctic Peninsula. These authors stated that air temperature had increased by 0.5°C per decade since the mid-1940s. The warning signs of climate changing were there some 50 years ago! We note that the

Bellingshausen Sea was devoid of sea ice in the austral summer of 2023 when visited by the German vessel *RV Polarstern* (Claus-Dieter Hillenbrandt, pers. com.). The latter stated that the 'missing sea ice was worrying because the widespread lack of sea ice felt as if a threshold had been crossed'. It is clear that absence of sea ice in the area today would see a very different set of temperature profiles, especially near the surface.

Figure 8.2.1 is a direct reproduction of Arctowski and Mill's (1908) plots of water temperature profiles with some additions made for clarity. For position of all the stations, refer to the publication of Arctowski and Mill (1908).

Once, the ship was outside the pack ice, in the open ocean, the temperature profile was very different. Water temperature near the surface (at 10 m) was 7.4°C and it eventually decreased progressively down to 3.4° C at 1,000 m.

It is necessary to point out that today oceanographers calculate 'potential temperature' (defined as the temperature of a water parcel that is raised adiabatically (without heat gain or loss) to the sea surface) in depth profiles, but here the data as discussed by Arctowski and Mill (1908) are presented.

There is no doubt about the veracity of the measurements made by Arctowski as all the instruments he took on the ship, and also after the expedition, were thoroughly tested in various laboratories. This is documented in great detail in Arctowski and Mill (1908) and below. On the ship, Arctowski had 19 thermometers made by the Chabaud House in Paris and five from the Negretti-Zandra House in London that also had a small propeller. The Chabaud thermometers

were triggered by a Rung messenger. The Negretti-Zandra thermometers were verified by the Kew Observatory and corrections were applied when the profiles were obtained. The Chabaud thermometers were verified by Mr. H. Walravens of the Royal Observatory of Uccle in Belgium. Upon the ship's return, thermometer Negretti-Zandra number 87387 was examined by the Bureau of Weights and Measures for comparison against the Chabaud thermometer number 68679. In the Negretti-Zandra thermometers, the distance between degrees was 2.7 mm and in the Chabaud thermometer it was 2 mm. Both thermometers listed above were examined periodically from October 1901 to the end of 1902 at the International Bureau of Weights and Measurements (Bureau international des poids et mesures at Breteuil near Paris in France). All measurements were made with a micrometer lens of 1/300 mm. Between February 27 1902 and October 1902, measurements with error over that period was 0.012°C for thermometer 68679 and 0.008°C for thermometer 87387. Several pages in Arctowski and Mill (1908) are dedicated to temperature calibration between the two thermometer types, once during a cooling of thermometers. These authors also state that it would have been desirable to maintain the thermometers at depth but the movement of the ship in open water did not render that task possible.

On several occasions, a slightly modified Sigsbee bottle (see Sigsbee, 1880) was used to obtain water samples and at the same time the reversed thermometers were deployed.

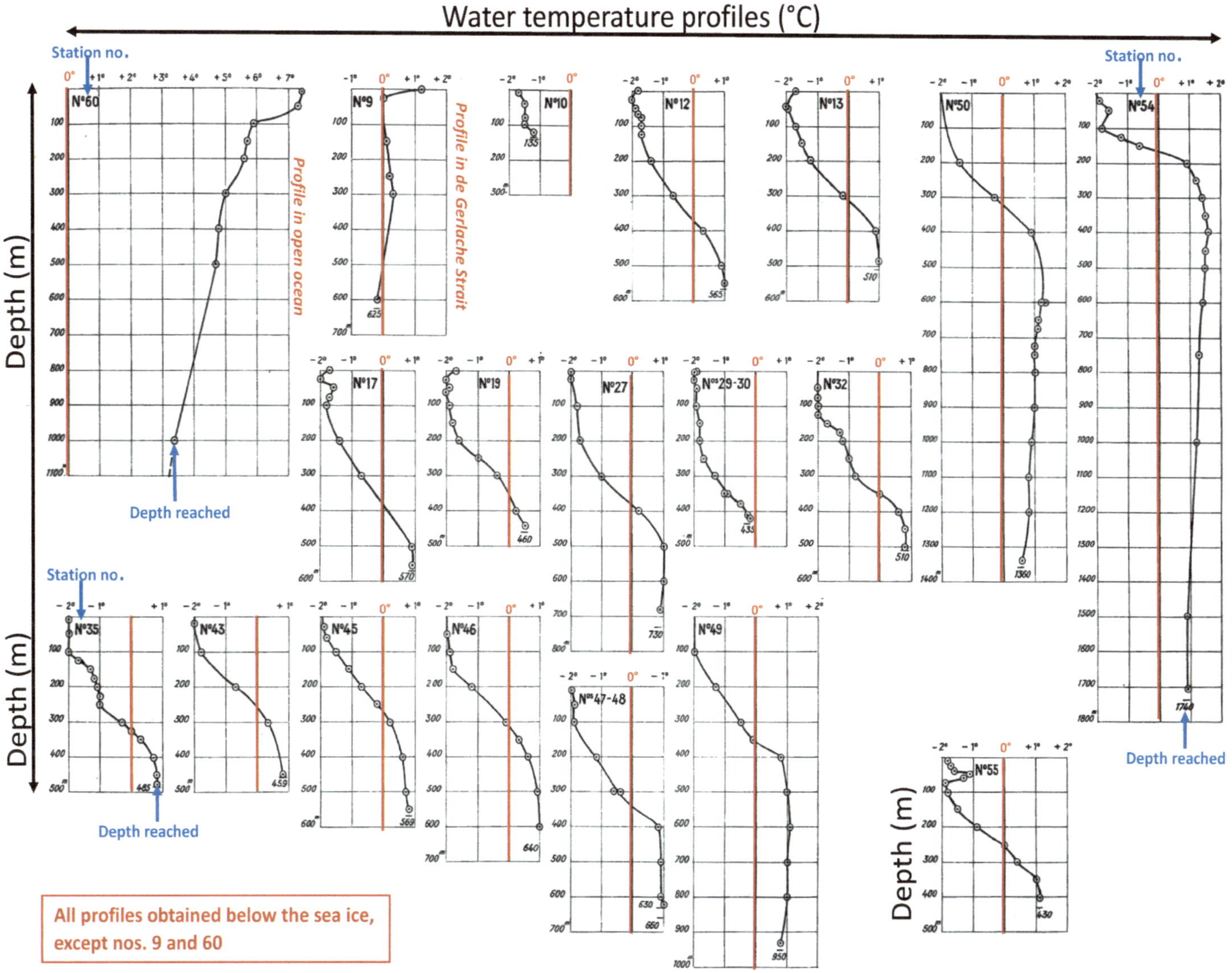

Figure 8.2.1 Reproduction of the temperature profiles in the Bellingshausen Sea presented in the monograph by Arctowski and Mill (1908), with small changes shown in colour to facilitate visibility.

93

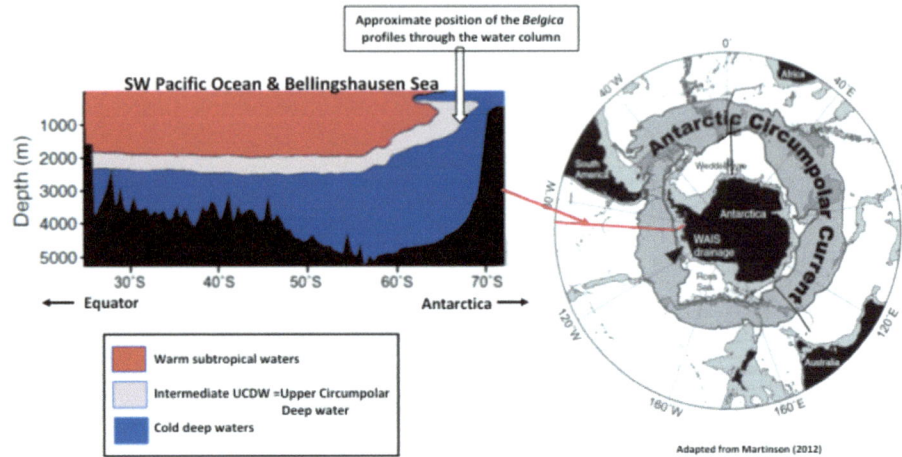

Figure 8.2.2 Cross section of the Southern Ocean in the SE Pacific Ocean sector and the Bellingshausen Sea to show the basic water masses (from Martinson, 2012) in order to explain the temperature reversals Arctowski and Mils (1908) saw in all their in-depth profiles, with surface waters (blue here) colder than those from the Intermediate Upper Circumpolar Deep water. This is no longer the case.

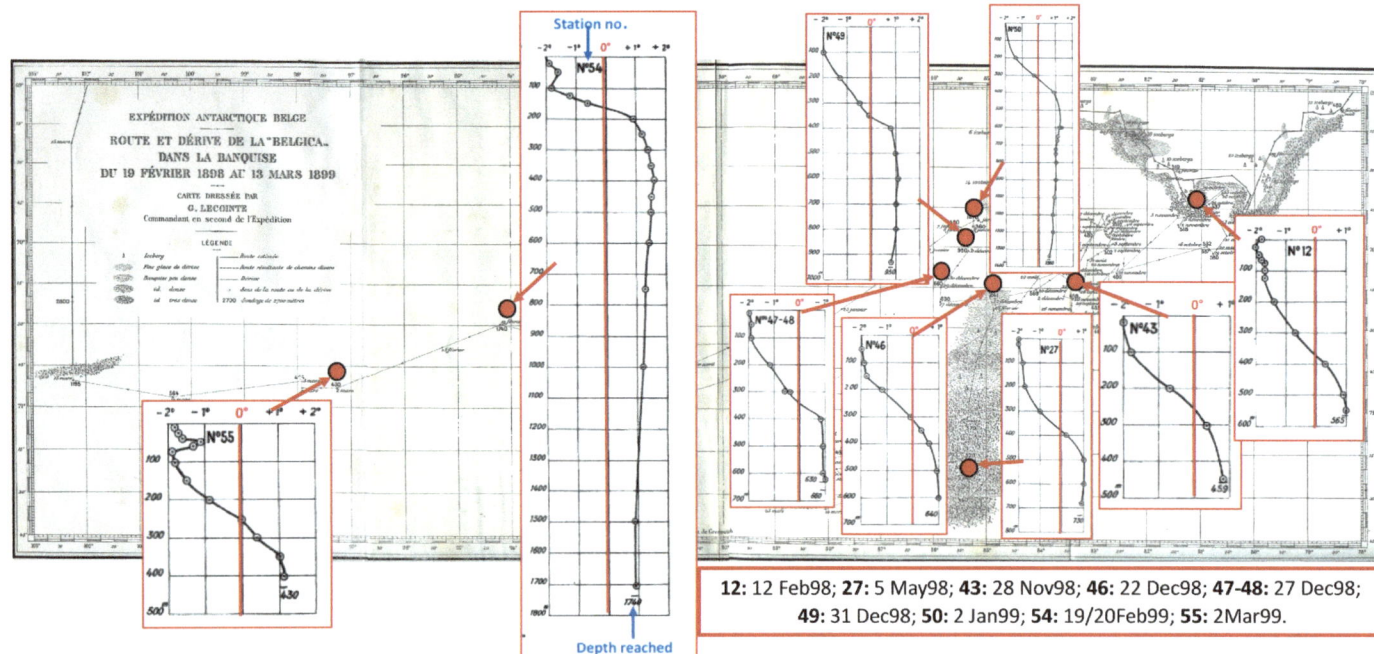

12: 12 Feb98; **27:** 5 May98; **43:** 28 Nov98; **46:** 22 Dec98; **47-48:** 27 Dec98; **49:** 31 Dec98; **50:** 2 Jan99; **54:** 19/20Feb99; **55:** 2Mar99.

Figure 8.2.3. Selected profiles made by H. Arctowski (see fig. 8.2.1) placed on the map produced by G. Lecointe for the Bellingshausen Sea during which time the ship was 'trapped' in the sea ice. This is to aid visualisation that near-surface water temperatures were all negative and this can be compared against modern findings presented in the figures overleaf. The profile numbers and thee dates they were obtained are listed in the bottom right hand corner rectangle.

8.3 Modern-day temperature profiles

There have been a large number of cruises along the Bellingshausen Sea over the last two decades during which CTD (Conductivity Temperature Depth) measurements were obtained. These must eventually be compared with the data obtained during the Belgica expedition profiles.

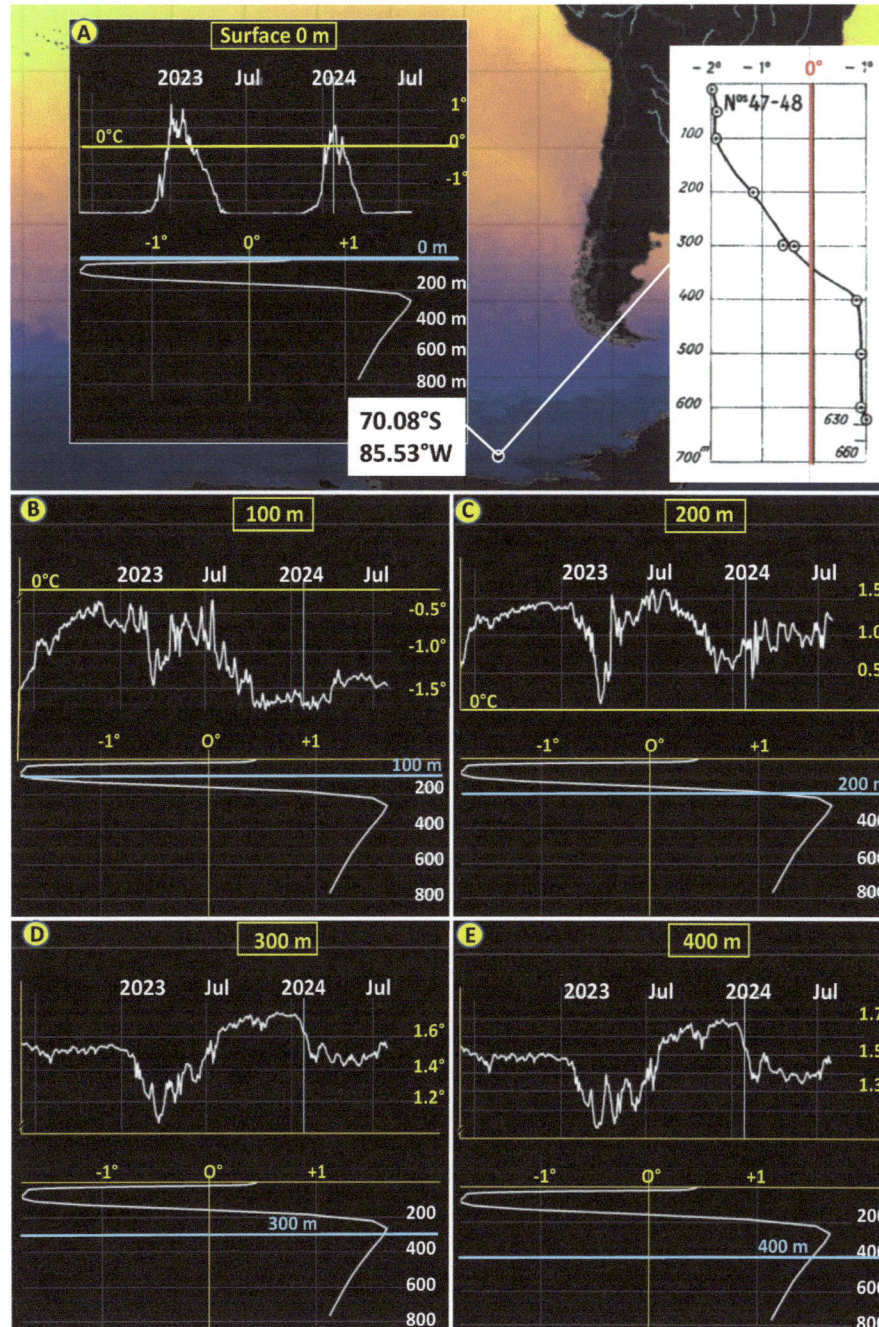

Figure 8.3.1 Sea temperature profiles for sites 47-48 combined measured by Henryk Arctowski on December 30, 1898 (top right diagram) compared to profiles obtained for the same sites using the Copernicus Marine Service program only for the upper 800 m of the water column, spanning the period January 1, 2023 to July 27, 2024. The plots A to E show the seasonal temperatures reconstructed for different depths (0, 100, 200, 300 and 400 m) over that period. Note that today's temperatures are very different from those measured by Arctowski and presented in Arctowski and Mill (1908).

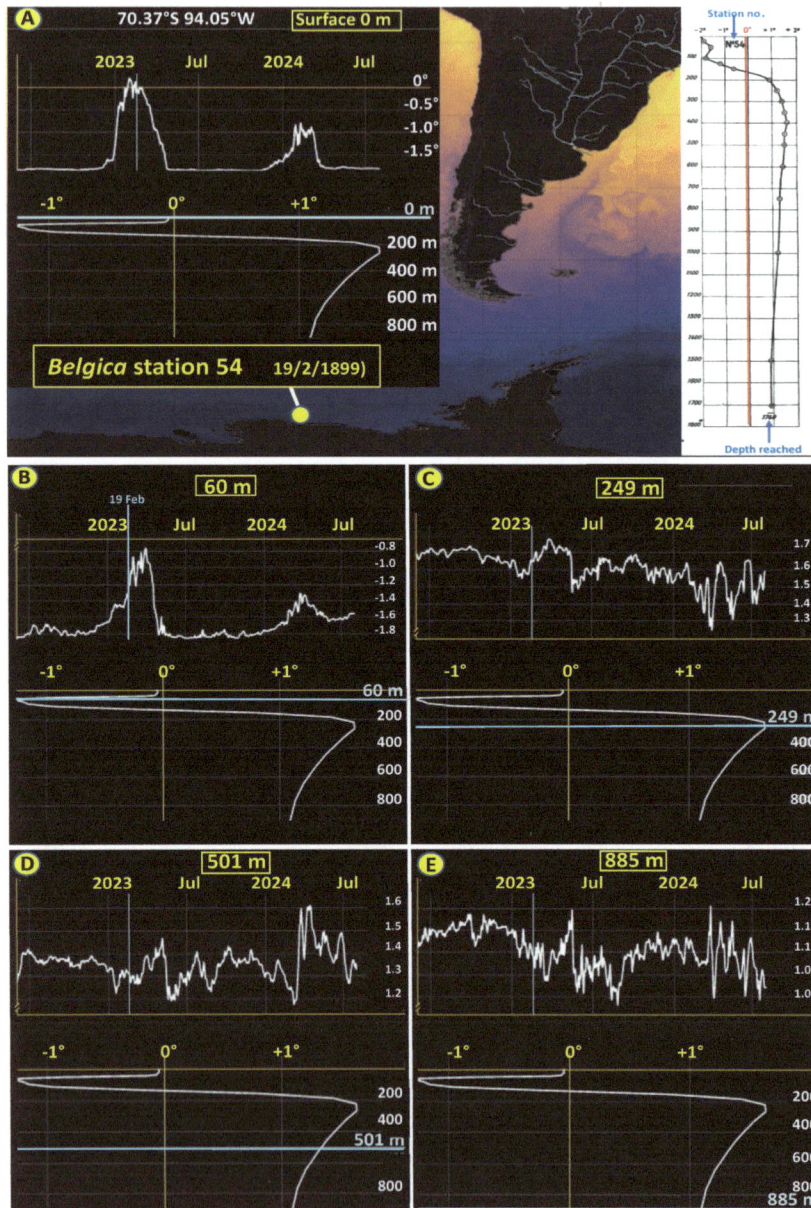

Figure 8.3.2 Sea temperature profiles for site 54 measured by Henryk Arctowski on February 19, 1899 (top right diagram) compared to profiles obtained for the same sites using the Copernicus Marine Service program only for the upper 800 m of the water column, spanning the period January 1, 2023 to July 27, 2024. The plots A to E show the seasonal temperatures reconstructed for different depths (0, 60, 249, 501 and 885 m) over that period. Note that today's temperatures are very different from those measured by Arctowski and presented in Arctowski and Mill (1908) except for those below ~250 m. Today's warming only occurs in the upper parts of the water column.

8.4 On seawater salinity and density in Bransfield Strait and the Bellingshausen Sea

KEY POINTS

- Only five samples were taken for their temperature and salinity in Bransfield Strait. Despite the fact that various samples were taken in depth profiles, Arctowski did not provide their salinities in this various monographs. It is interesting that de Gerlache in his 1938 monograph lists some bottom salinities in Drake Passage. Surface temperatures were always above 0°C but values decreased in a southerly direction. Too few samples were obtained for salinity for comparison with today's values.

- Fifteen water samples were taken once the ship left the de Gerlache Strait but she still remained free to move, and 38 more once she was 'trapped' in the sea ice. Salinity and temperature profiles were made but are not discussed any further, except that we know that since sea ice has recently disappeared in the Bellingshausen Sea, at least in summer, values taken by the *Belgica* in 1898-1899 would have differed significantly over 125 years.

Arctowski spent a vast amount of time in his specifically designed laboratory on the ship to measure water samples for their density, which was eventually translated into salinity. He used two aerometers built by Victor Chabaud in Paris and which were slightly modified and had been calibrated at the University of Nancy, where Professor Julien Thoulet was based and who collaborated with Arctowski on the publication of the results obtained while at sea. The aerometers were of different weight and volume (see Arctowski and Thoulet, 1908). Today, these instruments are called pycnometers.

Sampling for salinity measurements were taken almost always 3 times every 24 hours during the transect along the East coast of South America from October 2, 1897 near the equator until November 23, 1897 at latitude 45°35'S. The vessel used to take water samples at the surface was a small brass bucket 15 cm in diameter and 45 cm deep. The bottom was curved to allow easy cleaning and preventing salt deposits from forming during evaporation between sampling stations. A total of 179 samples were taken and measured for temperature, density which was then translated into salinity. A map and temperature and salinity plots are available in Arctowski and Thoulet (1908). Arctowski collaborated with Professor Julien Thoulet from the University of Nancy in France, who was an expert in oceanography and who also wrote a monograph on marine instruments (Thoulet, 1908).

Figure 8.4.1 Photo of Henryk Arctowski in his laboratory on the ship – in the process of measuring sea water density. He specially designed this laboratory that was based on the Challenger chemistry laboratory (see fig. 2.3 in chapter 2). Photo likely taken by F.A. Cook and reproduced with permission from the Emil Racovitza Archive, the Library of the Romanian Academy, Cluj-Napoca Branch. This photo was processed using Photoshop© to improve clarity and has been 'colorized' using palette.fm/color/filters.

Arckowski only took five samples on the western side of Bransfield Strait directly South of Drake Passage, and all were at the sea surface, despite the fact that many temperature profiles were taken down to great depths (see chapter 6). All temperatures were above 0°C and salinities ranged between 33.77 and 33.03, with salinities decreasing towards the tip of the Antarctic Peninsula due to the dilution from the melting icebergs and glaciers further South. Refer to the table on the next page.

Date	Latitude °S	Longitude °W	Water temperature °C	Salinity
22.1.98	63°05'	61° 48'	1.18	33.77
23.1.98	63°40'	61° 47'	0.7	33.77
idem	63°47'	61° 45'	1.1	33.53
24.1.1898	64°05'	61° 24'	1.8	33.17
idem	64°13'	61° 07'	2.47	33.03

Table 8.4.1 Details of the surface water samples taken in Bransfield Strait and measured on the ship by Henrik Arctowski.

No water samples were taken during the transit in the de Gerlache Strait and this is explained by the fact that Arctowski spent a large part of his time on the islands aiming at collecting rocks as well as examining glacial geomorphological features. The latter are discussed in chapter 12 on glaciology.

54 samples were taken by Arctowski when the ship was in the sea ice (see table 8.4.2). The samples this time were obtained by lowering a slightly modified Sigsbee bottle purchased from the instrument makers Knutsen in Copenhagen. However, when the ship was 'trapped' in the sea ice, a modified Buchanan bottle (refer to Buchanan, 1889) was used that had a large funnel at the bottom and with taps that could be closed with a Rung messenger. At some locations too samples were taken at different depths and the sounding numbers listed in the table below coincide with the station numbers mentioned when temperature profiles were taken (see chapter 8.2 on water temperatures). As noted

by Arctowski and Thoulet (1908), salinities were reduced at the sea surface but rapidly increased with depth. We now know that this results from the fact that there are different water masses at depth. Refer to figure 8.2.2 for more information and Martinson (2012).

In the table on the left the cells pasted in grey relate to samples when the ship was already in the sea ice but not yet 'trapped'. This commenced on February 28, 1898.

In their monograph, Arctowski and Thoulet (1908) plotted a diagram of surface sea water density as seasons progressed and they noted a slight increase in salinity during the winter months, and their discussion on this observation dealt with much care knowing that several phenomena could contribute to such an increase, like proximity to the coast as well evaporation due to stronger winds.

Today, oceanographers calculate potential density which is the density that a parcel of water would acquire if adiabatically (= a change that occurs with no transfer of heat) brought to the surface. This could be calculated for the Belgica samples, and the same could be calculated for potential temperature. By obtaining both parameters, one could then compare these with today's measurements obtained using CTD (conductivity temperature depth) profilers. We note that Arctowski's measurements were carefully obtained so they could be

compared with today's measurements, and therefore evaluate oceanographic changes in the region, especially since sea ice is now absent, at least in summer.

The increase in salinity at depth obviously relates to the different water masses that were encountered, especially the Upper Circumpolar Deep Water (UCDW) (see Martinson (2012) and figure 8.2.2 as well as information in Schubert et al. (2021)).

Date	Latitude °S	Longitude °W	Water temperature °C	Salinity	Depth (m)	Sounding no.
13.2.98	65°16'	64°33'	-1.12	30.55	surface	
14.2.98	65°31'	66°07'	-1.61	32.3	surface	
15.2.98	65°56'	68°58'	-1.65	32.49	surface	
16.2.98	65°59'	70°39'	-1.39	33.01	surface	10
idem	idem	idem	-1.2	33.71	120	
18.2.98	68°40'	76°55'	-1.68	31.99	surface	
19.2.98	69°06'	78°21'	-1.6	31.93	surface	11
same	same	same	1.2	33.23	465	
23.2.98	69°46'	81°08'	-1.79	32.4	surface	12
same	same	same	1	34.54	550	
24.2.98	69°30'	81°31'	-1.72	32.34	surface	13
same	same	same	1	34.27	488	
25.2.98	69°17'	84°39'	-1.52	31.65	surface	14
27.2.98	69°42'	84°41'	-1.45	30.81	surface	
idem	idem	idem	-1.4	31.99	surface	
1.3.98	71°06'	85°23'	-1.7	33.18	surface	17
idem	idem	idem	0.9	34.12	500	
idem	71°17'	85°26'	-1.7	33.31	surface	18
2.3.98	71°31'	85°46'	-1.73	33.35	surface	19
idem	idem	idem	0.2	33.86	400	
4.3.98	71°22'	84°55'	-1.5	33.31	surface	20
idem	idem	idem	0.75	33.47	450	
5.3.98	71°19'	85°28'	-1.7	33.33	surface	21
idem	idem	idem	-1.4	34.1	300	
3.5.98	70°37'	89°41'	-1.9	33.47	surface	
4.5.98	70°33'	89°22'	-1.87	33.55	3	26
5.5.98	70°38'	89°22'	-1.81	33.64	3.5	27
10.5.98	71°04'	89°16'	-1.82	33.62	surface	28
idem	idem	idem	-1.9	34.18	250	
19.5.98	71°16'	87°49'	-1.85	33.62	surface	
20.5.98	idem	idem	-1.88	32.92	surface	29
idem	idem	idem	-1.9	32.62	100	
idem	idem	idem	-1.8	33.9	200	
idem	idem	idem	-1	34.42	300	
21.5.98	71°45'	87°27'	-1.86	33.7	surface	
26.5.98	71°13'	87°44'	-2	33.77	5	30
idem	idem	idem	-1.9	34.05	100	
idem	idem	idem	-1.8	34.1	200	
idem	idem	idem	-1.3	34.15	300	
9.9.98	69°54'	82°36'	-1.9	34.03	surface	32
idem	idem	idem	-2	33.9	100	
idem	idem	idem	-1.2	34.13	200	
idem	idem	idem	-0.8	34.21	300	
idem	idem	idem	0.6	34.36	400	
29.9.98	70°21'	83°29'	-2	33.9	75	36
idem	idem	idem	-1.1	34.06	200	
idem	idem	idem	0.7	34.3	400	
29.12.98	70°15'	85°54'	-1.9	33.79	50	47
idem	idem	idem	-0.6	34.15	300	
idem	idem	idem	0.9	34.46	600	
19.2.99	70°29'	94°12'	-1.9	32.72	20	53
idem	idem	idem	1.2	34.38	1000	
idem	idem	idem	0.9	34.36	1500	
idem	idem	idem	0.9	34.33	1710	

Table 8.4.2 Information on the location of water samples and their ambient temperatures and salinities measured by H. Arctowski once the ship had left Drake Passage. The top 15 listed samples were taken when the ship was still free to move. The others were taken while the ship was 'trapped' in the sea ice and were obtained through a hole in the ice.

8.5 Meteorological observations in the Bellingshausen Sea

KEY POINTS

- The meteorological observations presented by Arctowski are the first of their kind for a complete set of 12 months for Antarctica, and even perhaps for the southern hemisphere. This was accomplished simply through hard work as measurements were made almost every hour for a year.

- The data presented in Arctowski (1904)'s lengthy report has been completely ignored by twentieth century meteorologists and oceanographers.

- The coldest winds come from the South, and the annual wind rose indicates that winds from NW to ESE increase temperatures above the mean, whereas winds SE to WNW engender a temperature drop.

- During the entrapment in the pack ice, when there were openings in the sea ice, the water would elevate air temperature, humidity and engender haze conditions.

- The atmospheric pressure was the highest during the polar night, and the broadest atmospheric pressure oscillations occurred during the equinox minima. The months of maximum solstice in summer was characterised by a relative stability of the barometric height.

- It would surely be very valuable to revisit Arctowski (1904)'s data and link it with the observations made later on by Jean-Baptiste Charcot's expeditions in 1904-1905 and 1908-1910 that visited the same area investigated by the *Belgica*. Equally, the Belgian- Australian Louis Bernacchi overwintered at Cape Adare (Bernacchi, 1901) and was part of a group collecting meteorological data (see Klovstad, 1902) over the 1898-1900 period.

- Arctowski's scientific legacy here is figure 8.5.4 which provides a continuous set of air temperature measurements made over one year from March 1898 to March 1899. It also includes his compilation of wind roses (Fig. 8.5.3) that ought to be compared with today's automated and satellite data to determine changes over 125 years.

Henryk Arctowski (1904) wrote an extensive report on his meteorological observations while the ship was trapped in the sea ice for close to 13 months. These included atmospheric pressure using a Richard continuous recording barometer, wind intensity and relative direction, air temperature measured almost always every hour of the day and night. Arctowski acknowledged that meteorological measurements were made by groups of people consisting of Arctowski, Dobrowolski, Lecointe, Amundsen, Cook and also de Gerlache. In general, although measurements were made hourly, this practice nevertheless changed when effort was made when attempting to release the ship from the pack ice.

These observations obtained in 1898 -1899 were the first of their kind for the Antarctic region and form very important meteorological information, especially since the French Charcot expeditions several years later used the same equipment (see Matha and Rey-Pailhade (1911) and devoted some 310 pages to meteorological observations between January 31, 1904 and February 14, 1905; note the longitude refered to in this report refers to that of Paris!). The meteorological investigations made at Cape Adare by members of the Southern Cross expedition (Klovstad et al. 1902) ought to be consulted. They cover the period of 1898 to 1900.

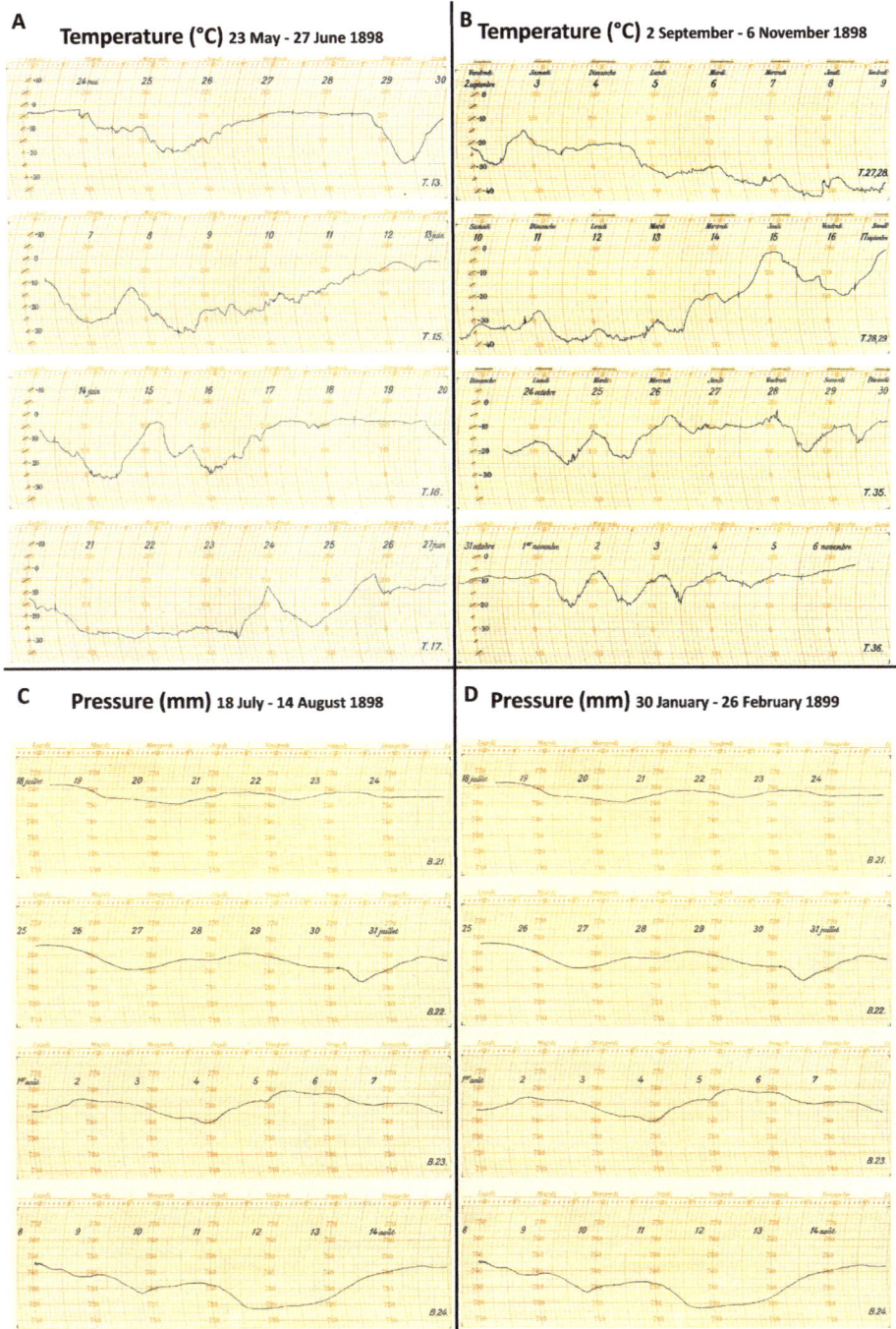

A Temperature (°C) 23 May - 27 June 1898

B Temperature (°C) 2 September - 6 November 1898

C Pressure (mm) 18 July - 14 August 1898

D Pressure (mm) 30 January - 26 February 1899

We are now well aware of that part of Antarctica is undergoing very rapid climatic changes. The monograph by Arctowski (1904) is voluminous because all the data obtained during his observations are tabulated and illustrated therein. An example of his charts is reproduced in Fig. 8.5.1. A photograph of the meteorological box that was permanently stationed at the front of the ship is shown in Fig. 8.5.2.

Figure 8.5.1 Example of the temperature and barometric recordings listed in Arctowski (1904) obtained using Richard recorders. Illustrations modified from Arctowski 's publication.

A: Temperature recordings from the Richard Thermometer Recorder for the period of 23.5.1898 to 27.6.1898;

B: Temperature recordings from the Richard Thermometer Recorder for the period of 2.9.1898 to 6.11.1898;

C: Atmospheric pressure recordings from the Richard Barometer Recorder for the period of 18.7.1898 to 14.8.1898;

D: Atmospheric pressure recordings from the Richard Barometer Recorder for the period of 30.1.1899 to 26.2.1899.

Arctowski (1904) also plotted summary wind roses data for the entire 12 months with one exception when he added the data for February 1899 to the period of March-April 1898 when assessing wind direction per trimester. It is a pity that recent research in the Bellingshausen Sea by Meredith et al. (2017) and Oehlerich et al. (2022) did not refer to the important work of Arctowski (1904) to identify changes in wind patterns over the last 120 years. This must be remedied in the near future to assess environmental changes in the area. Check also https://www.meteoblue.com/en/weather/week/bellingshausen-station_antarctica_6620740.

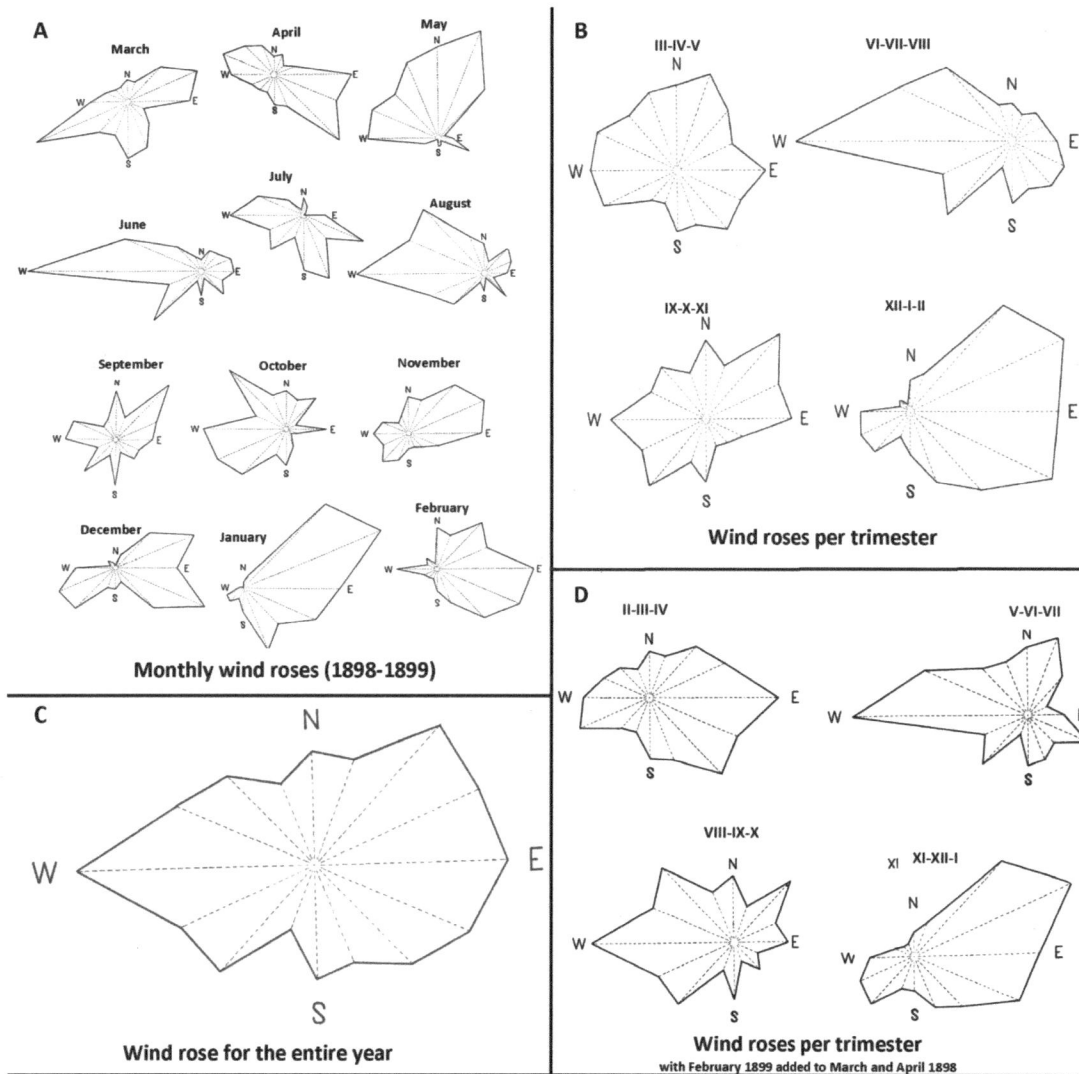

A: Monthly wind roses (1898-1899)

B: Wind roses per trimester

C: Wind rose for the entire year

D: Wind roses per trimester
with February 1899 added to March and April 1898

Figure 8.5.3. Salient wind roses plotted by Charles Leonard for Henryk Arctowski (1904) and rearranged here for better visualisation.

A: monthly wind roses for 1898 and part of 1899;

B: wind roses per trimester for 1898:

C: wind roses for the entire 1898 year;

D: wind roses per trimester for 1898-1899, with February 1899 added to March and April 1898.

March 1898 to March 1899

Most winds coming from many directions

SW + NE.   Mostly SE   NE + W + NW   Most winds coming from the West   Most winds coming

| March 1898 | April | May | June | July | August | September | October |

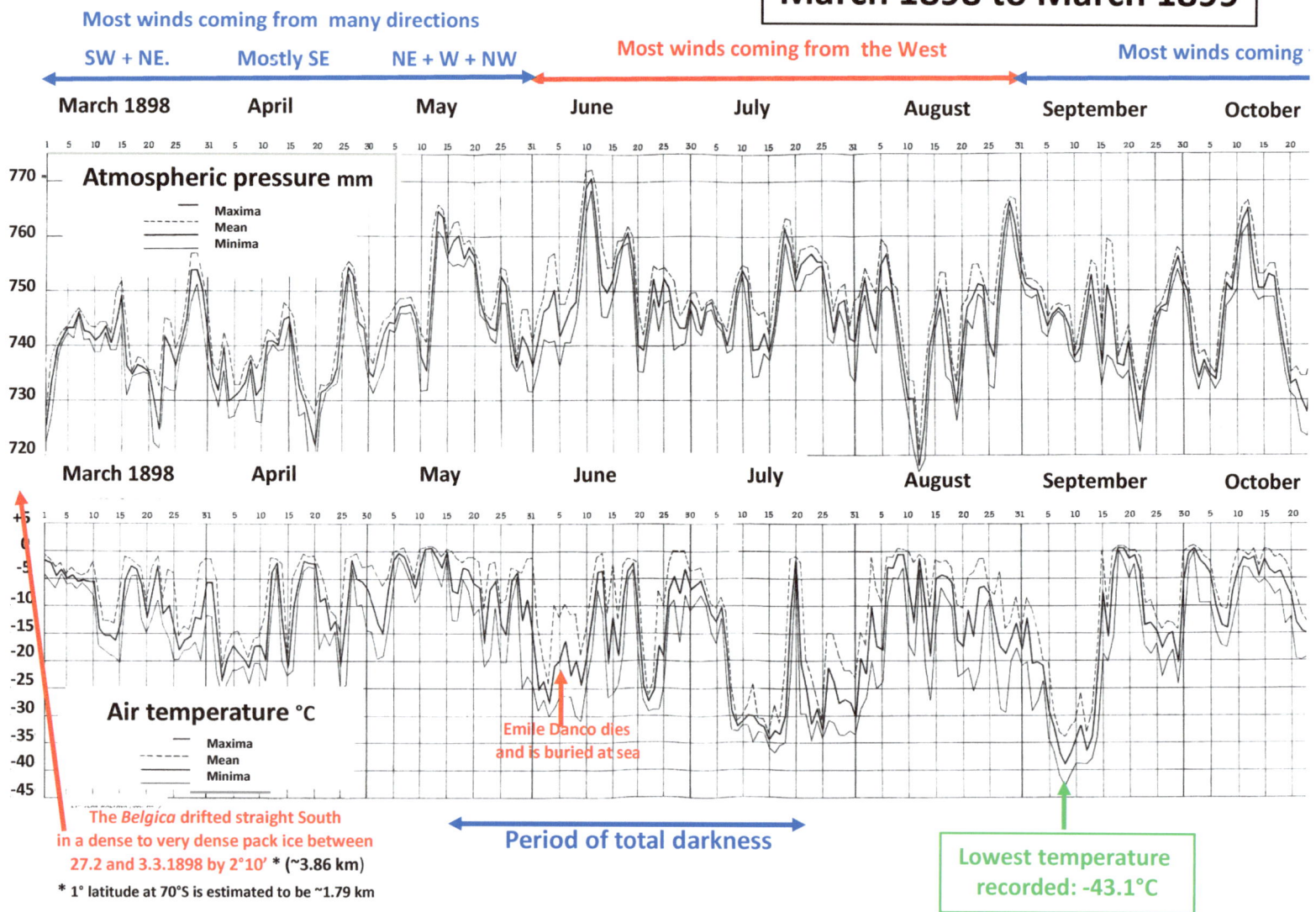

Atmospheric pressure mm

- Maxima
- Mean
- Minima

770
760
750
740
730
720

| March 1898 | April | May | June | July | August | September | October |

Air temperature °C

- Maxima
- Mean
- Minima

+5
0
-5
-10
-15
-20
-25
-30
-35
-40
-45

Emile Danco dies and is buried at sea

Period of total darkness

Lowest temperature recorded: -43.1°C

The *Belgica* drifted straight South in a dense to very dense pack ice between 27.2 and 3.3.1898 by 2°10' * (~3.86 km)

* 1° latitude at 70°S is estimated to be ~1.79 km

Measurements were made almost <u>every hour day and night for 12 months</u>, principally by Arctowski and Dobrowolski, but also by Amundsen, Lecointe, Cook and de Gerlache

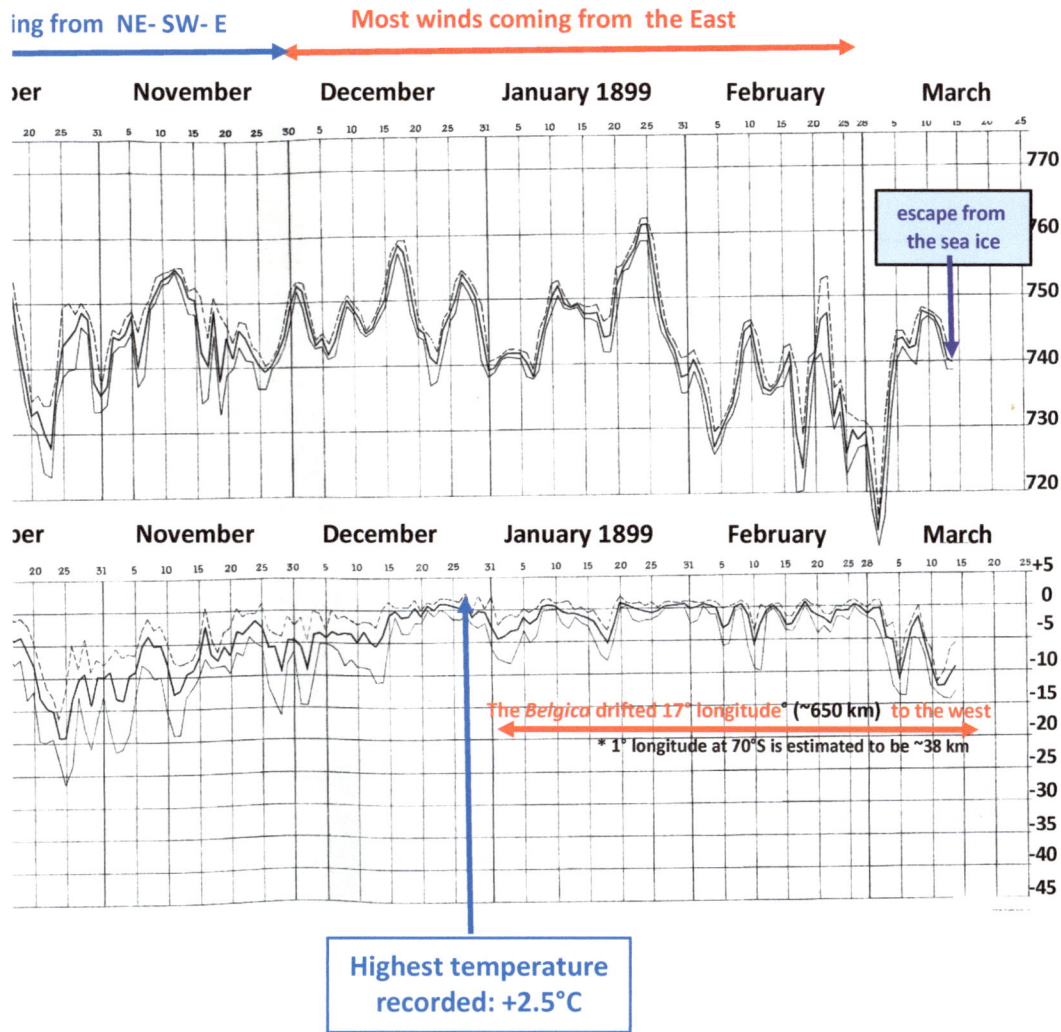

Figure 8.5.4 Annotated figure from Arctowski (1904) that summarizes for the period of March 1898 to mid-March 1899. In the upper panel, the atmospheric pressure recording in mm Hg, and air temperature in °C in the lower panel. On this figure, dominant wind directions for various periods are also indicated, as well as additional information on the lowest and highest temperature recordings. Note that when the ship was drifting in the pack ice in a westward direction, air temperatures showed little fluctuations and remained close to 0°C and winds came from the east.

Below is a summary of Arctowski (1904)'s important findings over an entire year. These are:

1. The coldest winds come from the South, with a mean -16.56°C and the least cold winds come from the NE, with a mean of -3.95°C;

2. The annual wind rose indicates that winds from NW to ESE increase temperatures above the mean, whereas winds SE to WNW engender a temperature drop;

3. Between June and August, the winds from NW to SW are the most frequent ones, whereas between December and February, the predominant winds are from NE to SE;

4. During the entrapment in the pack ice, when there were openings (called water streams by Arctowski, and looking like lakes and streams, the water would elevate air temperature, humidity and engender haze conditions;

5. The temperature of the ship did not affect readings made from instruments placed in the meteorological station at the front of the vessel (see Fig. 8.5.2);

6. Maximum atmospheric pressure of 772. 1 mm was recorded on June 11, 1898, and a minimum value of 711.7 mm on March 3, 1899. For the period of observations, the arithmetic mean was 744.4 mm with a 60.4 mm range;

7. During the polar night, the atmospheric pressure is at its highest, and the broadest atmospheric pressure oscillations occur during the equinox minima. The months of maximum solstice in summer are characterised by a relative stability of the barometric height;

8. The mean highest barometric reading of 749.11 mm coincides with winds coming from the West, whereas the lowest mean of barometric reading of 738.92 mm sees winds coming from the SE;

9. Concerning temperature readings, the lowest recorded value was -43.1°C and the highest +2.5°C. The difference between the mean of the coldest month and that of the warmest month was 22.6°C, thus justifying that the climate was not marine *per se*, but more like a coastal one.

The latter conclusion made by Arctowski (1904) is a very important one as it was unknown thus far for the Antarctic continent. As pointed out by Marchowski (2001), who tried to summarize the achievements of the two Polish scientists involved in the Belgica expedition, the meteorological observations made in 1898-1899 defined the wave character of cyclone movement around Antarctica long before the wave theory of frontal cyclones had been proposed. In addition, Arctowski (1904) established that the Antarctic is much colder that was originally presumed.

Disappointingly, again, is to determine that recent investigations by meteorologists and oceanographers in their discussions on the recent changing conditions of wind directions and salinity changes in the Bellingshausen Sea (Meredith et al., 2019) have ignored the important baseline data which Arctowski (1904) so carefully documented at great length. I hope this will be revised in the future. Equally, investigations of the extent of sea ice in the Bellingshausen Sea over the last century based on studies of an ice core on the Bruce Plateau on the Antarctic Peninsula failed to acknowledge the work by Arctowski (1904). These are by Porter et al. (2016), Goodwin et al. (2016) and Thomas and Tetzner (2018). The latter authors disappointingly stated: " the observational period for Antarctica is short. Observational records only began in the 1940s and much of our understanding of the wider spatial climate variability and glacial dynamics is limited to the satellite era (post 1979)".

It is noteworthy that, in his 1904 publication, Arctowski acknowledged his wife N. Arctowska for helping him during the preparation of this volume. Equally, he listed Professor Walthère Spring of the University of Liège for the loan of a calculator after the expedition, as well as for providing him with numerous meteorological equipments. M.A. Lancaster, Director of the Meteorological Service of Belgium, is also thanked for advice before the start of the expedition and later during the writing up process. Finally, Arctowski acknowledged that the calculations of the wind roses were made by Mr Engelbert Gutteman and the illustration shown here in Fig. 8.5.3 were prepared by Charles Leonard.

It is disappointing to see that Sippel et al. (2024), in their assessment of the early 20th century 'cold bias' in surface temperatures, did not use the continuous data acquired by the *Belgica* in the Bellingshausen Sea for the period of March 1898 to March 1899, that could have also been combined by the data also acquired by the Charcot expedition some 10 years later. Those data would have helped appreciate changes that have been happening since in the region. At least around the Antarctic Peninsula there is no 'bias', temperatures have been rising steadily since the Belgica expedition.

8.6 Aurora australis - southern lights

KEY POINTS

- The auroras in 1898-1899 were weakly developed and were close to being of minimal frequency as the area where the *Belgica* drifted was far from the zone where polar auroras pass through the zenith (the highest point on the celestial sphere). The year 1898 coincided with a minimum in sun spots, and thus a minimum is polar auroras.

- In total 61 sightings of the southern lights were made by Arctowski in 1898 between March 11 and September 11. A last observation was made just before the ship escaped from the pack ice on March 12, 1899.

- Arctowski described at length, and with the aid of sketches, 12 different types of auroras, ranging from a variety of arcs and rays, some undulating ribbons, darts, drapes, coronas and flames.

- Arctowski discussed the concomitance of auroras in both hemispheres. He also argued for the link between storms, barometric changes and auroras. He discussed at length the limitations of his observations due to the absence of necessary equipment to measure atmospheric electricity.

- Arctowski's scientific legacy here consists in his thorough descriptions of the aurora phenomena for the entire year of 1898.

Observations by Henryk Arctowski of the *'Aurores Australes'* also called *'Southern Lights'* are documented in his monograph published in 1901, fairly soon after the return of the expedition to Antwerp. In the introduction of this monograph, he pointed out that the ship drifted between 69°51'S and 71°36'S and 82°35'W and 92°21'W for a bit more than one year. Overall, the meteorological conditions were unfavourable for the observations of auroras as cloudiness was particularly strong. Nevertheless, he was able to observe the aurora some 62 times, always at night. The last time being on March 12, 1899, two days before escaping from the entrapment of the sea ice. All the other observations were made in 1898. Roald Amundsen was the first to see an aurora on March 11, 1898 and later F. Cook, G. Lecointe and R. Amundsen helped H. Arctowski with his observations and the crew often called him when the lights became visible. Nevertheless, Arctowski insisted on being present for all the sightings. The first 39 pages in the monograph describe each of the 61 observations. Apart from the last observation made in March 1899, the 61 observations spanned the period of March 11 and September 11, 1898.

Arctowski (1901a) described at great length the optical phenomena. For example, during the night of April 14 to 15, 1898, his observations commenced at 19:10 pm and concluded the next day at 01:35 am; they totalled 25 with ample descriptions of his observations. On another occasion, for the night of 25 to 26 of April 1898, he recorded 27 observations, sometimes quite detailed ones. His observations are also backed by sketches illustrating what he saw (see Fig. 8.6.1). For some observations, he used a variety of coloured glass plates loaned to him by his mentor at the University of Liège, Professor Walthère Spring. These allowed Arctowski to estimate the light intensity by using a series of glass plates over one another. In total, he described up to 12 features ranging from a variety of arcs and rays, some undulating ribbons, darts, drapes, coronas and flames.

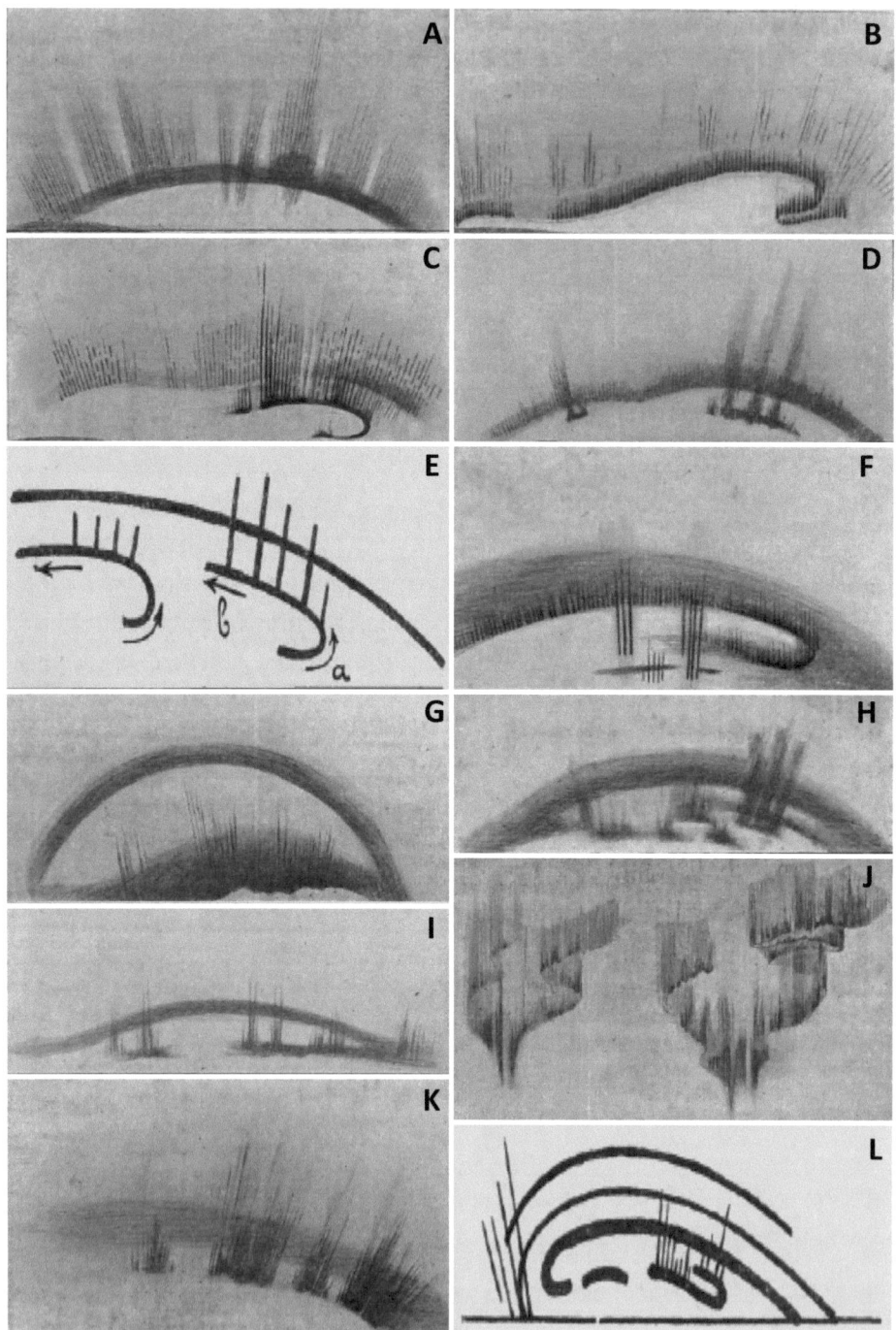

Figure 8.6.1. These sketches are reproduced from Arctowski (1901a) for which he provided dates (all 1898) and timing of observations with individual descriptions.

A: 14/15 March, 23H00, very hectic rays;

B: 14/15 March, 23H05, undulated and silvery, a little greenish, at times discontinued;

C: 14/15 March, 23H35, the aurora fades, little by little the radiation becomes less neat;

D: 14/15 March, midnight; a luminous point appears below a great luminous arc;

E: 19/20 March, 0H30, a is further away from the ship than b, more clarity at the right;

F: 19/20 March, 23H58, the arc does not reach the horizon and bends back on itself on the right;

G: 15/16 April, 20H50, the luminosity has the appearance of well illuminated clouds, the rays are clearly marked;

H: 14/14 April, 21H30, the arc has moved up; there are always many obscured rays so that the centre of the area is most luminous;

I: 22/23 June, 21H30, the area is concentrated in a homogeneous band highly luminous with neat rays on the right of the glow is confused;

J: 13/14 June, 19.15 to 19.30, above there is a yellow band but clear, the glow with weak drapes that are stretched;

K: 19/20 March, 20H45, the large arc is more regular, broad on the left and narrow on the right, rays emanate from the 2nd arc that is more luminous and appears at the front;

L: 2 September, 20H30; double arc; the external one whiter, the other is yellow and more luminous, with barbs of rays.

After those detailed observations, Arctowski (1901a) tried to summarise his observations. Overall, he was quite careful, noting the absence of equipment to measure atmospheric electricity which he thought would enlighten more on the southern lights. First of all, he attempted at discussing the link between storms and auroras, with the idea that the former could eventually even be predicted. He also noted the concordance between the most brilliant and longer auroras during the equinoxes compared to winter solstices. He also noted that barometric variations were more frequent and intense during equinoxes compared to polar nights and summer solstice.

Arctowski (1901a) also refers to the observations made by the Finnish-Swedish explorer Adolf Erik Nordenskiöld (1881) on the aurora borealis during the winter of 1878-1879 while on the *Vega* steamship which aimed at finding the Northeast Passage. This was a Swedish expedition funded by King Oscar II. In volume 2 of the expedition report, there are a number of descriptions of the aurora with

sketches of events in March 1878 (3, 20, 21) that are similar to those made by Arctowski (1901a). These were made when the *Vega* was trapped in the ice. Arctowski (1901a) showed some astonishment at the concordance between the Vega and Belgica observations, thus linking the similarities in both hemispheres.

Arctowski (1901a) believed that his monograph formed the first and complete set of observations for the aurora australis in the southern hemisphere. Later on, he discussed the observations made by Borchgrevinck made at Cape Adare in 1899 (Borchgrevink, 1900) but does not compare them except to say that the Cape Adare auroras were in the form of arcs like in the magnetic north. In fact, the latter author provided quite a bit of information which included that when there were well defined auroras, the magnets were significantly disturbed, thus linking the two phenomena. Borchgrevinck pointed out that during winter, the southern lights were seen nearly every night in winter, and that the diurnal period was between 6 pm and

3 am with maximum intensity between 8 and 9 pm, with some exceptions. Additional information is available in Borchgrevinck (1900) which unfortunately Arctowski did not discuss in his 1901 monograph.

In February 1901, Arctowski discussed in an article in Ciel et Terre as well as in his monograph (Arctowski 1901a) that the president of the Canadian Institute Mr. Arthur Harvey, a polymath who also became President of the Royal Society of Canada, observed the aurora borealis in Toronto between March and September 1898. These phenomena in fact are concomitant with the events documented by Arctowski in the southern hemisphere, especially since the longitude of Toronto is very similar (only 4° difference) to the position of the *Belgica* at that time. Harvey's investigations into solar-terrestrial relationships claimed to have discovered the emission in solar radiation of negatively charged particles and was the first to announce a 27.5 day periodicity in magnetic disturbances on earth. Arctowski (1901a,b) instead refers to a periodicity of some 26 days which was also noted for the northern hemisphere by Erkolm and Arrhenius in 1899.

In his monograph, Arctowski (1901a) compared observations made of northern hemisphere auroras with his, as well as annual variations. Refer to his publication for more information.

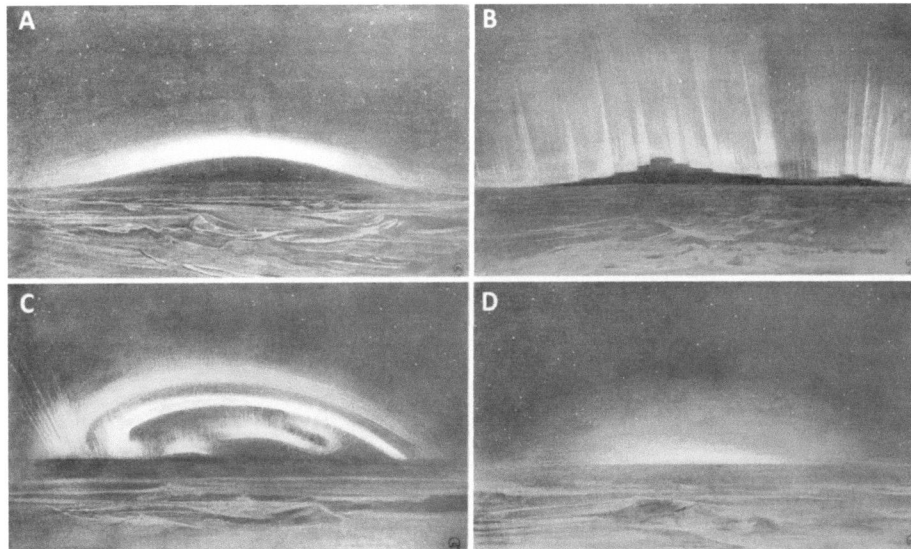

Figure 8.6.2 Different types of auroras illustrated in Arctowski's (1901) monograph.

A: Homogeneous arc;

B: Drapery;

C: Double arc;

D: Auroral glow.

Note no dates were linked to those drawings that were made by artist Auguste Donnay (whose acronym appears at the bottom right hand corner of each illustration) under the supervision of Arctowski.

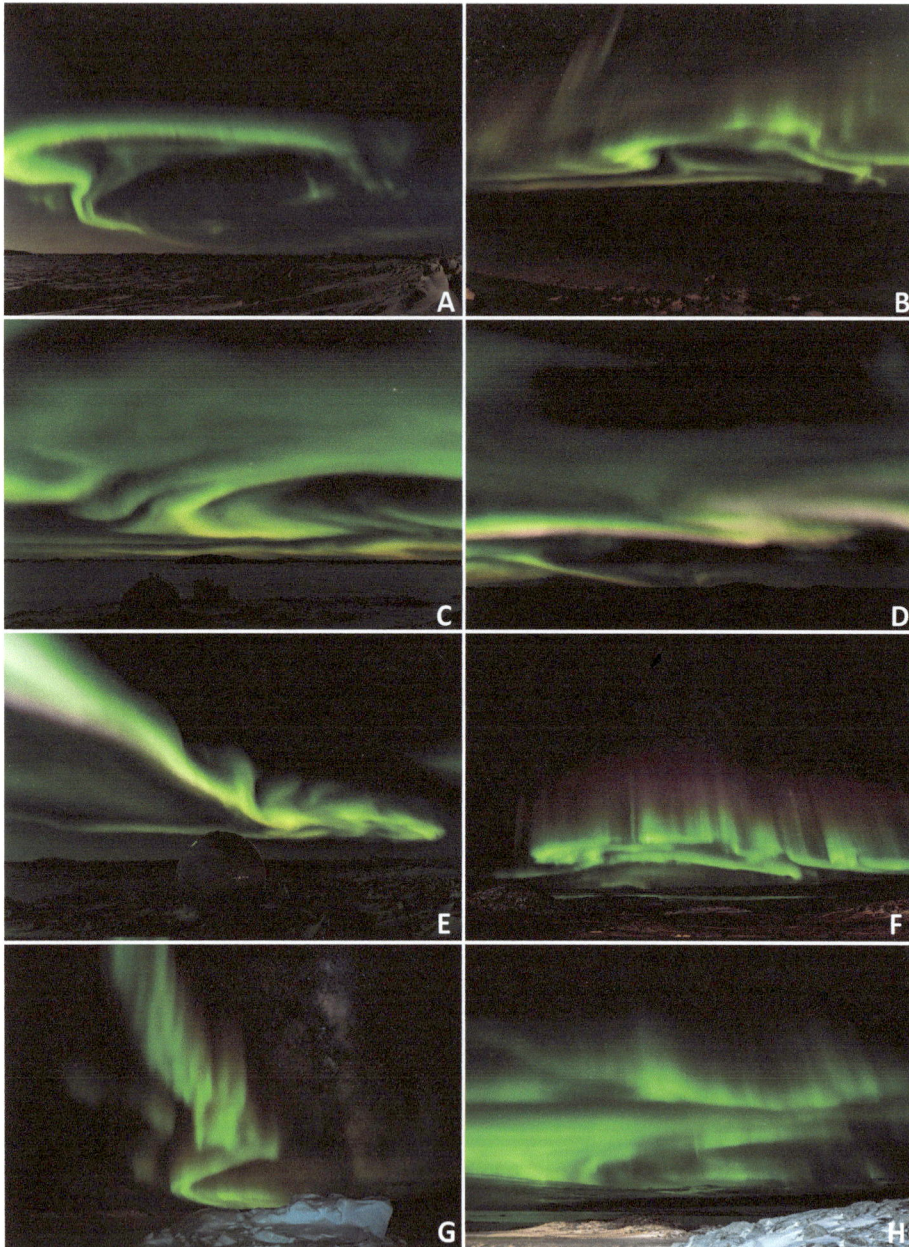

For more information on current knowledge of the southern lights or aurora australis, consult Crooker et al. (1977), Stern et al. (1996), Hamacher et al. (2013), Fox (2019) and the Australian Bureau of Meteorology website (BOM 2024).

Figure 8.6.3. Recent photographs of the aurora australis taken by Berend Becker at two Australian stations.
A-D: Davis Station in 2019;
E-H: Casey Station in 2022.
Reproduced with his permission.

8.7 Clouds

Antoni Dobrowolski joined the *Belgica* after she had to undergo some maintenance on its engine in Ostend harbour. He was welcomed to join the Belgica contingent at the very last minute at the insistence of Henryk Arctowski (a Polish compatriot) and this in the capacity of a sailor. He had only a few items of clothing with him, but because of his studies in the natural sciences undertaken at the University of Zürich – where he likely met Henryk Arctowski – and he also had studied at the University of Liège in Belgium. He was eventually asked to collaborate by collecting some meteorological data. He took the tasks of studying clouds and the formation of snow and hoar-frost. Dobrowolski (1903)'s observations commenced in April 1898 and ended on March 14, 1899. In the very extensive 48 pages of tables Dobrowolski placed quite a few question marks which are explained by the fact that, during winter especially, the ship although being trapped in sea ice, was not very far from the free ocean. This explained why fog was frequent, and that prevented from cloud observations. Equally, snow storms also prevented observations. On average, observations were made every hour, and at the end Dobrowolski summed up the type of clouds for each of the 13 months.

Figure 8.7.1 Photograph of Antoni Dobrowolski observing clouds on board the *Belgica*, reproduced with permission from Dr Pietrzak Agnieska, Ziemi Museum, Warsaw, Poland, later on processed using Photoshop© to improve its clarity and then 'colorized' using palette.fm/color/filters.

FORM AND STRUCTURE OF CLOUDS

1. He observed that clouds were very often organised in 'systems'; they formed groups where the characters vary in a defined way and always the same in their essence;

2. Fog and low clouds prevented observation of high clouds. All the entire systems and the majority of observed segments showed well-defined character variation;

3. Of all the characters of a system its thickness varied most for 2 different types: the first one, relatively rare, where the thickness decreased progressively from the anterior extremity to the rear; and the second, being very common, the thickness was at its maximum in the middle, and diminished towards both ends;

4. The systems showed local thinning. He then described this phenomenon for different types of clouds.

Figure 8.7.2 Photograph of Antoni Dobrowolski observing clouds on board the *Belgica,* reproduced with permission from Dr R.-M. Mocanu from the Ștefan cel Mare Vaslui County Museum, Vaslui, Romania, and then processed using Photoshop© to improve its clarity and 'colorized' using palette.fm/color/filters.

Note snow shoes partly visible on the left as well as the meteorological box behind. The ship was obviously trapped in the sea ice at that time.

In the 3rd part of the monograph which is labelled as an appendix, Dobrowolski described three principal cloud systems for each day seen during the period of April 1898 to March 1899 when the ship came out of the sea ice. These are: 1. Cirrus-type clouds; 2. Systems with clouds at middle levels (including stratocumulus-type clouds); and 3. System of low clouds. This amounts to 62 pages of detailed observations.

8.8 Snow and hoar-frost (givre)

Dobrowolski (1903) stated that in the absence of a specific microscope with an attached camera this prevented him from making accurate observations of ice crystals. He also wondered as to whether an observation pertained to a single crystal or an assemblage of crystals. Nevertheless, he made a large number of observations of snow crystals, most often with the help of a lens in combination with a microscope and, at other times, just with a lens. We must remember that these observations would have been made outside the ship at temperature close to 0°C or even much lower.

Concerning snow, he described two main types of crystals: **lamellar type** (length of the main axis very small relative to that of the secondary axes) and **rod type** (length of the main axis usually greater, rarely a little smaller). In total, observations were made on 454 crystals of the first type and 419 on the second. Dobrowolski was curious to determine why snow took one or the other forms. He discussed at length

both the form and structure of each type. He provided sketches of these but are not reproduced here. Consequently, a plate (Fig. 8.8.1) is presented here to give a flair of the type of crystals Dobrowolski would have seen and studied. The plate is a collage of photographs produced for an exhibition at the Ziemi Muzeum of the Earth which is part of the Polish Academy of Sciences in Warsaw. It consists of photographs of what were originally glass plates. He also made an attempt at describing lamellar formations related to prismatic crystals, in addition to acicular snow crystals and related granules, he listed snow powder and frost covering ice crystals, snow flakes and groupings of snow crystals. In the tables that follow, it is possible to determine the large number of Dobtwolski (1903)'s observations that were made at different temperatures as demonstrated in Tables 8.8.1 and 8.8.2.

Table 8.8.1 Relationship between air temperature and basic snow crystal form

	Lamellar snow	Prismatic snow	Acicular snow
Number of observations	454	213	206
1°C °C to -5°C	52.20%	62.50%	84.60%
-5°C to -10°C	23.60%	24.40%	12.90%
-10°C to -15°C	18.90%	13.10%	2.5 % combined
below -15°C	5.30%	none	2.5 % combined
from 1°C to -2.5°C	30.30%	43.20%	66.20%
Mean temperature	-5.9°C	-4.4°C	-2.4%
Minimum temperatrue	-21.9*	-14.7°	-17.6°C
Maximum temperature	+1.4%	+1°C	+1.1°C

Table 8.8.2 Relationship between air temperature and specific crystal form

	Stars without central field, well developed appendices	Stars without central field, rudimentary or absent appendices	Simple hexagonal lamellae, star-shaped lamellae with considerable central field relative to the rays
Number of observations	140	35	161
1°C °C to -5°C	43.6%	8.6%	59.6%
-5°C to -10°C	22.9%	34.3%	21.1%
-10°C to -15°C	27.8%	54.3%	13.0%
below -15°C	5.7%	2.8%	6.3%
Mean temperature	-7.3°C	-10.0°C	-5.1°C
Minimum temperature	-21.9°C	-19.8°	-19.8°C
Maximum temperature	+0.7°C	+0.5°C	+0.8°C

He also discussed at length the relationship between ambient temperature and ice crystals properties and this is further elaborated here, with some results in Table 8.8.3.

The second section of Dobrowolski (1903)'s monograph provides some extensive observations on frost, both as vertical and horizontal types. Many of these very detailed observations were made during the nights over several hours. Over 11 pages (pp. 61-72), he described at length the formation of crystals. These observations are also accompanied by sketches.

It is noteworthy that Dobrowolski continued the study of ice crystals and snow over two decades after the Belgica expedition. This led to the publication of an enormous treatise on snow already in 1923. Barry et al. (2011) have recognised Dobrowolski for having been the person to have coined for the first time the word **cryosphere**, a now commonly-used term, which even recently saw the creation of a new journal published by the European Geophysical Union (https://www.the-cryosphere.net/) bearing that name. Machowski (1998) reported on the fact that Dobrowolski, commencing during with his observations on the Belgica, discovered a new type of ice crystal which contributes to the halo phenomenon in the atmosphere that is linked to the special formation of clouds. Such a phenomenon was recently confirmed by satellite observations.

Temperature range	Number of observations	Mean diameter
+1.0 to -2.5°C	30	1.6 mm
-2.6 to -5.0°C	13	1.6 mm
-5.1 to -7.5°C	5	?
-7.6 to -10.0°C	9	1.4 mm
-10.1 to -12.5°C	6	1.3 mm
-12.6 to -15.0°C	6	1.0 mm
below -15°C	7	0.7 mm

Table 8.8.3 Relationship between air temperature and snow crystal diameter

Figure 8.8.1 Collage of photographs of snow crystals that were originally produced on glass plates and were on display at the Muzeum Ziemi in Warsaw. It is presumed that these photographs had been produced by Antoni Dobrowolski. Some cracks are visible on some photos which were later processed by myself using Photoshop©.

8.9 On ice, sea ice and their formation

At first, Henryk Arctowski reminded us that there was little known about sea ice in the southern hemisphere in contrast with the Arctic region by the time the Belgica expedition took place. He stated that Fabian Gottlieb von Bellingshausen, when he discovered the Alexander I Coast in 1821, found the sea ice was smaller in extent compared to the period of 1898-1899 when the *Belgica* was trapped in the ice (Arctowski and Mill, 1908).

It is during the last few days of 'free sailing' that they had decided to sail in a southerly direction. This proved somewhat fateful. They remained trapped for twelve and an half months with detrimental consequences for people's health, morale, but also during which time much scientific endeavour occurred.

Arctowski devoted a 64 pages long monograph entitled: *'Les glaces: glace de mer et banquises'* (Ice: sea ice and pack ice) to discuss his observations of sea ice and icebergs.

Over several pages, Arctowski described the nature of the ocean and when they encountered floating ice, and eventually became permanently 'trapped' in it on February 28, 1898. Prior to that time, Arctowski described the vagrancy of the sea ice and on how it was affected by strong winds.

Arctowski and Mill (1908)'s observations are multiple. As an example, already on February 23, 1898, just before reaching the pack ice, he ventured on the ice floe and he tried to drill though it (Fig. 8.9.1). At the top was 8 cm of snow, but already the bottom 4 to 5 cm were like perfect *névé* with ice grains 1 cm in diameter, then below were 15 to 16 cm of compact ice impregnated with sea water. This ice was yellow with vertical crystallisation. In total on 3.1 m of ice there was only 30 cm above the sea surface, thus being only 1/10th emerging (Fig. 8.9.2). In some places, the snow was 1 m thick. Later on, icebergs appeared when the ship entered the pack.

Arctowski wondered why the ice consisted of long bands, oriented E-W and in between these were large 'lakes' free of ice. Over one year of observations, he determined that the water 'bands' formed each time ice was pushed northward by the wind, to eventually become detached by ocean swell. He also mentioned the extensive openings at times in the ice where free water was seen, one of which had formed during a snow storm (see Fig. 8.9.6 E) and which was covered by whitish young ice which had been transported there. On the edge of the old ice, up to one metre of snow had accumulated. He also mentioned these areas as dangerous for venturing on the sea ice. He described the various aspects of the new ice, some of which was wrinkled, other smooth (see Fig. 8.9.6).

Arctowski separated his observations in several topics. These are: (1) the freezing of sea water, (2) speed of the growth of sea ice, (3) transformation of the young sea ice, (4) sea ice of 7 months, (5) blue ice and névé formation, (6) the role of wind, (7) ice fields and icebergs, water ways, and (8) crevasses and pressions.

We will discuss here some of the salient and significant observations.

THE FREEZING OF SEA WATER

Arctowski (in Arctowki and Mill, 1908) wanted to conduct experiments on the freezing of sea water but decided not to pursue these due to the lack of time. However, he made several observations as he examined on how different salts form and at what temperature, using a sample of sea water obtained at 1,500 m and with a salinity of 34.36. Later in January 1899, he laid down on the ice and observed what was happening in the water near an area which had been sawn off. This was a time when air temperatures were quite mild and the crew was trying to cut an opening in the sea ice in order to release the ship from its entrapment. He also discussed ice crystal formation and compared these results from those obtained in March 1898.

Figure 8.9.1 Photograph of Henryk Arctowski probing the sea ice near the *SY Belgica*. Photo courtesy of Dr Ramona-Maria Mocanu of the Vaslui Museum in Romania. Photo 'colorized' using palette.fm/color/filters.

Note also the magnetic observatory (black box) on the right of the ship and also the masts further on the right where the sounding through a hole in the sea ice remained while the ship was drifting with the sea ice.

RATE OF SEA ICE GROWTH

He made several observations in the hole near the ship which was used to collect water profiles and make several soundings. He also measured the thickness of the ice forming through time at different temperatures ranging from -32° to -41°C. Over a period of five days (3 to 8 of September 1898) (see Table 8.9.1), Arctowski assiduously assessed the way ice grows and the growth rate. It was an arduous task as outside temperature was very low, reaching -41°C and he performed his observations during the day as well as at night. He is to be commended for his amazing efforts, all on his own!

Arctowski said that his findings are very similar to those made by others in the northern hemisphere (see relevant references in Arctowski and Mill, 1908). It is noteworthy that Arctowski took a temperature profile in the same permanent hole that was located some 50 metres from the ship; soundings 31 and 32 in Arctowski and Mill (1898) (see also Fig. 8.2.1). The observations on ice formation coincide with the coldest period experienced during the entire expedition (Fig. 8.5.4). Figures 8.9.6 E, G show a water opening in the ice, which formed during a snow storm, that was covered with young whitish ice formed in great part by blown up ice (neige chassée).

Discussion continued with a brief note to say that 'pancake ice' which was only seen only once at midday on February 22, 1898. At that time, temperature was only -5.8°C. The plates were 5 cm thick, made of triangular crystals, arranged vertically. This ice was soft and was easily broken. Its saline taste was quite pronounced. Later at night, fresh ice formed into rounded plates ranging from 0.5

Table 8.9.1 Observations on sea ice growth during September 3-8, 1898 (data reproduced from Arctowski (1908).

Date	Time	Temperature	Ice thickness (mm)	Comment
3.9.1898	17:30 to 20	-22° to -23°	15	ice is flexible & moist, vertical axes in many directions
	23:30	-23° to -25°	18	
	2:30	**	25	
4.9.1898	9:00	-23° to -22°	38	in 9.5 hours
			50	in 15 hours. This is smooth and dry at the surface. 1 cm below the surface, the ice is more compact and contains air bubbles. Lower it has vertically oriented crystals
	11:30	-20° to -21°	12	in 2.5 hours
	15:15	-20°	15	in 3.5 hours
			22	in 6 hours
			58-60	in 21.5 hours
	midnight	-20°	75-78	in 31 hours
		thermometer down to -31°	100-102	in 39.5 hours
5.9.1898	17:30			hole cleared
	19:30	-34°	17	after 2 hours
	22:30		23	after 3 hours
		-32°	34	after 5 hours
	0:30		16	after 2 hours
		-32°	41-42	after 7 hours
6.9.1898	8:30		49	after 8 hours
		-32°	75	after 15 hours
	17:00			hole opened again
	19:00	-34°	15	after 2 hours
	22:00		21	after 3 hours
		-36°	30	after 5 hours
	midnight		15	after 2 hours
			30	after 5 hours
		-37°	40	after 7 hours
7.9.98	13:00			hole cleared at 13:00
	17:00	-36°	24	after 4 hours
	20:00		21	after 3 hours
		-39°	40	after 7 hours
	midnight		28	after 4 hours
			44	after 7 hours
		-41°	55	after 11 hours
8.9.1898	9:00		51	
	18:00	-41°	90-95	in this ice, 6-8 mm consisted of frozen 'rassol'* & below 30 cm were vertical crystals, friable and pointy at their end at the bottom
	19:00		65	after 12 hours
			97	after 21 hours
		-34° to -40°	130	after 30 hours, with temperare -34° to -40°

* Arctowski uses this term to define sea water brine (= saumure)

** It is assumed that the temperature listed above is the same as for the following measurement

to 1 m in diameter, barely emerging from the water and garnished by a small thickening engendered by plates rubbing against one another. Arctowski melted a fragment of pancake ice and fusion water was slightly white and the weight of the salts was 8.9 gram per kilogram in solution (= 8.9 salinity), whereas sea water was 32.34. Another melted fragment, yellowish and originating from a thinner ice, gave a salinity of 11.43.

TRANSFORMATION OF THE YOUNG SEA ICE

Arctowski examined pancake ice and noted that it contained between 7 and 11 grams per kilo of salts whereas sea water had a salinity of 33 (being for dissolved salts). He further noted that a piece ice with 11.43 per mil of its weight of salts left for two days to allow slow fusion had only retained 4.64 per mil, thus demonstrating that a certain amount of salts are linked to the ice crystals. He noted that young ice only keeps its salts (or brines) for a few days that at first it concentrates in large quantities, but that it eventually gets rid of it almost completely with time.

He went further into discussing on how small and very thin needles 1 to 2 cm long form from a single point, then develop further, often in a 'rassol' (brines) and that their tips are often very salty. More information is available in Arctowski and Mill (1908)'s monograph.

SEVEN-MONTHS OLD SEA ICE

Arctowski was able to make observations on the ageing of sea ice simply because the ship remained in the same place for many months and therefore he could monitor the evolution of sea ice. On January 30, 1899, after having been 'trapped' for 11 months, and when the crew decided to saw a channel in the ice, he made observations at a location which was originally open water in July

1898. Hence, the ice was thin in places and most of the thick accumulation of snow over it had disappeared. He then was able to describe in detail a profile through the ice that is reproduced overleaf. Several layers are distinct, some of which contain water.

SNOW COVER AND NÉVÉ

Arctowski made several important observations on the temperature of the ice below the snow cover which must have helped towards the end of the period when the ship was trapped. He observed that if the snow cover was removed, the ice below would warm up and become friable, leading to some melting. He also noticed that black colouring of the snow cover, such as what was left where the astronomical observation hut had been, caused melting and even later the formation of a water pool. In his report, Arctowski used a sketch to show such melting areas and identified the course of the vessel to escape from its imprisonment. He also presented some tables to clearly argue that the temperature of the snow cover, near the surface (some 10 cm down) changed according to air temperature fluctuations, but that lower down (at 50 cm), temperature changed very little and remained warmer that the layers at 10 cm above. Such measurements were made in early March 1899. We note that air temperature at that time had dropped somewhat since the warm air temperatures registered the month before.

BLUE ICE AND NÉVÉ FORMATION

Arctowski described observations on the importance of snow cover. He observed that on February 2, 1899, within a few days, some 50 cm ice had formed around the *Belgica* as a result of snow evaporation; water pools also had formed. He remarked on a cabin that had been placed in front of the ship during the period preceding the polar

night, and then disappeared completely under the snow. When it was uncovered, it had sunk by some 1.5 metres and its bottom was immersed in sea water. In November that year, the ship was engulfed in extensive snow drift, such that she had sank somewhat and snow had to be removed together by digging a trench as deep as possible along the ship which eventually raised again.

He went further into describing on how seawater can infiltrate the névé in winter. He also discussed the importance of sun light/rays to melt snow and eventually help forming ice.

When placing Arago actinometers on the snow, he observed at 11 am on March 12, 1898 a temperature of +48.2°C for the thermometer covered with smoked black and +38°C for the one with a brilliant bowl, whereas the thermometers placed in the meteorological shelter returned at the same time a measurement of -13.8°C. Later on, at 11 am on April 12, 1898, he used Arago actinometers which he placed on the snow and read temperatures of +28.3°C and +9.2°C whereas the air temperature was -22°C. Arctowski observed that the snow was powdery and perfectly dry and consequently the sun rays were unable to melt the snow to turn it into névé. Nevertheless, he concluded that at temperatures in the vicinity of -10°C, snow is not dry when the solar rays are intense. He noted on several occasions that snow can readiliy melt when air temperature is in the range of -4 to -7°C.

More information and discussions on these phenomena can be found in this monograph.

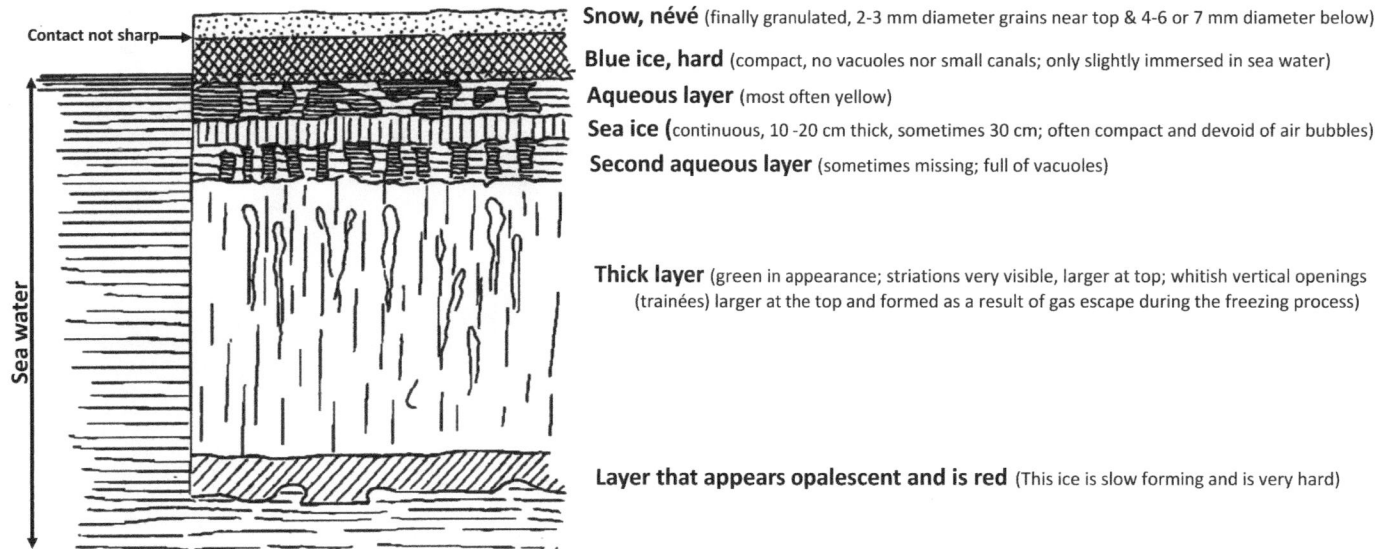

Snow, névé (finally granulated, 2-3 mm diameter grains near top & 4-6 or 7 mm diameter below)

Blue ice, hard (compact, no vacuoles nor small canals; only slightly immersed in sea water)

Aqueous layer (most often yellow)

Sea ice (continuous, 10 -20 cm thick, sometimes 30 cm; often compact and devoid of air bubbles)

Second aqueous layer (sometimes missing; full of vacuoles)

Thick layer (green in appearance; striations very visible, larger at top; whitish vertical openings (trainées) larger at the top and formed as a result of gas escape during the freezing process)

Layer that appears opalescent and is red (This ice is slow forming and is very hard)

Figure 8.9.2 Reproduction of the cross section through a block of sea ice made by Arctowski (1908) with interpretation of the different layers. For more information consult that publication. It is interesting that Arctowski did comment further on the red colouration, which likely was caused by different species of diatoms.

THE EFFECTS OF THE WIND

When temperature is low, snow is dry as observed by Arctowski who then said that it can be easily blown away. In fact, the *Belgica,* being an obstacle to the wind, snow accumulation was quite considerable. On two occasions, in October and November 1898, the ship was completely covered by snow (Fig. 8.9.6 B and compare with Fig. 8.9.7 F). Icebergs trapped in the ice formed the most important obstacles and snow drifts are most marked on them. Large banks of snow form around them. He further commented that snow drifts produced several patterns around hummocks as seen in Fig. 8.9.6 F,H, as well as the equivalent of 'ripple marks' (Fig. 8.9.6 F, H). He also noted that snow drifts can also form scaly deposits as seen in Fig. 8.9.7 B. And he extended his discussion on features associated to hummocks that are caused by the wind (Fig. 8.9.6 D,H).

ICE FIELDS AND ICEBERGS

Arctowski's discussion here dealt with the fact that, overall, sea ice moves around, but ice fields undergo continuous changes in their aspects. Modifications are caused by pressure occurring on the edge of the open ocean, such that the ice crust was often dislocated and therefore is always on the move. Winds coming from the E, SE and SW would eventually detach fragments from the pack ice and as a result start moving. Unfortunately, the crew was unable to make observations during the polar night - many also were suffering from anaemia and scurvy (see chapter 12) –. Arctowski noted that, at times, the ice field was quite uniform (see Figs. 8.9.1. and 8.9.5) but when hummocks were present there was evidence that they formed by compression of ice plates that had been isolated previously.

Concerning icebergs, Arctowski stated that whey were abundant in the early days when in the sea ice (just before the completed 'entrapment'), with Lecointe counting 147 icebergs on February 18, 1898 and Amundsen counting 320 icebergs on February 21 a few days later (Fig. 8.9.3). Towards the end of the entrapment, some large icebergs were seen moving towards the ship and these were moving in a southerly direction, which led Arctowski to suggest the presence of deep current moving from N to S.

On page 37 of his report, Arctowski stated that G. Lecointe would discuss in his monograph the drift (dérive) of the *Belgica.* However, while consulting this volume entitled 'Travaux hydrographiques et instructions nautiques' I found a note written by Lecointe which stated that its publication had been delayed and that a second 'fascicule' would appear at a later date. I failed to find it. It is worth mentioning that Georges Lecointe, on top of becoming in 1900 the Scientific Director of the Astronomical Survey of the Royal Belgian Observatory (and its Director in 1914) had taken on many tasks after the expedition, including the managing of all the publications resulting from the Belgica expedition. A formidable task for which Emil Racovitza did help a lot, but it is likely that those tasks unfortunately prevented the second volume to be published.

Figure 8.9.3 Detail of map 3 that appeared in the trio publication of G. Lecointe, H. Arctowski and E. Racovitza who extensively reported on the Belgica expedition to the Royal Belgian Geographical Society in Brussels on November 28, 1900. (Société royale belge de *Géographie,* vol. 24). This important map shows the position of the ship for two significant periods when she entered the pack ice after leaving the de Gerlache Strait. **Period 1** from 19.2.1898 until 1.3.1898 (coloured in pale blue) when it managed to sail in among pack ice and iceberg fields on 28.2.1898, just before becoming finally 'trapped' in the pack ice on 3.3.1898, and **Period 2** from 18.8.1898 until 12.1.1899 when the ship drifted with the pack ice. Note that during Period 1 the ship passed very close to many icebergs; those listed by Lecointe in his 1900 publication are shown in pale blue, with more listed in his 1903 publication appear in mauve. This number of icebergs is confirmed through examination of the translated diary of R. Amundsen (Declerc, 1999). Note that the largest field of icebergs between 80° and 82° W was standing above what is now known as the Latady Trough* (see Fig. 8.9.4) and the other field of icebergs sat around 85°W, about what is now known as the Belgica Trough*. During Period 2, when the ship was confined to the pack ice and could not move freely, she started moving in a westerly direction, to eventually zigzag around 83°30' and 84°30'W (above the Belgica Trough) for a bit more than two months, to then head further west to the region where it originally was in late February earlier that year (around 80°30'W, being above

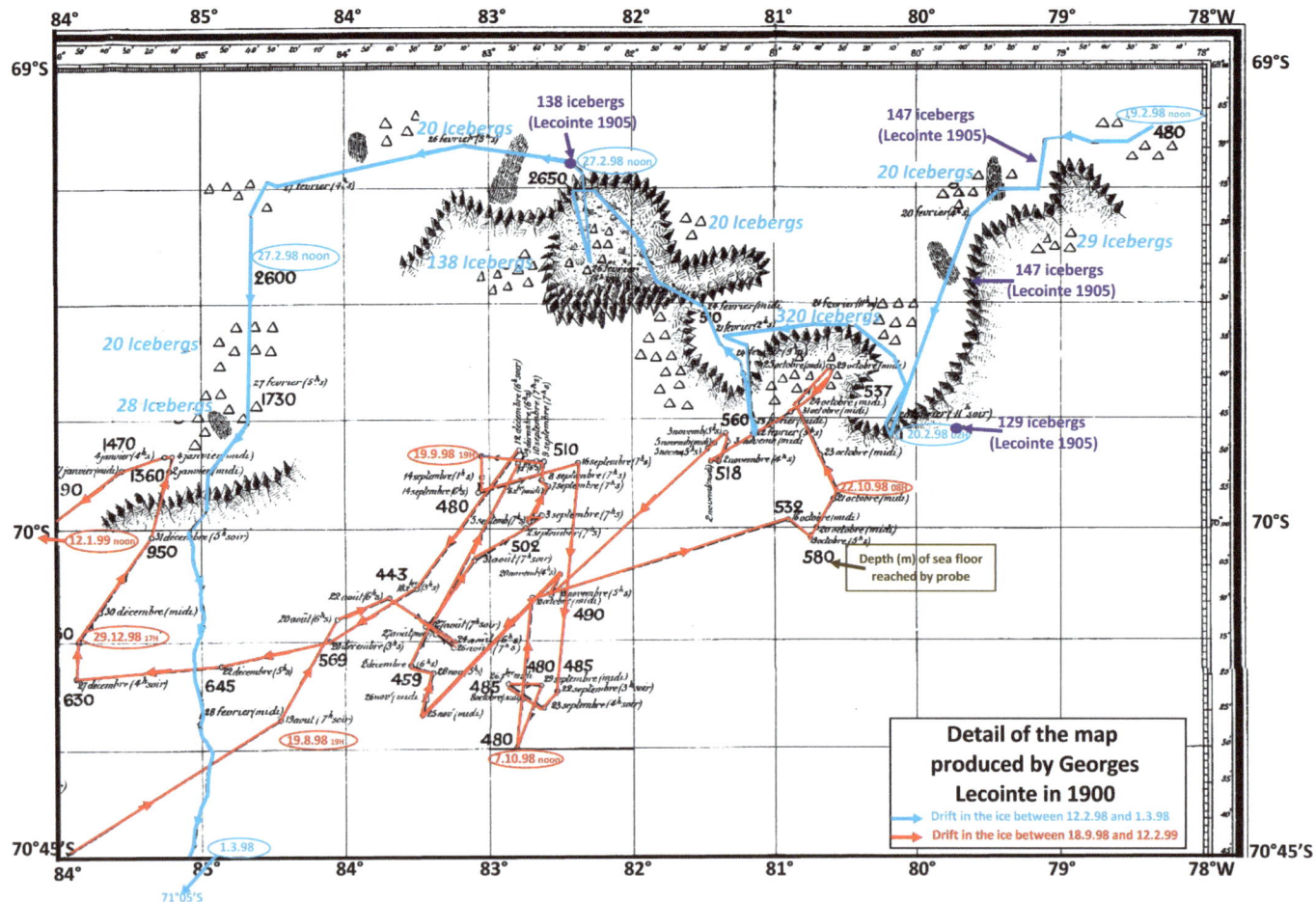

the Latady Trough). The position of the iceberg fields shown on this map only relates to period 1 as none of the expeditioners (namely Lecointe and Amundsen) mention the presence of icebergs in the area for October 19 to November 3, 1898). The latter must have drifted at sea. Of interest also is that for the period December 27 1898 to January 4, 1899, the ship drifted with the ice in a northerly direction above an area where icebergs were seen 11 months earlier. This is the area that directly sits above the Belgica Trough. Undersea currents moving northward must have forced the ship and pack ice to follow course. (see Fig. 8.1.8).

*Those undersea features where first coined by Dr Robert Larter from the British Antarctic Survey in 2004 in the British Antarctic Survey Report JR104 when using the RRS *James Clark Ross* (R. Larter, pers. comm.) and they appeared the following year in O'Cofaig et al. (2005). These authors postulated that the Belgica Trough was the site of the 'pathway for a major ice sheet outlet that was fed by ice draining from the southern part of the Antarctic Peninsula Ice Sheet as well as ice from the Western Antarctic Ice Sheet draining through Eltanin Bay' (O'Cofaig et al., 2005).

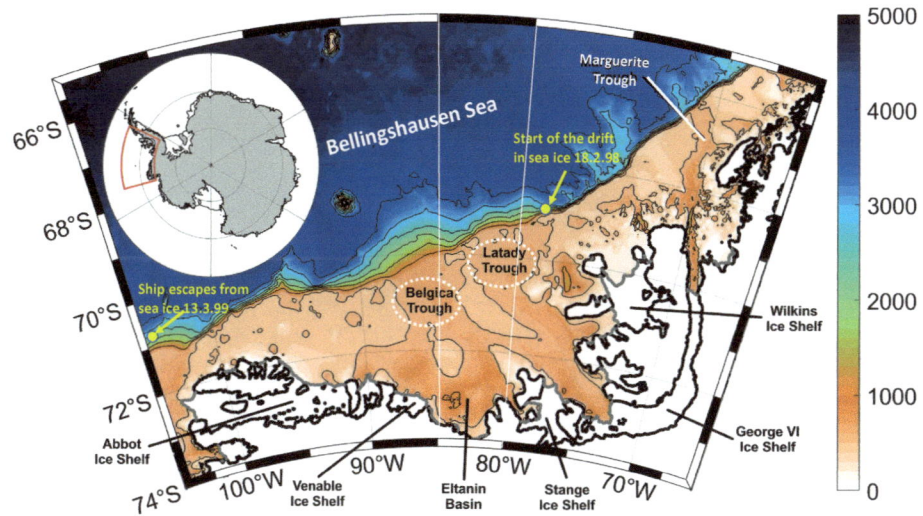

Figure 8.9.4 Modified map of the bathymetry of the Bellingshausen Sea and West Antarctic Peninsula continental shelves originally produced by Schubert et al. (2021) with emphasis on the Belgica and Latady Troughs above which the *SY Belgica* drifted while in the pack ice. Note that extensive fields of icebergs were seen in 1898 above both troughs. Thin black contours delineate isobaths between 0 and 3000 m, with a 500 m interval. Thick black and gray lines indicate the coastline and the edge of permanent ice shelves, respectively. Pay attention to the two meridian lines (shown in white) that pass over both Troughs.

Figure 8.9.5 Photograph showing four members of the crew in the process of using a saw to cut a channel in the sea ice so as to help release the ship from its entrapment. The person with the alpine beret is likely to have been E. Racovitza. Reproduced with permission from the Emil Racovitza Archive, The Library of the Romanian Academy, Cluj-Napoca Branch. This photo was processed using Photoshop© to improve clarity and 'colorized' using palette.fm/color/filters.

Figure 8.5.2 Photograph of the meteorological station that was permanently placed at the front deck of the ship. Photograph taken from Arctowski (1904)'s monograph.

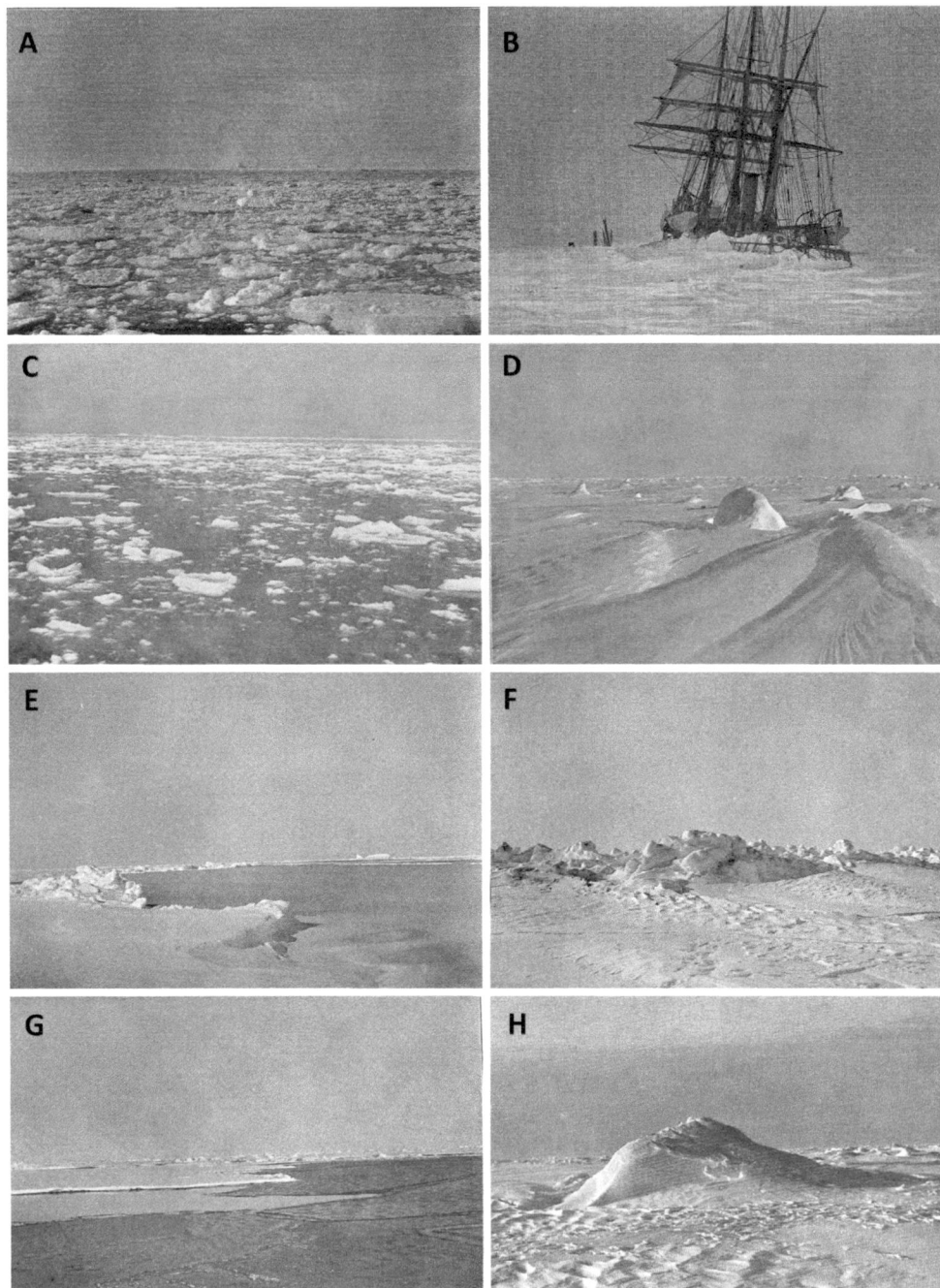

Figure 8.9.6 Combination of Arctowski's (1908) plates 1 and 2 scanned from the original publication as the original photos are missing.

A: View of the edge of the sea ice with iceberg in the background.

B: The *Belgica* after snow deposited after a storm (chasse neige) on November 19, 1898.

C: The last icicles and an opening in the background.

D: Aspect of the ice field on October 8, 1898.

E: Large water opening in October in front of the 'little iceberg'. A drifted snow paste covers the water surface.

F: Hummocks partially buried by the drifted snow. The snow surface at the front presents characteristic forms.

G: Water opening on the right. An old ice field in the background. Young ice at the front and ice flowers. Further on, the young ice is snow covered. Further on still, the ice is thicker and has not suffered from pressions.

H: Hummock which formed near the *Belgica* on May 22, 1898 and for which the transversal section was measured in January 1899. Note the scaly aspect at the snow surface produced during the snow storm during the night of October 6 to 7.

Figure 8.9.7 Combination of Arctowski's (1908) plates 3 and 4 scanned from the original publication as the original photos are missing.

A: Zigzag crevasse which is only slightly open and along which no pressions operated, then later on consolidated and strongly masked by blown up snow.

B: Long strings of blown up snow formed in front of hummocks. In this snow recently deposited wind has dug oblong bowls.

C: Isolated hummock. A ditch surrounds it. The dune which partially buries the hummock is elongate following the direction from which the snow drift (chasse-neige) originated.

D: Aspect of a chain of old hummocks following a snow drift.

E: Ice field and water ways on March 3, 1898.

F: Ice field and water ways on March 5, 1898.

G: February 3, 1899. Fusion holes formed close to the ship surrounding black objects.

H: Ice fields in which the *Belgica* advanced on February 16, 1899, having been tightened and showing signs of slight pressions.

8.10 The fear of the ship being crushed by the ice or being hit by an iceberg

KEY POINTS

- The fear of the Belgica crew with the ship becoming crushed either by compressing forces of the shifting sea ice or by moving icebergs ploughing through the sea ice must have been constant

- Comparison is made between two similar ships, both built in Sandefjord, the *Belgica* and the *Endurance*, and on how they behaved in the sea ice

- Ernest Shackleton purchased the *Endurance*, originally named *Stella Polaris* which had been built for Adrien de Gerlache and Lars Christensen, a ship magnate, for use as a tourist ship in polar regions

- The *Endurance* was crushed and Shackleton's team survived by undertaking a very long trek to the edge of the sea ice (and eventually reaching South Georgia Island

The *SY Belgica* survived the entrapment in the sea ice until then end in March 1899 when it started to sail in the free and open ocean. It is clear that the crew must have seriously and continuously feared its destruction by compressing forces of the ice, and/or possibly also by icebergs ploughing through the sea ice. At times, some of the people (Amundsen and Cook) ventured on the sea ice in the hope of determining the edge of the sea ice, but this proved extremely dangerous as in places, there were significant openings in the sea ice and they feared not being able to return to the ship.

However, the fate of a similar ship to the *Belgica* called the *Endurance* was completely crushed in the Weddell Sea on November 21, 1915 (Fig. 8,10.1B). This ship was originally built in the Framnæs shipyard in Norway and launched in 1912 from Sandefjord, the same harbour where the *Patria* (later on called *Belgica*) was built. The ship was actually designed by Ole Anderud Larsen, under the master wooden shipbuilder, Christian Jacobsen. At that time, the ship had originally been ordered and named *Stella Polaris* by Adrien de Gerlache and Lars Christensen, a Norwegian shipowner, whaling magnate and philanthropist. The ship was meant to be used for touristic purposes in the polar regions. However, de Gerlache, who had received financial endorsement from several people, including the philanthropist and supporter of science Ernest Solvay, entered into financial difficulty and eventually the ship was purchased in January 1914 by Ernest Shackleton who baptised her as *Endurance*. Of note is that the latter ship was

of very similar built to the *Belgica* that had survived a long period of entrapment in the Bellingshausen Sea, and this must have been a factor in guiding Shackleton to make such a purchase. Comparison of the two ships against a shift ice blocks (see Fig. 8.10.1C, D) is quite amazing and often led people to confuse the ships in such photographs. Fig. 8.10.1B shows the devastating effect on the *Endurance* by crushing forces of the ice. Fortunately, this did not happen to the *Belgica*. There are ample photographs of the fate of the *Endurance* in Frank Hurley book (1925).

Figure 8.10.1 (oppostite)

A: photograph of the *Endurance* having been pushed on its side in the sea ice in the Weddell Sea (note a person on the mast for scale);

B: photograph of the *Endurance* crushed by the ice floe;

C: photograph of the *Endurance* trapped in the sea ice with large blocks of ice on the port side of the ship;

D: photograph of the *Belgica* trapped in the sea ice with large blocks of ice on the starboard side of the ship. Note that this photograph was taken under moon light, with an exposure of 90 minutes, in very low temperatures (see Cook, 1938). A, B more than likely taken by Frank Hurley and published in Worsley (1931, which is out of copyright), C; taken by Frank Hurley and obtained from Wikimedia Commons Robertson-Cole Pictures Corporation (film), public domain; D taken by F. A. Cook (1901). Note the similarity between photos C and D that led some authors to be confused.

A

The Endurance
on its side

crushed by the ice

B

C *The Endurance*

D *La Belgica*

Photo of Emperor penguins wandering on the sea ice. Photo courtesy of the late Franz Gingele, used with his permission.

Chapter 9

Biota in the Bellingshausen Sea: whales, seals, penguins and other birds, fish and other organisms

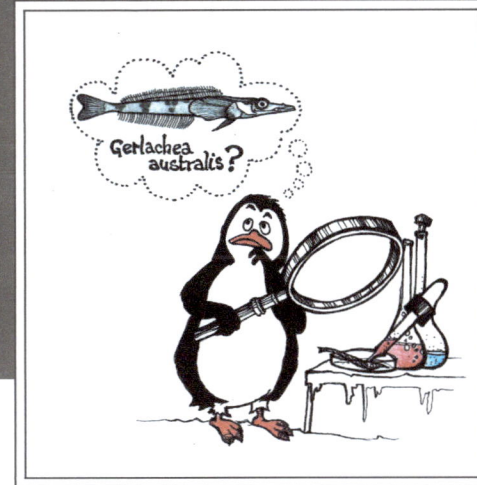

This chapter describes the animals encountered and studied by Emil Racovitza in the Bellingshausen Sea.

9.1. Emil Racovitza the biologist

Emil Racovitza was an amazing biologist who had almost an encyclopaedic knowledge of animals and plants. He collected assiduously not only in the de Gerlache Strait, where he participated in 15 out of the 20 landings, but likely did the same during the 24 landings in the Beagle Channel and Magellan Strait. For more information, refer to chapter 14 on the biota in the Beagle Channel. In addition, while 'trapped' in the sea ice, he collected a vast amount of plankton, netted fish and many other organisms such as jellyfish, in addition to sorting out organisms found in the muds on the sea floor at the bottom of every of the 60 soundings. He must have spent a huge amount of time in his dedicated laboratory on board the *Belgica*, identifying organisms, pressing plants, mushrooms, lichen and cryptogams, but also sorting organisms and preserving them in alcohol. Finally, he spent much time dissecting organisms including large ones (such as seals and penguins) and finally stuffing some. Racovitza was helped by the sailor Johan Koren who had a strong interest in animals, and in particular birds (Fig. 22.1.1) (see also chapter 14 on Johan Koren).

After his time on the *Belgica* collecting a vast number of plants and animals, and after that also spending much time curating his collections and dispatching them to specialists all around Europe, E. Racovitza commenced a new scientific 'venture': the study of caves and the organisms inhabiting them. He eventually dedicated most of his time studying biospeleology, a field which he developed with the aid of several French colleagues, some of whom joined him in Romania. This important field of specialisation in biology is still regarded as a very important one, and Danielopol and Tabacaru (2024) recently reviewed the importance of this field of science and the impact it still has.

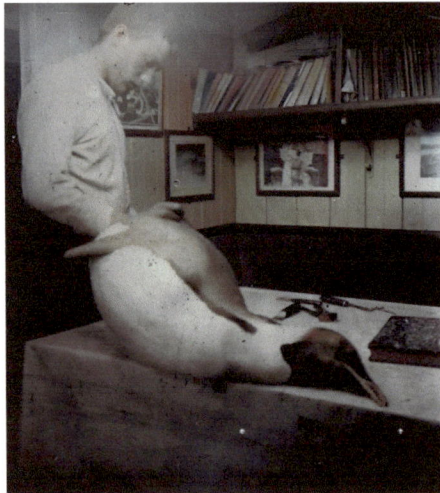

Figure 9.1.1 Photograph of Johan Koren helping Emil Racovitza dissect an emperor penguin. Original obtained from Rita Jalen from photos assembled for the first Belgica exhibition held at the MAS in Antwerp. Photo 'colorized' using palette.fm/color/filters.

Figure 9.1.2 Photograph of Emil Racovitza in his dedicated biological laboratory looking down a brass monocular microscope. Reproduced with permission from the Emil Racovitza Archive, The Library of the Romanian Academy, Cluj-Napoca Branch. This photo was processed using Photoshop© to improve clarity and 'colorized' using palette.fm/color/filters.

9.2. Cetaceans – whales

KEY POINTS

- Racovitza made a lot of observations on whales, especially in the de Gerlache Strait

- The observations principally deal with inspiration and expiration.

- The spout does not consist of water, but air saturated with moisture expelled during expiration.

- Expiration is completely separated from the digestive organ.

- The sound produced by whales is not a 'voice' but air passing through a narrow orifice during inspiration.

- The oily slick seen at the water surface results from excrements engendered by whales (mainly from plankton).

- Body fat in whales is to protect the animals against the cold, not as a food reserve.

- Racovitza's investigations have been completely ignored by subsequent experts on whales

- Racovitza provided an extensive literature review of the sightings and observations on whales since 1820 in latitudes below 50°S

- Racovitza's legacy deals with all his observations on whales which are listed here in 11 points.

Most of Racovitza's observations relate to respiratory movements of whales, as well movements not related to respiration. These observations were new at the time.

These are presented in eleven points that are listed below:

1. The movement at which the spout is produced is exactly the timing of expiration when the head reaches the surface. During that time, this movement is very rapid and the protuberance of the blowhole is very obvious. Nevertheless, in the blue whale *Balaenoptera musculus*, 'the median region of the back often appears before the protuberance of the blowhole' Racovitza (1904, p.628).

2. The duration of the spout is variable and depends on size of animal. The larger whales obviously spout longer than the small ones. Racovitza (1903) estimated it to last 5 to 6 seconds in blue whales and 3 to 4 in humpback whales. The spout always lasts longer than the inspiration (1904, p.628).

3. The noise of the spout is variable in intensity and this is related to the size of the animal. It is quite loud in small finback whales, louder with right whales and humpbacks and even stronger in blue whales. This noise is caused by vibration engendered by the expulsion of air under pressure. Even whistling sounds can be heard.

4. The form of the spout depends on the force of expulsion, and its appearance consists of a 'mass of white and pearly vapour' (Racovitza, 1904, p.629). The right whale emits a very large spout compared to that of finbacks which is small. Racovitza (1903) clearly demonstrates that previous accounts made by others were incorrect and that it was not water that was expelled, but air.

5. The nature of spout is such that no water is expelled, but instead air saturated with vapour (Racovitza, 1903). He quoted his colleague Professor Paul Portier, marine biologist at the time at La Sorbonne who suggested that the powerful thoracic cage contributes to the expulsion of air under strong pressure which also explains the high nature of the jet. In addition, he stated that the respiratory organs are completely separated from the digestive organs as the extremity of the larynx is prolonged into a very long appendage that completely fills the cavity. Water cannot penetrate into the larynx but food is actually passed into the esophagus that is separated from the larynx. He added that in humpback whales, the corners of the mouth are gutter-like features that are useful for expelling water in which food is mixed.

6. Racovitza (1903, 1904) discussed the body temperature of whales and disputed many of the prior observations and concluded it

to be lower that the average temperature of land mammals. He added that the insulating layer of fat in whales (and seals) is primarily to avoid loss of body temperature. He added further that the fat is not to be considered as matter for reserve and thus he disputed previous authors who held contrary views.

7. Racovitza (1903, 1904) also commented on the odour of the spout is simply 'nauseating' due to the decomposition of organisms in the whalebone of baleen whales. He further added that a source of infection in the respiratory apparatus needs to be looked at.

8. 'Inspiration is effected immediately after expiration, without an interval' (Racovitza (1903, 1904). He described at length which part of the blowhole appears at the surface. He also indicated that the duration of inspiration is always half of expiration. For the latter, the orifice of the blowhole is small and the air is expelled with 'violence' and this explains the height the jet can achieve. On the contrary, during inspiration, the orifice is wide open to allow air to be taken rapidly. Racovitza in his two publications states that he observed these phenomena in finbacks, humpbacks as well as porpoises. In his discussions, he compared his findings with that of other authors and contradicts some previous findings.

9. Racovitza (1904) claimed that the sound produced by whales is not a 'voice' but 'simply a sound produced by the strongly inspired air passing a narrow orifice' during strong inspiration.

10. An 'oily slick' spread on the sea surface left by whales is discussed and he disputed that the oil originates directly from the skin of the mammals. Instead, his observations in the de Gerlache Strait indicate that the oil is a biproduct of waste products of digestion of the whales that contains some oily products which therefore explain the observed 'slicks'. He further adds that penguins and seals' excrements principally consist of krill (*Euphausia* spp.) on which they feed.

11. Racovitza (1903) elegantly documented the movement of whales through three important sketches (Figs. 9.2.2 to 9.2.3) which were the first of their kind available in the scientific literature. He noted also that humpback whales were very prone to leaping out of the water, whereas the finback do not. He further added that 'right whales and humpbacks have been observed to remain motionless at the surface of the water' (Racovitza, 1904, p. 641), but disputed this as a sleeping position, having seen it only once during his time in the de Gerlache Strait where the ship was surrounded by humpbacks. He noted that whales were active day and night in the Strait, thus refuting that they slept near the surface. Photographs of whales taken recently are presented in Fig. 9.2.4.

Finally, Racovitza also briefly mentioned whale migration and diving depth but relied mostly on observations made by other authors.

There are ample notes of collections and animal behaviour made by Racovitza in two of his diaries that are duplicated in the Rameau d'Or prepared by Alexandru Marinescu with the collaboration of two others from the National Grigori Antipa Museum of Natural History in Bucarest (Racovitza, 1998). Disappointingly, a third diary is still missing despite many searches; it would have covered the period of February 12 to November 6, 1898, a great part when the *Belgica* was trapped in the pack ice and probably also informed on people's health, in particular during the period of complete darkness.

Nevertheless, two important and very comprehensive documents written by Racovitza on his observations are available. The first on is his lengthy monograph of some 147 pages which, in its first half of some 47 pages, forms the first set of scientific observations of whales and their behaviour in Antarctic waters (Racovitza, 1903) and the second one which is a succinct summary in 18 pages of his findings (Racovitza, 1904) (written by him in French and translated into English by Frederick W. True, a whale expert at the Smithsonian Institution). Racovitza (1903) was the first to provide photographs of whales in the wild (Fig. 9.2.1).

At the end of the first part of his monograph, Racovitza (1903) lists all the sightings made of whales during the Belgica expedition, one in the Beagle Channel, numerous ones in the de Gerlache Strait, some later in the sea ice and later on during the entrapment in the pack ice. Sadly, this is not reported by the British whale experts in their various articles on whales published in the Discovery Reports by Macintosh (1929, 1942), Sayer (1940) and Brown (1954, 1963) despite that the latter author acknowledges the work on whales by F.W. True from the Smithsonian Institution who, as mentioned earlier, had translated a summary of the work by Racovitza (1904). In addition, there is no mention of the work on cetaceans by Racovitza in the review on whales by Brown et al. (1974) in the important Antarctic map folio series. This is particularly disappointing and one question remains: were these omissions intentional?

Figure 9.2.1 A-H: (oppisite) *Megaptera* cf. *longimana* (*sic* Racovitza). All photos were taken by Frederick Cook for Racovitza (1903) and which appeared in Racovitza (1903)'s monograph.

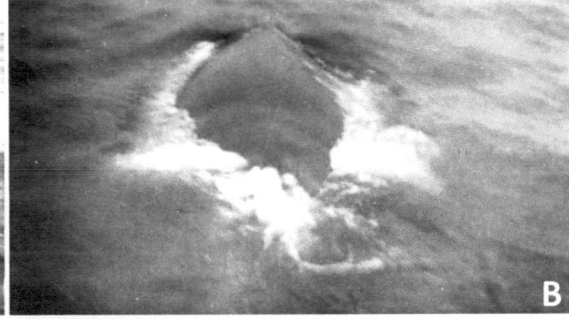

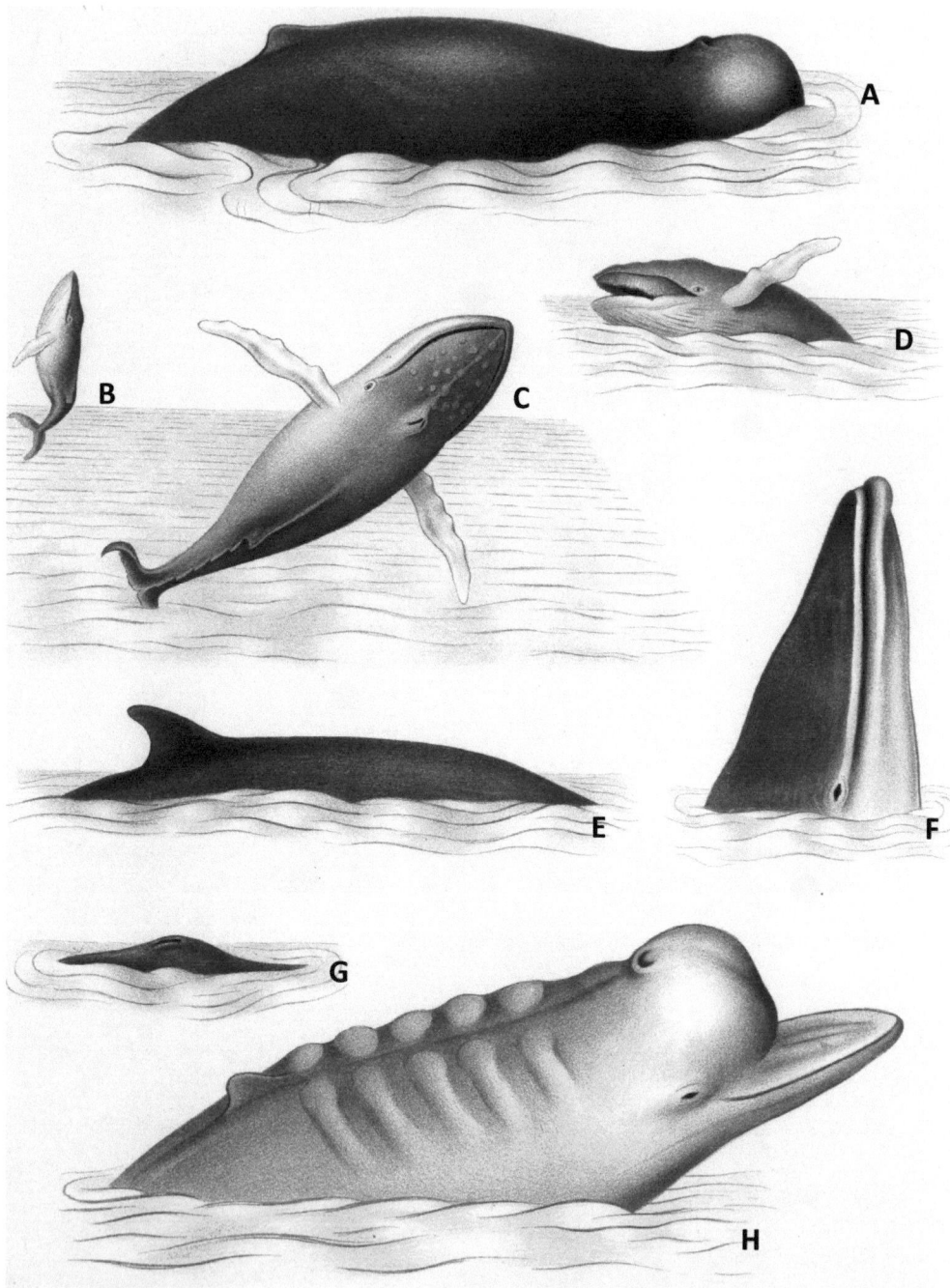

Figure 9.2.2 Original sketches by Racovitza (1903).

A: *Hyperodon* sp.:

B-D: *Megaptera* cf. longimana (*sic* Racovitza);

E-G: *Hyperodon* sp.;

H: *Hyperodon* cf. *varietas* (*sic* Racovitza).

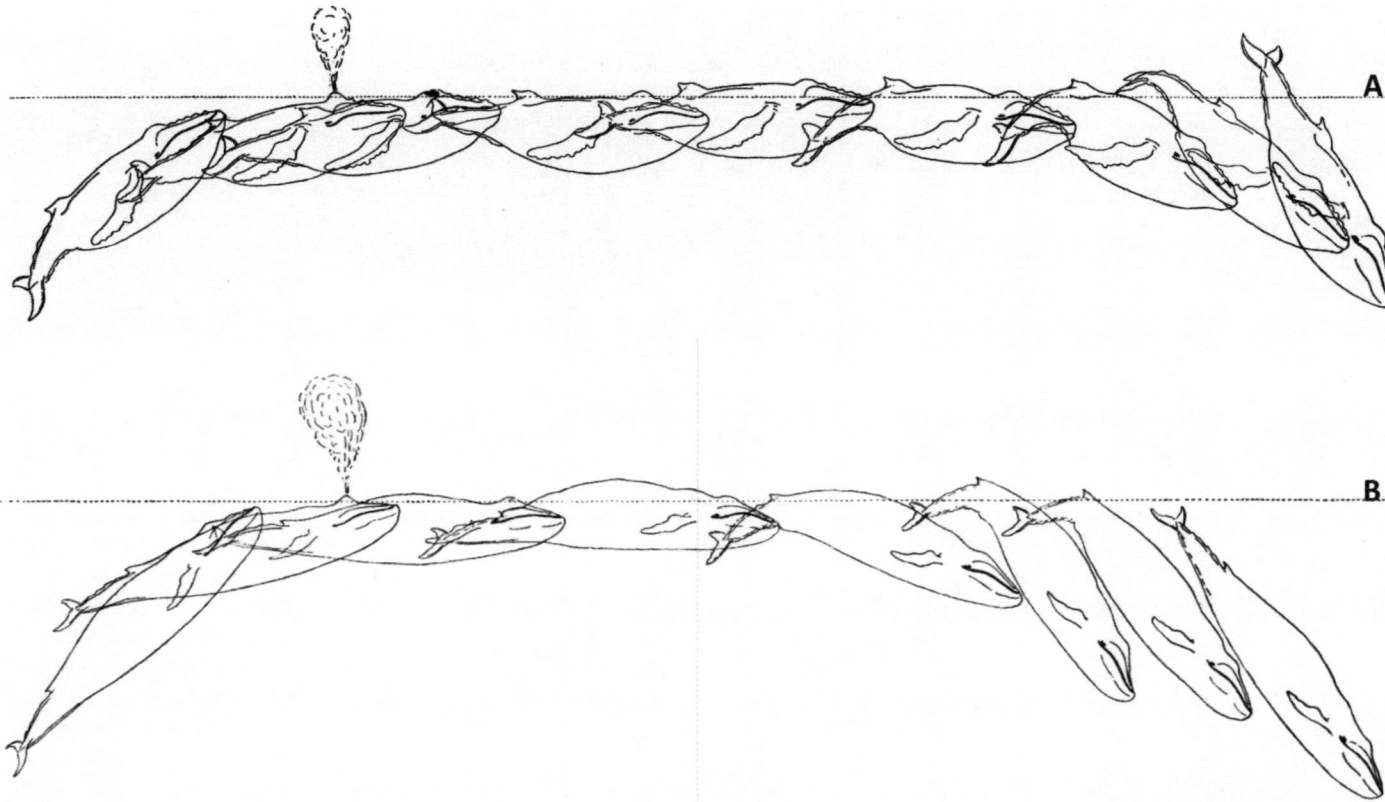

Figure 9.2.3 Original sketches
by Racovitza (1903).

A: Successive positions of a *Megaptera*
between the blow and plunge;

B: Successive positions of a *Balaeonoptera*
cf. *musculus* (*sic* Racovitza).

Note that in Racovitza (1903)'s monograph
there are additional sketches showing he
behaviour of whales near the surface. We
now know that Emil Racovitza was one of the
founding fathers of 'ethology', the science
of studying the behaviour of animals.

Figure 9.2.4 A-C: Recent photographs of humpback whales; **D**: Orca; **E-F**: Southern right whales. All photos by the late Franz Gingele and used with permission.

The second part of Racovitza (1903)'s monograph deals with a discussion of previous observations mentioned in what Racovitza refered to as 'Antarctide' below 50°S. This section is very detailed and covers most of the published records of exploration in the Antarctic region, including the Southern Cross expedition led by K. Borchgrevink in 1898-1900. The start of observations goes as far back as 1820. Obviously, Racovitza had done a fairly detailed research on past records and discussed at length their respective findings. He listed the records in some 9 comprehensive tables.

The last 25 pages of Racovitza's monograph on cetaceans deals with what he refered to as 'chorology', viz. the study of the causal relations between geographical phenomena occurring within a particular region, and the study of the spatial distribution of organisms, in other words, their biogeography. The latter discipline was fairly new at that time of his 1903 publication. He first discussed the necessity to have a better taxonomic knowledge of cetaceans and the same on their ecology. He went onto revising knowledge on the type of food they eat. He devised six different groups, but also mentioned exceptions to his categories, thus demonstrating some still poor knowledge at that time. Later on, he also discussed the ontogeny of cetaceans and concluded that much investigation was still needed. This chapter concluded with an extensive bibliography, demonstrating the thoroughness of Racovitza in his attempt at providing much assessment on whales. It is a pity that his comments had been ignored by later authors and would therefore helped them avoid duplication.

9.3. Pinnipeds - seals

KEY POINTS

- The original publication on seals in the Résultats series by the British seal expert Barrett-Hamilton in 1901 provided few details on the seals collected by E. Racovitza. Only a few specimens examined were by Barrett-Hamilton and little information on the seals anatomy and ecology of the seals were given.

- Fortunately, the recent lengthy publication by Murariu (2016, 521 pages) based the notes assembled by Racovitza have enabled us to determine many facets on the biology of the seals, going from foetuses to the adult stage. In total some 56 individual seals had been euthanised by Racovitza and studied in great details after dissections. These notes are perhaps the most prolific ones ever published on those Antarctic seals. They also contain information on the seals' diet.

- Notes are also provided on where and when the seals studied here rely on the sea ice to give birth and rearing their young. These bear significant implications since sea ice is rapidly vanishing, with the Bellingshausen Sea even recently becoming ice free in summer. An important questions remains as to whether these seals will shift their breeding grounds in the future, or already have.

- The presentation here of maps showing the distribution of the seals seen during the Belgica expedition will play an important control in determining where seal populations have shifted as a result of the significant climatic warming in the region of the Antarctic Peninsula and adjacent seas.

- Another important threat today concerning seal populations and their distribution is the findings that krill populations are significantly decreasing in some regions, including the Bellingshausen Sea. That large area will have to be surveyed in the future to determine where seals populations now are and where they will be in the future.

- Racovitza's scientific legacy here consists of his ample notes on the seals he examined during the expedition, and on the seals distributions shown in maps in Figs. 9.3.5 to 9.3.8. These maps will have to be compared against the modern-day seal distribution that occur now under 'warmer conditions'.

- Racovitza's notes presented in Murariu (2016) are now summarised and tabled in Appendix 1 at the end of this book.

This chapter is rather important as seals form a significant role in the food web of polar regions; the Antarctic Peninsula is no exception. The chapter presented here is quite long simply because the biologist Racovitza's impressive notes remained unpublished until Professor Dumitru Murariu of the Antipa Museum in Bucharest published them almost word for word in a monograph of the Editions Universitaires Européennes in 2016 (Murariu, 2016). As this facsimile volume is not only large (521 pages) and being a direct replica of Racovitza's notes, at times it proved difficult to sort through them. However, since Racovitza's notes are so detailed and informative they are well worth publishing here. Nine tables using all of Racovitza's notes presented in Murariu (2016) are now available in Appendix 1 of this book, together with some text on Racovitza's notes presented in that 2016 publication. They are rather important as no detailed notes of the quality written by Racovitza have even been published since the Belgica expedition. The important fact to note also is that since the recent disappearance of the sea ice in the Bellingshausen Sea - where some of the seal species lived during the time of the Belgica expedition - must affect their distribution today, and therefore Racovitza's notes ought to be very important.

Racovitza not only observed seals but he also collected numerous specimens; he euthanised at least 56 specimens, some of which were dissected and the bones (including cranium) were separated (Figs. 9.3.1 - 9.3.3); they are kept in the Museum of Natural Sciences in Brussels now part of the Royal Belgian Institute of Natural Sciences (= RBINS).

Racovitza also had preserved pelts which had been repatriated to Belgium (Fig. 22.5.2.3). Some of that material went to Major Gerald Edwin Hamilton Barrett-Hamilton who was a British/Irish natural historian who described in 1901 the material he had received. He compared the Belgica material against the material already held at the time in the British Museum of Natural History in London. Copy of his drawings of the skulls are show in Fig. 22.5.2.4. Overall, Barrett-Hamilton (1901) provided extensive tables giving measurement of skulls and dentition. The notes that follow pertain to Barrett-Hamilton (1901)'s notes published as part of the Belgica's 'Résultats' monographs. Concerning the **Ross Seal (*Ommatophoca rossii*),** for which he received 2 skulls and skeletons, Barrett-Hamilton stated that little variation was found apart from the cheek-teeth and the described the differences at length. He went onto saying that little was known (at the time) on the distribution of that species, but the data from the Belgica expedition confirmed that it is an inhabitant of the pack ice and, that during the winter, only 13 encounters occurred and also none in the de Gerlache Strait. He stated that this species exclusively feeds on cephalopods. Barrett-Hamilton (1901) then reported on the 'vocal powers' of this seal by reporting in French the text written by Racovitza that is translated here. 'Briefly, this species possesses a very curious voice and its sounds are very varied. The noise passing through the larynx sounds a bit like a bagpipe, with other sounds reminiscent of cooing of hoarse doves followed by the clucking of a frightened hen, and then an inharmonious sniff produced by the air violently expelled through the nostrils '(Barrett-Hamilton, 1901).

Concerning the **Leopard Seal (*Ogmorhinus leptonyx*),** Barrett-Hamilton received one juvenile skull collected on February 20, 1898 after leaving the de Gerlache Strait. Racovitza claimed this specimen to be more than 3 metres and its skin is dark grey with yellow spots.

Concerning the **Crabeater Seal (*Lobodon carcinophagus*),** Barrett-Hamilton received material from 7 specimens, even a complete skeleton, a skull, skin with complete skeleton or simply skin. All were obtained while the ship was entrapped in the sea ice. Once again, ample measurements of the skulls and teeth are provided with comments on the nature of preservation of the teeth. Comparison with some 11 British Museum specimens are also provided with a discussion on the sexual dimorphism of the teeth. Based on Racovitza's notes, Barrett-Hamilton stated that the crabeater seal is commonly found on the pack ice but also in the de Gerlache Strait. Its food consists of krill (*Euphausia*; Fig. 9.3.10) obtained with its mouth open like whales and thus can consume vast quantities of specimens. Racovitza (quoted by Barrett-Hamilton) suggested that the cheek-teeth cusps act as a sieve which strain the water taken into the mouth with krill, and this explains the lack of wear on the teeth which are not used for mastication. Young seals are brought forth on the sea ice and are 'clothed with a thicker coat than that of their parents'. The mother nurses the young only for a few days before leaving it alone.

Barrett-Hamilton (1901)'s last encountered species was the **Weddell Seal (*Leptonychotes weddelli*)** and he was only able to examine four specimens (two skins and skulls, a complete skeleton and a skull) all from the pack ice except one form 17th landing in the de Gerlache Strait (Bob Island). This material was compared against four specimens stored in the British Museum. He commented on the development of the sagittal crest which is poor and added a few comments on sexual dimorphism. He also commented on skin colouration and also said that its food consists of krill. One final remark on the young is that they are born in September.

Finally, one small skull was included in the collection sent to the British Museum and consisted of a young South American Sea Lion collected on January 9, 1898 near Staten Island at the tip of Argentina.

On page 4 of Barrett-Hamilton (1901), Racovitza inserted a note[1] to say that he was intending to write a memoir on the biology of Antarctic seals in which detailed dimensions of some 30 adults and 15 juveniles of the four described species by Barrett-Hamilton would be presented. This never happened, until the memoir by Murariu was published in 2016 containing all the notes assembled by Racovitza, some after the expedition. These are discussed at length below and Appendix 1 as they contain a vast amount of information thus far unknown until recently.

[1] Racovitza was able to insert this note as he was on the editorial board of all the publications (Résultats) of the Belgica scientific publications.

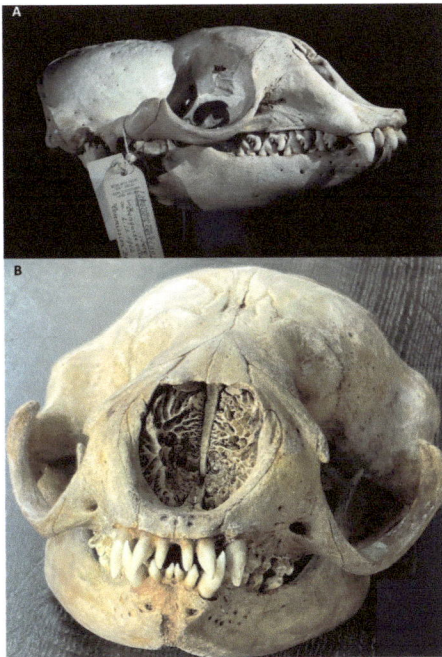

Figure 9.3.1. (left)

A: Side view of a skull of a Leopard seal obtained from the sea ice in the Bellingshausen Sea on 2.11.1898 and photographed in the MAS Museum in Antwerp (note the label stipulates a date of 1902, but this must be an error);

B: front view of a skull of a Ross seal obtained and prepared as mentioned above from the sea ice in the Bellingshausen Sea on 31.12.1898. Note the characteristic differences in the dentition of both species. All specimens are normally housed in the RBINS in Brussels.

Figure 9.3.2. (right)

A: Skull of the Weddell seal from the Bellingshausen Sea on 6.12.1898;

B: Bones of the flipper and shoulder blade of a Ross seal obtained from the sea ice in the Bellingshausen Sea on 31.12.1898;

C: digits of a flipper of a female Weddell seal obtained from the sea ice in the Bellingshausen Sea on 6.12.1898, note the nails are still attached;

D: skull of a male Weddell seal obtained from the sea ice in the Bellingshausen Sea on 7.12.1898 and photographed in the MAS Museum in Antwerp. All specimens are normally housed in the RBINS in Brussels and were originally prepared for storage on the *Belgica* in Racovitza's laboratory.

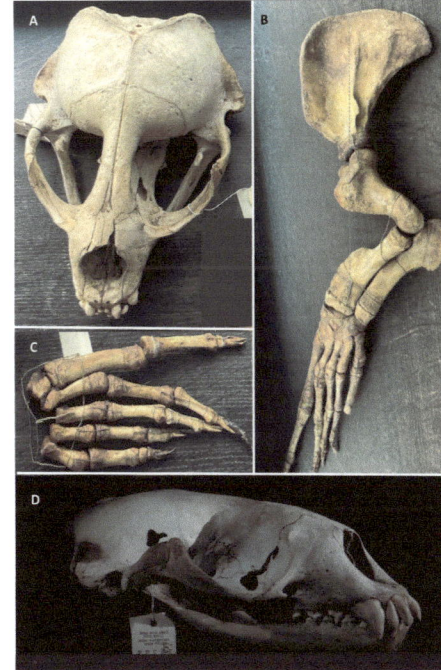

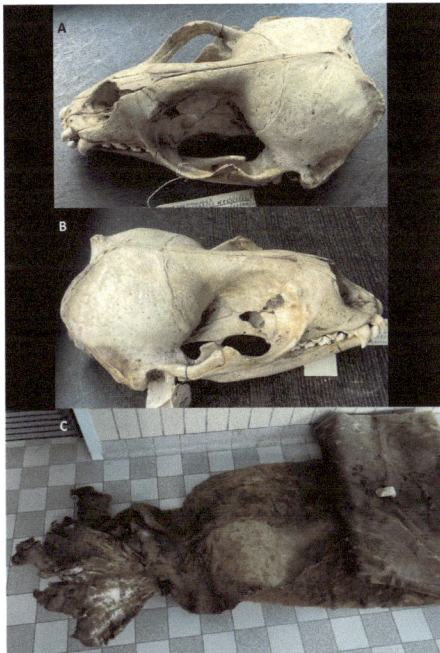

Figure 9.3.3. (left)

A: top side view of a female Weddell seal skull from the sea ice in the Bellingshausen Sea on 6.12.1898;

B: other view of specimen shown in A;

C: partly unwrapped skin of a Weddell seal skull obtained later from the sea ice in the Bellingshausen Sea on 7.12.1898. All skulls and skin (note the skin is covered with some arsenic salts to help with preservation). All specimens housed in the RBINS in Brussels and had been prepared for storage on the *Belgica* in Racovitza's laboratory.

Figure 9.3.4 (below) Skull of *Ommatophoca rossii* drawn by Barrett-Hamilton (1901) and re-arranged here.

A: lateral view,

B: vertex (=dorsal) view;

C: inferior (=ventral) view. The collection number was not stipulated.

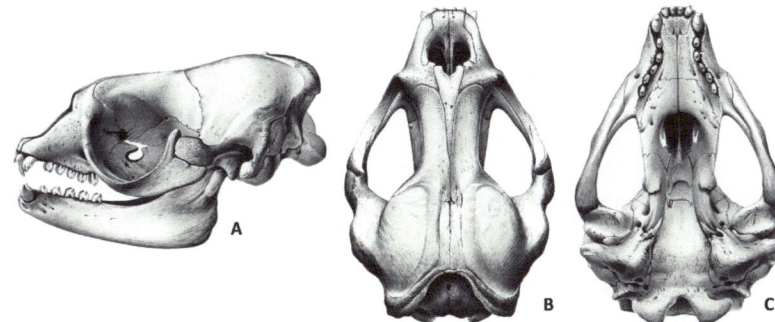

137

Barrett-Hamilton (1901) compared the measurements he made on the Belgica seals with those found at Cape Adare and environs (see Lankaster, 1902).

As for many other publications that were published in the 'Résutats du voyage de la Belgica' the publication by Barrett-Hamilton (1901) received no mention in the recent publications of Bester et al. (2020) nor Southwell et al. (2012); in addition, Bester et al. (2020) did not refer to Murariu's (2016) work reporting on Racovitza's notes (some 521 pages!). These authors did not mention the two conference papers published by Racovitza (1900a,b) that discussed seals.

In addition, Racovitza wrote ample observations on seals in the three conferences he gave soon after his return from the expedition. In 1900, he gave a conference to the Belgian Society of Geography (1900a)

and also to the French Geographical Society (1900b) as well to the French Zoological Society of Paris (1900c). Some of these notes are presented below. In his 1900a publication, Racovitza briefly discussed the Crabeater Seal with its sharp molar teeth that are curved backward (see Fig. 9.3.1A), a white pelt with a greenish reflection and with a size of 2 m. It moults easily on the sea ice and is quite aggressive displaying its teeth and blowing through its nostrils. These animals feed on krill (*Euphausia*), swim with an open mouth in among swarms of those crustaceans which they eat in great quantity. They give birth on the sea ice in September. The young, of already a good size, possess a pelt that is warmer than that of the parent. The female breastfeeds for only a few days, and then leaves the young alone. The other seal, much larger, fatter and more agreeable is the Weddell Seal (Fig. 9.4.5 B). It is a brave seal, lazy and complying ('bonasse' *sic),*

with an iron-grey pelt with small yellow rounded spots. Its teeth are small, its eyes round and moist. When approached it opens its large pink mouth, and normally reverses on its back while raising its head and backside, thus curving itself in an arc form. It is a simple way to frighten the enemy. Its food is the same as that of crabeater seals, and gives birth in September, the young resemble plump and furry bears. The Ross Seal was only seen in Summer and only 13 specimens were seen during the stay in the ice. It is a 'true seal' as its quadrupede form has disappeared. Its body is only a fusiform sac with very reduced limbs. Teeth are thin, pointed and useful to master large cephalopods which form is exclusive food. This seal has very curious voice and that emits very varied sounds. It is a real Antarctic virtuosity. Its larynx is swollen with a resonance box, and the roof of the palate very developed, distanced by air, such that it sounds like a bagpipe.

1. Four species of seals are described from the open water (some in the de Gerlache Strait) and then from the sea ice where the ship was 'entrapped' for a bit more than 12 months (from March 4, 1898 to March 13, 1899). These are the Ross Seal, the Leopard Seal, the Weddell Seal and the Crabeater Seal.

2. There are descriptions also of the Sea Lion seen on rock platforms of Staten Island.

3. There are extensive tables provided here that provide ample and very detailed observations of the seals made by Racovitza mostly on the ship, and later on preserved embryos kept in the Museum in Brussels.

4. The descriptions of the anatomy of the four seal species mentioned above were obtained through a thorough examination of numerous specimens going from foetuses to adults specimens.

5. In total, at least 56 seals were killed and examined in great detail for their anatomy, dentition, stomach content, parasites, presence of foetus in females, and pelt: 13 Ross Seals, 3 Leopard Seals, 12 (3 foetuses, 2 young and 7 adults) Weddell Seals, and 26 (6 males and 6 females, 12 foetuses (of which were 9 males) and embryos) of Crabeater Seals. In addition, it is likely that the anatomy of 2 Sea lions was examined; these were from the Beagle Channel and Staten Island.

6. Despite the fact that Racovitza's notes on the seals were written a long time ago (during and soon after the expedition), their summary is very, very important as none of the kind had been published before the time of the Belgica expedition.

7. Racovitza notes in Murariu (2016) remain a very significant set of observations on pinnipeds living in the vicinity of the Antarctic continent. More relevant also are these notes in line with the environmental changes that have occurred in the recent decades, with sea ice having disappeared from the Bellingshausen Sea, in which the *Belgica* ship sojourned during the austral winter of 1898-1899 and was able to observe the seals in winter.

At first, the cooing of a turtle dove, followed by a the cooing of a distraught chicken, and finally the sniffing without harmony produced by air violently expelled through the nostrils. Finally, the Sea Leopard with a size of more than 3 m and that merits its name of carnivore. Very agile when on land, it has very strong teeth and appears to be ready to use them. It is believed to eat penguins, with on one occasion seen two leopard seals eat the carcass of a penguin thrown overboard. In a footnote, Racovitza disputes a note by Sir George Newnes that during the *Southern Cross* voyage that new species had been seen (Strand Magazine, September 1899: The Southern Cross Antarctic expedition). Racovitza recognised the already known species based on photographs shown in Hansen (1902). Racovitza also determined body temperatures for penguins as 40°C and 37°C for seals, arguing that this is low for advanced mammals. This explains that insulation is warranted with a thick skin and fatty layer that both constitute a very efficient protection against the cold. He also described that a seal killed for 24 hours and exposed to an outside temperature of -20°C was still lukewarm.

In the 1900b publication of Racovitza ('Vers le Pôle Sud'), very similar descriptions to those listed above are given and therefore are not discussed any further. Similarly, the 1900c conference paper given in Paris only refers to seals in just three lines and will not be discussed any further.

To the left is a brief summary of Racovitza's descriptions of the seals he examined while in Antarctica which appeared in Murariu (2016). For more detailed information, refer to the Appendix 1 at the end of this book.

DISTRIBUTION MAPS OF THE SEALS ENCOUNTERED DURING THE BELGICA EXPEDITION

Four maps, originally drafted by Captain George Lecointe during and after the expedition (Lecointe, 1901) are reproduced here and slightly modified; on these maps, the location of all the seals mentioned by Racovitza (2016) is placed. These form the first-ever maps showing the distribution of the five species of seals discussed there. These maps ought to be used now to determine as to whether the distribution of the seals has changed over 125 years in the same region. For example, the disappearance of the sea ice in summer as witnessed over the last few years in the Bellingshausen Sea must have a profound effect on the presence of some seal species, especially since Racovitza (2016) stated that some female seals give birth on the sea ice.

Noteworthy is the fact that all the five species discussed here were encountered in the de Gerlache Strait, and three were seen in the pack ice (with only two encounters of Weddell seals). In the frozen Bellingshausen Sea, there were 14 sightings of the leopard seals, and 18 of the crabeater seals, at times in large numbers. Those seals appeared either on the sea ice, or in fissures that were common at times due to the continuous movement of the sea ice which, at times, was moving in a zigzag fashion over deep-sea troughs, such as the Belgica and Latida Troughs (see Graham et al., 2011, fig. 2). The likely oceanic circulation over the deep-sea troughs many have contributed to upwelling which would have contributed to significant biological productivity, on which the seals would have fed under the sea ice.

Apparently, there was no sightings of seals during the complete winter night between May 22 and July 22, 1898; see figure 4), either because the seals could not be seen, or perhaps because this period coincided with a time when many expeditioners suffered from polar anaemia and lacked energy and/or were sick (Cook, 1900).

TODAY'S KNOWLEDGE ON THE SEALS IN THE REGION AND COMMENTS ON THEIR FUTURE DISTRIBUTION

The four seals species discussed here are now much better known since the Belgica expedition, although there has not been any description as detailed since those carried out by Racovitza (2016) on the seals. The sea lion is not being discussed here as it does not pertain to Antarctic waters *per se*. Below I summarize what we now know of the seals and have added comments about possible changes that may have occurred around the Antarctic Peninsula that may impact on seal distribution and feeding.

Crabeater seals

Since the Belgica expedition, crabeater seals have been extensively recorded and studied, but never as extensively examined like Racovitza did (2016). On the SCAR Antarctic Biodiversity Portal (https://www.biodiversity. aq/), there are close to 150,000 recordings of crabeater seals all around Antarctica, meaning they are definitely not endangered. Many of the recent observations were made by recorders linked to satellites. We now know that crabeater seals spend their entire life on the sea ice in the pack ice zone all around Antarctica where they breed, moult, rest and also feed in nearby waters. They are the most common species in Antarctic waters and their population is estimated to reach well over 15 million (some figures go as far as 75 million (Bengston and Stewart, 2018). As crabeater seals spend so much time on the ice, they can drift long distances, but it is also known that they move southwards in the austral spring and go in the opposite direction in winter.

Breeding occurs from later September to early November. Females give birth to a single pup, and the lactation period lasts only 3-4 weeks while on the sea ice. Males do not contribute to pup care. Their main diet consists of krill (*Euphausia superba;* Fig. 9.3.10) which they trap in their mouth and sieve the water through the numerous sharp teeth that act like a sieve. They also eat small amounts of fish and squid. Those seals can swim down to ~250 m but feed mostly in the upper 20 m of the water column. Bryant (1945) recorded crabeater seals near the American East Base along Graham Land bordering the Antarctic Peninsula (for more information, check notes on Weddell Seals) when open water was close by, but later in the season they had disappeared except for two animals. Nevertheless, they did not return the following summer. Racovitza (2016) only made one recording of *Lobodon carcinophagus* in the de Gerlache Strait (Fig. 2), but since 1898 many more sightings have been made (refer to the Scar Antarctic Biodiversity Portal), whereas in the Bellingshausen Sea, 17 occurrences were noted (Fig. 9.3.8). No mention was made by him about the diet of Lobodon except that it feeds on *Euphausia.* Unfortunately, there is no mention of stomach contents for *Lobodon carcinophaga* in his 2016 book.

There is one alarming new factor in that krill populations are changing, with a very noticeable decrease in the Atlantic sector of the Southern Ocean (Kawaguchi et al., 2024) and a significant population contraction in higher latitudes. Nevertheless, figure 2 in Kawaguchi et al. (2024) shows that since 1926-1952, krill populations have significantly increased for the period of 1996-2016 around the Antarctic Peninsula, with apparently decreasing numbers in the Bellingshausen Sea. Kawaguchi et al. (2024) explains this phenomenon as a result of large-scale climatic oscillations, such that during La Niña

phases, the westerly wind belt brings warmer winds closer to the West Antarctic Peninsula. This causes the extent of the sea ice to be delayed and this recent phenomenon is critical not only for krill populations, but for the survival/presence of crabeater seals in the region of interest here. With the recent disappearance of the sea ice, at least in summer of the Bellingshausen Sea, one major question remains: is the region still frequented by crabeater seals since they spend much of their life on the sea ice, and in particular this is where females lay their pup, feed them through lactation until weaning after 3 to 4 weeks. Nevertheless, Kawaguchi (pers. com.) believes that the apparent lack of krill in that region is the paucity of sampling since 1996. However, the projections made by Piñones and Fedorov (2016) point out that the Bellingshausen Sea by 2100, as a result of oceanic warming, will support extensive krill populations. This region now needs to be revisited to determine where the crabeater seals live. I would postulate that, near the coast, there may still be some floating ice, possibly in large bays where the reproductions of those seals may occur. Satellite monitoring of the movement of those seals is urgently warranted.

Leopard seals

Again, more information is now available on leopard seals in the scientific literature. There are some 1900 recordings of leopard seals on the SCAR Antarctic Biodiversity Portal (*op. cit.*). We know that this is a solitary animal that is found on the pack ice all around Antarctica but it wanders further north with even sightings on either sides of Australia up to the Tropic of Capricorn (https://biodiversity.org.au/afd/taxa/Hydrurga_leptonyx). It is known to be an aggressive carnivore and there is even a record of one animal having killed a human in Antarctic Peninsula waters (Proffitt, 2003). It feeds not only on penguins, small fish and squid but its

diet consists also of krill. Its teeth are used to strain krill from ambient water. Little is still known about the biology of leopard seals which are solitary animals except that 6 years old animals or more give birth to a single pup on the sea-ice in November after a 9 month gestation, and then return to the ocean to feed. Racovitza (2016) said very little about feeding habits of this species. No specimens was found in the de Gerlache Strait in 1898, but 14 encounters were made in the Bellingshausen Sea (Fig. 4).

Despite the fact that this species is found on the sea ice, where it breeds, rest and moults, it is known to live in the coastal zone of Antarctica when sea ice is diminished (Meade et al., 2015). Indeed, with the more recent shrinking of sea ice around Antarctica, the home range of leopard seal has become restricted, especially since the abundance of krill is diminishing, especially in the Atlantic sector of the Southern Ocean (Kawaguchi et al. 2024. This is particularly important as females give birth from October to mid-November, and mother with pup live at least for 4 weeks together on the sea ice. Thus, with the current absence of sea ice in the Bellingshausen Sea in summer, I do not see that this will directly affect the distribution of leopard seals in the area in the future, but if krill populations further go down as a result of climatic modification, leopard seal distribution is at stake, except the projection for the future by Piñones and Fedorov (2016) provides some optimism for the presence of that species in the area.

Ross seals

During the Belgica expedition, there were 9 recordings of Ross seals in the Beagle Channel and Staten Island, and that included two in open water during the transit from the tip of South America before reaching Bransfield Strait (Fig. 9.3.5). Only one occurrence was made in the de Gerlache Strait and one more further to the west on February 15, 1898. No Ross seals were seen in the Bellingshausen Sea. In general, Ross seals are rare and dispersed and therefore poorly known and this is confirmed by the fact that there are only 1200 records of this seal on the SCAR Antarctic Biodiversity Portal (compared with crabeater seals sightings op. cit.). Racovitza (2016) determined the content of one of those seals that consisted of cephalopod beaks. This has been further confirmed by Southwell et al.(2012) and Skinner and Klages (1994) who indicated that these seals feed mostly on several species of squids as well as small fish and invertebrates, including krill (Ray, 1981). Ross seals are long distance travellers (reaching over 2000 km; Hügstädt, 2018a), but they need to return to the pack ice for breeding in October to December and they are known to moult from January to March. Populations are low, being estimated from 20,000 to 50,000 up to 220,000 individuals (Hügstädt, 2018a). Despite the fact that it is principally a solitary animal, larger numbers can be found in the pack ice when breeding and also moulting (Skinner and Klages, 1994). It is not known if that seal species which is not that common is likely to be affected by global warming, but we know for sure that sea ice is still important for their life cycle.

Weddell seals

Racovitza (2016) recorded the Weddell seal on 7 occasions in the de Gerlache Strait, and none elsewhere, especially the Bellingshausen Sea. Bryant (1945) reported that 'Weddell seals were present in the vicinity of East Base throughout the year in varying numbers'. East Base was located on Stonington Island and is the oldest American research station in Antarctica that was located off Graham Land along the Antarctic Peninsula. In one year, some 150 seals were killed for dog meat !! There, the pupping season occurred in October, with some 7 females found on the glacier tongue some 2.5 km inland. Bryant (1945) saw that the seals were infested with internal parasites, with some animals infested with nematode stomach worms and cestode intestinal worms, with some animals being severely infested. One examined young pups was free of parasites. Many males were affected by a skin disease especially near the opening of the penis and the 'armpits'. Racovitza (2016), on the other hand, claimed that birth during September and this always happens on the sea ice.

This species is very common with over 400,000 records of this seal on the SCAR Antarctic Biodiversity Portal. Its distribution is circumpolar, and lives near the coast although it can venture in the open ocean some 10 to 20 km. However, it remains on the sea ice to give birth, moult and rest. Its diet is varied depending on its dives: it relies on fish near the surface as well as at mid-depths that includes fish (such as the Antarctic silverfish and toothfish, some large up to 40 kg), squid, octopus, prawns and also krill; the latter in low quantities. It can also feed at great depths (as far down as ~700 m) on benthic fish.

The distribution of the Weddell seals is circum-antarctic on the sea ice but it is also found on land. More on their diet is found in Green and Burton (1987) and Heerah et al. (2013).

Pups are born from October to November (Hügstädt, 2018b), although Racovitza (2016) claims an earlier period such as September.

Despite the fact that the Belgica expedition did not record this species in the Bellingshausen Sea, it does occur there, and with the disappearance of the sea ice, it is likely to breed near the coast, probably in bays and spend time on land. Further investigations will eventually confirm this hypothesis. Climate warming in the area will not directly affect the distribution of this sea in the area of interest here.

Four maps showing the distribution of the seals along the route and drift of the *Belgica* ship are presented here (Figs. 9.3.5- 9.3.8) and must aid in establishing if these seal species today, some 125 years after the expedition, maintained the same distribution. This is particularly important in light of the disappearance of the sea ice in summer in the Bellingshausen Sea where the ship was trapped for a bit more than 12 months.

Despite the fact that Racovitza's notes on the seals took a long time to be published by Dumitru Murariu in 2016 (more than 100 years after they were written), their summary presented in this volume are very important as none of the kind had been published before the time of the Belgica expedition and soon after that, and remain a very important set of observations on pinnipeds living in the vicinity of the Antarctic continent. More relevant also are these notes in line with the environmental changes that have occurred in the recent decades, with sea ice having disappeared from the Bellingshausen Sea, in which the *Belgica* ship sojourned during the austral winter of 1898-1899 and was able to observe the seals in winter.

Today's knowledge on the seals in the region and comments on their future distribution

The four seals species discussed here (Figs. 9.3.5-9.3.8) are now much better known since the Belgica expedition, although there has not been any description as detailed since those carried out by Racovitza (2016) on the seals. The sea lion is not being discussed here as it does not pertain to Antarctic waters per se. We now know much more about the four seal species discussed here as summarized in the encyclopedia of marine mammals edited by Würsig et al., 2018, and associated publications) what we now know of the seals. In addition, the SCAR Antarctic Biodiversity Portal (https://www.biodiversity.aq/ allows us now to look at this huge database to determine the distribution of seals in the Southern Ocean through time. These are summarised in Appendix 1. However, the important feature is that the region around the Antarctic Peninsula and the Bellingshausen Sea is undergoing significant changes due to the substantial warming of the oceans there (Flexas et al., 2024). Importantly, the Bellingshausen Sea is already ice free in summer at least, so one important question arises: where are the seals which require sea ice for mating, giving birth, bringing up the pups and also resting go? In addition, krill populations are changing and it appears that over the last 2 decades, they are disappearing from the Bellingshausen Sea (Kawaguchi et al., 2024). It is certain that some of the seals that require sea ice for their life cycle must now move close to the coast in remote bays where sea ice must still occur. Nevertheless, there is a sign of optimism as Piñones and Fedorov (2016) predict that krill (Fig. 9.3.10) will benefit from a warming of ocean temperature close to the Antarctic coast, and this means ample food for seals as krill populations are to increase in number. Nevertheless, the seals will have to find some sea ice to complete part of their life cycle such as breeding, giving birth to pups, lactate and rest. Further investigations are required through visits in the Bellingshausen Sea.

Figure 9.3.5 (oppistie) Map showing the route taken by the Belgica expedition published by Lecointe (1901) encompassing Magellan Strait, the Beagle Channel, Staten Islands and then down through Drake Passage, Bransfield and de Gerlache Straits. This map shows the location of where Ross seals, sea lions and Magellanic penguins (one locality only) were seen by E. Racovitza. To aid with determining those locations, dates from Racovitza (2016) notes and accounts listed in Lecointe (1904) and Racovitza's diary (1998) were used.

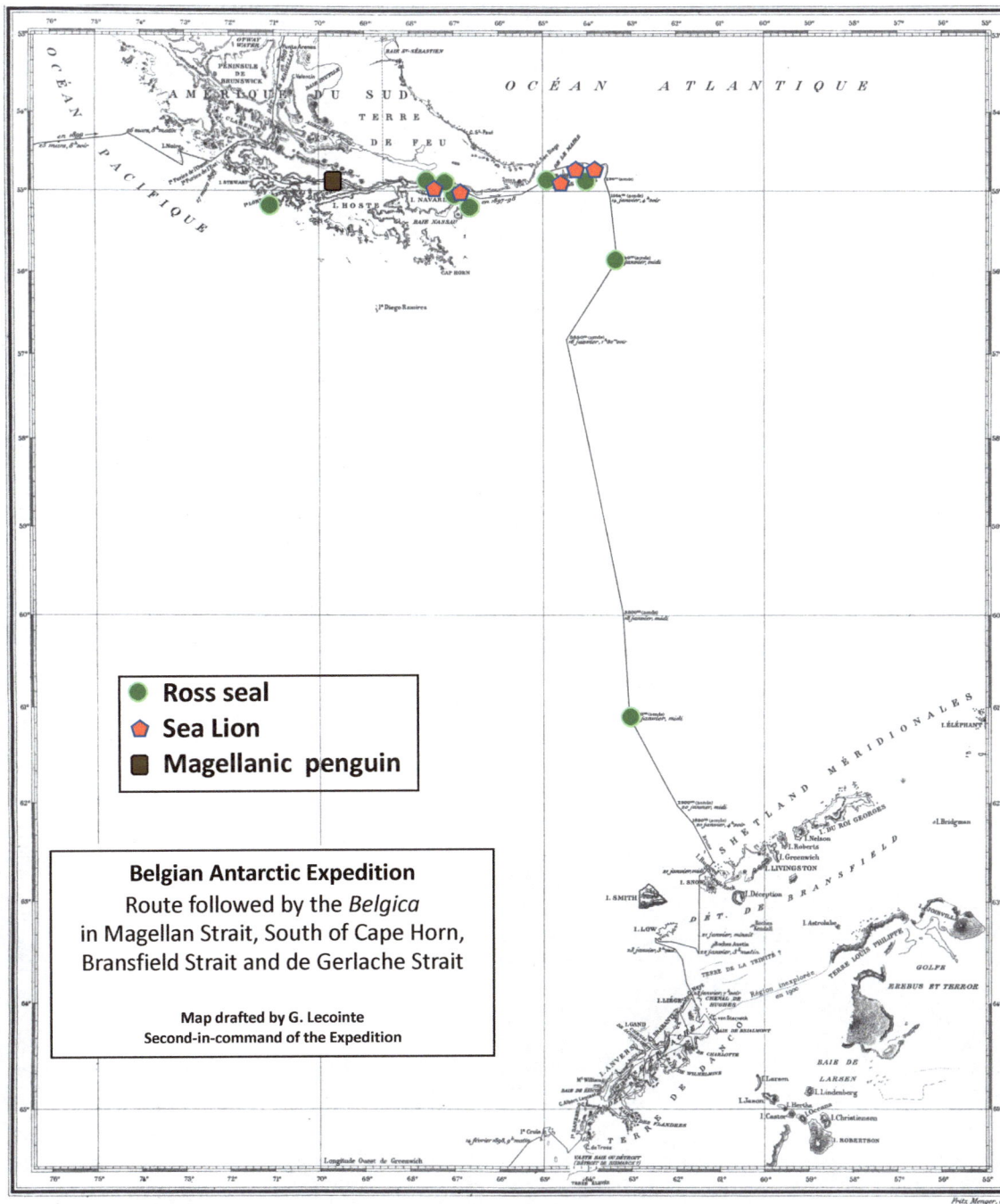

Belgian Antarctic Expedition
Route followed by the *Belgica*
in Magellan Strait, South of Cape Horn,
Bransfield Strait and de Gerlache Strait

Map drafted by G. Lecointe
Second-in-command of the Expedition

Legend:
- ● Ross seal
- ⬠ Sea Lion
- ■ Magellanic penguin

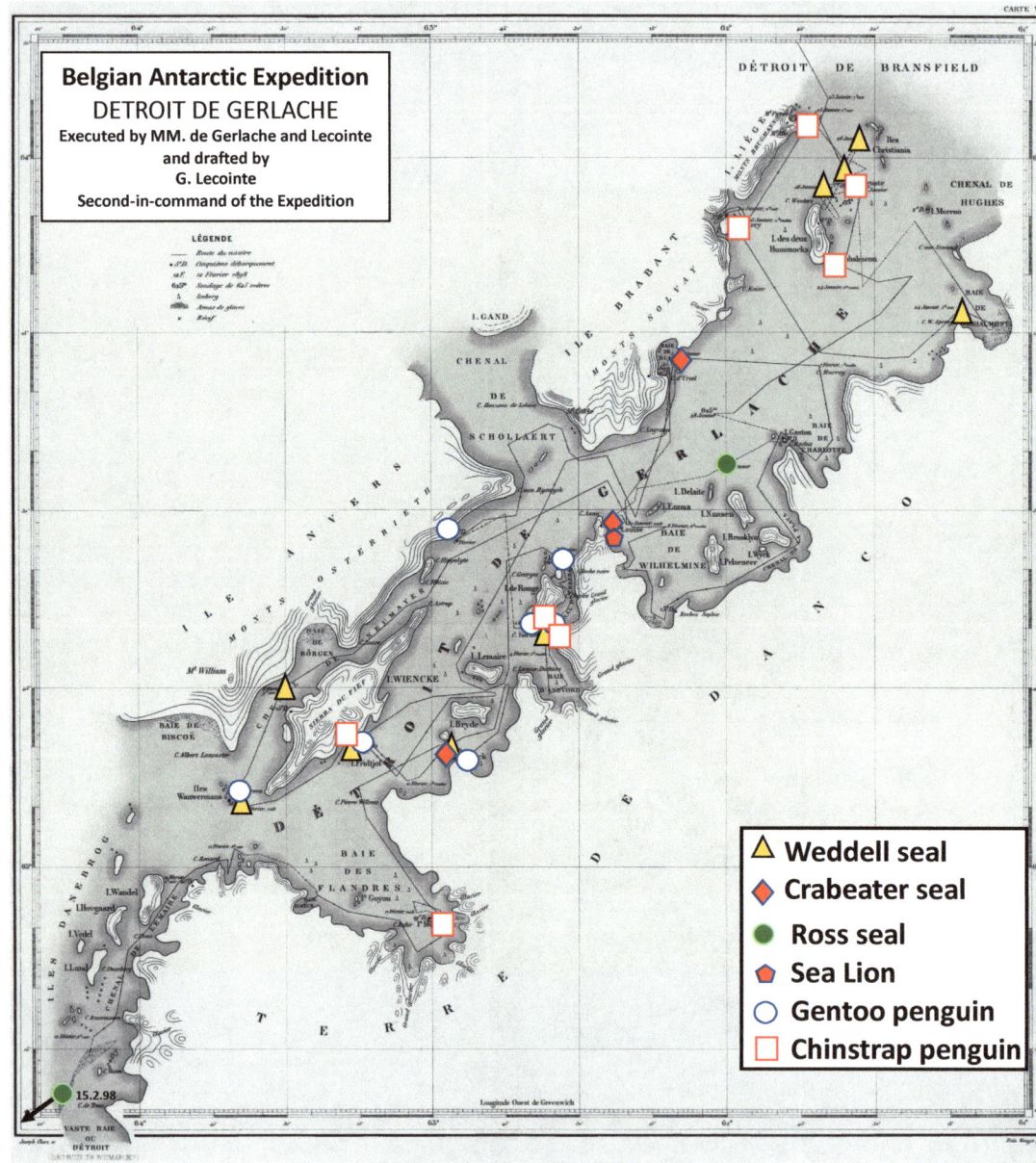

Figure 9.3.6 Map showing the route taken by the Belgica expedition, published by Lecointe (1901), detailing the de Gerlache Strait which Lecointe mapped with the help of de Gerlache. This map shows the location of where four seal species were found (crabeater seal, Ross seal, Sea Lion and Weddell seal) as well as two species of penguins (Gentoo and chinstrap penguins) were seen by Racovita (1938, 2016). The dates written on the original map, plus the landing numbers helped determine the location of where seals were seen and discussed in Racovitza (2016).

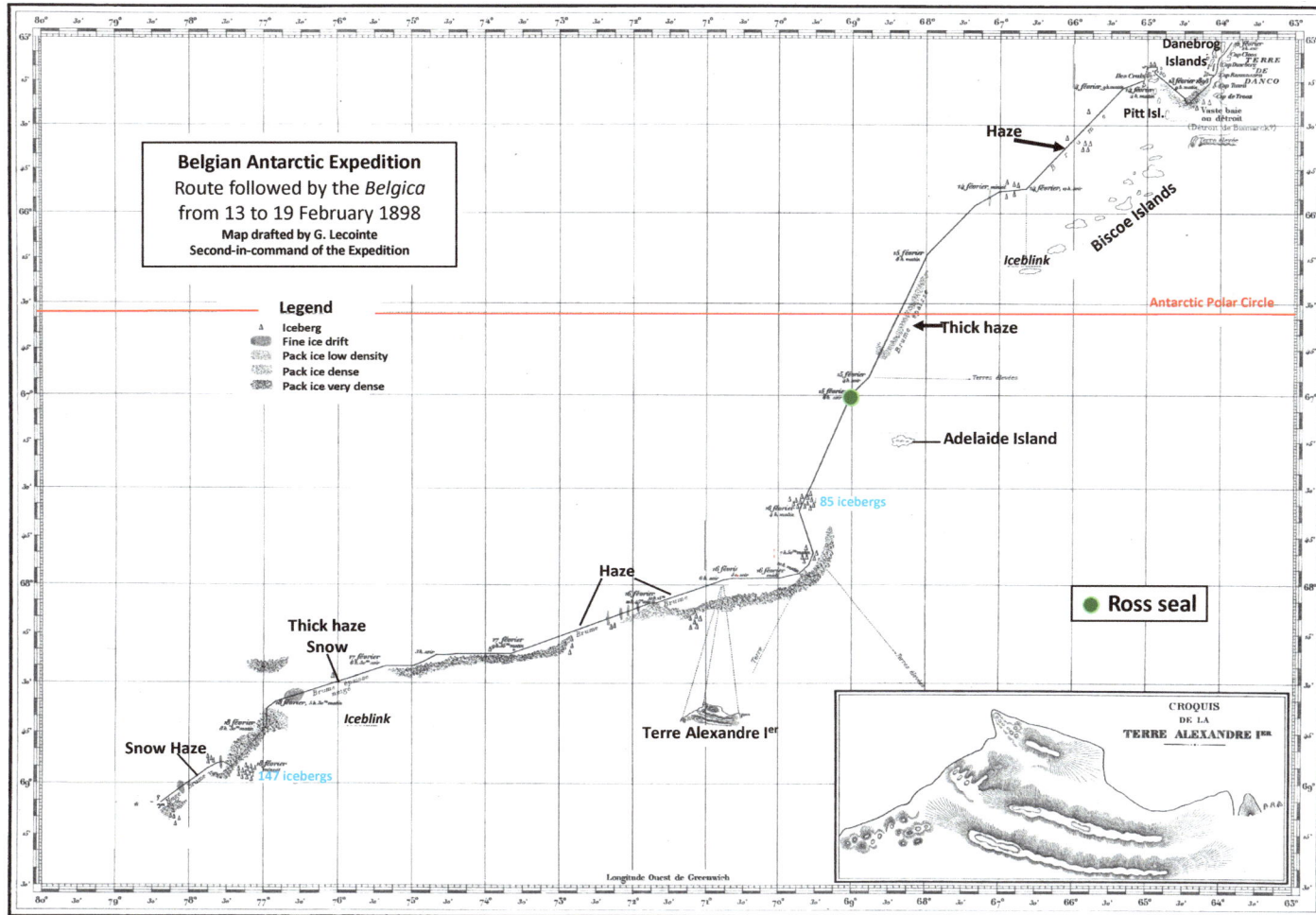

Figure 9.3.7 Map showing the route taken by the Belgica expedition, published by Lecointe (1901), between February 13 to 19, 1898 from the Danebrog Islands to 69°S 78°W. Only one sighting of Ross seals was made and this is based on Racovitza (2016)'s notes. It shows only one record pf Ross seals.

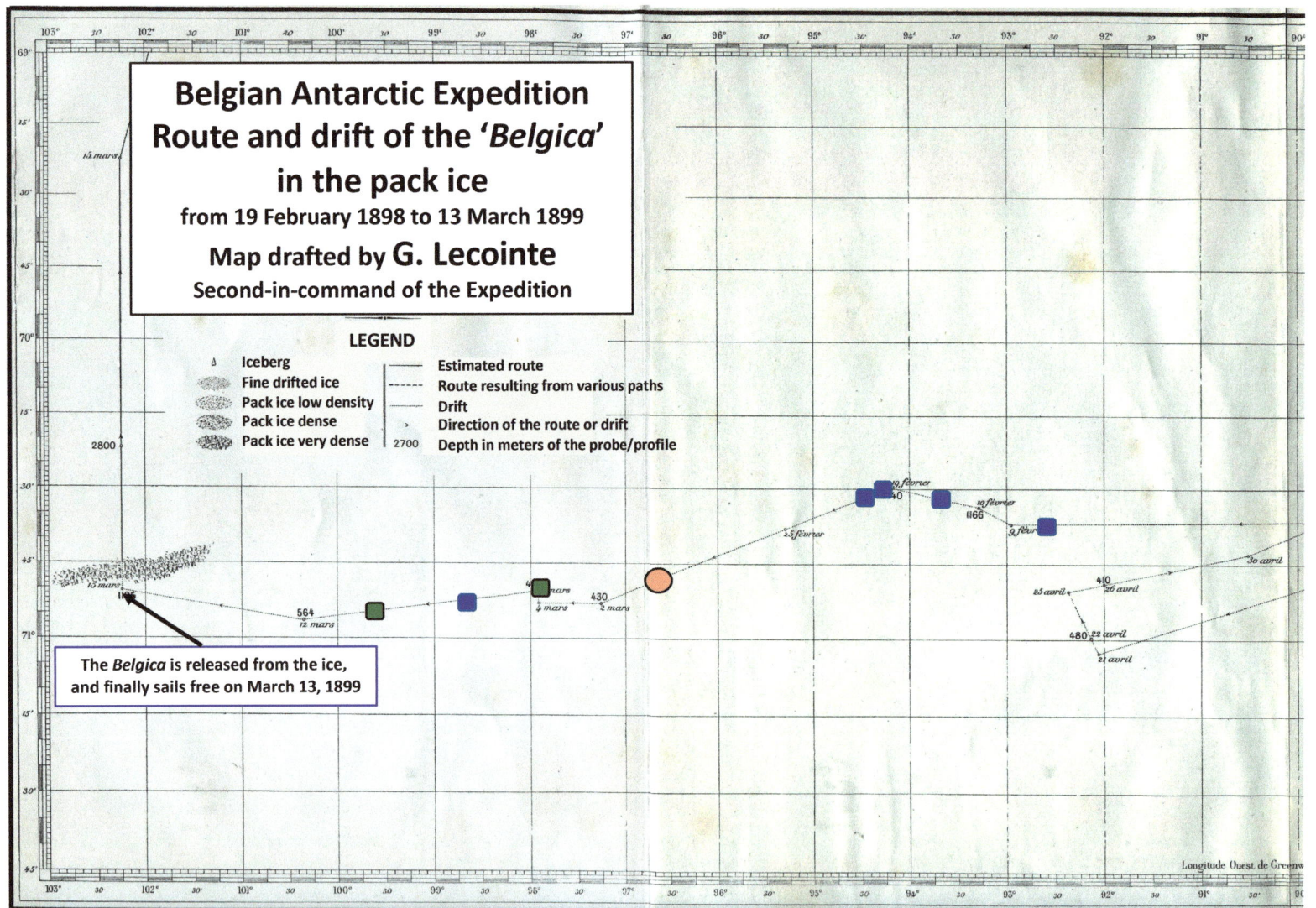

Figure 9.3.8 Map showing the route taken by the Belgica expedition during the February 19, 1898 to March 13, 1899 period and the location of were three seal species were encountered (crabeater seal, sea lion and Weddell seal) as well as Adélie and Emperor penguins. The dates written on the original map helped determine the location of where seals were seen and discussed in Racovitza (2016) and for penguins in Racovitza's (1998) diary.

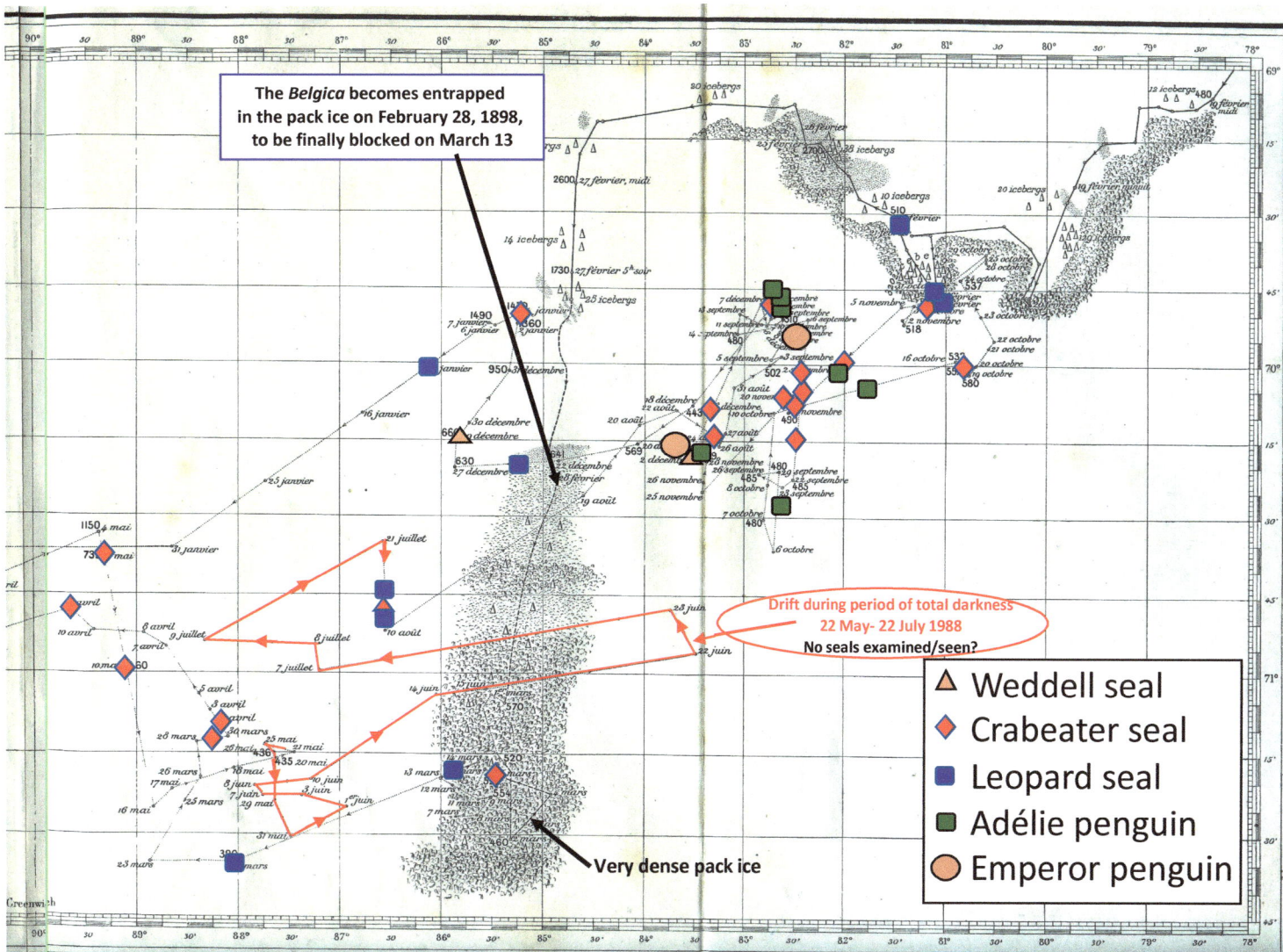

The *Belgica* becomes entrapped in the pack ice on February 28, 1898, to be finally blocked on March 13

Drift during period of total darkness
22 May- 22 July 1988
No seals examined/seen?

Very dense pack ice

△ Weddell seal
◆ Crabeater seal
■ Leopard seal
■ Adélie penguin
● Emperor penguin

147

Figure 9.3.9 Recent photographs of seals:
A-B: Weddell Seal, *Leptonychotes weddelli*;
C-E: Leopard Seal, *Ogmorhinus leptonyx*;
F-H: Crab eater seal, *Lobodon carcinophagus*.
All photographs published with permission from the late Franz Gingele.

Figure 9.3.10 Recent photographs of krill (*Euphausia antarctica*) provided by the Australian Antarctic Division (AAD) via Dr So Kawaguchi and published with permission. Top image photographed by Brett Wilks (AAD) with colours modified here and bottom one by Pete Harmsen (AAD). The specimens here are about 4 cm long, but can reach up to 6 cm (Kawaguchi, pers. com.).

The following photographs were all taken during the Belgica expedition and were obtained from a variety of sources.

Figure 9.3.11 A: Male Leopard Sea captured on February 28, 1898 lying on the ship's deck (photo A Racovitza Archives, Antipa Museum); **B:** three people pulling a dead seal (Amundsen on left, Racovitza in middle, 3rd person unknown), note also the magnetic observation hut on left and tripod on right from where soundings were made; **C:** men bringing a seal back to the ship deck (photo A from Racovitza Archives, reproduced with permission from Professor D. Murariu of the Antipa Museum, B-C reproduced with permission from the Emil Racovitza Archive, The Library of the Romanian Academy, Cluj-Napoca Branch. These photos have been processed using Photoshop©).

Figure 9.3.12
A: Ross Seal being examined by Racovitza and other person likely J. Koren;
B: Leopard Seal in front of de Gerlache on skis (photo A by Cook published with permission from Professor D. Murariu of the Antipa Museum, B reproduced with permission from Jan Parmentier, MAS Museum in Antwerp. These photos have been processed using Photoshop©).

A

B

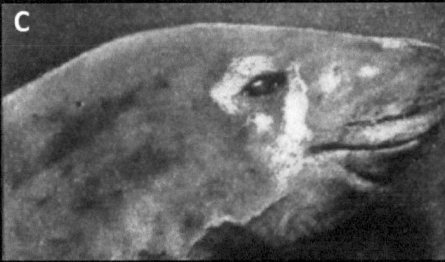

C

D

E

F

Figure 9.3.13

A: Weddell Seal photographed by Racovitza;

B: detail of A showing the head and folds in the pelt;

C: head of a Crabeater Seal photographed by Cook;

D: photo of a decapitated Leopard Seal to show the pointy and sharp teeth curved backward;

E: Racovitza and another person pulling a decapitated Leopard Seal with its head lying in front;

F: young Crabeater Seal photographed by Cook).

Photos A-E published with permission from Professor D. Murariu of the Antipa Museum, F reproduced with permission from Carol Smith from the Sullivan County Museum, Hurleyville, NY. These photos have been processed using Photoshop©.

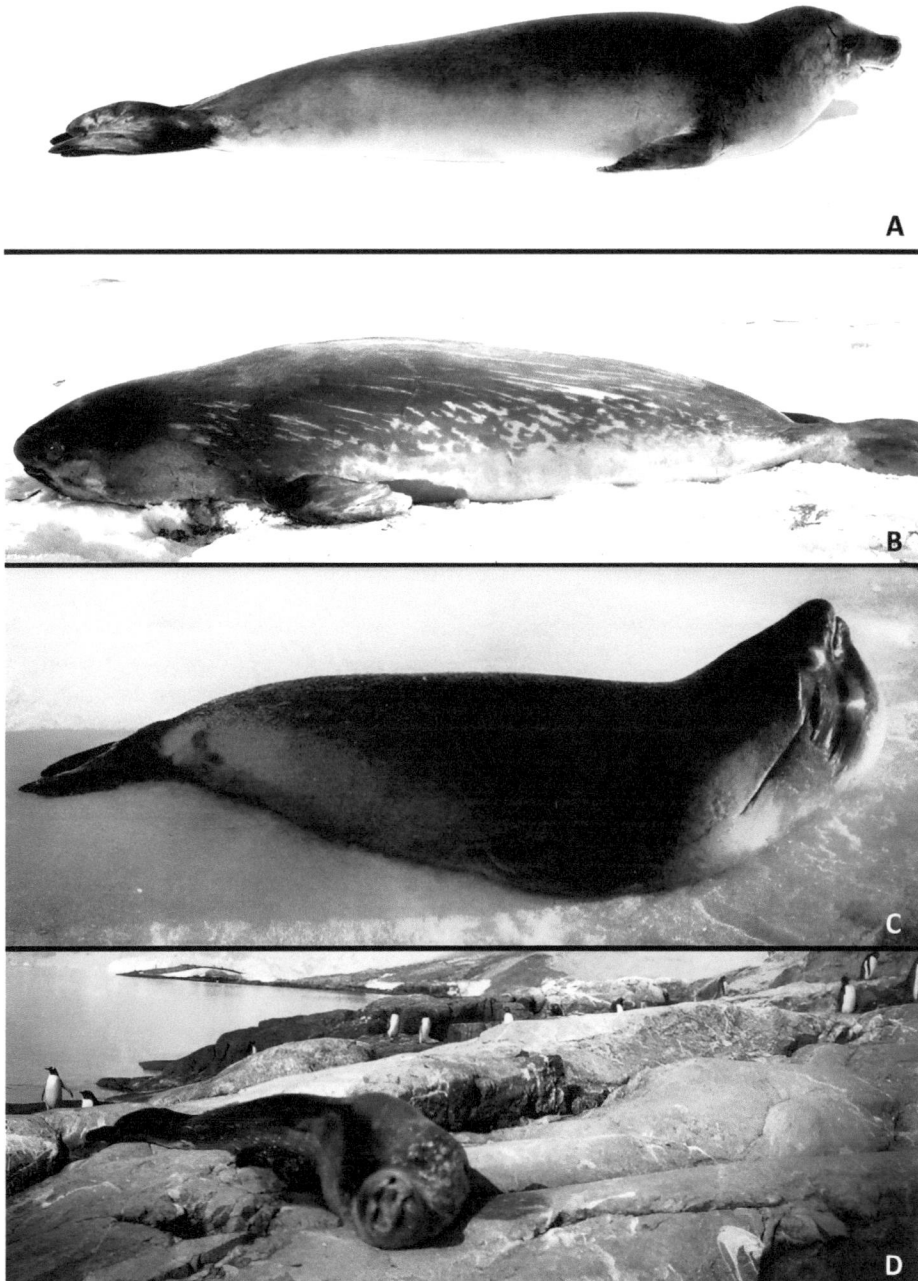

Figs.9.3.11 to 9.3.13 show evidence of the slaughtering of some of the seals that proved necessary for examining the seal in great details, even unborn foetuses. We are also aware that some of those seals were also consumed by the Belgica crew for sustenance, and also for combatting scurvy. For the latter, the flesh was eaten raw.

Figure 9.3.14

A: Crabeater seal with the characteristic muzzle;

B: Ross Seal with obvious yellow coloured pates on the pelt;

C: Ross Seal with inflated trachea;

D: Weddell Seal resting on rocks in the de Gerlache Strait.

Photos A,B, D reproduced with permission from the Emil Racovitza Archive, The Library of the Romanian Academy, Cluj-Napoca Branch, **C** photo by Cook reproduced with permission from Carol Smith from the Sullivan County Museum, Hurleyville, NY. These photos have been processed using Photoshop©.

9.4 Birds, including penguins

KEY POINTS

- The publication on penguins by C. Dupond in the Résultats series was the last one to appear in 1946, but little ecological notes were provided except for notes that Racovitza had published as a result of three conferences given in France and Belgium in 1900. Disappointingly, the notes on penguins in the publications of Cook, de Gerlache and Lecointe cannot be used as their reference to the penguins were rarely done at species level.

- The recent publication of Racovitza's diary (1998) provided additional information on a day-to-day basis on penguins, including additional data on their distribution. This permitted to place information on Lecointe's original maps, thus showing in the de Gerlache Strait of both Gentoo and Chinstrap penguins were found.

- Adélie and Emperor penguins were found in the frozen Bellingshausen Sea. The penguins must have appeared at the surface along cracks/openings in the sea ice. The highest concentration of those penguins occurred in an area between 82° and 83°W and around 70°S where the sea ice and entrapped ship zigzagged in 1898 due to under currents above deep-sea troughs. This region is located above the Latady and Belgica Troughs where upwelling of plankton, and especially krill (the main food of these penguins), must have been plentiful in the late 1890s.

- With recent observation that the Bellingshausen Sea is becoming ice free in summer, it is likely that new colonies will form along the coasts bordering that Sea. The suggested location will likely be opposite deep-sea canyons where biological productivity is high and krill will be abundant, despite the forecasted decrease in their population. This must be checked in the future.

- The de Gerlache Strait is predicted to see an increase in pygoscelid penguin colonies (at least Chinstrap and Gentoo), so it should be an area of significant conservation and protection of penguins, especially under climatic change predictions.

Originally, Howard Saunders was to prepare a volume on birds and Racovitza another on their biology. None of these two planned publications eventuated. The choice of Howard Saunders to publish on the Antarctic birds was obvious at the time as he had already published a chapter on Laridae (gulls, terns, noddies, skimmers, and kittiwakes) birds collected during the Challenger expedition. Charles Dupond, an ornithologist who was an associate ornithologist of the Royal Museum of Natural History of Belgium (RBINS) in Brussels eventually agreed in 1933 to write a monograph on the birds collected during the expedition. Unfortunately, he had many commitments and only commenced work in 1942 with the publication of the monograph on birds being eventually published in 1946. This was the very last of the publications in the series entitled 'Résultats du Voyage de la Belgica'. It is interesting that the publishing house J. Bushmann in Antwerp lasted close to 50 years to publish those volumes, which eventually totalled some 3246 pages!

Dupond was not happy with this project as he stated up front that the task was 'unrewarding' (ingrat) having to write on the morphological aspect. His publication is based on three parts: (1) the study of H. Saunders principally concerning synonymy; (2) results of Dupond's own research dealing with the morphological examination of the specimens (assumed to be all stored today at the RBINS) and relying on the important book entitled: The Oceanic Birds of South America by R.C. Murphy); and (3) the ornithological observations obtained during the Belgica

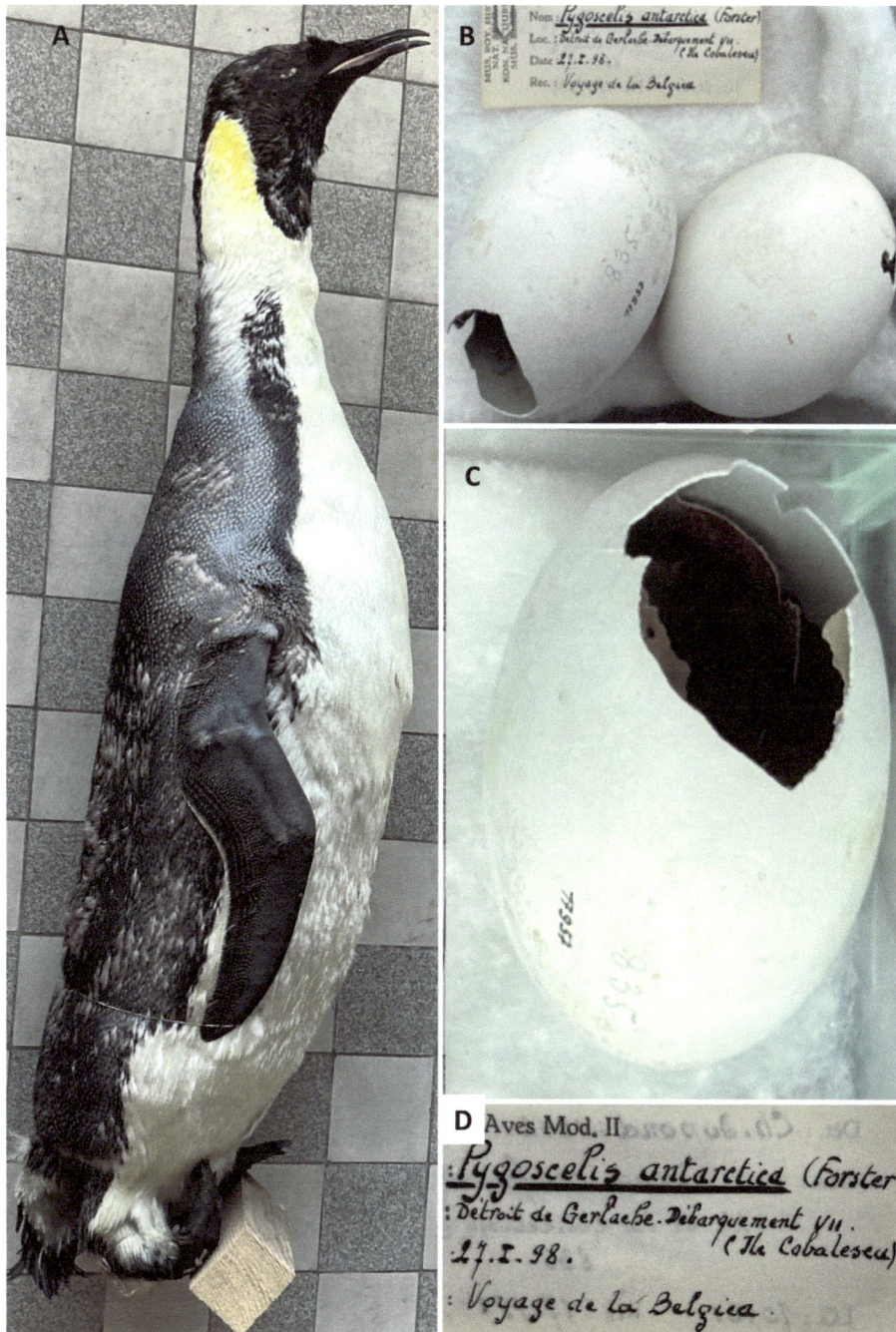

expedition, together with three publications of Racovitza (1900 a,b,c). He also relied on other publications, but these were not as important. Nevertheless, these were notes from Cook (1900) and notes by Racovitza therein,de Gerlache (1902, 1938), and Lecointe (1904).

Dupond listed all the species encountered during the expedition (both in the Magellan Strait and Antarctica), giving the coordinates of their location and types, specimen numbers stored at RBINS. This totals 44 catalogue numbers, and he also gave details of their nature (skin, skeleton, birds kept in alcohol) see Table 9.4.1.

In this chapter, I will only discuss penguins observed and collected by E. Racovitza. Those interested in finding more on the seabirds are recommended to directly consult the work of Dupond (1946).

Photographs of specimens held in the RBINS are presented in Figs. 9.4.1 and 9.4.2.

Figure 9.4.1.

A: The emperor penguin Astenodytes forsteri, fully stuffed specimen lying on the floor, specimen collected on the sea ice on 7.9.1898 at 68° 55'S 82° 36'W;

B: photograph of two eggs belonging to the Chinstrap penguin *Pygoscellis antarctica*;

C: additional cracked egg (same species) showing part of the preserved inner membrane;

D: label for the eggs.

Recent photographs taken by the late Franz Gingele of penguins (Figs. 9.4.3 and 9.4.4) and other birds species (Figs. 9.4.5 and 9.4.5) discussed here appear in Figs. 9.4.5 and 9.4.8, together with photos taken by Frederick Cook during the Belgica expedition.

Figure 9.4.2.

A: Side view of a stuffed specimen of the silver-grey petrel *Priocella antarctica* collected on the sea ice in the Bellingshausen Sea, 70°40'S 102° 15'W on 10.3.1899,

B: ventral view of same specimen,

C: detail of head,

D: label.

Scientific name	Common name	Nature of the collection	Number of specimens	Numbers in the register	Photos in this chapter
Aptenodytes forsteri	**Emperor penguin**	**bird with skin**	3	3	1 D-F
Pygoscelis adeliae	**Adélie penguin**	"	9	9	1 A-C
Spheniscus magellanicus	**Magellanic penguin**	"	1	1	
Megalestris antarctica	South polar skua	"	4	4	4 C-D
Ossifraga gigantea	Giant petrel	"	7	7	3 E
Thalassogeron culminatus	Yellow-nosed albatros	"	2	2	
Fulmarus glacialoides	Southern fulmar	"	1	1	3 B
Thalassoica antarctica	Antarctic petrel	"	1	1	3 A
Daption capensis	Cape petrel	"	1	1	3 F
Pagodroma nivea	Snow petrel	"	1	1	3 C-D
Oceanites oceanicus	Wilson's storm petrel	"	1	1	4 E-F
Larus dominicanus	Kelp gull	"	1	1	4 A-B
Phalocrocorax sp.	Cormorant	"	1	1	
Ossifraga gigantea	Giant petrel	**skeleton**	1	1	3 E
Pygoscelis adeliae	**Adélie penguin**	"	3	3	1 A-C
Aptenodytes forsteri	**Emperor penguin**	"	2	2	1 D-F
Turdus megellanicus	Austral thrush	**supplement to the list of birds in skin**	1	1	
Thalassoica antarctica	Antarctic petrel	"	2	2	3 A
Pagodroma nivea	Snow petrel	"	2	2	3 C-D
Oceanites oceanicus	Wilson's storm petrel	"	2	2	4 E-F
Pagodroma nivea	Snow petrel	**birds in alcohol**	3	1	3 C-D
Chloephaga magellanica, chicks	Magellan goose	"	2	1	
Vanellus occidentalis, chick	Southern lapwing	"	1	1	
Zonotrichia capensis	Rufous-collared sparrow	?		with crested bird with 2 eggs	
Aptenidytes forsteri	**Emperor penguin**	?		skeleton with limbs, crania	! D-F
Pygoscelis antarctica	**Chinstrap penguin**	?	2	eggs from nest	1 G-I
Pygoscelis papua	**Gentoo penguin**	?	1	eggs from nest	2 A-F
Megalestris antarctica	South polar skua	?	1	eggs from nest	4 C-D

Table 9.4.1 List of birds examined by Charles Dupond and which were stored at the Royal Museum of Natural History by E. Racovitza. Information on number of specimens and what is preserved and the type of medium is listed here. Names in bold are penguins.

DUPOND (1946)'S NOTES ON EACH OF THE PENGUIN SPECIES

Aptenodytes fosteri Emperor penguin

First of all, Dupond (1946) provided the synonymy list made by H. Saunders. The material the latter studied (3 females) were collected on the pack ice. Dupond (op. cit.) examined the same specimens and concluded that this species appears to moult in December and January and this is completed in February. He also provided measurements of the 3 specimens. In addition, he examined 2 skeletons, bones of anterior and posterior limbs, 2 skulls. He further indicated that this is a circumpolar bird found in the ocean circling the Antarctic continent. It reproduces on vast areas of firm ice in favourable localities of the Antarctic coasts, south down to 78°S and north up to latitudes of the South Orkney Islands, without reaching South Georgia. Concerning its food, Racovitza (1900a) stated that this species eats krill (Euphausia sp., see fig. 9.3.8 in chapter on seals) in large numbers by diving in krill 'schools' and, when its stomach is full, it returns to the surface on the sea ice and goes to a hummock so as to be protected from the wind. There, it will rest either in an up-straight position or lying down lazily on the snow. After digestion is completed, it will dive once more to seek food. In Racovitza (1900b), we are informed that this penguin can reach 40 kg and its size reaches 1.10m. There are more details on its plumage and colouration. de Gerlache (1902) claims that this penguin can reach 1.20 m. When diving, this animal already has its mouth open so as to catch krill. For their distribution found during the Belgica expedition refer to Fig. 9.3.6.

Pygoscelis adeliae Adélie penguin

Once more, Dupond (1946) provides a synonymy list originally generated by H. Saunders. He then follows on with additional notes on synonyms. He goes on to say the young generally appear in December and carry a juvenile plumage until the end of their second summer. Moulting of both young and adults occurs in February-March and is completed by March 15. He then goes on to describe the colouration of the plumage. Concerning their geographical distribution, it is also circumpolar and lives on favourable sites on the Antarctic coasts. After the nesting season, it migrates in floating sea ice, free ice but rarely reaches latitudes north of 60°S. Nevertheless, in the American quadrat (of Antarctica), this species resides north along the coast of the Antarctic Archipelago until the South Shetland, South Orkneys and South Sandwich Islands where they are found on vast and fixed sea ice fields. Racovitza (1900a) reported that it does not reach a size above 70 cm. Some are 60 cm tall. It is nervous, with lively movements and angry. It has an extraordinary curiosity and can jump out of the water up to 2 to 3 m with great success at landing. A the end of autumn, these animals congregate in large groups sheltering from a large icy hill to be ready for a delicate operation; viz. moultingso as to have a new fresh plumage in good condition to resist the harsh winter. Moulting lasts 2 to 3 weeks during which time they cannot seek food. During that time, they suffer from moult fever and their temperament is affected by that: they lie on the snow, head inside the shoulders, shivering and miserable and hides form other animals such as seals, or birds, penguins or humans. There are also additional notes from De Gerlache (1902, 1936) and Lecointe (1904) but they conform Racovitza's notes. For their distribution found during the Belgica expedition refer to Fig. 9.3.6.

Pygoscelis antarctica Chinstrap penguin

Dupond (1946) provided a short synonymy list and only described the 2 eggs in the collection (Table 9.4.1) with dimensions of 68 mm X 51.3 mm and 71.5 mm X 53.5 mm (see also Fig. 9.4.1). These are uniformly white slightly greenish, with a few yellow brown spots irregularly placed.

Concerning their geographical distribution, this species occurs exclusively in the American quadrat. It nests to the east as far as Bouvet Island (3° E) to the west as far as the western side of the Antarctic Archipelago; in the south it nearly reaches the Antarctic Polar Circle and to the north up to the Falkland Islands where it occasionally errs. It is more abundant in the South Orkney and Sandwich Islands to the south. It is very rare on South Georgia and unknown on the coasts of South America.

Racovitza (1900a) stated that this species is poorly known, but was found in the de Gerlache Strait. He stated that it resembles the Adélie penguin in both size and plumage, except for its white cheeks with a black streak. They quarrel a lot in their colonies and create a loud roar. A pair builds a round nest, very primitive consisting of a small circles of little pebbles and even bones, being the rests of penguins. In the nest are 2 young, little 'fellow' with a belly, vested with a little crest made of grey down with in the front a white bib. Parents watched the young while alternating to seek food. Around each nest, there was a little, separated from the others by a virtual border zone which made the 'family' property. For their distribution found during the Belgica expedition refer to Fig. 9.3.6.

Pygoscelis papua Gentoo penguin

H. Saunders (1946) only observed one egg which he described as having a remarkable form, nearly round, uniformly white, slightly greenish with here and there dirty yellowish brown spots.

Concerning this penguin's geographical distribution, Saunders stated that this species occurs all around Antarctica but not as near it compared to the other species. It is found on Staten Island and the Falkland Islands and appears the most abundant on Prince Edouard, Crozet and Kerguelen Islands. It approaches Antarctica being on South Georgia, Heard and Macquarie Islands. It does not frequent the temperate zone, unless as an errand.

Racovitza (1900a) described at length the plumage. He refers to the 'Papua city' in the de Gerlache Strait where he spent some time among the colony observing the birds. For there, he gave a lengthy description of what he saw. The colony was on a squarish rocky platform, located some 10 m above the sea, and fringing a high steep cliff. On the other side, there was a natural staircase, formed by small fallen rocks, leading to a gravel beach. The other two sides were bordered by a steep wall above the sea. The young were all grouped in the middle of the platform and adults were posted at the surroundings facing the sea or the little gravelly beach. He believed that this arrangement was perfectly intentional. The adults were placed at the edge of the platform to prevent the young from falling into the sea. Racovitza (1900a) went onto describing what does happen if a young approaches the cliff and other behaviour. He also believed that the organisation of these penguins is a collective one, and gave more examples to document this statement. In his 1900 publication, Racovitza (1900b) compared both the Chinstrap and the Gentoo penguins and noted that the former is noisy and a bad sleeper ('mauvais coucheur'), and is a strict individualist constantly quarrelling to defend its property. On the contrary, the brave and honest Gentoo penguin is a well-informed 'communist' with nothing to fend against the members of hits colony, having organised the site and economised the task of bringing up the colony which he referred to as a communal boarding school ('pensionnat communal'). De Gerlache (1936) recalls that Racovitza landed on the Cavelier de Cuverville Island (landing no. 12) where he saw Weddell and Crabeater seals as well as an agglomeration of Gentoo penguins amounting to some tens of thousands of individuals. He commented that this species is larger than the Chinstrap penguin, and reaffirmed Racovitza's description that the Chinstap peguin is very much individualist in behaviour compared to the more 'communist' Gentoo penguin that has nothing to fear from the other members of its colony.

For their distribution found during the Belgica expedition refer to Figs. 9.3.6.

Spheniscus magellanicus Magellanic penguin

After listing Saunders' synonymy, Dupond provided measurements for the adult individual collected from the French Canal in Tierra del Fuego in Chile. He provided a more up-to-date geographical distribution by saying that it inhabits the coasts and islands at the extremity of South America, including the Falkland Islands, and in the Atlantic coast of South America where it reaches up to 41°S, and on the western side in the Pacific along Chile it reaches up to 35°S. After nesting, it goes further north up to 30°S in the Pacific and 25°C in the Atlantic Ocean. No other notes are provided. For their distribution found during the Belgica expedition refer to Fig. 9.3.6.

Additional remarks

In among the Racovitza archives in the Antipa Museum in Bucharest in Roumania, there is quite a substantial set of notes on birds, including penguins. These include ample notes on external morphologies, such as plumage and its colouration, stomach contents, and numerous measurements that included length of tibia, length of digits, nails and much more. The latter appear on sheets that were specifically made for the Belgica expedition. On some sheets, weight, body temperature are also listed as well as locality and day of collection. These were not further consulted. Obviously, all these notes were meant for a publication on the biology of the birds and it is disappointing to know that Dupond did not have access to those data sheets and notes, although Racovitza was still alive at the time of preparation (1942) and eventual publication in 1946, but this understandable as this was the time of WWII. There are also notes on birds observed by Racovitza in his published diary in Rameau d'Or (1998). However, the diary is missing notes from a critical period when the ship was trapped in the sea ice; this period spans from February 12, 1898 to November 6, 1898.

Comments on today's distribution on penguins in the area visited by the Belgica[2]

Emperor penguins are up to 130 cm tall and are long-lived (up to 40 years at least) but only produce one egg per year that is incubated by the male. Their distribution is circumpolar between 54° and 78°S. They breed in mid/late December to April. They are found on stable fast ice in winter and mortality of the young is high once they leave the nest.

2 Notes on penguins from the Australian Antarctic Division (AAD) (https://www.antarctica.gov.au/about-antarctica/animals/penguins/) and the very valuable book also on penguins by De Roy et al. (2013) - that also contains many comments from penguin experts - have been used to contribute to this section.

Winter conditions can be variable, but storms and blizzards make take a severe toll on emperor penguins, and if the sea ice on which they live as a colony is extensive, they are faced to travel long distances. Numbers around Antarctica vary from a few hundreds to over 20,000 pairs, but recent estimates for 46 colonies reach up to 238,000 breeding pairs (De Roy et al., 2013). They are most common in the Ross Sea region, Weddell Sea and East Antarctica. It is postulated that populations may undergo a rapid decline due to the effects of climate change as well as krill fisheries. A reduction of the sea ice due to global warming is a direct threat to their survival. Due to their size and diet requirements, emperor penguins are near the top of the food chain. They mainly eat Antarctic silverfish, but other fish as well including krill and squid, but their prey is small so as to prevent a loss of body temperature when eating. They also eat much before returning to the colony to feed the young. Emperor penguins depend on the fast-ice for their long-term survival (AAD) and it must last long enough to enable chicks to be reared, otherwise survival is at great risk.

Adélie penguins are rather small and only weigh 3 to 6 kg. They are around 70 cm tall. They build nests on land, mostly on sloping platforms to enable melting snow to flow away from the nests. They can venture up to 50 km inland, and as far as 100 km on the sea ice to forage at sea (Cimino et al., 2013). In mid-November, they incubate 2 eggs and incubation may last up to 2 weeks. Colonies can vary in size from a few 100s to 100,000 (De Roy et al. 2013). Their diet consists of krill, fish and other small crustaceans (amphipods), but this depends on the location of the colony. Reduction in krill populations (see comments later referring to the work of Santora et al. (2020) and Kawaguchi et al. (2024)).

Their distribution is circumpolar all along the Antarctic coast. Global population is estimated to be 2.37 million pairs (de Roy, 2013).

Gentoo penguins have a large geographical range and are found on sub-Antarctic islands and the Antarctic Peninsula where there are the largest colonies (Figs. 9.4.4 A, 9.4.5 A,D), as well as on South Georgia. The colonies last the whole year round. They have 2 eggs every year and incubation last 34 to 37 days. They are opportunistic feeders and their diet consists of crustaceans (mostly krill), small fish and squid. It appears that their population is increasing on the Antarctic Peninsula, but populations are decreasing in the Indian Ocean sector of the Antarctic Ocean (AAD). Estimates extend up to 387,000 breeding pairs (Lynch in De Roy, 2013). Cimino et al. (2013) stated that Anvers Island is an area where Chinstrap populations have recently increased. Same comments as for Adélie penguins concerning reduction in krill populations.

Chinstrap penguins (Fig. 9.4.5B) can reach 75-90 cm in height and breed on the Antarctic Peninsula and on islands in the Atlantic sector of the Southern Ocean with some colonies extending as far as New Zealand, Heard Island and South Georgia. Their distribution is still regarded as being circumpolar. Population numbers are around 8 millions pairs (De Roy et al., 2013), and appear to be in decline around the Antarctic Peninsula due to shrinkage of sea ice and a decreasing krill populations (De Roy et al., 2013). Breeding occur occurs between November and March and breeding colonies are nearly all located below 60°S, but they spend winters north of the pack-ice zone. Each couple care for 2 eggs and brooding can last 20-37 days. They travel well north of the pack ice in order to feed (Cimino et al., 2013). However, the decline in krill populations may cause their own decline (see note

below). They lay 2 eggs and are near-shore feeders, so do not have to travel very far.

Magellanic penguins occur in the temperate regions of South America and feel on small fish such as anchovies, crustaceans and squid. Hence, the extensive anchovy fishing contribute to their threat. They live up to 20 years and produce 2 eggs. They are on average 70 cm tall.

The future of penguin colonies in the regions visited by the Belgica

Thompson et al. (1997) obtained information on past temperatures from 2 ice cores from the Dyer Plateau (70°40'16"S; 64°52'30"W; 2002 m a.s.l.; mean annual temperature: -21°C) on the Antarctic Plateau and determined that, at the time of that publication, "the last two decades have been among the warmest in the last five centuries". The period on the Dyer Plateau spanning 1500 to 1850 had been stable with no evidence of the Little Ice Age. However, from 1950, a prominent warming became noticeable. This ought to have provided signs of warning that climatic conditions were changing in the Antarctic Peninsula area and naturally would affect the biota in the area. Furthermore, Convey et al. (2009) identified that in the Bellingshausen Sea, the extent of the sea ice had already been significantly reduced as a result of changes in winds in the area; this may result from the fact that penetration of maritime air has been evident since the 1940's. Barnes and Peck in 2008 had already discussed the vulnerability of the Antarctic shelf biodiversity under a predicted regional warming since 1950.

This was confirmed by the long-term decline in krill stock coinciding with the increase in salps in the Southern Ocean (Atkinson et al., 2004) which then leads to a significant change in food webs that are to affect the large animals such as whales, penguins, seals and sea birds such as albatrosses. Such articles were followed by the very important work of Ducklow et al. (2007) dealing specifically with the Antarctic Peninsula. It indicated that the latter is "one among the most rapidly warming regions on Earth, having experienced a 2°C increase in the annual mean temperature and a 6° C rise in the mean winter". These authors also pointed out that heat transfer via the Antarctic Circumpolar Current that is causing a 0.6°C warming of the upper 300 m of shelf water. It is in that zone that penguins and seals feed.

In their important review paper, Ducklow et al. (2007) summarized the data obtained by others for Anvers Island which indicated that between 1975 and 2005, populations of the ice-dependent Adélie penguins significantly decreased by 65%, whereas chinstraps increased by 2730% and gentoos (between 1994 and 2005) increased by 4600%! Cimino et al. (2013) predict that chinstrap and gentoo populations that are ice-intolerant will increase in numbers around Antarctica in the future by colonizing new shorelines as a result of sea ice decreasing. Cimino et al. (2016) indicated already that Adélie about 20% of penguin populations may be decreasing by 2060 around Antarctica. It is also necessary to revisit the concept that the Antarctic Peninsula has been warming up with the recent study of Oliva et al. (2017) that indicates that this region has been undergoing a cooling trend of (-0.47°C/per decade) during 1999–2014 period.

Nevertheless, the alarming study of Kawaguchi et al. (2024) that clearly indicated a decrease in krill populations in the Bellingshausen Sea may severely affect not only seal populations but also penguins. Kawaguchi (pers. comm.) indicated that this area may need further investigations because it has been poorly studied thus far. Nevertheless, the recent absence of summer sea ice may in fact cause penguin colonies to increase in the area with new access to coastal areas, especially for those species that can establish a colony on land. Further exploration and visiting these areas are therefore warranted. Of importance also is the study of Santora et al. (2018) which indicated that submarine canyons have always been known to support much biological diversity by generating energy flow and trophic interactions are critical for krill populations. These areas are often referred to as 'biological hot spots' (Hudson et al., 2019). In Antarctic waters, Santora and Reiss (2011), examined two submarine canyons north of the Antarctic Peninsula and found that penguins concentrated closer to shore in the area due to high krill concentration in the submarine canyon where mesopelagic fish also occur. Santora et al. (2020) who collated surveys of penguins all around Antarctica also indicated that availability of breeding habitat and proximity of polynyas (= area of open water surrounded by sea ice) and submarine canyons where prey (mainly krill) is abundant. Examination of the maps in that study (Santora et al. 2020) and by concentrating on the Antarctic Peninsula and the Bellingshausen Sea, showed that: (1) emperor penguins are only found on three locations west of the Antarctic Peninsula per se (~ 63° to 69° S) in small colonies with two occurring in the Bellingshausen Sea on either sides of a large polynya with the one further east opposite a large canyon; (2) Adélie penguins occur in numerous colonies all along the Antarctic peninsula *per se* but are almost entirely absent in the Bellingshausen Sea; (3) Gentoo and Chinstrap penguins are abundant all along the Antarctic Peninsula *per se*.

It is clear now that the disappearance of the sea ice in the Bellingshausen Sea in summer at least will open 'new grounds' for pygoscelid penguin colonies (Adélie, Chinstrap and Gentoo) as coasts will become easily accessible. It is likely that the three troughs (Latady, Belgica and Pine Glacier Basin, see Fig. 11.7) are areas of extensive biological productivity that would include krill. Noteworthy already is that the map generated from Racovitza's penguin data (Fig. 9.3.6) clearly indicates that the largest occurrences of several penguin species occurred between 82° and 83°W and around 70°S, the area offshore the Latady and Belgica Troughs where the sea ice and entrapped *Belgica* underwent a large zigzag circuit in 1898. For more information, refer to chapter 8. Planktic biological activity would have been enhanced in that area. This area being ice free now in summer will see many more penguins foraging and with colonies being established opposite on land.

The more alarming note by Fretwell et al. (2023) is that emperor penguins have suffered immensely due to breeding failure in the central and western parts of the Bellingshausen Sea due to sea ice loss in 2022. That year, four out of five sites experienced total breeding failure! Refer to their figure 3. Does the same apply to all the other penguin colonies in the region? This needs to be urgently assessed.

Figure 9.4.3 Recent photographs of penguins.
A, B: Adelie penguins; **C:** juvenile Adelie penguin;
D-F: Emperor penguins; **G-H:** Chinstrap penguins;
I: juvenile Chinstrap penguin.
All photos by the late Franz Gingele,
used with permission.

Figure 9.4.4 Recent photographs of gentoo penguins.

A: large colony;

B: juvenile in the process of moulting;

C: Individual protecting an egg;

D: on the move, note the red stain caused by penguin faecal matter mostly from krill remains;

E: swimming and jumping in the ocean.

All photos by the late Franz Gingele, used with permission.

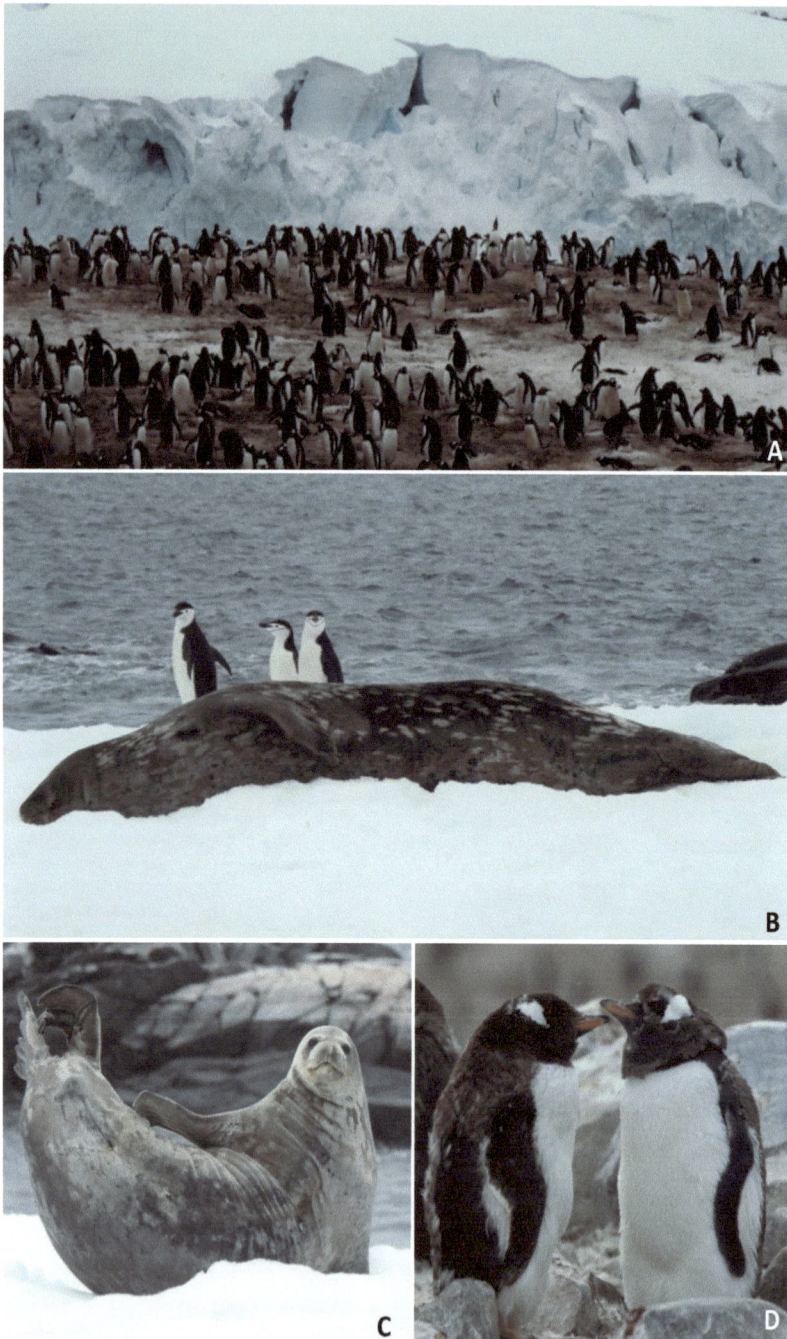

Figure 9.4.5 Recent photographs of penguins and seals photographed in the de Gerlache Strait by Mikołaj Golachowski.

A: Gentoo penguin colony on Couverville Island;

B: Weddell seal and Chinstrap penguins on Hydrurga Rocks;

C: Weddell seal in common curved postiion;

D: Moulting Gentoo penguins on Couverville Island.

Figure 9.4.6 Recent photographs of sea birds.

A: Antarctic petrel;

B: Southern fulmar;
C: Snow petrel;

D: Snow petrel chick;

E: Giant petrel;

F: Cape petrel.

All photos by the late Franz Gingele,
used with permission.

Figure 9.4.7 Recent photographs of sea birds.
A: Kelp gull;
B: Kelp gull juvenile;
C: Skua;
D: Skua carrying a stolen egg in its beak;
E: Wilson's petrel resting;
F: Juvenile skua. All photos by the late Franz Gingele, used with permission.

Figure 9.4.8 Photograph reproduced with permission from the Emil Racovitza Archive, The Library of the Romanian Academy, Cluj-Napoca Branch. The colony is likely to be that of Adélie penguins.

ARHIVA EMIL RACOVIȚĂ

Figure 9.4.9 Photograph of Racovitza holding a captured penguin (likely Adélie penguin) reproduced with permission from the Emil Racovitza Archive, The Library of the Romanian Academy, Cluj-Napoca Branch. This photo was processed using Photoshop© to improve clarity and 'colorized' using palette.fm/color/filters.

9.5 Fish

KEY POINTS

- Based on Racovitza's collections, Dollo (1904) described four new species of fish.

- Dollo benefitted from the very detailed notes taken by Racovitza during the collections of the fish, including associated organisms and plankton collected at the same time

- Dollo also described a skate egg case that has since been associated with the smallest skate found in Antarctic waters by Stehmann et al. (2021).

- Dollo provided extensive discussions on fish collections from the southern hemisphere, including the collections made by the Belgica expedition in the Magellanic Strait, Beagle Channel and the State Islands region.

- Dollo concluded that there is no shared deep fish species between the polar regions of the globe, thus correcting previous biogeographical misconceptions.

Louis Dollo who was curator of vertebrates at the Royal Belgian Institute of Natural Sciences in Brussels was provided with fish specimens collected by Emil Racovitza during the Belgica expedition. The specimens he received, and was asked to describe by the Belgica Commission, were the first one ever collected in Antarctic waters. Dollo was already well known for having reconstructed and displayed in the early 1890's at the Museum a significant collection of Early Cretaceous gigantic *Iguanodon bernissartensis* dinosaurs that were found in a coal mine in Bernissart in Belgium. This collection is still prominent today at the Museum in Brussels and already contributed to Dollo's international reputation.

Dollo's 1904 monograph on fish consists of some 253 pages; he not only described the *Belgica* collections he received but also discussed the biogeography of fish from Antarctic and subantarctic waters, their ecology and phylogeny. This was an impressive contribution to ichthyology. His illustrations of the fish are superb and only the specimens collected by Racovitza are displayed here in Figs. 9.5.1 and 9.5.2 in newly arranged plates. The first observation to make is that the specimens must have been extremely well preserved and this is due to the skills Racovitza had acquired by visiting specialists in Europe before the expedition. Exemplary also was Racovitza's dedication as we note that one new species of fish (*Nematonurus lecointei*, see Figs. 9.5.2C and 9.5.3) was collected at 2,800 m the day the ship was finally released from the ice. No time for celebration for the biologist, it seems.!

The other important note that has to be discussed here is the timing of the original diagnosis of the new species of fish. In science, the common practice (and international rule of taxonomic nomenclature) is that when a new species is described, the scientific name of the organism/plant is followed by the name of the descriptor, followed by the year of publication. Thus, priority prevails with the data of publication. In the case of fish fully described in his 1904 monograph (op. cit), Dollo lists all the new species with a 1900 date. The reason being that many of the Belgian scientists who received specimens for their respective scientific description were aware of the British expedition led by Karsten Borchgrevink on the *Southern Cross* that left London on August 22, 1898 and reached Cape Adare on February 17, 1899. On that expedition was the Norwegian biologist Nicolai Hansen whose duty was to collect biological specimens. Hence, the Belgian scientists feared that the collections made by the *Southern Cross* could jeopardize the priority of their scientific descriptions. Concerning insects, it was decided then to rapidly publish short but succinct diagnoses of many of the new species so as to retain scientific priority. These appeared in the Annales de la Société entomologique de Belgique in 1900 (see chapter 13 on insects). Dollo also rapidly published more lengthy descriptions of his new fish species which he still refered to as 'preliminary descriptions' in the Académie royale de Belgique, Bulletin de la Classe des Sciences in volumes 2,3, 4 and 6 (see Dollo, 1900a-d). Full descriptions appeared in his 1904 monograph discussed here. In fact, Dollo (1904, p. 12)'s fears were unjustified as he was able to assess that Borchgrevink's expedition collected some 171 fish but none from abyssal depths (see Boulenger GA, 1902).

In total, the *Belgica* fish collections in Antarctic waters consisted of four new species that were already described by Dollo in 1900, followed more thoroughly in 1904. These are: *Cryodraco antarcticus, Gerlachea australis, Nematonurus lecointei* and *Racovitzaia glacialis*. The latter species is quite small: 8.2 cm. Of those four species, Dollo (1904, p. 209) stated that *Nematonurus lecointei* is the only one that occurs at great depths (2800 m), whereas the others are found on the Antarctic continental plateau at depths around 400 m or a bit more. In his descriptions of the new taxa, Dollo (1904) provided an amazing amount of data for each of the collections. These even list the time of day/night of the collection, the type of collecting device and occasionally duration of trawling (some lasting 14 hours), water density and temperature, nature of current, and more importantly a list of the other organisms collected at the same time as the fish. Some of that information, especially the complete list that includes the type of plankton is provided and the type of bottom sediment at each station. This information would have been provided by Emil Racovitza. We are unaware of the location of these notes today.

In addition, Dollo (1904) described skate egg cases and illustrated one of them (shown here in Fig. 9.5.2 G), and provided details on three of those collections which contained them. Dollo had given a name for the egg case as *Raja arctowski* and, since then, extensive investigations by Stehmann et al. (2021) have conclusively identified that the eggs case belongs to the skate genus

Bathyraja. These authors stated that it was 'possible to connect captured specimens with the empty egg capsules and completely described it as Dollo's *R. arctowskii* with detailed external morphology, skeletal features, clasper morphology, and clasper skeleton and assign it to the genus *Bathyraja Ishiyama*, 1958'. It was eventually named as *Bathyraja arctowskii* which is one of the smallest known skate species that is 61 cm long.

In his 1904 monograph, Dollo discussed other collections made by the *Belgica*, this time in the Magellanic Strait, Beagle Channel and around the Staten Island at the very tip of South America. Racovitza's collection did not establish new species from those regions. Nevertheless, Dollo (1904) did a comprehensive review of what was known up to 1904 in those three regions (with information graphically displayed in his map (Fig. 9.5.3), and once again acknowledged the amazingly detailed descriptions of the collections made by Racovitza, despite the fact that at times the expedition encountered some bad weather conditions.

Dollo (1904) also went onto discussing body shape, the nature of the tail of all the fish collected in those regions as well as the fish scales. This was followed by a lengthy discussion on the biogeography of the fish species listed in his monograph and touched even on aspects of the palaeogeography of the most common group of fish in the southern hemisphere, viz. the galaxiidae. In Dollo (1904)'s monograph there are also superb illustrations of galaxiid fish from New Zealand and the Magellanic Archipelago. These topics are not discussed any further here as

there must be a vast array of publications discussing these aspects over the last 120 years and it is beyond the aim of this book.

Dollo (1904) went on to comment at great length on knowledge of up to 1904 of Antarctic fishes describing the various habitats, relying especially on Racovitza's notes.

Finally, he concluded that there are no similarities between Arctic and Antarctic fish. They form distinct entities and thus corrected some previous erroneous assumptions.

In addition, Dollo's work on fish from the Belgica expedition has been well quoted in the literature since his 1904 publication, likely because he was well known among ichthyologists and had already acquired a reputation as an expert on the subject. The subsequent investigators on fish collected during the Charcot expeditions (Charcot, 1905, 1911; Vaillant 1906) knew of Dollo's work further contributed to this widespread knowledge.

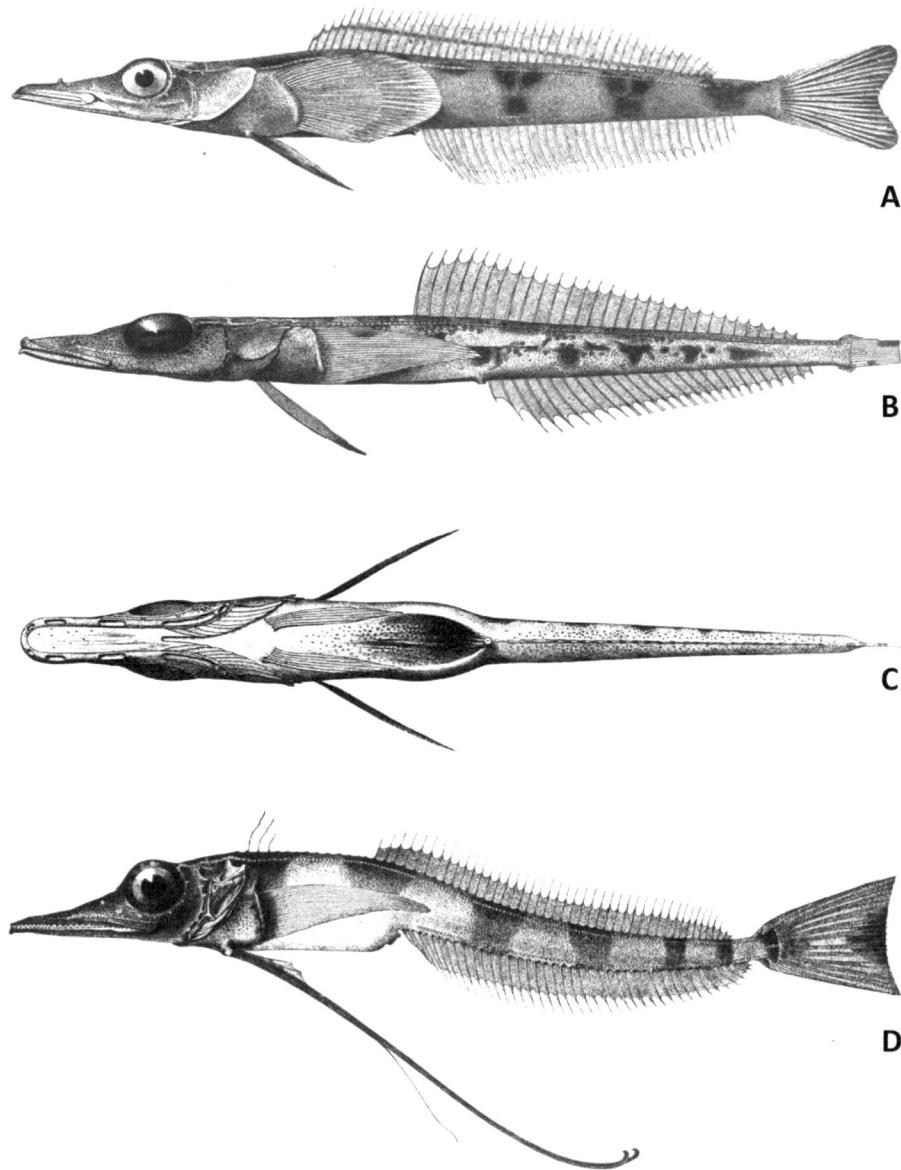

Figure 9.5.1

A: *Gerlachea australis* Dollo 1900 71°14'S 89°14W, 450 m, temp. 0.3°C, 12 May 1898, length 18 cm, colour grey blue with black bands, calcareous ooze little sand and terrigenous sediments; **B-C:** *Racovitzaia glacialis* Dollo 71°19'S 87°37'W, 435 m, 0.2°C, 28 May 1898, 8.2 cm, colour grey blue with black bands, sandy ooze and terrigenous sediments,

B lateral view to show reduced scales,

C ventral view showing the abdominal depression;

D: *Cryodraco antarcticus* Dollo, 450 m, Antarctic continental plateau below pack ice, temp. -0.3°C, length 20 cm, sandy ooze and erratic sediments.

Note that Dollo (1904) commented at length on the unusual ventral fins of this species and compared it for other bathyal fish species. For the abdominal pocket in *Racovitzaia glacialis* he considered it to be for egg incubation, although he did not find eggs there.

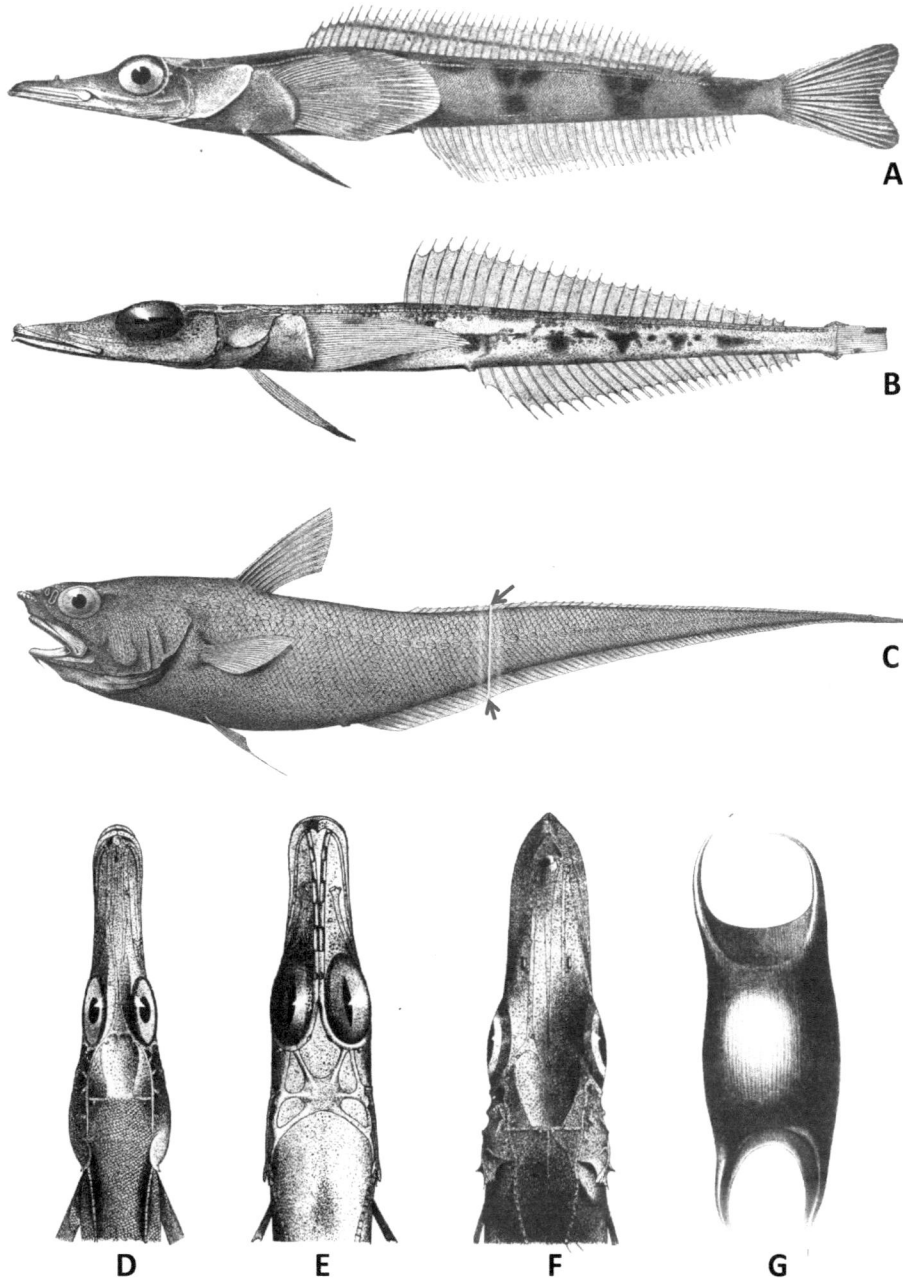

Figure 9.5.2

A: *Gerlachea australis* Dollo, 450 m, continental plateau below pack ice, calcareous ooze with little sand and erratic rocks, 0.3°C, length 18 cm;

B: *Racovitzaia glacialis* Dollo, 435 m, sandy ooze and terrigenous sediments; -0.2°C, length: 8.2 cm;

C: *Nematonurus lecointei* Dollo, 70°40'S, 102°15'W, 2800 m, 0.5°C, 14 March 1899, ooze and erratic rocks, just coming out of the pack ice, 48.2 cm, brown except for except the skin fold separating the pre-nostril from the post-nostril and the edge of the branchiostegeal membrane which are black; **D-F:** Dorsal views of head:,

D: *Gerlachea australis*, length of head 5 cm;

E: *Racovitzaia glacialis*, length of head 27.5 cm;

F: *Cryodraco antarcticus*, length of head 5.3 cm;

G: horny eggs shell of *Raja arctowski* Dollo, length 6 cm, depth 400-569 m, Antarctica.

Note in **C** the grey arrows show the fold in the large illustrated page that could not be removed.

171

Figure 9.5.3.

A, C: Fish specimens kept in alcohol in jars in the store room at RBINS; all specimens were described by L. Dollo, with top row showing labels and reverse side showing the specimens;

B-D: assembled photograph of the holotype of *Macrurus lecointei* prepared by the RBINS photographer Thierry Hubin (the specimen is now kept in a horizontal glass jar and restauration was made to the specimen which is tied to a transparent plate to regain its original shape. Originally, the specimen was kept vertically in a glass jar (like in C) and was partly bent/deformed, **B** showing the detail of the head, and **D** the entire specimen with label.

Figure 9.5.4 (right) Map produced by Louis Dollo to show the 30 locations in Antarctic waters and the subantarctic zone where fish have been observed in a detailed manner. Dollo (1904) referred all these species in his monograph. The red dots and line refer to locations of Belgica collections. Note the shape given to the Antarctic mainland (shown in brown) which was still poorly defined which Dollo and others refered to this area as 'Antarctide'.

ATLANTIQUE

AFRIQUE

AMÉRIQUE

INDIQUE

Tristan da Cunha

Limite Septentrionale de la Zone Subantarctique = Isotherme de Température moyenne annuelle de la Surface de l'Océan 45°=45°

Bouvet

Marion

Challenger

Valdivia

Challenger

Sandwich du Sud

Challenger

Géorgie du Sud

Challenger

Crozet

Cercle Polaire Antarctique

Orcades du Sud

Kerguelen

St Paul

Juan Fernandez

Melvinnes

Challenger

I. Dick Charritz

Balleny

ANTARCTIQUE

A. Magellanique

Challenger

Lutken

Belgica

Gauss

Belgica

I. Guillaume II

Pierre I

Challenger

Mowwan

Belgica

ANTARCTIDE

Challenger

Southern Cross

Dougherty

Erebus & Terror

I. Victoria

Challenger

Limite Extrême de la Banquise

Southern Cross

Erebus & Terror

Challenger

Marquarie

Campbell

PACIFIQUE

Auckland

AUSTRALIE

Chatham Warekauri

Tasmanie

Nouvelle

Zélande

173

9.6 Other biota

KEY POINTS

In this section, documentation on the following groups is presented after a list of all the groups covered in the Reports dealt by the 'Commission de la Belgica' is tabled.

These are:

- Jellyfish
- Micro-mollusks
- Free-living polychaetes
- Sponges
- Diatoms
- Hydroc orals
- Tunicates
- Brachiopods

The comprehensive list of publications that appeared as a result of the Belgica expedition (see Table 9.6.1) is indeed extremely impressive. The biological material makes a total of 2124 pages comprising of 512 pages dealing with the flora (7 volumes) and 1512 pages dealing with animals (54 volumes), plus an additional 512 pages when considering the book on seals based on Ravcovitza's notes published posthumously by Murariu in 2016. This compares with only 344 pages published in 1902 by the British Museum (Lankaster (editor), 1902) as a result of the *Southern Cross* expedition that returned from Cape Adare in Antarctica.

Table 9.6.1 Comprehensive list of all the publications that appeared (or were to appear but never did) in the "Résultats du voyage du *S.Y. Belgica* en 1897-1898- 1899 – rapports scientifiques" as published by the Commission de la Belgica, and funded by the Belgian government by order of the Belgian King Léolopld II. List modified from de Broyer and Kuyken (2001).

List of official scientific reports as scheduled by the "Commission de la Belgica"
Modified from de Broyer and Kuyken, 2001)

In 1900, members of the 'Commission" planned the publications of the expedition to appear in 10 volumes. Those published are marked here by an asterisk. Some were authored by different people, and some were never published. Note, for example, none of vol. X, all by F.A. Cook were never published.

Volume I

*Relation du voyage et résumé des résultats, by A. de Gerlache de Gomery.
*Travaux hydrographiques et instructions nautiques, by G. Lecointe.
Note relative à l'usage des explosifs sur la banquise, by G. Lecointe.

Volume II Astronomy & Magnetism

*Etudes des chronomètres (deux parties), by G. Lecointe.
Recherche des positions du navire durant la dérive, by G. Lecointe.
Observations magnétiques, by Ch. Lagrange and G. Lecointe.
*Notes relatives aux mesures pendulaires, by G. Lecointe.
Conclusions générales sur les observations astronomiques et magnétiques, by M. Guyou.

Volume III-IV Meteorology

*Rapport sur les observations météorologiques horaires, by H. Arctowski.
*Rapport sur les observations des nuages, by A. Dobrowolski.
*La neige et le givre, by A. Dobrowolski.
*Phénomènes optiques de l'atmosphère, by H. Arctowski.
*Aurores australes, by H. Arctowski.
Discussion des résultats météorologiques, by A. Lancaster.

Zoology

Foraminifères, by A. Kemna et E. Van den Broeck.
Radiolaires, by Fr. Dreyer.
Tintinoides, by K. Brandt.
*Spongiaires, by E. Topsent.
*Hydraires, by C. Hartlaub.
*Hydrocoralliaires, by E. von Marenzeller.
*Siphonophores, by C. Chun.
*Méduses, by L. Schultze.
Alcyonaires, by Th. Studer.
*Pénnatulides, by H. F. E. Jungersen.
*Actiniaires, by O. Carlgren.
*Madréporaires, by E. von Marenzeller.
*Cténophores, by C. Chun.
*Holothuries, by E. Hérouard.
*Astérides, by H. Ludwig.
*Echinides et Ophiures, by R. Kœhler.
*Crinoides, by J. A. Bather.
*Planaires, by L. Böhmig.
Céstodes,Trématodes et Acanthocéphales, by P. Cerfontaine.
*Némertes, by O. Bürger.
*Nématodes libres, by J. D. de Man.
Nématodes parasites, by J. Guiart.
Chaetognathes, by O. Steinhaus.
Géphyriens, by j. W. Spengel.
*Oligochètes, by P. Cerfontaine.
*Polychètes, by G. Pruvot et E. G. Racovitza.
*Bryozoaires, by A. W. Waters.
*Brachiopodes, by L. Joubin.
Rotifères et Tardigrades, by C. Zelinka.
Phyllopodes, by E. Hérouard.
*Ostracodes, by G. W. Müller.
*Copépodes, by W. Giesbrecht.
*Cirripèdes, by P. P. C. Hoek.
*Crustacés édryophthalmes, by J. Bonnier.
*Schizopodes et Cumacés, by H. J. Hansen.
Crustacés décapodes, by H. Coutière.
*Pycnogonides, by G. Pfeffer.
*Acariens libres, by A. D. Michael et E. Trouessart.
*Acariens parasites, by G. Neumann.
*Aranéides, by E. Simon.

Volume V Oceanography & Geology

Rapport sur les sondages et les fonds marins recueillis,
    by H. Arctowski and A.-F. Renard.
*Rapport sur les relations thermiques de l'océan,
    by H. Arctowski and R. Mill.
*Détermination de la Densité de l'eau de mer,
    by J. Thoulet.
*Rapport sur la Densité de l'eau de mer,
    by H. Arctowski and J. Thoulet.
Note sur la couleur des eaux océaniques,
    by H. Arctowski.
*Les glaces antarctiques (journal d'observations rela-
    tives aux icebergs et à la banquise),
    by H. Arctowski.
Note relative à la géographie physique des terres
    antarctiques, by H. Arctowski.
La géologie des terres antarctiques, by A.-F. Renard.
*Note sur quelques plantes fossiles des terres magel-
    laniques, by M. Gilkinet.

Volume VI-IX Botany & Zoology
Botany

*Diatomées (moins Chaetocérés), by H. Van Heurck.
Péridiniens et Chaetocérés, by Fr. Schütt.
*Algues, by E. De Wildeman.
*Champignons, by Ch. Bommer and M. Rousseau.
*Lichens, by E. A. Wainio.
*Hépatiques, by F. Stephani.
*Mousses, by J. Cardot.
Cryptogames vasculaires, by Ch. Bommer.
*Phanérogames, by E. De Wildeman.

*Myriapodes, by C. Attems.
*Collemboles, by V. Willem.
*Orthoptères, by C. Brunner von Wattenwyl.
*Hemiptères, by E. Bergroth.
Pédiculides, by V. Willem.
*Diptères, by J. C. Jacobs.
*Coléoptères, by H. Schouteden, E. Rousseau,
    A. Grouvelle, E. Olivier, A. Lameere, H. Boileau,
    E. Brenske, J. Bourgeois and L. Fairmaire.
*Hyménoptères, by C. Emery, J. Tosquinet, E. André
    and J. Vachal.
*Solénoconques, by L. Plate.
*Amphineures, Gastropodes et Lamellibranches,
    by P. Pelseneer.
*Céphalopodes, by L. Joubin.
*Tuniciers, by E. Van Beneden.
*Poissons et Reptiles, by L. Dollo.
Bile des oiseaux antarctiques, by P. Portier.
Oiseaux (Biologie), by E. G. Racovitza.
*Oiseaux (Systématique), by Howard Saunders.
*Cétacés, by E. G. Racovitza.
Embryogénie des pinnipèdes, by E. Van Beneden.
*Organogénie des pinnipèdes, by J. Brachet and
    H. Leboucq.
Encéphale des pinnipèdes, by J. Brachet.
Pinnipèdes (Biologie), by E. G. Racovitza.
*Pinnipèdes (Systématique), by E. Barrett-Hamilton.
Bactéries de l'intestin des animaux antarctiques,
    by J. Cantacuzène.
Biogéographie de l'Antarctide, by E. G. Racovitza.

Volume X Anthropology

Medical Report, by F.-A. Cook.
Report upon the Onas, by F.-A. Cook.
A Yahgan Grammar and Dictionary, by F.-A. Cook.

In this book, it is not possible to discuss all the organisms that are described in the 'Résultats' and only a select few illustrations are presented here to show their high quality. It appears that many of the plates with exquisite drawings, sometimes in colour, in those publications were in fact inserted separately in the volumes published by J. E. Buschman in Antwerp, the printer of all the volumes over some 45 years. These plates were made elsewhere by other expert printing houses, frequently outside Belgium.

Here, a selection of pages are reproduced but the reader is encouraged to examine many of the other publications, all of which are available in many libraries, but also on line for free at the Flanders Marine Institute (www.VLIZ. be) in Belgium.

The following figures give an example of some of the illustrations of Belgica material.

These are: Jellyfish (Medusae) by Otto Maas on Fig. 9.6.1, Micro-molluscs described by Paul Pelseneer on Fig. 9.6.2, Free polychaete worms by Pierre Fauvel on Fig. 9.6.3, Sponges by Emile Topsent on Fig. 9.6.4, Diatoms by Henri Van Heurck on Fig. 9.6.5, Hydrocorals by Emil von Marenzeller on Fig. 9.6.6, and Tunicates by Van Beneden de Selys-Longchams (1913) on Fig. 9.6.7 and brachiopods by Louis Joubin (1902) on Fig. 9.6.8.

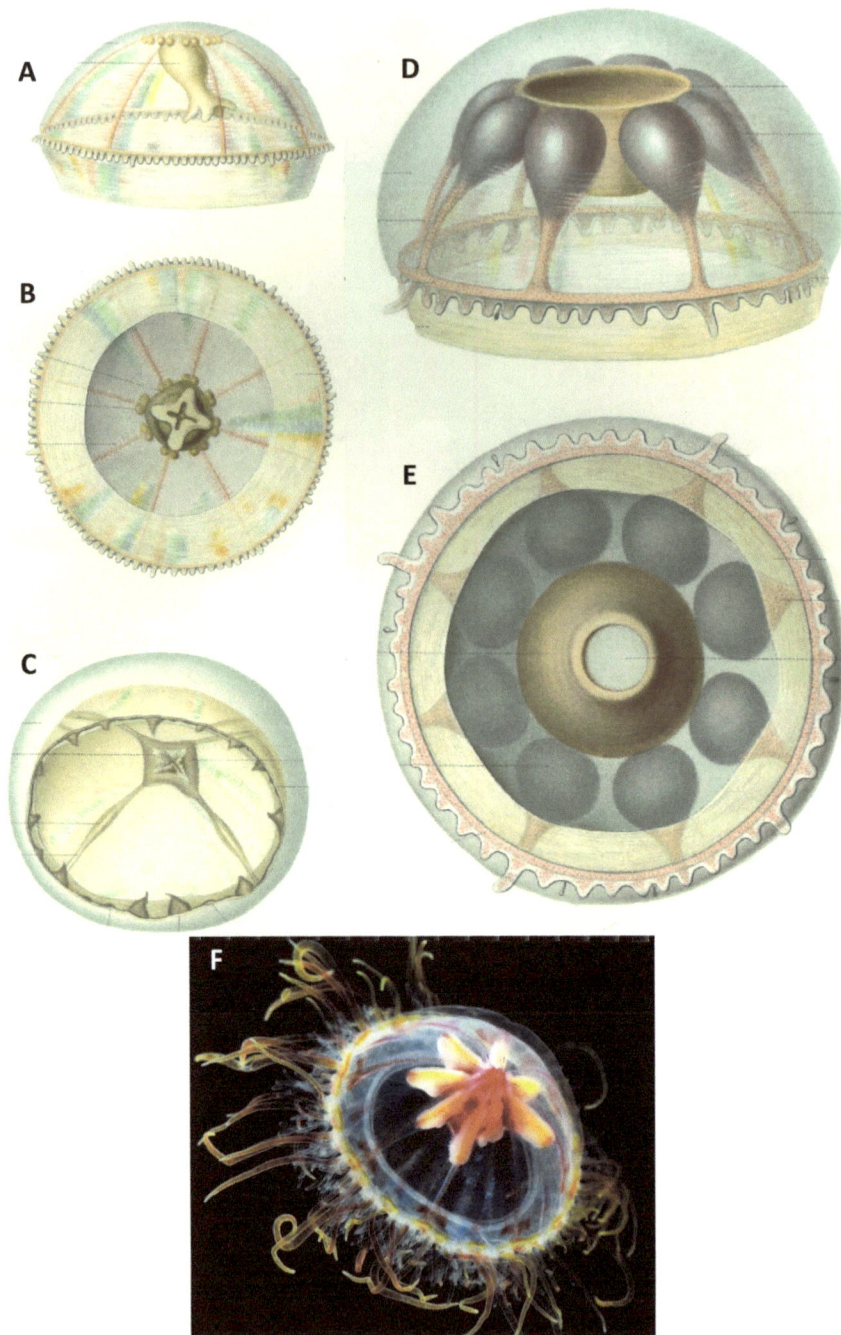

Figure 9.6.1. Reproduction of medusae (jellyfish) described and illustrated by O. Maas.

A, B: *Isonema amplum* Vanhöffen;

C: *Phialidium (Clytia) iridescens* Maas;

D-E: *Homoionema racovitzae* Maas;

F: *in situ* photograph of likely to be *Homoionema racovitzae* taken by Christoph Held (Alfred Wegener Institute for Polar and Marine Research) at 492 m water depth, near Racovitza Island at 64°24.345'S 61°54.986'W. This figure clearly shows that Emil Racovitza did preserve his biological material in excellent condition in that Otto Maas was able to illustrate the medusae's soft tissues very well. The modern-day photo indicates this superbly.

Note the specimens are extremely small, indeed some 2.5 mm.

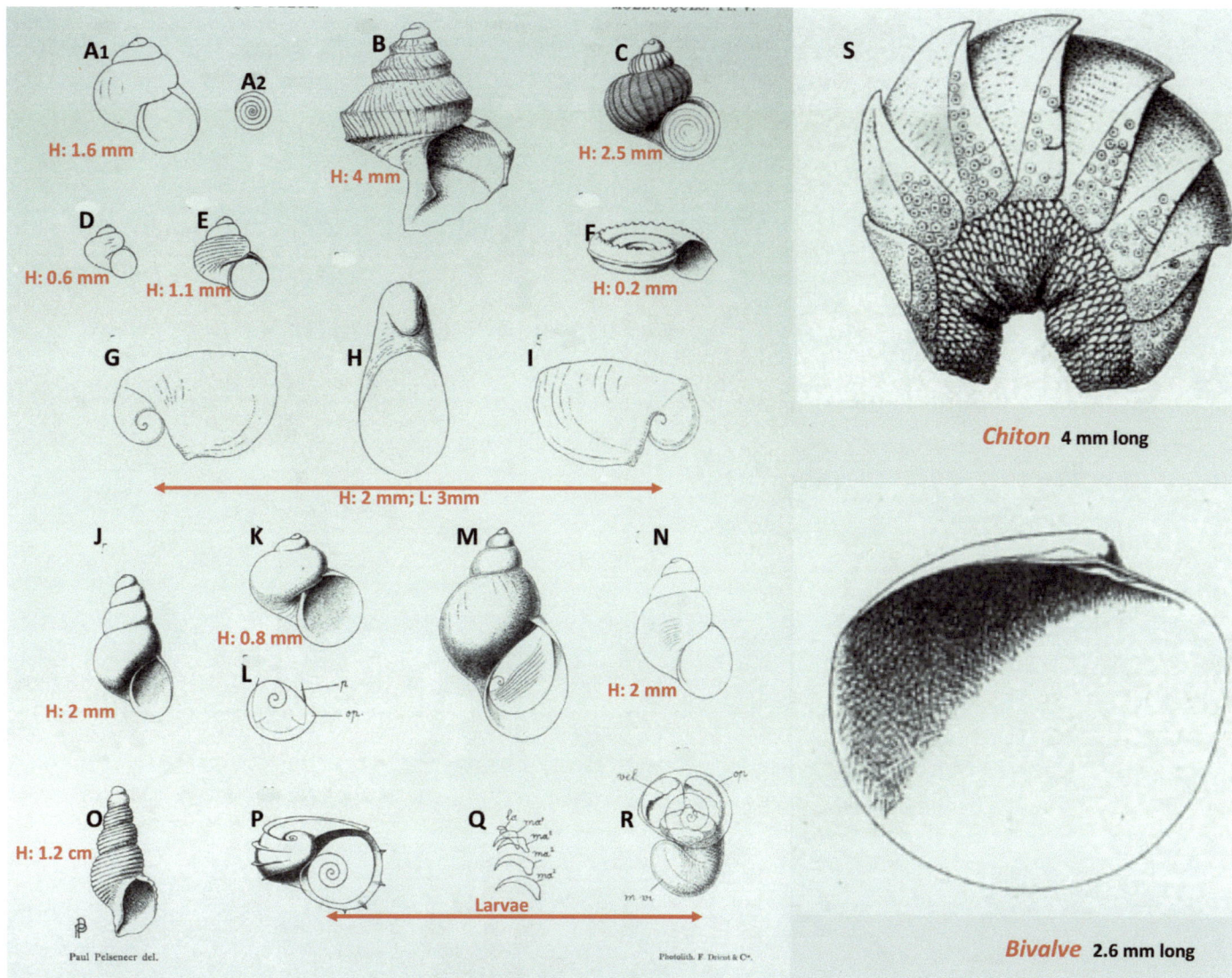

Figure 9.6.2 Micro-molluscs described by Paul Pelseneer:

A: *Tharsis globose* P.;

B: *Margarita lamellosa* P.;

C: *Cyclostrema decussatum* P.;

D: *Cyclostrema humile* P.;

E: *Cyclostrema liratulum*

P.; F: *Circulus perlatus* P.;

G: Capulus subcompressus P. side view;

H: *C. subcompressus* P. view from the opening side;

I: *C. subcompressus* P. left side;

J: *Rissoa (Setia) columna* P.;

K: *Rissoa (Setia) inflata* P. aperture view;

L: *R. (Setia) inflata* P. dorsal view with operculum attached to the foot;

M: *Lavilittorina elongata* P.;

N: *Rissoa (? Ceratia) subtruncata* P.;

O: *Sipho antarctidis* P.;

P: pelagic larva of *Streotoneure taenioglosse*;

Q: same larva radula teeth;

R: same larva taken out of the shell; **Other molluscs**

S: *Leptochiton belgicae* P.;

T: *Callocardia laevis* internal view of left valve.
(P. is an abbreviation for Pelseneer).

Note the small sizes of all specimens, indicating that Racovitza spent much time sorting this small material in his laboratory.

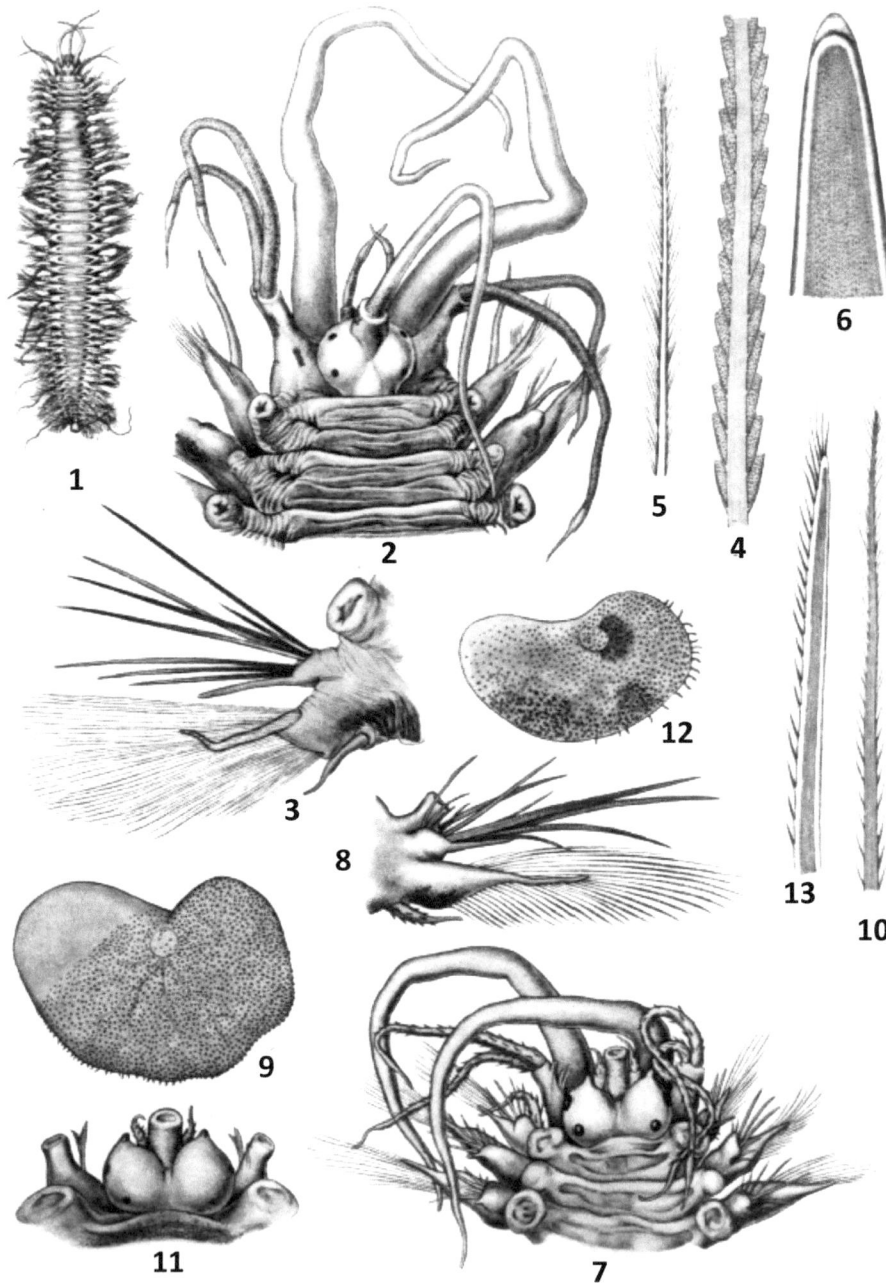

Figure 9.6.3 Free-living polychaetes.
1-6: *Antinoë hastulifera* Peuvot
1: entire animal;
2: anterior region;
3: parapod;
4: base of a ventral hair (soie);
5: extremity of a ventral soie;
6: extremity of a dorsal 'soie';
7-10: *Antinoë antarctica* Bergström,
7: anterior region;
8: parapod;
9: elytra;
10: extremity of a ventral 'soie';
11-13: *Antinoë antarctica* var. *fulges* Peuvot;
11: head;
12: elytra;
13: extremity of a ventral 'soie'.

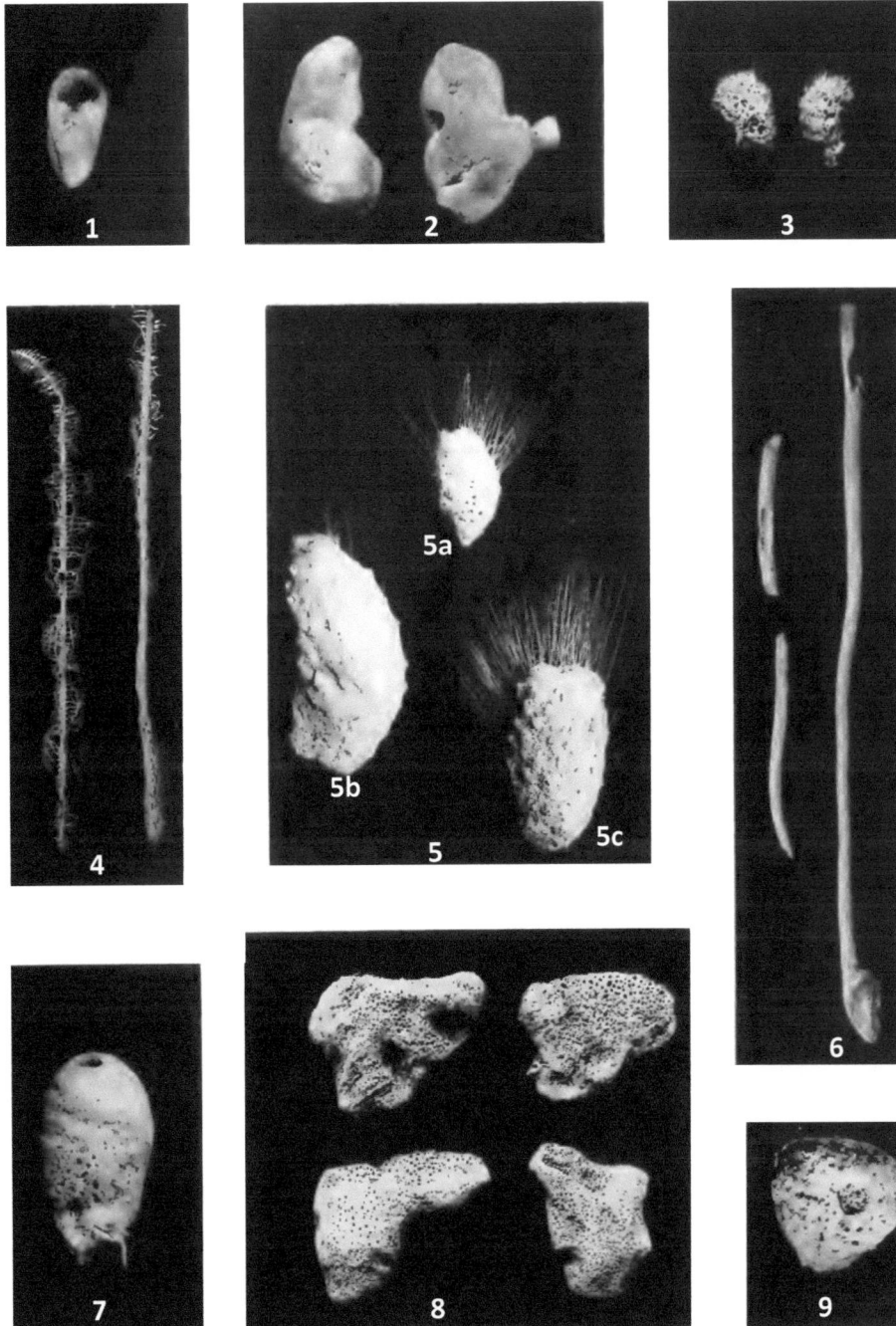

Figure 9.6.4 Sponges (rearranged plate)

1: *Bathydorus spinosus*;

2: *Halisarca dujardini* var. *magellanica*;

3: *Desmacidon setifer* Topsent;

4: *Cladorrhiza (Asbestopluma) belgicae* Topsent;

5: *Rossella racovitzae* Topsent (**5a-5c** are 3 different specimens); **6:** *Caulophacus ?* sp.;

7: *Rossella nuda* Topsent;

8: *Chonelasma* sp.;

9. *Gellius rudis* Topsen. All the new species named by Topsent bear his name.

Note that since the Belgica expedition, Cataneo-Vietti et al. (1996) have since described an amazing development of the *Rossella racovitzae* sponge that can reach up to 1 m in height and that filamentous green algae were found inside the sponge suggesting that light energy might reach the inside of the sponge. It was found that some sponge spicules bent to 90° angle do conduct red light. These authors showed that the siliceous spicules can act as optical fibres. In addition, diatoms were found adhering to the spicules and are helped by light transfer via the spicules. Those sponges were collected in the Ross Sea.

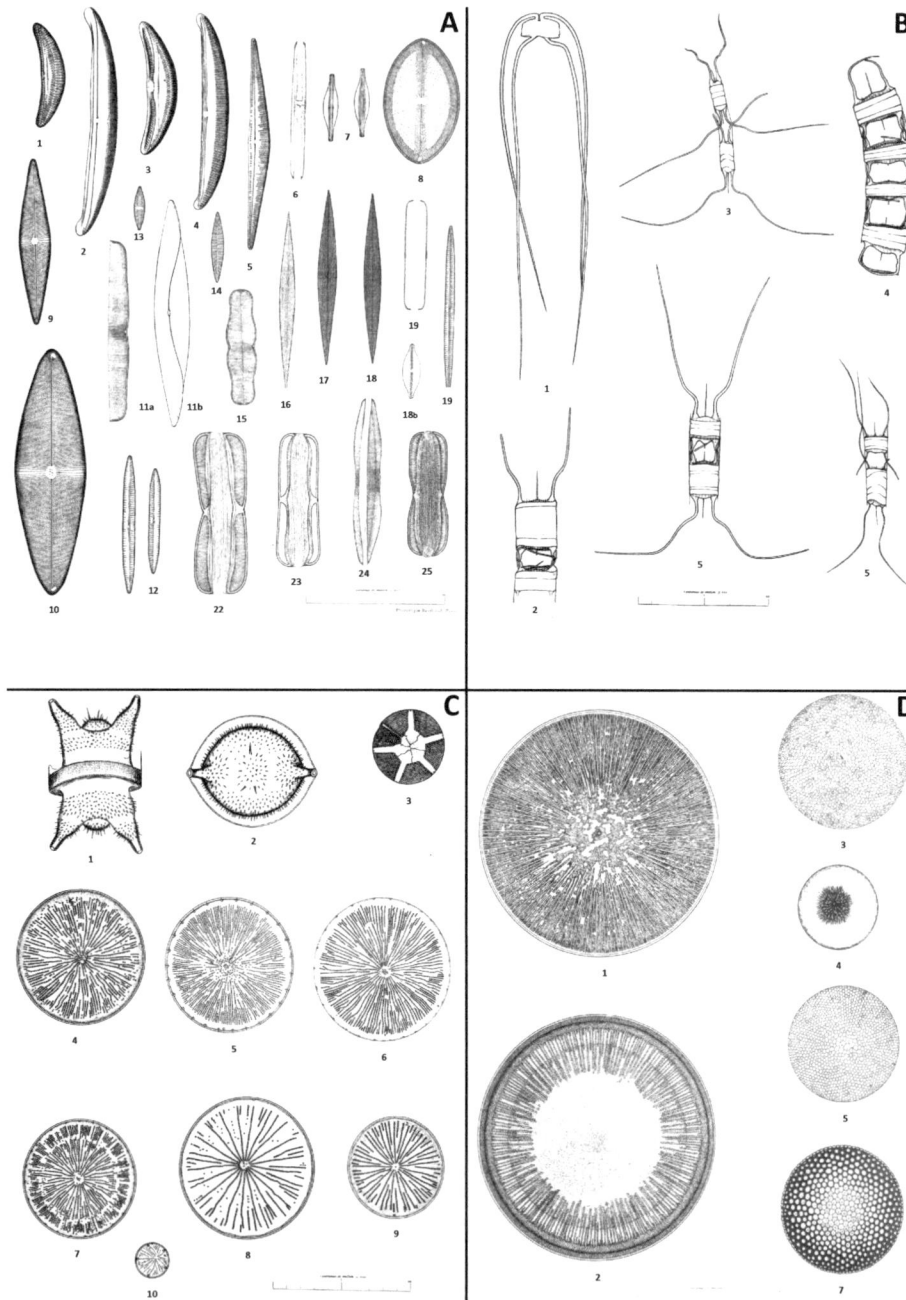

Diatoms secrete a siliceous frame, with two 'valves' looking a bit like a pill box. These remains are abundant in both marine and freshwater sediments and can help reconstruct past environments. Some diatoms thrive below the sea ice, so those species can help reconstruct the extent of the sea ice through time by identifying their remains in sediment cores taken from the sea floor. Diatoms are also an important part of the food web in the oceans, especially in polar oceans.

Figure 9.6.5

Diatom frustules A:

1,3: *Amphora racovitzae* VH;

2: *A. peragallorum* VH;

4: *A. peragallorum* var. *robusta* VH;

5: *A. angusta* Greg. var. *angustissima* VH;

6: *A. arcta* Schm.;

7: *A. cymbelloides* Grun.;

8: *Navicula praetexta* Ehr. var. *antarctica* VH;

9: *N. rhombica* Greg. var;

10: *N. schuetti* VH;

11a: *Amphiprora (Amphiropsis) belgicae* var. *major* VH;

11b: idem valval face;

12: *Navilula jejunoides* VH;

13: *N. glaciei* VH;

14: *N. frequens* VH;

15: *Amphiprora belgicae* VH;

16-18: *Navicula trompii* HV; —18b: *Van heurckia rhomboides* Breb. var. *crassinervis* forme *antarctica*;

19: *Amphipora ?;*

20: *Navicula jejunoides* forme *longissima* VH;

22: *Amphiprora oestrupii* HV;

23: idem var. *minor;*

24: *A. oestrupii ?;*

25: *A. kjellmanii* Cl. var. *subtilissima* VH.

B: 1: *Chaetoceras curvatum;*

2-6: *Chaetoceras dischaeta;*

C: 1: *Asteromphalus hookeri;* 2: *Coscinodiscus bifrons;* 3-4, 6-7: *Coscinodiscus chromoradiatus;* 5: *Coscinodiscus australis;* 8-9: *Biddulphia ottomulleri* VH var. *rotunda* VH; 10: *Actinocyclus polygonus* var.?.

D: 1: *Podosira?,* 2: *Hyalodiscus (?) pantocsekii* VH; 3, 5: *Coscinodiscus radiatus;* 4: ?; 6: *Coscinodiscus decrescens.*

Note: All species followed by 'VH' were named by Van Heurck.

Such collections of calcareous organisms are important nowadays so as to be able to reconstruct past ocean chemistries, but even past temperatures through the analysis of elemental ratios and oxygen isotopes in their skeletons that vary with water temperature. In addition, since the Belgica material was collected before atomic bombs were exploded, the isotopic carbon (C^{14}) composition of the biological carbonate making such hydrocorals can be identified and used for dating carbonate shells obtained from deep-sea sediment cores. (See https://www.radiocarbon.com/carbon-dating-bomb-carbon.htm).

Figure 9.6.6 Photographs of the hydrocoral *Errina gracilis* von Marenzeller.

A: original photograph shown in von Marenzeller (1903) publication;

B: same specimen photographed on its other side in among the RBINS collections.

Note the calcareous tube worm attached to the specimen. Material collected on the sea floor using a Faubert sampler in May 1898 in the Bellingshausen Sea.

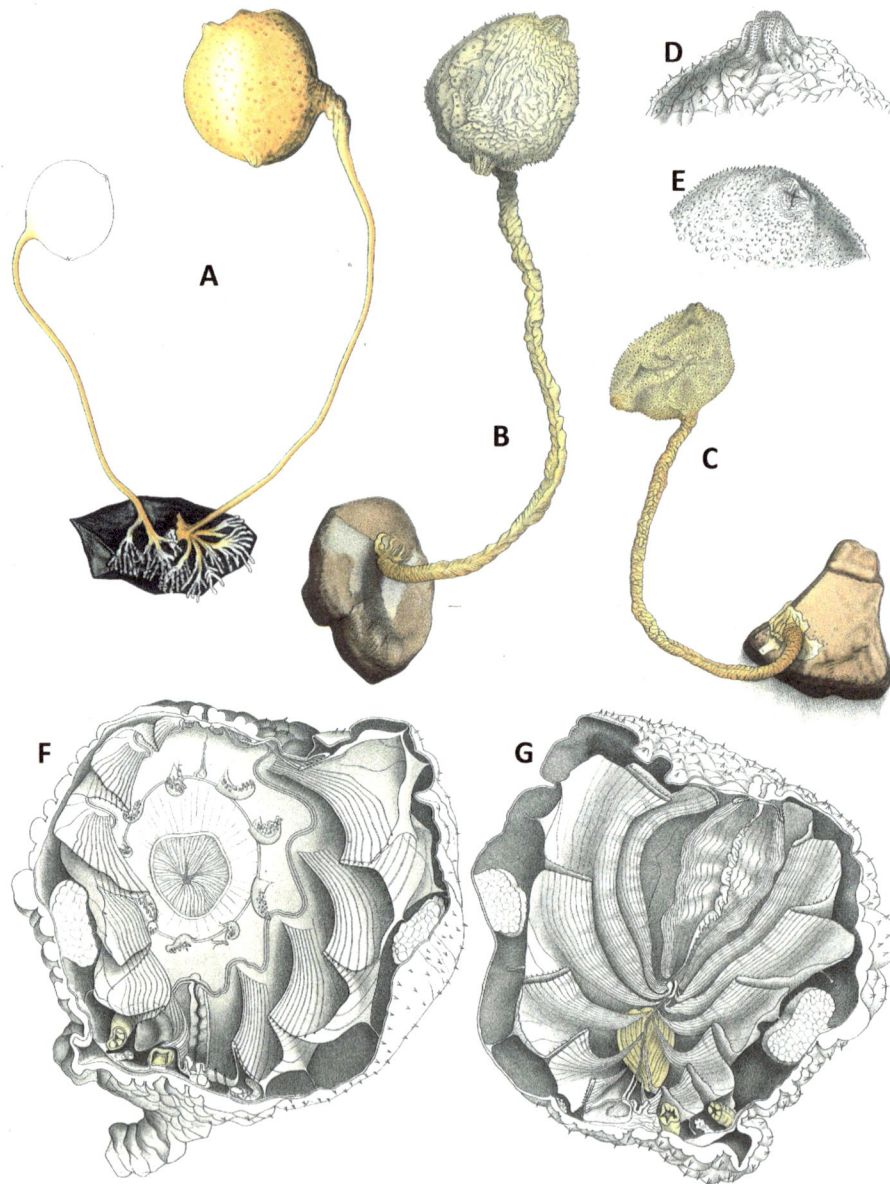

Figure 9.6.7 Tunicata (=Ascidians) *Boltenia antarctica* originally described as a new species by Van Beneden and de Selys-Longchams (1913), but now synonymised to *Pyura georgiana* (Michaelsen, 1898) by Clarke and Johnson (2003).

A: Two specimens fixed to a stone, based on a sketch of living organisms prepared by E. Racovitza;

B, C: individuals as preserved;

D: cloacal siphon of the right hand specimen;

E: buccal siphon of the left hand specimen;

F: anterior half of B, interior view:

G: posterior half of the same specimen seen from inside. Material collected on 18 October 1898, at 580 m water depth, at approximately 70°01'S, 80°48'W.

Note that Edouard Van Beneden was an important advisor during the preparations of the Belgica expedition and after it he sat on the Belgica Commission that was overseeing the publications of the results of that expedition.

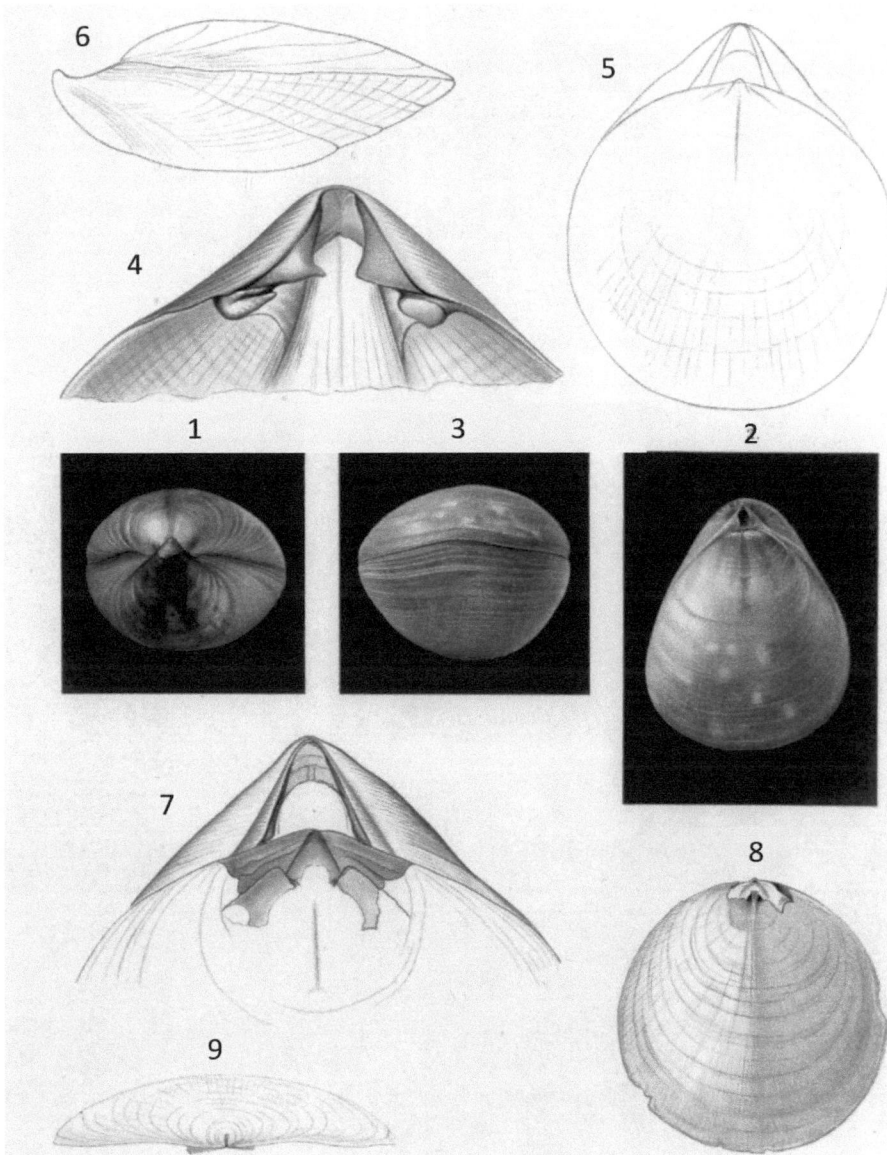

Brachipods have long history of evolution and were prominent during the Palaeozoic era. They are much rarer today. Nevertheless, Racovitza collected only a few small specimens which he sent to Professor Louis Joubin from the University in Rennes which the latter described in the 'Résultats' series.

All specimens were very small. *Rhynchonella racovitzae* was 12 mm long and obtained from a depth of 500 m at 70°S, 80°48'W on October18, 1898 when the ship was trapped in the sea ice. *Rhynchonella gerlachei* was only 4 mm long and obtained at a depth of ~450 m at 71°14'S, 89° 14" W on May 12, 1898, as well as the other station listed above. One of Joubin's plate is reproduced here (Fig. 9.6.8).

Figure 9.6.8 Brachiopoda **1-4**: *Rhynchonella racovitzae* **1**: posterior view showing its 'hook', **2**: dorsal view, **3**: anterior view showing the sinuosity of the commissure of both valves, **4**: internal view of the peduncle area. **5-9**: *Rhynchonella gerlachei* **5**: ventral view, **6**: side view of both valves seen from the right side, **7**: peduncle view; **8**: internal view of the dorsal valve, **9**: rear view of the dorsal valve.

Crew members in the process of using the winch through a hole in the sea ice to collect water samples, plankton, fish and sea floor sediments. Photo reproduced with permission from the Racovitza Archive, The Library of the Romanian Academy, Cluj-Napoca.

Chapter 10

Study of sea floor sediments by Arctowski and Renard

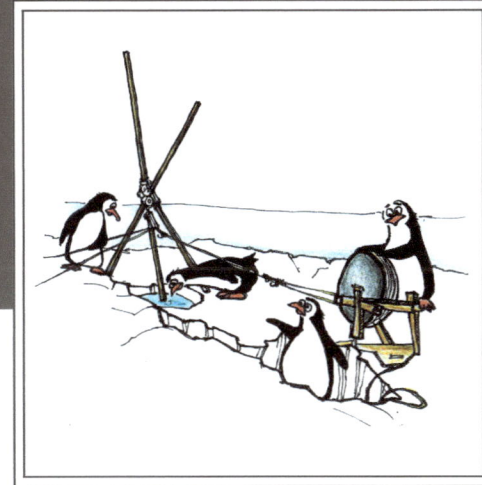

KEY POINTS

- The composition and granulometry of the 60 samples collected from the sea floor during the Belgica expedition has been assessed because the death of the main investigator Professor A.-F. Renard prevented completion of the work.

- Maps were produced for the first time to show the location of the samples using the data of Arctowski and Renard (1900, 1901).

- A map showing the percentage of gravel and coarse sand informs us of the iceberg traffic in the Bellingshausen Sea that may have occurred above the two deep-sea troughs (Latady and Belgica) where we know there are strong undercurrents, many of which are moving away from the coastline.

- Surprisingly, despite being in very cold waters, there is a large percentage of samples that contain remains of organisms with a $CaCO_3$ skeleton. An unexpected phenomenon seen in cold and CO_2-rich waters that would otherwise dissolve those skeletons.

Arctowski and Renard

With Henryk Arctowski having the responsibility of anything geological during the Belgica expedition, he consulted with his mentor Professor Alphonse-François Renard (Fig. 10.1) who was not only a geologist but also a supporter of the expedition. In chapter 2, mention is already made of his extensive study of deep-sea floor sediments published with John Murray after the Challenger expedition. This explains why sediments obtained by dredging for all the soundings in both Drake Passage as well as in the Bellingshausen Sea were sent to him by Arctowski on return to Antwerp after the expedition. All the samples were partly studied in Ghent where Renard held a Chair of Geology. Fairly rapidly, two publications appeared providing preliminary results of the investigations made on those sea floor sediments (Arctowski and Renard, 1900, 1901). However, the final results and their interpretation never came to light because Professor Renard died of cancer in 1903, leaving several tasks related to the Belgica expedition unfinished and that included the description of the rocks which Arctowski had collected on the Antarctic Peninsula

as well as in the Beagle Channel. It is likely that Renard with the help of Arctowski had intended to publish a geological map of both areas. Eventually, two Czech scientists (A. Pelikan (1909, for de Gerlache Strait) and D. Sistek (1912, for the Beagle Channel)) published the rock description as part of the expedition's 'Résultats" (see chapters 7.8).

A full account of the period towards the end of Renard's life is sadly reported by his young wife. Having been a Jesuit priest before marrying, Renard encountered vociferously nasty reactions to his decision to leave the Catholic Church from not only the ecclesiastic community in Belgium but also government people. In fact, after his death, a statue was erected in Ixelles in Brussels in his memory: (https://en.wikipedia.org/wiki/Alphonse_Fran%C3%A7ois_Renard#/media/File:Alphonse_Renard_by_Alphonse_de_Tombay_(Brussels)_-_september_2019.jpg,) but it was paid by the international community in recognition for his scientific achievements, not the Belgian community!

Figure 10.1 Photograph of Professor Alphonse-François Renard extracted from Henriette Renard pamphlet on her husband published after his death in 1907. The photo was 'colorized' using palette.fm/color/filters.

Figure 10.2. Photograph of Henryk Arctowski obtained from the Vaslui Museum Archive courtesy of Dr Oana Mocanu. The photo was 'colorized' using palette.fm/color/filters.

A total of 60 sea floor sediment samples had been collected by Arctowski during the expedition. Arctowski and Renard (1900) described on how the samples were obtained. A 'Leblanc sounding machine' (https://digitalcollections.lib.washington.edu/digital/collection/fishimages/id/53139 was used and it seems that it was a modified sampler originally designed by the Prince of Monaco for his sampling of the sea floor. We know that at least Racovitza went to Monaco to inspect the Prince's yacht and many of his oceanographic equipment. On the ship also instruments donated by the Commander Wandell from Copenhagen to collect bottom sediment were used. The equipment was lowered using surprisingly a very thin steel cable (0.9 mm in diameter). While in the sea ice, the equipment and cable were lowered though a hole in the ice using a winch (see Fig. 10.3) modified by Max van Rhysselberghe, the young engineer on the ship.

Figure 10.3 Photograph showing members of the crew in the process of lowering equipment down a hole in the sea ice in order to make a vast number of measurements (water temperature, salinity) as well as retrieve plankton, benthic organisms on the sea floor as well as collected bottom sediments. Note that the hole remained next to ship while it was trapped and drifted with the sea ice. Photo reproduced with permission from the Emil Racovitza Archive, The Library of the Romanian Academy, Cluj-Napoca Branch. This photo was processed using Photoshop© to improve clarity and has been 'colorized' using palette.fm/color/filters.

Station no.	Date	Lat. S	Long. E	Depth (m)	mud <0.1mm	very fine <0.2mm	fine <0.25mm	medium 0.5mm	coarse >0.5 mm	gravel >2mm	CaCO3 %	description
1	14.1.98	54°54'	63°37'	296								
2	14.1.98	55°0'3	63°29'	1564								
3	15.1.98	55°51'	63°19'	4010								
4	16.1.98	56°49'	64°40'	3850								
5	18.1.98	59°58'	63°12'	3800	83.37	4.5	9.37	1.4	1.36	0	19.34	
6	19.1.98	61°05'	63°04'	3690								calcareous mud, little sand
7	20.1.98	62°02'	61°58'	2900	95.86	0.59	0.1	0.59	2.96	4.52		mud
8	20.1.98	62°11'	61°38'	1880								
9	28.1.98	64°23'	62°02'	625	96.63	1.41	0.58	0.45	0.93	0		sandy mud
10	16.2.98	69°75'	70°39'	135								
11	19.2.98	69°06'	78°21'	480	45.59	19.99	9.84	13.05	11.53	1.67	0.05	
12	23.2.98	69°46'	81°08'	565	90.43	6.92	1.77	0.53	0.35	0	4.24	mud slightly calcareous
13	24.2.98	69°30'	81°31'	510								
14	25.2.98	69°17'	82°25'	2700	93.69	3.26	1.22	0.61	1.22	0	10.27	calcareous mud
15	27.2.98	69°24'	84°39'	2600	90.23	4.36	2.31	1.62	1.16	0	9.84	calcareous mud
16	27.2.98	6941'	84°42'	1730	81.75	7.2	6.17	2.44	0	0	0	mud, little sandy
17	1.3.98	71°06'	85°23'	570	76.6	10.68	4.71	3.9	4.11	1.81	11.98	calcareous mud, little sand
18	1.3.98	71°17'	85°26'	520	78.43	11.02	5.08	5.08	3.39	0	13.01	
19	3.3.98	71°31'	85°16'	460	78.18	9.39	4.42	4.14	3.87	4.11	7.21	
20	4.3.98	71°22'	84°55'	530	86.86	7.29	3.65	1.1	1.1	0.72	15.15	
21	5.3.98	71°19'	85°28'	520	84.6	6.65	3.8	2.38	2.57	2.32	16.26	
22	9.3.98	71°23'	85°33'	554	77.49	5.2	2.6	14.28	0.43	6.85	5.63	
23	20.3.98	71°35'	88°02'	390	66.56	12.31	5.82	6.82	8.49	6.24	1.59	sandy mud, little calcareous
24	22.4.98	71°02'	92°03'	480	83.78	5.86	4.73	3.38	2.25	1.33	7.45	calcareous mud, little sand
25	26.4.98	70°50'	92°22'	410	63.03	12.73	5.45	7.88	10.91	6.25	2.26	calcareous mud
26	4.5.98	70°33'	89°22'	1150	70.6	11.49	11.49	3.43	2.99	11.72	26.48	
27	5.5.98	70°33'	89°22'	730	61.1	17.75	7.83	6.27	7.05	3.04	7.94	
28	10.5.98	70°33'	89°22'	460	81.45	8.65	5.51	3.01	4.38	0.37	11.88	
29	20.5.98	71°16'	87°38'	435	59.66	10.64	7.79	7.79	14.15	0	0	
30	26.5.98	71°13'	87°44'	436	62.13	10.03	5.99	6.8	15.05	0	0	sandy mud
31	2.9.98	70°00'	82°45'	502								
32	9.9.98	69°51'	82°36'	510	71.03	11.21	4.67	5.61	7.48	5.23	0	
33	14.9.98	69°53'	83°04'	480	78.73	14.32	4.04	2.08	0.78	2.29	0	mud, little sand
34	22.9.98	70°23'	82°31'	485	64.74	11.32	7.08	8.11	8.75	9.23	1.13	sandy mud, sligntly calcareous
35	26.9.98	70°21'	82°52'	485	75.62	12.32	5.64	4.06	2.36	0	4.81	sandy mud, sligntly calcareous
36	27.9.98	70°21'	82°39'	480	80.87	10.46	4.48	3.59	0.6	0	0	
37	7.10.98	70°30'	82°48'	480	68.08	12.77	6.39	7.09	5.67	2.33	0.05	
38	16.10.98	69°59'	80°54'	532	76.63	10.05	5.03	4.52	3.77	1.48	1.63	
39	19.10.98	70°01'	81°45'	580	87.99	5.41	2.99	2.04	1.81	0	4.49	
40	24.10.98	69°43'	80°50'	537	70.45	9.55	3.64	5	11.36	2.65	0.05	little sandy mud
41	2.11.98	69°51'	81°24'	518	91.63	4.85	2.03	1.23	0.26	7.87	0	mud
42	10.11.98	70°09'	82°35'	490	75.74	12.5	5.88	4.41	1.47	0	0	mud little sandy
43	28.11.98	70°20'	83°23'	459	53.72	13.22	6.61	9.09	17.36	23.9	5.63	sandy, calcareous mud
44	18.12.98	70°08'	83°30'	443								
45	20.12.98	70°15'	84°06'	569								
46	22.12.98	70°18'	84°51'	645								
47	27.12.98	70°20'	85°52'	630	78.86	13.07	4.32	3.3	0.45	0	0.05	mud, little sandy
48	29.12.98	70°15'	85°51'	660	66.46	11.08	7.59	5.85	9.02	33.61	14.22	
49	31.12.98	70°01'	85°20'	950								
50	2.1.99	69°52'	85°13'	1360	87.54	6.13	2.67	2.08	1.58	0	9.32	mud little sandy
51	2.1.99	69°50'	85°12'	1470	77.35	7.35	2.86	3.77	8.67	5.77	3.08	mud with little sand and calcareous
52	7.1.99	69°52'	85°21'	1490	84.87	5.61	3.06	3.55	3.91	6.66	14.91	calcareous mud, little sand
53	10.2.99	70°34'	93°17'	1166								
54	19.2.99	70°30'	94°12'	1740	95.89	1.59	1	0.86	0.66	0.13	1.5	mud little calcareous
55	2.3.99	70°53'	97°17'	430	82.65	7.35	3.13	3.37	3.5	0.03	0.95	
56	5.5.99	70°51'	97°57'	425	62.76	14.85	6.23	6.51	9.65	2.83	7.56	sandy calcareous mud
57	12.3.99	70°56'	100°18'	504	78.42	11.8	3.88	4.44	1.45	0	5.1	calcareous mud little sand
58	13.3.99	70°50'	102°12'	1195	62.39	16.24	6.84	7.69	6.84	21.48	0.12	calcareous mud little sand
59	14.3.99	70°40'	102°15'	2800	99.35	0.41	0.08	0.08	0.08	0	0	mud
60	23.3.89	56°28'	84°46'	4800	82.92	10.56	4.52	1.5	0.5	0	0	red clay

Table 10.1 List of all sediment samples taken on the sea floor by the *Belgica* from Drake Passage through the de Gerlache Strait, Bellingshausen Sea, and back to the tip of South America giving all the information, especially granulometry as originally provided in Arctowski and Renard (1900). This is reproduced here as the original publication is not easily obtainable.

Already in the laboratory of Professor Renard in Ghent, samples from the 60 soundings were treated, following the protocol already used by Renard and Murray when examining the Challenger samples (see Chapter 2). In summary, the samples were weighed, then treated in hydrochloric acid to dissolve calcium carbonate ($CaCO_3$: principally consisting of remains of planktic organisms such as foraminifera, pteropods and gastropod molluscs) and forcing the precipitation of calcium using a solution of ammonium oxalate; the percentage $CaCO_3$ was then estimated. The remainder after dissolution would have been siliceous (diatom frustules and radiolarian skeletons), minerals as well as rock fragments, and finally an amorphous substance (~0.5 mm in size). Several sieves were used to determine the size of all these particles. All the information is revealed in Table 10.1, having been transcribed from Arctowski and Renard (1901, a publication not so easy to obtain).

Disappointingly, likely due to the illness and eventual death of Renard, the results were never properly assessed, in particular the description of the mineral particles recovered after the dissolution procedure. This was one of Renard's specialties.

Because of this incomplete study, maps using the data from Arctowski and Renard (1900, 1901)'s study are being produced below here. None of the like had been shown before and the data has never been examined by other researchers who have worked in the area. Nevertheless, the maps are very telling. Figure 10.4 provides the location of all the sea floor samples, and shows that the depths of collection varied much, but most frequently between 1,000 and 3000 m. Many of the samples taken in Drake Passage were taken a great depths. This had not been performed before, nor since then. Figure 19.5 shows the dates of the collections.

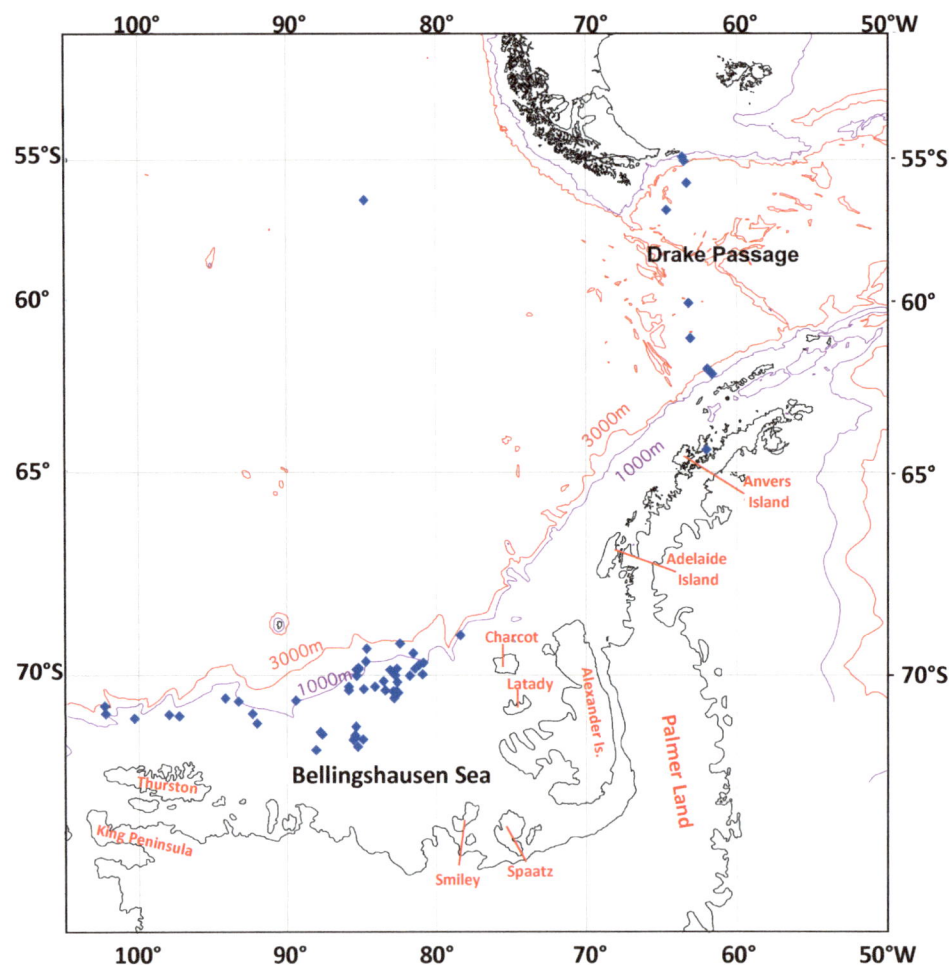

Figure 10.4 Map showing the location of all the sea floor samples taken by the Belgica expedition.

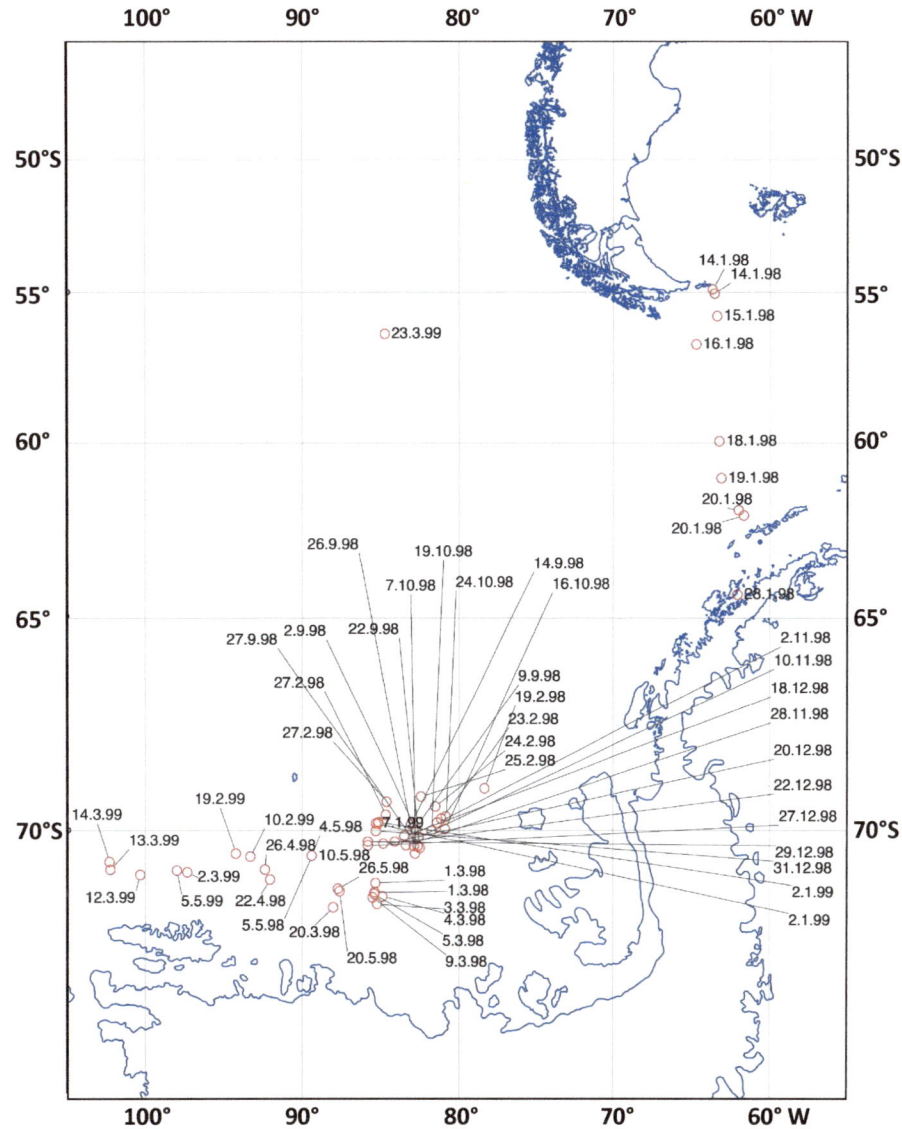

Figure 10.5 Map showing the location of the sea floor samples taken by the Belgica expedition and dates of their collection. Note the samples taken between 28.2.1898 and 14.3.1899 were taken by piercing a whole though the sea ice and lowering the sampling probe. The last sample taken on 23.3.1899 was taken when the ship was in open water on its way back to Punta Arenas. Sample labelled 14.3.1899 was taken as the ship was being liberated from the sea ice.

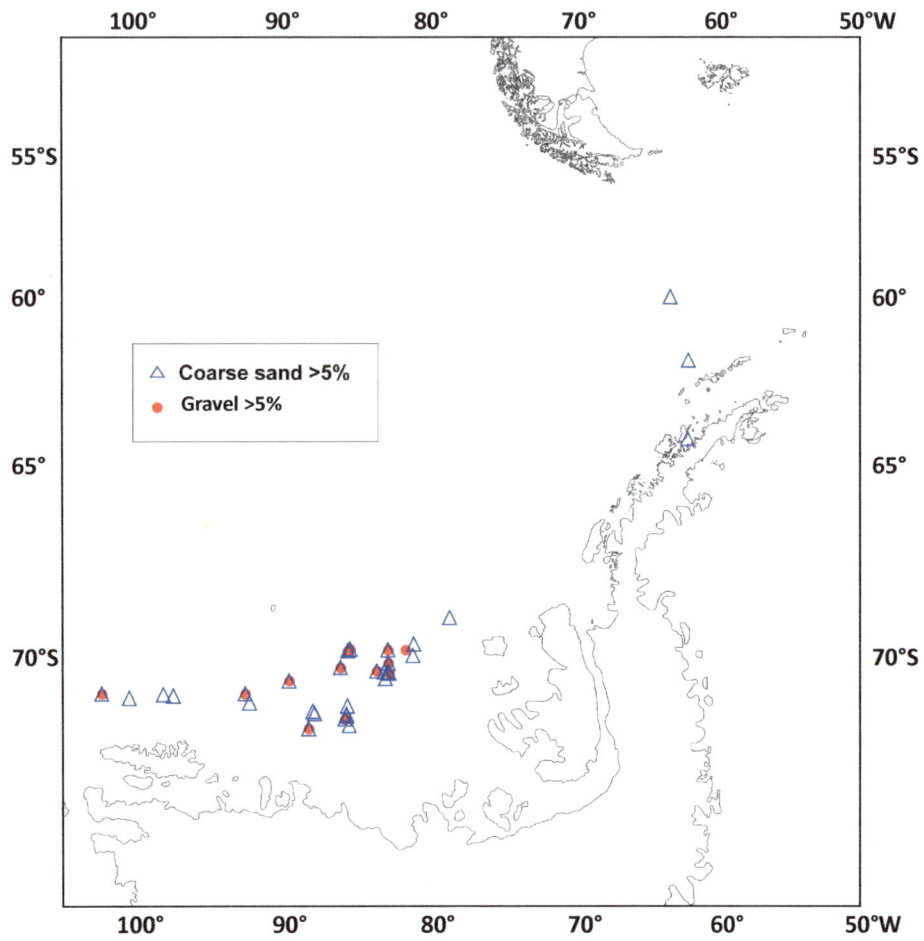

Figure 10.6 Map showing the location of the sea floor samples that contained some coarse material obviously resulting from erratics having been transported in the open was by icebergs and eventually dumped in the open water.

Legend:
△ Coarse sand >5%
● Gravel >5%

Figure 10.6 is very informative in that it shows the samples with a portion of the sediment containing gravel was not uniform in the Bellingshausen Sea. Examination of Table 11.1 tells us that only 10 samples had a large proportion of gravel (>10 % and reaching up 26%). The sea floor at those sample sites much have received a contribution of 'terrigenous' (= coming from the land) material that would have been transported by glaciers. We call these 'drop stones' that eventually fell to the sea floor after partial melting of icebergs. Already several members of the Belgica expedition had confirmed that icebergs were seen to plough through the sea ice (and at some stage were threatening to crush the ship). The second category of samples are those with less gravels, 17 with percentages between >1%and <10%. These indicate still the presence of icebergs that would have caused some drop stones to be deposited, but less frequently. The separation between these two types of samples may inform us the possible 'pathways' of icebergs. Unfortunately, we do not have sufficient data to see if the pathways of those icebergs would have coincided with the presence of the two major deep-sea troughs (Latady and Belgica) over which many undercurrents have today been found (see Schulze Chretien (2021 and Chapter 8.1).

Of interest also is that of the samples taken in Drake Passage only two had coarse sand, and these are on the Antarctic Peninsula side, which makes sense as the source of sandy erratics would be from Graham Land. Members of the Belgica crew in their respective diaries mentioned having seen icebergs very soon after entering Drake Passage, but these were scattered and would have lost the mineral portions underneath them before travelling north towards the tip of South America.

In addition, it is more than likely that the iceberg traffic in the Bellingshausen Sea is to change direction now as a result of the absence of sea ice, at least in summer.

Interestingly, a good percentage of samples were calcareous (see Table 10.1) and would have consisted of the calcite (for foraminifera) and aragonite (for pteropods and some gastropods), being both forms of $CaCO_3$. Normally, in the cold waters of the Antarctic region which are also rich in dissolved CO_2, one would expect a sediment depauperate in calcareous material

Photograph taken by H. Arctowski to show the rocks and the front of the glacier which extends between Landing IX and Cape Anna (Arctowski, 1908, Plate X).

Chapter 11

Glaciers – modern and ancient – in southern South America and the de Gerlache Strait

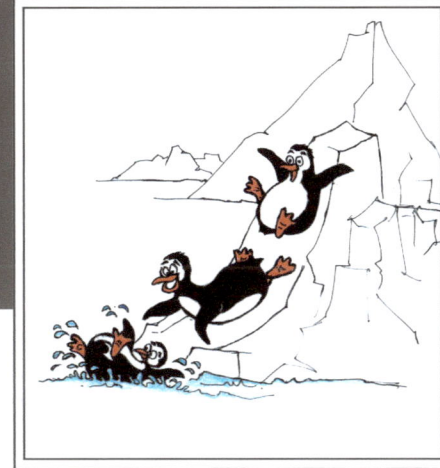

KEY POINTS

- Already in the Magellan Strait, Arctowski saw evidence of ancient glaciers in Peckett Harbour, some 30 km from Punta Arenas, and this was based on the recognition of large moraines.

- In Baie du Torrent (a name coined at the time and that does not seem to be used today), Arctowski saw further evidence of past glacial activity by identifying moraines and he provided sketches (Figs. 12.2, 12.3) to document his observations.

- In the de Gerlache Strait, Arctowski after examining outcrops in situ on various islands and seeing also ancient moraines containing boulders from different locations, referred to an extensive glaciation in the region. He also postulated that the de Gerlache Strait had been filled by a large glacier, but he was unclear about the direction it took. This extensive glaciation has been clearly documented by Canals et al. (2016) who recognized glacial features on the floor of the Strait (see Fig. 12.5) with the glacier travelling from the de Gerlache Strait towards the western Bransfield Basin.

- Arctowski argued for a temperature lowering of some 10 to 12°C to justify the presence of a very large glacier infilling the de Gerlache Strait. His argumentation was very detailed and not that far from today's reconstructions.

SECTIONS

11.1 Observations in South America

11.2 On glaciers and evidence of past glacial events

In 1908, Henryk Arctowski completed a 114 pages monograph on glaciers he visited in the vicinity of the Beagle Chanel at the southern tip of South America as well as along the de Gerlache Strait. He also made some extensive observations of features left by past glaciers such as moraines and striations on rock faces and came to postulate on past glacial events. We need to be aware that, prior to the expedition, Arctowski had visited Professor Eduard Suess in Vienna (at least twice) to seek information on glaciers and their morphologies. It is noteworthy that the same expert was also visited by Emil Racovitza who, in addition, had received a geological training from the Romanian Professor Grigore Cobalescu (whose name was given to one of the islands in the de Gerlache Strait). In addition, Arctowski consulted geologist Professor Alphonse-François Renard who not only had co-authored the major volume on 'Deep-sea sediments' with John Murray in 1891, but who also had translated into French Darwin's monograph on the formation of atolls (Renard 1902). It is more than certain that A-F. Renard influenced A. de Gerlache to spend time in the Beagle Channel to collect rocks (which H. Arctowski eventually did) and make geological observations. Although this is not written anywhere, as far as I know, it was the intention of A-F. Renard to publish a geological map with H. Arctowski of the Beagle Channel environments. Renard's premature death in 1903 prevented this from happening. Search through some of E. Racovitza's archives held in the Antipa Museum in Bucharest has enabled me to see a letter addressed to Racovitza as 'mon cher Raco' which stipulated that all the thin sections of the South American and Antarctic Peninsula rocks prepared at the University of Ghent were to be sent to Czech geoscientists A. Pelikan (who described the rocks from the de Gerlache Strait) and D. Sistek (who described the rocks from the Magellan Strait). Both geologists eventually wrote reports after their examination of the rocks and their thin sections (see chapter 7.8). No geological map based on the Belgica expedition was ever produced.

11.1 Observations in South America

Figure 11.1 Photograph taken by G. Lecointe depicting the 'Baie du Torrent' on Londonderry Island within the background O' Brien Island; Lecointe claimed it to be in the Beagle Channel.
Note that the photographer would have had to walk a long way from the bay to take this photo showing the *SY Belgica*.

After leaving Punta Arenas in Chile and during the transit to the southern tip of South America, the ship stopped in the fjord of the Grand Glacier, then it went to a little bay in Darwin Channel and eventually in the Beagle Channel.

The first examination of glacial features was in Peckett Harbour, some 30 km NW of Punta Arenas. There, Arctowski (1908) saw the first moraine, 38 m high located at 8 to 10 m above sea level. Its direction was NE-SW and its length about 700 m; it contained striated rocks, gravel and sheets of black 'shiste' [1]. Arctowski postulated that these features belonged to a glacier coming from the south.

In fact he proved to be correct as more recent work on glacial features in the area by McCollogh et al. (2005) and DeNuro et al. (2017) document twolateral morainal features near the sea (moraines B and C), north of Punta Arenas that have been dated to coincide with the local Last Glacial Maximum (see photographs in DeMuro et al. 2017).

In his 1908 monograph, Arctowski described the geomorphological features related to glaciers (past and present) which he encountered during the passage through the Beagle Channel and prior to that in the Canal Ballenero.

---

[1] The term 'shiste' in French could refer in English to either the metamorphosed rock called 'shist' or a 'shale'.

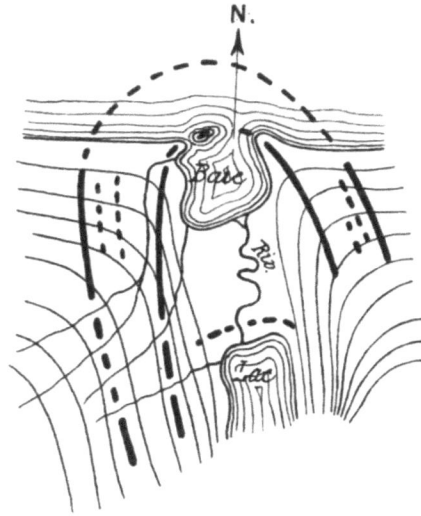

In this area, the *Belgica* scientists named an area as 'Baie du Torrent' although it seems that this name has not be used since. It is located near Londerrry Island which is facing the Atlantic Ocean. In this area (see figure 12.2), Arctowski undertook several reconnoitring missions during which he found evidence of prior glaciers. He for example stated that a valley was formed by erosive action of an immense glacier tongue ('fleuve') (Fig. 12.3).

Figure 11.2 Sketch made by Arctowski (1908) showing in bold the moraines interpolated moraines (mostly lateral moraines) and their continuation under water in the Channel as dotted lines. It is assumed that this is in Baie du Torrent.

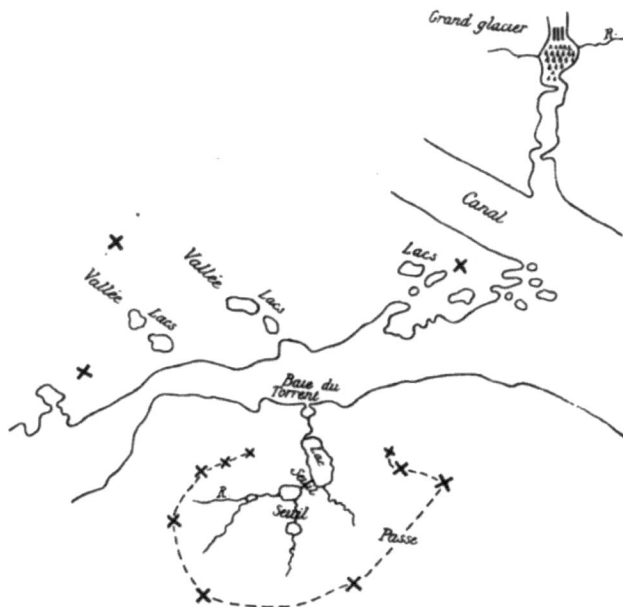

Figure 11.3 Sketch made by Arctowski (1908) to delineate the glacial cirque (where the glacier was originally located) bounded by a dotted line and crosses for a former glacier that drained down the Baie du Torrent, adjacent to the Beagle Channel seen on the top right hand corner.

A modern-day view of the Beagle Channel with views of the current glaciers and associated moraines is documented with the following photographs (Figs. 11.4 to 11.5).

Figure 11.4

A: Area of the Cape Horn Biosphere Reserve (pale blue dotted line), the glaciers, including the Cordillera Darwin, Beagle Channel, Magellan Strait, and Punta Arenas (taken from Rozzi et al. 2006, back cover);

B: Mount France, east of Glacier Italy;

C: Germany Glacier, note forest on frontal moraine on the edge of the sea;

D: Bahia Tres Brazos, Isla Gordon;

E: Romanche Glacier with Mt Darwin Range in the background;

F: view of Gordon Island with the North (Equatorial) facing slope as seen from the NW Arm of the Beagle Channel; note the rivers cascading from the glacier;

G: Eastern extension of the Glacier Pia Complex with an old moraine visible in the sea;

H: Chilean Yamana Navy Station, located east of the NW arm of the Beagle Channel. Names of glaciers confirmed by Professor Ricardo Rozzi (Universidad de Magallanes, Chile) with many thanks. Photos by P. De Deckker.

Figure 11.5

A: Overview of the Beagle Channel with *Nothofagus* forest in the foreground, just above Puerto Williams on Navaro Island. The mountains in the background are in Argentina. Photo taken from Cerro Bandera, in Chile.

B: View of the Beagle Channel looking South and Channel with *Nothofagus* forest in the foreground; the small islands are parts of an ancient morainic system;

C: Nothofagus trunk and foliage photographed at the base of Cerro Banderra;

D: cormorant colony on small rock in the Beagle Channel, opposite a glacier flowing down to the Channel. Photos by P. De Deckker.

11.2 On glaciers and evidence of past glacial events

Arctowski, during his talk presented to the Geographical Society of London on June 24, 1901, commented on glacial features he recognised in the de Gerlache Strait. For example, he stated that his discovery of the former extension of the Antarctic glaciers is 'very important to record' (sic Arctowski,1901, p. 372) for various reasons by alluding to climates of the glacial epoch with the aim at determining the mean temperature of the air during that period. He stated that the position of the moraine must have occupied the de Gerlache Strait which, near Cape Reclus, had a breadth of 10 miles (~16 km) and a depth of 342 fathoms. During the 17th and 18th landings where on Bob Island, not far from Wiencke Island, well-preserved fragments of moraines were found, 15 to 20 feet high (=5 to 6 m high) resting against a sloping shore at a height of 80 (~25 m) feet above the sea. Further, he indicated that this moraine had the same direction as the channel (meaning de Gerlache Strait which in his paper he called Belgica Strait) and that its height decreased towards the west. He also said that there were 'huge blocks of perfectly polished gneiss boulders (Arctowski, 1901, p. 372). He also mentioned rounded boulders of red granite whereas some diorite rocks were often angular. In addition, he commented that on the other side of the de Gerlache Strait, opposite the other spot, a fine moraine, 65 feet high (~20 m) was found on Bank Island and followed the same direction as the Strait. There, on the side of the mountains, he also recognized 'roches moutonnées' (= 'asymmetric bedrock humps or hills with

a gently sloping and abraded upglacier face and a quarried downglacier *(lee)* face that is typically blunter'; *see* www.antarcticglaciers. org). Arctowski (1901, p.373) deducted that these 'glacial features mentioned above mush have been the product of an immense glacier which must have flowed through the de Gerlache Strait westward, i.e. towards the Pacific Ocean'). He eventually listed the location on other islands of erratics (= transported rocks by glacial activity).

In his monograph published much later (Arctowski, 1908), he stated that erratic rocks were collected during landings 3, 5, 6, 9, 11, 14, 17 and 18 in the de Gerlache Strait (Table 7.1) , and recognition of their lithologies enabled him to identify their possible source. In fact, in this monograph he listed the composition of rocks he had examined at the various landings. He was able to do this being a qualified geologist from the University of Liège in Belgium and from La Sorbonne in Paris. It is disappointing that the geologists who went in the area later on such as Adie (1957), Hooper (1962) and Birkenmajer (1987, 1988) all failed to acknowledge the original observations of Arctowski. Refer to the discussion in chapter 7.8. Thus, Arctowski's postulated that there had been in the past some glaciers that covered part of /or many of the islands in the de Gerlache Strait. Hence, he did not hesitate to state that he obtained evidence of previous glaciers (moraines, erratics and roches moutonnées) that showed an extensive glaciation which he linked to the

'age glaciaire' which we now refer to as the Last Glacial period (peaking around 20,000 years ago; *note added by the author*).

On pages 60 to 65 in his 1908 monograph, Arctoswki provides a lengthy discussion on the geological nature of the erratics and is considering their origin, based on the many landings made in the de Gerlache Strait. First of all, he mentions the presence of extensive and highly located moraines on some islands. For example, on Bank Island (Landing 18, see table 7.1) facing Bob Island (see Figs. 7.1.3, 11.6), he examined a 20 m high moraine having the same direction as the Strait. This moraine is on the flank of the mountains which looks like roches moutonées. Arctowski postulated that the 'grand glacier' as he called it would have moved towards the south to join another in Bay des Flandres towards the west. He also discussed the possibility of this glacier to have flowed towards the Pacific Ocean having passed between Cap Renard and Cap Errera (see figs. 7.1.3, 11.6). This statement is somewhat confusing because modern studies by Canals et al. (2016, fig. 4) clearly indicate that the ancient glacier also moved eastward towards the Pacific Ocean but instead travelled through West Bransfield Basin and between Smith and Snow Islands, via Boyd Strait (see also Dowdeswell et al., 2016). Elsewhere, Arctowski (1908) found another moraine some 25 m above sea level, 5 to 7 m high, well preserved in between Bob and Wiencke Islands and having the direction of the Strait. There he thought the direction was slightly towards the west.

Arctowski (1908) went on to discussing as to whether the glacier reached the bottom of the de Gerlache Strait and considered that it probably had not. Nevertheless, he had too little time in the area and not enough data to justify this claim. We now know that the de Gerlache Strait was filled by a large glacier as glacier streamlined features as well as drumlins (= features formed under a glacier) that have been well documented by Canals et al. (2016, fig. 4) using multibeam-bathymetric compilations. Disappointingly the authors in Canals et al. (2016) do not acknowledge nor discuss the pioneering work of Arctowski

(1908) and this applies also of the earlier work by O'Cofaig et al. (2014). Perhaps, the moraines examined by Arctowski belong to a post Last Glacial event, some of which would fit with the models of O'Cofaig et al. (2014, fig. 11 and discussions). It would be possible for a geomorphologist to re-visit the islands Arctowski discussed and sample the moraines he mentioned and use some of the appropriate dating technique, such as exposure dating, to provide an accurate age of the moraines. Arctowski's description would be easy to locate the moraines.

Arctowski (1908) also provided an extensive discussion on the temperatures that would have been necessary to cause a major glaciation that filled de Gerlache Strait and left moraines high above sea level on some of the islands he visited. After a comparison of temperatures at different locations in the Magellanic Strait and for different altitudes, he came up with suggesting a temperature drop of some 10 to 12 °C for the glacial period (Arctowski, 1908, p.73). He was not very far off the reconstructions that have been postulated since worldwide. This is particularly impressive and well ahead of this time!

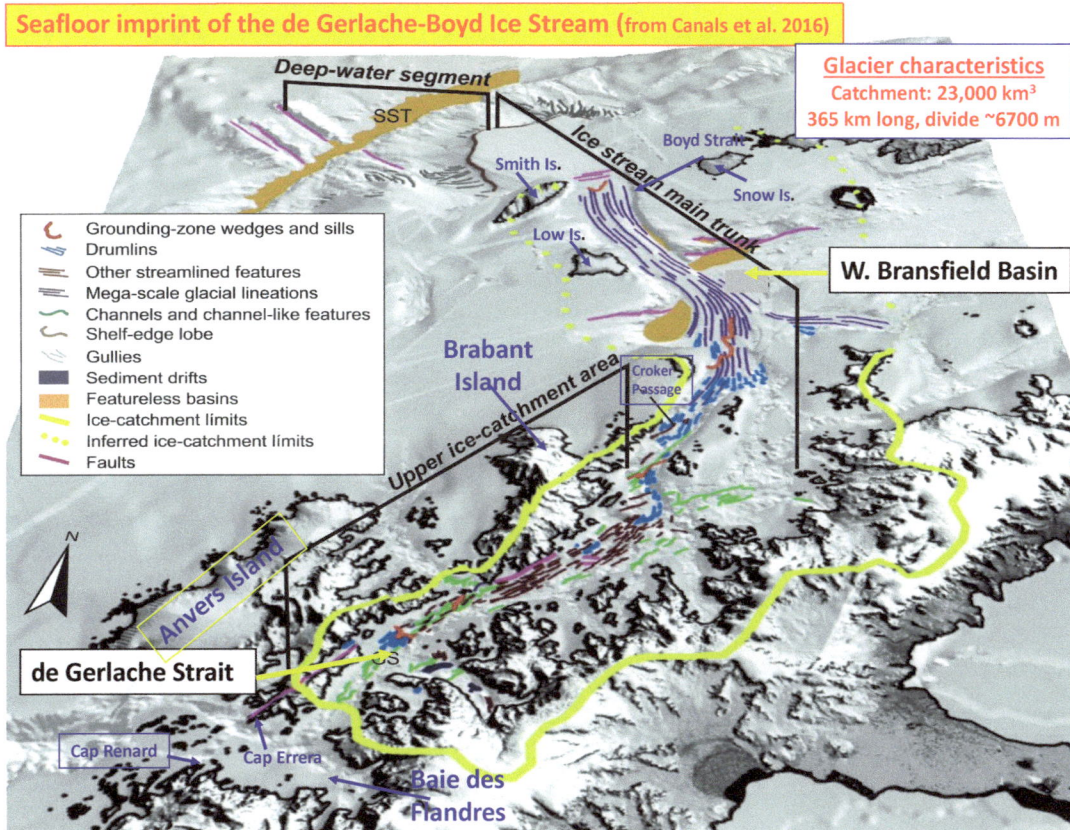

Figure 11.6 Reproduction of figure 4 of Canals et al. (2016) with significant additions to show the glacial features recognized on the floor of the de Gerlache Strai, listing also locations refered to by Arctowski (1908). Note the identified catchment of the glacier bounded by yellow lines that extended east of Baie des Flandres to the South Shetland Trench (SST). The glacier movement is from west to east, contrary to Arctoswki's earlier postulation. The characteristics of the glacier provided by Canals et al. (2016) are listed in the top right hand corner.

Photographs of members of the crew taken by Frederick A. Cook that show the effect of the polar 'anoemia on people's faces. For more details refer to the caption of figure 12.2.

Chapter 12

Polar 'anaemia' among the crew

An alarming situation arose during the expedition: people started to feel sick, some suffered from anaemia, dizziness, lacked appetite and also felt very weak.

Several crew members were breathless and realised that their heartbeat had become alarmingly irregular. Their skin was pale and in many cases turned yellow and was dry. The medical doctor on the ship, Frederick A. Cook (Fig. 12.1), was well aware of the situation and endeavoured to monitor people's health. Every day, he checked everyone's heart pulse, body temperature, skin behind the eye lids, the nature of gums and teeth as well as mucous membranes.

Disappointingly, his notes were never published, especially since polar medicine would have benefitted much for those continuous observations at the beginning of polar exploration, and which would have lasted more than six months; particularly also during a significant period (up to 3 to 4 months) when everyone on board lived in total darkness.

Figure 12.1 Photograph of Frederick A. Cook taken on the ship and obtained from the Racovitza archives (published with permission from the National Archives of Romania in Cluj). The photo was 'colorized' using palette.fm/color/filters.

The photos which Cook took during the voyage, especially before and after illnesses had appeared, tell a lot. These are displayed in Figs. 12.2 and 12.3 and have been 'colorized' here.

Examination of the diaries/books now available by Cook (1900), Amundsen (English translation in Decleir, 1999), de Gerlache (1902), Lecointe (1904) and Dobrowolski (1950) are indeed very informative. All the comments made in those four books are presented here in an abridged form in Table 18.1. However, since no dates are provided by Dobrowolski (1950) in his recollections of the time spent on the *Belgica*, a copy of the relevant text, translated by Ms Dagmara Bożek, is provided here:

'On humans, the polar night has a negative effect. Although we missed the terrible scurvy, nowadays unknown to polar expeditions, because it was solely a consequence of poor hygienic conditions and bad food. However, we did not miss the beginnings of the disease; our appetite disappeared, an irresistible distaste of canned food appeared; had it not been for the kind-hearted seals and penguins, some of us might not have returned from the ice. The lips, gums, nostrils and the inside of the eyelids turn white; the pulse is abnormal; hair and nails grow lazily; wounds heal slowly; some people's legs swell; drowsiness at first, and then insomnia; blunting of the physical and mental will - inactivity, apathy, a tendency to daydream; one feels an effort to perform the simplest movement, the simplest mental operation'.

Figure 12.2
Photographs taken by Frederick A. Cook (Cook, 1901) that show the effect of the polar 'anoemia on people's faces', on the left are photos physiological changes resulting from sickness.

A-B: F.A. Cook,

C-D: R. Amundsen;

E-F: E. Racovitza.

These photos have 'colorized' using palette.fm/color/filters.

Figure 12.3 Photographs of members of the crew taken by Frederick A. Cook that show the effect of the polar 'anoemia on people's faces. These photos have been rearranged from the original plate in Cook (1901) and then 'colorized' using palette.fm/color/filters.

A: Max van Rhysselberghe;

B: Louis Michotte;

C: Johan Koren;

D: Jules Melaerts;

E: Adam Tollefsen;

F: Henry Sommers;

G: Engelbret Knudsen;

H: Ludvig Johansen;

I: Jan Van Mirlo;

J: Gustave Dufour.

All other comments are presented in a chronological order to enable the reader to identify what different authors said about themselves as well as others. In many ways, examination of those comments clearly identify that the situation for many was very alarming. Even A. de Gerlache and G. Lecointe, who were first and second in command of the expedition, were so distressed that de Gerlache wrote his will which was co-signed by Lecointe, both thinking that death was near.

Examination of Table 12.1 shows that a large part of the poor health conditions occurred during the 'polar night' (grey column on the left) between May 27 and July 21, 1898. Cook had come up with a series of remedies, based on his observations made when he spent time in the Arctic where he found that eskimos were always in good health, despite being deprived of fresh vegetables, a source of vitamins B and C. He had concluded that eating raw (uncooked) meat was a likely treatment. Therefore, he eventually encouraged people to eat raw penguin and seal meat. Several members of the crew at first refused to do so, but several accounts listed in Table 18.1 inform us that people felt much better eventually after eating raw meat. This was not a discovery as this practice had already been applied during the German expedition near the Antarctic Peninsula when several sailors had been suffering from symptoms of scurvy and became much better after eating raw seal meat and drinking their blood. In fact, Cook (1894) had already written a note in the New York Journal of Obstetrics describing on how eskimos cope with the lack of vitamin C and survived from scurvy by eating raw meat.

In addition, Cook recommended that those affected spend one hour each day naked in front of an open flame of the ship's stove to be exposed to infrared light. I assume that the wooden planks that were to be used in the prefabricated huts in case of landing at Cape

Adare were used to this 'new' purpose. There is no doubt that Cook's remedies proved successful in many instances. Some crew members even stated that "Cook saved us".

It seems that everybody on the ship was affected in one way or another. The conditions that especially affected the scientists prevented them from performing the routine tasks of taking atmospheric and magnetic measurements (Arctowski, Dobrowolski, Lecointe), identify the ship's position (Lecointe), collecting animals and curating them (as well as dissecting them) (Racovitza). It is no surprise therefore to find that the diary of Racovitza dealing with the time of the polar night has been missing. Perhaps, in fact, it was never written for obvious reasons. People were well aware of their alarming health condition, such that Amundsen in his diary had written: "If we have to spend a second winter here, then not many of us would survive, according to the doctor". He further stated that "no one from the staff agrees with the commander's plan" as de Gerlache wanted to stay in the region for much longer.

This was surprising as he himself was very sick, and perhaps more than anyone else and for a much more extensive period of time! (see Table 18.1). de Gerlache remained unwell after the expedition and went to southern France to recover as mentioned in several of his cards addressed to Mrs. Léonie Osterrieth found in the Felix Archief held in Antwerp. Cook in his book published in 1900 stated also that there is "much indigestion, fermentation gastric intestinal and gastric pain, imperfect gastric action, and a general suppression of all digestive secretions. The heart is constantly, easily disturbed and mitral murmurs which I have not heard before, are audible. Temperatures almost without exception are subnormal, breathing is often difficult." He then summarised in Appendix 1 in his book that there were symptoms of chronic anaemia, and that he noticed discolouration of the

mucous membranes, dysphorea, acceleration of the pulse, dizziness, insomnia and complete incapacity for prolonged intellectual work, and even swelling of the legs". This was indeed very alarming and nearly all the members of the *Belgica* personnel eventually 'pulled through'. One exception is that Adam Tollefsen lost sanity and never regained full healthy conditions after the expedition eventually returned to Europe.

During the polar winter, Emile Danco (Fig. 12.3), the staff member who was taking daily magnetic measurements eventually died during the middle of the polar night. Frederick Cook had been monitoring his condition and had identified a poor heart condition that the former soldier must had had before joining the expedition, but which became aggravated likely due to the effects of isolation in the dark that enforced several of the conditions listed above.

Danco's death seriously affected the morale of all on the ship as he was very well liked and had been a close friend of both de Gerlache and Lecointe. Cook (1901) described on how he routinely prescribed, at the early stage of people sicknesses that affected their heartbeat, some strychnine to regulate the heart. He also devised a chemical treatment consisting of iron and arsenic.

Polar 'anoemia', the condition which Cook described was not unique to the Belgica crew. The French geologist E. Gourdon, who participated on both French expeditions to the Antarctic Peninsula led by J.-B. Charcot, related to the fact that many personnel of the two French expeditions had also suffered from the same conditions which Cook (1901) had referred to. He examined the conditions which he thought were related to the tinned food. He called it: 'la maladie des conserves' (the sickness cause by preserved food). This was indeed an issue with the Belgica

Figure 12.4 Photograph of Emile Danco taken before the ship's departure. Reproduced with permission from Anders Bache, Roald Amundsen's House, MiA – Museums in Akershus, Norway, and 'colorized' using using palette.fm/color/filters.

expedition as people consumed much food kept in tins that had been prepared in Norway. Several staff members vociferously complained about the nature of that food, especially Georges Lecointe. The latter described three kinds of food: (1) kjoedbollers, (2) kjoedpolkers and (3) Australian rabbit.

There was much humour spent trying to determine the nature of the first two foods: Arctowski thought the food belonged to the mineral realm, Racovitza to a combination of the animal and vegetal realms, Lecointe to a star without an atmosphere fallen in an infernal cascade and Cook escapers from the morgue! These comments show that food was not much appreciated despite quite a varied menu and did not contribute to a good morale.

Perhaps some compounds in the tin may have affected people's health (see Gully below).

It is of interest to learn that E. Racovitza spent countless hours in his laboratory making funny and sometimes sarcastic drawings, mostly of the scientific personnel so as to entertain people, often during the difficult period of isolation and frustration when the ship was trapped in the sea ice. It is assumed that this was a way of trying to raise the morale of the staff. Many of those drawings are displayed in Kløver' (2010)'s book but are not reproduced here so as not to contravene copyrights. Some of the drawings are coloured in.

The medical doctor H.R. Gully recently examined the conditions people suffered in a number of early Antarctic explorations, including that of the *Belgica*. He assessed the proper use of the words 'polar anaemia' and examined all the other possible conditions that may have affected people such as scurvy and beriri (Gurly, 2011). This author wrote a considerable amount of information on the conditions that affected people in the early days of Antarctic exploration. People on the *Belgica* were not uniquely affected. Many other expeditions underwent similar problems. Gurly (2011, 2012) discussed at length the various possibilities that affected not only people's health but also mental conditions. Nevertheless, the ample descriptions of the state of health and mind of the Belgica people is proving to be a treasure trove for assessing the nature of humans under very harsh conditions. A pity Cook's diary is missing.

In a letter dated April 14, 1900 written by Cook from New York and addressed to A. de Gerlache, he wrote that his intention was to write an account of the medical and physiological observations he made on the ship that would amount to about 20,000 words. He further stated that if 'however, I decide a general review of the whole polar question, and its bearing upon health and disease in the cold regions it will be much longer'. This report, although listed in the list of contributions to be published from the Belgica expedition, disappointingly never appeared (refer to Appendix 1). On January 8, 1900 Cook sent a letter to de Gerlache stating that 'I am at work, at present, looking up the medical notes which you have asked, to go into the official journal. This will be sent to you in the course of a month or so'. An attempt at contacting Mr Henri de Gerlache who is now overseeing the Belgica archives and equipment has remained unanswered. The medical diary of F. Cook is a very important document that would be of great importance to medical researchers interested in human performance and behaviour during a long period of isolation in Antarctic waters, and in particular during the lengthy 'Polar Night'.

It is my firm belief that all the documents (such as daily logbooks, magnetic measurements books collated by E. Danco and after his death by G. Lecointe that were generated during the Belgica expedition ought to be deposited in a Belgian State archive. After all, the Belgica expedition was entirely funded by Belgium, its government, its constituents and donors, and not by family members of the expeditioners, so its archives should be made public. If family members decide to retain those archives, at least good quality scans of those important documents ought to be made available to a library such as the one belong to the VLIZ (= Vlaams Instituut voor de Zee in Ostend, aka Flemish Marine Institute) which already holds a huge amount of publications related to the Belgica expedition and which are easily available for free.

Comments and diagnoses concerning people's health on the Belgica in 1898, especially during the Polar Night (15 May - 21 July)																
Date in 1898	Author of comment	Concerning all crew	Amundsen	Arctowski	Cook	Danco	de Gerlache	Dobrowolski	Lecointe	Raco-vitza	Johansen	Knudsen	Melaerts	Tollefsen	Van Mirlo	van Rhysselberghe
25-Apr	Lecointe	a certain apathy among us, some don't want to leave the ship for daily walk														
12-May	Lecointe						has melancholy for several days, appears rarely at the mess room; his health is not good; has violent impressions on his temples									
27-May	Lecointe					Cook says Danco is sick, extreme weakness, strong albuminaria										
5-Jun	Lecointe					receives morphine injection, panting respiration; died that evening										
26-Jun	Cook						pale & yellow with feeble almost imperceptible pulse 100 to 140; his recovery is uncertain									
30-Jun	Lecointe			weak pulse, stayed in bed all day on 26th; very nervous on 28th												
6-Jul	Lecointe			not well at all, status aggravating; talks about his 'immersion in the water' like Danco												
8-Jul	Amundsen	everyone has irregular heart beat														
9-Jul	Amundsen		heartbeat 133 pulse abnormal													
9-Jul	Lecointe	in the evening everyone is demoralised					complains of headache		legs are painful, ankles are swollen							
10-Jul	Lecointe		weak, but eats a raw penguin steak						had no sleep, head heavy like lead, temples beating with violence; legs swollen more and more as well as left hand, later all paralysed							
10-Jul	Amundsen	state of health onboard not good		I do not have strength												
11-Jul	Amundsen						is ill but not in danger		is ill but not in danger, face & feet swollen; is in much panic about his health and for his life; feels death is near & gave instructions to Amundsen							
11-Jul	Lecointe								am so weak, end is near							
12-Jul	Cook								health is suddenly failing, pulse intermittent, 1st sign of debility; his entire skin is dry, glossy appearance; is assuming a deathly parlour, difficulty at sleeping, puffiness under eyes, swollen anckles							
12-Jul	Amundsen		blood circulation gradually improving, pulse after short trip 118													
13-Jul	Amundsen								I am not dead; coma did not last long; ate penguin meat							
13-Jul	Lecointe								after coma that did not last long, felt better after eating penguin							

Table 12.1 Compendium of all the comments made by F. Cook, R. Amundsen, G. Lecointe and A. de Gerlache in their respective books that mention the state of health of many members of the *Belgica* crew. Parts of the left column that are coloured grey relate to the period when there was a complete polar darkness. The observations are presented in chronological order.

The comments by Arctowski in his 1903 Memoir entitled: Die Antarktishen Eisverhältnisse. Auszug aus meinen Tagebuch der Südpolarreiseder Belgica 1898-1899. *Petermanns Geographische Mitteilunge , Ergänzungsheft* 144, 1-121 are not mentioned here but confirm the comments made by other members of the expedition listed here.

Polar night = total darkness

Comments and diagnoses concerning people's health on the Belgica in 1898, especially during the Polar Night (15 May - 21 July)																
Date in 1898	Author of comment	Concerning all crew	Amundsen	Arctowski	Cook	Danco	de Gerlache	Dobrowolski	Lecointe	Raco-vitza	Johansen	Knudsen	Melaerts	Tollefsen	Van Mirlo	van Rhysselberghe
14-Jul	Cook								has given hope of ever recovery, has made his last instructions							
15-Jul	Amundsen		after outing to an iceberg, pulse 121, after 10 min. down to 90				pulse 131 & irregular									
18-Jul	Amundsen		pulse 108													
18-Jul	Lecointe				not brilliant		seriously threatened		getting better	not brilliant		legs very swollen legs, espec. ankles				
19-Jul	Cook		making slow recovery	in a bad way			making slow recovery	in a bad way								
19-Jul	Amundsen		pulse is getting better													
20-Jul	Amundsen		general state of health poor									is seriously ill				
21-Jul	Amundsen		pulse continues to improve													
22-Jul	Amundsen	we all look rather sickly & pale										condition improved				
22-Jul	Cook	after much physical, mental and moral depression, we are elated at the expectation														
23-Jul	Amundsen	everyone is getting better quickly	swollen limbs, irregular and weak heartbeat & depression													
23-Jul	Lecointe	we all need light and warmth									legs very swollen; heartbeat up to 150	legs very swollen				
24-Jul	Amundsen											not doing well; fear for the worst				
28-Jul	Amundsen											is slightly better				
31-Jul	Cook	we believed ourselves in fine trim but far from normal														
8-Aug	Amundsen	general state of health not good									state is worse				has gone out of his mind, cannot speak or hear, but calm	
8-Aug	Lecointe		suffering from heart issue	heartbeat 46-48/min.	languishing			weakens			languishing			suffering from heart issue		
9-Aug-	Amundsen														condition worsened	
11-Aug	Amundsen														condition unchanged but can speak/hear	
12-Aug	Amundsen														is better, can speak and hear	
19-Aug	Amundsen			mental state not so good			mental state not so good; plagued by headaches							suffers from insanity (sic H. Decleir)		
Sept-Oct	Cook	we failed more and more in strength and developed alarming symptoms, one man was terribly insane														
no date provided	de Gerlache	Our skin became greenish yellow; our sleep was interrupted by long insomnia; one sailor was hysterical with loss of hearing and speech; Cook thought we had scurvy		suffered from stomach pain			am seriously suffering	in danger for several days		suffered from stomach pain						got cardiac troubled

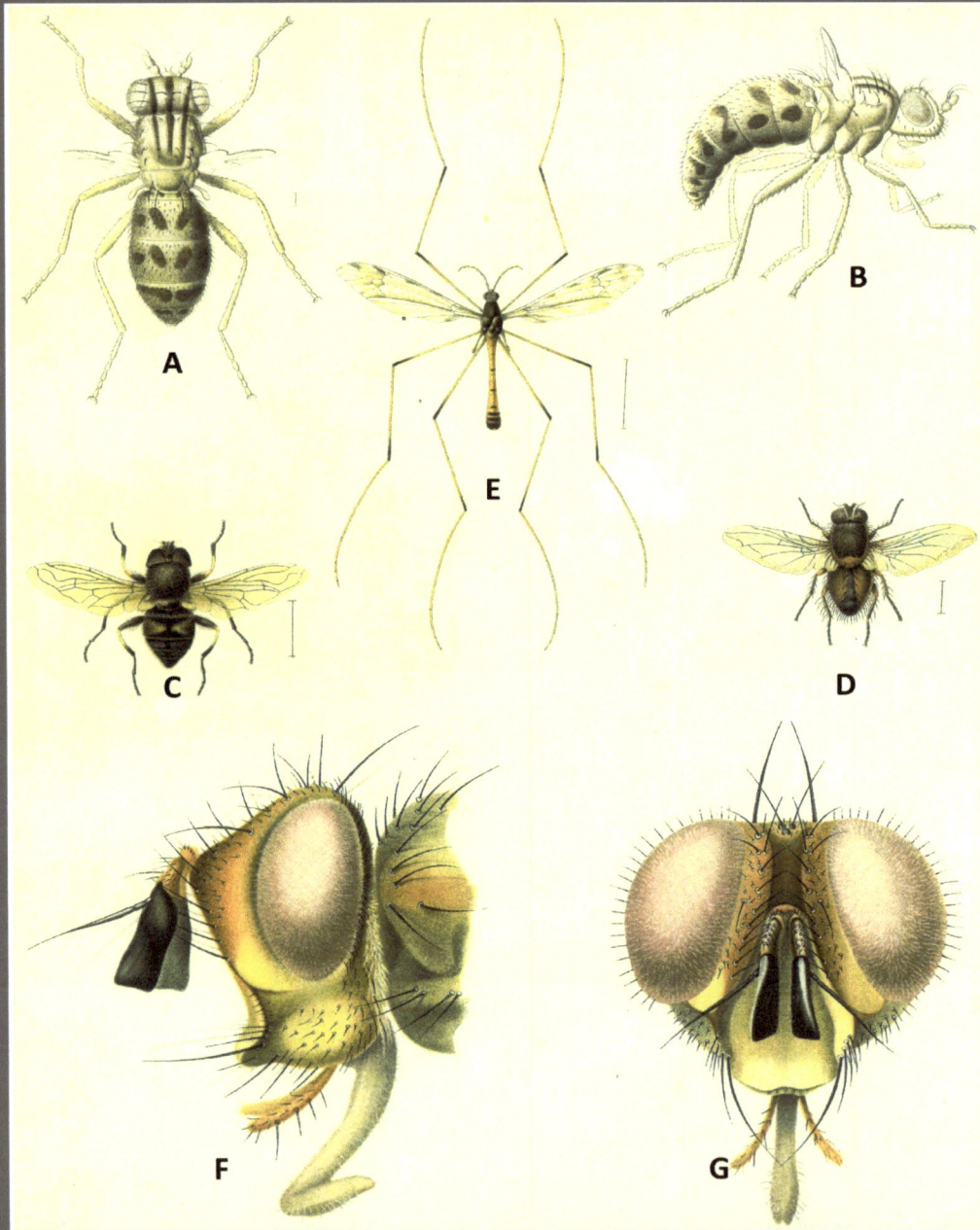

Illustrations of various insects collected by E. Racovitza in the surroundings of the Beagle Channel. For more details refer to the caption of figure 13.4.1.

Chapter 13

Investigations in the Beagle Channel

The Belgica expedition spent quite a substantial amount of time in the Magellan Strait that included the Beagle Channel.

The ship left Punta Arenas after purchasing many supplies and reorganising the crew after several were asked to leave for various reasons, including insubornation and illness. The crew now amounted to a total of 19 people. The ship left Punta Arenas on December 14, 1897, and sailed through the Magellan Strait to eventually reach the Pacific Ocean close to one month later. Time spent in that area was already seriously delaying the prospect of reaching Cape Adare as originally planned and dictated by the Royal Belgian Geographical Society. There were some 24 landings (débarquements) in the Magellanic area, a list of which is provided in Table 13.1.

It is likely that the influence of Professor A.F. Renard who had been a great supporter of the Belgica expedition and had eventually translated into French Charles Darwin monograph on the geology of the Beagle Channel (Darwin 1902). He obviously had encouraged Henryk Arctowski to collect rocks in the area, some of which were eventually studied by Sistek (1912). All rocks and thin sections are housed in the RBINS collections in Brussels.

13.1 Sites visited and species richness

Emil Racovitza was ever busy collecting plants and animals wherever he went. As mentioned before, he had visited several institutions in Europe before the expedition in order to learn the best possible techniques to preserve plants and animals. For example, the preserved plants shown in Figs. 13.2.1, 13.2.2 which are all kept in the National Belgian herbarium of the Meise Botanic Garden, are a testimony of Racovitza's skills, and he same applies for the preservation of organisms which have been illustrated in this book.

Nevertheless, E. Racovitza was able to make substantial collections in the Magellanic Straits which eventually were described by numerous experts and appeared in several of the *Résultats du voyage du S. Y. Belgica en 1897-1898- 1899 – rapports scientifiques.* Some of these are discussed in this chapter as they have been little publicized since their original publications and deserve much attention. These are already listed in Table 9.6.1.

Of interest also is to determine the vast number of new genera and species described by taxonomists who studied biological material collected by Emil Racovitza. This clearly indicates the astonishing biological discoveries made during the course of the Belgica expedition. This list is presented below in Table 13.1.2. It amounts to 348 new species and 25 new genera, many of which bear names associated with the ship or some members of the crew.

Of note also is that three members of the scientific crew (H. Arctowski, E. Racovitza and F. Cook) spent a few days visiting Dawson Island because of their genuine interest in the native people there with at least some 250 Indians (mostly Onas) under the 'care' of Salesian Brothers. This will be further discussed in chapter 15.

List of the landings and sites visited by the Belgica in the Magellanic area of South America

Number	Location name	Additional details	Country
1	Mc Donald Station	Cabeza del Mar. Magellan Strait	Chile
2	Morro Chico	Rio Gallegos Valley, Magellanes	Chile
3	Cabo del Monte	Rio Coy Basin. Territorio Santa Cruz	Argentina
4	Farmer's Galpon	Ultimo esperanza Bay, Magellanes	Chile
5	Gregory Cap	Magellan Strait, Magellanes	Chile
6	Saint Elisabeth Island	Magellan Strait, Magellanes	Chile
7	Punta Arenas	Magellan Strait, Magellanes	Chile
8	Chabunco	Near Punta Arenas, Magellanes	Chile
9	Rio de las Minas	Near Punta Arenas, Magellanes	Chile
10	Punto Carrera	Brunswick Promontory, Magellan Strait	Chile
11	Port Famine	Brunswick Promontory, Magellan Strait	Chile
12	Harris Bay	Dawson Island, Magellan Strait	Chile
13	Hope Harbour	Clarence Island. Magellan Strait	Chile
14	Basket Island	Magellanes	Chile
15	Baie du Torrent	Londonderry Island, French Channel, Magellanes	Chile
16	Baie du Grand Glacier	Darwin Channel, Tierra del Fuego	Chile
17	Baie des Astéries	Darwin Channel, Tierra del Fuego	Chile
18	Lapataïa	Beagle Channel, Tierra del Fuego	Argentina
19	Acigami Lake	Lapataïa. Beagle Channel, Tierra del Fuego	Argentina
20	Ushuwaïa	Beagle Channel, Tierra del Fuego	Argentina
21	Harberton Harbour	1st and 2nd gulf, Beagle Channel, Tierra del Fuego	Argentina
22	Ile des Lapins	Harberton, Beagle Channel, Tierra del Fuego	Argentina
23	Porto Toro	Navarin Island, Magellanes	Chile
24	Saint Jean Gulf	Staten Island	Chile

Table 13.1.1 (left) List of the landings and sites visited by the *SY Belgica* in the Magellanic area.

Table 13.1.2 List of all the new taxa collected by Emil Racovitza during the Belgica expedition bearing the names of members of the crew (Racovitza 21, Lecointe 4, Danco 3, Wiencke 1, Arctowski 1, de Gerlache 18) or associated with the name of the ship (Belgica 16).

Genera & species named after Racovitza		Organism	Author & publication date
Racovitzanus	*antarcticus*	copepod	Giesbrecht 1902
Racovitziella	*antarctica*	alga	de Wildeman 1935
Racovitzaia	*glacialis*	fish	Dollo 1904
Belgicella	*racovitzana*	starfish	Ludwig 1903
Rhipidothuria	*racovitzai*	holothurian	Herouard 1906
Idya	*racovitzai*	copepod	Giesbrecht 1902
Gamarus	*racovitzai*	free acarian	Trouessart 1903
Homoeonema	*racovitzae*	jellyfish	Maas 1906
Pecten	*racovitzai*	mollusc	Pelseneer 1903
Rhynconella	*racovitzae*	brachiopod	Joubin 1901
Rosella	*racovitzae*	sponge	Topsent 1901
Trinacria	*racovitzae*	diatom	Van Heurck 1909
Amphora	*racovitzae*	diatom	Van Heurck 1909
Sarcoscypha	*racovitzae*	fungus	Bommer & Rousseau 1905
Lecanoreae	*racovitzae*	lichen	Wainio 1903
Verrrucaria	*racovitzae*	lichen	Wainio 1903
Amphiporus	*racovitzai*	nemertine worm	Burger 1904
Thynnus	*racovitzai*	hymenopteran	André 1906
Antarctia	*racovitzai*	carabid insect	Rousseau 1906
Webera	*racovitzae*	moss	Cardot 1902
Colella	*racovitzai*	tunicate	van Beneden & de Selys-Longchamps
Salpa	*racovitzai*	tunicate	van Beneden & de Selys-Longchamps

Species named after Lecointe			
Crania	*lecointei*	brachiopod	Joubin 1901
Trinacria	*lecointei*	diatom	Van Heurck 1909
Amphiporus	*lecointei*	nemertine worm	Burger 1904
Nematonurus	*lecointei*	fish	Dollo 1904

Species named after Danco			
Reniera	*dancoi*	sponge	Topsent 1901
Sibylla	*dancoi*	ceramicid insect	Lameere 1906
Lecanoreae	*dancoënsis*	lichen	Wainio 1903

Species named after Wiencke			
Trechus	*wiencki*	carabid insect	Rousseau 1906

Species named after Arctowski			
Raja	*arctowski*	fish	Dollo 1904

Genus & species named after de Gerlache		Organism	Author & publication date
Gerlachea	*australis*	fish	Dollo 1904
Cheiraster	*gerlachei*	starfish	Ludwig 1903
Metridia	*gerlachei*	copepod	Giesbrecht 1902
Pronemia	*gerlachei*	mollusc	Pelseneer 1903
Rhynconella	*gerlachei*	brachiopod	Joubin 1901
Mononchus	*gerlachei*	free nematode	de Man 1904
Serolis	*gerlachei*	isopode	Monot 1926
Eurete	*gerlachei*	sponge	Topsent 1901
Coscinodiscus	*gerlachei*	diatom	Van Heurck 1909
Lecanoreae	*gerlachei*	lichen	Wainio 1903
Amphiporus	*gerlachei*	nemertine worm	Burger 1904
Nymphon	*gerlachei*	pycnogonid	Giltay 1934
Myrostoma	*gerlachei*	polychete worm	Fauvel 1936
Cryptocoda	*gerlachi*	siphonophore	Leloup 1938
Bryum	*gerlachei*	moss	Cardot 1902
Nörneria	*gigas var. gerlachei*	free acarian	Trouessart 1903
Pronemia	*gerlachei*	mollusc	Pelseneer 1903
Salpa	*gerlachei*	tunicate	van Beneden & de Selys-Longchamps

Genera & species named after the Belgica			
Belgica	*antarctica*	chironomid fly	Jacobs 1906
Belgicella	*racovitzana*	starfish	Ludwig 1903
Anasterias	*belgicae*	starfish	Ludwig 1903
Psolus	*belgicae*	holothurian	Herouard 1906
Cyclopina	*belgicae*	copepod	Giesbrecht 1902
Conchoecia	*belgicae*	ostracod	Müller 1906
Notopsis	*belgicae*	free acarian	Michael 1903
Leptochiton	*belgicae*	mollusc	Pelseneer 1903
Plectus	*belgicae*	free nematode	de Man 1904
Campanilina	*belgicae*	hydroid	Hartlaub 1904
Amphiura	*belgicae*	echinoid	Koehler 1901
Tetrastemma	*belgicae*	nemertine worm	Burger 1904
Paraperioculode	*belgicae*	amphipod	Ruffo 1949
Chilota	*corralensis var. belgicae*	oligochete worm	Cernosvitov 1935
Paraonis	*belgicae*	polychete worm	Fauvel 1936
Cladorhiza	*belgicae*	sponge	Topsent 1901

13.2 The ship's misadventure near Haberton

The ship decided to stop at Haberton (see chapter 15 on Yaghan and Ona people) but it nearly sank at night on January 1, 1898 having hit a large underwater bank of rocks (Figure 13.2.1). Cook (1900) reported on this incident as well as Lecointe (1904), see below.

Eventually, with help of locals (mostly natives) after having off-loaded the ship's freshwater and coal supplies, combined with a high tide, the ship became afloat once more. Arctowski had brought a Belgian flag that was to be waved as is traditionally done before a ship sinks! "It was a close call" as mentioned by George Lecointe in his 1904 book.

A similar event had already happened offshore The Netherlands in 1897 when the ship was on its way to Antwerp and hit a large sand bank. The *Belgica* at the time was then towed by a Dutch vessel and de Gerlache had to pay a substantial fee for that rescue. This is rarely mentioned in the annals of the *Belgica*.

13.3 Flora

In this chapter, most of the specimens collected by Emil Racovitza originated from the Beagle Channel region, nevertheless, quite a few plants also came from the de Gerlache Strait. Hence, those plants which came from the Beagle Channel and environs will be presented in the section dealing with South America. Fortunately, all the specimens collected by Racovitza and originally preserved by him are in excellent conditions and are now curated at the Herbarium of the Meise Botanic Garden in Belgium. It is possible to download the digitised images available from the Meise Botanic Garden and are produced here with permission of Dr F. Leliart. Various specimens were originally described by several specialists: Bommer and Rousseau (mushrooms) in section 13.3.2, Cardot (mosses) in chapter 7.5, De Wilderman (phanerogams = flowering plants) in chapter 7.2, Stephani (liverworts) in chapter 7.7 and A. Wainio (lichen) in chapter 7.6.

Extracts of some of these works are presented here and key illustrations are provided and many of specimens have been re-studied by various experts since the Belgica expedition. Evidence of this is found directly on some of the pressed sheets that are adorned with comments from those specialists.

Figure 13.3.1 Photograph of Emil Racovitza sitting on a log in the Beagle Channel taken by Georges Lecointe and published with permission of Anders Bache from the MIA Museum near Oslo (from a photographic album given to R. Amundsen by G. Lecointe). Photograph enhanced using Photoshop© and then 'colorized' using palette.fm/color/filters. Note the dense vegetation (with many *Nothofagus* trees and shrubs) near the water's edge so characteristic of the region.

Figure 13.2.1 (left) Photograph of the *YS Belgica* on the sandy flats on January 1, 1898 near Harberton Mission in the Beagle Channel after she hit a large rock bank. The large canoe visible behind the 3 men belonged to the local 'brig' *Phantom* which was in Harberton Harbour at that time (Lecointe, 1904). A storm followed during which time the wooden supports (called béquilles (=crutches) by Lecointe) seen on the photo eventually crushed. Photo 'colorized' using palette.fm/color/filters. Note the original photo is likely to have been made by G. Lecointe. Published with permission from Anders Bache, Follo Museum, Museene i Akershus, Norway.

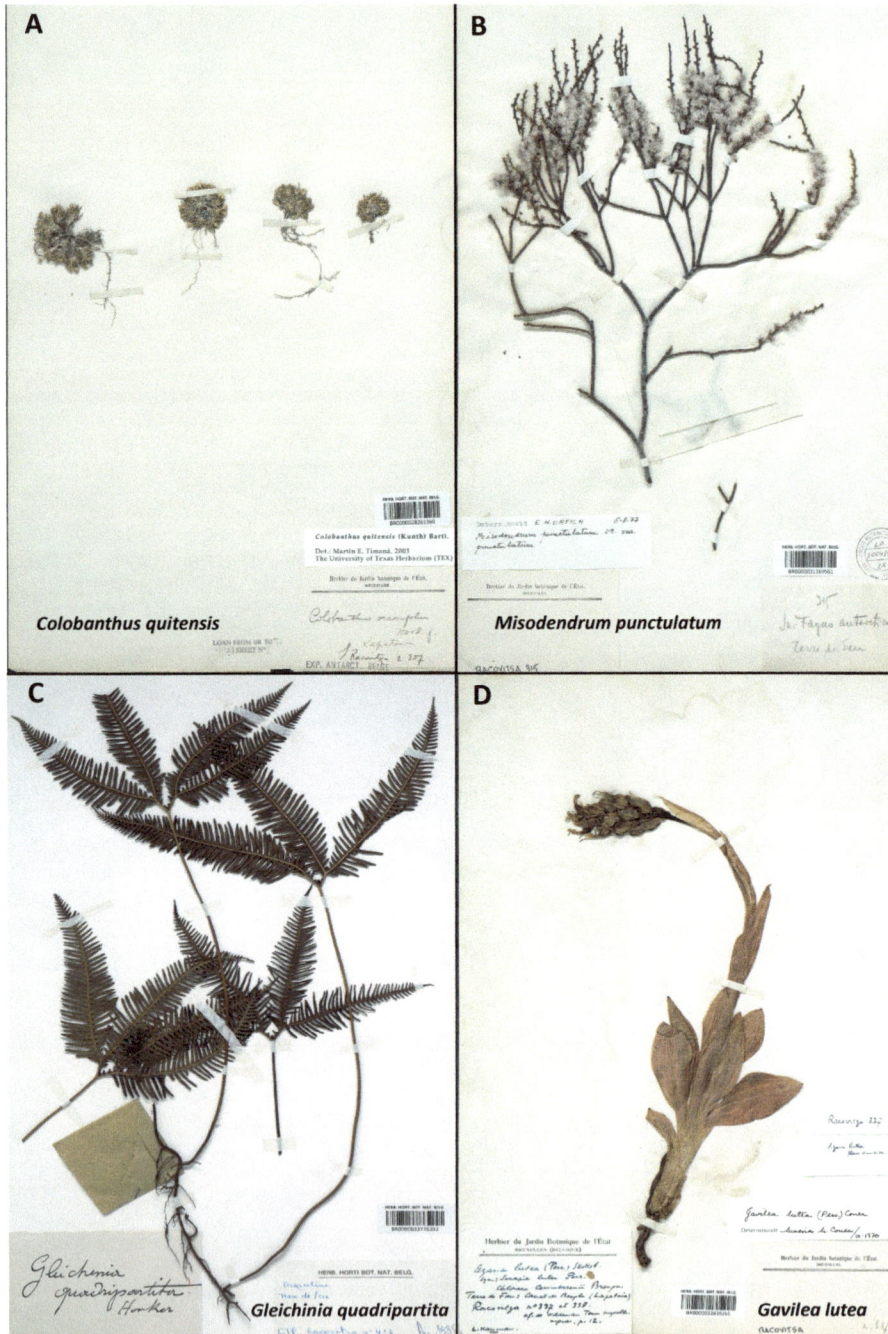

A

Colobanthus quitensis

B

Misodendrum punctulatum

C

Gleichinia quadripartita

D

Gavilea lutea

13.3.1 PHANEROGAMS (PLANTS WITH SEEDS)

De Wilderman (1905) produced an extensive monograph in the Résultats de la *Belgica* series that covered some 246 pages. He discussed some 539 plant species and varieties and concluded that none of the material collected by Racovizta who did spend quite an extensive amount of time collecting and preserving (pressing) material. There had been extensive collections and descriptions made by other botanists prior to the Belgica expedition. Of note was the work of Alboff (1896) on the plants from the Beagle Channel, and another important one by the same author that was published posthumously (Alboff, 1903). On the flora of Tierra del Fuego. In his extensive monograph, De Wilderman (1905) simply lists the two plants which Racovitza had collected in the de Gerlache Strait: *Aira Antarctica*, the Antarctic hair grass, and *Collobanthus quitensis* also referred to as the Antarctic pearlwort. For illustrations of the latter species, refer to Fig. 13.3.1.2A . The genus *Aira is* now replaced by *Deschamsia* a genus of grasses described by the young and brilliant French botanist Étienne Émile Desvaux who sadly died at the age of 24. He published a monograph on Chilean grasses entitled: *Flora Chilena*. Illustration of a conspecific taxon of *Deschampsia* is illustrated in Fig. 13.3.1.2A. For photographs of both flowering plants taken in the Antarctic Peninsula area, refer to Fig. 7.2.1.

Figure 13.3.1.2 Examples of plants collected and pressed by E. Racovitza and kept at the Meise Botanic Garden in Belgium.

A: *Colobanthus quitensis* Loc. 307, Beagle Channel, hills near the coal depot of the Argentinian government;

B: *Misodendrum puntulata* Loc. 315, Tierra del Fuego, on *Nothofagus antarctica;*

C: *Gleichinia quadripartite* Loc. 423, Tierra del Fuego;

D: *Gavilea lutea* Loc. 337-338, Beagle Channel.

All illustrations downloaded with permission from Dr F. Leliart from the Herbarium of the Meise Botanic Garden, Belgium.

A: *Deschampsia flexuosa*

B: *Ranunculus minutiflorus*

C: *Charex banksii*

D: *Baccharis patagonica*

The astonishing surprise in that De Wilderman (1905) did not comment on the presence of those two flowering plants on the Antarctic Peninsula, viz. *Deschampsia antarctica* and *Collobanthus quitensis*. These represented to be the first occurrence of flowering plants in Antarctica, and some 1300 km from the Beagle Channel !! Seeds of those plants would have had to travel across an ocean (Drake Passage) where winds are extremely strong and predominantly travel latitudinally. Surprising also is the lack of comment from De Wilderman knowing what Racovitza said at public conferences published in 1900 such as: *"on a particularly well-sheltered ledge, we found a small herb, a grass, the only flowering plant in this inhospitable region. All other terrestrial plants collected are part of the group of mosses, lichens and algae, lower plants…"* (Racovitza 1900a, pp. 37-38). Also, Racovitza in 1900b (p. 189) said: *"a single flowering plant, Aira antarctica, a tiny grass hiding between tufts of moss and seeking well-sheltered ledges on the side of cliffs"*.

Figure 13.3.1.3 Examples of plants collected and pressed by E. Racovitza and kept at the Meise Botanic Garden in Belgium.

A: *Deschampsia flexuosa* Loc. 346, Beagle Channel, Hills near the coal depot of the Argentinian government;

B: *Ranunculus minutiflorus* Loc. 121, Prairie *humide*;

C: *Charex banksii* Loc. 44, Dawson Island, Harris Bay near the sea in woods;

D: *Baccharis patagonica* Loc. 332, Beagle Channel, Hills near the coal depot of the Argentinian government, shrub in humid field.

All illustrations downloaded with permission from Dr F. Leliart from the Herbarium of the Meise Botanic Garden, Belgium.

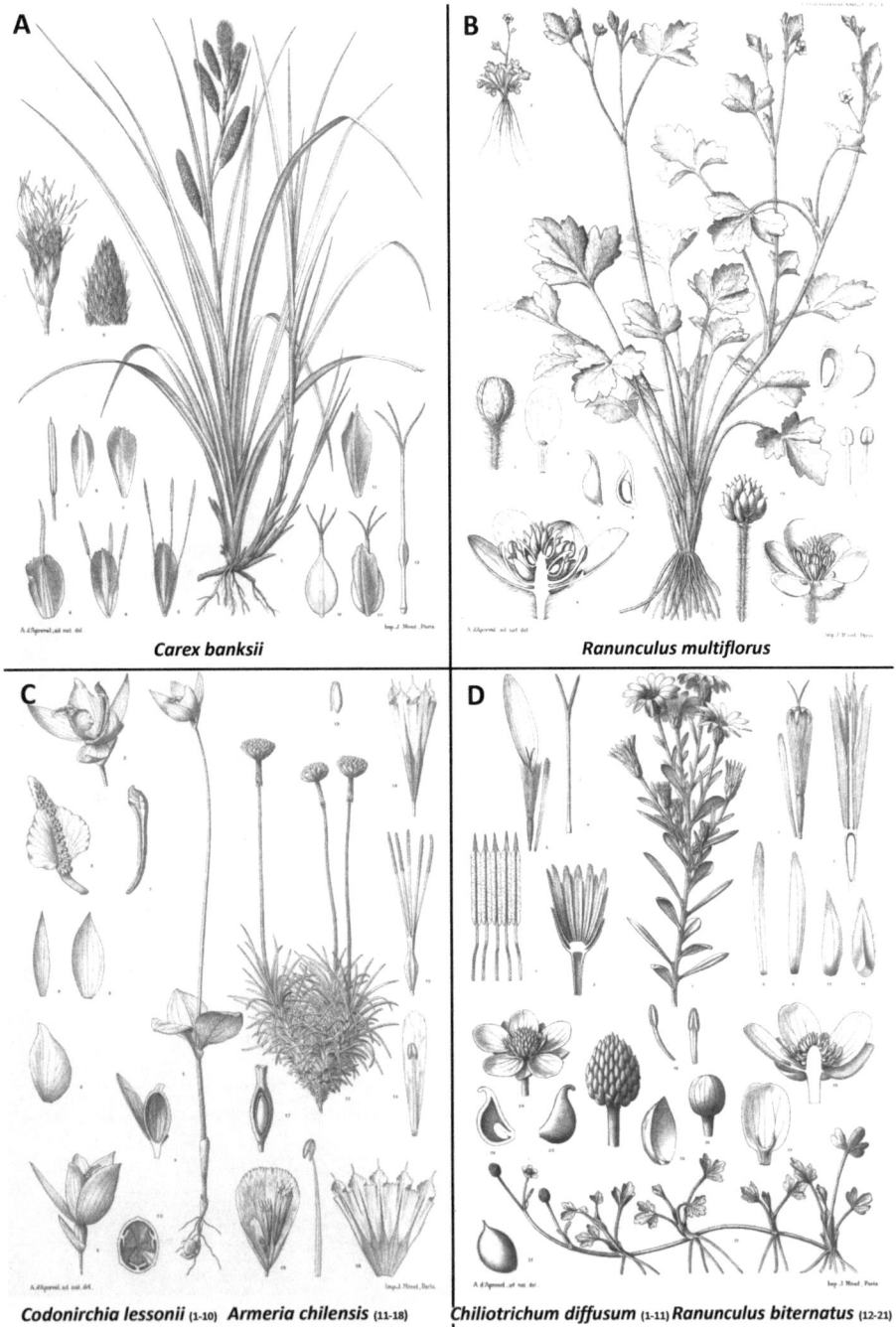

A: *Carex banksii*

B: *Ranunculus multiflorus*

C: *Codonirchia lessonii* (1-10) *Armeria chilensis* (11-18)

D: *Chiliotrichum diffusum* (1-11) *Ranunculus biternatus* (12-21)

Figure 13.3.1.4 Examples of phanerogams collected by E. Racovitza in the Beagle Channel area and illustrated by De Wilderman (1903).

A: *Carex banksii*, Loc. 44, 45, Dawson Island, Harris Bay near the sea and woods, 18.12.1897;

B: *Ranunculus multiflorus*, Loc. 37, on hills around Punta Arenas, 6.12.1897: Loc. 121, 128, in the woods and humid fields surrounding the town, 9.12.1897;

C: *Codoronirchis lessonii* (1-10), Loc. 108, woods and fields around Punta Arenas; Loc. 384b, Londonderry Island, Torrent Bay, French Canal, hills bordering the bay, 17.12.1897, and *Armeria chilensis* (11-18), Loc. 403, Clarence Island, Hope Harbour (Magdalena Sound), on sandy beaches, 14,12,1897;

D: *Chiliotrichium diffusum* (1-11), Loc. 53, Dawson Island, Harris Bay, in forest near the sea and hills near Punta Arenas, 10.12.1897; *Ranunculus biternatus* (12-21), Loc. 39b. 109, hills surrounding Punta Arenas, 6 and 9.12.1897.

All illustrations adapted from De Wildeman (1905).

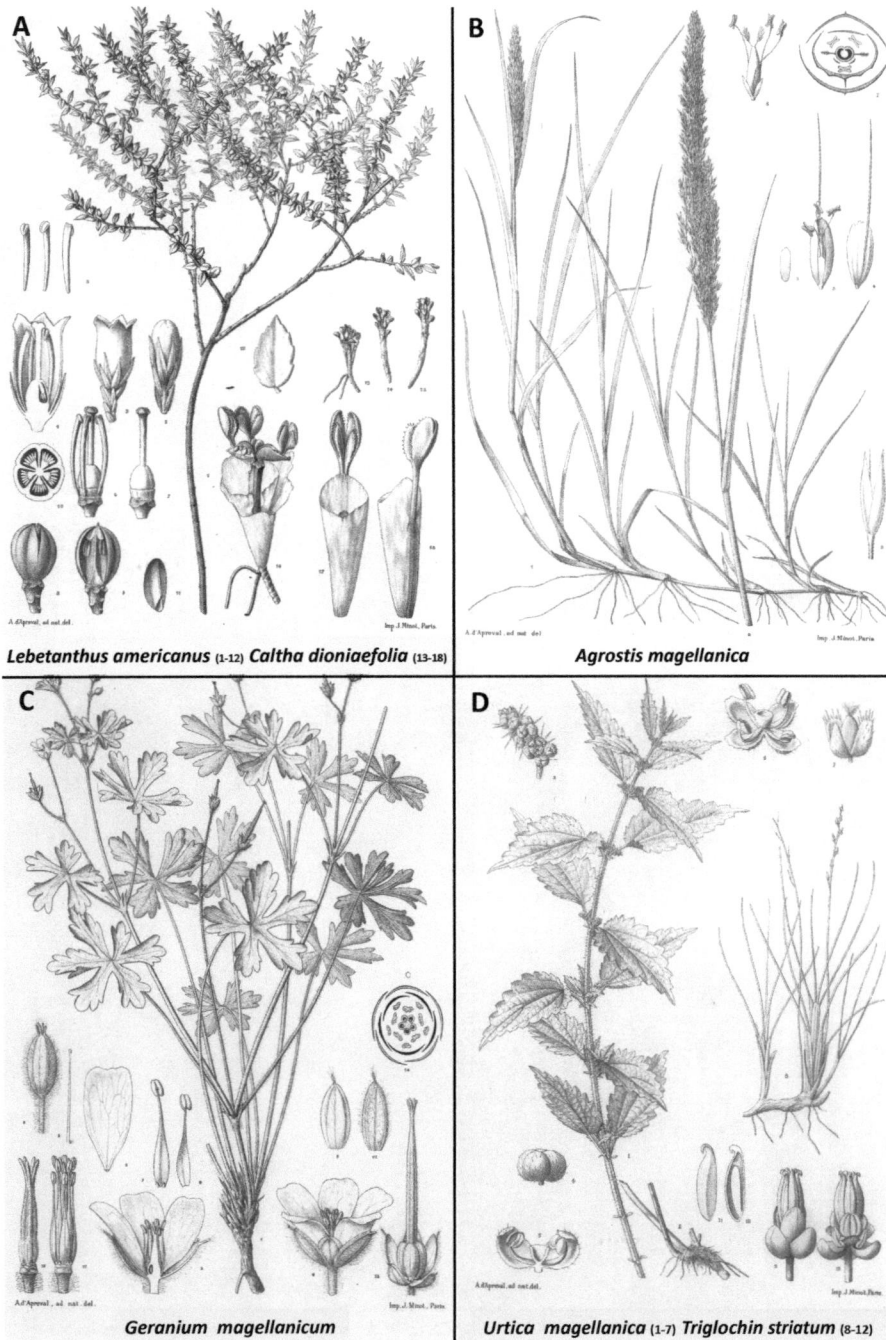

A: *Lebetanthus americanus* (1-12) *Caltha dioniaefolia* (13-18)

B: *Agrostis magellanica*

C: *Geranium magellanicum*

D: *Urtica magellanica* (1-7) *Triglochin striatum* (8-12)

Figure 13.3.1.5 Examples of phanerogams collected by Racovitza in the Beagle Channel area and illustrated by De Wilderman (1903).

A: *Lebetanthus americanus (*1-12), Loc. 404, Clarence Island, Hope Harbour (Magdalena Sound) and *Caltha dionaefolia (*13-18), Clarence Island, Havre Hope (Magdalena Sound), 14.12.1897;

B: *Agrostis magellanica,* Loc. 287-290, St. John Gulf, Staten Island, 8.1.1898;

C: *Geranium magellanicum,* Loc.47, Harris Bay, Dawson Island, 10.12.1987; Loc. 336, Lapataïa, Beagle Channel, hills surrounding the coal depot of the Argentinian Government, 23.12.1897;

D: *Urtica magellanica* (1-7), Loc. 402, Clarence Island, Hope Harbour (Magdalena Sound), entrance of a creek in the moist plain, no date recorded, and *Triglochin striatum* (8-12),Loc. 326, Lapataïa, Beagle Channel, hills near the coal depot of the Argentinian government, 23.12.1897.

All illustrations adapted from De Wildeman (1905).

13.3.2 MUSHROOMS

Emil Racovitza was vigilant in his collecting of the flora during the Belgica expedition and did not miss the fungi (mushrooms). Nevertheless, his collections which were mostly obtained from the Beagle Channel area were passed onto two women friends Elisa Bommer and Mariette Rousseau-Hannon. Together, they had already published several papers on the mushrooms of Belgium in the Journal de la Société royale de Botanique de Belgique. They described ten new species from the Beagle Channel area. These experts also mentioned having obtained a specimen from the de Gerlache Strait, which they described as a new species *Sclerotium antarcticum* which was found in among *Deschampsia antarctica* plants on Danco Land. These authors had already published a diagnosis for this new species in 1900 in the Bulletin de l'Académie royale de Belgique on page 165 (for reasons, check comments in chapter 9.5). The material which Bommer and Rousseau described in 1905 is splendidly illustrated with 5 plates, one of which is presented below. Their material could not be found among the *Belgica* specimens housed at the Herbarium of the Meise Botanic Garden in Belgium.

Figure 13.3.2 Examples of mushrooms collected by E. Racovitza and illustrated by Bommer and Rousseau (1905)

A: *Cyttaria darwinii,* Loc. 104, Beagle Channel, Lapataïa, all tumerous specimens on *Nothogagus antarctica,* 1-4 at the same scale;

B: *Cyttaria darwinii,* Loc. 104, Beagle Channel, Lapataïa;

C: *Puccinia cingens* (1-4), Loc. 96, Harberton Harbour, Beagle Channel; *Aecidium jacobsthalii-henriei* (5-7), near Punta Arenas, 6.12.1897; **D:** *Cyttaria darwinii* (1-5), Loc. 104, Beagle Channel, Lapataïa, and *Podocrea deformans* (6-7), Loc. 97, Harberton Harbour, Beagle Channel, 8.1.1898.

All illustrations adapted from Bommer and Rousseau (1905).

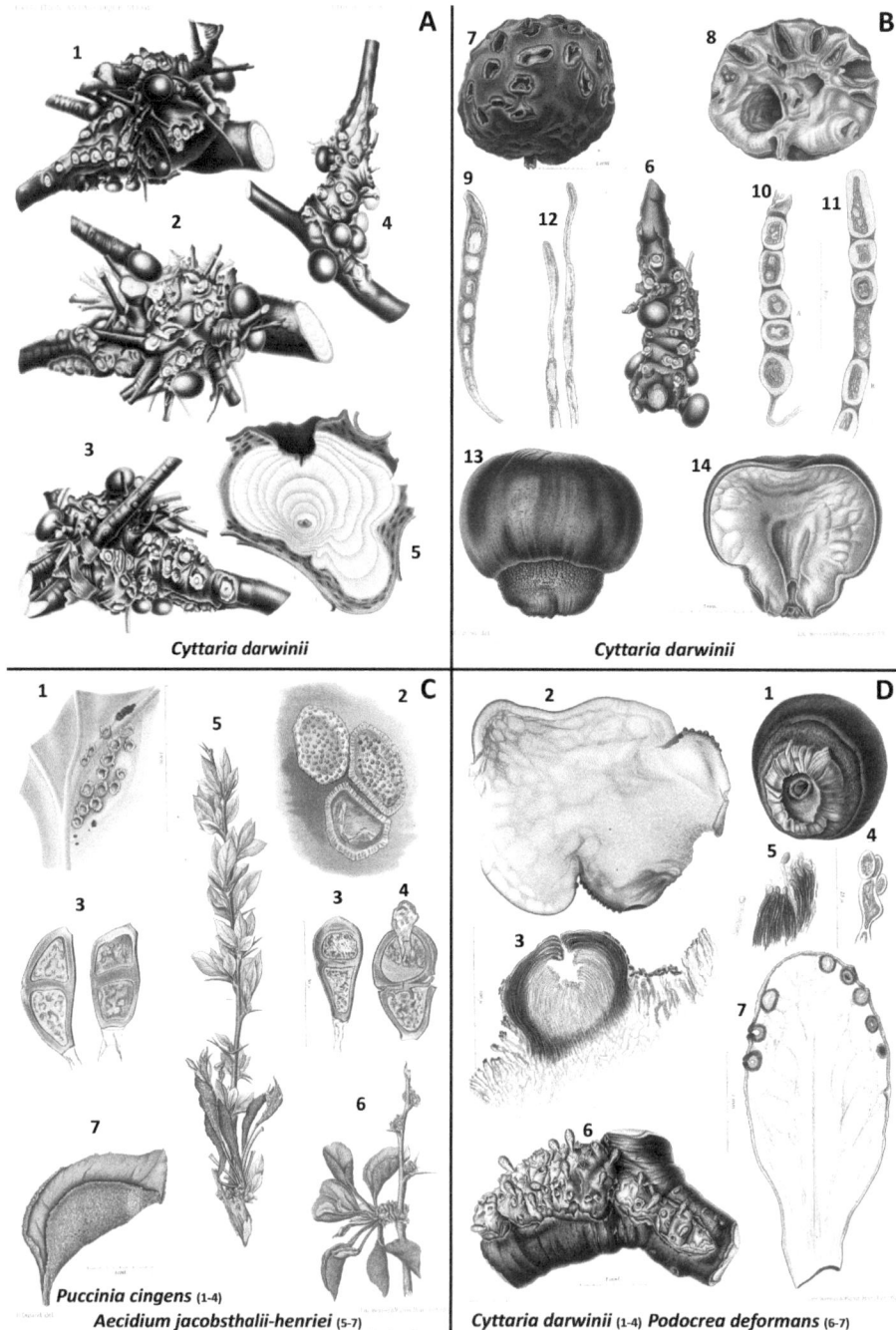

Cyttaria darwinii

Cyttaria darwinii

Puccinia cingens (1-4)
Aecidium jacobsthalii-henriei (5-7)

Cyttaria darwinii (1-4) *Podocrea deformans* (6-7)

13.4 Invertebrates in the Beagle Channel area

Racovitza made extensive collections in the Beagle channel, especially of insects and he must have preserved them extremely well as numerous monographs were published in the Scientific Reports of the SY Belgica expedition. Only a small representation of these are presented here as to discuss them all would take too much space in this book. The reader is advised to consult all the scientific reports published in the Résultats du voyage du S. Y. Belgica en 1897-1898- 1899. A complete list is available in Table 9.6.1.

Naturally, the spectacular illustrations are favoured here for display.

In total, Racovitza brought back to Belgium some 48 insect species, 20 of which were new. 18 species had been collected at Ultima Esperanza and surroundings in the Chilean Patagonia until November 26, 1897, when he accompanied Don Francisco Moreno who was at the time Director of the Museum of La Plata. The latter was the President of the Argentinian Commission designated to trace the boundary between Chile and Patagonia. The two travelled together for some 20 days on horseback to collect biological material. For more details, refer to Racovitza's letters addressed to his parents on November 2 and 25, 1897 (Racovitza, 1998).

Four insect species were found in the 'Canal Anglais' in the Beagle Channel (Magellan Strait) on December 20, 1897, 19 others were found at Lapataïa during a long stay between December 23 and 20, 1897, and finally six species were found in the Staten Island on January 8, 1898.

And of course, the most important finding was that of the flightless chironomid *Belgica antarctica* already discussed and illustrated in Chapter 7.3.

Since, it is considered here that the illustrations of the insect collections are so outstanding, several of these are reproduced here. It may be that that the taxonomy of some of these insects has seen been revised since 1906, but no attempt was made to search for evidence, simply as I am not an expert on insects.

The original insect volume was introduced by G. Severin, and then various experts described members of the Orthoptera, Hemiptera, Coleoptera, Hymenoptera and Diptera. The names of these experts are to be found in the monograph introduced by Severin (1906). All the illustrations shown here were of new species (labelled as n. sp.) at the time of publication in 1906).

Collections made in Patagonia consisted of *Udenus W-nigrum, Antarctica subamaroides*, Collections made in Patagonia consisted of *Udenus W-nigrum, Antarctica subamaroides, Listronyx hirsutus, Nyctelia longeplicata, Nyctellia bremei, Otiorhynchus (Tournieria) antarcticus, Thynnus racovitzai, Thynnus holomelas, Tipula flavo-annulata* (Rio Gellegos).

Lapataïa: *Trechus winckei, Antarctica racovitzai, Microcara fuegensis, Tolmerus longipennis, Sybilla dancoi. Meteorus australis.*

Baie du Grand Glacier, Canal Anglais, Tierra del Fuego: *Jacobsiella magellanica.*

Harberton Harbour, Beagle Channel: *Phorocera triangulifera.*

Terre Saint Jean, Staten Island: *Hemiteles antarcticus, Eristalis croceïmaculata, Scatophila curtipennis.*

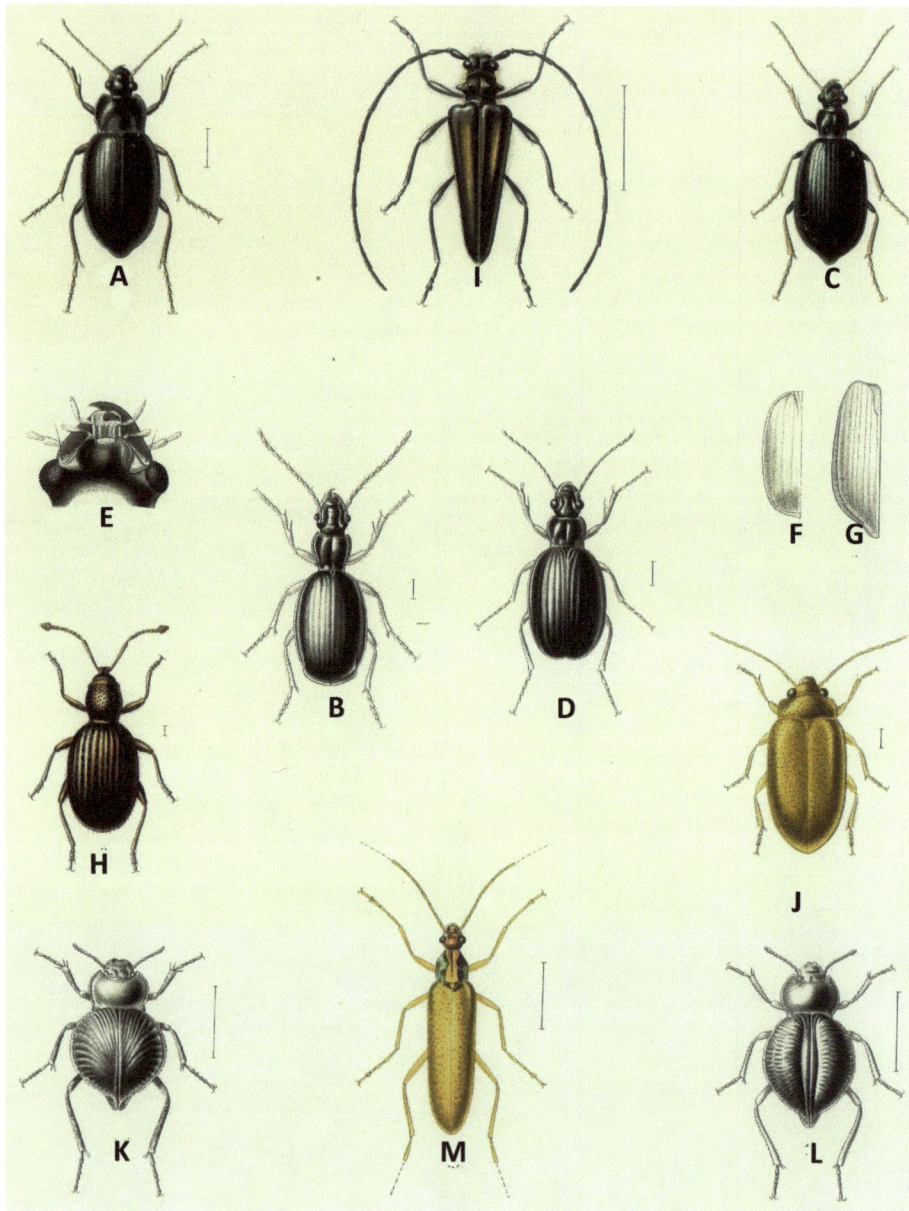

Figure 13.4.1

A: *Antarctia subamaroides* n.sp.;

B: *Trechus einclei* n.sp.;

C: *Antarctia racovitzai* n.sp.;

D: *Trechus antarcticus* Dej.;

E: Head of *A. racovitzai;*

F: Elytra of *R. winckei;*

G: Elytra of *A. racovitzai;*

H: *Otiorrhynchus antarcticus* n.sp.;

I: *Sibylla dancoi* n. sp.;

J: *Microcara dancoi* n. sp.;

K: *Nyctelia bremei* Waterhouse;

L: *Nyctelia longeplicata* n. sp.;

M: *Tolmerus longipennis* n. sp.

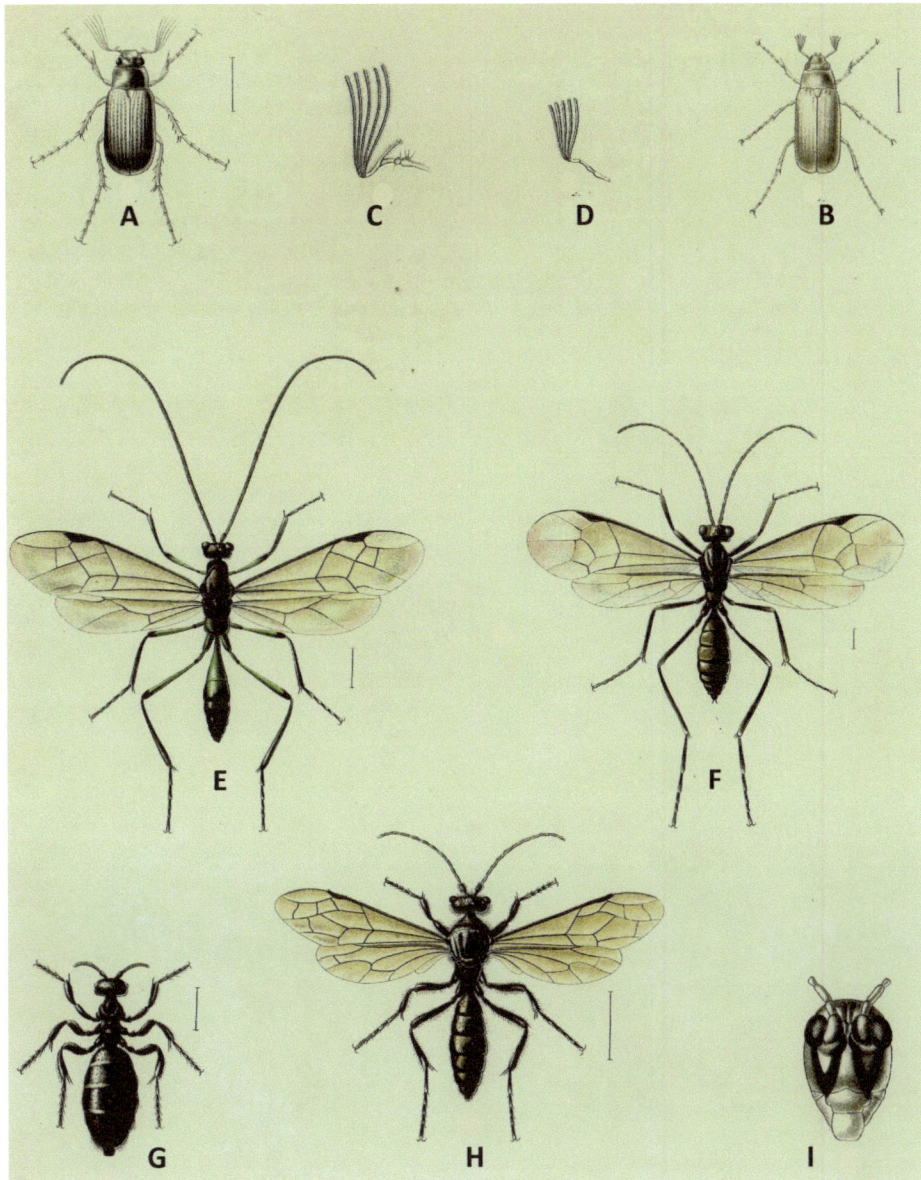

Figure 13.4.2

A: *Listronyx antarcticus* n.sp.;

B: *Listronyx hirsutus* n.sp.;

C: Antenna of *L. antarcticus;*

D: Antenna of *L. hirsutus;*

E: *Hemiteles antarcticus* n. sp.;

F: *Meteorus australis* n.sp.;

G: *Thynnus racovitzai* n. sp.;

H: *Thynnus holomelas* n. sp.;

I: Head of *Udenus W-nigrum* n. sp. (the latter illustration was quite controversial, refer to Severin (1906) pp. 1–11).

221

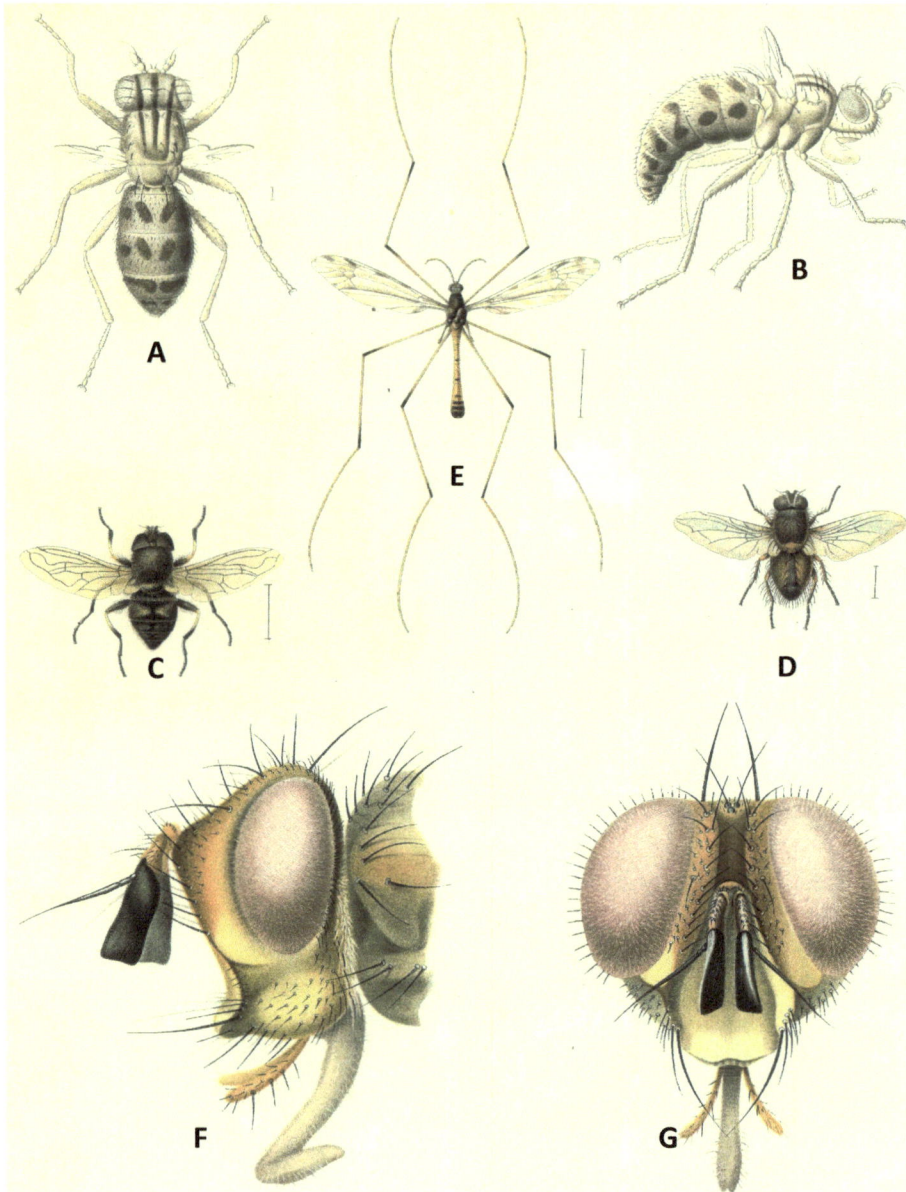

Figure 13.4.3.
A: *Scatophida curtipennis* n. sp. dorsal view;
B: idem side view;
C: *Eristalis triangulifera* n. sp.;
D: *Phorocera triangulifera* n. sp.;
E: *Tipula flavo-annulata* n. sp.;
G: *Phorocera triangulifera*, head side view;
H: idem facial view.

The original name of the flightless midge *Belgica magellanica* (Fig. 13.4.4) given by Jacobs in a rapid publication aimed at gaining taxonomic priority (see Chapter 9.5) that was collected by E. Racovitza changed several times. Already, when all the insects collected by Racovitza were described in the volume edited by Severin (1906), Rübsaamen (in Severin, 1906) changed the name to *Jacobsiella magellanica*. Since then, its final name of *Telmatogeton magellanicus* has been accepted. Simões et al. (2020) rediscovered the species at several locations on Navaro Island where Puerto Williams is now located along the Beagle Channel as well as the Omora Ethnobotanical Park (Puerto Williams, Chile, 2000), the UNESCO Cape Horn Biosphere Reserve (5 mill. hectares, 2005) founded by the eminent Chilean ecologist and philosopher Professor Ricardo Rozzi. Simões et al. (2020) provide many details on the ecology of this midge.

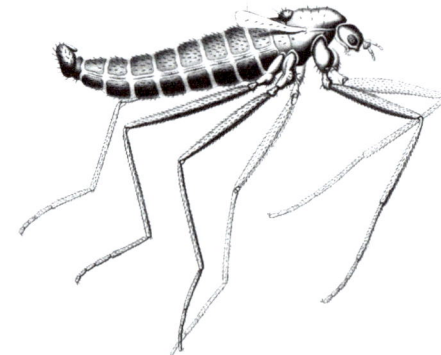

Figure 13.4.4 (right)*Jacobsiella magellanica* (Jacobs), now called *Telmatogeton magellanicus* (Jacobs).

13.5 Brief mention of whales and seals seen in the Beagle Channel area in the Staten Islands

Whales and seals were seen by all members of the Belgica crew, including Emil Racovitza who made a number of observations which are all assembled in the chapters dealing with both the descriptions of the biota in both the de Gerlache Strait (see chapter 7) and in the Bellingshausen Sea (see chapter 9).

Figure 13.5.1 Recent photographs of whales and seals

A: Humpback whales (*Megaptera novaeangliae*) blowing offshore Carlos III Island; photo Jardi Plana;

B: Tail of humpback whale seen in a fjord of the Cape Horn Biosphere Reserve; photo Jordi Plana;

C: Humpback whales in Beagle Channel; photo Jorge Herreros;

D: Colony of Southern Elephant Seals (*Mirunga leonina*) in Ainsworth Bay; photo Jordi Plana. All photos reproduced with permission from Professor Ricardo Rozzi and scanned from Rozzi et al. (2018).

Skarve koloni — Phalacrocorax carunculatus.

Chapter 14

Johan Koren – naturalist sailor

KEY POINTS

- Johan Koren was not only a sailor on the *Belgica* but had a great interest in the animal life. This is apparent through examination of his diary written in Norwegian that contains a large number of sketches of birds, seals and whales, many of which are reproduced here.

- After the expedition, Koren pursued his interest in travels to polar regions and also collected a vast number of birds which he sold to museums around the word.

- Koren also unsuccessfully tried to organise expeditions in the polar regions and sadly died of the Spanish flu in Vladivostok in 1919.

The Norwegian sailor Johan Koren was only 17 years of age when he joined the Belgica expedition (Fig. 14.1).

Figure 14. 1. Photograph of Johan Koren in his Belgica outfit, likely taken on his return to Antwerp after the expedition as he is wearing a medal (not shown here). Photograph obtained from the MAS Museum and used with permission from Mr Jan Parmentier in 2017. The photo was 'colorized' using palette.fm/color/filters.

He was distantly related to Roald Amundsen who looked after all the Norwegian sailors, even after the expedition. Koren wrote a 60 pages diary which contains many of his own illustrations, some of which dealt with activities on the ship (Fig. 14.2) which are so delicate that it has been decided to reproduce many of them as a collage picturing the many of the wildlife he illustrated (see Figs. 14.4 to 14.7). His diary was written in Norwegian and is now available digitally at the Norwegian National Archives where I examined the original. A good deal and interesting of information concerning Johan Koren is available at the following we site: https://amundsen.mia.no/en/person/johan-koren-2/, including one book in Norwegian about Koren (see Wikan, 2000), his travels and achievements, plus numerous articles were written about him and are listed at the following site: https://nbl.snl.no/Johan_Koren_-_1879%E2%80%931919. We learn that he gave another diary to Amundsen and is now available at Amundsen's House in Uranienborg in Norway.

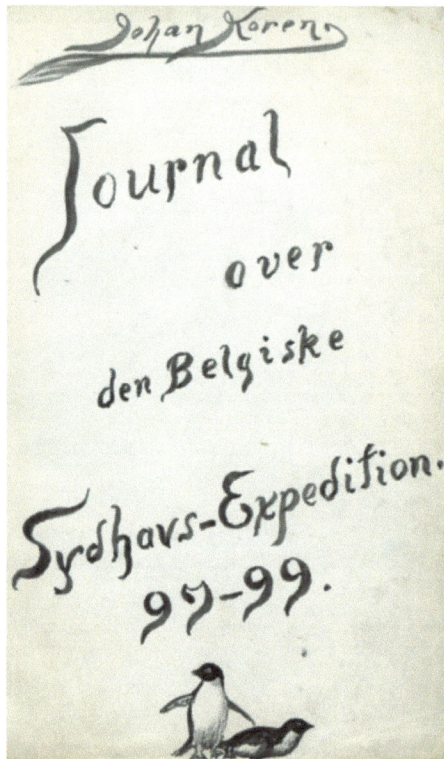

Figure 14.2 (above) Front cover of Johan Koren's diary held in the Archives of the Library of Norway.

Figure 14.3 (above) Sketch by Koren of the celebrations organised on the *Belgica* during the crossing of the equator in the Atlantic Ocean. Copied from his diary used with permission from the MIA Museum. Compare this sketch with the photograph displayed in Fig. 14.4.

Figure 14.4 (right) Reprocessed photograph taken by G. Lecointe which he donated to R. Amundsen as part of an album that is housed at the Follo Museum, Museene i Akershus, Norway. The original photo 'colorized' using palette.fm/color/filters. Published with permission from Anders Bache, Follo Museum, Museene i Akershus, Norway.

Koren provided much assistance to the biologist Emil Racovitza, especially in the ship's laboratory where he helped prepare, dissect, stuff and curate animals which eventually were deposited after the expedition in the Museum in Brussels and which were subsequently used for description by numerous experts, including E. Racovitza himself. The photo of Koren preparing a penguin in Racovitza's laboratory is shown in Fig. 9.1.

Figure 14.5 Illustrations of the avifauna encountered by J. Koren during his travels on the *Belgica* copied from his digitatised diary.

A: the wandering albatross *Diomedea exulans*;

B: the kelp gull *Larus dominicanus* - winter plumaged:

C: cormorants in flight;

D: Magellan geese (male and female), also called Upland geese *Bernicla magellanica*; dolphin from Cape Horn;

E: Magellan geese (male and female), called *Bernicla antarctica* by Koren;

F: heron;

G: colony of King shags (*Phalacrocorax carunculatus*) held in the Archives of the Library of Norway.

Figure 14.6 Penguins.

A: Adelie penguin (*Pygoscelis adeliae*):

B: chinstrap penguin (*Pygoscelis antarcticus*);

C: Gentoo penguin (*Pygoscelis papua*);

D: ? northern rockhopper penguin with yellow feathers as labelled on drawing;

E: ? chinstrap penguin staying afloat (labelled as forster penguin by Koren), held in the Archives of the Library of Norway.

Figure 14.7

A: Whales in de Gerlache Srait (called *Belgica* Strait at the time for the drawing);

B: Weddell seals with typical Antarctic ice field;

C: men in small boat and sea lion seals around the Staten Island at sunset, copied from the Archives of the Library of Norway.

Upon returning to Belgium at the end of the expedition (see Chapter 18), Koren was presented with medals, one in Antwerp by the local chapter of the Royal Geographical Society and also in Brussels by the Royal Geographical Society. On December 9, 1899, Koren received a formal letter from Jean Du Fief, Secretary General of the Belgian Royal Geographical Society based in Brussels and also its resident General C. Peny, accompanying a diploma and a medal offered to him by the Society and the city of Brussels.

Copies of his two medals are shown in the figures on the opposite page (Fig.14.9).

After the *Belgica* expedition, Koren travelled extensively and collected many animals for various museums. For example, Mehlum and Potapov (1995) reassessed some of Koren's collections from the Arctic that are kept in the Oslo Museum. He even tried to organise his own expedition which never anticipated due to the lack of financial support. More information on this amazing person with a great interest in natural history is available on the web site listed above. Sadly, Koren died of Spanish flu in the American Red Cross hospital in Vladivostok in 1919.

Several books were published on Koren whom people referred to as 'The Boy Norway Forgot'. He was a very much liked individual who was very much interested in the natural environment.

Figure 14.8 Sketch of the two Polish scientists on the Belgica. Sketch processed by Photoshop©. Note his spelling of their names. Taken from Koren's diary held at the Archives of the Library of Norway.

Figure 14.9 (oppostie) Photographs of Koren's medals (recto and verso) awarded by

A-B: the Royal Belgian Geographical Society in Antwerp upon the return of the *Belgica* in that city;

C-D: the Royal Belgian Geographical Society and the city of Brussels. The moto in A reads: 'Overwintering at 71° 36'; in B '1876' is the date of the foundation of that society; in C the protector of Brussels the Archangel Saint Michael killing the dragon is shown; in D it reads: 'The city of Brussels, to Mr Koren, sailor onboard of the Belgica 1899'. Reproduced with permission from Åshild Haugsland, The National Archives Services of Norway, item RA-PA-0337 - Koren-familien.

A

B

C

D

Photograph of a person sleeping outside the ship waiting to make meteorological measurements, likely to be A. Dobrowolski. For more details refer to the caption of Fig. 15.4. Published with permission from the archives of the Vaslui Museum in Romania.

Chapter 15

Illustrations of activities of the personnel during the expedition

KEY POINTS

In this chapter a series of photographs, taken mostly by Frederick Cook, are displayed to show the activities during the expedition, simply to give a glimpse of what people did at times of relaxation, during excursions on the sea ice, and also towards the end of the expedition in the Bellingshausen Sea when there was a serious attempt at delivering the ship from the sea ice.

These photographs have been 'colorized' for the first time.

There is a surprisingly vast record of photographs detailing many of the activities by members of the crew during the Belgica expedition.

Many of these are reproduced here simply to give a glimpse of what people did at times of relaxation, during excursions on the sea ice and also towards the end of the expedition in the Bellingshausen Sea when there was a serious attempt at delivering the ship from the sea ice. We note that in the early months of 1899, the air temperatures remained close to 0°C (see Fig. 8.5.4) and the sea ice started to crack and move. Frederick Cook was instrumental in planning the organisation of cutting channels to enable the ship to be released from its entrapment. In addition, members of the crew used a large amount of explosives called tonite placed in drums in the sea ice too help break it but results proved unworthy. Craters were formed, but to no avail. R. Amundsen and H. Arctowski prepared a large amount of tonite in the staff room on the ship. This was a very dangerous operation as tonite is a very unstable compound, especially in the presence of water.

Many of the photographs obtained from a variety of sources (mentioned in the captions) have been 'colorized' using the program palette.fm/color/filters.

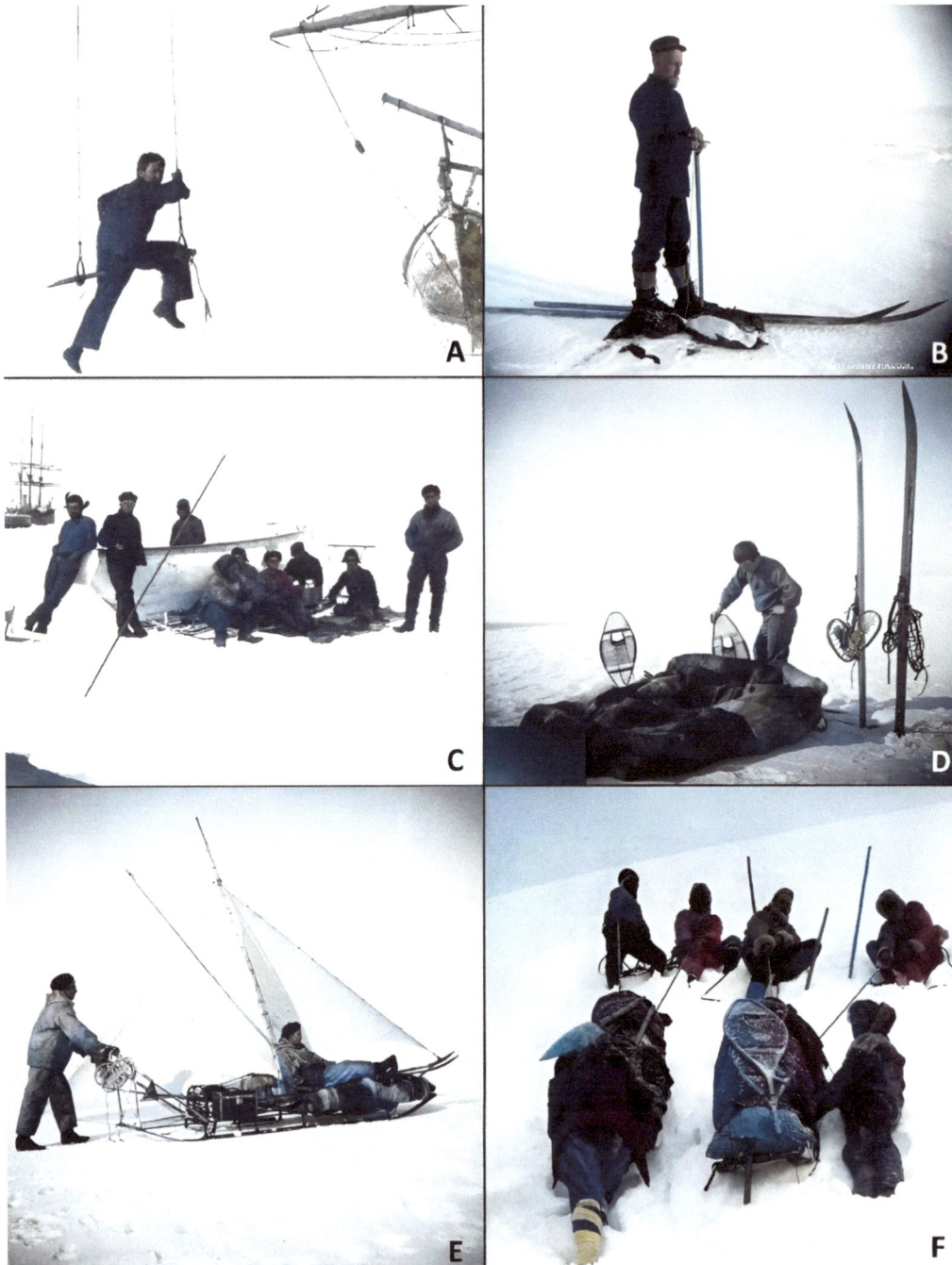

Figure 15.1

A: a sailor relaxing on a swing;

B: Amundsen on skis with 3 dead penguins;

C: men bivouacking during the time spent trying to cut the ice to free the ship from the sea ice;

D: Lecointe in the process of trying the 3-men sleeping bag, with the smallest section for him due to his short height;

E: man pulling the sled with a sail with another person sitting on it;

F: men in the process of pulling sleds uphill, likely to be Brabant Island. Photo A reproduced from F.A. Cook's 1901 book, B-F reproduced with permission from the Emil Racovitza Archive, The Library of the Romanian Academy, Cluj-Napoca Branch. These photos have been processed using Photoshop© to improve clarity and have been 'colorized' using palette.fm/color/filters.

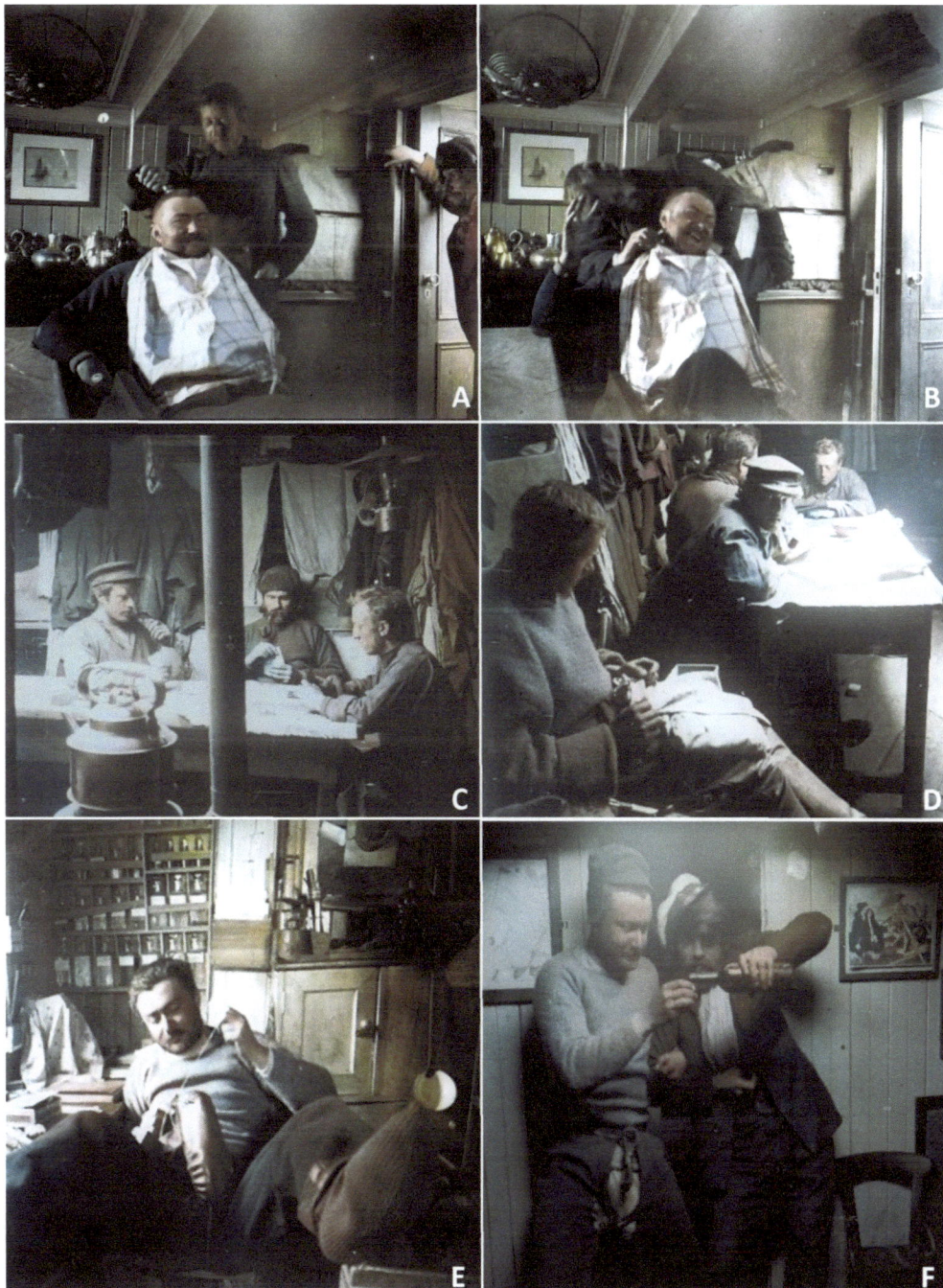

Figure 15.2

A-B: Amundsen giving a haircut to Racovitza;

C-D: men relaxing in the mess room;

E: Racovitza repairing his (traditional leather) shoes in the laboratory;

F: Racovitza and Arctowski enjoying a drink.

Photos **A-B, F** reproduced with permission from Dr R.-M. Mocanu from the Ștefan cel Mare Vaslui County Museum, Vaslui, Romania;

C-D: provided by Ms Rita Jalen, formerly of the MAS Museum, Antwerp, Belgium (C: AS1971.049.011 showing sailors Dufour, Van Mirlo, Michotte);

E: reproduced with permission from the Emil Racovitza Archive, The Library of the Romanian Academy, Cluj-Napoca Branch. These photos have been processed using Photoshop© to improve clarity and have been 'colorized' using palette.fm/color/filters.

Figure 15.3 Newly conceived tent made by R. Amundsen and F. Cook that consisted of sail material after the original oiled silk tent brought from Belgium was destroyed in a storm in the de Gerlache Strait. This new tent survived many meteorological events and a copy of the original dimensions of this tent are available in the Norwegian National Library archives. It is of interest also that a similar type of tent was used by R. Amundsen in his attempt at reaching the South Pole. Photo processed using Photoshop© to improve clarity and later on 'colorized' using palette.fm/color/filters.

Figure 15.4. Photograph of a person sleeping outside the ship waiting to make meteorological measurements. The photo is said to portray Emil Racovitza in the archives of the Vaslui Museum in Romania, but it is more than likely that it was Antoni Dobrowolski who was making hourly meteorological observations during the period of 'entrapment in the sea ice'. Behind the person lying on a sled, is the special hut dedicated to magnetic observations. Photo processed using Photoshop© to improve clarity and later on 'colorized' using palette.fm/color/filters.

Figure 15.5 Georges Lecointe taking magnetic measurements with members of the crew in the background hauling equipment through the sea ice as discussed in Chapter 9. Photograph obtained from the Lecointe Family collection, courtesy Terence Lecointe and processed using Photoshop© to improve clarity and later on 'colorized' using palette.fm/color/filters. In several publications by members of de Gerlache family, Lecointe has been misidentified as representing Frederick Cook. The correct identification was confirmed by the Belgian surveyor Jean-Jacques Derwael.

Figure 15.6 Photograph of the young engineer Max Van Rysselberghe who had modified a burner for melting blocks of snow in order to produce freshwater for human consumption, but also to have sufficient water reserves to enable fighting a potential fire on the ship. Photo processed using Photoshop© to improve clarity and later on 'colorized' using palette.fm/color/filters. Published with permission from the Emil Racovitza Archive, The Library of the Romanian Academy, Cluj-Napoca Branch.

Figure 15.7 Photograph of Emil Racovitza relaxing on the snow, reproduced with permission from Dr R.-M. Mocanu from the Ștefan cel Mare Vaslui County Museum, Vaslui, Romania. Photo 'colorized' using palette.fm/color/filters'.

Figure 15.8 Collage of photographs showing people's activities aiming at releasing the ship from its 'entrapment' in the sea ice. **A:** A man attempting at cutting a channel in the sea ice using a large metal saw; **B:** Lecointe and Melaerts next to an already enlarged channel; **C:** four men using a metal saw to cut the sea ice; **D:** effects of a tonite explosion while attempting to make an opening in the sea ice. A and B were provided by Rita Jalen, formerly of the MAS in Antwerpen, C obtained from the Emil Racovitza Archive, The Library of the Romanian Academy, Cluj-Napoca Branch, and D copied from F. Cook's book. All photos processed using Photoshop© to improve clarity and later on 'colorized' using palette.fm/color/filters.

Photograph taken by Frederick Cook of a woman covered by a guanaco pelt. Published with permission from Laura Kissel, Polar Curator at Ohio State University and Carol Smith of the Sullivan County Museum in Hurleyville, New York where some of the F.A. Cook archives are held.

Chapter 16

Frederick Cook and the First People of Patagonia

Charles Darwin visited what is now called the Beagle Channel in 1832 (Fig. 15.1) and later on the *Belgica* returned to it and personnel made observations in contradictions with those of Darwin.

16.1 Charles Darwin and HMS Beagle

Charles Darwin visited what is now called the Beagle Channel in 1832 (Fig. 15.1) during his voyage around the world and he mentioned at length the indigenous people he saw there. Revisiting Darwin's Voyage, Catlin and Kelly (2009) stated that in 1832 Darwin wrote the following: *"their language does not deserve to be called articulate. He further stated that it is like a man clearing his throat, to which may be added another very hoarse man trying to shout and a third encouraging a horse with that peculiar noise which is made in one side of the mouth. Darwin also stated that their food chiefly consists in limpets & muscles, together with seals & a few birds; they must also catch occasionally a Guanaco. They seem to have no property excepting bows and arrows and spears. I shall never forget how savage and wild one group was. 4 or 5 men suddenly appeared on a cliff near to us – they were absolutely naked and with long steaming hair... their appearance was strange, that it was scarcely like that of earthly inhabitants"* (see also Catling and Kelly, 2009). Darwin was accompanied by the artist Conrad Martens who painted the Channel and also the 'natives'. Two paintings appear overleaf and it is interesting to note that the sketches are somewhat 'romanticised', especially the surroundings of the Channel. Compare for example recent photographs of the area shown in Chapter 13.

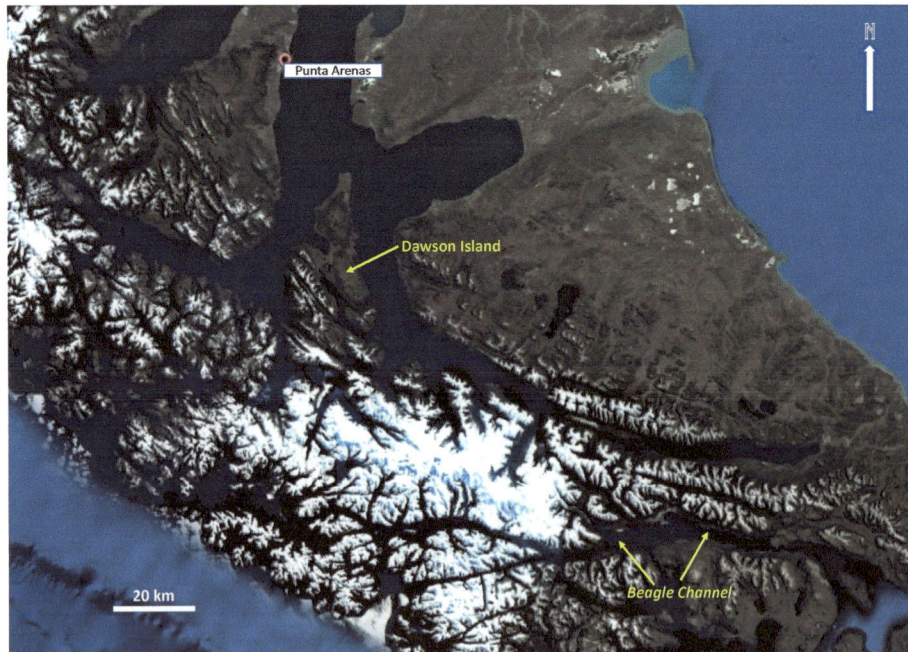

Figure 16.1.1 Google Earth© satellite imagery of Patagonia showing the location of Dawson Island and the Beagle Channel visited by the Belgica expedition.

Figure 16.1.2 Painting of the Beagle Channel made by Conrad Martens in 1833, who was the artist who accompanied Charles Darwin and Captain Fitz Roy on the *HMS Beagle* in the seaways of Tierra del Fuego (now referred to as Beagle Channel). Reproduction from Wikimedia Commons. Note the Indigenous People pictured in their canoe (in which they lived) at the front on the left.

Figure 16.1.3 Reproduction of a water colour painting made by Conrad Martens when he accompanied Charles Darwin the Beagle Channel (see more details in Fig. 15.2) between 1831 and 1836. Reproduction from Wikimedia Commons.

243

16.2 Frederic Cook's interest in the Native People of Patagonia

The opinion of the Belgica people differed extensively from those of Charles Darwin. After spending several days in Punta Arenas, Arctowski, Cook and Racovitza boarded a small boat called *Toro* loaned to them by the Governor to go to Dawson Island, the Catholic mission of the Salesian Brothers, with instructions to allow the party to take anthropological measurements on the Fuegians. Arctowski described the small ship as horribly dirty. The sailing trip took all night and they arrived at 7am. The Chilean Government had given the island to Salesian brothers with the condition that they look after the people who were brought there. The Fuegians had been forced to leave by the colonist sheep farmers who had chased them out of Tierra del Fuego. Arctowski stated that the Jesuits knew how to profit from them. They used them as labour while looking after their material goods. Arctowski wrote that his impression after his visit to Dawson Island was painful (=pénible). He stated that it is 'a penitentiary of innocent people, poor devils who do not understand their fate, who do not know why they are detained, nor why they are forced to work. They all suffer, complain all the time and women cry. 'These natural men die as a result of the misery of our civilisation (Arctowski, 1901). There is not land left for them and soon they will be exterminated, like other Indian people have already been. There were altogether eight Salesian brothers and some sisters with 200 Fuegians. On the left there is an alignment of several huts where the 'savages' (*sic* Arctowski 1901) (Fig. 15.4) and on the right is a steam sawmill, some shops and other wooden constructions'

Figure 16.2.1 Photograph of the wooden huts provided to the Fuegian Indians on Dawson Island which Cook (1900a) refer to as Rio Grande Mission. Photograph taken from Cook (1900)'s book.

All the Salesians were Italian, other than a Polish cook originating from Prussian Salesia. Arctowski learned from the cook that there was no real interest in the Fuegians. Eventually Cook, aided by his companions took numerous anthropological measurements and photographs of the Indians. Arctowski eventually got to talk to a young man who had been in Europe and who spoke Spanish and, through the intermediary of one of the brothers, was able to make a vocabulary of some 100 words. These are listed at the end of Artctowski (1901)'s article.

He stated that the pronunciation of the words is extremely difficult, and some sounds are completely unknown. He also mentioned the Ona language which he claimed to be extraordinary guttural. Artctowski (1901) finished by saying that he firmly believed that the Ona people would soon disappear, with people dying on Dawson Island of contagious illnesses, such as pulmonary tuberculosis.

Racovitza in his diary (reprinted in Marinescu et al. 1988) devoted four pages to describe his trip to Dawson Island. Some of his notes differ somewhat from those of Arctowski (1901), but he mentioned more about people's activities, especially once a parent dies. He also listed a dictionary consisting of 47 words, many of which relate to plants and animals. He also mentioned the presence of Alacaluf people (also referred to as Yaghan) who live in the canals and who have a totally different language. He confirmed that the Indians were suffering from tuberculosis, but added that syphilis was also common.

Figure 16.2.2 Coloured drawing of young children that appeared in Cook's 1900 book.

Figure 16.2.3 Processed photographs of Ona Indians taken by Frederick Cook held in the Ohio State University, Byrd Polar and Climate Research Center Archival Program, Frederick A. Cook Society Collection. The photos were sharpened using Photoshop© and then 'colorised' using palette fm.

A: Ona chief;

B: Wife of an Ona chief,

C: person deploying a bow and arrow;

D: group of people with the Beagle Channel in the background. Note all people wear guanaco pelts.

Figure 16.2.4 (opposite) Processed photograph of Ona people found in Koren's diary. The photo was originally very faded, but was 'improved' using Photoshop using Photoshop© and then 'colorised' using palette fm. It shows the type of clothing they wore consisting of guanaco pelts. Copied from Koren's diary and used with permission from the MIA Museum. Note that this photograph seems to have been taken impromptu whereas those displayed in 15.6 A-C may have been taken after the people were asked to pose for the photo.

Cook was obviously the driving force behind visiting Dawson Island as he definitely had an interest in native people after having spent some time with Eskimos in the Arctic prior to joining the Belgica expedition. It is understood that he took many measurements of the First People of Patagonia, not only on Dawson Island, but later on near Harberton along the Beagle Channel and also after the return of the *Belgica* from the overwintering period. In an article published in The Century Magazine, Cook (1900b) described what he called three different races inhabiting Tierra del Fuego: (1) the short-statured Aliculufs who are living in the western Chilean channels who live in beech-bark canoes and in dugouts feeding principally mussels, snails, crabs and fish, (2) the dwarf Yaghans who are (were) the most numerous people inhabiting the islands around Cape Horn and northward to the Beagle Channel, and like the Aliculufs, live in canoes and feed on products of the sea, and (3) the giant Onas, who have refused contact with the colonists, are meat eaters, feeding principally on the local guanacos. Since the arrival of Europeans who brought sheep, conflicts occurred between the two ethnic groups as Onas were known to prey on easier targets which they called the 'white guanacos'. They lived on the main island of Tiera del Fuego on the southern coastal fringe of the Beagle Channel and principally use bows and arrows for hunting. In that Magazine, Cook (1900b) provided more information of the Ona customs and way of life.

Cook spent quite some time studying the anatomical features of these First Nation People and had promised a publication on his investigations, but it never appeared, like the other two volumes listed in the original list of *Résultats of the Belgica* expedition (see bottom right hand corner in Table 9.6.1; it was entitled 'Report on the Onas'). Attempts by Ms R. Fenstermacher at locating Cook's notes (as well as his medical diary) in the Library of Congress, where his archives were donated by his granddaughter Janet Cook Vetter, unfortunately failed

Nevertheless, Cook produced several stunning photographs of Ona people which are reproduced here. The originals are held by the Ohio State University Archives and permission to publish them here in a modified form was granted by Laura Kissel, archivist at that University as well as Carol Smith from the Frederick A. Cook Society Museum in Hurleyville, New York. For more information on Cook's use of photographic equipment and developing methods, some of which he had to improvise using dangerous chemicals, refer to his short article written for photographic experts (Cook, 1938).

More recently in an essay Glausiusz (2021) tried to understand the attitude Darwin had towards the First Nation People inhabiting the Beagle Channel. This is in contrast with the interest mentioned above of members of the Belgica expedition who showed much sympathy towards these people. Glausiusz (2021) identified that at the time of Darwin there was a racist attitude towards indigenous people of all nations. To quote Glausiusz (2021), she said that Darwin described, those people as "wild," "savage," "cannibals" and "idle"; also "retard[ed] in their civilization." This attitude has now changed but sadly members of the three groups of people who were inhabitants of the Beagle Channel have now vanished as a result of illnesses brought by the early European who arrived in the area and also contributed to their genocide. Thus, the archives brought back by the members of the Belgica expedition are proving a great interest for not only humanity, but also science. It is a great pity that Cook's anatomical measurements have never been found nor published.

16.3 A case for the vanished Yaghan dictionary

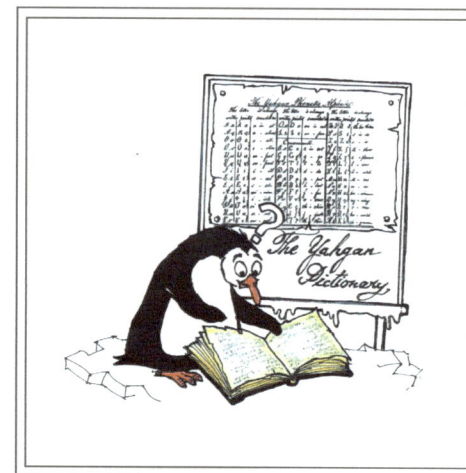

In the list of proposed Résultats, there is an item entitled: 'A Yaghan grammar and dictionary.' This proposed publication has had a very convoluted history worthy of commenting here, but not to be fully disclosed as it would consist of many pages. There is also a significant episode labelled as the 'Vagrant Dictionary' in a book published by E. Lucas Bridges and translated in French in 2013 by Michel L'Honoret entitled: 'Aux confins de la Terre: une vie en Terre de Feu (1874-1910)'. In this book, the grandson of Reverend Thomas Bridges who had met Frederick Cook on January 1898 in Harberton on the edge of the Beagle Channel (where the *Belgica* ship was marooned, see chapter 13.2) and discussed with him a manuscript that had taken him some 30 years to compile and which consisted in an English-Yaghan dictionary consisting of some 32,000 words. Thomas Bridges was originally an English missionary who eventually left his church so as to become the owner of a large Ranch with many sheep having received a large property from the Argentinian government. Cook offered Bridges to help him publish his dictionary in the US as he knew of a society

there that was interested in publishing all American Aboriginal languages. Bridges showed an interest in this offer but told Cook that he would give him his manuscript on his return from Antarctica. In the meantime, Thomas Bridges died in Buenos Aires in late 1898, but his family agreed to hand over the manuscript to Cook when he returned from his voyage. Lucas Bridges described in his book (chapter 51), the peregrinations of the manuscript which Cook had submitted for publication in the Resultats 'series' of the Belgica expedition. Georges Lecointe who was handling the Belgica manuscripts had already prepared the first proofs of the dictionary volume when a descendant of the Bridges family went to Brussels to claim the manuscript back, arguing that Cook had little to do with its preparation. At this stage, the manuscript was lost but eventually resurfaced as a publication in Modling, Austria in 1933 as part of a series of studies on poorly-known languages.

The initiator of this publication was Professor Ferdinand Hestermann from the University of Münster in Germany who co-edited it

with Martin Gusinde. Nevertheless, with the difficult times generated by WWII, the original manuscript was again lost and eventually was to be found after the war. It is now held in the British National Library in London with two other original manuscripts prepared by Thomas Bridges. More details are available in the publication by E. Lucas Bridges. Under its catalogue, this dictionary reads as 'Dictionary of the Yamana-Yaghan Language (b. 1898) Superintendant of of the South America Missionary Society in Tierra del Fuego; 1865-1933' (catalogue MS 46177-46181).

Copy of two pages from the original dictionary prepared by Thomas Bridges in 1865 that is now available in the British Library is presented in Fig. 16.3.1. Due to its age, there was no longer a copyright on this volume. Note that the original dictionary was deposited in the British Museum before being transferred to the British Library. Note that members of the Lecointe family are in possession of some 30 letters to and from Lecointe that pertain to the peregrinations of the dictionary, some of which contradict some of the material published by the Bridges family.

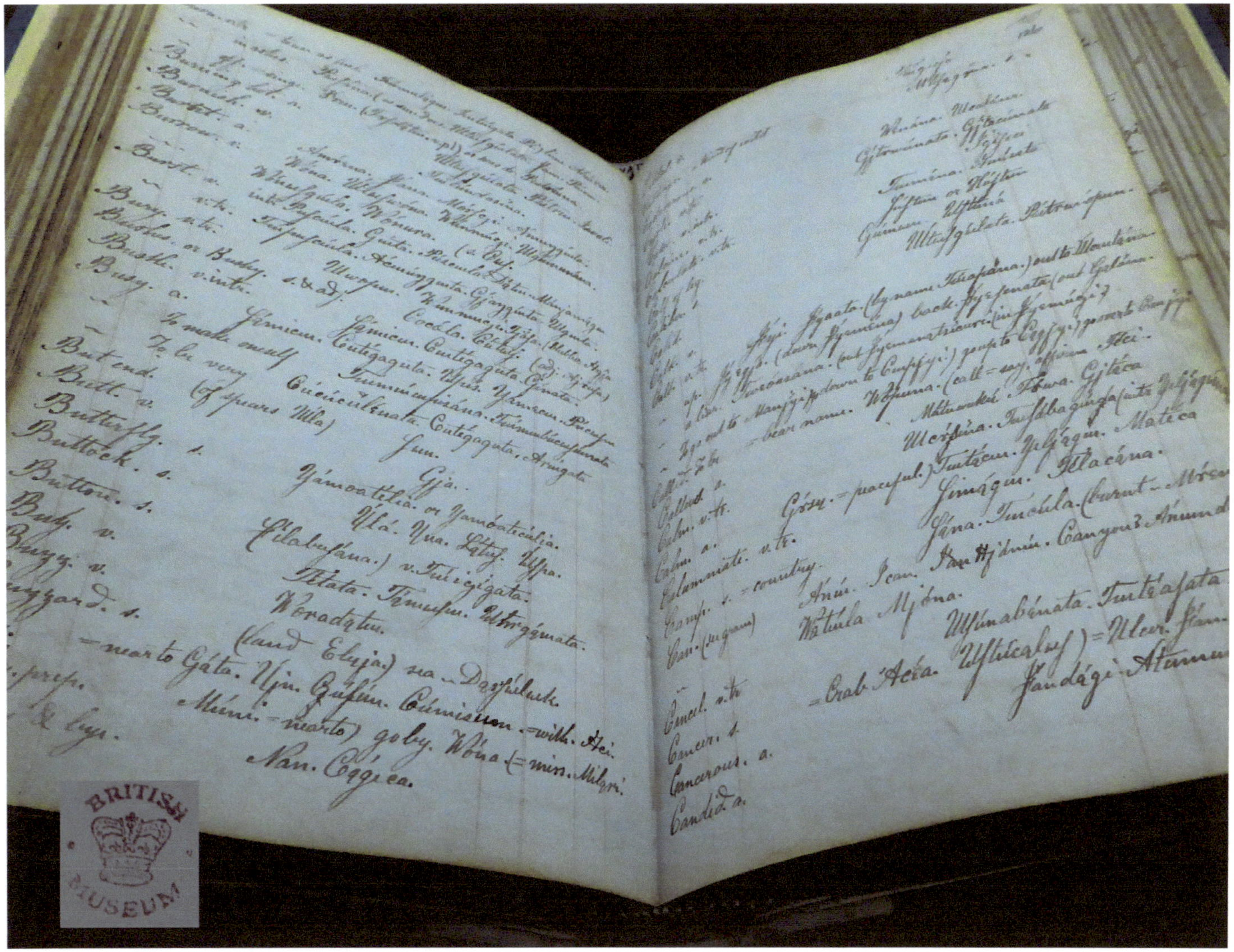

Figure 16.3.1 Two pages from the original dictionary prepared by Reverend Thomas Bridges. The stamp place on the bottom left corner confirms that the original dictionary was deposited in the British Museum and later transferred to the British Library.

6 Novembre 1899

Banquet
offert par le
Yacht Club d'Anvers
à Monsieur le Commandant A. de Gerlache
et a ses Compagnons.

Menu

Huîtres Royales
Potage d'Orléans
Petites Timbales Médicis
Turbot Normande
Filet de Bœuf à la Portugaise
Epigrammes d'Agneau Périgueux
Petits pois à la Française
Râble de Chevreuil 6ᵉ Veneur
Faisan de Bohême Truffé
Salade Laitue
Pâtisseries
Glace Belgica
Fruits — Dessert

L'ordre des Toasts est réglé

Vins

Graves — St Julien
Champagne Bertrand
Château Latour Pibran
Mâcon ou Beaune
Moët & Chandon

Menu of the official banquet held at the Yacht Club of Antwerp to celebrate the successful return of the SY *Belgica* (see more details in the caption of Fig. 17.3.4).

Chapter 17

The return to Antwerp and celebrations

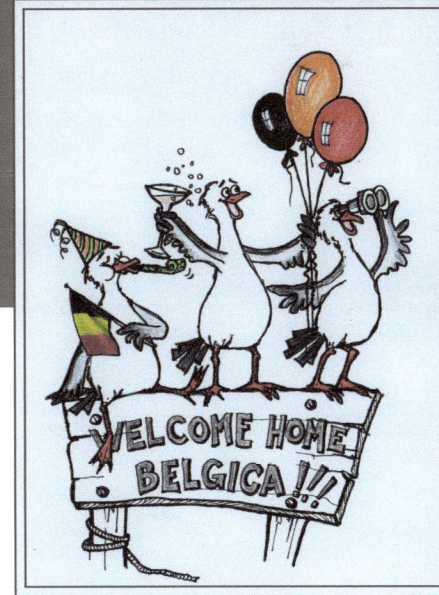

KEY POINTS

- On March 15 1899, the *Belgica* was finally freed from the sea ice.

- However, just the day before, an iceberg got very close to the ship and she was in great danger of being hit. Luckily this did not happen.

- The ship returned via the Cockburn Canal and is was a dangerous route but this was done to avoid meeting other ships to keep the news of the return away from the press.

- The ship and its crew reached Punta Arenas on March 28 but there were no celebrations. All enjoyed much scrumptious food, new clothes and a clean shave. They all stayed in the Hotel de France visited later by other polar expeditions.

- Arctowski, Dobrowlski and Racovitza boarded a fast ship to return to Europe and work on their collections/data. Amundsen also returned to Norway with a sick Norwegian sailor.

- Cook returned to Tierra del Fuego to fetch the Yaghan dictionary from the Bridges Family and acquire more anthropological information.

- Lecointe returned to Patagonia to take addition geomagnetic measurements. He re-joined the *Belgica* later in Buenos Aires, but embarked on a fast ship for Belgium.

- The return in the Atlantic Ocean proved to be very slow having to only use sails due to the lack of funds that prevented the purchase of coal.

- The *Belgica* reached Boulogne-sur-Mer in France on October 29, where Lecointe, Arctowski and Racovitza re-joined the ship, and all entered the Escaut/Schelde River on November 5, amidst amazing celebrations, some which continued in Antwerp with a lavish banquet.

- Eventually, more celebrations with the award of medals followed both in Antwerp and Brussels, including the Royal Palace.

17.1 Into the open water and return to Punta Arenas

On March 15 1899, the Belgica was finally freed from the sea ice. There was total relief and joy among all the members fo the *Belgica* ship. Even on the last day while trapped in the ice, Amundsen relates to a very frightening event. He said that '*this was one of the most critical situations in which we have ever found ourselves. We were getting closer and closer to an iceberg. We just managed to avoid a smaller iceberg by a few metres. The iceberg was twenty meters from the big one... everyone was standing on deck... we drifted closer and closer to the large iceberg... the situation was undoubtedly particularly tense... our stern no more than four metres from the iceberg... the engine was running at full steam ahead and we got a few meters away ...the ship crept forward, inch by inch, foot by foot, metre by meter.. We were free!*'' (Amundsen in Decleir, 1999, p. 198). It is interesting that no other authors from the Belgica expedition mentioned this scary event, except for Racovitza (1988, p. 150).. who wrote: '*the ship is drifting too close to an iceberg. She can almost touch it, which can constitue a great danger knowing the strength of the swell. We finish by leaving it with pain and overtaking behind ... a large lake of free water and many birds..*' He then stated that they went into open ocean. The date is a little different from Amundsen's.

de Gerlache then decided to head up north towards the Cockburn Canal which was a dangerous route but the aim was to avoid a busy seaway where they could meet other ships but wanted to avoid news being released of their return from Antarctic waters. The Commander wanted to be able to announce himself of the death of their two companions.

During the rest of the voyage the ship still collected data at sea, including doing a depth profile and collecting material from the sea floor.

On March 26, during the night they faced huricane conditions and the anchor did not hold on the sea floor and they drifted dangerously near rocks of Black Island. Visibility was poor. Nevertheless they escaped once more and finally reached Punta Arenas on March 28. There was no celebrations as the ship and its crew were almost unnoticed. Cook (1900), in his book, stated that the personnel had curious physionomies (see Figs. 12.2, 12.3), 'their clothes were in a good state of repair, they had long hair and their skin was rough'. In Punta Arenas, all members of the crew did require a decent haircut and new clothes, and also had very welcome meals cooked for them and to their delight in the Hotel de France [1]. While in Punta Arenas they were able to carry out some repair to the ship.

---

[1] The Hotel de France, which operated between 1890 and 1950, was located on the centre of Punta Arenas. It was the favourite of French citizens and travelers who came to the docks of Punta Arenas. Jean-Baptiste Charcot and his crew also stayed there (information obtained from Dirección Regional de Turismo Magallanes y Antártica Chilena). The owner of the hotel was Mademoiselle Euphrasie Dufour, originally from Marseille. Racovitza had already stayed in that hotel while waiting for the *Belgica* to arrive in Punta Arenas after having spent time in Patagonia with Professor Francisco Moreno, then Director of the La Plata Museum, collecting biological specimens.

17.2 The slow return to Antwerp

Arctowski, Dobrowlski and Racovitza boarded a fast ship to return to Europe and work on their collections/data. Cook returned to Tierra del Fuego in search of the Yaghan disctionary and acquire more anthropological information. Amundsen also returned to Norway with a sick Norwegian sailor. On April 1st, de Gerlache sent a letter via a fast ship addresssed to the Geographical Society with a brief summary of the achievements of the expedition and announcing the deaths of Danco and Wiencke. This letter arrived in Belgium 27 days later.

In Ria de Santa Cruz, the ship once again was marrooned on a large sand bank where there was a huge tidal range (some 18 m?) and this permitted to examine the underneath of the ship.

It came to my attention that, in unpublished archives held at the Royal Belgian Institute of Natural Sciences, A. de Gerlache had made enquiries to the Argentinian Government and had requested, on a personal basis since this was not part of the expedition programme, two of the following: a 'concession' to

establish a cetacean and pinniped oil smelter in Ushuaia Bay, and the other for land in the western part near the Argentian lakes region [assuming for either sheep or bovid farming].

de Gerlache had suggested that Lecointe make a reconnaissance for such ventures while making his trip on horseback in Argentina to install a series of geomagnetic stations along the way. Lecointe and the two sailors J. Koren and L. Johansen left the Belgica and were accompanied by two French explorers and two assistants.

Less than two weeks later, Johansen complained of an illness similar to the one he had experienced in Antarctic waters dealing with blood circulation. Given the rigours of winter that were beginning to be felt, Lecointe ordered the two sailors to re-join the Belgica. Together with the surveyor French G. Gex and an assistant, Lecointe carried out a reconnaissance as far as Lakes Argentino and Viedma, both in Argentina, which lasted more than 2 months, before finally embarking on an Argentinian war ship on 16 August 1899.

Lecointe then headed for Buenos Aires where he boarded a fast ship bound for Antwerp.

At the end of September, G. Gex wrote from Buenos-Aires to A. de Gerlache saying that 'Mr Lecointe will certainly have given you all the details of our expedition. To sum up, there is good land near the lakes. Requests for concessions were presented to the Argentinian Congress, with the one relating to fisheries exploitation was refused as unconstitutional, and the other was postponed.

There were many celebrations along the way, such as one in Buenos Aires with members of the Belgian and French communities.

The return in the Atlantic Ocean proved to be very slow having to use only sails due to the lack of funds preventing the purchase of coal. The itinerary can be seen on the map in Fig. 5.4. Eventualy, the ship arrived in Boulogne-sur-Mer on October 29 where Lecointe, Arctowski and Raovitza were all waiting. Eventually, she reached the Escaut/Schelde River on November 5 where they were met by Jules de Trooz and the Belgian royal boat *Clementine*.

17.3 Celebrations in Antwerp and Brussels

Jules De Trooz, who at the time was Minister of the Interior and Public Institution, was very enthusiastic about the expedition and, in fact, this proved very fortunate as he eventually authorised the funding for the publication of the 'Résultats' of the Belgica expediton with public funds following the recommentation of King Leopold II. De Trooz was accompanied by Fernand De Jardin the President of the Royal Geographical Society of Antwerp and stated: "*Anvers vous attend. Anvers qui est la métropole des arts et des sciences*" (Antwerp is waiting for you. Antwerp the metropolis of the arts and sciences).

Ample celebrations in Antwerp followed with the signing of the Golden Book of the city Antwerp (Fig. 17.3.1), and a lavish banquet at the Yacht Club (Fig. 17.3.3). In fact, in an article prepared by Georges Lecointe in 1901, there is a list of all the celebrations in Antwerp that included: (1) the royal yacht *Clémentine* was loaned to the Geographical Society of Antwerp and on board were numerous political and other dignitaries, including the de Gerlache family, (2) the President of the Geographical Society of Antwerp made a lenghty speech, (3) followed by another made by Minister Jules De Trooz, who announced that the King had awarded a Knighthood of the Order of Leopold to de Gerlache, Lecointe, Amundsen, Racovitza, Arctowski and Dobrowolski, (4) De Trooz further announced that Melaerts, Somers were to receive the Civic Cross (1st class), and the other members of the expedition the Civic Cross (2nd class), and (5) this was followed by a reception at the Town Hall where Mayor Jan Van Rijswijck gave a speech.

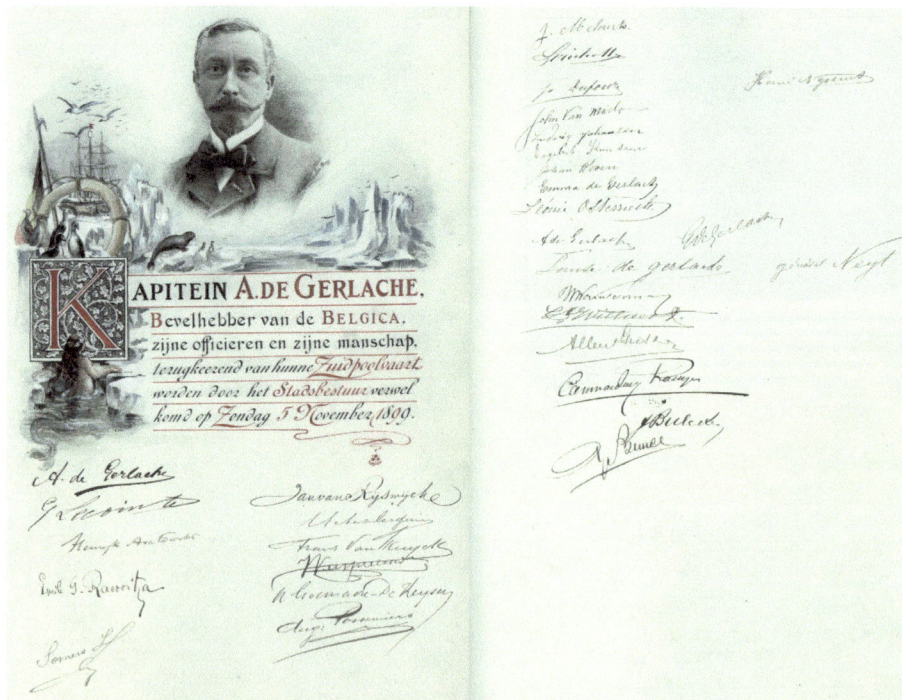

Figure 17.3.1 Copy of the two pages in the City of Antwerp Gold Book acknowledging the return of the *Belgica* and its crew on November 5, 1899. All the crew have signed this book except Roald Amundsen who was already back in Norway.

Notable additions bear the names:

- Jan Van Rijswijck – Mayor of Antwerp,
- Henri-Emmanuel Wauvermans – first president of the Royal Geographical Society of Antwerp,
- Léonie Osterrieth – the socialite and supporter of the expedition, and
- General Neyt – the first person to subscribe to the call for a Belgian expedition to Antarctica.

Permission to reproduce this was granted by Ms Nelle Van Bedts, FelixArchief, Antwerp, Belgium.

Medals were also awarded to all members
of the expedition (see Fig. 17.3.2) by the
Geographical Society fo Antwerp.

Figure 17.3.2 Photographs (recto and verso) of the gold medal awarded to Georges Lecointe by the Royal Belgian Geographical Society in Antwerp. Note on the right are the names of Mercator and Ortelius who were figured on the logo of the First International Geographical Society held in Antwerp in 1871. Photographs provided by Terence Lecointe.

Figure 17.3.3 Menu of the official banquet held in the Antwerp Yacht Club on November 6, 1899, to celebrate the successful return of the expedition. The extraordinary menu reads as: Huitres royales, Potage d'Orléans, Turbot Normande, Filet de Boeuf à la Portugaise, Epigrammes d'Agneau Périgueux, Petits pois à la Française, Râble de Chevreuil Grd Veneur, Faisan de Bohême Truffé, Salade Laitue, Patisseries, Glace Belgica, Fruits – Desserts, and wines as: Graves – St Julien, Champagne Bertrand, Château Latour Pibran, Mâcon ou Beaune, Moêt & Chandon.

Later on, there were also celebrations in Brussels, with an invitation to the Royal Palace, plus as a ceremony at the Royal Geographical Society of Brussels as well as the city of Brussels with additional medals being awarded in the presence of Prince Albert, who later became King.

In addition, on November 25, 1899, Georges Lecointe gave a long talk to the Royal Society of Antwerp that provided the first lenghty summary of the expedition; it included early maps with the original name of Belgica Strait on one of them (Lecointe, 1901).

Figure 17.3.4 Photograph of Jules Melaerts silver medal awarded to him by the Royal Belgian Geographical Society in Brussels. On the left is the box with the medal inside and on the right is the outside of the box holding the medal. Both items are kept in the MAS collections in Antwerp, item AS.1973.007.025 photographed by Waander Delivillé, and on the left by the author. Note a photo of the medals awarded to Johan Koren are shown in Fig. 14.9.

PART
THREE

Figure 18.1 The elegant *SY Belgica* trapped in the sea ice in the Bellingshausen Sea, a phenomenon that would no longer happened today as the sea ice has vanished. Photo courtesy of the MAS archives in Antwerp provided by Rita Jalen, reference AS AS1957.051.009 and sharpened using Photoshop© and then 'colorised' using palette fm. Note the presence of an observer in the crowsnest.

Chapter 18

Conclusions and lessons for the future

1897 – 1899

KEY POINTS

- The expedition was extremely well prepared and equipped. It proved to be an outstanding scientific success and was a display of amazing human endurance.

- Despite the fact that the expedition never reached Cape Adare, it became trapped in the sea ice for close to 13 months.

- During that time, despite the fears of the ship being crushed by the forces engendered by sea ice and shifting icebergs, the scientists were helped by the other members of the crew and gathered an amazing amount of scientific information in the Bellingshausen Sea and surroundings, especially in the de Gerlache Strait.

- Much of this information is particularly relevant today in light of the significant climatic changes that are occurring around the Antarctic Peninsula. Sadly, this information gathered some 125 years ago has long been ignored, and this book is aimed at informing the scientific community of its important and significant value.

- There is a need to return to the many sites visited by the *Belgica* and assess the changes that have already occurred and model future changes. This is urgent.

- Many of the Antarctic biota are under an imminent threat because of the disappearance of the sea ice, oceanic temperature increases and changes in water currents as well as atmospheric conditions that will be (and already are) affecting numerous species.

- The introduction of non-native species to the Antarctic Peninsula may cause likely irreversible environmental impacts on Antarctic ecosystems and biodiversity. There is an urgent need to monitor these.

- The impact on refractory black carbon on rapid snow melt introduced by ships taking tourists in the Antarctic Peninsula region is alarming, and ships ought to use different fuels or diesel filters. Eco-tourists should demand these changes.

The Belgica expedition was inspired by the Challenger expedition that started 25 years earlier. Acclaimed Belgian scientists strongly supported as well as helped towards the preparation of the Belgica expedition; some of those scientists had worked on material collected by the Challenger, such as the zoologist Paul Pelseneer and the geologist Alphonse-François Renard. They eventually sat on the Belgica Commission with other academics after the expedition to ensure the propagation of results from the expedition be successful.

The expedition was extremely well prepared and equipped. It took more than one year for the ship to be refurbished with two laboratories designed by Henryk Arctowski. Emil Racovitza purchased much necessary equipment and visited numerous laboratories and experts to learn about sampling and specimen preservation techniques. Arctowski also visited experts in Austria and received much advice from members of the Royal Geographical Society of London. That society also provided important maps.

The prime aim of the Belgica expedition was to reach Cape Adare in Antarctica and leave four people there to winter to make magnetic and meteorological measurements while the rest of the part with the ship would travel to Melbourne in Australia and eventually explore the Pacific Ocean. However, this did not happen as the ship became trapped in the sea ice for close to 13 months.

Nevertheless, the Belgica expedition proved to be a great scientific success, and the crew was very resilient, especially during the winter season when the ship was trapped in the sea ice. During that time, there was much fear among the men that the ship would be crushed by the forces engendered by the moving of sea ice as well as the drifting of large icebergs that could eventually crush the ship. Nevertheless, despite this endless fear of annihilation and possible drowning (in case of the ship being crushed), plus the potential loss of all the collected material and data, the scientific crew, helped by some of the sailors, continued their task assiduously. All worked endless hours, and at times spent many of the nights gathering data, even when outside temperatures were extremely low. Eventually, the ship drifted with the sea ice for close to 13 months before venturing into the open ocean.

This was the first time that a ship and its crew spent so much time in Antarctic waters and the scientific observations made were unrivalled. The scientific results of the expedition were published in 3767 pages that appeared (mostly in French) in a series of monographs entitled: 'Résultats du voyage du SY Belgica en 1897-99 – rapports scientifiques' and published in Antwerp, Belgium. Exquisite illustrations adorned some of the reports and were printed elsewhere by specialist printers in several European countries.

Key observations and data gathered during the expedition

In the Antarctic region:

1. Continuous meteorological observations (air temperature, atmospheric pressure, wind intensity and directions) lasted over 12 months, and this for the first time in the Southern Hemisphere. These were made by Henryk Arctowski.

2. Observations of sea ice, snow formation and clouds were made over one year by Henryk Arctowski and Antoni Dobrowolski, except perhaps during the period of total darkness.

3. Important oceanographic data were gathered that included water temperature profiles down to great depths. The thermometers were extremely well calibrated before and after the expedition. Sea water salinity was estimated in the laboratory on the ship by measuring water density.

4. It is now clear that the ship and the sea ice drifted together, and this was due to important undercurrents. The ship did not drift as a result of wind, except perhaps during the latter part of its entrapment when air temperatures were close to zero °C and the sea ice started to open up.

5. Definition for the types of icebergs were made and compared against those found in the Arctic Ocean.

6. Ample observations of penguins, seals, and whales were made and these were based on many dissections of seals at all stages of their life. Many descriptions of these animals made by previous observers were proved to be incorrect.

7. Many other animals were collected and described from all parts of the water column, including new fish species and many invertebrates. These relied on extremely well-preserved specimens collected and curated by Emil Racovitza.

8. A new passageway was discovered, mapped and described by Georges Lecointe. It is now called the de Gerlache Strait.

9. Many important discoveries were made in the de Gerlache Strait. These included the description of the first insect inhabiting the Antarctic region, as well as two flowering plants. Numerous other organisms, especially plants were collected and eventually described by experts on return of the expedition.

10. Geological observations were made in the de Gerlache Strait by Henryk Arctowski, with rocks subsequently analysed in great detail. Arctowski also identified evidence of a past and extensive glaciation in the de Gerlache Strait and even postulated the air temperature required to facilitate such glaciation.

11. Frederick Cook, the medical doctor, took extensive notes on people suffering from 'polar anaemia' and recommended as a remedy that people eat raw meat (penguins and seals) and stay in front a flame to regain good health condition. Unfortunately, Cook's medical report has not been found.

In the Magellanic Straits and the Beagle Channel of Patagonia:

12. A great variety of flowering plants were collected, pressed by Emil Racovitza and eventually described by experts.

13. Equally, numerous insects were collected a collected and carefully curated by Emil Racovitza and eventually described.

14. Evidence of a former glaciation was found by Henryk Arctowski and his rock collections were also described in detail.

15. Frederick Cook, at some stage was aided by Henryk Arctowski and Emil Racovitza on Dawson Island, made elaborate annotations on the First Nation People of Patagonia and provided some stunning photographs of those people. Unfortunately, his detailed anatomical observations of these people have not been found. All three researchers *believed that those people were soon to face extinction.*

It is now hoped that publication of this book with alert scientists of the great importance of the data collected during the Belgica expedition. This is particularly important in line with the awareness that the area visited by the *Belgica* and its crew is now facing significant changes as a result of global warming. Already, in the Bellingshausen Sea where in the ship was trapped fin the sea ice for close to 13 months, there is no longer sea ice in Summer. This has important implications for the survival of the biota that lives there. The sea ice (banquise) which seals that rely on for breeding and raising young is now absent; krill – an important part of the diet of seals, penguins and whales – is decreasing in numbers. Seals will have to find new locations to breed.

Hence, the data acquired by the *Belgica* scientists ought to form an important base line spanning some 125 yeas of observations. Importantly also, is that the French Charcot expedition that visited the same area where the *Belgica* had been some 10 years later - using similar instruments - ought to be re-examined and compared with the Belgica data against modern-day observations. Equally, on the other side of Antarctica, at Cape Adare meteorological data were obtained by the Southern Cross expedition in 1898-1900.

It is worth investigating the genetic material preserved in some of the specimens collected during the Belgica expedition that are currently stored at the Royal Institute of Natural Sciences of Belgium in Brussels to determine possible changes that may have occurred over 125 years in around the de Gerlache Strait and the Beagle Channel.

There is also a need to monitor the 'effects' of tourist visitors, as well as scientists, in the Antarctic Peninsula to prevent the possible introduction of 'pests', as well as viruses such as the H5N1 strain of bird flu that could have devastating effects on the avifauna. For a good but alarming review, refer to Hughes et al. (2023) which documents many issues already at stake in the Antarctic Peninsula regions and adjacent islands, and it also gives ample references. Antarctic ecosystems are significantly at risk and the Antarctic Peninsula is part of an extreme and fragile environment that deserves much more monitoring and modelling for a better future.

In addition, the impact on refractory black carbon (rBC), engendered by the long-range atmospheric transport of the bi-products of biomass fires in the southern hemisphere, as well as by local tourism and human (research) activities, was recently discovered to have an important impact on snow melt in the Antarctic Peninsula by Magalhães et al. (2024). These authors suggest that the use of low-sulfur fuels that produce less black carbon as well as biofuels which ships to be used by ships or filters on diesel particulate filters on chimney of ships would effectively reduce the emission of black carbon that otherwise cause rapid snow melt. Perhaps eco-tourists should insist on the ships that transport them to the Antarctic Peninsula to modify their destructive practices. It is urgent!

The recently published study of Landsat satellite images by Roland et al. (2024) (see discussion in Chapter 7.5) that identified a significant expansion of moss fields on the Antarctic Peninsula resulting from global warming is like the *'canari in a coal mine'*: entire ecosystems on the Antarctic Peninsula are about, if not already, to change, These need monitoring assiduously and we must make sure that invasive plants and other organisms do not reach this pristine environment, and ecotourists must be informed of the potential dangers they may cause.

In conclusion, this **very successful Belgica expedition was funded by Belgium,** its government, its people, many of its cities and benefactors, and more importantly, for the first time, it was **a truly international venture with people from Belgium, Norway, Poland, Romania and America.**

View of the tail flukes of a humpback whale at sunset. Photograph by the late Franz Gingele, used with his permission.

Appendix Seal descriptions made by Racovitza

ROSS SEAL *Ommatophoca rossii*

As stated by Racovitza, no exact measurements had been made before the Belgica expedition. In the book edited by Murariu (2016), there are a few low quality photos and some sketches of seals and dissections, and also listed are the physionomic characters of the species, and it stipulated that the eyes are quite small compared to what was said before in Barrett-Hamilton (1901) who reported on notes given to him by Racovitza accompanying the specimens he received from the Museum in Brussels. He went onto saying that little was known (at the time) on the distribution of that species, but the data from the Belgica expedition confirmed that it is an inhabitant of the pack ice and, that during the overwintering, only 13 encounters occurred and also none in the de Gerlache Strait. Barrett-Hamilton (1901) then reported on the 'vocal powers' of this seal by reporting in French the text written by Racovitza that is translated here: *'Briefly, this species possesses a very curious voice, and its sounds are very varied. The noise passing through the larynx sounds a bit like bagpipe, with other sounds reminiscent of cooing of hoarse doves followed by the clucking of a frightened hen, and then an inharmonious sniff produced by the air violently expelled through the nostrils'*. Racovitza (2016)[1] further added that the anatomy of the nasal cavity and mouth and illustrated the larynx and photographed a dissection of the oesophagus although the scale next to it is illegible. He also gave a diameter of the cornea to be only 35 mm. There are also details on scars, the tail, hair (10-11

mm thin and long with the fur less furnished than other Antarctic seals; after moulting the hair is dark grey to eventually turn to brown and reddish), nails (reduced, especially on posterior limbs) and teeth (providing a sketch of 5 different pointed teeth), digestive tube (not very distinct and its diameter is small, thus allowing confusion with the stomach, and both muscly) and parasites in the stomach that is filled with large nematodes and with its pyloric region covered with flatworms ('botriocephales') of all sizes (see Table 1), penis (relatively long and thin with full description), dental formula provided, muzzle (fully described).

Racovitza (2016) also commented on the behaviour of these seals, especially when a young came near the boat to see a large female that had been killed by Dr Cook. Racovitza (2016) also gave details of the encounters of *O. rossii* and the data are tabulated in Table 1. This is provided here to enable people to determine changes of occurrence in today's waters near the de Gerlache Strait and Bellingshausen Sea. Racovitza (2016) also commented on occurrences made by previous researchers, including Louis Bernacchi and Nicolai Hanson participants on the Southern Cross expedition to Cape Adare that occurred about the same time. He also corrected some misleading reports/description including some by Barrrett-Hamilton (1901).

Racovitza (2016, p. 95) reported that the female udders encountered on January 8, 1899, contained a very thick pale yellow juice that tasted of a very pronounced cod liver oil. Based on his observations,

he suggested that coupling must occur in January, that milking must last at least one month, and that the female caught on January 8 must had abandoned its young recently (*sic*) and must have given birth towards the end of November 1898.

Racovitza (2016) added that 13 specimens climbed on the sea ice to sleep, lying close to cracks not far from free water. They preferably sleep on their stomach and are slow and heavy when moving. Racovitza (2016) went on to describing in more detail the sound produced by this species and even experimented on sound production on dead animals by blocking their nostrils and he also described the buccal groove and the nature of the palate. In addition, he added that this seal is a bottom feeder and feeds on cephalopods which are very agile and is aided with the capacity of withholding a large quantity of air. Only on three occasions was Racovitza able to examine the stomach content of the seals. On December 17, he found a large number of cephalopod beaks, and based on their dimensions must have belonged to large animals, including a large number of cephalopod spermatophores. On January 6, he found cephalopod beaks and eyes belonging to large animals. In January, the stomach was nearly empty but remains of eyes and cephalopod crystallines. All the other seals had empty stomachs.

Racovitza (2016, p. 104-104) stated that no *Ommatophoca* was ever encountered on land or a beach, and the sea ice is the only place of occupation, but not necessarily everywhere. This seal seems to prefer floating sea ice, the

---

1 Racovitza's notes presented in Murariu (2016) are referred to here as Racovitza (2016) for simplification and avoid any confusion.

likely reason being its food preference for cephalopods. Racovitza (2016) also indicated that it seems to be isolated and never in flocks. Only twice were two specimens found, but still at a far distance from the other. He also confirmed that it is only found in summer (refer to Table 1.) in the area visited by the *Belgica*, but 8 specimens were also found in the Ross Sea offshore the Balleny Islands and one specimen by the Gauss expedition (81°, 65° S) on the edge of the sea ice. Thus, Racovitza suggested that this species is distributed all around the 'Antarctide' *sic* Racovitza.

Comment: the recent observations by members of the *RV Polarstern* in the Bellingshausen Sea in the summer of 2022-2023 of absence of sea ice in the Bellingshausen Sea (Gohl, 2023; C-D. Hillenbrand, pers. com. 2024) are alarming since *Ommatophoca rossii* probably relies on the sea ice and its edge to rest during parts of its life.

LEOPARD SEAL *Hydrurga leptonyx*

Once again, Racovitza (2016) discussed previous encounters of leopard seals in the literature and provided coordinates for the period of 1829 to 1900, including the observations of Bernacchi (1901) and Hanson (1902) near Cape Adare at about the same time of the Belgica expedition.

Racovitza (2016) stated that he was unable to make many observations on this species. Nevertheless, he noted that the muzzle has a considerably developed upper lip; the distance of 53 mm from the top of the muzzle to the furrow marks the middle of the upper lip was measured on a young male 1.97 m long. He went onto describing this feature even further. He also commented on aspects of the urinary bladder of a young female captured on March 7, 1899. Finally, he observed that the fatty layer (lard) in a young male was 35 mm thick and that overall, this amount was lower compared to other species.

Based on observations of others, Racovitza (2016) stated that birth must occur at the end of September but coupling and giving birth is unknown but must occur on the ice.

Concerning its behaviour, Racovitza also said that this species likes to sleep in the sun, often lying on its ventrum with the body in line, and the chin and neck resting on the ice and the anterior limbs stuck to the body. He further states that this species can rapidly become angry and gets furious and can be considered as being ferocious and even dangerous; he provided additional remarks on its behaviour when seeing people on the ice. Concerning its movement on the ice, it is clumsy but more confident and rapid than other species and can also glide on the ice. There are additional comments on its movement on the ice, on how it climbs on it. He finally stated that this specie is an excellent swimmer that can also stand vertical in the water up to the beginning of its anterior limbs so as to assess the surroundings and can do so for a long period of time.

Date	Specimen	Pathology
17.12.1898	1 female, moulting, caugt by F. Cook and brought alive at the back of the ship	very large nematodes in the stomach, large number of 'botriocephales' tapeworms in the intestine and the pyloric part of the stomach
29.12.1898	1 female killed with complete change of hair	
31.12.1898	1 male, killed, having got out of a crack in the ice and was rolling on the snow, started moulting	numerous 'botriocephales' tapeworms in the the pyloric part of the stomach and some penetrated probably by piercing the stomach
4.1.1899	1 specimen killed	
6.1.1899	2 captured specimens, 1 male, 1 female, both with old pelt	in female: large 'botriocephales' tapeworms in the median region of the stomach, but in the pyloric part they are small but extremely abundant; in male, only few nematodes in the stomach
8.1.1899	1 adult female captured; the liver is unedible as 5 hours after its ingestion we all had violent headaches, ejected eyes and some with diarrhea, others vomiting, in full moult	the pyloric part of the stomach and intestine are infested by a large number of 'botriocephales' tapeworms
11.1.1899	1 male killed, old hair, 195 cm body length, normal dental formula, no ectoparasites, stomach content with crystalline fragments of cephalopods	part of the stomach is infested by parasites and 'botriocephales' tapeworms
14.1.1899	one specimen seen thought to be a large *Ommatophoca*	
19.1.1899	2 females killed not fecund, of fairly large size	
29.1.1899	one male killed	
15.2.1899	one male killed, thin and of small size.	

TABLE 1 List of observations made by Racovitza (2016) related to the Ross seal *Ommatophoca rossii*.

On August 1, 1898, Racovitza (2016) observed a flock of sea leopards in a large channel, and the seals seemed to prefer to break 8 cm thick ice with a vigorous hit by their formidable neck. This was not a game, he insisted, but a way to rest their chin on the edge of the ice and respire. This behaviour could be done due to the low specific gravity of their body in the water. Racovitza never heard their call but reported that Bruce (1894) had described it, but descriptions are unclear.

Concerning their feeding habits, Racovitza (2016) stated that their choice is eclectic. He described an account on February 21, 1899, when several cadavers of emperor penguins were left floating in the water by the crew after removal of the pectorals for human consumption. Two leopard seals fought for these remains with a description provided by Racovitza. He also stated that the seals eat krill and fish but doubts that they feed on cephalopods and prefer larger preys. Racovitza disputed a description to the contrary made by Borchgrevink (1901) with an 'Octopus' sic found in the stomach of a leopard seal. He finally stated that leopard seals eat penguins and birds, the latter obtained from the water. He also mentioned that the seals are generally solitary and prefer to live near the edge of sea ice but rarely ventures in channels and cracks in the ice.

Racovitza (2016) found trematodes in the stomach of a young male and a taeniid worm in the intestine. He also found brown to black ice, especially on the neck and anterior limbs considered by Racovitza to be sites which the seal cannot scratch. Racovitza mentioned that cestodes, trematodes and acanthocephale parasites would be described in the Résultats. However, no publication was found, although in an earlier version of the list of publications prepared by the Belgica Commission, there is mention of a future volume listing the organisms mentioned above by Paul

Cerfontaine, an expert in parasitology working in the laboratory of Professor Edouard Van Beneden at the University of Liège. Apparently and disappointingly, this was never published. Racovitza (2016) finished by discussing the paucity of sightings of leopard seals and the lack of information on their migration but did not offer any plausible explanation. He also listed detailed measurements of one male specimen collected on November, 22, 1898 (Racovitza, 2016), pp. 144-145).

WEDDELL SEAL *Leptonychotes weddellii*

This species of seal as mentioned by Racovitza (2016) is common in Antarctic waters, and this is the reason its presence has been remarked by many Antarctic explorers. He lists those encounters going from 1825 with Weddell to Bernacchi in 1901. At the end of the 19th century, it was hunted. Racovitza (2016, p. 154) gives measurements made by others to which he adds his own measurements made on a fecund female (2.3 m) on January 16, 1898 and on a female with embryo (2.67 m) and another (from muzzle to big toe: 3.07 m) on February 10, 1899. Based on these measurements relying on what Racovitza (2016) calls 'serious measurements', this seal does not exceed 2.7 m, but can be slightly larger, but its size does not exceed the 3 m size of *Ommotophoca*. In addition, there is no size difference between the sexes. Newly-born must be between 1.3 and 1.4 m to reach 1.7 m after 10 to 12 weeks. Adolescents must reach 2 m, and, in the third year, the adult reaches about 2.3 m. In fact, Racovitza (2016) found in January and February two non-fecund females reaching 2.3 and 2.3 m, and a third one with an embryo and was 2.36 m long. The maximum circumference in adults is at the level of the xyloid appendage and, in young, it is at the posterior of the armpits.

Date	Specimen	Location
19.2.1898	evening, appeared on an ice block, likely a leopard seal, muzzle very elongated, yellow spots on the ventrum	sea ice
20.2.1898	killed a young male with narrow eye orbits, large lips, covered with lice (especially neck and hands) always on 2 hair, which can be cleaned by the hind legs, the lice is very slow, 2 adults, one male had already moulted and its hair short and shiny	sea ice
22.2.1898	2 specimens large than from previous day, the neck is enormous	sea ice
6.3.1898	head and shoulders seen of an enormous specimen in the channel, seem to want to observe people and ship	channel in the sea ice
20.3.1898	Koren seemed to have seen one black specimen	sea ice
1.8.1898	enormous specimen in a crack in the ice, able to easily break 8 cm thick ice, attempt to shoot him, 3 adults	sea ice & channel in the sea ice
2.8.1898	seen one in a fissure in the ice	channel
24.11.1898	Dr F. Cook claims to have seen one specimen	sea ice
12.12.1898	two sightings in the channel, 1 male 2.8 m long with hair solidly stuck to the skin	channel
8.2.1899	one female killed	channel
14.2.1899	on large specimen seen in the water with its round back appearing first followed by the posterior limbs	channel
20.2.1899	3 specimens seen by the crew	sea ice
21.2.1899	one specimen swims around *Lobodon* seals; at night, 2 large specimens seen grabbing the carcass of an *Aptenodytes* penguin and fighing for it. Question asked: how does the seal obtain the penguin? In the water or the sea ice?	
7.3.1899	one female specimen killed, likely a juvenile as the oracle is not resorbed and the uterus is virgin. Meat as red as Lobodons	

TABLE 2. List of observations made by Racovitza (2016) related to the Leopard seal *Hydrurga leptonyx*.

Date	Description of the animal(s)	Size (m)	Stage
2.2.1898	completely white, no hair, white whiskers 1 mm long, white nails on anterior limbs, nail 1 & 5 subterminal	1.13	foetus
8.2.1898	completely white, no hair, white whiskers 1 mm long, white nails on anterior limbs, nail 1 & 5 subterminal, anterior nails black and best developed compared to posterior ones which are white	1.2	foetus
12.2.1898	epidermis completely white, hair only visible on the head, black whiskers with white tips, white and more reduced on subterminal on posterior limbs nails	1.72	foetus
2.12.1898	black muzzle and lips, orifice of the penis sheath, eye lid, umbilicus and anus all black, pink oral mucus and tongue, brown iris, hair black on the dorsal side, grey black with silvery reflection on the ventral face, spots more numerous and larger on the sides and ventrum compared to the back, hair are obvious but no down, black whiskers and nails black and no sign of wear	1.55	young male ?8 weeks old
30.12.1898	black muzzle and lips, pink oral mucus and tongue, eye lids, opening of anal sheath and anus and orifice all black, brown hair, on the dorsal side of the face black and grey black and shiny on lateral side, white spots on the body except on limbs, no down	1.675	young female 12 weeks old
24.1.1898	all with pale yellow spots over dark grey or brown background, number of spots very variable and overall colour variable, one relatively small specimen is dark grey on its back and on this part of the body are numerous spots, on the ventrum the colour is brown or grey and spots appear to be lacking		a dozen resting on a rock
26.1.1898	mucus buccal cavity pink and vagina black, fur is pale brown almost blond on the sides and the ventrum is faintly covered with yellow spots	2.3	adult female
29.1.1898	the smallest youngest individuals appear darker than the adults with yellow spots on the fur more resorbed on the adults		17 individuals of both sexes resting on a moraine
2.2.1898	black skin as well as muzzle and lips, oral mucus and tongue pink, vagina, umbulicus and anus all black, brown iris, dark grey hair, fresh and brilliant with silvery reflection on the doral region and less dark on the ventrum. Muzzle hair and chin pale grey, almost white, numerous yellow spots on the ventrum and rare on the back	2.67	female
2.2.1898	dark bron pelt with barely visible spots		adult female
8.2.1898	skin black, muzzle and lips black, oral mucus and tongue pink; eye lids, vagina, umbiliicus and anus all black, brown iris, at the end of its moult	2.36	female
9.2.1898	black muzzle and lips, pink oral mucus and tongue; eye lids, vagina, umbilicus and anus all black, brown iris, dorsal side of face pale brown faded and dirty and ventral side pale grey; the fur appears dull, dark tint and dirty general aspect, whiskers and nails black	2.03	adult female
9.2.1898	on an island the specimens display great variations in colouration due to the various moult stages. The hair is grey alsmost black, darker on the back compared to the ventrum and the spots have a straw yellow colour, the old hair is brown and have many different tints.		3 males, 1 female
7.11.1898	black skin as well as muzzle and lips, oral mucus and tongue pink, vagina, umbulicus and anus all black, clear brown iris, hair on dorsum darker mousey grey than ventrum, hair on muzzle and chin whitish, elongated fresh yellow spots on all the body, black whiskers mixed with a few white ones, nails whitish at the base	2.695	male
8.12.1898	black skin, black muzzle and lips, oral mucus and tongue pink, eye lids, opening of the penis sheath black, pink penis, umbilicus and anus black, light brown iris, hair grey black on the dorsal side and lighter grey on the ventral side, rare yellow spots on the back and very numerous on the ventrum	2.595	male
9.12.1898	black skin, black muzzle and lips, oral mucus and tongue pink; eye lids, opening of the penis sheath black, pink penis, umbilicus and anus black, brown iris, in full moult, old hair dirty brown, new hair iron grey on the dorsal side, lighter grey on the ventral side; yellow spots, very brilliant in the new fur, very dark in the old fur, few on the back, numerous on the ventrum	2.51	adult female of 16 months?

TABLE 3. List of observations made by Racovitza (2016) related to the Leopard seal *Hydrurga leptonyx*. List provided by size as done by Racovitza.

However, this species appears to be more cylindrical compared to the other seals examined by him. The weight must extend over 400 kg; young ones at 6 to 12 weeks 90 kg with the newborn likely to reach the same weight. Racovitza also discussed prior encounters mentioned in the literature between 1834 and 1892.

All measurements provided by Racovitza (2016) include those made on foetuses. These are summarised in Table 3 on the previous page.

In addition, Racovitza (2016) provides ample information on this species having been able to examine and dissect numerous specimens.

On the epidermis, he said that the 3 young specimens had a colourless epidermis but already the embryo (1.72 m, 3 months old) had already back spots on the head. In adults, the skin and parts that surround the orifices are completely black but the buccal mucous, tongue and penis are always pink.

The iris of the eye is always brown but its tint is more or less dark.

Concerning the hair, the (1.72 m, 3 months old) embryo had visible hair embryo. He had not seen down on young compared to specimens obtained during the Southern Cross expedition After the first moult in young and moult in adults, the hair is very dark; the colour varies from black velvety to steel grey. The ventral side and sides are paler than the sides which are a little clearer than the dorsum. A silvery reflection is noticeable in full light due to the tips of hair which are very pale compared to the rest that is very dark. The body is covered with spots which are rarely round or oval, but more often irregular. The spots are more or less clear yellow, rarely white and they are more abundant on the ventrum and sides. They can sometimes be missing on the back and are rarely found on the limbs. The extremity of the muzzle and chin

are often white of yellow. The brilliant nature of the pelt does not resist to severe weather with colours fainting and are more or less clear brown tint that replaces the primitive dark colour until moulting occurs. The animals have a dull brown or grey pelt with barely visible spots.

On the whiskers, the youngest embryos have white whiskers; the 1.72 m (3 months old) embryo had whiskers with a black base and white tips. Youngs as well as adults generally have black whiskers often with mixed white and black ones, rarely brown.

The nails are white in embryos but become black in more advanced embryos. Adults nearly always have black nails, rarely of a clearer tint.

Anatomy: *Nostrils* are very narrow when at rest and can be hermetically closed when the animal dives. They diverge near the top and at the bottom from a point located exactly at the level of the superior extremity of the internasal groove. It is from that point that Racovitza considered the extremity of the muzzle to be from which he took all his measurements. *Whiskers* form a single group composed of seven rows from which the last one overtakes the level of the middle of the nostril of the first row. The one that borders the lip has the largest number of hair, but this number decreases in number from the second row. A little group of whiskers occurs at the internal edge of the eyebrow and a and a few isolated whiskers also occur on other parts of the muzzle. The whiskers are spiral but less so than on *Lobodon* seals. The lip is a median depression is little depressed and has no fold.

Dentition: Racovitza (op. cit.) provided the dentition formula and also stated that the two supplementary teeth are molars as, when comparing the skull with a normal one (*sic*), it was easy to determine that the new teeth were

simply added to the normal dentition past the 9th post-canine one. Those supplementary molars, in fact, resemble in form and dimensions to the 9th post-canine one. Racovitza then discussed the work of others and also listed a table giving dentition formulae (Racovitza, 2016, p.200).

Genital-urinary organs: *the bladder* taken from an adult female and blown up has an elongated form with a posterior region that is ovoid and large, separated by a slight narrowing from a rounded and smaller anterior region. Its length is 36 cm and its maximum circumference 46 cm. The *urine* has a very bad smell in those animals. *Penis:* it is already formed in the youngest specimens, and an illustration is used to show this in a 3.4 cm embryo. It is clear that this organ is free, the penal sheath forms later. The body of the penis is cylindrical and covered by a mucus folded longitudinally. More information is also listed and a diagram is provided for a young in Racovitza (2016, p. 167). In adults, the penis has undergone some transformations such that it does not resemble a juvenile penis. It is the glans that is modified by being longer and considerably swollen. The corona is the glans is now halfway through the organ. The external urethral orifice is subterminal with more information provided in p. 168. The same for its orifice and the penial bone and dimensions of the erectable part of the penis are also provided.

Fat (lard): is already visible from birth to adult age. In 3 month old young specimens, it is 3.9 to 4 cm thick; in adults it is 8.9 cm thick. The maximum thickness is at the centre of the stomach and often the dorsum has a considerable thickness; the fatty layer is the thinnest on the head and limbs. Racovitza (2016) mentioned that dimensions are quite variable between specimens and that, in autumn, the 'lard' is more abundant than in spring.

Flesh: its colour is very dark sombre red almost black and differs from *Lobodon* which is less coloured but more oily and therefore less tasty.

Physiological traits: ***The temperature*** of only on a two-month-old young in poor condition gave 39.1°C in the rectum, nevertheless the animal had a fight just before.

Moult: no information on newly born. Table 4 below details all of Racovita's observations.

To sum it up:

1. the period of moulting is not very constant, it varies with limitation;

2. the normal moulting period is the first half of February,

3. moulting starts first on the back and head.

These observations were made in the de Gerlache Strait (thus a terrestrial region), so the normal mean moult period in the sea ice region may be either be a little later or a little earlier. On December 2, 1898, the large male that had a brilliant and sombre pelt had the appearance of having formed new hair. However, all the skin with hair was elevated on the back at a simple traction, whereas the horny layer when removed in lumps was black like the normal epidermis. No further comment was provided.

Sexual differences: there are no differences between the sexes which show differences in size, length and pelt colouration. Males appear to reach the size of females. Out of 31 individuals with determined sex, 11 were males. Nevertheless, he discussed counts made by Hanson (1902) near Cape Adare.

Reproduction: Racovitza (2016) claims to have been the first to have examined an embryo on February 2, 1898, in the de Gerlache Strait that measured 4.13 cm. On December 12, 1898, he captured a young likely to have been born just a few weeks before, so he concluded that coupling must occur around January 1st and birth at the end of September. The following year, he obtained in February 1899 embryos only 3 to 4.4 cm long. It occurred in the free sea ice. He then tried to explain the differences with previous catches by suggesting that 'near land occurrences' embryos appear earlier. Racovitza (2016) then compared his notes with those obtained during the *Southern Cross* expedition and then concluded that:

1. coupling must certainly occur before February knowing the size of embryos found at the beginning of that month. Coupling must occur at the end of December and beginning of January,

2. birth occurs during September, (30 makes and females do not form permanent unions; like Lobodon, this must be haphazard; in the region of the de Gerlache Strait, the animals are generally in small groups and it is possible that an old male may take the lead, but in the sea ice, individuals appear isolated with males likely searching for females,

3. the female must be pregnant for 9 months at least, perhaps more. Giving birth occurs as well as on the sea ice or beaches on Antarctic land,

4. there is no information on milking but it is likely that this period is short like in Lobodon; the young seen in December were alone on the sea ice; milking cannot take more than two months with knowledge of what Lobodon does,

5. maternal love must be fairly well developed as on December 30 , Racovitza found a young full of krill in the stomach as much as in an adult,

6. he observed females without embryos in January and December and compared his notes with those of Hanson (1902).

Development: Racovitza (2016) claims there are few data on embryos and then discussed his data against that of Hanson (1902) and related once more the belief that embryos born in the sea ice appear later than those on land. He also stated that the youngest embryos he collected nearly all had well developed characters. He never saw rudiments of the external ear in two embryos; the auditory canal is simply opened in a small dimple. The whiskers are already perfectly visible; there are two groups at the internal corners of the eye lashes and one group on each side at the extremity of the muzzle. The longitudinal axis of the limbs form a 90° angle to the length of the body and the already formed nails are terminal. The posterior limbs

Date	Comments concerning moulting
24.1.1898	some 10 individuals of different sex and age with no trace of moult
26.1.1898	1 large female with its old coat
26.1.1898	17 specimens of both sexes and different age with old fur and trace of moult
2.2.1898	adult female 2.67 m already moulted with no trace of old hair
8.2.1898	adult female 2.36 m at the end of its moult, still with old hair on its side and ventrum
9.2.1898	adult female 2.03 m (~16 months old) not yet moulted but old hair not resisting to traction
9.2.1898	adult male 2.91 m in full moult, with on its side and back old hair having fallen in chunks
9.2.1898	1 large moulted male, 3 females in different moulting stages
2.12.1898	no trace of embryonal hair in the youngests

TABLE 4 List of observations made by Racovitza (2016) related to the Weddell seal *Leptonychotes weddellii moulting.*

only take their position later. As with the largest embryos, eye lids are closed. For the 17.2 cm embryo pigment started to appear in the skin at the same time as hair, but these form only on the head. Only one embryo was found in a uterus like found by Hanson (1902). The foetal envelopes and placenta are like in *Lobodon*.

Chorology: At first, Racovitza (2016) discussed findings of others and summed up his results while comparing weddell seals with crabeater seals. These descriptions are very lengthy (7 pages) and relate to the behaviour of the seals when the crew tried to bring the seals to the ship. These are not discussed any further here. On page 190, he stated that the preferred habitat is definitely land compared to free sea ice; they like resting on rocks or gravely platforms near the sea (grève *sic*) and reluctantly rest on sea ice. More information gathered by others are also discussed in Racovitza (2016).

Voice: juveniles are often noisier than adults; Racovitza (op. cit.) describes some of the sounds at length on pages 183-184 and compare his results with other reported ones.

Food: information is provided in Table 5 but later compared with information from Bernacchi (1901) and Hanson (1902) from the *Southern Cross* expedition.

Sociability: It is clear that this species is the most social of stenorhynchinid seals. It is more often seen in bands than in isolation, and this rule applies more to young ones. In near land regions, it is very rare not to see in groups compared to on the sea ice. This species appears to be the only one to be found in groups, sometimes in large proportions., but this Racovitza (2016) never saw compared to Bernacchi (1901)'s observations. The largest flock was seen in the de Gerlache Strait consisting of 17 individuals. Those groups are not social organisations. There is no hierarchy between the members of the group. Individuals form groups and disperse without any reason, except for following food or the attraction of forcing an animal lying down on other seals of its own species that seek a resting place. They show no interest in protecting others when danger occurs. Racovitza (2016) never saw weddell seals fight among themselves; they only display affection towards the young.

Parasites: *Ecto-parasites*: the animals are covered with lice and this is not the same as in *Lobodon*. On two very young (around 8 weeks) individuals did not have lice, but a slightly older one had numerous ones. Adults without lice are very rare except for some living on the

sea ice. To get rid of these the animal scratch themselves vigorously such that skin was seen to be scratched and bloody. Lice occurs on sites the animal cannot reach such as back and forelimbs. *Endo-parasites:* the two young individuals had none, but the stomach of adults were stuffed with them. The nematodes are found in the stomach and are, at times, free or fixed on the wall of that organ. Cestodes are found in the intestine, but on December 6 during autopsy of a female Racovitza saw in the piloric region of the stomach it was voluminous and hard and, when opened, was filled with a large quantity of cestodes. These were bothriocephalids with a faint green tint and which were fixed by bundles in the hollow folds of the stomach mucus. They were strongly attached and broke when attempting to remove them, with all contracted which was possibly normal since they were still alive despite the seal having been recently killed. In between bothriocephalid puffs, there were very small trematodes, being so abundant, the mucus could not be seen. In the rectum, one small sized acanthocephalid was seen.

Enemies: not even humans who can cause destruction; in addition, specimens are too few for a commercial exploitation (Racovitza, 2016). He also noted that specimens on the sea ice were more worried than on land as in the de Gerlache Strait, perhaps because on the sea ice they settle more frequently. In water, these seals must fear orcas, but Racovizta never encountered them.

Scars: this species has less scars than *Lobodon*, but on January 24, on 17 specimens on the de Gerlache Strait, half of them had a zebra-like skin with long cuts. The old wounds are always limited to the sides likely caused by sharp ice blocks.

Date	Specimen	Stomach content
26.1.1898	adult female	7 fish half digested, ~40 cm long
2.2.1898	adult female	filled with *Euphausia*, same species as found in *Pygoscelis* penguins
8.2.1898	adult female	fish debris and *Euphausia*
8.2.1898	adult female	5 to 6 fish, ~39 cm long, 2 pairs of cephalopod beaks, one brachial crown with 10 arms
9.2.1898	adult female	fish debris and *Euphausia*
12.2.1898	adult female	4 large fish (20-40 cm) and debris of small decapod cephalopods, one of the fish is *Nototheuria* or of analoguous form; others had very close projecting eyes, large head, body covered with transversal bands, alternatively yellow, reminiscent of coastal fish living between algae along the coast.
1.8.1898	adult male	fish debris of small size and numerous scales very similar to those found in the stomach of *Pagodroma* petrels, but the largest mass that filled the stomach were two forms of *Euphausia*, the largest found in penguin stomach and *Lobodon*

TABLE 5 List of observations made by Racovitza (2016) related to the Weddell seal *Leptonychotes weddellii* stomach content.

Death: no cadaver was ever seen, nor bones and debris belonging to that species. This can be explained as, on sea ice, dead animals can eventually fall in the water, but in the de Gerlache Strait careful exploration there failed to find any; this cannot be easily explained except that perhaps they die on narrow rocky bands that may be washed by avalanches or movement of ice and snow.

Hunting: These animals can easily be killed with a stick without any danger, but they show a remarkable resistance that do not affect (?) the brain or heart. Several gun shots do not seem to inconvenience them at the time with no sound nor appearance of suffering. The quantity of lost blood is really prodigious. If the animal is hit on the heart, the reaction is such that eyes turn on their orbit (white eyes shown), the head retreats in the shoulders and reverses backwards and thick folds of the skin form around the neck; then the body slowly stretches and he animal dies without any other movement. When the wound has affected other organs, the animals never takes that position. The hemorrhage produced by the wounds causes intense thirst and the animal- to calm itself - eats snow. It becomes more and more weak, yawns nervously several times and dies after a final contraction.

Frequency: with *Lobodon*, this species among stenorhynchinids is the most widespread in Antarctica. It also appears to be the only one forming large herds, but the number of individuals is lower than for Arctic seals, but nevertheless it can reach two to three hundreds. Again Racovitza discussed at length the findings of others; (1) his conclusions are that the habitat extends from 50° S as far as the pole to Patagonia, but the Land of Fire cannot be considered to be the normal habitat of this species; individuals that have been seen there must be have been lost; (2) this species occurs all along the periphery of Antarctica; (3) the large population centres are the shores of Victoria Land and the shores of the South American Antarctic lands, notably Graham Land more than isolated archipelagos (4) the small centre is Kerguelen and Heard Island; (5) *Leptonychotes* is a species that inhabits almost exclusively the vicinity of land and avoids the free sea ice. This explains its pronounced ichthyophagous diet.

Migration: there is nothing to suggest that this species has regular migrations. Reasons for this assumption are: (1) they are found at the same place in summer and winter, (2) they give birth in isolation on the sea ice, (3) in contrast to fur seals and sea lions rookeries when compared with what some authors said, this does no say that some individuals move alone, (4) it is even certain that they exercise long voyages in part to follow groups (of fish?) that it feeds on while searching for open water. In summer, they certainly venture further in the sea ice and in winter. This is proven by the lack of variation for specimens from different regions. There is no evidence of geographical variation in this species.

Behaviour: Racovitza (in Murariu, 2016) provided some 9 pages of notes with sketches of *Leptonychotes weddellii* and compared them with *Lobodon carcinophaga* but are not duplicated here.

CRABEATER SEAL *Lobodon carcinophaga*

On pages 206-207, Racovitza (op. cit.) made a calculation of the progressive growth of embryos to the adult stage. He then provided a lengthy table listing sightings and types going from sightings in Dumont d'Urville (1842) to many others until Hanson (1902).

External characters: these are based on 26 specimens (12 young and adults, 6 males, 6 females) and 12 foetuses and embryos; 6 males and 8 females). All young and adults were measured soon after death, but foetuses were measured after the expedition and had been kept in alcohol. All the details are presented in Table 22.5.2.6 parts 1 and 2.

In the zoological registry (assuming this is in the Royal Institute of Natural Sciences in Brussels), Racovitza (in Murariu, 2016) stated that he added sex, date of capture and presumed age; he also stated that the longest specimen (extremity of muzzle to end of tail) is inscribed in the left column and the others by decreasing length. He then concluded:

1. The maximum length is 2.5 m; there may be larger specimens, but they do not overtake this length by much;

2. females appear to be slightly larger than males and this difference if already noted in foetuses. Therefore, on May 8, Racovitza gathered 9 male foetuses and 1 female; on March 29, 2 males and 4 females and, in both cases, the female length was superior to males; additional notes are added and mention of an observation made on January 29, 1898, of a full female of 1.36 m ad an adult male of 2.44 m;

3. the young, at time of birth, must be around 1.3 m in length; three months after, it reaches 1.7 to 1.8 m; in its second year, it must be above 2 m and the *Lobodon* male like female in the third year must be 2.3 m. He in fact found one female of 2.36 m and a male apparently not fully developed of 2.29 m;

4. the maximum circumference occurs at the extremity of the xyphoid appendix in both sexes; females appear larger than males in the foetus, young and adults; these animals are neatly fusiform; the measured voluminous female had a ratio of 1:1.38 between width and height; this ratio is higher for other species;

5. the variation in proportions is considerable between individuals; this is manifested in the length of the toes and tail; it appears that males have longer, especially posterior ones, compared to females and are better developed;

6. the maximum weight of this species must be more than 200 kg; Racovitza was unable to weight the largest captured individual males; a large 2.15 m male that certainly had not reached full development weighed 162.5 kg and was relatively skinny; 2 or 3 months after birth, the young weight is around 70 kg and certainly weight at birth must not be too inferior to 50 kg;

7. the brain of a 8 weeks old young weighed 430 g; the ratio of the between brain weight and the total of the body in the young is of the order of 1:166.28; in adults, the brain must not increase in weight by much, but the body can reach 3 times more; the ratio must be approximately 1:400 to 450; when comparing the following proportions (human 1:47, big dog 1:110, horse 1:400, elephant 1:500, bull 1:750), Racovitza argued that *Lobodon* fits between the horse and elephant; this ratio does not tell much with the latter but is certainly more intelligent; in the case of *Lobodon*. It weighs much due to its enormous fatty layer. Racovitza thought that the latter is more intelligent than the ratio shows.

General aspect: *Lobodon* is a seal with muscles and is agile. Its form is slender and even elegant compared to *Ommatophoca and Leptonychotes*. More comments are provided on this remark. Limbs are short and more so in anterior limbs.

Detailed descriptions of many animals appear in Tables 6 parts 1 & 2.

Colouration: all the explorers were struck by the pale tint of *Lobodon*, stated Racovitza.

Epidermis and mucous membranes: in the foetus, it is colourless, pigmentation starts towards the end of the third month when the length of the embryo has reached 15 cm; the darkish colouration is pale at first, then darker, then pitch black which appears at the extremity of the muzzle and the palpebral regions and later on invades the rest of the body in the following order: (1) muzzle and palpebral region towards the 4th month, (2) head towards the 4th month, (3) neck by same time, (4) front back at the end of the 4th month, (5) ventral face and anterior limbs towards the 5th month, (6) posterior limbs towards the end of the 5th month. Pigmentation, therefore, extends from the head towards the tail and proceeds with spots more to less tightened and more and more dark. At the end of the 6th month, the procedure is completed. The newly born foetus is completely black in places, around the orifices where the epidermis proper is transformed into a mucous membrane (translation correct?). Therefore, the lips, the edge of the eyelids, the umbilical scar, the penial sheath, the entrance of the vagina and anus are always black. During moulting, the pigmented epidermal layer falls off and if, artificially removed, the new epidermis layer is already formed but not pigmented. The buccal mucus membrane presents very variable colourations, uniform pink, with black, brown spots that does not absolutely depend on age nor sex. It seems that with age pigmentation increases; nevertheless, fully formed foetuses are with a black mucous membrane. It is only in young of that year that no pigmentation was found. The penis is in general pink and not pigmented; only the extremity can be pigmented, and age does not play a role. The vaginal mucus appears to be pink, non-pigmented; the

pigmentation of the mucus varies. between individuals; there are melanic individuals and other albinos and this is confirmed by the mucus in the most coloured ones.

Racovitza (2016) further summarized those results for various aspects:

Iris: always brown although can vary for pale to dark brown.

Fur: *in embryos*, it is very pale blond; in foetuses at full term, it can be an abundant fur with the following details: the hair is reminiscent of the brilliant aspect of trestle of hemp but the colour is dark blond or clear depending on individuals with green reflection in the back, yellowish on the sides, ventral face and head. Addition information is provided.

Hair: grey and rapidly darken with growth. There are many addition aspects discussed by Racovitza (2016) followed by observations made by others.

Whiskers: blond in small embryos, then becoming dark, brown, white, black and white, or brown and white with those variations not related to age, sex or colouration of the hair or the general pigmentation; often the base differs in colour from the tip.

Nails: very small and colourless in embryos; the nails of the anterior limbs which are more developed are pigmented first. Near month 6th, posterior nails start with a tint, with individual variation; some embryos have white anterior and posterior nails; full-term embryos have black nails with white tips; in adults, the colour is generally black; rare are those individuals with white nails but more frequent on those with more or less clear spots on the organs. Colour variation depends on individuals.

Date	Length (cm)	Sex	Epidermis	Iris	Hair	Whiskers	Nails
5.3.1898	15.3	female	completely white		barely visible pale blond		blackish on anterior limbs 1 mm long, white on posterior
29.3.1898	18.5	male	white with sombre stain on the head, but more marked on end of muzzle and eye lids		none	white and blond	on anterior limbs white with black tips; on rear toes 1 and 5 less developed than others
29.3.1898	18.5	male	white with faint sombre stain on head		none	blond	on anterior limbs 2mm, more developed than on posterior ones, white
29.3.1898	19.0	male	muzzle, face and head blackish, inferior jaw and rest of body white		distinct on head only	black with blond extremity	2 mm and black on anterior limbs, more developed than posterior ones that are white
29.3.1898	19.3	female	white with muzzle and superior region of the head covered with faint black spots		barely visible	blond	on anterior limbs 2 mm, sombre with black extremity, less developed on posterior ones, those of nail 1 are black, others white
29.3.1898	21.5	female	white with sombre stain on head that extends into neck; front, palpebral regions and extremity of muzzle uniformly black		starts to appear	blond	on anterior limbs 2 mm, sombre with black extremity, less developed on posterior ones, those of nail 1 are black, others white
29.3.1898	22.5	female	white with extremity of muzzle and palpebral regions black, the start of the neck and part of the back are covered with a sombre stain which fades towards the back		barely visible on the head	blond	2 mm and black on anterior limbs, on posterior limbs less developed and white
2.4.1898	22.8	female	white, muzzle extremity and top of head faintly somber		barely visible on the head	blond	2 mm and black on anterior limbs, on posterior limbs less developed and white
11.4.1898	25.5	male	muzzle, face and head blackish, all the back is covered with sombre spots that fade towards the posterior region and ventral face, anterior an posterior limbs and ventral face		visible on all the body, but only with an apreciable length on head and anterior region, lacking on limbs	blond	on anterior limbs, 3 mm, darkish tint with black extremety, reduced on posterior limbs and clearer tint
8.5.1898	31.5	male	black muzzle and palpebral region, head and back covered of black bands that decrease in extent towards the back, ventral face and anterior limbs covered with faint sombre stain, posterior limbs white		neartly visible on all the body, pale blond	black	on anterior limbs 4 mm, black, on posterior limbs more reduced and white
8.5.1898	42.8	male	extremety of muzzle black, all the body is covered with stains that are less abundant on head and back		pale blond, really neat on the whle body	black	blackish on anterior limbs 5 mm, on first anterior subterminal digits, on other limbs more reduced, white, subterminal
8.5.1898	53.5	female	black muzzle and head, rest of body covered with large spots		on the head 1 mm long, shorter on the rest of the body, body colour pale blond	black	white on anterior limbs, the subterminal digits and other terminal ones; the nail of digit 1 is 6 mm, the others a little shorter, of decreasing length from first to last; on posterior limbs more reduced and white also
18.10.1898	127.0	female	black, nostrils and buccal mucus black, pink tongue with black spots, pink mucosal papillae which cover the teeth, black nipple, vagina and anus. Foetus with darker tint than other listed below	pale brown	brilliant, reminiscent of a pale tint hair, darker than the limbs, and presenting a green fluffy reflection on the back, pale yellow on the sides, ventrum and head	lightly curled, white in the 2 rows closest to the lips, others black	black with extremity white
18.9.1898	129.0	female	black, nostrils and lips black, palate blackish, pink dental area and tongue , black nipples, vagina and anus. Foetus lighter in tint		brilliant, reminiscent of a pale tint hair, darker than the limbs, and presenting a green fluffy reflection on the back, pale yellow on the sides, ventrum and head, muzzle and posterior limbs completely covered	lightly curled, white in the 2 rows closest to the lips, others black	black with extremity white
1.11.1898	150.0	female 4-5 weeks	brownish black, pink buccal mucous pink, black nipple, vagina and anus	dark brown almost black	covered with embryonal hair, overall colour grey yellow with fluffy aspect, the new hair remains sombre grey in places where the embryonal hair is gone, lighter grey under the persisting	black except for a few white ones	black

TABLE 6 PART 1 List of observations made by Racovitza (2016) related to the Crabeater seal
Lobodon carcinophaga. List of observations classified by length made by Racovitza.

Date	Length (cm)	Sex	Epidermis	Iris	Hair	Whiskers	Nails
6.12.1898	157.5	female of 8 weeks?	black, muzzle, lips, buccal mucus all black, pink tongue with black spots, eye lids, nipple, vagina, anus all black		definitive hair, blond colour with silvery reflection, limbs sombre grey with white spots on limbs, posterior ones darker and anterior ones	white in their proximal hals, twisted in spiral	black
9.12.1898	160.0	female of 8 weeks?	black muzzle and lips, palate blackish, pink tongue with black spots, eye lids, opening to the penial groove black, anus black	brown	definitive hair, blond hair with silvery reflection, limbs are sombre grey with blond spots, posterior limbs darker thant the anterior ones.	white base and etremity brown	black
20.11.1898	170.5	male 6-8 weeks?	black, muzzle and palate black, pink penis, on the back the corny of the skin can be removed with in lumps with hair, the new cover below is white	brown	definitive hair, blond colour with silvery reflection, limbs are sombre grey with spots of blond in bundle, posterior ones darker	brown with white base	black
11.11.1898	175.0	male 5-6 weeks?	black muzzle, pink mouth and tongue, eye lids and opening of the penial sheath black, anu black	brown	embryonic, yellowish or greenish grey with fluffy aspect, in some places appears to be definitive sombre grey	brown with white base	black
4.1.1899	211.5	adolescent male 1.5 years old?	black, muzzle and lips black, buccal mucus pink with black spots, blackish tongue, orifice of the penial sheath black, pink penis with black extremity, black anus	brown	yellowish white with silvery reflections with darker stain almost brown on the posterior side	brown with white base	black
8.11.1898	229.0	adolescent male >1 year old?	black, muzzle and lips black, buccal mucus pink with black spots, blackish tongue, orifice of the penial sheath black, pink penis with black extremity, black anus	dark brown	silvery white with uniform greenish reflection, no stain	white except for a few black hair	black
10.5.1898		adolescent male 1.5 years old?	silvery white with pale maroon stains on the posterior extremity and posterior limbs; the posterior limbs are very dark				
29.1.1898	236.0	adult female	black, muzzle black, buccal muscus brownish, black nipples and vagina, vaginal mucus pink, black anus	brown	yellowish white with silvery reflection as dark at the base than at the top and with the same tint on all the body		black
2.11.1898	240.0	old adult female	black, muzzle, buccal mucus, tongue, vagina and anus all black	light brown	blond with silvery reflection, limbs pale brick-red with white spots. The tint is darker that usual	white	white with black spot at base
29.1.1898	244.0	old adult male	black, muzzle black, buccal mucus brownish, pink penis, black anus	brown	yellowish white with silvery reflection darker than at the top and of the same tint on all the body		
18.9.1898	245.0	adult female	white with silvery reflection at the top, clear pale brown at the base, spots very marked in the posteriror region of the body, posterior limbs dark brown almost black; so similar to the previous one but a little darker				
18.9.1898	250.0	adult female	white with silvery reflection at the top, dark brown at the base, spots very marked in the posterior region of the body, posterior limbs dark brown almost black. So similar than the previous one but a little darker				
5.3.1898		adult female	white with silvery reflection as dark at the base than the top and with the same tint on all the body; no spots				
29.3.1898		adult male	silvery white at the top, white at the base, posterior limbs pale brown with white spots				
10.5.1898		old adult male	white with silvery reflection at the top like at the base, similar tint on all the body				
10.5.1898		3 adult females			white with silvery silvery at the tops, blond at the base, posterior limbs darker than the rest of the body, appearing black when the hair is dry, brown spots pale and dark on the side of the neck, in the anterior limbs and especially on the back side		
10.5.1898		adult female			pale brown with silvery reflection on all the body, no spots		
25.8.1898		adult male			silvery bands as dark at the base than at the top of the same tint on the whole body, no spots		

TABLE 6 PART 2 List of observations made by Racovitza (2016) related to the Crabeater seal *Lobodon carcinophaga*. List of observations classified by length made by Racovitza.

Anatomical notes: *nostrils*: the slit of the nostrils is narrow in this species, and 2 diverging slits on the anterior and posterior from a point which is located exactly at the level of the superior tip of the internasal furrow; this point of divergence corresponds also to the extremity of the muzzle (with more information supplied); in adults this furrow is 4 cm long; in a full term foetus, the periphery of the nostrils is covered with air that disappear at the first moult. Internasal furrow: in this species it has a median notch on the lip where it is very large and shortens towards the extremity of the muzzle. Whiskers: those tactile hair for 2 groups on the muzzle of *Lobodon* (one of 2 and the inferior one of 4) on either side, the inferior points of the nostrils and a second group on the superior lip consisting in 4 rows on either side of the median line; those groups are absolutely constant and always arranged in the same fashion. At the extremity of the inferior jaw and on other regions of the muzzle they are also isolated but do not follow the consistency nor the invariability of the first ones; a bunch of whiskers occurs also above the eyes above the internal extremity of the eyebrow; the spiral structure of the whiskers is neatly pronounced in this species; their length is very variable and is not related to sex nor, to a certain extent, to age. Around 3 months, the embryo already has 1 mm long whiskers; the full-term foetus has 40 to 45 mm long ones; finally, the adult can have up to 80 mm long ones. Superior lip: shows a very near median notch, forming an open rounded angle and, in addition, a fold is well marked on either side which is not found in other species. Hair at the time of birth, the young is covered with special hair, a down differs from the final hair and which Racovitza studied on 2 full-term foetuses and on several young found during November and December;

the down covers the entire body of the young even on parts which moult in adults, therefore the periphery of the nostrils and posterior limbs are completely covered. The hair of the down is longer, finer and silkier than the permanent hair; they are 3.2 cm long on the entire body, except the posterior limbs that are shorter, on the other hand, they are more numerous than the final hair. The down, therefore, constitutes a real fur very efficient against the cold, but less so against humidity because it wets more easily and retains water more avidly, but this is not necessary as it does not have to go into water to find food; the largest part of the downy hair have a straight extremity and a curvy base; others that are also numerous and curly and form a felt at the base of the others (more information provided); the down is replaced during the last month and is replaced with final hair; when moulting is completed, these have a maximum length of around 1.2 cm; two forms are found: strait hair with a bulb deeply buried in the skin, and between these curly hair are more superficial and form a felt at the base of the first ones (more discussion provided).

Dentition: the dental formula is typical of the Phocidae, thus 2+1+5/2+1+5, with no encountered variation. Racovitza (2016, p. 232-234) provides 4 pages of descriptions for foetuses to adults. Urinary bladder: after blowing it, it is 27 long and 8.5 cm wide, and more information is also provided. Male genital organs: the external organs are already developed in the embryo during the second month; the penis, at first free, is small and surrounded by an epidermal fold that makes its sheath; in 6-8 weeks young, it is reminiscent of a dog with the free extremity formed by a glans limited at the back by a rounded and circular crest thicker on the dorsal

side; the external urethral orifice is subterminal and, in one animal, Racovitza (2016) noted a little membrane-like and thin tongue that overlapped the opening (more discussion follows); in adult males, the penis has a totally different form and similar to *Leptonychotes* with a difference that it is shorter, less swollen and thinner in its middle; in an adult male, in a state of flaccidity, is 26 cm, the glans circumference is 12 cm and at the base 13 cm; the penial bone is well developed and in male in a state of flaccidity it was 24.5 cm long and the penial bone 19 cm; the bone is located near the middle of the penis, the 3 cm at the base is boneless, then 19 cm for the bone and a 2.5 cm extremity overtaking the bone. Testes: as in the Phocidae, they are covered with skin and there is no scrotum; in an adolescent male, its form was 211.5 cm (error by Racovitza?), is ovoid and there is a difference between the testes: the right is 7 cm long and 2.5 cm wide and weighs 22.8 g, whereas the left one is 7.2 cm long, 2.8 cm wide and weighs 24.4 g. Not having seen enough specimens, Racovitza cannot state if this is the rule. Fat: it is a true organ destined to protect against the cold, so it appears early in the embryo; in foetuses, it is 2 cm thick and in adults it has the same disposition. The fat (lard) layer appears rapidly in the milk-fed young that receives a very efficient protection on top of what the down offers; after breastfeeding, the fat layer diminishes; it varies between individuals, and this depends on the more or less large capacity to capture a prey; this is therefore a remarkable isolating layer. Flesh: *Lobodon* flesh is dark red, paler than that of *Leptonychotes* but the same as *Ogmorhinus*. Moult: the down rapidly disappears after birth; the final hair forms underneath and the old is removed by plates first on the back, then the ventrum and there it progresses from the front to the back; on the base sits the final hair that is already about 1.2 cm long. Observations made that year on young are presented in Table 7 below. Racovitza also stated that the first moult must occurs between the 4th and 6th week after birth and occur in November. The adult moult appears to occur during January. The only information in his possession was at the end of January. He added information on another unusual specimen.

Racovitza (2016) further reports that on March 29, 1898, 6 *Lobodon* were killed at 14:00; the next day at 15:00, he examined them, the cadavers had been for 25 hours on the sea ice with an outside temperature of -20°C; the limbs and muzzle were frozen hard but it was different for the opened body with lukewarm viscera, blood liquid; nematodes and cestodes in the stomach and intestine were perfectly alive (additional comments provided on death in the cold). A 162.5 kg male had a head and neck weighing 18 kg, the dorsal muscles (which are used as food by explorers) weighs 15 kg and the carcass 84 kg and the skin 45 kg. On pages 283-286 listed 124 occurrences (with coordinates) but it is not clear what animal species they belonged to.

Date	Comments concerning moulting
24.1.1898	some 10 individuals of different sex and age with no trace of moult
26.1.1898	1 large female with its old coat
26.1.1898	17 specimens of both sexes and different age with old fur and trace of moult
2.2.1898	adult female 2.67 m already moulted with no trace of old hair
8.2.1898	adult female 2.36 m at the end of its moult, still with old hair on its side and ventrum
9.2.1898	adult female 2.03 m (~16 months old) not yet moulted but old hair not resisting to traction
9.2.1898	adult male 2.91 m in full moult, with on its side and back old hair having fallen in chunks
9.2.1898	1 large moulted male, 3 females in different moulting stages
2.12.1898	no trace of embryonal hair in the youngests

TABLE 7 Observations on moult stages for young adults made by Racovitza (2016) related to the Crabeater seal *Lobodon carcinophaga.*

Date	Location	Observations
5.1.1898	Harburton Harbour Beagle Channel	produce a fairly strong blow, dull snoring; voluminous head out of the water, 20 m from ship, then more observations listed before swimming away
6.1.1898	Beagle Channel	on a rock near Picton Island covered with cormorants and among them a sea lion that raises its head then jumps in water
7.1.1898	Staten Island	coming from the west, near the entrance of San Juan Harbour, 2 large rookeries of *O. byronia* , both on a rocky platform of the cliff, 5-6 m above sea level. Each rookery with 100 inhabitants, lazily resting on rock, most are of a dirty yellow colour, few are more or less dark brown, hair like hemp tow, additional information provided. The Argentine Governor informed us that *O. byronia* live on the northern side of the island and Falkland Island fur seals live exclusively on the southern side in grottos
9.1.1898	Staten Island	at the entrance of San Juan, on a rocky platform inclined towards the sea, about 200 *O. byronia* lying in all positions; a yellow female; very long set of information follows, one young removed and brought to the ship, crustaceans abundant in the water
10.1.1898	Staten Island	a group *of O. byronia* feeds in San Juan Gulf, followed by more description on produced sounds; crustaceans plentiful in the water

TABLE 8 Observations made by Racovizta (2016) for *Otaria byronia* in the Beagle Channel and the Staten Island.

SOUTH AMERICAN SEA LION *Otaria byronia*
(originally called *O. jubata* by Racovitza)

Oliva (1988) confirmed the valid scientific name of this species.

Racovitza (2016) provided a list of information on the South American Seals which were observed in the Beagle Channel and Staten Island of southern South America. These are listed in Table 8 below.

In addition, on January 10, 1898, he made the following observations in Staten Island on one female and a young of that year: colouration is very variable that goes from blond tow (filasse) to dark brown, males are darker than females; solitary ones have much paler hair, especially on the mane that makes them look grey; females and young older than one year have a blond or clear pale yellow tow; on some individuals clearer spots are noted. The young of that year, until the first moult, are black but the ventrum and the extremity of the muzzle are a little less dark and look like a brownish reflection. The female had brown irises, with pink buccal mucus, black skin; ears, nostrils, anus, vagina, soles and hands, interdigital membranes, predigital appendices naked and black. The hair on the back are blond tow or whitish yellow, on the ventrum a little darker, going brown especially on the armpits. The whiskers are white.

Concerning rookeries: the sea lion rookeries occur on the northern side of Staten Island where they occur most especially at the base of exposed cliffs. The two visited rookeries were installed on the caps at the entrance of San Juan Gulf. One platform was 40 m and 130 m long and inclined towards the sea to eventually reach it closely. On one side, it next to the cliff and the rest presented steep sides reaching 5-6 m. The rock surface was polished due to the friction caused by the seals and, on top of that, it was greasy and shiny; the animals could then slide when jumping in the sea. However, they had difficulty to climb and applied their 'hands' gain a larger surface of adhesion and the predigital limbs played a great role in this performance. In the rocks grooves and drains, urine, orangey and murky accumulated and spread a nauseous smell. However, excrements were rare (more comments added); food debris were completely absent due to the presence of skuas and gulls which must remove the detritus from the colony.

Families: the rookery is inhabited by about 200 sea lions; there were some 20 families with a large male surrounded but a certain number of females and young of that year and the preceding one. It seems that no more than 5 to 6 females were in a family. Females certainly had 2 young but it is not certain if this is the norm as seals generally have one young at a time. (Additional discussion follows).

Behaviour: ample notes are provided. Voice: the adult males have a formidable voice reminiscent at the same time of a lion and a bull; the female voice is less noisy and a yelp that is reminiscent of the attenuation of the male sound; the young yelp like females and the young of that year wail like a lamb. When the seals are in the water and fish, they continuously make a deafening sound like that of kittens; when they emit sounds, they lift their head and open they mouth wide open.

Swimming: there is no need to comment on their ability to swim and, when they are hunting, they jump out of the water like dolphins. In order to inspect the environs, they raise themselves vertically in the water, the body emerges up the shoulders and maintain this position for a long time; they blow noisily when returning to the surface after a long dive.

Temperature: the rectal temperature of the young mentioned before (?) and obtained 37.2°C.

Measurements: on pages 295 to 297, numerous measurements are provided for an adult female and a young of that year, including the dental formula.

In addition, in pages 303 to 312, there is a list of observations (48) made by Racovitza (2016) for the period of January 21, 1898, to March 12, 1899, but unfortunately it is not possible to identify which seal species he is referring to on most occasions. After that, he provided an exhaustive list of specimens (some listed in the registry of what is now called the Royal Belgian Institute of Natural Sciences) of many seals belonging to different species with ample measurements and collection dates; these cover pages 315 to 417! Following that, Racovitza (2016) provided again an exhaustive list of seals recorded in many publications going from Captain J. Cook (1779) to Hanson (1902) and Barrett-Hamilton (1902), both dealing with *Southern Cross* material published in Lankaster (1902). This list encompasses pages 418 to 515!

Additional information on *Lobodon* and *Leptonychotes*

Finally, additional information on *Lobodon* and *Leptonychotes* is available in Racovitza's notebooks which appear Murariu (2016) on pages 271-279. These are presented in Table 9 on the following page.

Date	Landing	Description	Colour
24.1.1898	II	10 leopards are lying comfortably on the rock. They do not move when approached. A large female is there, I sit next to her and touch her feet, she raises her backside, breathes slightly and closes its nostrils but does not shift place. A leopard arrives while swimming, goes on land and comes to check us up curiously and very close. Elsewhere, there are in the water at our feet. They roll lazily, scratch their back with their forelimbs but do not appear scared by our presence. The female mentioned earlier which I had touched ealier appeared very emotional and its heart was beating violently. The beating was visible on the left side	All have yellow spots on the grey or brwon background, with the periphery of the lips yellow, but these tints are very variable in intensity and the spots are more or less numerous. A little individual was dark grey with very large spots which are found on the back. The ventrum is uniformy coloured brown of dirty grey. The body of these false leopards was covered with scars. Saw some false leopards lying on small
25.1.1898	IV	4 or 5 leopards on ice blocs in front of our landing. F. Cook signals some 30 a bit further	
	V	17 false leopards (*L. weddellii*) lying on the moraine. Their favourite position is lying either on the side or on the ventrum, with neck and head stretched. When touched on the tail, they fold into two; another opens its mouth faking to bite; when disturbed they make a chuckle soun. They scratch their back frequently with forelimbs which informs that they have parasites. Their aspect is completey different when they are in the water or when they are wet. The hair is stuck to the body and the tint appears clearer as the root of the hair is darker that the tips. They have a great difficulty to move on land, especially old ones which have a tripple chin and a formidable belly. They jump, doing the carp jump et at the same time crawl with a vertical undulated movement like done for a sea snake	Young are darker than adults and have more obvious yellow spot. The colour of adults varies much, it is almost brown, grey of pale yellow with many alternate tints; often the spots are completely absent on the back and sides. The colour is generally confused with the rocks which makes them difficult to see, It is not a protecting resemblance as on land they have no enemies and they in fact often lie ice and in this case can be seen from very far
25.1.1898	Ia	1 female of false leopard lying on its side, I shot it and the animal died without moving (description follows); 2.3 m long, dentition described; pale brown colour, blond on the sides, yellow spots barely visible, pink mouth, vagina black, thick fatty layer; the stomach with debris of 7 fish some 40 cm long and 2 typrs of nematode parasites completely covering the stomach; not fecund; brown ticks on body, inside the epidermis with bleeds in certain spots likely where the animal scratched	
20.1.1898		near the coast, large animal on ice	
30.1.1898	X	one leopard on ice	
31.1.1898	X	leopards on ice which fail to move when the ship is close; lying on their side or back or ventrum (20?) but never mixed with *Lobodon* which are frequent here	
2.2.1898	XII	2 female leopards lying on snow; very sombre colour; I killed one with a large embryo in the uterus	
4.2.1898	XIII	a few leopards on ice, urinating and jumping in the sea	
8.2.1898	XiV	on female leopard moulting on rocks; a young embro inside; stomach full of fish and decapods (sic!) *Euphausia*	
9.2.1898	XVII	3 male and 1young female with large colour variations due to the different moult stages; new hair is blackish grey with yellow spots, more sombre on the ventrum, old hair brown of many different shades	
11.2.1898		leopards and *Lobodon* isolated in 4, 5 or 6 on ice all day; leopards look at us without moving (50?)	
12.2.1898	XX	1 female *Leptonychotes* on rock with a well developed embryo without hair but with whiskers already; this tends to indicate (translation uncertain ?) that hair around the mouth are those lost last (v. cetaceans? *sic*) indiicates that in mammal ancestry hair must have started around the mouth,' these hair must have true sensory organs, a role still used today. The embryo was inside the distal horny part odf he uterus; in stomach 4 large fish (20-40 cm) ans several cephalopods of small size; one od hte fish resembles Notothenia, the others with projecting eyes, very close, round head with brilliant yellow with bown alternating streaks, whose colouration is reminiscent of coastal fish inhabiting algae. All day saw *Lobodon* and *Leptonychotes* on ice (20?)	
13.2.1898		saw several *Lobodon* and *Leptonychotes* on ice (10?)	
18.2.1898		1 leopard just moved on ice black near the ship, with blowing the ship horn, animal panics and jumps in the slush	
23-30.7.1898		seals blow in holes in the water; possibility that one *Leptonychotes* among them	
31.7.1898		1 *Leptonychotes* in a water hole	
1.8.1898		1 *Leptonychytes* demolishes the hole in 3 strikes; one of those mentioned above is an old male with a beautiful winter coat similar to the female of landing XII with the same size; stomach contained remains of digestion of a fish of large size and numerous very thin scales similar to those found in the stomach of a *Pagodroma* petrel (which contained fish remains and *Euphausia*); however the largest quantity of the food in the stomach was composed of 2 sorts of schizopod crustacean (added here), one being identical to those found in the stomach of *Lobodon*, the other smaller	
3.8.1898		1 *Leptonychotes* in a water hole	
6.8.1898		lengthy description of a *Leptonychotes* found near a water hole in great panic; *Lobodon* does not show this behaviour	
17.9.1898		1 seal blowing in a water hole, it is *Leptonychotes* based on its muzzle	

Date	Landing	Description	Colour
2.11.1898		1 large *Leptonychotes* female near a crack with its winter coat very nice still; moves away despite 4 bullet holes below the armpit; more discusssion added; the body of *Lobodon* does not toss as much while walking; *Leptonychotes* easily sleep on their side and when disturbed or curious move on their sides and raise their heads	
7.11.1898		1 male *Leptonychotes*	
11.11.1898		1 *Leptonychotes* in a water hole	
2.12.1898		1 young *Leptonychotes* of this year, 1.55 m long which indicates a 3 to 3.5 month old based on the majority of seals with well developed teeth and alone on the ice	
3.12.1898		killed an old female *Leptonychotes* of large size but no fecund, very big but with nevertheless small longitudinal dorsal muscles, stomach empty	
6.2.1898		1 very fat female *Leptonychotes* killed and not fecund; one medium size female *Leptonychotes* likely 2-3 years old, cannot be brought back to the ship, its stomach only with numerous *Taenia* parasites, uterus with no trace of inflamation and not fecunded	
7.12.1898		1 female *Leptonychotes* and a young of that year (same species), no evidence of being united; 1 very large male killed with 5 bullets in the heart region	
8.12.1898		1 large male seen yesterday, killed that afternoon	
11.12.1898		2 females and 1 male *Leptonychotes* killed	
12.12.1898		2 *Leptonychotes,* killed one male	
16.12.1898		1 female *Leptonychotes* killed	
30.12.1898		1 captured young female *Leptonychote* s of that year	
6.2.1899		1 female *Leptonychotes* killed with the right conea of the uterus containing an embryo of 0-3 cm, already resembling a seal with clearly visible drafts of whiskers and eye lashes, no external ears	
10.2.1899		one very large female 3.7 m *Leptonychotes* killed with an embryo in the cornea of the uterus of similar size to the one from 6.2.1899	
13.2.1899		1 *Leptonychotes* seen blowing in the channel	
17.2.1899		1 *Leptonychotes* seen on the ice	
20.2.1899		about 10 *Leptonychotes* seen isolated or in small groups on the sea ice	
5.3.1899		1 female *Leptonychotes* killed with a 25 cm male embryo on the right in the uterus	
8.3.1899		1 skinny male *Leptonychotes* killed	

TABLE 9 List of additional details which Racovitza (2016, p. 271-279) provided on both *Lobodon* and *Leptonychotes* seals encountered in the de Gerlache Strait and later on in the open water and when entrapped in the sea ice.

References by chapter

Introduction

Brechon D. 2024. Shackleton, mon amour. Biographie amoureuse d'un explorteur polaire. 175 pp. L'Harmattan, Paris, France .

Chapter 1 Setting the scene for the exploration of the 'unknown Antarctica'

Barr S., Lüdecke C. (Eds.). 2010. The History of the International Polar Years (IPYs). 320 pp. Springer-Verlag, Berlin, Heidelberg. doi. org/10.1007/978-3-642-12402-0.

Buchanan A. 1891. The meteorological results of the 'Challenger' expedition in relation to physical geography. Proceedings of the Royal Geographical Society and Monthly Record of Geography n.s. 13. 137- 158].

Cook J. 1777. A voyage towards the South Pole, and round the world performed in His Majesty's ships he Resolution and the Adventure in the years 1772-1775, 2 volumes . London W. Strahan and T. Cadell, London, UK.

Dumont G.H. 1977. Histoire de la Belgique. 566 pp. Librairie Hachette, France.

Dumont-d'Urville J.S.C. 1846. Voyage au Pôle Sud et dans l'Océanie sur les corvettes l'Astrolabe et la Zélée sous le commandement de M. Dumont-d'Urville, capitaine de vaisseau. Tome 2, 1837-1949. Département de la Marine. Paris, France.

Fifth International Geographical Congress, published in 1892. Compte rendu du Congrès international des sciences géographiques tenu à Berne. 2 volumes, Kraus, Nendeln, Liechtenstein.

Hunt S., Terry M., Thomas N. 2002. Lure of the Southern Seas. 141 pp. Historic Houses Trust of New South Wales, Sydney, Australia.

Lüdecke C. 2004. The First International Polar Year (1828–83) – A big science experiment with small science equipment. History of Meteorology 1, 54–63.

Markham C. 1895. The need for an Antarctic expedition. The Nineteenth Century 224, 706-712.

Mills HR. 1905. The siege of the South Pole. The story of Antarctic exploration with maps, diagrams, and other illustrations, and maps by J. G. Bartholomew. 455 pp. Alston Rivers, London, UK.

Murray J. 1984. The renewal of Antarctic exploration, The Geographical Journal 3, 1-27.

Murray J., Renard AF. 1891. Report on Deep-Sea Deposits Based on the Specimens Collected during the Voyage of HMS Challenger in the Years 1872 to 1876. Report on the Scientific Results of the Voyage of HMS Challenger during the Years 1873-76, Part 3, 525 pp., 43 charts, 22 diagrams, 29 plates and 3 appendices. Her Majesty's Stationary Office, London. UK.

Neumayer G. 1891. Berghaus' Physikalischer Atlas. Atlas des Erdmagnetismus - 5 kolorierte Karten in Kupferstich mit 20 Darstellungen, Gotha, Germany. Available at https://doi.org/10.3931/e-rara-71028.

Tammiksaar E. 2016. The Russian Antarctic Expedition under the command of Fabian Gottlieb von Bellingshausen and its reception in Russia and the world. Polar Record 52, 578–600 (2016). doi:10.1017/S0032247416000449.

Chapter 2 The Challenger expedition 1873-1876; the first exploration of the world's ocean

Buchanan J.Y. 1884. Specific gravity of samples of ocean water. *Volume 1, Part 2 of Report on the scientific results of the voyage of Challenger: Physics and chemistry.* 599 pp. Report on the scientific results of the voyage of H.M.S. Challenger during the years 1873–76 under the command of Captain Georges S. Nares and the late Captain Frank Tourle Thomson. . Published by Order of Her Majesty's Government, London, UK.

Huxley T.H., Pelseneer P. 1895. Report on the specimen of the genus *Spirula* collected by H.M.S. Challenger. 32 pp. Report on the scientific results of the voyage of H.M.S. Challenger during the years 1873–76 under the command of Captain Georges S. Nares and the late Captain Frank Tourle Thomson. Published by Order of Her Majesty's Government, London, UK.

Murray J., Renard A.-F. 1891. Report on the deep-sea deposits based on the specimens collected during the voyage of *HMS Challenger* in the years 1873-1876. 686 pp. Report on the scientific results of the voyage of H.M.S. Challenger during the years 1873–76 under the command of Captain Georges S. Nares and the late Captain Frank Tourle Thomson. . Published by Order of Her Majesty's Government, London, UK.

Murray J., Renard A.-F. 1891. Carte des Sédiments de Mer Profonde avec Notice Explicative. Bruxelles, Société Belge de Librairie, 45 pp., map. (can be downloaded from the web).

Pelseneer P. 1887. Report on the Pteropoda collected by H.M.S. Challenger. 74 pp. Report on the scientific reslts of the voyage of H.M.S. Challenger during the years 1873–76 under the command of Captain Georges S. Nares and the late Captain Frank Tourle Thomson. . Published by Order of Her Majesty's Government, London, UK.

Pelseneer P. 1888. Anatomy of the Deep-Sea Mollusca. 42 pp. Report on the scientific results of the voyage of H.M.S. Challenger during the years 1873–76 under the command of Captain Georges S. Nares and the late Captain Frank Tourle Thomson. Published by Order of Her Majesty's Government, London, UK.

Pelseneer P. 1888. Report on the Pteropoda. First Part. Gymnosomata. 132 pp. Second Part. Thecosomata. 132 pp. Third Part. Anatomy 97 pp. Report on the scientific results of the voyage of H.M.S. Challenger during the years 1873–76 under the command of Captain Georges S. Nares and the late Captain Frank Tourle Thomson. Published by Order of Her Majesty's Government, London, UK.

Renard A.-F. 1882. Report on the petrology of St. Paul's Rocks. 30 pp. Report on the scientific results of the voyage of H.M.S. Challenger during the years 1873-76 under the command of Captain Georges S. Nares and the late Captain Frank Tourle Thomson. Published by Order of Her Majesty's Government, London, UK.

Chapter 3 A dream to conduct a Belgian Antarctic expedition

Cabay A. 1996. L'expédition Antarctique belge 1897-1899. Mémoire présenté sous la direction du professeur G. Kurgan, en vue de l'obtention du grade legal de license en histoire. 128 pp. + annexes. Faculté de Philosophie et Lettres, Université Libre de Bruxelles.

de Gerlache A. 1938. Fragments du récit du voyage. Résultats du voyage de la Belgica en 1897-99 – rapports scientifiques. 75 pp. Imprimerie J.-E. Buschmann, Antwerp, Belgium (this was edited and seen through its publication by Anton Dobrowolski).

Chapter 4 Preparations for the voyage to Antarctica

de Gerlache A. 1902. Quinze mois dans l'Antarctique. 1st edition. 302 pp. Hachette et Cie, Paris, France, and G. Lebègue et Cie, Brussels, Belgium.

de Gerlache A. 1938. Fragments du récit du voyage. Résultats du voyage de la Belgica en 1897-99 – rapports scientifiques. 75 pp. Imprimerie J.-E. Buschmann, Antwerp, Belgium (this was edited and seen through its publication by Anton Dobrowolski).

Demarée G.R., Verheyden R. 2016. Walthère Victor Spring – A forerunner in the study of the Greenhouse Effect. Papers on Global Change 23, 153-158. cejsh.icm.edu.pl, Polish Academy of Science. doi: 10.1515/igbp-2016-0011.

Janzing, J. 2020. High Tide, Blue Moon – Antwerp Antarctica. (partly translated into English by Paul Vincent). 290 pp. Vrijdag Publishers, Anterpen, Belgium.

Marinescu A. 2019. Le voyage de la "Belgica". Premier hivernage dans les glaces antarctiques. (Traduction by Matei Marinescu, but previously by Dumitru Purnichescu). 337 pp. L'Harmattan, Paris, France.

Spring W., Roland L. 1886. Recherches sur les proportions d'acide carbonique contenues dans l'air de Liége. Ciel et Terre 6, 217–227.

Chapter 5 The Belgica personnel, celebrations in Antwerp prior to departure and departure to Antarctic waters

Cook F.A. 1900. Through the first Antarctic night 1898-1899. A narrative of the voyage of the "Belgica" among the newly discovered lands and over an unknown sea about the South Pole. 478 pp.Doubleday & McClure Co., New York, USA.

de Gerlache A. 1938. Fragments du récit du voyage. Résultats du voyage de la Belgica en 1897-99 – rapports scientifiques. 75 pp. Imprimerie J.-E. Buschmann, Antwerp, Belgium (this was edited and seen through its publication by Anton Dobrowolski.

Declerc H., De Broyer C. 2001. (editors). The Belgica Expedition Centennial: Perspectives on Antarctic Science and History. 367 pp. VUB University Press, Brussels, Belgium.

Lecointe G. 1897a. *La navigation astronomique et la navigation estimée.* 410 pp. Berger-Levrault Publishers, Paris, France.

Lecointe G. 1897b. *La création d'une marine nationale belge.* 208 pp. Berger-Levrault Publishers, Paris, France.

Chapter 6 Drake Passage

Arctowski H., Thoulet J. 1902. Rapport des densités de l'eau de mer observées à bord de la Belgica. 23 pp. Résultats du voyage de la Belgica en 1897-1898-1899 – rapports scientifiques. Océanographie. Imprimerie J. Buschmann, Antwerp, Belgium.

Cunningham S.A., Alderson S.G., King, B.A., Brandon, M.A. 2003. Transport and variability of the Antarctic Circumpolar Current in Drake Passage. Journal of Geophysical Research 108, 8084, doi:10.1029/2001JC001147, C5.

Decleir H. 1999. (Editor). Roald Amundsen's diary. The first scientific expedition to the Antarctic. 208 pp. The Cromwell Press, Wiltshire, UK.

de Gerlache A. 1902. Quinze mois dans l'Antarctique. 292 pp. Imprimerie Ch. Bullens, Bruxelles, Belgium.

Gordon A.L., Goldberg T.D. 1970. Circumpolar characteristics of Antarctic waters. Antarctic Map Folio Series. Folo 13. American Geographical Society New York, USA.

Gutierrez-Villanueva M.O., Chereskin T.K., Sprintall J. 2023. Compensating transport trends in the Drake Passage frontal regions yield no acceleration in net transport. Nature Communications **14**, 7792. https://doi.org/10.1038/s41467-023-43499-2

Jackett ßD.R., McDougall T.J., 1997. A neutral density variable for the world's oceans. Journal of Physical Oceanography 27, 237-263.

Jacobs S.S., Comiso J.C. 1997. Climate variability in the Amundsen and Bellingshausen seas. Journal of Climate 10, 697–709.

Lecointe G. 1904. Au Pays des Manchots. Récit. Voyage de la Belgica. 368 pp. Société belge de librairie O. Schepens & Cie, Bruxelles, Belgium.

Sigsbee C.D. 1880. Deep-sea sounding and dredging; a description and discussion of the method and appliances used on board the Coast and Geodetic Survey Steamer, "Blake". 221 pp., 41 plates. Government Printing Office, Washington DC. USA.

Sprintall J. 2008. Long-term trends and interannual variability of temperature in Drake Passage. Progress in Oceanography 77, 316–330.

Xu X., Chassignet, E.P., Firing Y.L., Donohue, K. 2020. Antarctic Circumpolar Current transport through Drake Passage: wat can we learn from comparing high-resolution model results to observations? Journal of Geophysical Research Oceans 125, 2020–016365.

Chapter 7 The de Gerlache Strait
7.1 The discovery of the de Gerlache Strait

Arctowski H. 1901. The Antarctic voyage of the "Belgica" during the years 1897, 1898, 1899. The Geographical Journal 58, 353-390.

Arctowski H. 1908. Les glaciers. Glaciers actuels et vestiges de leur ancienne extension. 74 pp.Résultats du voyage de la Belgica en 1897-1898-1899 – rapports scientifiques. Géologie. Imprimerie J. Buschmann, Antwerp, Belgium.

Arctowski H., Mill H.R. 1908. Rapport sur les relations thermiques de l'océan. Rapport sur les observations thermométriques faites aux stations de sondage. Océanographie. 36 pp. Résultats du voyage de la Belgica en 1897-1898- 1899 – rapports scientifiques. Imprimerie J. Buschmann, Antwerp.

Barr W.I., Krause R., Pawlik P.-M . 2004. Chukchi Sea, Southern Ocean, Kara Sea: The polar voyages of Captain Eduard Dallmann, whaler, trader, explorer 1830-96. Polar Record 40, 1 - 18. 10.1017/S0032247403003139.

Cook F.A. 1900. Through the First Antarctic Night, 1898-1899: A Narrative of the Voyage of the "Belgica" Among Newly Discovered Lands and Over an Unknown Sea about the South Pole. 478 pp. Doubleday & McClure Company, New York, USA.

Cornet Y., Derwael J.-J. 2023. La carte du Détroit de Gerlache en Antarctique. Analyse de l'incertitude des coordonnées astronomiques levées pendant l'expédition de la Belgica en janvier et février 1898. Bulletin de la Société Géographique de Liège 81, 5-30. doi:10.25518/0770-7576.7073.

Decleir H. (ed.) 1999. Roald Amundsen's Belgica Diary. The First Scientific Expedition to The Antarctic. 208 pp. Bluntisham Books, The Cromwell Press, Wiltshire, UK.

De Deckker P. 2018. On the long-ignored scientific achievements of the Belgica expedition 1897–1899. Polar Research, 37:1, 1474695, DOI: 10.1080/17518369.2018.1474695.

de Gerlache A. 1902. Quinze mois dans l'Antarctique. Voyage de la 'Belgica'. Imprimerie scientifique Ch. Bulens, 303 pp. Bruxelles, Belgium.

Derwael J.-J. 2013. La méthode de l'Amiral Mouchez - Revue XYZ 134, 61-66.

Derwael J.-J. 2023. Antarctique. La carte du détroit de Gerlache. Description d'un levé cartographique effectué en 21 jours. Revue XYZ 174, 51-59.

Federaal wetenschapsbeleid 2008. Four maps representing Belgian typonyms in Antarctica (2008). https://www.vliz.be/en/imis?module=ref&refid=208684.

Koren J.(no date) Journal over den Belgiske Sydhavs Expedition 97-99. Johan Korens håndskrevne dagbok fra *Belgica* ekspedisjonen. 60 pp. The National Library of Norway, Oslo, Norway. https://media.digitalarkivet.no/en/view/77494/48.

Lecointe G. 1900. Aperçu des travaux scientifiques de l'expédition antarctique belge. Bulletin de la Société Royale Belge de Géographie (Bruxelles). 24, 29-52.

Lecointe G. 1903. Travaux hydrographiques et instructions nautiques. Cartes.– rapports scientifiques. Hydrographie. Résultats du voyage de la Belgica en 1897-1898- 1899. 8 maps. Imprimerie J. Buschmann, Antwerp, Belgium.

Lecointe G. 1905. Travaux Hydrographiques et Instructions. Résultats du Voyage du S.Y. Belgica en 1997 – 1898 – 1899. 110 pp. Imprimerie J. Buschmann ,Antwerp, Belgium.

Pawlik P.-M. 1996. Von Sibirien nach Neu Guinea: Kapitän Dallmann, seine Schiffe und Reisen 1830–1896. Ein Lebensbild in Selbst- und Zeitzeugnissen. 208 pp. Hauschild Verlag, Bremen, Germany.

Racovitza, E. 1900a. Expédition Antarctique Belge. La vie des animaux et des plantes dans l'Antarctique. Conférence faite à la Société belge de Géographie. Bulletin de la Société Royale Belge de Géographie (Bruxelles) 24, 177-230.

Racovitza E. 1900b. Résultats généraux de l'Expédition Antarctique Belge. La Géographie. Bulletin de la Société de Géographie (Paris), 2 (15 février 1900), 81-92.

Racovitza E. 1903. Cétacés. Résultats du voyage du S.Y. Belgica en 1897-1898- 1899. 142 pp. Imprimerie J. Buschmann, Antwerp, Belgium.

Verlinden J. 2008. Discovery and exploration of Gerlache Strait. Belgian Antarctic Expedition 1897-1899. 172 pp. Privately published by Asteria Expeditions, Bruges, Belgium.

7.2 Flowering plants

De Wilderman E. 1903. Les phanérogammes des terres magellaniques. Résultats du voyage du S. Y. Belgica en 1897-1898- 1899 – rapports scientifiques. Botanique. 246 pp. Imprimerie J. Buschmann, Antwerp, Belgium.

Kozeretska I.A., Parnikoza I.Yu., Mustafa O., Tyschenko O.V., Korsun S.G., Convey P. 2010. Development of Antarctic herb tundra vegetation near Arctowski station, King George Island Polar Science 3, 254-261.doi: 10.1016j/j.polar.2009.100001.

Kozeretska I.A. Parnikoza I.Yu., Mustafa O., Tyschenko O.V., Korsun S.G., Convey P. 2010. Development of Antarctic herb tundra vegetation near Arctowski station, King George Island. Polar Science 3, 254-251. doi. org/10.1016/j.polar.2009.10.001.

Nuzhyna N., Parnikoza I., Poronnik O.O., Kozeretska I., Kunakh V. 2019. Anatomical variations of Deschampsia antarctica É. Desv. plants from distant Antarctic regions, in vitro culture, and in relations to Deschampsia caespitosa (L.) P. Beauv. Polish Polar Research 40, 361-383. 10.24425/ppr.2019.130903.

Parnikoza I.Y., Maidanuk D.N., Kozeretska I.A. 2007. Are Deschampsia antarctica Desv. and Colobanthus quitensis (Kunth) Bartl. migratory relicts? Cytology and Genetics 41, 226–229. doi.org/10.3103/S0095452707040068.

Parnikoza I., Convey P., Dykyy I., Trokhymets V., Milinevsky G., Tyschenko O., Inozemtseva D., Kozeretska I. 2010. Current status of the Antarctic herb tundra formation in the Central Argentine Islands. Global Change Biology 15, 1685-1693. doi.org/10.1111/j.1365-2486.2009.01906.x

Parnikoza I., Kozeretska I., Kunakh V. 2011. Vascular Plants of the Maritime Antarctic: Origin and Adaptation. American Journal of Plant Sciences 2, 381-395. doi: 10.4236/ajps.2011.23044.

Parnikoza I., Convey P., Dykyy I., Trokhymets V., Milinevsky G., Tyschenko O., Inozemtseva D., Kozeretska I. 2015. Comparative analysis of Deschampsia antarctica Desv. population adaptability in the natural environment of Admiralty Bay (King George Island, maritime Antarctic). Polar Biology 38, 1401–1411. doi. org/10.1007/s00300-015-1704-1.

Parnikoza I., Rozhok A., Convery P., Veselski M., Esefeld J., Ochyra R., Mustafa O., Braun C., Peter H.-U., Smykla J., Kunhak V., Kozeretska I. 2018. Spread of Antarctic vegetation by the kelp gull: comparison of two maritime Antarctic regions. Polar Biology 41, 1143-1155. oi.org/10.1007/s00300-018-2274-9.

Podolich O., Prekrasna, I., Parnikoza I., Voznyuk, T., Zubova G., Zaets, I., Miryuta N., Myryuta G., \Poronnik O.O., Kozeretska I., Kunakh V., Pirttilä A.M., Dykyi E., Kozyrovska N. 2021. First record of the endophytic bacteria of Deschampsia antarctica É. Desv. from two distant localities of the maritime Antarctic. Czech Polar Reports 11, 134-153. doi:10.5817/CPR2021-1-10.

Upson R., Newsham K.K., Read D.J. 2008. Root-fungal associations of Colobanthus quitensis and Deschampsia antarctica in the maritime and subantarctic. Arctic, Antarctic, and Alpine Research 40, 592-599.

Racovitza E. 1900a. Expédition Antarctique Belge. La vie des animaux et des plantes dans l'Antarctique. Conférence faite à la Société belge de Géographie le 22 décembre 18999. Bulletin de la Societé Royale Belge de Géographie (Bruxelles) 24, 177-230.

Racovitza E. 1900b. Vers le Pôle Sud. Conférence faite à la Sorbonne sur l'Expédition Antarctique Belge, son but, ses aventures et ses résultats. Causeries scientifiques de la Société zoologique de France (Paris) 6, 175-242.

Santiago I.F., Rosa C.A., Rosa L.H. 2017. Endophytic symbiont yeasts associated with the Antarctic angiosperms Deschampsia antarctica and Colobanthus quitensis. Polar Biology 40, 177-183.

Xiong F.S., Ruhland C.T., Day T.A. 1999. Photosynthetic temperature response of the Antarctic vascular plants Colobanthus quitensis and Deschampsia antarctica. Physiologia Plantarum 106, 276-286.

Yevchun H., Dykyi, E., Kozeretska I., Fedchuk A., Karamushka V., Parnikoza I. 2021. Minimizing tourist impact on the Argentine Islands ecosystem, Antarctic Peninsula, using visitor site guidelines approach. Ukrainian Antarctic Journal 98, 116. doi:10.33275/1727-7485.1.2021.669.

7.3 The amazing chironomid fly: Belgica antarctica

Baust J.G., Edwards J.S. 1979. Mechanisms of freezing tolerance in an Antarctic midge, Belgica antarctica. Physiological Entomology 4, 1-5.

Courtney-Mustaphi C.J., Steiner E., von Fumetti S., Heiri O. 2024. Aquatic invertebrate mandibles and sclerotized remains in Quaternary lake sediments. Journal of Paleolimnology 71, 45–83. doi.org/10.1007/s10933-023-00302-y.

Dollo L. 1900a. Cryodraco antarcticus, poisson abyssal nouveau recueilli par l'Expédition Antarctique Belge. Communication préliminaire. Académie royale de Belgique, Bulletin de la Classe des Sciences (Bruxelles) 2, 128-137.

Dollo L. 1900b. Gerlachea australis, poisson abyssal nouveau recueilli par l'Expédition Antarctique Belge. Communication préliminaire. Académie royale de Belgique, Bulletin de la Classe des Sciences (Bruxelles) 3, 194-206.

Dollo L. 1900c. Racovitzia glacialis, poisson abyssal nouveau recueilli par l'Expédition Antarctique Belge. Communication préliminaire. Académie royale de Belgique, Bulletin de la Classe des Sciences (Bruxelles) 4, 316-327.

Dollo L. 1900d. Macrurus Lecointei, poisson abyssal nouveau recueilli par l'Expédition Antarctique Belge. Communication préliminaire. Académie royale de Belgique, Bulletin de la Classe des Sciences (Bruxelles) 6, 383-401.

Gerke G. 1889. Vorläufige Nachricht über die Fliegen Süd-Geogiens, nach der Ausbeute der Deutschen Station 1882-83. Jahrbuch des Hamburgishes Wissensschaftlichen Anstalten 6, 153-154.

Greene S.W., Gressitt G.L., Koop D., Llano G.A., Rudolph E.D., Singer R., Steere W.C., Ugolin F.C. 1967. Terrestrial life of Antarctica. Map 8. Diptera and Siphonaptera (Midges and fleas). Antarctic Map Folio Series, Folio 5. American Geographical Society of New York, New York, USA.

Ihtimanska M., Kovalenko P., Michailova P., Parnikoza I. 2023. Larval morphology of Belgica antarctica Jacobs, 1900 (Diptera, Chironomidae, Orthocladiinae) from central part of the maritime Antarctic and deformities found in the larvae. Zootaxa. 5311. 405-416. doi:10.11646/zootaxa.5311.3.5.

Jacobs J.C. 1900. Diagnoses d'insectes recueillis par l'expédition antarctique beige (partie Chironomidae). Annales de la Société entomologique de Belgique 44, 107– 108.

Jacobs J.C., Becker T., Rübsaamen E.H. 1906.

Insectes. Diptères. Résultats du voyage de la Belgica en 1897-1898- 1899 – rapports scientifiques. Zoologie. 67-85 pp., figs. 4-5. Imprimerie J. Buschmann, Antwerp, Belgium.

Kelley J L,. Peyton J.T., Fiston-Lavier A-S., Teets N.M., Yee M-C., , Johnston J.S., Bustamante C.D., Richard E. Lee R.E., Denlinger D.L.,2014. Compact genome of the Antarctic midge is likely an adaptation to an extreme environment. Nature Communications 5, 4611; doi: 10.1038/ncomms5611

Kozeretska I., Serga S., Kovalenko P., Gorobchyshyn V., Convey P. 2022. *Belgica antarctica* (Diptera: Chironomidae): A natural model organism for extreme environments. Insect Science 29, 2–20.doi: 10.1111/1744-7917.12925.

Michailova P., Kovalenko P., Serga S., Parnikoza I., Kozeretska I., Convey P. 2023. A chromosome map of *Belgica antarctica* Jacobs (Diptera: Chironomidae) from Antarctica, including chromosome variability. Antarctic Science 35, 1-17. doi: 10.1017/S0954102023000202.

Racovitza E. 1900a. Expédition Antarctique Belge. La vie des animaux et des plantes dans l'Antarctique. Conférence faite à la Société belge de Géographie le 22 décembre 1899. Bulletin de la Societé Royale Belge de Géographie (Bruxelles) 24, 177-230.

Racovitza E. 1900b. Vers le Pôle Sud. Conférence faite à la Sorbonne sur l'Expédition Antarctique Belge, son but, ses aventures et ses résultats. Causeries scientifiques de la Société zoologique de France (Paris) 6, 175-242.

Racovitza E. 1998. (Eds. Marinescu A., Banarescu A., Iftimie A.). Belgica (189701899). Lettres, journal antarctique, conférences. Fondation Culturelle Roumaine, Collection Le Rameau d'Or 2 (7), 1-207.

Richard K.J., Convey P., Block W. 1994. The terrestrial arthropod fauna of the Byers Peninsula, Livingston Island, South Shetland Islands. Polar Biology 14, 371–379.

Siegert M., Atkinson A., Banwell A.,Brandon M., Convey P., Davies B., Downie R., Edwards T., Hubbard B., Marshall G., Rogelj J., Rumble J., Stroeve J, Vaughan D. 2019. The Antarctic Peninsula under a 1.5°C global warming scenario. Frontiers in Environmental Science 7:102.. doi: 10.3389/fenvs.2019.00102.

Usher M.B., Edwards M.E. 1984. The terrestrial arthropods of the grass sward of Lynch Island, a specially protected area in Antarctica. Oecologia 63,143—144.

7.4 Acarid mites

Dalenius P. 1965. The acarology of the Antarctic regions. In: Van Mieghem J., Van Oye P. (eds). Biogeography and ecology in Antarctica. pp 414–430. Junk Publishers, The Hague, The Netherlands.

Dalenius P., Wilson O. 1958. On the soil fauna of the Antarctic and of the sub-antarctic islands. The Oribatidae (Acari). Arkiv för Zoologi series 2, 11(23), 393-415

Hogg I.D., Stevens M.I. 2002. Soil Fauna of Antarctic Coastal Landscapes. In: Beyer, L., Bölter, M. (eds). Geoecology of Antarctic Ice-Free Coastal Landscapes. Ecological Studies, 154, 265-280. Springer, Berlin, Heidelberg. doi. org/10.1007/978-3-642-56318-8_15.

Michael A.D. 1903. Acarida (Oribatidae). Résultats du voyage du S. Y. Belgica en 1987, 1988, 1989. Rapport Scientifiques. – Zoologie. 6 pp., 2 plates. Imprimerie J. Buschmann, Antwerp, Belgium.

Racovitza E. 1998. (Eds. Marinescu A., Banarescu A., Iftimie A.). Belgica (189701899). Lettres, journal antarctique, conférences. Fondation Culturelle Roumaine, Collection Le Rameau d'Or 2 (7), 1-207.

Wallrock J.A. 1962. A redescription of *Notapsis antarctica* Michael, 1903. (Acari: Oibatei). Pacific Insects 4, 869-880.

7.5 Mosses

Cardot J. 1900. Note préliminaire sur les mousses recueillies par l'Expédition Antartique Belge. Revue de Bryologie 27(3), 38-47.

Cardot J. 1902. Mousses et coup d'oeuil sur la flore bryologique des Terres Magellaniques. Résultats du voyage du S. Y .Belgica en 1897-1898- 1899 – rapports scientifiques. Botanique. 61 pp. Imprimerie J. Buschmann, Antwerp, Belgium.

Roland T.P., Bartlett O.T., Charman D.J., Anderson K., Hodgson D.A., Amesbury M.J., Maclean I., Fretwell P.T., Fleming A. 2024. Sustained greening of the Antarctic Peninsula observed from satellites. *Nature Geoscience* **17**, 1121–1126. doi.org/10.1038/s41561-024-01564-5.

7.6 Lichen

Wainio E. A. 1903. Lichens. Résultats du voyage du S. Y. Belgica en 1897-1898- 1899 – rapports scientifiques. Botanique. 52 pp. Imprimerie J. Buschmann, Antwerp, Belgium.

7.7 Bryophytes (Hépatiques – Liverworts)

Bednarek-Ochyra H., Váňa J., Ochyra R., Smith R.I.L. 2000. The liverwort flora of Antarctica. 258 pp. Polish Academy of Sciences, Institute of Botany, Cracow, Poland. ISBN: 83–85444–74–2.

Douin C. 1920. La famille des Céphaloziellacées. Mémoire de la Société Botanique de France 28/29, 1-90.

Gottsche C. M. 1890. Die Lebermoose Süd-Georgiens. In: G. Neumayer (ed.), Die Internationale Polarforschung 1882–83. 449–454 pp. Die Deutschen Expeditionen und ihre Ergebnisse, 2. Berlin, A. Asher, Germany.

Gradstein S. 2006. Stephani's Species Hepaticarum revisited. Willdenowia 36.,10.3372/wi.36.36152.

Stephani F. 1901. Hépatiques. Résultats du voyage du S.Y. Belgica en 1897-1898-1899 – rapports scientifiques. Botanique. 6 pp. Imprimerie J. Buschmann, Antwerp, Belgium.

7.8 Seals and penguins in the de Gerlache Strait

No reference see chapter 9.3

7.9 Geological observations in the de Gerlache Strait

Adie R.J. 1957. The petrology of Graham Land. Falkland Island Dependencies Survey. Scientific Reports 20, 1-31.

Birkenmajer K. 1987. Report on the Polish geological investigations in the Antarctic Peninsula sector, West Antarctica, in 1984–85. Studia Geologica Polonica 93, 113–122.

Birkenmajer K. 1988. Report on the Polish geological investigations in the Antarctic Peninsula sector, 1987–1988. Polish Polar Research 9 (4), 505–519.

Birkenmajer K. 1994. Evolution of the Pacific margin of the northern Antarctic Peninsula: an overview. Geologische Rundschau 83, 309–321.

Birkenmajer K. 1995. Geology of Gerlache Strait, West Antarctica. I. Arctowski Peninsula. Polish Polar Research 16 (1–2), 47–60.

Brinkenmajer K. 1999. The tectonic structure of Gerlache Strait. In: Repelewska- Pêkalowa, J. (ed.), Polish Polar Studies. 26th International Polar Symposium. The 25 Jubilee of the Polar Club of the Polish Geographical Society. Lublin, 18–20 June 1999. 45-50 pp. Maria Curie Sklodowska University Press, Lublin, Poland.

Birkenmajer K. 2001. Polish geological research in Antarctica after the *Belgica* expedition. In H. Decleir and C. De Broyer (eds.). pp. 235-246. The Belgica Expedition Centennial. Perspectives on Antarctic Science and History. VUB University Press, Brussels, Belgium.

British Antarctic Territory geological map 1979. British Antarctic Survey prepared for multi-coloured reproduction at 1:500,000 by the Directorate of Overseas Surveys, sheets 2 and 3.

Craddock C. et al. 1969-1979. Geologic maps of Antarctica, Folio 12. Geologic maps of Antarctica. In: Antarctic map folio series. (VC Bushnell ed.). Geographical Society of New York, New York, USA.

Hooper P.R. 1962. The petrology of Anvers Island and adjacent islands. Falkland Island Dependencies Survey. Scientific Reports 34, 1-62.

Pelikan A. 1909. Petrographische untersuchung der Gesteinproben. I Theil. Résultats du voyage de la Belgica en 1897-1898- 1899 – rapports scientifiques. Géologie. 56 pp. Imprimerie J. Buschmann, Antwerp. Belgium.

Chapter 8 In the Bellingshausen Sea – physico-chemical observations

8.1. Trapped in the sea ice

Arctowski H. 1906. Les glaces. Glace de mer et banquises. Résultats du voyage du S.Y. Belgica en 1897-1898- 1899 – rapports scientifiques. Océanographie. 62 pp. Imprimerie J. Buschmann, Antwerp, Belgium.

Cornet Y., Derwael J.-J. 2023. La carte du Détroit de Gerlache en Antarctique. Analyse de l'incertitude des coordonnées astronomiques levées pendant l'expédition de la Belgica en janvier et février 1898. Bulletin de la Société Géographique de Liège 81, 5-30. doi:10.25518/0770-7576.7073.

Graham A.G.C., Nitsche F.O., Larter R.D., 2011. An improved bathymetry compilation for the Bellingshausen Sea, Antarctica, to inform ice-sheet and ocean models. The Cryosphere 5, 95-106. doi:10.5194/tc-5-95-2011.

Lecointe G. 1901. Astronomie – Etude des chronomètres – Première partie, Méthode et Conclusions. Expédition Antarctique Belge. Résultats du voyage du S.Y. Belgica en 1897-1898- 1899 – rapports scientifiques. Astronomie. 72 pp. Imprimerie J. Buschmann, Antwerp, Belgium.

Lecointe G. 1903. Travaux hydrographiques et instructions nautiques. Cartes. Résultats du voyage de la Belgica en 1897-1898- 1899 – rapports scientifiques. Océanographie. 8 pp. Imprimerie J. Buschmann, Antwerp, Belgium.

Schubert R., Thompson A.F., Speer K., Schulze Chretien L., Bebieva Y. 2021. The Antarctic Coastal Current in the Bellingshausen Sea. The Cryosphere 15, 4179–4199. doi. org/10.5194/tc-15-4179-2021.

Schulze Chretien L.M., Thompson A.F., Flexas M.M., Speer K., Swaim N., Oelerich R., Ruan X., Schubert R., LoBuglio C. 2021. The shelf circulation of the Bellingshausen Sea. Journal of Geophysical Research: Oceans, 126, e2020JC016871. doi. org/10.1029/2020JC016871.

Web sites: A worrying absence of sea ice. (https://125yearsbelgica.wordpress. com/2023/02/17/a-worrying-absence-of-sea-ice/)

Belgica Trough and the West Antarctic Ice Sheet, 21/02/2023. (https://125yearsbelgica. wordpress.com/2023/02/21/belgica-trough-and-the-west-antarctic-ice-sheet/)

8.2 On oceanic temperature measurements made by Henryk Arctowski

Arctowski H. 1900. Géographie physique de la région antarctique visitée par l'Expédition de la Belgica. Bulletin de la Société royale belge de Géographie (Bruxelles) 24, 93-175.

Arctowski H., Mill HR. 1908. Rapport sur les observations thermométriques faites aux stations de sondage. Résultats du voyage de la Belgica en 1897-1898- 1899 – rapports scientifiques. Océanographie. 36 pp. Imprimerie J. Buschmann, Antwerp, Belgium.

Arctowski H., Renard A-F. 1901. Notice préliminaire sur les sédiments marins receuillis par l'expédition de la Belgica. Mémoires couronés et autres mémoires publiés par l'Académie royale de Belgique. (Bruxelles), 61, 30 pp., 1 plate.

Bigg G.R. 2024. The Southern Ocean marine ice record of the early historical, circum-Antarctic voyages of Coo and Bellingshausen. Climate of the Past 20, 2045-2054.

Dailaden Q., Goosse H., Rezsöhazy J., Thomas E.R. 2021. Reconstructing atmospheric circulation and sea-ice extent in the West Antarctic over the past 200 years using data assimilation. Climate 57, 3479–35

Debenham F. (editor). 1945. The voyage of Captain Bellingshausen to the Antarctic Seas 1819-1821. Translated from the Russian. Volume 1. Hakluyt Society, London, UK.

Fogt R.L., Dalaiden Q, Zarembka M.S. Understanding differences in Antarctic sea-ice-extent reconstructions in the Ross, Amundsen, and Bellingshausen seas since 1900. Past Global Changes Magazine.30 (22), 74-75

Jacobs S.S., Comiso J.C. 1997. Climate variability in the Amundsen and Bellingshausen seas. Journal of Climate 10, 697–709.

Martinson D.G. 2012. Antarctic circumpolar current's role in the Antarctic ice system: An overview. Palaeogeography Palaeoclimatology Palaeoecology 335-336, 71-74.

Schmidtko S., Heywood K.J., Thompson A.F., Aoki S. 2014. Multidecadal warming of Antarctic waters. Science 346 (6214), 1227–1231.

Schubert R., Thompson A.F., Speer K., Schulze Chretien L., Bebieva Y. 2021. The Antarctic Coastal Current in the Bellingshausen Sea. The Cryosphere, 15, 4179–4199.

Schulze Chretien L.M., Thompson A.F., Speer K., Oelerich R., Swaim N., Ruan, X., Schubert R., LoBuglio C., Heywood K.J. 2021. The circulation of the Bellingshausen Sea: heat and meltwater transports, Journal of Geophysical Research 126, e2020JC016871.

Sigsbee C.D. 1880. Deep-sea sounding and dredging; a description and discussion of the method and appliances used on board the Coast and Geodetic Survey Steamer, "Blake". 221 pp., 41 plates. Government Printing Office, Washington DC, USA.

Venables H.J., Meredith M.P., Brearley J.A. 2017. Modification of deep waters in Marguerite Bay, western Antarctic Peninsula, caused by topographic overflows. Deep-Sea Research Part II 139, 9-17.

8.3 Modern-day temperatures profiles
No references. See 8.2

8.4.On seawater salinity and density in Bransfield Strait and the Bellingshausen Sea

Arctowski H., Thoulet J. 1908. Rapport sur les densités de l'eau de mer. Résultats du voyage de la Belgica en 1897-1898- 1899 – rapports scientifiques. Océanographie. 28 pp. Imprimerie J. Buschmann, Antwerp, Belgium.

Buchanan J.Y. 1889. Report on the Specific Gravity of Samples of Ocean-Water, observed on board H.M.S. Challenger, during the years 1873-1876. 44 pp., 11 diagrams. Published by Order of Her Majesty's Government, Printed by Her Majesty's Office, London. UK.

de Gerlache A. 1938. Fragments du récit du voyage. Résultats du voyage de la Belgica en 1897-1898- 1899 – rapports scientifiques. 74 pp. Imprimerie J.-E. Buschmann, Antwerp (this was edited and seen through its publication by Anton Dobrowolski).

Sigsbee C.D. 1880. Deep-sea sounding and dredging; a description and discussion of the method and appliances used on board the Coast and Geodetic Survey Steamer, "Blake". 221 pp., 41 plates. Government Printing Office, Washington DC. USA.

Martinson D.G. 2012. Antarctic circumpolar current's role in the Antarctic ice system: An overview. Palaeogeography Palaeoclimatology Palaeoecology 335-336, 71-74.

Schubert R., Thompson A.F., Speer K., Schulze Chretien L., Bebieva Y. 2021. The Antarctic Coastal Current in the Bellingshausen Sea. The Cryosphere, 15, 4179–4199.

Schulze Chretien L.M., Thompson A.F., Speer K., Oelerich R., Swaim N., Ruan X., Schubert R., LoBuglio C., Heywood K.J. 2021. The circulation of the Bellingshausen Sea: heat and meltwater transports, Journal of Geophysical Research 126, e2020JC016871.

Thoulet J. 1902. Détermination de la densité de l'eau de mer. Résultats du voyage de la Belgica en 1897-1898- 1899 – rapports scientifiques. Océanographie. 29 pp. Imprimerie J. Buschmann, Antwerp, Belgium

Thoulet J. 1908. Opérations et instruments d'océanographie pratique. 186 pp. Librairie militaire R. Chapelot et Cie. Paris, France.

8.5 Meteorological observations in the Bellingshausen Sea

Arctowski H. 1904. Rapport sur les observations météorologiques horaires. Résultats du voyage de la Belgica en 1897-1898- 1899 – rapports scientifiques. Métérologie. 249 pp. Imprimerie J. Buschmann, Antwerp, Belgium.

Bernacchi L. 1901. To the South Polar regions : expedition of 1898-1900. 348 pp. Hurst and Blackett, London, UK.

Charcot J. 1905. The French Antarctic expedition. The Geographical Journal 26, 497-516.

Charcot J-B. 1908. Expédition antarctique française (1903-1905). Journal de l'expédition. Masson et Cie, Paris, France.

Charcot J. 1911. The second French Antarctic expedition. The Geographical Journal 37, 241- 257.

Charcot J. 1913. Autour du pôle sud : expédition du Pourquoi-pas? 1908-1910. Masson et Cie, Paris, France.

Goodwin B.P., Mosley-Thomson E., Wilson A.B., Porter S.E., Sierra-Hernandez M.R.. 2016. Accumulation Variability in the Antarctic Peninsula: The Role of Large-Scale Atmospheric Oscillations and Their Interactions. Journal of Climate 27, 2579-2596. doi: 10.1175/JCLI-D-15-0354.1.

Klovstad H., Hanson, N., Evans H.B., Tongmer A., Bernacchi L.C., Colbeck W. 1902. Meteorological observations taken by the staff of the "Southern Cross". Royal Society of London, UK.

Matha A., Rey-Pailhade J-J. 1911. Expédition antarctique française (1903-1905) commandée par Jean Charcot. Hydrographie, physique du globe. Gauthier-Villars, Paris, France. 4 volumes, 619 pp.

Meredith M.P., Stammerjohn S.E., Venables H.J., Ducklow H.W., Martinson D.G., Iannuzzi R.A., Leng M.J., vanWessem J.M., Reijmer C.H., Barrand N.E. 2017. Changing distributions of sea ice melt and meteoric water west of the Antarctic Peninsula. Deep-Sea Research II 139, 40–57. dx.doi.org/10.1016/j.dsr2.2016.04.019.

Oelerich R., Heywood K.J., Damerell G.M., Thompson A.F. 2022. Wind-induced variability of warm water on the southern Bellingshausen Sea continental shelf. Journal of Geophysical Research: Oceans, 127, e2022JC018636. https://doi.org/10.1029/2022JC018636.

Porter S.E., Parkinson C.L., Mosley-Thompson E. 2016. Bellingshausen Sea ice extent recorded in an Antarctic Peninsula ice core/ Journal of Geophysical Research, Atmospheres 121, 13,886–13,900, doi: doi:10.1002/2016JD025626.

Sippel S., Kent E.C., Meinshausen N., Chan D., Kadow C., Neukom R., Fisher E.M., Humphrey V., Rohde R., de Vries I., Knutt R. 2024. Early-twentieth-century cold bias in ocean surface temperature observations. Nature 635, 618-624. https://doi.org/10.1038/s41586-024-08230-1.

Thomas E.R., Tetzner D.R., 2018. The Climate of the Antarctic Peninsula during the Twentieth Century: Evidence from Ice Cores. In: The Climate of the Antarctic Peninsula during the Twentieth Century: Evidence from Ice Cores. doi: http://dx.doi.org/10.5772/intechopen.81507. Published online.

8.6 Aurora australis – southern lights

Arctowski H. 1901a. Aurores australes. Journal des aurores polaires observées pendant l'hivernage de la Belgica. Résultats du voyage de la Belgica en 1897-1898- 1899 – rapports scientifiques. Métérologie. 67 pp. Imprimerie J. Buschmann, Antwerp, Belgium.

Arctowski H. 1901b. Sur les aurores australes et boréales. Ciel et Terre 21, 553-556.

Boller W. 1895. Das südlicht. Gerlands Beiträge zur Geophysik 3, 55-130, 550-608. Porter S. E., Parkinson C.L., Mosley-Thompson E. 2016. Bellingshausen Sea ice extent recorded in an Antarctic Peninsula ice core. Journal of Geophysical Research, Atmospheres 121, 13,886–13,900, doi: doi:10.1002/2016JD025626.BOM 2024.

SWS - Aurora - Australian Space Weather Forecasting Centre. https// www.sws.bom.au/Aurora (accessed 26.4.2024).

Borchgrevinck K. 1900. The "Southern Cross" Expedition to the Antarctic, 1899-1900. The Geographical Journal 16 (4), 381-411.

Crooker N.U., Feynman J., Gosling J.T. 1977. "On the high correlation between long-term averages of solar wind speed and geomagnetic activity". Journal of Geophysical Research 82 (13), 1933. doi:10.1029/JA082i013p01933.

Ekholm N., Arrhenius S. 1898. Ueber den einfluss des mondes auf die polarlichter und gewitter. Proceedings of the Swedish Academy of Sciences 31 (2), 77 pp.

Fox A. 2019. The northern and southern lights are different. Here's why. Science doi: 10.1126/science.aaw8037. Reporting on an article by Ohma A. et al. (2018) in Journal of Geophysical Research Space Physics 123, 10,030-10,063.

Hamacher D.W. 2013. Aurorae in Australian Abiriginal traditions. Journal of Astronomical History and Heritage 16, 207–219.

Stern D.P. 1996. A brief history of magnetospheric physics during the space age. Reviews of Geophysics 34, 1–31.

Nordenskiöld A.E. 1881. The voyage of the Vega round Asia and Europe, with a historical review of previous journeys along the north coast of the Old World. (Translated by A. Leslie) 2 volumes, Macmillon and Co, London. UK.

8.7 Clouds

Dobrowolski A. 1903. Observations des nuages. Résultats du voyage du S.Y. Belgica en 1897-1898- 1899 – rapports scientifiques. Météorologie. 161 pp. Imprimerie J. Buschmann, Antwerp, Belgium.

8.8. Snow and hoar-frost (givre)

Barry R.G., Jania J., Birkenmajer K. 2011. A. B. Dobrowolski – the first cryospheric scientist – and the subsequent development of cryospheric science. History of Geo- and Space Sciences 2, 75-79.

Dobrowolski A. (1903) La neige et le givre. Résultats du voyage du S.Y. Belgica en 1897-1898-1899 – rapports scientifiques. Métérologie. 84 pp. Imprimerie J. Buschmann, Antwerp, Belgium.

Dobrowolski A B .1923. Historia naturalna lodu (The natural history of ice), 940 pp. Warszaa: Kasa Pomocy im. Dr. J. Mianowskiego, (in Polish with French summary, 926–940).

Machowski J. 1998. Contribution of H. Arctowski and A. B. Dobrowolski to the Antarctic Expedition of Belgica (1897–1899), Polish Polar Research 19, 15–30.

8.9 On ice, sea ice and their formation

Arctowski H. 1908. Les glaciers. Glaciers actuels et vestiges de leur ancu=ienne extension. Résultats du voyage du S.Y. Belgica en 1897-1898- 1899 – rapports scientifiques. Géologie. 111 pp. Imprimerie J. Buschmann, Antwerp, Belgium.

Arctowski H., Mill H.R. 1908. Rapport sur les relations thermiques de l'océan. Rapport sur les observations thermométriques faites aux stations de sondage. Résultats du voyage du S.Y. Belgica en 1897-1898- 1899 – rapports scientifiques. Océanographie. 64 pp. Imprimerie J. Buschmann, Antwerp, Belgium.

Debenham F. (editor). 1945. The voyage of Captain Bellingshausen to the Antarctic sea 1819-1821 (translated from the Russian). 2 volumes, 474 pp. Hakluyt Society, 2nd series no. 91-92. London, UK.

Cook J. 1777. A Voyage Towards the South Pole and Round the World: Performed in His Majesty's Ships the Resolution and Adventure, in the Years 1772, 1773, 1774 and 1775. 1st edition, 2 vols. London, UK.

Declerc H. (editor). 1999. Roald Amundsen's Belgica diary. The first scientific expedition to the Antarctic. 208 pp. Bluntisham Books, Erskine Press, Norwich, UK

Lecointe G. 1903. Travaux hydrographiques et instructions Nautiques. Résultats du voyage de la Belgica en 1897-1898- 1899 – rapports scientifiques. Hydrographie. 146 pp. Imprimerie J. Buschmann, Antwerp, Belgium.

O´ Cofaigh C., Larter R.D., Dowdeswell J.A., Hillenbrand C.-D., Pudsey C.J., Evans J., Morris P. 2005. Flow of the West Antarctic Ice Sheet on the continental margin of the Bellingshausen Sea at the Last Glacial Maximum. Journal of Geophysical Research 110, B11103, doi:10.1029/2005JB003619.

Société royale belge de Géographie. 1900. Expédition antarctique belge sous le Commandement de Adrien de Gerlache 1897-1899 Conférences faites par Mm. G. Lecointe, H. Arctowski et E. Racovitza, Membres de l'Expédition. Conférence donnée à la Société royale belge de Géographie, le 18 Novembre 1899, Vol. 24. Including: Lecointe, G. Aperçu des travaux scientifiques de l'expédition antarctique belge. pp. 29-52. Lecointe G. L'hydrographie dans le détroit de de la Belgica et les observations astronomiques et magnétiques dans la zone australe. pp. 53-92. Arctowski H. Géographie physique de la region antarctique visitée par l'Expédition de la Belgica. pp. 93-175. Racovitza G. Expédition Antarctique Belge. La vie des animaux et des plantes dans l'Antarctique. pp. 177-230.

8.10 The fear of the ship being crushed by the ice or being hit by an iceberg

Cook F.A. 1938. My experiences with a camera in the Antarctic. Popular photography 2(2), 12-14, 90-92.

Hurley F.A. 1925. Argonauts of the south. 290 pp. London, G.P. Putnam's sons, London, UK.

Worsley F.A. 1931. Endurance; an epic of polar adventure. 316 pp. Philip Allan & Co. London, UK (out of copyright).

Chapter 9 Biota in the Bellingshausen Sea: whales, penguins and other birds, fish, other organisms

9.1 Emil Racovitza the biologist

Danielopol D.L., Tabacaru I.G. 2024. Emile G. Racovitza (1868-1947: His views on the advancement of biospeleology are still useful today. Travaux de l'Institut de Speologie "Emile Racovitza" 63, 3-14.

9.2 Cetaceans - whales

Brown S.G. 1954. Dispersal in blue and fin whales. Discovery Reports 26,355-384.

Brown S.G. 1963. The movements of fin and blue whales within the Antarctic zone. Discovery Reports 33, 1-16.

Brown S.G., Brownwell RL Jr., Erickson AW, Hofman, R J, Llano GA, Mackintosh NA. 1974. Antarctic mammals. In: Antarctic map folio series. (VC Bushnell ed.). American Geographical Society of New York, New York, USA.

Mackintosh N.A. 1929. Southern blue and fin whales. Discovery Reports 1, 257-540.

Mackintosh N.A. 1942. The southern stocks of whalebone whales. Discovery Reports 22, 197-300.

Racovitza E. 1900. Expédition Antarctique Belge. La vie des animaux et des plantes dans l'Antarctique. Conférence faite à la Société belge de Géographie. Bulletin de la Société Royale de Géographie (Bruxelles) 24, 177-230.

Racovitza E. 1903. Cétacés. Résultats du voyage de la Belgica en 1897-1898- 1899 – rapports scientifiques. Zoologie. 147 pp. Imprimerie J. Buschmann, Antwerp, Belgium.

Racovitza E. 1904. (FW True translator into English). A summary of general observations on the spouting and movements of whales. Smithsonian Report for 1903, 627-645.

Racovitza E. 1998. Lettres, Jounal antarctique, Conférences. (Marinescu A., Banarescu A., Iftimie A. (eds)). Fondation Culturelle Roumanine Le Rameau d'Or 2 (7), 1-207.

Sayner G.W. 1940. Whale markings. Progress and results to December 1939. Discovery Reports 19, 245=284.

9.3. Pinnipeds - seals

Barrett-Hamilton G.E.H. 1901. Seals. Résultats du voyage de la Belgica en 1897-1898- 1899 – rapports scientifiques. Zoologie. 21 pp. Imprimerie J. Buschmann, Antwerp, Belgium.

Barrett-Hamilton G.E.H. 1902. Seals in: Report on the collections of Natural History made in the Antarctic region during the voyage of the "Southern Cross". 344 pp. British Museum (Natural History), London, UK.

Bester M.N., Wege M., Oosthuizen W.C. , Borneman H. 2020. Ross seal distribution in the Weddell Sea: fact and fallacy. Polar Biology 43, 35-41 https://doi.org/10.1007/s00300-019-02610-4.

Flexas M.M., Thompson A.F., Robertson M.L., Speer K., Sheehan P.M.F., Heywood K.J. 2024. Pathways of inter-basin exchange from the Bellingshausen Sea to the Amundsen Sea. Journal of Geophysical Research: Oceans, 129, e2023JC020080. https://doi.org/10.1029/2023JC020080.

Hanson N. 1902. In: Lankaster ER. Report on the collections of Natural History made in the Antarctic region during the voyage of the "Southern Cross". British Museum (Natural History), London, UK.

Kawaguchi S., Atkinson A., Bahlburg D., Bernard K.S., Cavan E.L., Cox M.J., Hill S.L., Meyer B., Veytia D. 2024. Climate change impacts on Antarctic krill behaviour and population dynamics. Nature Reviews Earth and Environment 5, 43–58. https://doi.org/10.1038/s43017-023-00504-y.

Murariu D. 2016. Les pinnipèdes antarctiques. Recherches d'Emile Racovitza. 521 pp. Editions universitaires européennes, Saarbrücken, Germany. EAN 978-3-8416-1148-2.

Piñones A., Fedorov A.V. 2016. Projected changes of Antarctic krill habitat by the end of the 21st century. Geophysical Research Letters 43, 8580–8589. doi:10.1002/2016GL069656.

Racovitza E. 1900a. Expédition Antarctique Belge. La vie des animaux et des plantes dans l'Antarctique. Conférence faite à la Société belge de Géographie le 22 décembre 1899. Bulletin de la Societé Royale Belge de Géographie (Bruxelles) 24, 177-230.

Racovitza E. 1900b. Vers le Pôle Sud. Conférence faite à la Sorbonne sur l'Expédition Antarctique Belge, son but, ses aventures et ses résultats. Causeries scientifiques de la Société zoologique de France (Paris) 6, 175-242.

Racovitza E. 1900c. Résultats généraux de l'Expédition Antarctique Belge. La Géographie. Bulletin de la Societé de Géographie (Paris) 2, 81-92.

Southwell C, Bengtson J, Bester MN, Blix AS, Bornemann H, Boveng P, Cameron M, Forcada J, Laake J, Nordøy E, Plötz J, Rogers T, Southwell D, Steinhage D, Stewart BS, Trathan P. A review of data on abundance, trends in abundance, habitat use and diet of ice-breeding seals in the Southern Ocean. CCAMLR Science 19, 49–74.

Würsig B., Thewissen J.G.M., Kovacs K.M. 2018. Encyclopedia odfmarine mammals. 1157 pp. Academic Press and Elsevier, San Diego, USA.

9.4 Birds, including penguins

Amesbury M.J., Roland T.P., Royles J., Hodgson D.A., Convey P., Griffiths H., Charman D.J. Widespread Biological Response to Rapid Warming on the Antarctic Peninsula. Current Biology 27, 1616–1622. dx.doi.org/10.1016/j.cub.2017.04.034.

Atkinson A., Siegel V., Pakhomov E.A., Rothery P. 2004. Long-term decline in krill stock and increase in salps within the Southern Ocean. Nature 432, 100–103

Barnes D.K.A, Peck, L.S. 2008. Vulnerability of Antarctic shelf biodiversity to predicted climate change. Climate Research, 37, 149–163.

Cimino M.A., Fraser W.R., Irwin A.J., Oliver M.J. 2013. Satellite data identify decadal trends in the quality of *Pygoscelis* penguin chick-rearing habitat. Global Change Biology 19, 136–148. doi: 10.1111/gcb.12016.

Cimino M.A., Lynch A.J., Saba V.S., Oliver M.J. 2016. Projected asymmetric response of Adélie penguins to Antarctic climate change. Scientific Reports 6, 28785. doi: 10.1038/srep28785

Convey P., Bindschadler R., Di Prisco G., Fahrbach E., Gutt J., Hodgson D.A., Mayewski P.A., Summerhayes C.P., Turner J., and The Acce Consortium. 2009. Antarctic climate change and the environment. Antarctic Science 21(6), 541–563. doi:10.1017/S0954102009990642.

Cook F.A. 1900. Through the first Antarctic night. 1898-1899. A narrative of the voyage of the "Belgica" among newly discovered lands and over an in known sea about the South Pole. 478 pp. Doubleday & McClure Co. New York, USA.

de Gerlache A. 1902. Quinze mois dans l'Antarctique. 303 pp. Imprimerie scientifique Ch. Bullens, Bruxelles, Belgium.

De Roy T., Jones M., Cornthwaite J. 2013. Penguins. Their world, their ways. 240 pp. CSIRO Publishers, Colingwood, Australia.

Ducklow H.W., Baker K., Martinson D.G., Quentin L.B., Ross, R.M., Smith R.C., Stammerjohn S.E., Vernet M., Fraser W.2007. Marine pelagic ecosystems: the West Antarctic Peninsula. Philosophical Transactions of the Royal Society B 362, 67–94. doi:10.1098/rstb.2006.1955.

Dupond C. 1946. Oiseaux. Résultats du voyage de la Belgica en 1897-1898- 1899 – rapports scientifiques. Zoologie. 92 pp. Imprimerie J. Buschmann, Antwerp, Belgium.

Fretwell P.T., Boutet A., Ratcliffe, N. 2023. Record low 2022 Antarctic sea ice led to catastrophic breeding failure of emperor penguins. Nature *Communications Earth Environ*ment **4**, 273 (2023). https://doi.org/10.1038/s43247-023-00927-x

Hudson K., Oliver M.J., Bernard K., Cimino M.A., Fraser W., Kohut J., Statscewich H., Winsor P. 2019. Reevaluating the canyon hypothesis in a biological hotspot in the Western Antarctic Peninsula. Journal of Geophysical Research Oceans 124, 6345–6359. doi. org/10.1029/2019JC015195.

Kawaguchi S., Atkinson A., Bahlburg D., Bernard K.S., Cavan E.L., Cox M.J., Hill S.L., Meyer B., Veytia D. 2024. Climate change impacts on Antarctic krill behaviour and population dynamics. Nature Reviews Earth and Environment 5, 43–58. https://doi.org/10.1038/s43017-023-00504-y

Lecointe G. 1904. Au pays des Manchots. Récit du voyage de la "Belgica". 368 pp. Société belge de Librairie, Bruxelles, Belgium. (an English translation now exists and was published by Erskine Press, Norwich, UK in 2020 and is entitled: 'In the Land of the Penguins'.)

Murphy R.C. 1936. Oceanic birds of South America: a study of species of the related coasts and seas, including the American quadrant of Antarctica, based upon the Brewster-Sanford collection in the American Museum of Natural History. 1245 pp. Macmillan Co., New York, USA.

Oliva M., Navarro F., Hrbáček F., Hernández A., Nývlt D., Pereira P., Ruiz-Fernández J., Trigo R. 2017. Recent regional climate cooling on the Antarctic Peninsula and associated impacts on the cryosphere. Science of the Total Environment 580, 210–223. dx.doi.org/10.1016/j.scitotenv.2016.12.030.

Racovitza E. 1900a. Expédition Antarctique Belge. La vie des animaux et des plantes dans l'Antarctique. Conférence faite à la Société belge de Géographie le 22 décembre 18999. Bulletin de la Societé Royale Belge de Géographie (Bruxelles) 24, 177-230.

Racovitza E. 1900b. Vers le Pôle Sud. Conférence faite à la Sorbonne sur l'Expédition Antarctique Belge, son but, ses aventures et ses résultats. Causeries scientifiques de la Société zoologique de France (Paris) 6, 175-242.

Racovitza E. 1900c. Résultats généraux de l'Expédition Antarctique Belge. La Géographie. Bulletin de la Societé de Géographie (Paris) 2, 81-92.

Racovitza E. 1998. (Eds. Marinescu A., Banarescu A., Iftimie A.). Belgica (1897-1899). Lettres, journal antarctique, conférences. Fondation Culturelle Roumaine, Collection Le Rameau d'Or 2 (7), 1-207.

Santora J.A., LaRue M.A., Ainley D.G. 2020. Geographic structuring of Antarctic penguin populations. Global Ecology and Biogeography 29, 1716–1728.doi:10.1111/geb.13144.

Santora J.A., Reiss C.S. 2011. Geospatial variability of krill and top predators within an Antarctic submarine canyon system. Marine Biology 158, 2527–2540. Ddo:10.1007/s00227-011-1753-0.

Santora J.A., Zeno R., Dorman J.G., Sydeman W.G. 2018 Submarine canyons represent an essential habitat network for krill hotspots in a Large Marine Ecosystem. Scientific Reports 8:7579. Doi: 10.1038/s41598-018-25742-9.

Thompson L.G., Peel D.A., Mosley-Thompson E., Mulvaney R., Dal J., Lin P.N., Davis M.E., Raymond C.F. 1994. Climate since AD 1510 on Dyer Plateau, Antarctic Peninsula: evidence for recent climate change. Annals of Glaciology 20. 420-426. doi: org/10.3189/199 4AoG20-1-420-426.

9.5 Fish

Boulenger G.A. 1902. Report on the collections of natural history made in the Antarctic regions during the voyage of the "Southern Cross". British Museum Natural History 5, 174-189.

Charcot J. 1905. The French Antarctic Expedition. The Geographical Journal 26, 497-516.

Charcot J. 1911. The Second French Antarctic Expedition. The Geographical Journal 37, 241-257.

Dollo L. 1900a. *Cryodraco antarcticus*, poisson abyssal nouveau recueilli par l'Expédition Antarctique Belge. Communication préliminaire. Académie royale de Belgique, Bulletin de la Classe des Sciences (Bruxelles) 2, 128-137.

Dollo L. 1900b. *Gerlachea australis*, poisson abyssal nouveau recueilli par l'Expédition Antarctique Belge. Communication préliminaire. Académie royale de Belgique, Bulletin de la Classe des Sciences (Bruxelles) 3, 194-206.

Dollo L. 1900c. *Racovitzia glacialis*, poisson abyssal nouveau recueilli par l'Expédition Antarctique Belge. Communication préliminaire. Académie royale de Belgique, Bulletin de la Classe des Sciences (Bruxelles) 4, 316-327.

Dollo L. 1900d. *Macrurus Lecointei*, poisson abyssal nouveau recueilli par l'Expédition Antarctique Belge. Communication préliminaire. Académie royale de Belgique, Bulletin de la Classe des Sciences (Bruxelles) 6, 383-401.

Dollo L. 1904. Poissons. Résultats du voyage de la Belgica en 1897-1898- 1899 – rapports scientifiques. Zoologie. 253 pp. Imprimerie J. Buschmann, Antwerp, Belgium.

Dollo L., Traquair M.R.H. 1909. *Nematonurus lecointei*, poisson abyssal de la Belgica, retrouvé par l'Expédition Nationale Ecossaise. Proceedings of the Royal Society of Edinburgh (Edinburgh) 29(6), 488-498.

Stehmann M., Weigmann S., Naylor, G. 2021. First complete description of the dark-mouth skate *Raja arctowskii* Dollo, 1904 from Antarctic waters, assigned to the genus *Bathyraja* (Elasmobranchii, Rajiformes, Arhynchobatidae). Marine Biodiversity 51, 10.1007/s12526-020-01124-1.

Vaillant L. 1906. Poissons. In: Expédition antarctique française (1903-1905) commandée par le Dr. Jean Charcot. 52 pp. Masson et cie, Paris. France.

9.6 Other biota

Cataneo-Vietty R., Bevestrello G., Serano C., Sara M., Benatti U., Giovini M.. Gaino E. 1996. Optical fibres in an Antarctic sponge. Nature 383, 397-398.

Clarke A., Johnston, Nadine M. 2003. Antarctic marine benthic diversity. *Oceanography and Marine Biology: an Annual Review* 41, 47-114..

Fauvel P. 1936. Medusen. Résultats du voyage de la Belgica en 1897-1898- 1899 – rapports scientifiques. Zoologie. 36 pp. Imprimerie J. Buschmann, Antwerp, Belgium.

Joubin, J. 1902. Brachiopodes. Résultats du voyage de la Belgica en 1897-1899 – rapports scientifiques. Zoologie. 14pp. Imprimerie J. Bushmann, Antwerp. Belgium.

Lankaster E.R. 1902. Report on collections of the natural history made in the Antarctic regions during the voyage of the 'Southern Cross'. 344 pp. Printed by order of the Trustees of the British Museum (Natural History), Longmans and co., London, UK.

Maas O. 1906. Medusen. Résultats du voyage du S.Y. Belgica en 1897-1898- 1899 – rapports scientifiques. Zoologie. 36 pp. Imprimerie J. Buschmann, Antwerp, Belgium.

Pelseneer P. 1903. Mollusques (Amphineures, Gastropodes et Lamellibtranches). Résultats du voyage du S.Y. Belgica en 1897-1898- 1899 – rapports scientifiques. Zoologie. 93 pp. Imprimerie J. Buschmann, Antwerp, Belgium.

Topsent R. 1902. Spongiaires. Résultats du voyage du S.Y. Belgica en 1897-1898- 1899 – rapports scientifiques. Zoologie. 60 pp. Imprimerie J. Buschmann, Antwerp, Belgium.

Van Beneden E., de Selys Longchamps, M. 1913. Tuniciers, Caducichordata (Ascidiacés et Thaliacés) – Rapports scienitfiques. Zoologie. 122 pp, Résultats du Voyage du S.Y. Belgica en 1897-1898-1899: Rapports Scientifiques (1901-1913). Buschmann: Anvers. X

Van Heurck H. 1909. Diatomées. Résultats du voyage du S.Y. Belgica en 1897-1898- 1899 – rapports scientifiques. Botanique. 138 pp. Imprimerie J. Buschmann, Antwerp, Belgium.

von Marenzeller E. 1903. Madreporia und Hydrocoralia. Résultats du voyage du S.Y. Belgica en 1897-1898- 1899 – rapports scientifiques. Botanique. 10 pp. Imprimerie J. Buschmann, Antwerp, Belgium.

Chapter 10 Study of sea floor sediments by Arctowski and Renard

Arctowski H., Renard A.-F. 1900. Notice préliminaire sur les sediments marins reccueillis par l'expédition de la Belgica. Mémoires couronnés et autres Mémoires publiés par l'Académie royale de Belgique (Bruxelles) 61, 1-30.

Arctowski H., Renard A.-F. 1901. Le sédiments marins de l'expédition de la *Belgica*. Bulletin de la Société Géologique, Paléontologique et Hydrologique (Procès Verbaux) (Bruxelles) 15, 420-423.

Renard H. 1907. Alphonse Renard – Souvenirs. Published privately, 15 pp. Available online through VLIZ.be (Vlaams Institut voor de Zee, Ostende, Belgium.

Pelikan A. 1909. Petrographische untersuchung der Gesteinproben. I Teil. Résultats du voyage de la Belgica en 1897-1898- 1899 – rapports scientifiques. Géologie. 56 pp. Imprimerie J. Buschmann, Antwerp. Belgium.

Schulze Chretien L.M., Thompson A.F., Flexas M.M., Speer K., Swaim N., Oelerich R., Ruan X., Schubert R., LoBuglio C. 2021. The shelf circulation of the Bellingshausen Sea. Journal of Geophysical Research: Oceans, 126, e2020JC016871. doi.org/10.1029/2020JC016871.

Sistek D. 1912. Petrographische untersuchung der Gesteinproben. II Teil. Résultats du voyage de la *Belgica* en 1897-1898- 1899 – rapports scientifiques. Géologie. 28 pp. Imprimerie J. Buschmann, Antwerp. Belgium.

Chapter 11 Glaciers – modern and ancient – in southern South America and the de Gerlache Strait

Adie R.J. 1957. The petrology of Graham Land. Falkland Island Dependencies Survey. Scientific Reports 20, 1-31.

Amblas D., Canals M. 2016. Contourite drifts and canyon-channel systems on the Northern Antarctic. In: Dowdeswell J.A., Canals M., Jakobsson M., Todd B.J., Dowdeswell E.K., Hogan, K.A. (eds). *Atlas of Submarine Glacial Landforms: Modern, Quaternary and Ancient*. Geological Society, London, Memoirs. 46, 393–394.

Arctowski H. 1901 A propos de la question du climat et des temps glaciaires. Ciel et Terre 22, 27-35.

Arctowski H. 1908. Les glaciers. Glaciers actuels et vestiges de leur ancienne extension. Résultats du voyage du S.Y. Belgica en 1897-1898-1899 – rapports scientifiques. Géologie.14 pp. Imprimerie J. Buschmann, Antwerp, Belgium.

Canals M., Amblas D., Domack E.W., Lastras G., Lavoie C., Casamor J.L., Smith C. 2016. The seafloor imprint of the Gerlache–Boyd Ice Stream (65–62°S), northern Antarctic Peninsula. . In: Dowdeswell J.A., Canals M., Jakobsson M., Todd B.J., Dowdeswell E.K., Hogan, K.A. (eds) *Atlas of Submarine Glacial Landforms: Modern, Quaternary and Ancient*. Geological Society, London, Memoirs. 46, 477-484. doi:10.1144/M46.174.

Canals M., Lastras G., Urgeles R., Casamor J.L. Mienert J., Cattaneo A., M. De Batist M. et al. 2004. Slope failure dynamics and impacts from seafloor and shallow sub-seafloor geophysical data: case studies from the COSTA project. Marine Geology 213, 9-72.

Cofaigh C. and 17 co-authrs. 2014. Reconstruction of ice-sheet changes in the Antarctic Peninsula since the Last Glacial Maximum. Quaternary Science Reviews 100. doi:10.1016/j.quascirev.2014.06.023.

Darwin C. 1846. *Geological observations on the volcanic islands and parts of South America visited during the voyage of H.M.S. 'Beagle'*. 279 pp. Smith Elder, London. UK.

DeMuro S., Brambati A., Tecchiato S., Porta M., Ibba A. 2017. Geomorphology of marine and transitional terraces and raised shorelines between Punta Paulo and Porvenir, Tierra del Fuego, Straits of Magellan – Chile. Journal of Maps, 13, 311-321, doi: 10.1080/17445647.2017.129540.

Dowdeswell J.A., Canals M., Jakobbsen M., Todd B.J., Dowdeswell E.K., Hogan K.A. 2016. Introduction: an Atlas of Submarine Glacial Landforms. . In: Dowdeswell J.A., Canals M., Jakobsson M., Todd B.J., Dowdeswell E.K., Hogan, K.A. (eds). *Atlas of Submarine Glacial Landforms: Modern, Quaternary and Ancient*. Geological Society, London, Memoirs. 3-14.

Henriet .JP. 2010. The face of the ocean: Alphonse-François Renard (1842-1903) and the rise of marine geology. Sartoniana (Gent) 23, 47-80.

McCulloch R.D., Bentley MJ., Tipping RM., Clapperton, CM. 2005. Evidence for late-glacial ice dammed lakes in the central Strait of Magellan and Bahia Inútil, southernmost south America. Geografiska Annaler: Series A, Physical Geography 87, 335–362.

Pelikan A. 1909. Géologie: Petrographische Untersuchungen der Gesteinsproben, I Teil. Résultats du Voyage du S.Y. Belgica en 1897-1898-1899 sous le commandement de A. de Gerlache de Gomery: Rapports Scientifiques (1901-1913). 49 pp. and 2 plates. Buschmann, Antwerp, Belgium.

Renard A-F. 1902. Observations géologiques sur les îles volcaniques explorées par l'expédition du "Beagle" et notes sur la géologie de l'Australie et du Cap de Bonne-Espérance par Charles Darwin. 246 pp. Librairie C. Reinwald, Paris, France.

Rozzi R., Heidinger K., Massardo F. 2018. Tracing Darwin's Path in Cape Horn. 350 pp. University of North Texas Press. 350 pp. Denton, Texas, USA.

Rozzi R., Massardo F., Mansilla A., Anderson C.B., Plana J. 2006. The virgin landscapes of the Cape Horn Biosphere Reserve. 226 pp. Gobierno Regional de Magallenes y Antarctica Chilena. ISBN 956-7189-36-6.

Sistek D. 1912. Géologie: Petrographische Untersuchungen der Gesteinsproben, II Teil. Résultats du Voyage du S.Y. Belgica en 1897-1898-1899 sous le commandement de A. de Gerlache de Gomery: Rapports Scientifiques (1901-1913). 20 pp. and 1 map. Buschmann, Antwerp, Belgium.

Chapter 12 Polar 'anaemia' among the crew

Cook J. 1777. A voyage towards the South Pole, and round the world performed in His Majesty's ships he Resolution and the Adventure in the years 1772-1775, 2 volumes . London W. Strahan and T. Cadell, London, UK.

Charcot J.-B. 1931. La maladie des conserves. La Presse Médicale 55 1057-1058.

Cook F.A. 1894. Medical observations among the esquimaux. New York Joutrnal of Obstetrics and Gynecology October 4, 1893 to October 20, 1894, 171-174.

Cook F.A. 1900. Through the first Antarctic night 1898-1899. A narrative of the voyage of the "Belgica" among the newly discovered lands and over an unknown sea about the South Pole. 478 pp. Doubleday & McClure Co., New York, USA.

Decleir H. (editor) 1999. Roald Amundsen's diary, The first scientific expedition of the Antarctic. 208 pp. Bluntisham Books, Erskine Press, Wiltshire, U.K.

Dobrowolski A.B. 1950. Wspomnienia z wyprawy polarnej. (Memoirs from the polar expedition). Warsawa. Wydawnietwo « Prasa Wajkowa » 102 pp. (in Polish).

de Gerlache A. 1902. Quinze mois dans l'Antarctique par le Commandant de Gerlache.303 pp. Imprimerie Scientifique Ch. Bulens, Bruxelles, Belgium

Gourdon E. 1936. Hivernage dans l'Antarctique en 1904. In: Jean-Baptiste Charcot 1867-1936. Paris: Yacht Club de France, pp. 131-133.

Gurly H.R. 2011. 'Polar anaemia': cardiac failure during the heroic age of Antarctic exploration. Polar Record 48 (245): 157-164. doi:10.1017/S0032247411000222.

Gurly H.R. 2011. Psychology during the expeditions of the heroic age of Antarctic exploration. History of Psychiatry 90(2), 194-205. doi:10.1177/0957154X11399203.

Kløver, G.O. (Editor) 2010. Antarctic Pioneers. The Voyage of the Belgica 1897-1899. 119 pp. The Fram Museum. Oslo, Norway.

Lecointe G. 1904.Au pays des manchots. Récit de la 'Belgica'.368 pp. Société belge de Librairie, Bruxelles, Belgium.

Chapter 13 Investigations in the Beagle Channel

13.1 Sites visited and species richness

Darwin C. 1902. Observations géologiques sur les îles volcaniqueves on Antarctic Science and Histroys explorées par l'expédition du «Beagle» et note sur la géologie de l'Australie et du Cap de Bonne-Espérance. Traduit de l'anglais sur la troisième édition par A.-F. Renard. C. Reinwald and Schleicher Frères éditeurs, Paris, France.

De Broyer C., Kuyken T. 2001 Bibliography of the Belgica Antarctic expedition 1897-1899. In Decleir H. and De Broyer C. (editors) 'The Belgica Expedition centennial: Perspectives on Antarctic Science and History' pp. 329-360, VUB University Press, Brussels, Belgium.

Sistek D. 1912. Petrographische untersuchungen der Gesteinsproben. Résultats du voyage du S. Y. Belgica en 1897-1898- 1899 – rapports scientifiques. Géologie. 28 pp. Imprimerie J. Buschmann, Antwerp, Belgium.

13.2 The ship's misadventure in Harberton

Cook F.A. 1900. New Antarctic Discoveries. The Century Magazine 59 (3) 408-427.

Lecointe G. (1904). Au Pays des Manchots. Récit. Voyage de la Belgica. 368 pp. Société belge de librairie O. Schepens & Cie, Bruxelles, Belgium (an English translation has recently been published by Erskine Press).

11.3 Flora

Alboff N.M. 1896. Contributions A La Flore De La Terre De Feu V1-2: Observations sur la végétation du Canal de Beagle et énumeration des plantes du Canal de Beagle. 96 pp. Reprinted in 2010 by Kessinger Publishing, Whitefish, Montana, USA.

Alboff N.M. 1903. Essai de flore raisonnée de la Terre de Feu. 85 pp., 23 appendices. Anales del Museo de La Plata, Argentina.

Bommer E., Rousseau M. 1905. Résultats du voyage du S. Y. Belgica en 1897-1898- 1899 – rapports scientifiques. Botanique. 52 pp. Imprimerie J. Buschmann, Antwerp, Belgium.

Cardot J. 19002. Mousses. Coup d'oeil sur la flore bryologique des Terres Magellaniques. Résultats du voyage du S. Y. Belgica en 1897-1898- 1899 – rapports scientifiques. Botanique. 62 pp. Imprimerie J. Buschmann, Antwerp, Belgium.

Darwin C. 1902. Observations géologiques sur les îles volcaniques explorées par l'expédition du «Beagle» et note sur la géologie de l'Australie et du Cap de Bonne-Espérance. Traduit de l'anglais sur la troisième édition par A.-F. Renard. C. Reinwald and Schleicher Frères éditeurs, Paris, France.

De Wilderman E. 1903. Les phanérogammes des terres magellaniques. Résultats du voyage du S. Y. Belgica en 1897-1898- 1899 – rapports scientifiques. Botanique. 246 pp. Imprimerie J. Buschmann, Antwerp, Belgium.

Racovitza E. 1900a. Expédition Antarctique Belge. La vie des animaux et des plantes dans l'Antarctique. Conférence faite à la Société belge de Géographie le 22 décembre 18999. Bulletin de la Societé Royale Belge de Géographie (Bruxelles) 24, 177-230.

Racovitza E. 1900b. Vers le Pôle Sud. Conférence faite à la Sorbonne sur l'Expédition Antarctique Belge, son but, ses aventures et ses résultats. Causeries scientifiques de la Société zoologique de France (Paris) 6, 175-242.

Rozzi R., Heidinger K., Massardo F. 2018. Tracing Darwin's Path in Cape Horn. 350 pp. University of North Texas Press. 350 pp. Denton, Texas, USA.

Rozzi R., Massardo F., Mansilla A., Anderson C.B., Plana J. 2006. The virgin landscapes of the Cape Horn Biosphere Reserve. 226 pp. Gobierno Regional de Magallenes y Antarctica Chilena. ISBN 956-7189-36-6.

Sistek D. 1912. Petrographische untersuchungen der Gesteinsproben. Résultats du voyage du S. Y. Belgica en 1897-1898- 1899 – rapports scientifiques. Géologie. 28 pp. Imprimerie J. Buschmann, Antwerp, Belgium.

Stefani F. 1902. Hépatiques. Résultats du voyage du S. Y. Belgica en 1897-1898- 1899 – rapports scientifiques. Botanique. 63-67 pp as published in Cardot's monograph. Imprimerie J. Buschmann, Antwerp, Belgium.

Wainio A. 1903. Lichens. Résultats du voyage du S. Y. Belgica en 1897-1898- 1899 – rapports scientifiques. Botanique. 52 pp. Imprimerie J. Buschmann, Antwerp, Belgium.

11.4 Invertebrates

Racovitza E. 1998. Belgica (1897-1899). Emile Racovitza. Le naturaliste de l'expédition antarctique "Belgica". Le Rameau d'Or. Fondation Culturelle Roumaine 2 (7), 1-207.

Severin G. 1906. Insectes. Résultats du voyage du S.Y. Belgica en 1897-1898- 1899 – rapports scientifiques. Zoologie. 120 pp. Imprimerie J. Buschmann, Antwerp, Belgium.

Simões F.L., Contador-Mejías T., Rendoll-Cárcamo J. ,Pérez-Troncoso C., Hayward S.A.L., Turner E., Convey P. 2020. Distribution and Habitat Preferences of the Newly Rediscovered Telmatogeton magellanicus (Jacobs, 1900) (Diptera: Chironomidae) on Navarino Island, Chile. Insects 11(7), 442, https://doi.org/10.3390/insects11070442.

13.5 Brief mention of whales and seals seen in the Beagle Channel area in the State Island

No references, see chapter 9.

Chapter 14 Johan Koren

Mehlum F., Potapov E. 1995. Small mammals from the Koren Arctic Expedition to the Kolyma River, northeast Siberia 1914-1918. Polar Research 14(1), 1–14. https://doi.org/10.3402/polar.v14i1.6647.

Wikan S. 2000. Johan Koren: feltzoolog ofgpolarpioner. ∤° Schibsted Publisher, Oslo, Norway.

Chapter 15 Illustrations of the activities of the personnel during the expedition

Cook F.A. 1900. Through the First Antarctic Night, 1898–1899: A Narrative of the Voyage of the "Belgica" among Newly Discovered Lands and over an Unknown Sea about the South Pole. 478 pp. London: Heinemann.

Chapter 16 Frederick Cook and the first people of Patagonia

Catling D., Kelly M. (eds.) 2009. Darwin for the love of science. 280 pp. Bristol Cultural Development Partnership, Bristol, UK

Cook F.A. 1900a. Through the first Antarctic night 1898-1899. A narrative of the voyage of the "Belgica" among newly discovered lands and over an unknown sea about the South Pole. 478 pp. Doubleday & McClure Co. New York, USA.

Cook F.A. 1900b. The giant Indians of Tierra del Fuego. The Century Magazine (New York) 59, 72-729.

Cook F.A. 1938. My experiences with a camera in the Antarctic. Popular photography 2(2), 12-14, 90-92.

Glausiusz J. 2021. Savages and Cannibals: Revisiting Charles Darwin's Voyage of the Beagle. An essay available at https://www.whatisemerging.com/opinions/savages-and-cannibals

Hestermann, F., Gusinde M. (Editors) 1933. Yamana-English, a Dictionary of the speech of Tierra del Fuego, by the Reverend Thomas Bridges Missionsdruckerei St. Gabriel, Mödling, Austria.

L'Honoret M. (translator). Aux confins de la Terre: une vie en Terre de Feu (1874-1910), originally by E. Lucas Bridges. 656 pp. Nevicata Editions, Brussels, Belgium.

Marinescu A., Bănărescu A., Itftimie A. 1988. Belgica (1897-1800). Emile Racovitza. Le naturaliste de l'expédition antarctique "Belgica". Lettres, journal antarctique, conférences. Le Rameau d'Or, Fondation Culturelle Roumaine 2 (7), 1-207.

Chapter 17 The return to Antwerp and celebrations

Decleir H. (editor) 1999. Roald Amundsen's Belgica diary. The scientific expedition to the Antarctic. 208 pp. Bluntisham Books, Erskine Press, Huntingdon, UK. (this is a translation of Amundsen's diary but, as pointed out by several Norwegian colleagues, there are several paragraphs missing from the original that was written in Norwegian!).

Lecointe, G. 1900. Expédition Antarctique Belge. Réception solenelle des explorateurs à leur arrivée à Anvers. Conférence donnée par M. Georges Lecointe. Bulletin de la Société Royale de Géographie d'Anvers 24, 5-51.

Racovitza E. 1998. (Eds. Marinescu A., Banarescu A., Iftimie A.). Belgica (1897-1899). Lettres, journal antarctique, conférences. Fondation Culturelle Roumaine, Collection Le Rameau d'Or 2 (7), 1-207.

Chapter 18 Conclusions and lessons for the future

Hughes K.A., Chwedorzewska K.J., Molina-Montenegro M.A., Pertierra L.R. 2023. Terrestrial non-native species in Antarctica: introduction, impact and management response. Antarctic Environments Portal https://doi.org/10.48361/qbtd-qt57

Magalhães N., Evangelista H., Gonçalves S.J., Alenca A.S., Alves dos Santos E., Cataldo M., McConnell J.R., Silveira R.S. Mayewski P.A., Potocki M., Simões J.C., Jana R. 2024. on the Antarctic Peninsula due to rising shipborne tourism and forest fires. Science Advances 10(42): eadp1682. doi: 10.1126/sciadv.adp1682.

Roland T.P., Bartlett O.T., Charman D.J., Anderson K., Hodgson D.A., Amesbury M.J., Maclean I., Fretwell P.T., Fleming A. 2024. Sustained greening of the Antarctic Peninsula observed from satellites. Nature Geoscience 17, 1121–1126. doi.org/10.1038/s41561-024-01564-5

Appendix Seal descriptions made by Racovitza

Barrett-Hamilton G.E.H. 1901. Seals. Résultats du voyage de la Belgica en 1897-1898- 1899 – rapports scientifiques. Zoologie. 21 pp. Imprimerie J. Buschmann, Antwerp, Belgium.

Bengston J.L., Stewart B.S. 2018. Crabeater seals. Lobodon carcinophaga. In: (Eds. Würsig BG, Thewissen JGM, Kovacs KM) Encyclopedia of marine mammals 3rd edition, 230-232 pp. Academic Press, an imprint of Elsevier. San Diego, USA. doi.org/10.1016/C2015-0-00820-6.

Bernacchi L.C. 1901.To the south polar regions Expedition of 1898-1900. 348 pp. Bluntisham Books, Denton, UK.

Dumont d'urville J.S.C. 1842. Voyage au pole sud et dans l'Océanie : sur les corvettes l'Astrolabe et la Zélée, exécuté par ordre du roi pendant les années 1837-1838-1839-1840, sous le commandement de M.J. Dumont d'Urville - publié par ordonnance de sa Majesté sous la direction supérieure de M. Jacquinot. 10 volumes (1842-1846). Gide, Paris, France.

Hamilton-Barrett G.E. 1902. In: Lankaster ER. Report on the collections of Natural History made in the Antarctic region during the voyage of the "Southern Cross". 66 pp. British Museum (Natural History), London, UK.

Hanson N. 1902. In: Lankaster E.R. Report on the collections of Natural History made in the Antarctic region during the voyage of the "Southern Cross". British Museum (Natural History), London, UK.

Lankaster Er. 1902. Report on the collections of Natural History made in the Antarctic region during the voyage of the "Southern Cross". 344 pp. British Museum (Natural History), London, UK.

Murariu D. (2016). Les pinnipèdes antarctiques. Recherches d'Emile Racovitza. 521 pp. Editions universitaires européennes, Saarbrücken, Germany. ISBN 978-3-8416-1148-2.

Index

Photograph of F. Cook on the left holding a camera and R. Amundsen near the tent which they both designed.
Photo from an album gifted by G. Lecointe to R. Amundsen and used with permission from Anders Bache,
Follo Museum, Museene i Akershus, Norway. Photo enhanced using Photoshop© and 'colorized' using palette.fm.

www.ingramcontent.com/pod-product-compliance
Lightning Source LLC
Chambersburg PA
CBHW041550030426

42335CB00004B/176